BETSY ROSS AND THE MAKING OF AMERICA

# BETSY ROSS

## *and the*

# MAKING *of* AMERICA

MARLA R. MILLER

HENRY HOLT AND COMPANY   NEW YORK

Henry Holt and Company, LLC
*Publishers since 1866*
175 Fifth Avenue
New York, New York 10010
www.henryholt.com

Henry Holt® and $\blacksquare$® are registered trademarks of
Henry Holt and Company, LLC.

Library of Congress Cataloging-in-Publication Data

Miller, Marla R.
   Betsy Ross and the making of America / Marla R.
   Miller.—1st ed.
      p. cm.
   Includes bibliographical references.
   ISBN 978-0-8050-8297-5
   1. Ross, Betsy, 1752–1836.   2. Revolutionaries—United States—Biography.
3. Flags—United States—History.   4. Philadelphia (Pa.)—History—Revolution,
1775–1783.   I. Title.
   E302.6.R77M54 2010
   973.3092—dc22
   [B]
                                                             2009035385

Henry Holt books are available for special promotions and
premiums. For details contact: Director, Special Markets.

First Edition 2010

*Designed by Kelly S. Too*

Printed in the United States of America
1   3   5   7   9   10   8   6   4   2

*To my parents
and my husband,
with love and gratitude*

# CONTENTS

Prologue         *1*

### PART I: SIX HUNDRED MILES NEARER THE SUN

1: The Light Within    *19*

2: A Nursery to the Lord    *36*

3: Pins and Needles    *50*

4: Crafting Comfort    *61*

### PART II: THE FURNACE OF AFFLICTION

5: Combustible Matters    *77*

6: Domestic Rebellions    *98*

7: Union and Disunion    *106*

8: Mr. and Mrs. Ross    *127*

9: Meditations in Trouble    *143*

### PART III: TRUE COLORS

10: Crafting Colors    *155*

11: Signals of Independence    *167*

12: The Mariner's Bride    *182*

13: The Occupied City    *196*

14: Privateer to Prisoner    *212*

## PART IV: PEACE AND PROSPERITY

15:  Third Time's a Charm                    223

16:  For Lord and Empire                     237

17:  Brotherly Love                          253

18:  Fever                                   269

19:  The Federal Edifice                     286

## PART V: ENDINGS AND BEGINNINGS

20:  War, Redux                              309

21:  A Port in the Storm                     327


Epilogue                                     343


Key Figures                                  363
Notes                                        367
Acknowledgments                              445
Index                                        449

BETSY ROSS AND THE MAKING OF AMERICA

# Prologue

The number of bidders responding to the auctioneer's call collapsed to a handful within moments, the audience watching closely the expressionless faces of men and women whispering into their phones, waiting to see who would act next. Like spectators at a tennis match, the 150 heads gathered in Sotheby's fifth-floor gallery looked to the left, to the right and back again. Bidding—tracked on huge screens at the front of the room in dollars, euros and yen—quickly reached the presale estimate, and moments later hit twice that figure. When the gavel fell, the first lot—the red-and-white-striped battle standard of the Second Connecticut Continental Light Dragoons—had sold for a staggering $11 million ($12.36 million if you include the fee the auction house takes for making the sale). When the second lot came up—three battle flags of the American Revolution comprising the so-called Waxhaws colors— the same thing happened. Sold! To the same buyer, this time for $4.5 million. The audience paused to catch a breath. In just fourteen heart-stopping minutes— less time than it took me to park my car—the assembled collectors, historians and curiosity seekers watched as a single unseen buyer spent $17.4 million (far and away more than the auction house had predicted) to acquire four surviving flags from the Revolutionary War.[1]

Seized by the noxious British cavalry officer Banastre (pronounced ben-*az*-ter, not banister, like the railing along the stairs) Tarleton in the throes of the Revolutionary struggle, the four flags spent the intervening centuries hang-ing in the Tarleton estate in the south of England, trophies of victories long past. They are among only about thirty battle flags known to have survived from America's struggle for independence, and as such, as Sotheby's Vice Chairman David Redden observed, are "sacred and vivid relics of the birth of our nation."[2] The Connecticut standard was captured in summer 1779, when the twenty-four-year-old Tarleton led his Green Dragoons in a surprise attack on a Continental regiment stationed at Pound Ridge, New York. Nine months later, in May 1780, Tarleton claimed the "Waxhaws colors" in a clash with the Virginia regiment of Lieutenant Colonel Abraham Buford in the Waxhaws, a region of the Piedmont Carolinas named after the local native community. For the next 225 years, they remained spoils of war. By the turn of the twenty-first century, they were rare and valuable totems of our nation's origins.

The colors are stunning for their beauty and craftsmanship. The flag carried at Pound Ridge is a spectacular silk standard of thirteen red and white stripes (which makes it perhaps the earliest extant American flag to employ the field of thirteen red and white stripes so familiar to us today). At the center, a painted panel shows a winged thundercloud, ten golden thunderbolts shooting in every direction, over a banner that reads PAT:A CONCITA FULM:NT NATI, or "When their Country calls, her sons answer in tones of thunder." Thirty inches at the hoist and thirty-six inches on the fly, the whole is bordered with silver fringe. On the field of battle, it must have made a dazzling display.

The regimental colors of the Virginia detachment—the only intact set, or *stand*, of Revolutionary colors known to have survived—are just as impressive. A scrolling banner carries the motto PERSEVERANDO, while the battle flag's field of gold silk is ornamented on both sides with the painting of a broad-tailed beaver felling a palmetto (a symbol of perseverance since at least 1597, when Joachim Camerarius included the image in his dictionary *Symbolorum ac Emblematum Ethico-Politicorum*; Benjamin Franklin consulted his edition of Camerarius when he designed currency for Pennsylvania and the United States, and he too favored the noble beaver).[3] In the *canton* (the upper corner of the flag nearest the staff), thirteen tin-glazed five-pointed stars scatter across a blue silk field.[4] Two secondary colors (called *ground colors*, they helped direct troop action) accompany the flag, one of gold silk, the other sky-blue. A ribbon bearing the word *Regiment* occupies the center of each. Both are self-fringed at the fly end; that is, the maker, after assembling the panels of fabric, frayed the edge for added effect as the standard flew in the Carolina breeze.

Sotheby's scheduled the auction for June 14, 2006—Flag Day—a date chosen to reference another moment in United States history. Flag Day (first proclaimed by Woodrow Wilson in 1916 and established by Congress in 1949) honors an act undertaken by the Continental Congress on that date in 1777, when the assembled delegates from the thirteen British colonies that had joined in rebellion resolved that "the flag of the United States be thirteen stripes, alternating red and white, that the Union be thirteen white stars in a blue field representing a new constellation." For generations, that flag has been associated, at least in popular historical imagination, with Betsy Ross, a Philadelphia upholsterer whose family claimed her to be the maker of the very flag endorsed by Congress on that June day. In May 2006, as Sotheby's prepared for this landmark sale, the auction house contacted the museum on Philadelphia's Arch Street now dedicated to telling Ross's story to see whether there was any chance that Ross might have had a hand in any of these four flags as well.

The case was certainly plausible. There's no doubt that Ross was working as a Philadelphia flag maker by 1777, and over her sixty-year career she made hundreds of flags—archival references can be found for dozens she fabricated for state and federal forces. But it is impossible to know today who the makers of almost any battle standards were, in part because such artifacts are unsigned, and also because records documenting flag construction are so rare. Unbeknownst to Sotheby's, however, New York auction houses had handled objects associated with Ross before, several times, and these, too, were record-setting sales. In 1999, a carved mahogany side chair—its trademark paw-feet so hairy you can feel their scratch—made in Philadelphia around 1769 for the wealthy merchant John Cadwalader went to auction at Sotheby's competitor, Christie's. One of only seven known to have survived from a set that initially numbered at least twelve (and possibly as many as twenty), this chair was expected to bring $1 million at auction.[5] The total, including the buyer's premium, crested $1.4 million.[6] Twelve years earlier, in January 1987, the twenty-nine-year-old antiques dealer Leigh Keno paid $2.75 million—at that time the highest price ever paid for a piece of American furniture—for a winged armchair once owned by Cadwalader and his wife, Elizabeth Lloyd, bought for their home on Philadelphia's Second Street. "This chair is a piece of history," Keno remarked. "It was made for one of the grandest residences in Philadelphia in 1770, when Philadelphia was the center of the colonial interpretation of rococo, for a patriot who entertained George Washington." "Americans," he added, "are beginning to appreciate furniture made by their craftsmen more than ever."[7]

Indeed, it was the confirmed association, through extant bills and receipts, with well-known and now-celebrated craftsmen that in part accounts for these tremendous values (or at least the high prices). The side chair auctioned in 1999 is believed to be from the Philadelphia shop of Benjamin Randolph, and the carving done by the London-trained craftsman John Pollard, possibly with the help of another carver named Richard Butz, who worked alongside Pollard for a time at his shop at the Sign of the Chinese Shield.[8] The winged armchair (or easy chair) came from Thomas Affleck, a Quaker furniture maker whose shop stood not far from the Cadwalader mansion. The ornate carving on the chair's frame has been attributed to James Reynolds, Nicholas Bernard and Martin Jugiez, all Philadelphia carvers whom Affleck regularly employed to embellish his work. Once the chair's frame was completed, a London and Philadelphia upholsterer with the memorable name Plunket Fleeson applied foundation upholsteries and stuffing and covered the whole with a sturdy plain canvas.

When the Cadwalader furniture was sold, no comparable calls were made to see whether there was any whiff of association with the Philadelphia seamstress Betsy Ross. But we know that she too contributed to the elegance of the Cadwalader suite, because surviving receipts document Cadwalader's relationship with another London-trained upholsterer, John Webster, for whom Betsy Ross (then a young woman named Elizabeth Griscom) worked as one of several employees. Webster's shop made Venetian window blinds, sofa cushions and bolsters for the Cadwalader home; it supplied the canvas and curled hair that supported some of the furniture upholstery, yards of fabric to cover the seats, and tassels to give them added panache.[9] The shop assembled and hung bed and window curtains, made and stuffed mattresses, and finished carpets. Betsy Griscom and the women who labored alongside her in Webster's workrooms, with materials that Cadwalader had ordered from the London firm Rushton and Beachcroft, labored to ornament and protect the expensive furniture when they cut, assembled and trimmed chair cases and sofa covers of silk damask as well as more serviceable check. To some cases, they stitched linings and applied yards of fringe. In the end, Betsy and her coworkers employed some 165 yards of silk and worsted lace to enliven the Cadwalader interior.[10] Though those items are long gone today—intact eighteenth-century chair covers are far more rare than the furniture they once protected—they helped ensure the survival of furniture now worth millions. In her long life, Betsy Griscom would make hundreds of chair cases, window curtains, mattresses, blinds and—yes—flags. But cases and curtains will never bring millions at auction, and those objects that might—rare and spectacular flags of the American Revolution—are almost impossible to attribute to any particular maker because craftswomen like her, usually employees of someone else's enterprise and the makers of objects that never bore labels, worked in anonymity. That we know the name of the Philadelphia upholsterer Betsy Ross is the work of chance, an artifact of another era, one that she did not live to see.

Betsy Ross comes to us today in story, song and pageantry as the maker of the first United States flag. As legend has it, George Washington, Robert Morris and George Ross, as representatives of the Continental Congress, appeared unannounced at Ross's upholstery shop and requested her help creating a new standard for Britain's colonies recently united in rebellion. The group retreated to Ross's parlor to discuss the matter further, and the ingenious needlewoman noted that the six-pointed stars the general had in mind were more difficult to construct than five-pointed stars; taking a piece of paper in hand, she folded it just so and demonstrated the fact with a quick snip of her scissors. A "specimen" flag was produced, to universal acclaim, and Ross commenced production in earnest. Her work—a flag of thirteen stripes with thirteen stars encircled on a blue field—became (so the story continues) the first official flag of the new nation. Decades after Ross's death, her children and grandchildren, nieces and nephews, under the leadership of grandsons William and George Canby (and with the help of a nation eager to embrace a patriotic seamstress), established her larger-than-life place in the mythology of the American Revolution.[11] Affectionate descendants and relatives signed affidavits affirming stories recollected by the family, and in public lectures and in the press family memory was converted to national history. After the United States celebrated its 1876 centennial and then the Columbian Exposition in 1893, interest in Ross mounted; a massive campaign emerged to save her Arch Street home from demolition. Among the few female figures to emerge as compelling characters in our national origin stories, Ross was embraced by teachers and schoolchildren, civic leaders, artists and authors of children's literature.

For most of the twentieth century, the making of the first flag remained an essential episode in any popular history of the Revolution. Ross has been commemorated in an array of products from dolls, sewing machines and dishes to (less predictably) cigars, brandy decanters, pocketwatches and pianos. One of the earliest biopics in American film history—the 1917 drama *Betsy Ross,* starring a young Alice Brady (who would go on to win an Academy Award for her portrayal of another historical character, Mrs. Molly O'Leary, in the film *In Old Chicago*)—took up her story. Betsy Ross enjoys the dubious distinction of being one of only four figures from United States history (together with Paul Revere, Daniel Boone and Elvis Presley) immortalized as a

Pez head. Her story is so familiar that Hanes Underwear introduced an advertising campaign for its "Barely There" line of foundation garments that tapped Ross's presumed frustration with being kept to the fringes of the Revolutionary circle; in the TV commercial, the Canadian supermodel Shalom Harlow, wearing only the product and no other visual cue suggesting her identity as Betsy Ross, complains about her exclusion from post-Declaration fireworks, and cryptically assures viewers that if she *had* been there, she'd have been "barely there."

Today, while many Americans have come to take the legend and its romance with a grain of salt, Betsy Ross's popularity is nevertheless undiminished. Some quarter of a million people visit her Philadelphia home every year. Dozens of books about Ross crowd shelves in the children's and young adult sections of libraries and bookstores. College students asked to name any person from pre–Civil War America who is *not* a politician or military figure consistently have included Ross among their top ten, year after year.[12]

This outpouring of cultural interest in Ross thrives despite the fact that no historical record confirms the alleged meeting in her parlor. Thousands of pages of records survive from Philadelphia's Revolution, but only a handful name the makers of the first flags required by the rebellion. When the records of the War Department were destroyed in 1800, consumed by fire, the veil between us and the past thickened.[13] That we today have any notion of Betsy Ross at all is the product of family pride and the considerable effort of two adoring grandsons. The story of the first flag as we know it rests in the testimonies captured in those nineteenth-century affidavits, when, at William Canby's request, various relatives made their way to lawyers' offices and set down their recollections in front of a notary. The shaky signature of an aged Rachel Claypoole Fletcher, by those years Betsy's only surviving daughter, captures the fragility of the enterprise.[14]

But human memory is deeply fallible. It didn't take long for professional and avocational historians, in the wake of both the nineteenth- and twentieth-century Betsy Ross hoopla, to question the story's veracity. Some researchers championed more plausible designers of the "first flag"; others challenged whether the house preserved at 239 Arch Street was actually Ross's residence at the time. It was easy to find places where the story as the children recalled it simply didn't hold up to scholarly scrutiny.[15]

This of course should not surprise us. As the historian Richard White so elegantly suggests, "Memory itself dies with its creator. We can record memories, but then they are fixed on the page, pinned like insects in a collection, bodies of what was alive."[16] When Ross's descendants affixed their signatures to those affidavits, they pinned to a page stories that had once vibrated with life, tales that they had all heard, but just a handful among the many passed down, and that were vulnerable to slips here and there. As they are handed from one generation to the next, facts get muddled, misremembered, forgotten, diminished or embellished. Among the descendants of Betsy Ross, some elements of their family stories were well preserved and can easily be confirmed in the usual historical sources; others became distorted through the lens of retrospection. The infelicities aside, enough consistency persists across the narratives to suggest that something tangible rests at the bottom of them, but retrieving what that might be means peeling away layers of misapprehensions and apocrypha and laying in their place new insights rooted in the historical record.[17]

If you poll Americans today and ask them about Betsy Ross, you will find both affirmation and doubt. Some believe that the story of the first flag that they've known since their childhoods is essentially correct. Others dismiss it altogether, believing Betsy Ross to be an all-but-fictional character made up by late Victorians and embraced so widely not because her story is true, but because it is charming, and because it served a practical purpose for a nation grappling with the women's suffrage movement, contributing a female figure to the company of founders without endorsing female political engagement or undermining the importance of the domestic sphere.[18] As we shall see, the family stories are neither altogether right nor altogether wrong. The truth is found in its usual place: somewhere in between.

In part, then, this effort to recover the life of Betsy Ross is a story about stories. If the affidavits are to be believed, Ross planted the seeds of her own mythology in the 1820s and '30s as she regaled her children and grandchildren with stories from her youth, her work and life in Revolutionary Philadelphia. She boasted about how she got her first job in Webster's upholstery shop, immediately impressing him with the neatness and beauty of her stitches. And she laughed as she recounted a dream she had had in her youth—and since she was her parents' seventh daughter, superstition attached some importance to it—in which she saw "the letters GRAC in looking through a handkerchief toward the sky." Her friends had teased her that she was missing the *e* to spell *grace*, "but she replied that she had that in her first name, Elizabeth," and then happily explained to her listeners the vision's true meaning, how she couldn't have known then what she would in time, that "these letters were the initials of her various names after her three marriages": Elizabeth Griscom Ross Ashburn Claypoole.[19]

She had other stories, too, but her best one—the one she told most often—was about General Washington's visit and the making of that flag. Grandmother Claypoole, as she recounted these events for her descendants, clearly believed in her own historical importance, grounded firmly in one moment in the birth of her nation. She beamed with pride as she described improving on Washington's design with a snip of the scissors, demonstrating the superiority, from a production standpoint, of the five-pointed, rather than six-pointed, star that the general had in mind. With that single slice of the shears, she asserted, she had made her own contribution to the fate of a nation. For the remainder of her days, she wore a silver hook at her waist with two silver chains. Attached to these were a small pair of scissors and a pincushion encircled in a silver band, reminders of good days long past. Between tales, out of a deep pocket would sometimes come a small silver snuffbox marked with her initials, from which she'd take the occasional dose; she claimed to dislike having to do it, but it was medicinal—good, she said, for her failing eyesight. The events surrounding the making of one of the earliest flags of the independence effort became essential to her sense of herself and, later, to her family's sense of its own history. Betsy's granddaughter Sophia Wilson Hildebrandt—who had come to work alongside her mother and grandmother in the Claypoole upholstery and flag-making shop—remembered hearing Ross "frequently narrate" the story of the first flag. One wonders whether she wore her family out with that old chestnut, an artifact of the deep pride the aging craftswoman harbored in her personal connection with the most important people and events of her age.[20]

It was not the flag story that first attracted me to Ross's life. I was never among the fourth graders bedecked in patriot costume at grade-school pageants (though on one memorable class trip, to a local garden inspired by those in Colonial Williamsburg, I did get a turn at a mob cap). I have no recollection of having formed any early opinion about Betsy Ross one way or another, even as I completed my doctorate in U.S. history. It wasn't until years later that, as a historian of women and work in early America and a university professor who teaches courses on the American Revolution, I was drawn to the Ross story, and particularly to the larger narratives hinted at in the margins of the affidavits. In many ways, it is the story of Elizabeth Griscom, not Betsy Ross, that so engages me. (That I refer to her here as "Betsy" is mainly a concession both to the name by which she became famous and to the need to distinguish her from the many other Elizabeths who populated her world, but I remain uneasy with the informality that the diminutive form implies.) I wanted to know more about the teenage girl working in an upholstery shop, like her counterparts in craft shops across the city; the young bride widowed before independence was even declared, who would venture to marry again while the war was at its highest pitch only to find herself widowed for a second time before peace was achieved; the new mother who gambled on marriage yet a third time when she wed the war veteran John Claypoole; the birthright Quaker who accepted dismissal from the Society of Friends in order to marry John Ross, but who as an early member of the Free Quaker meeting helped reinvent the faith for Revolutionary times, and was among the last members of that congregation to survive; the matriarch of a growing family whose fortunes declined as the nation's improved, casting the aging craftswoman's household on the charity of her fellow Friends in the final years of her life. I was intrigued by what the testimonies suggest were long evenings of storytelling. It was apparently easy to get Grandpa Claypoole to talk about his days as a soldier, and especially the day when the frigate on which he sailed as a privateer, the *Luzerne*, was outgunned by the British privateer *Enterprise* somewhere off the coast of Ireland, and the hard months he spent in an English prison. Years later, he would recount for his grandchildren how he had asked a wounded Hessian soldier why in the world he had come to America to fight men who would otherwise be his friends. The man replied, "Hesse no kill; Hesse shoot low." You can almost see the twinkle in his eye; that story was one of his favorites and opened yet another window for me on how everyday Pennsylvanians experienced the American Revolution.[21]

Within the family stories are other lines, too, more sober tales that hint at the scars left by the Revolution and the upheavals that followed. For instance, as refugees from revolutionary Haiti flooded into Philadelphia in 1793, they brought with them a ravenous yellow fever epidemic that would claim both Betsy's parents and her sister within a matter of days. Betsy apparently harbored resentment over her loved ones' failed care for the rest of her life. And then there are the mysteries, the stories that I now know could have been told—and perhaps were, quietly, on a rare evening, when Grandmother Claypoole was in a more contemplative mood—but were left unrecorded. How and why, exactly, did John Ross die, and why are the circumstances surrounding his death so cloudy? Who was the African American child living with the newlyweds in 1775, and how might he or she figure in the contradictory but simultaneous patterns of both slaveholding and antislavery activism that trace through the family's history? Who was the privateer Joseph Ashburn, and how did she come to remarry so quickly? How did Betsy and her struggling family survive after husband John Claypoole's stroke rendered him an invalid, just as the young nation braced for war once again? Surely there were other powerful stories to tell, many as compelling as the making of the flag, but no one thought they were important enough to record at the time. Why did only one narrative survive so robustly in the oral tradition of Betsy's children, when clearly her life brimmed with dramatic events?

At least part of the answer lies in the American obsession with George Washington. Like many Americans who came of age during the Revolution, both Betsy and John Claypoole sustained a lifelong admiration—even adoration—of General Washington. After the president's death, they were among the thousands of American households to acquire some memento of his life: a large framed engraving depicting a statue of the fallen leader upon a pedestal carrying the famous words from his funeral oration, FIRST IN WAR, FIRST IN PEACE, FIRST IN THE HEARTS OF HIS COUNTRYMEN. "We loved him as we shall never love another," Grandmother Claypoole told her grandchildren.[22] These were not just expressions of patriotic affection; Betsy Claypoole took exceptional pride in having known the president personally. William Canby would report that Betsy's daughter Rachel once pointed to an engraving of Adolph Ulrich Wertmuller's 1795 portrait of the nation's first citizen and boasted that it was her own mother who made the very ruffles cascading so prominently down his presidential chest.[23] Grandmother Claypoole's flag story put her in her own parlor with the Father of Our Country; nothing else could compete.

Many families in Revolutionary Philadelphia passed down accounts of their own brushes with greatness—including memories of encounters with Washington. And so the story of the making of the flag might be easily dismissed as the Claypoole family's own republican stargazing. But it is possible, too, that this esteem ran both ways: when Martha Washington's granddaughter, Eleanor Parke Custis Lewis, visited Philadelphia in 1820, she noted among the list of people to see, "Mrs. Claypoole I do not wish omitted or the others as they all called."[24]

This line—to date the only archival evidence of any possible relationship between the president and the flag maker—is a tantalizing point of contact between Ross's life and her legend. Moments like this one permit us to check the fables that lace through popular historical memory against the historical record itself. They also reveal aspects of the craftwoman's life absent from oral tradition. While descendants went to some trouble to set down one particular tale, and in so doing preserved what they misremembered alongside what they had once heard, other stories about their grandmother and her family were omitted altogether—things that they did and said that did not become part of the family tradition but that have been there all along in the documents that preserve our national memory. Looking for Ross in the considerable archival detritus of eighteenth-century Philadelphia, I often recalled the young Betsy Griscom, gazing through a handkerchief at the sky. My vision too is obscured, and it is hard to make sense of the things I see. I have spent years trying to recover the history of women who labored in early America's artisanal crafts, and needle trades in particular, and much of that history—not unlike that of Betsy Ross—is likewise clouded by a haze of myth and nostalgia. As I have written elsewhere, "mythologies surrounding women's work have made it difficult to imagine women as artisans," while "popular imagery surrounding early American crafts has made it difficult to see artisans as female. Longfellow's brawny vision of the village blacksmith, and Copley's elegant portrait of the silversmith Paul Revere, leave little imaginative space for village craftswomen."[25] My fascination with Ross began as an effort to grasp why disseminators of the flag maker's tale preferred to obscure her artisanal skill and training (her work as an upholsterer over some six decades) in favor of vaguer and more stereotypical notions about early American housewifery (the "seamstress" of myth and pageantry). What was it, I wondered, about women making furniture that seemed so hard to reconcile with our historical imagination?

As I delved into that question, I discovered not only that the life Ross led was compelling in its own right, in ways far and above the single episode captured in popular culture, but also that tracking this woman over the course of her life opened a new view onto Revolutionary America. From her vantage point we can sense how very painful the political protests were as they ripped through families and communities, driving some people apart while binding others together. We feel the deprivation that visited Philadelphia during the enemy occupation of the city. We hold our breath alongside Betsy and other women whose husbands were at sea, privateers vulnerable to any number of maritime predations. And we sense the relief, resolve and optimism that suffused the Claypoole household in the early years of the Republic, restored to unity with like-minded Quakers and eager to throw themselves into the building of the new nation in their own way, as reformers devoted to the welfare of enslaved and free blacks as well as the inmates of the city's prison, embracing the commitment to service that formed the foundation of their faith.

Each of her three quick marriages, too—an extraordinary fact itself—opens avenues of insight into how families survived the violence of Revolution and its long aftermath. Her craft skill obviously suggests opportunities and constraints among early American working women, but also how politics and commerce intersected during the resistance movement, how a family's economic assets shaped their household's choices, and how aging women coped with declining fortunes in the early Republic. The daughter of the house carpenter Samuel Griscom, Betsy Griscom was born in the mid-eighteenth century to a comfortable artisanal family that was thriving in one of the largest and most cosmopolitan cities in Britain's colonial empire. By the end of her life, her family's onetime prosperity had been sacrificed to the ravages of war and political upheaval, and the widow Claypoole struggled to keep her own family afloat. Yet through it all she nurtured pride, not bitterness, about the ways these more sweeping events shaped the course of her own life.

There is another story here, too, that bears notice. At its heart, this book celebrates the working men and women who "made" Revolutionary America. In the metaphorical sense of course, it was artisanal families like Betsy Griscom's who in so many ways forged our nation: they embraced the protest movements that converted a temporary breach between Britain and its North American colonies into a permanent rupture, they dismantled their colonial governments and replaced them with states that in time were knitted together as a nation, and they nurtured that fledgling apparatus through the uncertainties of the early Republic. But they built it, too, in a more tangible sense. Early America was, quite literally, made by this family and thousands of families like them. The Griscom men were house carpenters, generation after generation. They raised Philadelphia, the nation's first capital city. Griscom women cut and assembled the gowns that clothed Philadelphia's women, and applied the trimmings that made them stylish; they stitched the stays that gave shape beneath, and cleaned and dyed the fabrics of which they were constructed. Betsy, her sisters and two of her three husbands worked for decades as upholsterers, creating the fashionable interiors that we admire today. Her brother George, a silversmith, also forged Pennsylvania's gentility. Betsy's husband John Claypoole grew up in a tanyard, converting animal hides to leather for everything from the boots the colonists wore to the books they read and the chairs they sat on. When he joined his wife in the upholstery shop, the couple continued to provide the beds on which the city slept. The most spectacular of these works today command fabulous prices on the antique market, but every time someone lay down at the end of a hard day on a comfortable mattress wrought by Betsy's shop, they were just as pleased with their purchase.

This book, then, seeks to understand not (or not merely) the Betsy Ross of patriotic pageantry, but the woman behind the tableaux. There's no doubt whatsoever that Ross was one of Philadelphia's most important flag makers of the Revolution; on the eve of the War of 1812, she would be the primary flag maker contracting with the U.S. Arsenal on the Schuylkill River. But Ross's life merits attention not only because it has something to tell us about the history of the American flag, but because it offers a glimpse into the events of the American Revolution from a point of view that we do not yet have: neither John nor Abigail Adams, nor George or Martha Washington, nor fellow Philadelphians Thomas Paine, Benjamin Franklin or Dolley Payne Madison, but an ordinary woman who went to work as a teenager and labored in the furniture trades for the rest of her life, until she retired in her seventies, the mother of seven and grandmother of thirty-two. While contemporary readers can view the American Revolution through the eyes of everyday New Englanders Deborah Sampson, Martha Ballard and a Boston shoemaker with the unlikely name George Robert Twelves Hughes, Betsy Ross shows us the Revolution at its geographic and political nucleus, the streets of Philadelphia, from the perspective of a woman whose family ties put her a handshake away from the revolt's epicenter, but who nonetheless remained a working daughter, sister, wife, mother, aunt and grandmother before, during and long after the political drama subsided.[26]

When I told people that I was writing the first scholarly biography of Betsy Ross, they usually expressed considerable surprise—surely there's something out there somewhere? Stunningly, no scholarly biography of Ross has ever been published; her legend looms so large that her life itself has been largely overlooked.[27] Of the books that do exist on Ross, the majority, far and away, are children's literature. In part, the void is the result of an almost total absence of papers. Their familial pride notwithstanding, her descendants saw no need to preserve the letters she wrote, the shop accounts she kept, or any other record of her thoughts or actions. A potential cache of papers was lost in the 1880s when an inhabitant of the Arch Street home that today houses the museum found an old satchel filled with papers, some dating back to the early seventeenth century, which were mistaken for trash and burned.[28] Other papers have been similarly lost, misplaced and even stolen through the years. Today, very little remains. A pair of spectacles tells us something about her fading vision, and a silk petticoat hints at her size; descriptions of her startlingly blue eyes and trademark chestnut hair begin to fill in a picture of her appearance.[29] The recollections of her children, grandchildren, nieces and nephews contribute other small facts about her—that she liked her snuff dark, that she was fond of tomatoes—but her interior life is not preserved in journals or letters.[30]

Some small glimpses into her personality do survive. By all accounts, Betsy Ross, at least at the close of her life, and in the eyes of her grandchildren, was a quiet, retiring woman—modest, gentle, generous. Granddaughter Susan

Satterthwaite Newport, though, remembered her also as outspoken and intelligent, and grandson William Canby—who was eleven years old when his grandmother died in 1836—called her "bustling" and "active." In his now-celebrated 1870 talk before the Historical Society of Pennsylvania, Canby observed that she "drove a thriving trade" and was "prudent and industrious," with no time to "spend in the street gaping" or gossiping, and so was "consequently very much respected by her neighbors."[31] She of course could not always have been the aging saint so fondly recalled by a loving family eager to affirm her importance to the nation's birth. Her flaws (we should all be so fortunate) are well and truly cloaked now in the mists of time. Having spent several years on her trail, I have developed my own sense of her character— hunches based on small things said and unsaid rather than assessments based on archival evidence. I suspect she was headstrong, doggedly loyal and practical, perhaps even shrewd. She thought long and hard about matters of faith. I think she liked a good joke, but that her own sense of humor was more subtle. More than anything else, her choices in life also suggest a steely resolve, perhaps a smidge of obstinance. If her confidence ever slipped toward arrogance, if hardworking became demanding, or if the telling of her stories ever set the children's teeth on edge, the record of it is now lost; history can sometimes be forgiving that way.

In the absence of her own letters and diaries, Betsy's world must be reconstructed by gathering tiny shards of evidence from a wide range of disparate places: newspaper advertisements, household receipts, meeting minutes, treasurer's reports, shop accounts and ledgers, probate records, tools and artifacts of her trade, and oral traditions. The bread and butter of genealogists and antiquarians, family histories, too, hold often-unrecognized value for understanding more sweeping narratives. Today, we can map Betsy Ross's world much as her husband the ship captain charted his course at sea, marking points that she and her family also recognized and then, drawing on angles and projection, locating Ross within them as both she and the emerging nation struggled to find their place in a tumultuous world. Our cartography necessarily tracks the Revolutionary leadership of John Ross's uncles John and George Ross and George Read as well as the resistance of uncles Abel James and Giles Knight; the decisions made by Betsy Ross's husbands John Ross, Joseph Ashburn and John Claypoole; and the devotion of daughter Clarissa Wilson and niece Margaret Donaldson Boggs. Indeed, the picture of Betsy Ross would be incomplete without drawing in Betsy's large family. "Aunt Claypoole" was deeply embedded in a large, close-knit family whose lives were all altered by the Revolution and its aftermath: to understand her life, we must grapple with the fortunes of her several sisters and brother, whose joys and losses were every bit Betsy's own. Betsy's own signal resonates most clearly in the records of the Free Quaker meeting and the many receipts and ledger entries from the flag-making work that so long sustained her. Marking all of these points reveals how the men and women of this large family—some politically influential men of commerce, others everyday artisans—responded to their colony's crisis and the ensuing demands and opportunities that accompanied life in the young Republic.

This account of the craftswoman's life neither begins nor ends with the sewing of a single flag. Setting Betsy Ross's full story straight is important not least because the legend is too central in our culture and history for the life to be so egregiously misunderstood. But coming to grips with Betsy Ross also reminds us that the Revolution's success, taken in the broadest terms, hinged not just on eloquent political rhetoric or character displayed in combat, but also on Betsy Ross and thousands of people just like her—women and men who went to work every day and took pride in a job well done.

# PART I

---

# SIX HUNDRED MILES

# NEARER THE SUN

# The Light Within

Elizabeth "Betsy" Griscom's story begins on a New Jersey farm near the Delaware River, on a tract of land along Newton Creek. Five thousand tons of Bethlehem steel shadow the spot today: the house, fields and waterfront that sustained the first American Griscoms have given way to the towering eastern pier of the Walt Whitman Bridge and the deck truss spans that support its approach. But stare hard enough, and it is possible to gaze out from the Pennsylvania shore and imagine the empty banks of the Delaware when Betsy's great-grandfather, Andrew Griscom, arrived in the Quaker colony at West Jersey in 1680, a year before William Penn founded the City of Brotherly Love.[1] It was not long before Griscom felt Philadelphia's gravitational pull; by the time Betsy Griscom was born seven decades later, four generations of Griscoms had made their lives and livelihoods in the city and its environs. Understanding Andrew Griscom's roots in the city establishes Betsy's own, and not just because, over a century later, she would come to live in a house he built. As he laid the foundation for a new colony, he created the tangible world into which his great-granddaughter would enter, while also setting the family on the artisanal course that she too would travel. Her story, then, rightfully begins with Andrew's, in the migration of thousands of Protestant dissenters seeking relief, opportunity and adventure in the New World.

Andrew Griscom's exact origins are clouded in family memory that was already fading by the time his great-grandchildren tried to recall them in the nineteenth century. They weren't altogether sure where Andrew had lived before making the decision to migrate. Betsy's sister Sarah had always told her daughter that the Griscom family came from Wales, and cousin Deborah Griscom Stewart thought so, too. Another cousin agreed that it was Wales—or was it Scotland?—while yet another thought it was England.[2] Apparently by the time Betsy's generation reached adulthood, the memory of the family's Old World origins was already becoming foggy, indistinct.

If he cannot be grounded in space, he can be placed only slightly more closely in time. Andrew Griscom's life began about 1650, just around the time Charles I was beheaded in the Puritan ascendancy that accompanied England's civil war. His childhood unfolded during Oliver Cromwell's Protectorate, and as an adult he watched as Charles II regained the throne, unleashing the excesses of Restoration England. The appearance and growing availability of the first English-language Bible around the turn of the seventeenth century—a watershed development in European history—had prompted unprecedented theological innovation.[3] Griscom felt drawn to one group of religious, political and social dissenters whose vigorous critique of the Church of England was transforming lives across Europe. These religious radicals wanted to return Christianity to its most primitive origins. Among the most influential was George Fox, who left his home in Leicestershire at the age of nineteen to pursue a spiritual quest. Finding little inspiration among his country's religious leaders, the by-then twenty-three-year-old seeker became increasingly disillusioned. At last, however, he heard a mystical voice speaking to him, saying, "There is one, even Christ Jesus, who can speak to thy condition." Fox came to believe that God's spirit is present within everyone, that each person has an intrinsic capacity to apprehend God's word and to cultivate and share opinions on spiritual matters. The principle was shocking in an age that had long located spiritual authority elsewhere—in the clergy, according to the Church of England, or the Bible, according to the adherents of the Puritan effort to reform the Church. What Fox and his followers proposed would prove anathema to both.

Fox developed a theology grounded in the presence of Inward Light, that is, in the direct access between laity and deity. "It is not enough," wrote one adherent, "to hear of Christ, or read of Christ, but this is the thing—to feel him my root, my life, my foundation."[4] That core principle led naturally to other beliefs, including a radical commitment to equality (for the light of God's presence glimmered within all); a disdain for ceremonies, rituals or other "empty forms" that gestured toward artificial hierarchies; and a belief in human potential. Adherents to the emerging faith refused to pay tithes to the state Church. They would not take oaths in court, and they rejected social customs that implied deference to superiors. Discarding the extraneous trappings of religious practice, Fox and his followers worshipped largely in silence; people spoke only when moved by the Holy Spirit. They refused to engage in combat during wartime or in any way to support state-sanctioned violence. The belief that there is "that of God" within all also gave rise to an intense concern for the disadvantaged, including (in time) slaves, prisoners and residents of asylums, prompting Friends to agitate for social change in ways that their neighbors sometimes found agitating indeed. Because the clutter of the material world could distract them from attending to the light within, they embraced simplicity in all things, eschewing holidays, theater, wigs, jewelry and other types of ornamentation. They disapproved of alcohol and other forms of high living. In speech, too, they strove for simplicity of expression and preferred the biblical cadence of *thee* and *thou* to the common English usage of their day.

As "Friends of Truth" (from John 15:15), these dissenters came to consider themselves as the Society of Friends. Critics, however, had another term for them: Quakers. Given the quiet nature of their worship, the term seems a misnomer. The term was allegedly coined after an incident in which Fox was hauled into court and had the temerity to suggest that the judge "tremble at the word of the Lord." The judge sarcastically referred to Fox as a "quaker," and the term stuck, even to today. He was not alone in his derision; adherents, in rejecting the authority of both the Church of England as well as the Puritan critics who had gained control of the government in the decades around midcentury, threatened the social order, while many countrymen simply found their in-your-face piety abrasive, taking offense at men and women who seemed to think themselves, literally, holier than thou.

Reaction to the emerging faith was not limited to mere contempt. During the second half of the seventeenth century, thousands of Friends were jailed for their beliefs. Hundreds died. Many of Fox's followers, Andrew Griscom among them, began leaving Britain to escape persecution; that the New World offered unprecedented opportunity in more temporal concerns as well was the carrot that came with the stick.

By the time Andrew Griscom emigrated about 1680, he was an able and experienced carpenter, motivated by faith and fortune to try his luck in North America.[5] In 1675, the first shipload of Quakers sailed up the Delaware—a river as broad as the Thames at Woolwych, colonists noted with satisfaction— and came ashore in West Jersey.[6] Over the course of the next five years, the *Griffen*, the *Kent*, the *Willing Mind*, the *Martha*, the *Mary* and the *Shield* and other English vessels made their way from British ports to Jersey shores, bringing some fourteen hundred migrants in just five years' time.[7] From one of those ships stepped Andrew Griscom, who purchased land in the West Jersey colony, perhaps fifty to a hundred acres of it, north of Newton Creek around present-day Camden.[8]

About thirty when he made this move, Griscom was a man of conviction, confidence, optimism and ambition. By 1681, the West Jersey colony was reporting (in necessarily upbeat literature intended to impress readers back home) flourishing herds of cattle and hogs, crops "considerably greater" than England's (from which colonists obtained good bread, beer and ale) and "plentiful" natural provision of fish, fowl and fruit. Flax, hemp and wool were already being converted to cloth and then clothing, and animal hides to leather for shoes and hats. The soil was better, the winter shorter and the trees more varied and abundant. The latter was most important to artisans like Andrew Griscom, who were already converting the native oak, chestnut, cedar, walnut and mulberry trees to furniture, barrels, fences and houses. Structures rose across the settlements, some of brick, some of wood, that were "plaister'd and ceil'd" just as in England.[9] Timber by timber, colonists recreated in West Jersey the English towns they had left behind.

When William Penn—among the most influential Englishmen to embrace the community of Friends—launched his own venture, Pennsylvania, on the opposite bank of the Delaware River, the Friends' fortunes expanded once again, and so too did Andrew Griscom's. Penn's father, Sir William, had been a celebrated admiral, and in 1681 King Charles II gave the younger Penn, out of "regard to the memorie and merits of his late father" (and to discharge a large debt due the Penn family) a huge tract of land in North America, honoring the admiral by naming it Pennsylvania, or Penn's Woods. Penn also persuaded his friend the Duke of York (about to become King James II) to grant him title to the three counties of Delaware in order to secure access to the sea. Fox's followers, anxious to practice their faith in peace, finally had a refuge. Religious tolerance would prove the colony's most cherished achievement. In promotional tracts that circulated across Europe, Penn reminded readers that his new colony—which lay "six hundred miles nearer the Sun" than dreary old England—would need not just merchants, mariners and farmers to succeed, but also men of the "laborious handicrafts," especially carpenters, masons, sawyers, hewers, joiners and other building and timber tradesmen.[10]

The house carpenter Andrew Griscom knew an opportunity when he saw one: when Penn began offering land in his large grant across the Delaware River with plans to build a city there, Griscom acquired close to five hundred acres, which also entitled him to a town lot on what would become South Second Street.[11] At first, Penn's agent Thomas Holme assigned lots by lottery, but Penn eventually took over this task and brought a decidedly different approach to the matter. Penn cherished commitment over chance. In determining the all-important question of who would get which lots in his new city—assignments that would shape the fortunes of families for generations—he weighed a number of factors, including the assets (tangible and intangible) a person brought to the colonization effort, the size of the investment they chose to make, the quality of life they had given up in England to migrate, and how fast they were likely to improve any property they acquired.[12] Men who bought ten thousand acres would receive 204 feet of choice river frontage on the city's two waterfronts, the Delaware and the Schuylkill, as well as four interior lots, each 102 feet in breadth and the depth of a full city block. Five thousand acres secured a riverfront property half that size and a city lot on High Street; a thousand acres netted a waterfront lot running twenty feet for every thousand acres purchased, and a High Street lot calculated the same way. In September 1682, Griscom bought a tract just a sliver shy of five hundred acres, so he, alongside other artisans like fellow carpenter John Parsons, the brazier William Smith and the linen draper John Moon, received a comparatively modest lot on Second Street, some 51 by 300 feet—Penn's logic apparently being that tradesmen like these would add depth, figuratively and literally, to his project as their craft skills accelerated Philadelphia's development into a comfortable colonial city.[13]

Carpentry would prove an especially useful and lucrative occupation in a bubbling new settlement.[14] In those first five years of Andrew Griscom's life as a colonist, close to ninety ships disembarked some eight thousand immigrants on the banks of England's colonies in North America's Mid-Atlantic—a "population buildup unmatched in the annals of English colonization," according to the historian Gary Nash.[15] Fifty ships sailed in 1682–83 alone.[16] William Penn cautioned those thousands of migrants to "look for a Winter before the Summer comes," but summer came soon enough. Penn's city rose quickly and comfortably, thanks in part to the sweat of Andrew Griscom's determined brow.[17]

Griscom's skills were indispensable. In the earliest years of the settlement, he built dozens of timber houses for English families eager to move from the makeshift caves along the Delaware River that sheltered rich and poor alike in the province's earliest years. The first houses were only slightly more elaborate affairs: Griscom and other builders erected post-and-hole houses as well as small, sixteen-foot-square, one-room cottages.[18] The colony's leaders carefully managed the natural resources being so quickly harvested throughout the countryside. On one occasion, for instance, Andrew Griscom petitioned on "Behalf of John Murray" to be allowed two additional trees "to help finish the said Murray's house."[19] By February 1684, about 150 such houses were up in and around Penn's fledgling city, all of them wooden.[20]

But Penn and his fellow colonists had another vision for Philadelphia, one shaped in large part by the disastrous fire that had consumed London in 1666. More than thirteen thousand houses and almost ninety churches had been reduced to ashes; close to four hundred acres—fully 80 percent of the city—lay in ruin. London authorities responded quickly with measures that favored brick construction over timber. When Robert Turner hired builders for his new brick house in Philadelphia, he had the London Rebuilding Act of 1667 in mind.[21]

Claims to the building of the first brick house in Philadelphia are oddly reminiscent of claims to making the nation's first flag: there are several, and just enough evidence to support all or none of them. Most histories of early Philadelphia credit the Dublin linen draper (and Penn agent and ally) Robert Turner as the builder of the city's first brick house. Descendants of Andrew Griscom claim that the first three brick houses to rise in Philadelphia were their ancestor's handiwork. Descendants of the brickmason Richard Cantril make a similar claim. But these assertions need not necessarily compete or contradict one another, since clients, carpenters and bricklayers alike—and more than one of each—would have been necessary to erect such a large and impressive house, and everyone involved in such a landmark undertaking would surely have noted that fact to their children and grandchildren. What's surprising is not that there are three competing claims, but that there are not more.[22]

Andrew Griscom had his own Second Street lot surveyed in April 1683, at the start of the year's building season.[23] No description of the house Griscom built for himself survives today, but the building that rose next door to the south was a "large house of double front," with a "great display of dormer windows" and "five or six steps ascent." Twenty-five years later, that dwelling was still fashionable enough that it continued to be sought after; in the early eighteenth century, Philadelphia's Samuel Preston was house hunting on behalf of Jonathan Dickinson and wrote to advise him that he was "most inclined" to this house, which he described as much like Edward Shippen's (another impressive structure), "but larger—a story higher, and neatlier finished, with garden, outhouses, &c.," all down to Dock Creek. "I know it will suit," Preston assured Dickinson, "or none in Philadelphia."[24]

Andrew Griscom was in good company and was fast becoming an influential man in the city's community of builders. Among the grandest homes to rise in the new colony was Penn's own estate, Pennsbury, and though Andrew Griscom was not among the men employed to build the manor house, he was the man engaged to "measure" it—that is, to inspect the carpentry and determine what wages were due his fellow craftsmen.[25] As Penn's home rose, so too did Griscom's prospects.

The number of buildings multiplied quickly in the new city, to the public benefit of the city and to the private benefit of Andrew Griscom. Raising and dismantling scaffolding alone could make a man rich. Timber frames, roofing, doors, windows—there was possibly no better place for a house carpenter in the whole of the British Empire than Philadelphia in the 1680s and '90s. By 1684, Philadelphia boasted "three hundred and fifty-seven Houses," many of them "large, well built, with good Cellars, three stories, and some with balconies."[26] In 1689, Charles Pickering could easily predict that "Philadelphia will flourish," adding that "more good houses" would be built the coming summer "than ever was in one year"; the following season, another observer confirmed that "the people go on building very much," and houses were rising rapidly "on the Front, at least twenty this year."[27] No fewer than six cartmen were employed all day every day simply carrying timber, bricks, stone and lime to and from building sites. By 1698, one observer would exclaim that the "Industrious (nay Indefatigable) inhabitants have built a Nobel and Beautiful City . . . which contains above two thousand Houses, all Inhabited; and most of them Stately, and of Brick, generally three Stories high, after the mode in London."[28]

The pace strains credulity; could Griscom and his fellow builders—indefatigable though they surely were—have erected so many buildings during those first fifteen years of settlement? Perhaps. Certainly Griscom found enough work to generate considerable profit, since his newfound prosperity enabled him to accumulate more than three hundred acres of land in Germantown, as well as some four hundred acres around Poquessing Creek, northeast of Philadelphia.[29] In 1680, Griscom had possessed sufficient assets to buy a toehold in the New World, but in fifteen years' time he had amassed an estate that would have been unthinkable at home.

Griscom benefited from the need for a city's worth of public buildings as well. In 1685, for instance, the Society of Friends hired him to do the timber work, including the floor and roof beams, for the so-called Center meetinghouse, named for its placement at a midpoint between the Delaware and Schuylkill rivers—a structure the optimistic (overly so, it would turn out) Quakers believed would be necessary as the colony expanded westward.[30]

Though he contracted to do the work in April, the 1685 building season came and went without the frame going up, perhaps because Griscom was already in over his head building homes for the steady shiploads of new arrivals. The raising was at last organized in summer 1686, but still, in August, the impatient Friends urged Andrew to "forthwith come to finish the hipping of the roof that workmen may goe on with shingling the same."[31] That same month, Robert Turner reported to William Penn that his colonists were "now laying the foundation of a large, plain Brick house" at the Center site, and "hope to have it soon up, many hearts and hands at Work that will do it."[32] Apparently Andrew's heart and hands finally rallied, as in September, enough was done that two fellow carpenters came out to measure the work, so that Andrew could be paid.[33] When finished, the Center meetinghouse together with the Bank meetinghouse that rose about the same time would be the two largest religious structures yet built in the Delaware River valley or Maryland.[34]

Perhaps he fell behind on the meetinghouse because he was engaged in institution building elsewhere, this time at the behest of the colony's government; that same year, the Court of the Quarter Sessions addressed the subject of building a prison. The court reported that they "have treated with workmen about the many qualities and charges of a prison, and have advised with Andrew Griscomb [sic], carpenter, and William Hudson, bricklayer, about the form and dimensions." Griscom proposed a "house twenty feet long and fourteen feet wide in the clear, two stories high—the upper seven feet, and the under six and a half feet, of which four feet under ground, with all convenient lights and doors, and casements—strong and substantial, with good brick, lime, sand and stone, as also floors and roofs very substantial; a partition of brick in the middle through the house, so that there will be four rooms, four chimneys, and the cock-loft, which will serve for a prison; and the gaoler may well live in any part of it, if need be." The whole could be built, the tradesmen judged, for £140, including the wages due to the workmen.[35]

Whatever comfort Griscom found in the spiritual community of Friends was matched no doubt by the contentment conferred by financial success. But he did not do it alone. A few years after his arrival in the colonies, Andrew married Sarah Dole, a young Quaker who had emigrated some years earlier as an indentured servant. She, like many migrants, had traded future earnings against the price of passage. The cost of emigration could run to five pounds sterling (children under twelve traveled for fifty shillings, and "sucking children" sailed free of charge); unable to meet the expense, Sarah entered into a contract in which she pledged, in exchange for the cost of her passage, to work for four years as a servant.[36] Upon completion of her term of service, she would receive fifty acres of land and would come to acquire another fifty as well—an outcome she too would have found unthinkable in England.[37] In December 1684, John Dole presented a certificate to the Philadelphia Monthly Meeting indicating that the Bristol meeting had found his sister Sarah "clear" to marry. In February 1685, she and Andrew passed their second meeting with the Philadelphia Friends, and soon thereafter they wed.[38]

A glimpse of the lives led by these early couples is given by Elizabeth Hard, who arrived with her husband, William, in October 1683. Elizabeth later described how "all that came wanted a dwelling, and hastened to provide one. As they lovingly helped each other, the women set themselves to work they had not been used to before; for few of our settlers were of the laborious class, and help of that sort was scarce." Elizabeth went so far as to take up the other end of William's saw, and to carry buckets of water to help make the mortar needed to build their chimney. One day, a worn-out William turned to his bone-tired wife and said, "Thou, my dear, had better think of dinner." Elizabeth immediately burst into tears and "walked away weeping as she went, and reflecting on herself for coming here, to be exposed to such hardships, and then not know where to get a dinner, for their provision was all spent." Berating herself for regretting a move that had secured their precious religious freedom, she fell to her knees and prayed for forgiveness. Soon, a cat appeared with a large fine rabbit, which she promptly prepared for dinner. When William returned and heard the tale, he too burst into tears. "And thus," the story concludes, "did our worthy ancestors witness the arm of divine love extended for their support."[39]

Sarah Dole Griscom's tears are unrecorded, but she surely shed plenty in those years. The young couple would have five children, but only their first, Tobias, and a later daughter, Sarah, survived childhood.

The Griscom household also included at least two other women. One was Andrew's mother, Grizell. (*Grizell* bears an unfortunate resemblance to the word *grizzled,* though there's no reason to imagine her as the graying crone the name tends to conjure today.) Now married to the mariner Richard Morris, Grizell had also settled in the colonies and boarded with Andrew and Sarah while Morris was at sea.[40]

The other was an enslaved African, a woman of late middle age or older, one of two hundred slaves who constituted the "first generation of black Philadelphians."[41] She, too, had every reason to shed tears over her unwilling arrival in Penn's colony, the liberty enjoyed by women like Elizabeth Hard and Sarah

Griscom having come at the expense of her own. Given that only about one in fifteen Philadelphia households between 1682 and 1705 owned slaves, it is notable that the Griscoms were among them. The size of the black population in those years is unknown; the first significant influx of slave labor into the city was the shipload of 150 Africans who arrived in December 1684, and by 1693, enough slaves were present that the Provincial Council was looking for ways to keep a lid on their "tumultuous gatherings" every Sunday.[42] Both the age and the sex of the Griscom family's slave are unusual, since most of the city's captive labor force were younger men, bought to help settlers clear land and build houses.[43] How this woman found herself in Pennsylvania, and why she was purchased by the Griscoms, remains among the family's mysteries.

The home the Griscoms built was well appointed, reflecting the wealth that the household together accumulated, and the values of artisans who knew what it meant to make and enjoy beautiful things.[44] Their best room was a comfortable place to entertain guests and to display the trappings of their success. A chest of drawers held the family's linens, while woolens were stored in a trunk on the floor. Four windows lit the room, and each could be darkened with curtains—domestic accoutrements that, as we shall see, conferred privacy while displaying affluence, setting them decidedly apart from their less-fortunate neighbors. Two punch bowls allowed them to dine with style, with various pieces of earthenware and glassware for more common use.

At the end of a long day, Andrew and Sarah retired to a comfortable bed in the room's corner, the bedstead enclosed by curtains, their bodies cradled by a bolster and pillows and warmed by a quilt as well as a bed rug, a pair of blankets and a pair of sheets. Of all the various categories of domestic goods in the seventeenth century, textiles were among the most precious. No object revealed a family's prosperity better than the best bed, which, placed in the best room of the house, reported to all visitors the couple's ability to afford unusual comfort and style. The Griscoms were no exception; in fact, Andrew and Sarah's bed was worth more than the sixteen-acre parcel of land they owned in the Northern Liberties. (If we need any help remembering the tremendous gap that separates then and now, today sixteen acres in Philadelphia's Northern Liberties neighborhood would run into the tens of millions, while even the Westin hotel chain's "Heavenly Bed" will only set you back $3,420, though it would not come with bed curtains.)

In the chamber over the kitchen (a likely place for Grizell Morris to sleep when she was in the house), five joined stools and three chairs sat around an oval table. A bedstead complete with a bed, bolster and two pillows was again surrounded by a set of bed curtains; three blankets, two pairs of sheets, a rug and a coverlet could be drawn up to the chin of the bed's occupant. More linens were stored in a chest of drawers here, while a box atop held the documents important to the family, including Andrew's accounts. Brass andirons at the hearth glittered by the fire, luminosity amplified in a looking glass, a rare amenity acquired not simply to check one's appearance but also to distribute light. In the garret stood another bedstead with a bolster and pillows; though the blankets and sheets here were a little worn, warmth was provided by two rugs and curtains. Perhaps this was a convenient room to house Andrew's servant, Matthias Jewell.[45]

In the kitchen, flexibility reigned. Seven joined stools, six chairs, three tables and a screen allowed Sarah Griscom to configure the workspace any way she liked. Brass and pewter candlesticks provided portable sources of light, and a brass warming pan softened the shock of cold sheets elsewhere in the house. Yet another chest of drawers held still more linens—these being the most serviceable of the household's textiles. Finally, the Griscom buttery stored no fewer than seventeen pewter dishes, four porridge bowls, a close stool pan (a close stool was a chair with a hidden chamber pot—no word where the stool itself sat, but perhaps behind the aforementioned screen), bedpan, some dozen plates, a chamber pot and four quart pots. Five kettles (one copper) and plenty of iron and brass pots and pans stood ready to supply the cook's needs. Lastly, a separate wash house contained frying pans and iron kettles, a gridiron, shovel and tongs. Another small garret here contained the bed where the enslaved woman slept, above Andrew's shop and his tools.

Of some dozen carpenters active in the city while Andrew and Sarah lived there, no one approached them in terms of the total value of their estate.[46] In an age when the typical Philadelphia house sheltered four rooms, and many around five or six, Andrew and Sarah Griscom enjoyed no fewer than nine.[47] By any measure, they were among the most comfortable families in Philadelphia.

Andrew and Sarah had found in Penn's colony a prospect of religious tolerance that was unmatched in England, but faith and fortune remained braided together as tightly in the New World as they had been in the old. Andrew's encounter with both entwined can be glimpsed, if obliquely, in a series of events that scholars have dubbed the Keithian Schism, an event little known today outside the communities of specialists who study colonial Pennsylvania or early American religion but one that had threatened to unravel the young colony. George Keith had come to Pennsylvania early on, in 1685. One of the most educated intellectuals in the colony, he was also among the most volatile.[48] Keith looked around Britain's North American possessions and feared that the Pennsylvania Quakers—without the threat of persecution that in the Old World effectively discouraged all but the most dedicated—would become spiritually flabby. Perhaps the migrants, so focused on observing the Inward Light, now overlooked other sources of insight. Most worrisome, Keith felt they tended not to know scripture particularly well. In an effort to monitor and enforce theological uniformity, Keith wanted to require adherents to sign statements that would articulate the contours of their belief. Differences of opinion emerged, too, over the nature of the body of Christ; Keith insisted that Christ would be physically present at the resurrection, but this notion of "two christs"—one spiritual, one corporeal—was unconvincing to many in the Society of Friends.

These various critiques accelerated in 1690, when Keith articulated his proposals—including a formal profession of faith, the election of elders within each meeting and greater emphasis on the Bible as a guiding text—to the Yearly Meeting of Friends from Pennsylvania and West Jersey. But, in a faith founded on the primacy of the Inward Light, Keith's ideas were unwelcome. The meeting rejected his proposals as "downright popery." In the months that followed, the controversy escalated as the Quaker leadership and Keith tried to outshout one another, and men and women throughout the settlements chose sides. Much of the battle occurred in a series of publications that aired various observations, accusations and dissatisfactions—a breach of the peace that was especially objectionable to the Quaker preference for orderliness and consensus. The 1692 Yearly Meeting formally disowned Keith "for his vile Abuses and ungodly exposing of them in print." Congregations argued and divided. Finally, early in 1693, the battle came to a head at Philadelphia's largest meetinghouse when Keith's supporters snuck in under cover of darkness to build a gallery from which Keith—who had been banned from the building's proper gallery—might speak at the morning services. As the historian Gary Nash tells it: "The next day, as the Quakers filed into the meetinghouse for the weekly devotions, they found themselves caught in the cross fire of two groups of impassioned Friends. Accusations and counter-accusations filled the air as each side struggled to be heard. But the verbal exchanges paled before the physical demonstration that followed. Axes appeared from nowhere as each group sought to destroy the other's gallery. Posts, railings, stairs, seats—all went down before the angry blows of the two opposed camps."[49]

The violence of this scene is shocking enough to picture today; imagine how unnerving this schism was to the Friends, who seemed to be watching the whole colonization project and all of its promise crumble before their very eyes. Andrew Griscom, smack in the middle of it, was one of close to ninety known Philadelphia artisans and shopkeepers who gravitated toward Keith.[50] As a carpenter who supported Keith's reforms, did Andrew Griscom wield a midnight hammer to help build Keith's ad hoc pulpit? Since Griscom had been among the men who built the Center meetinghouse just a few years earlier, it seems possible that he had some hand in raising this one as well. Did he now swing an ax in an effort to "renovate" both the building and the faith it sheltered and nourished?

Griscom's position in the rupture may have been as much political as theological. The camps that emerged in support of and in opposition to Keith mirrored the political camps that had developed around the colonial government. What began as a dispute over the theological underpinnings of the Quaker colony became a vehicle for pursuing more worldly concerns.[51] Many of the men who rallied behind Keith could more accurately be said to have opposed Keith's opponent, Governor Thomas Lloyd, whose administration, many feared, was accumulating too much power. In May 1692, 260 men—Griscom among them—signed a petition, *To the Representatives of the Free Men of This Province of Pennsylvania*, opposing the provincial tax. These same men turned out in the following months to support the governor's adversary George Keith.[52] Lloyd's enemies in the political arena became his critics in the spiritual realm as well. It may also be significant that Griscom had been among the first purchasers of land in the West Jersey colony, since that settlement had embraced a much more radical and encompassing government than Penn preferred for his own colony. Where Penn was more comfortable with a system of government that preserved the authority of the settlement's most privileged members, the West Jersey settlers enjoyed a measurably more democratic structure, including a unicameral legislature. When the crisis erupted in Pennsylvania, Andrew Griscom may well have found the establishment's grip on the colony to be too tight. Whatever his reasons, he found good company in Keith's camp, which tended to attract Philadelphia's master craftsmen and shopkeepers.

In February 1693, Griscom joined a group of Keith's supporters at the annual meeting of Friends in Salem, New Jersey. The men submitted a series of proposals to the meeting that they hoped would speed reconciliation among the factions. They suggested that the judgments against Keith be withdrawn, particularly those of the Philadelphia Monthly Meeting that condemned him for having suggested that the "light within" was insufficient to salvation without "the man Christ Jesus." They proposed that both sides retract and forgive the personal insults that had been hurled back and forth, and urged that Keith's followers who had been acknowledged as leaders before the schism be restored to their positions.[53]

Griscom may also have been among the few Keithians to later alter his position.[54] When the vast majority of Keith's followers left the Quaker faith and became Baptists and Anglicans, Andrew eventually withdrew his support for Keith's reforms.[55] But although he had second thoughts about Keith's agenda, he did not reconcile with the community of Friends. When Andrew Griscom died, he was buried in Philadelphia but listed among those "such as are not Friends."[56] Andrew's willingness to dissent from the more orthodox Friends may have opened a door; decades later, when Betsy Griscom and her sisters, one after the next, began rejecting the tenets of the Quaker faith, they may well have looked to Andrew's apostasy as precedent.

In the years to come, Pennsylvanians found ways to heal the various breaches caused by the rupture. But Andrew would not live to see it; he died in July 1694. Death did not catch him by surprise. "Sick and weak of body" and "considering the certainty of death," Griscom penned a will by which to distribute his considerable estate. In his forty-some years, he had accumulated an impressive amount of property, including two lots on Philadelphia's Second Street (worth £300), some acres "with buildings and improvements thereon" on the border of Philadelphia and Sudsbery (£60), 150 acres in Germantown (£50), 395 acres at Poquessing (£65) and two parcels of 16 and 12 acres in the Northern Liberties (£10 and £10).[57] A man of property in one of the fastest-growing cities of the British Empire, he had come a long way by any measure. In his will, he bequeathed the land in Germantown to his mother, Grizell. His brother-in-law, John Dole, got the city lot. Sarah and the children got most of the goods—including the enslaved African, now a "negro old woman" valued at £20. Interestingly, though the Keithians had been among the earliest Friends to articulate an antislavery position, Andrew Griscom apparently never embraced this among their several reforms. Opposing slavery would remain a task for other Griscoms to tackle.

What happened in the aftermath of Andrew Griscom's death reminds us that complex, blended families are no invention of modern times. Having buried her husband in July, just two months later Sarah buried her mother-in-law, Grizell, too.[58] Though men and women in the late seventeenth and early eighteenth centuries lost spouses to death rather than divorce, remarriage and the amalgamation of stepparents and stepchildren, half brothers and half sisters,

were common features of early American life. Families sprawled across sur-
names are hard to track today but were entirely unremarkable then. Left with
her eight-year-old son Tobias and infant daughter Sarah, the widow Griscom
moved back to New Jersey and became the wife of John Kaighn, another
house carpenter, who had lost his wife about the same time Sarah lost her
husband. Kaighn (whose birth on the Isle of Man may account for some of
the confusion over Griscom's origins there) had a little girl, named Ann, from
his own first marriage.[59] In time, Sarah and John added two boys, John and
Joseph Kaighn, to their blended family. As this generation of siblings married
and raised families of their own in New Jersey, the Griscoms joined a large
and deeply entrenched network of families across the Delaware River from
Philadelphia who would become important resources in times of trial.

Tobias Griscom, Andrew's son and Betsy's grandfather, grew up in New
Jersey's Newton Township, raised by his mother and new stepfather on and
around land that his father had bought upon his arrival.[60] Once grown,
Tobias envisioned the family's future not in Philadelphia but east of the Delaware River; in time he sold the family's remaining property in Philadelphia
and bought land in New Jersey.[61] After the Burlington Friends' meeting granted
Tobias permission to marry Deborah Gabitas in January 1711, the couple
began a family that would come to include four boys: Andrew, Tobias, William and Betsy's father Samuel.

But Tobias and Deborah's marriage would prove even briefer than
Andrew and Sarah's; when Tobias died after just eight years of marriage,
Deborah was left with four sons under the age of ten. The thirty-five-year-old
widow remarried in 1724, to Tobias Holloway. Together Deborah and this
second Tobias raised the four Griscom boys, and also had a daughter together,
whom they named for her mother. Samuel Griscom, just two when his natural father died, would remember Tobias Holloway, not Tobias Griscom, as the
man who shaped his childhood. When in 1730, Deborah, too, died (perhaps from complications following childbirth), Tobias Holloway was left
with a flock of children to care for. He remarried two years later, and Samuel
Griscom learned to accept a stepmother, just as he'd come to accept his stepfather eight years before. His oldest brothers, twenty-one-year-old Andrew and
nineteen-year-old Tobias, were out or all but out of the house by this time, but
seventeen-year-old William and fifteen-year-old Samuel would consider this
household—which included stepsisters Mary, Abigail and Sarah—as the family
of their youth.

If the Griscom family had largely returned to its New Jersey roots, some
still gazed over the Delaware and took note of developments there. In the 1730s,

Samuel's brother Tobias moved across the river into Philadelphia and followed his family's craft, enrolling in the newly formed Carpenters' Company, a tradesmen's organization designed to protect and advance builders' interests in the city. Philadelphia was at the beginning of another building boom, prompted in part by the steady stream of German and Scots-Irish immigrants; the city's population would increase by some 75 percent in a short period. The flood of newcomers was good news for artisans of all sorts, since it meant "full employment for brickmakers, carpenters, masons, bricklayers, painters, plasterers, glaziers, joiners, carters, stonecutters, and laborers—almost everyone associated with the building trades."[62] Aunt Sarah Griscom—already a successful businesswoman in Philadelphia, having moved back to the city of her birth by the 1720s—introduced her nephews around, helping them meet key figures in the local business community, including her neighbor, Benjamin Franklin. The city was booming, and Tobias, like his grandfather before him, knew an opportunity when he saw one: we glimpse the beginning of his Philadelphia enterprise in a simple ledger entry, "Tobias Griskim [sic] for a blank book," after he walked into Deborah and Benjamin Franklin's print shop on a November morning late in 1735 and bought an empty ledger in which he would record his first sales.[63] By the end of the decade, his younger brother Samuel had joined him, too, in both the city and the Carpenters' Company.[64]

It was outstanding timing for the aspiring builders. As young Samuel Griscom walked the city's streets, he could look up and see the buildings his grandfather Andrew had offered its citizens. He would have his own chance to make a mark on that landscape; between 1750 and 1775, as many as three thousand houses rose across Penn's City of Brotherly Love.[65] By the 1740s, Philadelphia surpassed Boston to become the largest port in Britain's North American colonies, and it continued to grow and flourish. Each week, ships sailed in and out, bound for Europe, the West Indies, Asia and other parts of the British Empire; goods and people from around the world outbound and inbound crossed the numerous wharves along the Delaware River. But the city remained small enough that people stayed well acquainted with one another. One resident recalled that, even by the 1750s, he "not only knew every gentleman in town," but "every gentleman's servant and dog" as well.[66]

In July 1736, Tobias joined the ranks of Franklin's Library Company, spending some forty shillings (no small sum) for his share, making him one of just over seventy members that year—good company for an ambitious young builder. That year, the library moved from its home on Pewter Platter Alley (near Sarah Griscom's staymaking shop) to new quarters in William Parsons's house. By 1739, the collection would migrate once more, to the colony's statehouse, where it would remain for more than thirty years.[67] To browse the collection or to borrow a volume, Tobias ascended the stairs to rooms over the offices of the colonial government, enjoying the prestige that came with sharing a library with Pennsylvania's legislators. He surely made good use of titles collected there, which included books like *Architect: by And^w Palladio* and *Everyln's Parallels of Ancient and Modern Architecture*.[68] Buying the share seems like a mark of optimism, a hint at the sort of man Tobias was and the sort of future he envisioned for himself and his younger brother—the lives he thought they'd lead, and the people he thought they'd know. But Samuel, it seems, was less bookish; at least he didn't follow his brother into the library, preferring insights born of experience to those pressed to a page. It would not be the first time that Samuel chose a path that led away from Pennsylvania's statehouse.

# 2

# A Nursery to the Lord

Elizabeth Griscom was born on New Year's Day, 1752. Prior to that time, the official calendar across the Atlantic world—the Julian calendar—had considered March the first month of the year. As of 1752, the Gregorian calendar was adopted, and January became the first month. As her family would later observe with considerable pride, Betsy Griscom "was born on Sunday, January 1, 1752. By this circumstance her birthday became the first day of the first week of the first month of the first year of a new era."[1]

Betsy Griscom's entrance into the world was accompanied by the arrival of another future icon of American history: just as her grateful parents celebrated this new addition to their growing family, Pennsylvanians observed the jubilee of religious tolerance in their settlement by acquiring a large bell for the colony's statehouse. Purchased from London's Whitechapel Bell Foundry and commissioned to celebrate the fiftieth anniversary of the Pennsylvania Charter of Privileges, which guaranteed an extraordinary degree of religious freedom for the early modern Atlantic world, the bell was inscribed with words from Leviticus 25: PROCLAIM LIBERTY THROUGHOUT ALL THE LAND UNTO ALL THE INHABITANTS THEREOF.[2]

Today we give broad meaning to the liberty proclaimed by that bell, but at its inception a very particular liberty was referenced. William Penn's charter had given him free reign to govern as he might, and he had extended extraordinary freedoms to his colonists, including freedom of conscience, as well as a markedly generous access to the vote, extended to all white male taxpayers.

The frame of government, however, was comparatively conservative. Penn created a bicameral legislature in which the members of the upper house, or council, proposed legislation, which the lower house, or assembly, could just veto or amend. The latter body met only when the governor (Penn or his appointee) called it into session. But eventually, in the vicissitudes of colonization, the assembly accrued more and more power. In twenty years' time, it had claimed the authority to initiate legislation and to call its own meetings. By 1701, Penn had been forced to concede these developments in a new charter, termed the Charter of Privileges. "In less than two decades," one historian remarked, "the Pennsylvania Assembly had become the most powerful and independent colonial legislature in America."[3] In 1729, it built the Pennsylvania State House to house the government, and in 1747, it raised a steeple on the building's south side—in fact, family memory holds that the carpenter Samuel Griscom helped raise it. In 1752, as Samuel and Rebecca Griscom welcomed baby Betsy to the family, the statehouse received the two-thousand-pound bell that celebrated the achievements of both the colony and its elected assembly.

But the bell cracked almost immediately—it had to be recast, not once but twice. A superstitious observer might well wonder what the omen meant. Was there reason to doubt that the colony's achievement was secure?

It was in the bustle and swirl of the colonial city that a decade earlier Samuel Griscom had met Rebecca James, the daughter of a Quaker shopkeeper.[4] Her father, George James, had been moving between Philadelphia and its environs for some years when his youngest daughter met and married her husband. Once the indentured servant of a Philadelphia tailor, James completed the terms of his contract in 1715 and put down stakes in Byberry, a village north of the city.[5] Just over a year later he married, the newlyweds living near enough to the county line to fall within the compass of the Quakers' Abington Monthly Meeting.[6] But the place proved painful for George James, who buried his first wife and seven children in the Byberry meeting graveyard. Eventually George decided to give Philadelphia—where his son Joseph was now working as a tailor—another try. He remarried, and in May 1739 requested and received a certificate from the Byberry meeting transferring his family to the care of their Philadelphia counterparts.[7] His daughter Elizabeth would stay behind, but teenagers Rebecca and Abel went to Philadelphia, settling into their new home and exploring the opportunities their new situation offered.

George's Philadelphia shop was a success, its inventory a marvel of colors and textures for young Rebecca and Abel, and a geography lesson as well.[8]

Shelves groaned with fabrics from around the world: lawn and linen from Holland, India cottons, German serges and "foirrest cloth" and a panoply of kearseys, camblets, silks, paduasoys, taffetas, oznabrigs and damasks. Reams of writing paper hinted at letters yet to be written, accounts yet to be opened. Dozens of small looking glasses glittered in the right light, alongside the steadier glow of pewter porringers, kettles, pans, plates, dishes and basins. Knives and forks rattled in boxes and bins alongside buckles and buttons for shoes and sleeves; locks for boxes, chests and cupboards; and hardware of all sorts. The scent of green and Bohea tea filled one corner of the room; in another wafted pepper, cinnamon, nuts and cloves, coffee and cocoa—perfumes of empire that masked the more serviceable smells of sulphur and brimstone that also drifted across the room.[9]

Sulphur and brimstone were indeed in the air, and George James may have sensed something burning, too, in the choices his daughter Rebecca was making since she traded the wooded paths of Byberry for Philadelphia paving stones. When it came time for the James girls to contemplate marriage, Elizabeth had wed in orderly fashion the Bucks County farmer Giles Knight. Because there is no distinction between laity and clergy among Quakers (who believe ministry to be a gift conferred on some of their members, rather than an office to be held), couples married themselves—that is, the union occurred when the couple spoke to each other and pledged their troth. A wedding certificate signed by those present at the exchange affirmed that witnesses saw the couple marry themselves to each other. Given the obvious risks associated with marrying via the mere exchange of words, by the 1730s, the Society of Friends had developed an elaborate system to guide couplings among members, designed to preserve the much cherished tranquility of the Quaker community. The faith's discipline (that is, the body of principles guiding Quaker conduct) required that prospective couples first seek permission to court. Should things go well, they must then gain further permission from their parents to begin discussing marriage. Having decided to marry, they must then announce their intent before the larger community. Committees of members were assigned the couple's case—two men to investigate the prospective groom, and two women the bride—and charged with confirming that each was of sound "conduct & conversation," free to marry, possessed the full consent of their parents or guardians, and could demonstrate that no other obvious obstacle prevented the marriage.

If the couple passed these various tests, the committees also attended the wedding, to ensure that it, too, was a happy but orderly occasion. At the marriage ceremony, all who gathered signed the large marriage certificate, a document that gave physical and enduring form to the Quaker view of marriage as one relationship firmly embedded in the larger community of Friends. "Passing the meeting" this way ensured the present (in time as well as space) control over the future; as Friends monitored the unions formed by their children, they strove to guarantee their faith's security, stability and prosperity. The procedures also had the effect, whether intended or not, of ensuring that no couple could rush into marriage to conceal an unsanctioned pregnancy, since haste was incompatible with the deliberative nature of the proceedings.[10]

Elizabeth James and her beau, Giles, conformed altogether to the Friends' discipline, just as her father had before her—not once, but twice, for as it happens, the Friends present at the February 24, 1738, Abington Monthly Meeting that granted Elizabth and Giles permission to wed also passed George James, who had chosen Sarah Townshend as his new bride and stepmother to his children. The meeting further notes that "whereas Giles Knight & Elizabeth James, having declared their intentions of Marriage with each other before two monthly meetings, enquiry being made by persons app'd & found clear of all others, Nothing appearing to obstruct, they are at liberty to consummate their marriage."[11]

Rebecca James proved less cooperative. In February 1741, she and Samuel Griscom eloped to New Jersey and married, without the permission of their parents and by a "hireling priest" (egregious both because the "priest" or minister was of a different faith and because an official presided at all).[12] For their actions, the love-struck pair was censured by the Society of Friends for "Marrying contrary to Discipline."[13] But there was more to it than a simple breach of order. Family history has it that Samuel and Rebecca's mutual attraction was "so strong that their public displays of affection attracted comments of disapproval from the ladies of the Society of Friends."[14] It is tempting to imagine the smitten young couple holding hands and exchanging forbidden kisses when they thought no one was looking. But it was not merely the ardor of their courtship that drew critical attention; surviving records of the Society of Friends note that, in August 1742, "Samuel and Rebecca Griscom brought in a paper condemning their unchaste intimacy before Marriage which was read & sent to the Women Friends which this meeting directs to be publicly read at the close of one of our First day morning meetings betwixt this and the next meeting."[15] The reference to an "unchaste intimacy" (documents also refer to their "joynt acknowledgment" of having taken "disreputable freedoms") indicates sexual activity.[16] Perhaps the young couple was no longer in a position to wait for the Society's long prenuptial process. To be sure, there's no tangible evidence that Rebecca was pregnant (no child is recorded as having been born a few short months later), though it seems possible that the couple rushed to marry believing that to be the case. A significant gap elapsed between the error and the reprimand: eighteen months passed between the couple's February 1741 elopement to New Jersey and the September 1742 notice of their transgression, time that the couple spent—in part because of the death of Samuel's stepfather—on the family farm in New Jersey. In any event, in April 1743 their first known child was born on the Newton farm. They named their daughter Deborah, in honor of Samuel's mother.

The "joynt acknowledgment" indicates that Samuel and Rebecca did not wish to remain at odds with their community of faith. Whatever the reasons behind the elopement, the apology for it, too, was part of the Quaker discipline; errant Friends could reestablish unity with the Society by asserting their heartfelt regret before the other members. If the meeting found their remorse to be convincing, they would restore them to full membership. Samuel and Rebecca satisfied the Friends that they understood the error of their ways, regretted it and aimed to do better in the future.

Elizabeth James affirmed Quaker discipline in all the usual ways; Rebecca more notably did not. Brother Abel conformed as well, and, more spectacularly, also leaped up the community's social hierarchy when he married the daughter of one of the faith's most revered lights, Thomas Chalkley. Chalkley was one of those "public friends" to whom the gift of ministry had been given; he was also a ship captain and merchant. Errands on behalf of his faith easily combined with those on behalf of his fortune. He toured all of Britain's colonies on the North American mainland and traveled extensively throughout the Caribbean, as well as to Ireland and Scotland, Holland and Germany. By his own account, he found it "not easy to be idle," and felt constantly called to proselytize.[17] It was a dangerous life. On one trip, as his ship approached the coast of Barbados, a privateer appeared on the horizon. The mariners quickly began cursing the pacifist Quakers aboard ship, since at their insistence the vessel carried no guns. The earnest minister tried to assuage the men by pointing out that it was for their very safety that the Friends steered clear of weapons; he'd rather lose the whole ship than the life of a single sailor. Unpersuaded, the sailors replied that they'd rather lose the ship, and their lives, than be taken to France. Chalkley pressed on: but wouldn't they rather go to France than Hell? (Death, Hell and France seem to have been the only options considered, France landing somewhere in the middle.) Luckily, the question remained unresolved; when both ships got within gunshot of the port, the privateer abandoned chase.[18]

Between voyages, Chalkley kept a home in Philadelphia, and later Frank-ford, a mile north of the city. It was easy for young Abel James to make the family's acquaintance, since Chalkley visited Byberry in the course of his ministrations and Byberry people regularly stopped in at the Chalkley home when traveling to and from Philadelphia. After Thomas Chalkley died on the Caribbean island of Tortola in 1741, Abel was asked (even before he wed Chalkley's daughter) to edit Chalkley's journals for publication; Chalkley's text, which first appeared in 1749, sold briskly.[19] Abel's respect—even admiration—for his father-in-law, even though he had died six years before the wedding, was palpable. The 1747 wedding of Abel James and Rebecca Chalkley, attended by both of his sisters and their spouses, conformed closely to Quaker disci-pline (not least because her father's will stipulated that any deviation would alienate her from her considerable bequest).[20] Abel's first son was named Chalkley; his last, Thomas Chalkley. The family's country home in Frankford was called Chalkley Hall. Through the years no fewer than three of James's trading ships would be christened *Chalkley*. Abel James was acutely aware of how his marriage, and the wealth and position it conferred, had altered his life course. No one could say he was not grateful.[21]

These three James family weddings would prove decisive for Betsy's fam-ily. Elizabeth and Giles had married by the rules; Rebecca and Samuel had not. And Abel had formed a union with one of the most influential families in the international Quaker community in a wedding witnessed by an impressive collection of Philadelphians, including Powells, Logans and Pem-bertons.[22] Abel would remain closer to his sister Elizabeth's family, the Knights, than he ever was to Rebecca's relatives, the Griscoms.[23] Years later, in the middle of the nineteenth century, family genealogist Anna Griscom would describe one of her Griscom ancestors as tall, dark and irritable—the final trait she believed to be an unfortunate hereditary attribute that she hoped would fall away in time.[24] It is certainly tempting to ascribe these qualities to Samuel Griscom, who did not join his brother in the Library Company, did not accept offices within his community of faith and did not do so many other things that leave the usual traces in the documentary record. Whatever the reason, when we look at the James family from the perspective of its most successful member, Samuel Griscom seems an odd man out.

As the first half of the eighteenth century gave way to the second, Betsy's mother, Rebecca, her aunt Elizabeth and her uncle Abel each chose paths that would shape their children's lives in the tumultuous years ahead. Elizabeth and Giles settled on some two hundred acres on Poquessing Creek in Bensa-lem Township—about seventeen miles northwest of the James family home

in Philadelphia—where in time Giles would become one of the most prosperous and influential men in his community.[25] Giles's grandfather had himself been a respected figure in the early colony, having immigrated in 1682
with Penn; he would serve a number of terms in the early colonial assemblies.
His son Joseph was decidedly less ambitious. He preferred instead to work
little and live frugally. When a neighbor once asked Joseph how to make
money, he was famously remembered to have replied, "Thou knowest how to
make it better than I do, but thou dost not know how to keep it."[26] Giles
appears to have known how to do both. The Knights ran a large farm in Bucks
County, and Giles augmented their income by lending money at interest.
Described in one source as "prosperous but not rich," the family was certainly more than comfortable; to take just one measure, Giles Knight's 1742
tax assessment ranked in the eighty-second percentile of township taxpayers;
some years that ranking reached as high as the ninety-fourth percentile. By the
time Joseph, the first of their ten children, arrived, Elizabeth and Giles had
aquired both slaves and indentured servants.

Giles Knight took after his grandfather in other ways, too, and made good
use of his extensive library on government. Soon after his marriage he began
to accept posts as a public servant. He served as Bensalem Township constable
in 1742, an overseer of the poor in 1743, and, the following year, as supervisor
of the highways. In 1747, he was elected county tax assessor, the first of seven
consecutive terms. In 1754, he added county commissioner to his stable of
offices and titles. In 1760, he was elected to represent Bucks County in the
Pennsylvania Assembly. He soon found himself appointed to committees
charged with tackling a range of issues in the colonial government, from the
relief of Pennsylvania's poor to the structure of the provincial tax assessment.
When, in the middle of the French and Indian War, the assembly refused (by
a narrow vote) to raise additional troops to assist General Jeffery Amherst in
the defense of the colonies, Knight was among those charged with drafting a
message to the governor explaining why. Years later, Byberry neighbors would
still remember the "venerable patriarch" in his suits of velvet and broadcloth,
silver ornaments from head to toe, from the buttons on his jacket to the buckles of his shoes. Atop his head sat a full-bottom wig under a "first-rate beaver
hat, turned up behind and on each side before." Neighbors found him austere
and commanding. Giles Knight, it would be said, possessed a "dignity of manner and deportment" that "induced an apprehension and belief" that he "was
one of the great men of his day and his generation."[27]

If Giles Knight was the picture of gravity and decorum, Abel James struck
people as a man of action: "He would buy any thing—he would sell any

thing—he would transact any thing, rather than have nothing to do."[28] If someone mentioned that he was going on a trip to the country, people said, Abel James would sell him a horse for the road. You wouldn't have known it to see him at his desk or to meet him on the street—his pace never seemed particularly hurried. (However, like other "men of genius," he did sometimes seem a little distracted. In "paroxysms" of absence of mind, he had a tendency to abandon conversations midsentence, having already moved on in his mind to other things.) Like the young Benjamin Franklin, whose autobiography James would be among the first to read and admire, he was always looking for opportunity, for the next Big Idea. "These qualities explain his ascent to the summit of Philadelphia's commercial community," an acquaintance would later muse, and would prove his undoing as well.[29]

How the gap between the marriages of Elizabeth and Abel and that of Rebecca affected Betsy Griscom can never be known for sure, but there's no doubt that Abel James remained close to his sister Elizabeth and her husband, Giles, throughout his life, both families becoming politically influential and financially successful, while Rebecca and Samuel seem to have drifted away from their more prosperous siblings and their more important friends. Romance and religion would prove important forces in the life of young Betsy, too, but choices made a generation earlier would set her course in ways she would see only in hindsight, if at all.

In the early 1750s, when Betsy was born, her family was still rooted on the Jersey side of the Delaware River. Andrew Griscom's widow, Sarah, had left Philadelphia, and by midcentury her grandson Samuel owned an old farmhouse—its timbers raised by the Irishmen who settled the land seventy years earlier—along the banks of Newton Creek about a half mile from the Delaware River.[30] It was likely that home to which the newlyweds retreated after their unsanctioned wedding, and under that well-weathered roof that Betsy was born on the first New Year's Day of modern record a decade later. The winter of 1752 was so memorably cold in and around Philadelphia that people were still writing about it almost a century later; cattle and deer froze where they stood, and provisions were so scarce that families resorted to these animals' ice-covered carcasses for food. As late as April, fully three feet of snow still lay on the ground.[31] The baby's safe arrival amid such punishing weather surely brought joy and relief to the Griscom family. Rebecca named her newest daughter Elizabeth after her sister, Elizabeth Knight. Betsy already had five older sisters, from nine-year-old Deborah to fourteen-month-old

Mary. Four more brothers and five more sisters would follow. Though not all of Rebecca's children survived infancy, there would be eighteen in all.

While his brothers-in-law plunged into public affairs, Samuel Griscom appears to have concentrated his energies on work. Samuel may simply have been too busy advancing Philadelphia's midcentury building boom to think much about politics; in the 1750s, more than two thousand houses ("most of them brick, and well built") housed a city of thirteen thousand.[32] Before 1770, about two hundred houses rose every year; in particularly prosperous years, the number might double. (As one man would write in 1774, "There have been *only* four hundred and seventy-three houses built in Philadelphia this year.")[33] Griscom's investment in Philadelphia had begun as early as 1743, when he acquired property on the east side of Second Street. Four years later, he bought land in Northern Liberties at Shackamaxon Street and the Bristol Pike.[34] But it seems to be in the early 1750s, right around the time of Betsy's birth, when Samuel began investing seriously in city lots. By 1754, he and Rebecca appear to have been living in rented space near the city's waterfront, on Coomb's Alley (later called Cuthbert Street), which ran between Market and Arch streets from Front to Second. He also rented a lot on the north side of Cox's Alley between Front and Second, and around the same time bought a lot on the west side of Second between Mulberry (eventually known as Arch) and Sassafras (Race).[35] Ready to commit to a career in the city, he sold the Newton Township farm and joined his brother Tobias in the Carpenters' Company.[36] Soon the Griscoms could be found on Front Street, near the wharves that daily received lumber from New Jersey forests.[37]

Samuel was doing better than average among his neighbors, and a good bit better than his competitors around town. According to a 1756 list of "Taxables" in Philadelphia, the median tax bill in the High Street Ward, where the Griscoms lived, was £20, when Samuel was assessed at £24. Of more than fifty carpenters throughout the city that year, the median tax bill was just £16.[38] In time, he would build a large, two-story carpenter's shop behind his house, and a "good Smith-shop, well accustomed" that fronted on Cherry Street.[39] Clearly there was every reason for the Griscom home to ring with optimism.

When it came time for Samuel to build a permanent home for his growing family, he chose a lot on the north side of Arch Street between Third and Fourth streets, just west of the Second Presbyterian Church and across from the Quaker burying ground. By 1764, the house carpenter had raised his own home there, an impressive affair. Like other Philadelphia row houses of its day, the Griscoms' substantial house fronted sixteen feet along the street but stretched more than thirty feet deep and was three stories high. Its eleven rooms were warmed by nine fireplaces. A piazza (the broad porch that is a trademark feature of Philadelphia architecture) provided a place to enjoy a summer's breeze on a steamy day, and a separate kitchen with a chamber above afforded extra lodging.[40] The family needed the space for the household by now included the ever-growing number of Griscom children and perhaps Samuel's half sister Deborah Holloway and his seventy-one-year-old aunt Sarah, too.

By the time Betsy was twelve, and her father in the midst of moving the family to these larger and more permanent quarters, her parents had added another daughter, Hannah, to the fold, but also welcomed and buried three-year-old Samuel, three-year-old Martha and a second Samuel who also died just around his third birthday. Baby Ann lived just seventeen months. Particularly crushing must have been the loss of the twins, Joseph and Abigail, who were also three—like both Martha and Samuel, almost to the day—when they both died in the 1762 smallpox epidemic that ravaged the city. The whole family likely watched nervously as toddler George approached his third birthday just as they were preparing to move, and little Rachel took her first steps as she hurtled toward two.

As it happened, while Samuel's family blossomed and flourished, life had not worked out quite as planned for Betsy's uncle, Samuel's brother Tobias. Active alongside Samuel in the Carpenters' Company, Tobias had married Grace Rakestraw, the sister of a fellow craftsman. The optimism glimpsed in his Library Company membership was eclipsed by years of disappointment. He and Grace buried two infant sons in three years' time. Though their daughter, Rebecca, arrived in 1745 and seemed healthy and strong, something irreversible had happened to the grieving craftsman, who began to withdraw from his family, his business and Philadelphia society. In 1748, he sold his twelve-year-old share in the Philadelphia library to Benjamin Loxley, a fellow carpenter whose career was then on the rise.[41] Tobias's decision might have reflected not just a lapsed enthusiasm for the association but also his financial difficulties, since, as membership in the Library Company expanded, the value of its shares rose. By 1741, five years after Tobias bought in, shares that were once worth forty shillings apiece were valued at £6.10—an increase of 300 percent. (Franklin was quick to point out that this was nothing compared to the £500 in books the share provided access to, "whereby knowledge in this city render'd more cheap and easy to be come at, to the great Pleasure and Advantage of the Studious Part of the Inhabitants.")[42] The following year, the Quaker community censured Tobias for having "conducted himself disrespectably in his conversation and management of affairs," and, despite warnings, for abandoning his wife and family "in a clandestine manner being involved in debt." A month later, having appointed two Friends to look into the situation, the meeting determined that Tobias had for some time "accustomed himself to keep loose and idle company," and neglected his business. As a result, he had "absconded privately from his family to the prejudice of his creditors." Tobias had gone to Duck Creek, near Smyrna, Delaware. The Friends, anxious to distance themselves from any ill will Griscom was generating, chose to disown him until he reformed and made amends. But he never did; Grace died alone in Philadelphia in 1750, and Tobias in Duck Creek in 1751.[43]

The most important effect of these events for little Betsy was that six-year-old Rebecca came to live with her aunt and uncle, and so was living there the year she was born. In fact, Betsy never knew a period before Rebecca—a cousin who was more like a sister—was part of her family. By the time the last of the trunks were unpacked in the new house, the Griscom children in it numbered nine.

In time, young Betsy Griscom began venturing beyond her parents' home. In most Quaker families, children started to attend meeting for worship and school somewhere around the age of six (perhaps as early as four, or as late as eight or ten). In the late 1750s, probably about 1758, Betsy began going to school. Family memory places her in Rebecca Jones's school for Quaker children (on Drinker's Alley near her home), and later the Friends Public School on South Fourth Street below Chestnut.[44] No one yet knew it, but the training she would receive in her Quaker school would lay the foundation for the iconic status she would one day achieve.

When little Betsy Griscom took the hand of an older sister and headed off to her first day of school, Rebecca Jones was not yet the celebrity that she would become in Quaker circles of the late eighteenth century, but rather a young woman who had just buried her mother, the teacher Mary Porter Jones, and had taken over the school for lack of any other real option.[45] She was not, as people say, a "birthright" Quaker. Her mother had been born in another of Britain's colonial outposts—Barbados—and migrated to Philadelphia after her husband was lost at sea. Raised in the the Anglican Church, Rebecca was drawn to the Friends' faith as a girl. Mary had sent her daughter for a time to the school of the prominent Quaker Anthony Benezet, and later Rebecca began accompanying Friends to worship in order to be with her playmates.[46] A turning point came when the Quaker ministers Catharine Peyton and Mary Piesley visited from England and Ireland. Rebecca was sixteen. "I was at divers meetings in this city with the aforesaid Friends," she would later write, "and heard divers testimonies . . . with which I was much pleased," but it wasn't until she heard Peyton "speak so pertinently to [her] situation, in showing the consequences of trifling with Divine conviction, and proclaiming God's love through Christ to all returning sinners, that [she] cried out in the bitterness of [her] heart, 'Lord, what will thou have me to do be saved?'"

Rebecca slipped Peyton a note. Peyton wanted to reply but didn't know who had sent the message. Someone suggested that it may have come from "that wild Becky Jones, who has got to coming to meeting and sets by black Rose." (Rose, it seems, was a "goodly colored woman who sat on the bench near the door," and Rebecca Jones, "in her humility," chose the vacant seat beside her when she attended Quaker meetings.) Peyton's reply had to be sent in secret; Mary Jones, the Friends well knew, disapproved vehemently of her daughter's drift toward the Quaker faith. Once, when Rebecca was coming downstairs with her bonnet and cloak on, her mother grabbed hold of her cloak, trying to physically restrain her daughter from attending meeting. Quick-thinking Rebecca "untied the string and walked out, leaving her mother in silent astonishment." So Rebecca's friend Daniel Trotter took Peyton's reply to Rebecca at the "close of school." He chatted amiably with the mother and daughter, and when he saw a chance, passed Peyton's letter to Rebecca on the sly. Rebecca "kept it for two days before she had opportunity to read it in private, and then ripped a seam in her skirt, and concealed the letter in the quilting, as her pockets, drawers &c, were frequently searched."[47]

In time Mary Jones relented and allowed her daughter to join the Society of Friends. Just a year later Mrs. Jones died, leaving Rebecca, now entering her thirties, alone. Now Rebecca was, as she put it, "in a strait": "I had often thought that if it should please Providence to remove my mother, I would think of some other way than keeping school for a livelihood. But [eventually] in waiting to know what was best, I seemed easy to continue in the same way, as being what I was most used to: and a suitable friend offering, made it the easier." The friend was Hannah Cathrall, a "religious, prudent young woman" who joined Jones in the business. "We soon had a large school," she later wrote, "and were blest with a sufficiency to live comfortably."[48]

If Betsy Griscom entered Rebecca Jones's classroom sometime around this time, it was a room alive with the faith that Jones was finally free to pursue with vigor. Quaker education was different from what Jones herself had known. Students were trained to adhere to the distinct values of their faith, even if it meant setting themselves apart from society. Reading, writing, ciphering—all of these were desirable skills, as long as they advanced Quaker values: plainness, harmony, witness.

Betsy entered school during a time when education among Quaker children was changing to better encompass feminine perspectives. The foundational tenets of the Quaker religion, embedded as they were in belief in an Inward Light present in all God's children, necessarily conferred on women a form of equality absent from other faiths. The women's meeting, like the men's, helped transact essential business and administer relief to poor Friends, and women could serve in positions of leadership, too—even preaching during mixed-gender meetings. Women's authority was respected in the home, where they took a vigorous role in parenting, and their skills and perspectives were valued in the commercial realm, too. For these reasons, the education of girls occupied the increasing attention of Quaker elders during the eighteenth century.

Girls of Betsy's mother's era had been unlikely to attend formal school. Rebecca James Griscom appears never to have learned to write; when asked to acknowledge legal documents, she marked them with an $X$.[49] But in the late 1740s, '50s and '60s, after Anthony Benezet and Rebeckah Birchall began taking in students, more and more girls were found sitting at Quaker desks. Sometimes, the instruction they received was the same for members of either sex. For instance, all schoolchildren were asked to master principles like the "rule of three," the basic algebraic equation that allows one to calculate a fourth value if three others are known (for example, if one pound of sugar costs sixpence, how much will three pounds cost?).[50] Math problems given to boys often involved the purchase and sale of quantities of commercial goods (land and tobacco, bricks or lumber), while girls might be asked to puzzle out problems involving domestic goods, and in smaller quantities (measures of butter, linen or sugar). A math book aimed at boys might ask students to calculate the amount of wainscoting needed to finish trimming a room, and girls to determine the yardage needed for curtains. But whatever the nature of the variables, be they pounds of sugar or board feet of lumber, the skills conferred were the same, and prepared Quaker girls alongside Quaker boys to find places in the commercial arena as shopkeepers, mantua makers (dressmakers), printers, tavernkeepers—and upholsterers.

The curriculum at Rebecca Jones's school included reading, writing and basic mathematics, and for some students, needlework as well. Typically, students concentrated on their academic subjects in the mornings, and those taking sewing lessons stayed into the afternoon. But Jones's "firm commitment to 'plainness' precluded instruction in ornamental needlework."[51]

Indeed, a set of "testimonies of Friends against Superfluous Needlework" published in 1766, just about the time Betsy would have been in school, warned against various forms of ornamental stiching. "In thy Youth," one treatise advised Quaker daughters about Betsy's age, "learn to read, and write a little, and sew, and knit, and other Points of good Labour that belongs to a Maid," but do not "tempt vanity" by indulging in colorful, merely decorative work.[52] In order to allay Jones's concerns, Hannah Cathrall "attend[ed] to the sewing department in a separate room" at the Drinker's Alley school.[53] As a girl, Cathrall had attended Mary Jones's school, and along the way, mastered needle skills. Because Rebecca Jones went on to become a celebrated Quaker leader, her own girlhood needlework (completed before she had embraced the Quaker faith) has since become the object of curatorial attention (examples are preserved in Philadelphia's Atwater Kent Museum); less is known about Cathrall's skills, but we know enough about Quaker needlework more generally during this time to have a sense of what young Betsy Griscom learned in her sewing classes, tutorials that would pay off in the years to come.[54]

Young Betsy Griscom took all this in as she went about life alongside her sisters in and around their Arch Street neighborhood. Betsy and her schoolmates cultivated a sense of themselves as fourth-generation Pennsylvanians. They were the inheritors of a religious tradition that, transplanted in the New World, had flourished remarkably. The inventories of the city's shops were testaments to the success of the British Empire, and they had the great good fortune to live in its largest colonial city. Betsy's family claimed no small place in those achievements. Her aunts and uncles were influential members of the colony's political, religious and commercial leadership, and her father was a successful artisan who had offered his family a home every bit as comfortable as the many he was building around the city—perhaps more so. But with such prosperity came responsibilities and risks. Betsy's elders assumed the "Weighty care" to "train up" the children well, to help Quaker youth to navigate the world's temptations. "Your families ought to be as young nurseries to the Lord," one essayist wrote, and take care to help children choose wisely not only the food that they eat and the clothes that they wear, but also "that which you teach them for the Employment of their Hands."[55] Samuel and Rebecca would take that latter charge seriously. And as fortune would have it, opportunity for their daughter Betsy was about to appear, marked in upholsterer's chalk.

# 3

# Pins and Needles

Family legend holds that one day in the mid-1760s, young Betsy Griscom walked from her family's Arch Street home to the workshop of the Philadelphia upholsterer John Webster "to visit her sister." "While there," the story continues, "a piece of difficult work was given to one of the girls who failed in it and Betsy said she could do it, and surprised Mr. Webster by the neatness and beauty of her work. He at once went to her mother's and asked her to let him have Betsy [who] was unwilling at first to let her go. Mr. Webster offered to pay grandmother [Rebecca Griscom] the wages of a woman in the kitchen & give Betsy a thorough knowledge of the business. So her mother yielded."[1]

This anecdote—recalled by Betsy's youngest daughter Rachel, the only one of her children to survive to see grandson William Canby's effort to gather the family testimonials—is meant to preserve the image of an intelligent, quick-witted young Betsy, the needlework prodigy, to foreshadow the heroic contribution her stitchery would later make to the fledgling war effort. But it also offers an intriguing glimpse of artisanal work in colonial Philadelphia. One of Betsy's older sisters—Susannah, Sarah, Rebecca or Mary (Deborah being already out of the house, having married Everard Bolton, the proprietor of a cloth dying and scouring firm)—was already working in Webster's shop when Betsy visited her there, and, since "one of the girls" was struggling with an assignment—someone who was not Betsy's sister—then at least three girls, and perhaps more, were employed by the London-trained upholsterer. The upholsterer is remembered to have approached Rebecca Griscom rather than

Samuel to inquire about the girl's interest in taking a job and learning something of the trade. And the upholsterer was willing to pay the Griscom family a kitchen servant's wages—perhaps some £10–12 a year—in exchange for the novice's labor under his supervision.[2]

The men and women of the Griscom family were deeply steeped in craft tradition. Given the number and variety of artisans who populate the family tree, the question before young Betsy was not whether she would enter a trade, but which one it would be. Griscom men had prospered in the building trades, and Betsy's brother George would in time become a silversmith. Betsy's aunt Sarah had more than thirty years under her belt as one of the city's staymakers, and cousin Rebecca was just embarking on a career as a mantua maker (a maker of women's gowns). Betsy's education had included instruction in needlework; she had already begun to observe properties of color and design, and learned how to make a good firm stitch. Her family and her schooling had helped her develop an eye for the beautiful as well as an appreciation for the practical and the serviceable. Artisans like the Griscoms produced the extraordinary masterworks that we now appreciate in historic houses and museum galleries; they also (and more often) made simple, everyday objects that never gained the notice of collectors, historians or curators, but provided a thousand small comforts to men and women in eighteenth-century America.

Upholsterers were an integral part of that effort. Looking around any room, we today appreciate the comfort afforded by cushions, the privacy conferred by curtains or blinds, or the warmth of a soft throw. If you are reading now with the support of a good pillow, curled up in a well-made chair or resting on a comfortable mattress, with the blinds up to let in the morning sun or the curtains drawn for a more cozy effect, you're enjoying the work that was once (and often is still today) performed by skilled upholsterers. In eighteenth-century Philadelphia, conjuring such artifacts into existence demanded a stunning variety of skills cultivated by an array of artisans on both sides of the Atlantic. When Betsy Griscom first sat down to learn to sew upholstery goods in Webster's shop, she entered a trade that would maintain her over the course of some sixty tempestuous years. In fact, the skills she first cultivated there would prove more stable and enduring than any other source of identity, sustaining her through three marriages and three widowhoods, through the raising of seven daughters and the children they brought home, and alongside a religious life that would in time embrace four separate Quaker and Anglican congregations across the city. These are the skills that provided a livelihood for herself and her family over six decades, and positioned her to take up flag making when a fledgling independence movement demanded it.

To appreciate the meaning of Betsy Griscom's needle skills, we have to look closely at the world of fashionable interiors in eighteenth-century Philadelphia. As we walk behind the counters that greeted early American consumers and move toward a shop's rear workspaces, we enter the extraordinary world that colonial craftswomen and men inhabited, where making things that were both beautiful and functional demanded skill, ingenuity, deep knowledge of materials and processes, and attention to detail. By the time Betsy went to work, Pennsylvania was almost a century old; no longer a rugged outpost of the British Empire, it was instead a center of colonial sophistication, filled with residents whose access to fashionable goods was better than ever before.[3] Buildings, clothing and furniture were elegant, comfortable— and above all, genteel. Few things mattered more to eighteenth-century English Philadelphians than the achievement of gentility, and Betsy Griscom was at the heart of the effort.

Among young Betsy's many artisanal relatives, the most significant was the staymaker Sarah Griscom, Andrew Griscom's daughter and so Betsy's great-aunt. Sarah had been raised in New Jersey by her mother and stepfather John Kaighn, and returned to Philadelphia sometime about 1720.[4] She was among Philadelphia's earliest businesswomen, her enterprise firmly established behind the shop of the pewterer Thomas Byles, a shop which may account for the name Pewter Platter Alley (either that, or the "great pewter platter" that "hung out as a sign of a fashionable tavern at the Corner of Front Street").[5] Among her neighbors there was the printer Benjamin Franklin. When Sarah placed her advertisements in the *Pennsylvania Gazette*, it was an easy walk up the street into Benjamin and his wife Deborah's shop. In 1736, she placed just such a notice, alerting anyone whose debts were outstanding to settle up or expect to hear from a lawyer. She used the occasion, too, to remind readers that "any Person may be furnished with Stays of different Sorts, at very reasonable Rates, and Cyder by the Barrell or larger Quantity, by the sd Sarah Griscom."[6]

Staymakers could be found all around the city. The "Sign of the Stays and Childs Coat" on Second Street, and the "Sign of the Stays" in Arch Street both marked such shops. A pair of green stays hung over Chestnut Street, white stays on Second Street, and blue stays on Front Street, all signaling to the city's inhabitants sites where they might find someone to help them obtain a genteel appearance.[7] To look fashionable, successful and sophisticated (and few things were more important to colonial Philadelphians than looking fashionable, successful and sophisticated), it was essential to carry the body in a certain way, to be erect but not stiff, formal yet still graceful and easy. Stays reflected both position and accomplishment. A modern analogy might be high heels; our culture appreciates the effect they have on a woman's posture and appearance, and truly fashionable women wear them effortlessly, signaling along the way that they have the means and lifestyle that go with the shoes.

Stays, likewise, allowed women to demonstrate their ability to achieve this everyday grace. In order to control bodies, stays comprised a series of boned panels. Several layers of linen or canvas beneath a final, top fabric were stitched together to provide support, though the stays' shape was primarily provided by closely spaced channels filled with reed, whalebone or some other stiff material. Sarah's work making foundation garments for women seems natural to us today, but in the first half of the eighteenth century, since a good deal of force was required to push whalebone through the stitched channels, or to stitch through the leather with which the stays were bound, staymaking was generally considered men's work. In the *London Tradesman*, a guide book designed to help parents select appropriate trades for their children, Robert Campbell asserted that "the Work is too hard for Women, it requires more Strength than they are capable of."[8]

A quick glance at the advertising columns of the *Gazette* appears to confirm Campbell's claim. But such sources are misleading; many more women worked as staymakers than we can recover today. Eighteenth-century legal and commercial practices conceal women's work in a number of occupations, and staymaking is no different. While men availed themselves of tools like business directories or newspapers to attract clients, women (who typically had less access to advertising budgets) tended to find customers through word of mouth. Many women also routinely worked alongside their husbands and so are likewise hidden in traditional records.

Sarah Griscom never married; for her, staymaking proved her sole source of support through her life.[9] And, given Sarah's success, it is unsurprising that Betsy's cousin Rebecca Griscom would take up another occupation within the fashion trades: mantua making (later known as dressmaking). The two occupations were closely related, and it is worth noting that cousin Rebecca never married, either. For both Sarah and Rebecca Griscom, in the absence of male providers, craft skill proved essential to their livelihoods.

When she gained her training, Rebecca Griscom was participating in phenomena transforming opportunities for women across the Atlantic world. Just as we might have assumed that staymaking was always an appropriate occupation for women, it is hard to imagine that women have not always been the preferred makers of gowns for other women. But before the middle of the seventeenth century, the production of women's finest apparel was still considered the appropriate province of male specialists in the clothing trades. When a new fashion, the mantua, emerged in the mid-seventeenth century, it represented nothing short of a "revolution in women's apparel" (originally a sort of loose coat, the garment became a close-fitting bodice worn over stays and a stomacher, falling open to reveal either a matching or contrasting petticoat that was worn separately).[10] Previously, women's best gowns had involved a heavily structured bodice and a long-trained skirt that was attached to the bodice with hooks or buttons. Such garments involved skills traditionally protected by tailors' guilds. The mantua transformed gowns for both makers and buyers. Support was no longer a fixed part of each garment but was instead supplied by a separate article, the stays. These garments were easier to make and less expensive to buy, and a tremendous demand for them quickly ensued among women consumers who could for the first time participate in emerging fashions. At the same time, women producers, long shut out of the women's clothing trades by men anxious to protect their craft, seized this moment to assert their right to make clothing for other women. Suggesting that modesty demanded that women employ other women in the making of their clothing, craftswomen claimed a new place in the clothing trades. By 1675, the first such guild emerged in Paris, and others quickly followed throughout Europe and Britain. The mantua had transformed not just fashion but the clothing industry itself, creating opportunities that women like Rebecca Griscom continued to embrace a century later.

For Philadelphia craftswomen of the mid-eighteenth century, mantua making meant cultivating an understanding of and familiarity with many different fabrics. Skilled gown makers knew, for example, how to turn the special properties exhibited by expensive materials—stiff silks, heavy paduasoys, lustrous satins or stout ducapes—to best advantage. Robert Campbell's guide to the trades noted that the best craftswomen also possessed an ability to "flatter all complexions," to "praise all shapes" and be the "compleat Mistress of the Art of Dissimulation"—that is, deceit. Bound to discover her client's "deformities," she must have the prudence to keep silent about flaws in a given figure along with the ability to conceal—and transform—them.[11] Another manual, *The Book of Trades*, attests to the importance of word-of-mouth testimonials from satisfied clients: "Young women ought, perhaps, rarely to be apprenticed to this trade unless their friends can, at the end of the term, place them in a reputable way of business, and can command such connections as shall, with industry, secure their success." Happily for prospective artisans, because the materials were supplied by customers rather than crafts-women, the "business requires, in those who would excel in it, a considerable share of taste, but no great capital to set up in it."[12] The heir to generations of craft skill, assets transmitted by Sarah and Rebecca, Betsy would certainly learn how to supply the style and grace that elite Philadelphians so wanted.

In the 1760s, yet another Griscom girl at work in yet another allied trade was Betsy's sister Deborah, whose husband Everard Bolton's shop at the Blue Hand on Race Street between Front and Second scoured and dyed "all sorts of Silks, Velvets, Ducapes, Paduasoys, Tabbies, Lutestrings, Brocades, Sattins, &c." Like modern-day dry cleaners, the Boltons helped eighteenth-century Philadelphians extend the life of their garments by offering specialized clean-ing techniques and other treatments appropriate to their care. They also cleaned and dyed camblet and scarlet cloth cloaks, and cleaned "Gentle-mens Clothes . . . either wet or dry." "Damaged Cloth of any Sorts," they boasted, was "cured after the best methods now practiced in London, as they have the best Conveniences for carrying on that Business to the greatest Per-fection of any in America."[13] To be sure, the women of the Griscom family knew almost everything there was to know about the fabrics on offer at the city's shops, and could convert them to any variety of purposes.

In acquiring formal training and pursuing craftwork, Betsy, then, was by no means unusual; Griscom's Philadelphia was filled with women in busi-ness. Her great-aunt's successful enterprise surely modeled for all the Griscom girls the life of an established craftswoman, but in the middle decades of the eighteenth century, women could be found in any number of trades.[14] Together artisanal women like the Griscoms helped shape what came to constitute taste, gentility and refinement in the North American colonies' leading city. Well-heeled families may have transmitted the latest fashions from across the Atlantic to the streets of Philadelphia, but as Betsy Griscom and her counter-parts translated consumer preferences through their own skills and sensibili-ties they helped construct a particular vernacular gentility unique to their city and their clientele.[15]

Betsy was about seven when her cousin Rebecca began learning the man-tua maker's craft, and eleven when her sister married Everard Bolton; her great-aunt Sarah (born the year before Andrew Griscom died, in that well-appointed Second Street home) was verging on sixty when Betsy was born. As Betsy looked around at the work these women embraced, she anticipated the day when she would enter some sort of trade of her own. The visit to her sister at the Webster shop simply determined which it would be. As young Betsy

Griscom began contemplating her own future work in life, a city full of possibility lay before her.

In Betsy's lifetime, the upholstery trade was among the most lucrative and prestigious craft professions. Today, upholstery is generally assumed to refer mainly to the covering of furniture with stuffing and cloth, but in fact the trade has always encompassed an array of skills related to the decoration of domestic interiors. Modern-day Philadelphia upholsterers provide custom furniture, drapes, slipcovers, bedspreads and headboards. Likewise, in the eighteenth century, upholsterers also made and sold mattresses and bolsters, bed curtains and Venetian blinds. They sold and applied wallpaper, imported textiles and dry goods for resale and carried out a number of tasks intended to make parlors, sitting rooms and bedrooms more pleasing and comfortable. The products of their craft were largely things desired but not necessary to enhance one's domestic comfort, and so they tended to cater to the more affluent of the city's residents. Both these goods and the materials involved to create them were substantial: feather mattresses might weigh up to sixty pounds; curtains could consume between thirty and forty yards of expensive materials. Indeed, the high cost of textiles ensured that customers sought out skilled practitioners, rather than risking their expensive goods in the hands of an amateur.

Given its market, upholstery is necessarily an urban enterprise; it needs a population the size of a city in order to find enough business to sustain itself. In the 1740s, Campbell's *London Tradesman* described the work for the uninitiated. He noted that this "tradesman's Genius must be universal in every Branch of Furniture though his proper Craft is to fit up Beds, window-Curtains, Hangings, and to cover Chairs that have stuffed Bottoms." "He was originally a species of Taylor," the guidebook observed, "but, by degrees, has crept over his Head, and set up as a Connoisseur in every Article that belongs to a House. He employs Journeymen in his own proper Calling, Cabinet-Makers, Glass-Grinders, Looking-Glass Frame-Carvers, Carvers for Chairs, Testers, and Posts of Bed, the Woolen-Draper, the Mercer, the Linen-Draper, several Species of Smiths, and a vast many Tradesmen of the other mechanic Branches."[16] While the "stuffing and covering of a Chair or Settee-Bed is indeed the nicest Part of this Branch," these skills "may be acquired without any remarkable Genius," since "All the Wooden-work they use is done by the Joiner, Cabinet-Maker, and Carver."[17] Upholsterers, then, found themselves immediately enmeshed in networks of artisans and laborers that included a "vast many" sorts of tradesmen, as well as female employees.

Women were essential to the work. The prospective upholsterer "must handle the Needle so alertly as to sew a plain Seam and sew on the Lace without Puckers; and he must use his Sheers [*sic*] so dexterously as to cut a Valence or Counterpain with a genteel Sweep, according to a Pattern he has before him." "All this Part of the Work," trade manuals further explained, is in fact frequently "performed by Women, who never served an Apprenticeship to the Mystery as well as Men."[18] By "apprenticeship to the mystery," the author meant that women, unlike men, did not enter into a formal contractual agreement in which the artisan agrees to train the novice over a set period of years in the most specialized knowledge needed to practice the craft, trading labor for instruction. Young women like Betsy Griscom were excluded from the training needed to undertake the most complex tasks of the work, knowledge that would allow them to set up as full-fledged competitors. But they would nevertheless be taught the range of skills unique to the fabrication of upholstery goods; mastery of simple sewing techniques was the beginning, but not the end, of these shop employees' expertise.

As cities flourished in Britain's North American colonies, Boston, Massachusetts, became the first to amass the wealth and population necessary to support an upholstery trade. Between 1725 and 1760, at least 224 furniture makers, including 23 upholsterers, set up shop in New England's largest port.[19] In Philadelphia, the first man to formally identify himself as an upholsterer was John Budd, whose occupation was noted on a 1693 tax list. Perhaps it was he who furnished the elaborate curtains and bedding enjoyed by Andrew and Sarah Griscom. Between that date and 1760, at least eleven upholsterers can be found in the city, including the redoubtable Plunket Fleeson, who opened his Philadelphia shop at the Sign of the Easy Chair about 1739, the first such craftsman of substance and a man whose aesthetic and political influence would persist into the 1790s (and whose role in the production of the Cadwalader furniture would prove so important two centuries later).[20] Fleeson would achieve extraordinary success; to cite just one indicator, in surviving tax records from the period between 1754 and 1782, Fleeson never ranked below the eighty-second percentile among taxpayers in Philadelphia's Middle Ward, and all but one of those years his ranking ranged between the eighty-sixth and the ninety-fifth percentile.[21] He enjoyed the services of both servants and slaves, and traveled about the city in a riding chair. With clients from the best families in town, and access to the government contracts they controlled (window curtains for statehouse rooms, bedding for soldiers and so on), his future seemed assured from the moment he arrived.

Although before 1760 the city's population apparently could not support many expert upholsterers, the decades that followed saw a steady influx of such specialists.[22] Most were immigrants from European centers of style and manufacturing, men like Hyns Taylor, who enjoyed a nearly fifteen-year career as an upholsterer and cabinetmaker in London before moving to the colonies in the mid-1770s (though he arrived only to learn that the name of his London shop, the Crown and Cushion, had already been taken by competitor Blanch White for his warehouse on Front Street).[23] Almost half of the Philadelphia upholsterers who announced their skills in the local advertising columns between 1760 and 1810 claimed to be either recent immigrants or men who had trained abroad—important currency in a city eager to assert its membership among the empire's leading port cities.[24]

Philadelphia's upholstery market was shaped not just by the size and affluence of its population, but also by the Quaker sensibilities that colored almost every aspect of life there. Today we are familiar with what's called Quaker "plain" style, but what this meant to eighteenth-century Friends is open to interpretation. As one scholar aptly observes, "Quaker documents suggest that Quakers were plain; surviving artifacts suggest that they were not."[25] Ever since the Philadelphia merchant John Reynell famously ordered a "Handsome plain looking glass . . . and 2 raised Japan'd Black Corner Cupboards, with 2 door to each, no red in 'em, of the best sort, but plain," this phrase—the "best sort, but plain"—has been embraced to explain the apparent discrepancy between Quaker prescription and the elegant lifestyle many Friends enjoyed.[26] Close studies of Quaker clothing and Quaker furniture have found no obvious difference between objects bought by Friends and those chosen by "the world." Plain, it appears, was truly in the eye of the beholder.

Plainness, in fact, was not originally part of the Friends' radical critique; indeed, some early converts felt that this excessive attention to detail was in itself vain and distracting. But over time a set of policies emerged condemning the consumption of unnecessarily fashionable goods, mostly in terms of apparel. William Penn's *No Cross No Crown* railed against such fripperies. "How many pieces of riband [ribbon], and what feathers, lacebands, and the like did Adam and Eve wear in paradise, or out of it?" Penn asked. "What rich embroideries, silks, points, etc. had Abel, Enoch, Noah, and good Old Abraham! Did Eve, Sarah, Suzannnah, Elizabeth and the Virgin Mary use to cure, powder, patch, paint, wear false locks of strange colours, rich points, trimmings, laced gowns, embroidered petticoats, shoes with slipslaps laced with silk or silver lace?"[27] As the Pennsylvania settlement matured, Friends began to gather "Christian and Brotherly Advices" in a *Book of Discipline*, essentially guides to help Friends monitor their behavior, and these often mention particular abuses in dress (and are sometimes perhaps overly alert to detail: "at various times," one historian notes, "Friends condemned any apron that was not green or white, plaids and ruffled neckcloths, even prescribing the size of buttonholes"), but discussion of houses and furniture remained comparatively rare, and vague.[28]

But if injunctions to the faithful more often addressed errors in clothing than furnishings, from time to time the decoration of houses, too, troubled the most vigilant Friends. Once she had taken her position in the Webster shop, young Betsy and her family would have attended most carefully to passages in the 1762 *Discipline* that had been carried over from earlier editions: a stipulation that "further care be taken to discourage all superfluity in furniture, of houses & apparel whatsoever," and an appeal for "moderation and plainness in gesture, speech, apparel, or furniture, of houses."[29] By and large, Quaker discipline laid the blame for transgression on the consumers who could not resist extravagant goods, rather than the artisans who produced them. (In this they differed from the Shakers, who specifically instructed tradesmen to eschew engaging in unnecessary ornamentation.) One seventeenth-century statement (incorporated into later editions) did single out tailors as a source of concern: after prohibiting "long lapped sleeves, or coats gathered at the sides or superfluous buttons, or broad ribbons about their hats or long curled periwigs," and stipulating that no women, children or servants "dress their heads immodestly, or wear their garments indecently, as is too common, nor wear long scarves, and that all be careful about making, buying and wearing, as much as they can striped and flowe'd stuffs, or other useless and superfluous things," the authors went on to note that "all Taylors professing truth," who nevertheless fabricated such articles, should "be dealt with and advised accordingly."[30] But no other Quaker artisans were cautioned in this way; no furniture makers, house carpenters or upholsterers were put on notice that they were not to manufacture such goods.

Instead, Friends were warned not to succumb to temptation in the marketplace. In 1762, the *Discipline* specifically discussed plainness in furniture— evidence itself that excessive purchases had become worrisome among Quaker leadership.[31] The guide's compilers devoted ten pages to "Plainness," urging Friends to forego "needless things," and to avoid "Superfluity & Excess in Buildings and Furniture," preferring household furnishings that conformed to preferences for simplicity.[32] The injunction against "excess in eating, drinking, gaiety of apparel and furniture" hints at what at first glance appears to be a gap between word and deed, given that the furniture, silver and other artifacts that survive from eighteenth-century Quaker collections include some of the finest examples of the decorative arts made in early America. There is "scarce a new fashion comes up," the Friends opined, "or a fantastic cut invented, but some one or other who profess Truth is ready with the foremost to run into it." It was one thing for families whose diligence and piety had been rewarded with wealth to enjoy the comforts prosperity confers, but quite another to go rushing after one senseless fashion after another. The distinction is subtle but helps explain the survival of such extraordinarily rich objects made by Quaker artisans for Quaker consumers. Perceiving a tangible difference between quality and gaiety, as the *Discipline* continued, the Friends "earnestly caution[ed] and advise[ed] against the inordinate pursuit of worldly riches." Such things, when "sought within due bounds for the comfortable subsistence of ourselves and families, and the charitable relief of others in necessity," were "not only lawful but commendable," but when the "mind is carried away with the love of these things" they then become "a clog and hindrance," an excess which ought to be guarded against, "the love of money being the root of all evil."

But what good Quaker commissions lacked in ornament was offset by investment in the highest-quality materials and workmanship. Reynell's "Handsome, plain" looking glass indeed reflected the distinct sensibilities of wealthy Friends who appreciated the comforts the best of the city's artisans had to offer. Upholsterers, like other furniture tradesmen, helped aspiring Philadelphians draw distinctions between haves and have-nots. Immersed in luxury, they converted the elegant and expensive textiles flowing from European looms into objects that defined homes of privilege. As one resident remembered, "couches of worsted damask" were found "only in very affluent families," while "plain people used settees and settles."[33] As Betsy Ross joined the community of Philadelphia upholsterers, her handiwork enabled families who could afford it to soften the harder edges of life in the colonies. Her mattresses cradled tired bodies; her pillows cushioned the knees of the pious. She supplied color, patterns and textures in upholstery fabrics and fringes that enlivened otherwise drab rooms. The work of her needle gave colonial hands something soft to caress, and made possible other sensations, too, like the sense of security and snugness conveyed by bed curtains that blocked cold drafts or unwanted light while affording a precious bit of privacy in a crowded city.[34] Any young woman with an eye for the beautiful and fashionable textiles folded in large, luxurious bolts on the city's merchants' shelves would have found upholstery appealing. It's no wonder young Betsy felt their pull.

# · 4 ·

# Crafting Comfort

Betsy Griscom would spend some five or six years between 1767 and 1773 working for John Webster. When Webster first arrived from London, he found space in a house on Arch Street near Second—he must have been no more than a few doors away from the Griscoms' new house, which certainly helps explain how the girls came to work for him.[1] Betsy was about fifteen on the day she walked into his shop and landed the offer of a position. She would enter her twenties while still in Webster's employ, exchanging the preoccupations of girlhood for those of a young woman. It was during these years that she would make, among many other things, the fabulous accoutrements for the Cadwalader home, mastering the skills that would sustain her over the next sixty years.

John Webster is nearly as elusive as Betsy herself, but enough evidence survives in household ledgers and receipts, newspaper columns, extant artifacts and eighteenth-century trade guides to reconstruct some sense of his practice, and so also what Betsy's working life was like at the outset of her long career. Pause for a moment and imagine the tips of your fingers passing over smooth silks, sturdy linen, heavy damasks and coarse buckram. These are the sensations that most engaged Betsy Ross as she sat down in the work-room of John Webster's upholstery shop.

———

A rich sense of the material culture of the trade about the time Betsy entered it can be found in an advertisement of Blanch White's upholstery warehouse on Front Street near the London Coffee House. The list is long (in an era before marketing emerged among the business arts, most advertisers simply posted in the newspaper long lists of their present inventory or recent shipments), but worth reading slowly, item by item. Read slowly enough, and you can begin to imagine yourself walking through White's shop, peering into the bins and shelves for the most stylish, the most desirable goods, and the best deals, lingering over each item—just as Philadelphians did when the new edition of the paper came out. At White's warehouse in the summer of 1759, craftsmen and consumers alike could find:

Harrateens, cheneys, stamped linseys for bed furniture, with suitable binding; Upholsterers buckrams, furniture checks, erminettas, 3 qr. 7 8ths, yd. and 3 8ths linen and cotton apron checks, blankets, rugs, bed tickings, quilts, counterpanes . . . regimental worsted hat lace, white and yellow, tent hooks and eyes, 6, 8 and 10d nails, 14 ounce tacks, and 2d clout nails, house bells, bell bolts and pullies, cranks and wire, brass mounted swords, washed ditto, striped harrass for servants beds, globe lamps for stair cases or passages, sconces, brass fendors, shaving boxes and brushes, brass chair nails, lacquered ditto, lignum vitae, bed castors, brass and leather ditto. brass cloak pins, iron ditto, brass desk hinges, strong iron butt hinges, japanned boards and waiters, mahogony ditto, bottle boards, split bone knives and forks, sham buck ditto, steep capt ditto, buck pen knives, horn ditto, women's scissors, taylors shears, [and] sword belts.

Looking up, one found the wall lined with shelves, piled high with "cotton hollands, ginghams, calimancoes, shaloons, cambleteens, brilliants, bombazeens, Norwich crape, white serge and flannels, Scotch gartering, cherriderries, gowns, fine diaper, blue and white handkerchiefs, cross barred stuffs, silk poplins, hairbines, camblets, white and brown buckram, check handkerchiefs, Dutch sprigs, women's cotton hose, men's fine white, and black and grey worsted ditto." The young upholsterer's glance would have particularly noticed the "thread lines and tassels, all colours, and mix, with small rings for festoon or other window curtains." The house carpenter's eye would likelier be drawn to the batches of ink powder, iron hinges of all shapes and sizes, saws, compasses and vizes, black lead pencils, mathematical instruments and cases of razors. Craftsmen needing to stock up on tools found rulers, gimblets and spike bitts, rasps and files, plaisterers trowels, box hinges, screw pullies, table butts, plate saws, padlocks, all sorts of saddlers' tacks and nails, a variety of screws, screw buttons, chest handles, fine wrought handles and escutcheons and curling tongs. For the discerning shopper White carried both mahogany and painted telescopes, mahogany tea chests, Persia carpets and "steel mounted swords gilt with gold." White added a postscript to his notice to attract members of local militia units: "Drums and colours, halberts, spontoons, field bedsteads, mattresses, valances, and all kinds of military accoutrements and field equipage, ready made, at the lowest prices, as in London." Lastly, he reminded readers that they'd find "A Variety of Paper hangings, and all kinds of Upholstery work done as usual."[2]

In time, White's Crown and Cushion would be bought by John Mason, who offered Philadelphians "an assortment of paper hangings and FURNI-TURE CHECKS; likewise mattress beds, the utility of which is not duly attended to, for as they strengthen and brace up the nerves in summer, so they keep the body warm in winter, provided the person sleeps under them." Mason also advertised the "best of sacking bottoms, and wet and dry merchandize, very reasonable, and suitable to any season."[3] Just blocks away Plunket Fleeson offered "crimson, green, blue and yellow Harrateens and Cheneys [two sorts of woolen fabrics popular for bed hangings], best Cotton Chints [chintz] Bed Patterns, with suitable Trimmings, silk Bed lace, Furniture Check, Flanders and other Bed Ticks," and "a Variety of the best English Tossels."[4] Consumers might also choose "Polack Linnen" or "netted linens" for "Moschetto" or "Musqueto Curtains."[5] Another craftsman was William Martin, whose Front Street shop next door to the City Vendue (the city auction house) offered "all sorts of chairs, sofas, couches and deception beds (an innovation suited to an age that appreciated both wit and riddles, these beds, when folded, appeared to be a chest of drawers or a sofa), and every thing in the Upholder way; he hangs paper, and has some handsome patterns." Perhaps as a nod toward the city's Quaker clientele, he added that he could provide "the newest fashions, both elegant and plain."[6]

These notices remind us that a major aspect of any upholsterer's enterprise was the provision of bedding. Few eighteenth-century household goods were as desirable among consumers, or as lucrative for makers, as beds. Bedsteads enveloped in expensive textiles were a way to show wealth, to conspicuously consume obviously excessive amounts of materials and resources. Such amenities were of course rare. In Philadelphia before the Revolution, many households possessed bedding, but only half appear to have contained bedsteads, and only about a third of those were embellished with hangings.[7] In houses across the city, furnishing the best bed had been the family's largest single household expense.[8]

Betsy's family had been fortunate in this regard; as we've seen, even in the 1690s, Andrew and Sarah had also owned not one, but two beds fitted out with a bedstead, bed, bolster, two pillows and bed curtains, valued at £23 at a date when their sixteen-acre lot in the Northern Liberties was worth just £10.[9] For that reason, midcentury beds were placed in public rooms, like a family's best parlor—rooms that were otherwise devoted to the display of taste, wealth and style. By enclosing the bed on four sides, bed curtains became almost an architectural feature, creating another room in the house, a room-within-a-room that extended the home's living space for the bed's occupants. As one historian suggested, beds were "as much a place as a thing."[10]

At the foundation of many beds, and a staple of any upholsterer's inventory, was the sacking bottom. Some mattresses were supported by ropes or cords that passed through the bedstead's rails, but a more comfortable rest was supplied by sacking bottoms, lengths of heavy fabric (typically made of tow or hemp) with eyelets created along the edges through which cords passed, allowing the maker to lace the edges of the cloth to the frame of the bed. Not only did the maker of a sacking bottom join lengths of heavy fabric to get the correct width; a sacking bottom also might have some forty or more eyelets to engage the cording. Creating an eyelet in such heavy materials meant using very heavy needles, not to mention the strength necessary to push them through one side, and more, to pull the needle through again on the other.[11]

With the sacking bottom in place, one needed a mattress. A wide range of shapes and fillings was possible. Sea beds were particularly important in Philadelphia, the largest port in Britain's North American colonies, while households across the city demanded mattresses in a wide range of qualities. The fabrics chosen for the exterior of the mattress commonly included the Flanders and English bed ticking regularly advertised among the city's shopkeepers—striped fabrics that are still familiar to us today.[12]

More significant, from the maker's perspective, was the material selected for the filling, typically hair, wool or feathers.[13] The latter, the only one of the three still wanted today, traveled to the city in ships' holds as well as farmers' wagons together with other agricultural products from the Pennsylvania countryside. (By the early nineteenth century, an upholsterer's shop might dedicate a full room, or loft, to the work of drying, weighing and storing feathers, and a kiln for drying them.)[14] Before and during her marriage to Henry Drinker, for instance, Elizabeth Sandwith together with her sister Mary imported feathers from Ireland. (Today most of the down and feathers that fill American pillows and comforters come from breeders in southeast China's Anhui Province.)[15] As early as 1740, Plunket Fleeson advertised "Choice Live Geese Feathers . . . likewise Sea Beds, curled Hair Matrasses, Sacking Bottoms, all kind of Upholsterer's Work, done reasonably"; he further noted that "Any Person having such Feathers to sell, may apply to the said Fleeson."[16] "Live" feathers (feathers harvested from living birds considered superior to those otherwise gathered) continued to be a desirable filling throughout the century (there were plenty around Philadelphia when it came time to repurpose them in the political theater of the resistance movement), but Fleeson offered "Ready Money for Horse Hair and Cow Tails," too.[17] The upholsterer Edward Weyman provides another glimpse into the trade in fillings when he published a notice reminding the city's tanners and others who might "have cows, horses, and mare's tails to dispose of, that said Weyman gives the best prices for those sorts of hair."[18]

The work undertaken by the maker of a mattress suggests the extraordinary effort that lay behind a good night's sleep in colonial America. As Fleeson's notice suggests, among the best fillings of a quality mattress was curled animal hair. Horse tails were preferred for this purpose, though mane hair, cattle tail hair and hog hair were possibilities (shorter hair, however, usually contained less curl and was less resilient). Once the animal's hair was collected, it was curled and sterilized by twisting it into ropes and applying steam; alternatively, the maker might curl the hair around wooden cylinders which were then plunged into boiling water. Next, the ropes or cylinders were dried in ovens in order to set the curl. Given the threat posed by insects, ensuring that the hair was completely dry before proceeding was crucial to the successful preparation of the materials. Sometimes extra care was taken, and the hair dyed or bleached for good measure.[19]

With the curled hair in hand, the upholsterer then filled the mattress. Feathers were easily stuffed, a handful at a time, into small openings left in the tick. An alternative, and a better choice for mattresses filled with hair, was to construct the tick like a box without a lid, and then set in the hair, layer by layer, before stitching on the top. Once the stuffing material was inside the fabric, another series of steps ensured that it was distributed for good effect, the craftswoman teasing the filling through the tick using a regulator, making sure that slightly more filling lay in the center, but also that it had spread completely into the corners. Finally, the stuffing was stitched into place using a double-pointed mattress needle (needles with sharp cutting edges helped smooth their passage through especially compact filling materials) and twine; otherwise, over time the filling would move around, eventually becoming uncomfortably uneven. Stitches made on the diagonal of the fabric grain distributed the stress and prevented any tearing of the tick's fabric.[20]

The steady need to make and refresh mattresses created ongoing work for upholsterers. Many years after Betsy received her training, Elizabeth Drinker's diary captures glimpses of Betsy's younger sister Rachel (perhaps the third Griscom girl to work in an upholstery trade) at work: "Rachel Griscomb [*sic*] work'd here yesterday, she made up a Bed tick and put in the feathers, preparatory to our going out of town." Another summer, Rachel was again at the Drinker home "making up a bedtick and putting in the feathers." Later that year, she returned: "Rachel Griscomb [*sic*] here putting up beds."[21] One fall, Hannah Marshall Haines was so preoccupied with the state of her mattresses while traveling that she wrote her sister, asking her to "send for Rachel Brown . . . and get her to go to our house and brush all the bedsteads and Examine them that no Bugs get in, as I am uneasy about them, there being no person to have the necessary care, and I am uneasy about those in the Garrett."[22]

Indeed, because mattresses so often became infested with insects, upholsterers sold various remedies to expel them. Parents today still send their children to bed with the cheerful wish "Sleep tight [a reference to the tautness of rope supports]; don't let the bedbugs bite." Bedbugs were a serious problem for early Americans (as they remain today; U.S. cities at the turn of the twenty-first century continue to battle resurging infestations). Some people thought that applying a solution of vitriol (a metal sulphate) prevented insects and bugs from "harbouring therein"; others boiled coloquintida apples in water, dissolved vitriol into the mixture and then washed the bedsteads with the solution. The *Pennsylvania Gazette* published another remedy, advising readers to "take of the highest rectified Spirit of Wine (viz. Lamp Spirits that will burn all away dry, and leave not the least Moisture behind) half a Pint; newly distilled Oil, or Spirits of Turpentine, half a Pint; mix them together, and break into it, in small Bits, half an Ounce of Camphire, which will dissolve in it in a few Minutes; shake them well together." Even if your pests "swarm ever so much," a thorough dousing of the bed and bedding "will infallib'y kill and destroy both them and their Nitts." The recipe, the notice assured readers, will "neither stain, soil, or in the least hurt the finest Silk or Damask Bed that is." Even a bed teeming with bugs could be salvaged with this course of treatment: "To but touch a live Bugg with a Drop of it, and you will find it to die instantly." Nonetheless, the author braced potential users for the solution's side effects and potential danger: "The Smell this Mixture occasions, will be all gone in two or three Days, which yet is very wholesome, and to many People agreeable. You must remember always to shake the Mixture together very well, whenever you use it, which must be in the Day-time, not by Candle-light, lest the Subtlety of the Mixture should catch the Flames as you are using it, and occasion Damage."[23]

In addition to comfortable and clean mattresses, families of privilege desired the privacy, warmth and beauty of both bed and window curtains. While it was the sheer yardage of these objects that immediately greeted the eye—and, make no mistake, it was the purchase of dozens of yards of costly and fashionable fabric that was meant to strike observers—bed hangings also involved complex construction that demanded technical skill from the makers. The valances, for instance, that often decorated each side of such beds while concealing the top of the drapes had to be nailed to the frame of the bed without compromising the expensive fabric on display; instead, a maker might apply whatever stylish fabric the client had selected or supplied—silk and/or wool damask, copperplate or whatever visually arresting material was at the moment in vogue—to a coarser weave like buckram or linen that the artisan might happily pound nails through. The inside of a valance, where the panel was visible to the occupant of the bed, might be lined with another fabric, perhaps a glazed wool—something that would be pleasant to the eye of those within, but did not need to impress guests. The edges were then bound with a silk tape, and some additional ornament was sometimes added for still more effect—perhaps gimp, fringe or tassels, which themselves might also have been handmade in the upholsterer's shop.

Window curtains, closely related to bed hangings, were also rare. Fewer than one in ten Philadelphia households in the years Betsy entered her trade had them. (Years earlier they had been still more rare, and yet, again, her great-grandfather had been among the very few Philadelphians, in those heady days of city building, to possess them, having at the time of his death as many as four.)[24] The most common window treatment in colonial Philadelphia, far and away, was no treatment at all.[25] When people had window curtains, it was usually in the bedroom, sometimes en suite with the bed hangings. One 1761 household, for instance, included "a Sett of yellow and a Sett of green Worsted Bed and Window Curtains, fitted in the best Taste by Mr. Fleeson."[26] Lucky readers could sometimes achieve a posher environment than they could otherwise afford if they were willing to buy secondhand; Fleeson, for example, offered "a VALUABLE green English Silk Damask Bed and Window Curtains with Feather Bed, Sattin Quilt, &c." that "has been some Time in use."[27]

For consumers who could afford it, three sorts of window dressings were possible: straight hangings, Venetian curtains and festoon drapes.[28] Straight curtains were tacked directly to the window frame and held open by tiebacks. (French rod curtains suspended from rings connected to pulley cords—a precursor to the traverse rods that today allow the curtains to be drawn open and closed horizontally—were not yet available, though they would emerge in the years following the American Revolution.) For most of the century, those who wished to open and close their curtains did so vertically. So-called Venetian curtains were created by craftswomen who sewed tapes and loops or rings down the back of a panel of material of a width that covered the window. Cords lacing through these loops allowed the whole curtain to be drawn up, folding at each interval. Other makers sewed tapes and rings diagonally on the back from the bottom center to the outer top so that when the cords were pulled, the curtain gathered up from the center of the window in festoons, with tails hanging down each side of the window frame.

Webster's enterprise also featured a new item in the domestic landscape of fashionable Philadelphians: Venetian blinds. Blinds were already popular by the time Betsy went to work, not least because the product, as Webster noted, "moves to any position, so as to give different Lights, screens from the scorching Rays of the Sun, and draws a cool Air in hot Weather." In a city of close quarters, that blinds could admit light yet also "prevent being overlooked"— that is, thwart the curious glances of passersby into one's private spaces—was surely appealing. In the humid Philadelphia summers, blinds kept out the hot sun while still admitting the occasional cool breeze. Importantly, blinds were also "the greatest Preserver of Furniture of any Thing of that Kind ever invented."[29] Given the tremendous cost of genteel furniture fabrics, window treatments that, like chair cases, limited the damaging effects of sunlight were valuable investments by themselves.

To create them, wooden slats formed by lathes, typically an eighth of an inch thick (though the first and last had to be thicker, to support the weight in both the raised and lowered positions), were assembled together with tapes woven of a heavy linen or cotton. Blinds then as now could be purchased in a range of qualities. Some were painted to match the room, but most displayed their natural wood, from poplar to mahogany, the quality and cost varying by where the blinds were intended to go: cheap canvas blinds might do in a kitchen, while for better rooms, some sort of wooden blinds were in order. In some cases, the functional fabric of the tapes was concealed behind a more decorative selection—a step that again invoked the labors of a shop's needlewomen.

Upholstery seamstresses like Betsy Griscom also routinely supplied chair cases, that is, slipcovers for side chairs, easy chairs and sofas, for both functional and decorative effect. Men and women in the eighteenth century knew as well as we do today that sunlight damages textiles; they also saw how everyday use caused wear and tear. Chair cases protected one's investment in expensive fabrics (and, on occasion, had the added benefit of concealing inferior fabrics, too). Purchasing a set of chair cases was also a way to create a feeling of unity among a constellation of pieces acquired over time, creating the impression, too, of a simultaneous outlay of funds. Wool serge was preferred at midcentury, but in time, as new fabrics became increasingly available, consumers more often chose washable linens or cottons, usually of a color or pattern to match the rest of the furnishings in the room. "Checks and stripes," the textile curator Linda Baumgarten notes, "were preferred for public rooms such as libraries or parlors, whereas printed cottons were favored for bedchambers where the slipcovers often matched the bed hangings."[30]

Webster's firm charged a shilling each for Betsy's work constructing these fashionable and functional accessories. The stuffing and covering of furniture—the kind of work we most closely associate with the contemporary trade—was generally undertaken by men, but fabricating mattresses, bed curtains, window curtains, chair cases and trimmings was the sort of work that would most concern Betsy Griscom when she entered Webster's employ. The work was not necessarily less physically demanding; sewing a sacking bottom or stuffing a sixty-pound mattress demanded a good bit of strength. But because some of the work depended largely on tools associated with women, those tasks had come to be regarded as best executed by them.

We know that a woman named Ann King "had the care of the women's work" in Webster's shop from 1768 or 1769 to 1775, the years when Betsy worked there, affirming the picture hinted at in Rachel Claypoole Fletcher's recollection of her mother's childhood memory, of shops with three or four girls at work at any given time.[31] In this the shop was not unusual; when the upholsterer Samuel Benge advertised his ability to supply military equipage, he also noted that he was seeking "several women . . . to work at the above branch."[32] In some shops women worked alongside their husbands, and, if need be, carried on alone in widowhood. Not long after the funeral of the upholsterer Thomas Lawrence, his widow, Elizabeth, notified readers of the city's advertising columns that she would be "carrying on some branches" of the business "at her dwelling house, a few doors above Market Street, in Second Street, such as making feather beds, mattresses, sacking bottoms, bottoming chairs, cleaning the feathers of old beds, &c. &c."[33] The branches that Mrs. Lawrence elected to carry on (and she would remain among Betsy's competitors for many years to come) give us a rare glimpse into the particular tasks she had mastered in the shop while her husband was living, and would now undertake separately as an independent craftswoman: the stuffing and stitching of beds and mattresses, the refurbishing of mattresses made dirty or uneven by years of hard use, the construction of sacking bottoms on which they rested, the making of chair seats. Looking at these tasks and others in turn suggests the kinds of activities women performed in shops like John Webster's, and so begins to sketch the shape of the upholstery trades as they were encountered by Betsy Griscom.

For the craftswomen who made them, chair covers were not especially challenging, but did involve some opportunity to display advanced skills. If patterned fabric was involved, for instance, a thoughtful craftswoman took care to cut the material so that the chair seat displayed the key elements of the design.[34] Flounces along the sides should be gathered evenly. Adding tape or fringe, too, engaged another set of labors that had long been the province of female hands.

The creation and application of trimmings also occupied the women who worked in Webster's shop. When John Cadwalader ordered twenty-four yards of fringe, for example, the staff set to work to apply and perhaps produce it.[35] Fabricating trim was part of the "women's work" of any upholstery shop. Fringe is easy to take for granted today, but the making of fringe, tassels, tapes and other trimmings consumed hours of labor. Fringe was an element needed not only by upholsterers but also by saddlers and coach makers. Saddles in the eighteenth century were often ornamented with silk, worsted and even gold fringe. (In the Philadelphia saddler William Tod's 1769 advertisement, he boasts "ladies hunting side saddles, with scarlet, green and blue covers, trimmed with gold and silver lace, and gold fringes, ditto with silk and worsted fringes" as well as men's hunting saddles with holsters, also both plain and trimmed, "with double and single rows of gold and silver lace"—just the thing to go with the silver-mounted whips he also offered fashionable Philadelphians.)[36] Coaches, too, needed curtains to ensure the privacy and comfort of those within. Almost anywhere one looked, inside or outside, stood edges that could be improved with the flutter of a little fringe.

Embellishments like tassels, braids, gimps, laces and fringes might seem like shiny afterthoughts in the world of home furnishings, but they were not. They covered raw edges and accentuated outlines, enhancing the accom-plishment of the furniture maker; the best achieved an artistry of their own, the subtle movement of fringe and tassels creating three-dimensional effects that offset the monumentality of upholstered furniture, beds, window curtains and draperies, giving them the more human feel that was essential to their aes-thetic success. When she struck out on her own in the spring of 1775, King would boast that she was the "first American tossel [sic] maker that ever brought that branch of business to any degree of perfection"; she invited readers to browse her stock of fringes, cord and mattresses "of every sort" that she now offered.[37] In emphasizing her status as the first *American* tassel maker, she distinguished herself from George Richey, the Edinburgh upholsterer whose Front Street shop—the "Crown and Tassell" no less—offered "lines and tassels to answer any furniture or chariots."[38] As King worked to perfect tassel making in Pennsylvania, she trained Betsy and the other women in the shop in the art and mystery of *passementerie,* or the making of trimmings.[39]

The creation of such fine ornaments required remarkable skill and patience. To fabricate the tassel's shape, for instance, the maker chose a turned wooden mold, or created a combination of molds, which she covered closely with laid threads. Next, a mesh cover, spun-covered straps or knotted gimps could be applied. At the base she might add a cut ruff (a tufted pile of either silk or wool) or a gallery of rosettes. The tassel's fringe, called its skirt, was attached to the base of the mold. Among the most traditional fringes were those made of loose cords, sometimes knotted at ends or looped and twisted, though sometimes hangers (short strings or chains of decorative items like small spun-covered wooden molds, rosettes, bundles and bows, and the like) might be inserted at intervals. Some skirts might be made up entirely of hangers, with no real fringe at all. Tassels might then be joined in pairs, connected by a cord that passed through the mold's center and knotted invisibly beneath, to be used as tie-backs.[40]

This is the sort of sewing and fabricating that Betsy Griscom and women like her tackled, work that was the bread and butter of any upholsterer's shop: women cut cloth and assembled panels; they made and applied braid, binding and trimmings; they manipulated stitches, hardware and fabrics to create pleasing drapes and folds; they created eyelets and grommets and applied linings. For the upholsterer at the shop's head, such laborers were both necessary and inexpensive. Griscom's Boston counterpart, Elizabeth Kemble, for instance, cut the cloth, assembled and lined panels, and applied braid and binding for as many as forty to sixty sets of bed hangings in any given year, earning just over a shilling per day for her time and skill. According to Campbell's *London Trades-man,* "The Upholder's own Branch is paid Twelve to Fifteen Shillings a Week; and the Women, if good for any thing, get a Shilling a Day."[41]

Having launched his Philadelphia enterprise on Arch Street, John Webster soon relocated, first to Front Street and then Chestnut, and enough information survives about his shop to get a feel for Betsy Griscom's life during her years of training.[42] Like the shops of other London-trained craftsmen, Webster's appealed to the city's wealthiest citizens. A 1767 notice assured readers that he had been working "with applause for several of the nobility and gentry of England and Scotland." Now Philadelphians could avail themselves of his talents as well.

> JOHN WEBSTER, Upholder, [sic] Late of LONDON; BEGS Leave to acquaint his good Customers, and others, who shall please to employ him in the Upholstery Business, that he is removed from Front street, to the next Door below Doctor Bond, and nearly opposite Christopher and Charles Marshall, in Chestnut street, where may be had all Sorts of UPHOLSTERY WORK, in the newest and neatest Manner, on the most reasonable Prices. Also the best and newest invented Venetian SUN BLINDS for Windows, on the best Principles, stained to any colour, moves to any Position, so as to give different Lights, screens from the scorching Rays of the Sun, and draws a cool Air in hot Weather, draws up as a Curtain, and prevents being overlooked, and is in the greatest Preserver of Furniture of any Thing of that Kind ever invented. Said WEBSTER humbly begs Leave to return his most grateful Thanks to those benevolent Gentlemen and Ladies who have been pleased to honour and favour him with their Commands. A BUG WASH may be had, for entirely destroying that destructive Vermin.[43]

One of Webster's early ads noted that he was seeking an apprentice; he had found enough work that he was already looking for more help. Webster apparently kept a fairly large shop during these years, employing several men and women of various levels of skill and experience. Griscom labored alongside men like William Fleming and John Ross, who worked for Webster as they advanced their own training toward a future career in the trade.[44] George Haughton, a journeyman in Webster's shop, had completed his apprenticeship in London before coming to the colonies, and when he struck out on his own boasted that he had "done the principal work" in Webster's enterprise.[45] And of course Betsy's immediate supervisor was Ann King.[46] On any given day some half-dozen men and women bustled about Webster's shop filling orders large and small for the city's more prosperous residents.

Among the most notable products delivered by John Webster (and so also Betsy Griscom) are the sizable orders of John Cadwalader, whose elegant home near the corner of Second and Spruce streets was among the city's showplaces.[47] Cadwalader, a successful Quaker merchant, married Elizabeth

Lloyd, one of the wealthiest women in North America, in 1768. The couple began embellishing their home in high style. From Thomas Affleck, the city's leading cabinetmaker, they acquired card tables (today in the collections of the H. F. du Pont Winterthur Museum and the Philadelphia Museum of Art) and an easy chair (now in the Philadelphia Museum of Art, the mahogany and upholstered easy chair with carved hairy paw-feet that made history when it sold in 1987 for $2.75 million).[48] Cadwalader hired Plunket Fleeson to trim out a bedstead that he had also bought from Affleck. The astronomical prices that early American furniture brings today belie its relative cost in its day; the bed Affleck made cost Cadwalader £12, but Fleeson's bed hangings and window curtains ran more than four times that amount. Fifty-six yards of red copperplate were needed for the Cadwaladers' bedroom. The festoon bed hangings and Venetian window curtains (Affleck had also been engaged to make carved and pierced cornices for both the bed and the windows) were "splendid indeed," ornamented as they were with nineteen large tassels and twenty-eight small ones, finished up with neat trimmings, borders and fringes, and topped with plumes.[49]

So when Cadwalader strolled into Webster's shop late in May 1771, Betsy Griscom and everyone else inside snapped to attention. By July, she had helped complete three sets of Venetian blinds, two sofa cushions and a pair of bolsters, cases and four tassels for Cadwalader's home; twenty-one pounds of curled hair and a dozen yards of canvas suggest that a mattress was in the works as well.[50] Cadwalader must have been pleased with the shop's work; his next order did not disappoint. In January 1772, the women employed in Webster's shop made silk and check cases and covers for the sofas as well as some twenty chairs with fabric that Cadwalader had ordered from a London firm, Rushton and Beachcroft, the summer before. "Although Webster's bill was somewhat vague," writes the textile curator Linda Baumgarten, "an entry in Cadwalader's waste book recorded a payment for 'making Curtains in front & back Rooms, Covers to Settee's & Covers to Chairs in front & back Rooms.'" The covers and curtains for the front room were of a blue silk damask; fabric for the back parlor was yellow. Since the slipcovers Webster's staff produced "fit rather snugly against the seat rails," special care was needed to ensure that the narrow fringe attached to the edges fell just above the carving.[51]

While Betsy Griscom lined and fringed silk damask chair covers and window curtains and helped fabricate Venetian blinds, Webster and the men in his employ assembled pulley lathes and other hardware required to mount them. Betsy also worked to protect the expensive furniture Cadwalader had already acquired when she cut, assembled and trimmed their cases and covers.

But the showplace was yet incomplete. Over the winter and spring Cadwalader would return again and again to Webster's shop, giving Betsy and her companions the opportunity to produce still more goods for the finest domestic interior the city had yet seen. They made bed and window curtains, assembled four carpets (binding pieces to create carpets of the desired size and shape) and fabricated still more blinds. They installed a bit of wallpaper and border to ornament a china cabinet, and made three more mattresses from some fifty pounds of curled hair and not quite two dozen yards ticking.[52]

The bills to Webster's shop alone totaled just over £40—substantial when a typical Philadelphia laborer's annual wages hovered at around £50.[53] The effect created by Betsy and her artisanal counterparts around the city was jaw-dropping. When Silas Deane, in the city in 1775 to represent Connecticut in the Continental Congress, visited the house, he wrote to his wife, "[The] furniture and house exceeds anything I have seen in this city or elsewhere"—an impression surely shared by anyone lucky enough to cross the threshold.[54]

In 1773, two events dramatically altered Betsy's world. First, Great-Aunt Sarah died.[55] Born in the twilight of the seventeenth century, Sarah had witnessed nearly the whole career of Penn's colony. She had seen much of the prelude to the American Revolution but died before Britain's mainland colonies united in an independence movement, and so missed the rebellion that would see her niece made a legend in a nation that did not yet exist. She was Betsy's best and last tie to Andrew Griscom, the founding of the colony, and the city. Did her death feel to the young craftswoman like an unmooring of sorts? Did it leave her feeling rootless and adrift? Or somehow lighter, more weightless?[56] Whatever the answer, Betsy, it turns out, was thinking about more than family history or colonial politics, or even chair cases and bed hangings. She had formed a romantic attachment to one of the other workers in the shop, and the two were contemplating a future together. As the city and the wealth of its most prosperous residents grew, the already thriving market for the tassels, chair covers, bed hangings and valances that Betsy made so beautifully would only expand. The future seemed as bright as the dazzling silk damask she held in her hands.

# PART II

# The Furnace of Affliction

# 5

# Combustible Matters

Young Betsy Griscom was on the edge of adulthood and alert to all of the implications that brings when a series of crises in imperial relations embroiled her family—as artisans and consumers, men and women, leaders and laborers—in turbulence like they had never before seen. Between 1765 and 1770, two wrenching episodes—first the protests that erupted in the wake of the Stamp Act, and then renewed upheaval accompanying the Townshend Duties—washed over Pennsylvania. Together with her mother and sisters, Betsy would find herself among the targets of political rhetoric designed to persuade women to confront the political implications of their choices in the marketplace. After she secured work in an upholstery shop, her political awakening grew acute while she and her coworkers, gathered around worktables, spent hours hashing out the political scene as they braided lace and assembled valances.

For most of these years, Betsy was too young to be directly involved in the debates washing over the city, but one uncle (the venerable Giles Knight, a member of the colonial assembly) would be deeply engaged in the throes of political debate, while another (Abel James) would with his partner Henry Drinker find themselves at the very epicenter of the controversy, as merchants who had the most to gain, and to lose, from the outcome. As tempers flared, there's little chance that either the Griscom dinner table or Webster workroom offered shelter from the storm.

———

"The City of Philadelphia," Lord Adam Gordon noted during his 1764–65 tour of His Majesty's colonies, "is perhaps one of the wonders of the world, if you consider its Size, the Number of Inhabitants, the regularity of its Streets, their great breadth and length . . . their Spacious publick and private buildings, Quays and Docks, the Magnificence and diversity of places of Worship . . . The plenty of provisions brought to Market, and the Industry of all its Inhabitants, one will not hesitate to call it the first Town in America, but one that bids fair to rival almost any in Europe."[1]

Little did Philadelphians know, as Lord Gordon penned his sunny description of their hometown, that the world he so happily described was becoming increasingly fragile. Indeed, little did anyone know. Just at that moment, Britons everywhere swelled with pride at their membership in the world's most powerful empire. They had finally beaten France—decisively, at last—in the battle for supremacy in North America. With the Seven Years' War over, England's glorious future seemed secure. Among the few to perceive an alternate view was the French general Montcalm; as he lay dying on Quebec's Plains of Abraham, Montcalm glimpsed what lay ahead: "I console myself," he said, "that in my defeat and in her conquest, England will find a tomb."[2]

What Montcalm saw was that, without the constant threat of France to bind Americans to the mother country, the relationship between England and its colonies would take quite a different tone. He was right. The same years that saw Betsy Griscom mastering the skills of her trade would be years of confusion, fear and tumult across Britain's Atlantic colonies, but particularly its "first Town." As England struggled to pay for the war, which had saddled the nation with a staggering debt, large populations of men and women whose livelihoods were particularly tied to the trade and taxation measures that so surprisingly ensued were fast to protest (and loudly) what was quickly interpreted as threats to their liberty. Mass public meetings, political violence, street chaos—the years that followed the 1763 Treaty of Paris were punctuated by one political crisis after another. Together these events would lead to the American Revolution. But in the 1760s, they would engage Betsy's uncles, Abel James and Giles Knight, more than the budding craftswoman. When controversy over the Stamp Act erupted in 1765, twelve-year-old Betsy had a child's eye view of these momentous events, overhearing shouts as well as whispers with only a dim understanding of who was angry at whom and why. But the adults all around her knew exactly what was at stake, and Betsy Griscom spent her teenage years listening to her parents, uncles and sisters contend with a succession of crises in the political sphere. The ten years between her first appearance at Webster's shop (as an adolescent starting her first job) and her last (as a confident young craftswoman about to leave childhood behind for marriage and motherhood) would see Betsy Griscom's education in her trade, in politics, in romance, her future forged in a furnace of affliction.

The exhilaration that had accompanied Britain's triumph over France was quickly tainted by confusion and suspicion as residents of the empire's Atlantic possessions began to perceive a change in the imperial temperament. The cost of evicting France from North America had been steep: between 1754 and 1763, the British national debt nearly doubled, jumping from £75 million to £133 million. Taxes in England skyrocketed, and imperial administrators began looking to the two dozen or so colonies they administered across the North American mainland and Caribbean Sea—colonies whose safety the war had helped secure—for a larger share of the revenue required to manage and protect them.

Early signs hinted that something unwelcome was stirring. The so-called Revenue or Sugar Act, passed by Parliament in 1764, cut in half the tax colonists paid on molasses imported from the French West Indies, but it also strengthened measures to enforce compliance. For years, England had looked the other way when colonial smugglers evaded paying duties on foreign molasses, to the tune of close to £200,000 per year in lost revenue.[3] Now administrators needed the money. The English colonists were less alert to the reduction in the duty than the threat enforcement posed to what had been a lucrative extralegal trade with their counterparts in France's Caribbean possessions. Why was the administration suddenly buckling down? And since when did Parliament use these duties not just to steer buyers toward British providers (which most agreed was appropriate) but also to generate income? Then, the Currency Act, which prohibited southern colonies from issuing paper money, came close behind and also seemed to constrain colonial trade. Both new policies implied, to many Americans, that their fellow Britons did not consider them altogether equal members of the realm. There seemed to be a new wind in the air—even a conspiracy afoot—to reduce colonists to second-class citizenship. The most hotheaded observers went so far as to compare these policies to slavery.

British politicians shouldering the weight of taxation and the accompanying public protests saw matters in another light entirely. Their constituents at home in England had watched their tax burden escalate: while taxes per capita in America averaged about eighteen shillings, in England they'd reached a crushing £18—in other words, the English in England were paying almost twenty times the taxes of their counterparts in the American colonies.[4] And now, with the territorial gains made in the war, the empire would have a still-larger area to protect; in time as many as ten thousand men might be stationed in North America to ensure continued peace, if not with competing European nations, then with the Native nations that controlled the territory in and beyond colonial outposts. Why shouldn't the Americans, whose protection cost a small fortune, assume more of the burden?

Searching for solutions, imperial administrators proposed a stamp act. Stamp acts per se were no innovation. They had been implemented as early as the 1690s, when the monarchs William and Mary created an "Act for granting to Their Majesties several duties on Vellum, Parchment and Paper . . . towards carrying on the war against France," and they survive in the United Kingdom today. The operation of the tax was fairly straightforward: to generate revenue for the state, fees were assessed on certain documents or transactions, and a stamp issued when the duties were received, attesting to payment. Government-issued stamps were routinely required in England for paper goods, from newspapers and legal documents to playing cards, and several of the various colonies had already used stamp taxes as a tool to raise funds for their own governments. What was innovative in 1765—and worrisome, if not offensive, to colonists—was that stamp taxes had always been more or less local; they had not been used to collect money in the colonies for use by administrators abroad. If they allowed this door to be opened, colonists feared, there was no telling what might follow.

Imperial managers saw nothing wrong in asking colonies to contribute to the cost of their protection, but colonists necessarily perceived these policy shifts very differently. Drawing what they believed to be a fundamental distinction, they conceded that Parliament had the authority to impose duties designed to regulate trade (import and export taxes, for instance, that influenced prices in ways that favored the British economy and disadvantaged its foreign competitors) but insisted that only colonial legislatures had the power to direct levies designed to raise revenue. Accustomed to the Crown's long-standing hands-off approach to colonial administration, provincials viewed the attempt to meddle directly in colonial affairs by extracting taxes as threatening to the comfortable autonomy they had long enjoyed. Who knew where these new measures might lead? Anxious to nip the troubling developments in the bud, colonists objected strongly.

As a member of the Pennsylvania Assembly, Betsy's uncle Giles Knight was deeply enmeshed in the ensuing debate.[5] Indeed, Pennsylvania's response—political, commercial and popular—would eventually involve Betsy Griscom and every member of her family. But it was another uncle, the merchant Abel James, who would be dragged in first, and deeply. After his father's death in 1746, Abel had entered into a partnership with another aspiring businessman, the twenty-three-year-old John Smith.[6] For three years the two men enjoyed a highly successful enterprise. James bought large shares in four trading ships, importing English dry goods and Irish indentured labor. After James and Smith dissolved their partnership, Abel opened his own store on Water Street, where he sold West Indian rum, sugar, coffee, ginger, cocoa and dry goods. He invested in six more ships and became the sole proprietor of the 140-ton *Tryal*. By 1756, he had decided once again to take on a partner, and chose his father George's onetime apprentice, Henry Drinker. The son of a Philadelphia scrivener, at nine Henry began working in the James family's shop; in turn, George tutored him in "retailing goods & bookkeeping."[7] Now, twenty years later, James & Drinker owned one of the city's largest mercantile houses, exporting the commodities of Britain's colonies on the North American mainland (naval stores, tallow, beeswax, beef, pork and animal hides as well as wheat and flour from Pennsylvania, New York and North Carolina) and importing the products of the West Indies (rum, sugar, molasses, mahogany, coffee and limes). They also imported an enormous amount of finished goods from England. Any visitor to their Water Street store would find a stunning array of produce and wares from around the globe.[8]

When news of the Stamp Act arrived, the Pennsylvania Assembly was pressed to respond. Some might say that colonists overreacted; if all went as planned, the Sugar and Stamp acts together would fund only a third of the cost of the colony's ongoing defense.[9] But for their part, colonial assemblymen worried about both the actual impact of these new revenue tools and the implications for the future if even modest measures were accepted. In September 1765, Pennsylvania legislators, "taking into Consideration the Condition to which the Colonies are, and must be, reduced" should the Stamp Act be executed, appointed a committee charged with drafting resolves in opposition, and asked Giles Knight to serve. Knight had also been appointed, during the same session, to the committee that would draft instructions for the delegates to the Stamp Act Congress planned for New York—an ironic move, since Knight himself appears to have voted against sending delegates at all.[10] Knight was there to keep an eye on things, his appointment meant to reassure those who opposed opposition. Pennsylvania's delegates to the meeting (nine of Britain's North American outposts would send men), as per the instructions that Knight and his colleagues drafted, were permitted to join in a "most decent and respectful" address that sought the Stamp Act's repeal. And no more.

Knight's committee asserted that Pennsylvania's assemblies had always contributed, cheerfully and liberally, to their own defense when the Crown asked for funds, and that they would continue to do so in the future. At the same time, however, "the Inhabitants of this Province are entitled to all the Liberties, rights and Privileges of His Majesty's Subjects in *Great-Britain*, or elsewhere, and that the Constitution of Government in this Province is founded on the natural Rights of mankind, and the notable principles of *English* Liberty, and there is, or ought to be, perfectly free." Since it is both the right and the privilege of British subjects, the representatives argued, to be taxed only with their own consent or that of their elected representatives, and the only legal representatives of Pennsylvanians are those elected annually to serve in the colony's assembly, it follows that the "Taxation of the People of this Province by any other Persons whatsoever . . . is unconstitutional, and subversive of their most valuable rights." In the end, the members of the the Pennsylvania Assembly found it to be their duty to insist that any taxes to be levied on them come only from their own representatives, and hoped their words would stand as a "Testimony of the Zeal and ardent Desire of the present House of Assembly to preserve their inestimable rights, which, as *Englishmen*, they have possessed ever since this Province was settled, and to transmit them to their latest Posterity."[11]

Formal protestations aside, the threat of violence also hung in the air. On the first Saturday in October, the *Royal Charlotte* approached the city, carrying on board the stamped papers for Maryland, New Jersey and Pennsylvania. The matter was soon to become more than an abstract debate over political or economic philosophy, and once implemented, the policy would be that much harder to reverse. The ship had to be stopped. As the *Royal Charlotte* rounded Gloucester Point, others in the harbor lowered their colors to half-mast. Bells throughout Philadelphia were muffled and rang through the day. Faces were frozen in tension, or mourning, "for the approaching loss of Liberty."[12] By late afternoon, thousands of residents had drifted to the statehouse yard to talk about how best to prevent the act from being executed. First, the crowd sent a committee to the office of the stamp distributor John Hughes, asking him to resign his position. Hughes refused but agreed that he would not implement the act in Philadelphia until or unless it was implemented elsewhere. The gathered crowd was dissatisfied with this answer, to say the least; not until the committeemen reported that Hughes (who was already ill when events took this unwelcome turn) seemed to be facing death did their rage subside. By the end of the day, Hughes received a written request again seeking his resignation, first thing Monday morning.

On October 5, when Hughes's commission arrived, another mob converged. Muffled drums beaten through the streets by two black drummers alerted the city that there had been a development. Muffled bells at the statehouse, too, told residents to gather. The assembled citizens sent a deputation to Hughes, again demanding his resignation. Believing that the "Ring Leaders and promoters of this meeting" had "declared and vow'd destruction to [his] person and property" if he "refused to gratify them in this their demand," Hughes submitted his resignation accordingly; his compulsory declaration appeared in the *Gazette* and *Journal* on October 10.[13]

Abel James and partner Henry Drinker fired off a letter to their London suppliers. "You will be alarmed," they guessed, "with repeated Accounts from the several Colonies . . . of the riotous Proceedings of many of the People" aiming to prevent the Stamp Act from being implemented; the "better disposed" did not "Countenance such Tumultuous proceedings," but for the moment, their hands were tied.[14] At the end of October, publishers of the *Pennsylvania Gazette* were regretfully "obliged to acquaint our Readers, that as the most UNCONSTITUTIONAL ACT that ever these Colonies could have imagined, to wit, THE STAMP ACT, is feared to be obligatory upon us, after the First of November ensuing (the FATAL TOMORROW) the Publishers of this paper, unable to bear the Burthen, have thought it expedient to stop a While, in order to deliberate, whether any Methods can be found to elude the Chains forged for them, and escape the insupportable Slavery."[15] Not long after, Assemblyman Joseph Galloway wrote Franklin: "It is difficult to describe the distress to which these distracted and violent measures have subjected the people of this province and indeed all North America. Here are Stamp papers, but the mob will not suffer them to be used, and the public officers of justice and of trade, being under obligation of their oaths and liable to the penalties of the statute, will not proceed in their duties without them." "A stop is put to our commerce," he continued, "and our Courts of Justice is shut up. Our harbors are filled with vessels, but none of them, save those cleared out before the 2d of November dare to move, because neither the Governor or Collector will clear them out, and if they would, the men of war threaten to seize them as forfeited for want of papers agreeable to the laws of trade. Our debtors are selling off their effects before our eyes, and removing to another country, with innumerable other mischiefs brought on us by this fatal conduct, from which I can see no relief but from an immediate repeal of the Act."[16]

The city's importers and retailers agreed to boycott British goods from January 1 to May 1, 1766, and longer, if need be. The upholsterer Plunket Fleeson (who had recently been ejected from the Pennsylvania Assembly, in the same election that affirmed Giles Knight's seat) was among the signers.[17] Committees were appointed to manage the effort, circulating printed copies of the agreement, securing signatures and inspecting ships' holds and shop inventories for contraband goods. Abel James was elected to the eleven-member committee of merchants charged with enforcing the agreement among their peers. He and his counterparts were given public authority to pressure other merchants for their signatures; perhaps more important, they were also authorized to enter the shops and warehouses of men suspected of violating the agreement and, if offensive goods were found, to do whatever they had to do to prevent their sale.

A political gesture, the boycott had the added benefit of advancing the prospects of colonial merchants and artisans, who noted, "There is a full sufficiency of English goods now on the continent for at least seven year's consumption, and it would be for our advantage (the Stamp Act aside), if none were imported for half that time; then we might collect and pay our debts, which are already so heavy that we groan under them."[18] Withholding their commerce would remind Parliament how important the American market was to the British economy; at the same time, it would wean Pennsylvania consumers from imported goods and so promote American manufactures— and manufacturers. Put another way, the less fringe and fewer tassels that Philadelphians bought from European firms, the more work could be had by the girls in John Webster's upholstery shop.

The protestors' argument offered new meanings, with two sides: On one hand, an essay in the *Pennsylvania Gazette* asked readers to consider "the dependent state they must ever be in, if they do not engage in, or encourage Manufactories," but the tremendous consumption of British goods was also proposed as a source of strength: "It is well known that by our consumption of her manufactures we maintain a large proportion of her people."[19] By asserting both arguments simultaneously to uncertain observers, the historian T. H. Breen has proposed, advocates "made it seem almost inevitable that this colonial tail might soon wag the imperial dog."[20]

Though the authors of these polemics, and most of their readers as well, were the men of property most likely to control the government and to be invested in it, implementing nonimportation meant engaging the support of another audience not heretofore considered relevant to the political arena: the city's women. At the front lines of any boycott, the "approbation and assistance" of "the *American Ladies*"—as one essayist noted—was essential. Betsy, her mother and her sisters were constantly urged to "Buy American." To cite just a handful of examples, the owner of a Front Street shop at the "Sign of the Boot and Spatterdash" placed an advertisement seeking to "inform such of the Ladies of Philadelphia [who] are resolved to distinguish themselves by their Patriotism and Encouragement of American Manufactures," that he "makes and sells all Sorts and Sizes of Worsted Shoes, as neat and cheap as any imported from England; he likewise makes the best Calimancoe Shoes . . . allowed by such as have wore them to be equally neat, strong, and lasting with those that come from Bristol." A vendor of rye coffee published his "hope" that "all the fair sex, who have their breasts warmed with love to their country, will admit no foreign coffee to their tables, but ever give their native product the preference."[21]

Young Betsy, then—just shy of her fourteenth birthday—was barraged with public pleas to support the boycott. For the first time in the history of the colony, women like the Griscoms were asked to engage in political discussion—told, even, that their participation was essential to the movement's success. As one essayist insisted, "Great and good examples are certainly powerful inducements to virtue, and when such examples are inforced by the tender persuasions of amiable women they cannot fail to produce wonderful effects"; English tyrants would abandon their "plan of Tyranny and abuse in America," if only they understood how "the Ladies so universally encourage virtuous patriotism in all their conduct and conversation." Women "have been remarkable for sagacity and quick discernments. It is not therefore to be wondered at that so general and patriotic a disposition appears among them to give up tea and finery for Homespun and Liberty, when both reason and experience prove that good Husbands, generous Lovers and faithful Friends are not to be found in a Land of Slavery."[22]

The political currents soon overran their banks. Through the *Gazette*, Betsy discovered that young women in New York were making political statements within the context of courtship by insisting that they forgo marriage licenses rather than acquiesce to the hated law.[23] In New England, a "laudable Zeal for introducing Home Manufactures" caused eighteen women to haul spinning wheels to a local doctor's home, where they sat "spinning from Sunrise until Dark" and "displaying a Spirit for saving their sinking Country rarely to be found among Persons of more Age and Experience." Unafraid to speak frankly about the political nature of their critique, "before they separated, they unanimously resolved that the Stamp Act was unconstitutional." Not only did they affirm their resolve not to purchase any objects manufactured in Britain until the act was repealed; they also declared that they would entertain no romantic overtures from men who did not share their commitment to the boycott.[24]

The social pressure shaping responses to the crisis was strong. One's private views aside, in public it was difficult to do anything but conform. For the record, James and Drinker joined the chorus of voices condemning "those Badges of Slavery—Stampt Papers." Meanwhile, they assured their London contacts that they had little choice but to comply with the groundswell of protest; "our situation is truly alarming," they reported as they canceled their orders from a London supplier, "as no person dare Attempt to use a Stamp Paper, or in the least Degree propose any Thing short of the most fix'd Opposition to it."[25]

With attention riveted on the flow of international goods, artisans everywhere noted—and availed themselves of—the opportunity the political crisis presented to American manufacturers. Betsy's sister Deborah and her husband, Everard Bolton, chose just this moment to open a shop dedicated to the maintenance of imported textiles already in the city. In May 1765, Everard placed his notice announcing that "EVERARD BOLTON and COMPANY," at the Blue Hand, "scours, dyes, cleans and repairs a wide range of imported fabrics for household furnishings as well as genteel apparel." In the middle of a cross-colonial crisis over the importation of goods, the Boltons shrewdly offered Philadelphians a service by which they might prolong the usefulness of cloth and clothing they already owned, cleaning what had been soiled, and dying when the fabric's condition (or style) demanded it.[26] A March 1766 advertisement announces that they had also had "on hand some cloths for sale, and intend to continue to manufacture more, if they meet with suitable Encouragement, which they hope for, as their constant Endeavor will be to please their Customers."[27] The family business was deeply tied to the political crisis; here, in the middle of the nonimportation effort, the Boltons' firm offered to refurbish textiles that needed it. Interestingly, the enterprise—or at least the Boltons' involvement in it—did not extend beyond the crisis; Bolton sold the firm by the end of the year.[28]

Economic pressure and the threat of social upheaval together proved decisive. Parliament capitulated, and voided the Stamp Act. After the brig *Minerva* arrived in the city's harbor in mid-May carrying news of the act's repeal, the celebration in Philadelphia, as elsewhere across the colonies, was effusive. The ship's captain was led to the London Coffee House "with colours flying," and presented with a gold laced hat "for having brought the first certain Account of the Stamp Act being totally repealed." An illumination—a popular act of celebratory observance in early America, in which each family lit the windows of their home, making for an impressive collective display—was quickly organized, and the city's women, deemed so essential to the success of the resistance movement itself, were also congratulated for making the celebration successful: "the Houses made a most beautiful Appearance," editors of the *Pennsylvania Gazette* observed, "to which the Regularity of our Streets contributed not a little; the Scene was, however, variegated, by the different Manner of placing the Lights, Devices, &c. for which the Publick is indebted to the Ladies, who exercised their Fancies on the Occasion."[29] A bonfire was lit; bells pealed across the city; glasses were filled and raised. Abel James was so excited that he instructed one of his apprentices to take his best horse and ride at full speed with a note to New Jersey's governor William Franklin (Benjamin's son). James's personal messenger delivered the news just before Pennsylvania's official express rider arrived at Franklin's door.[30]

To cap the celebration, the statehouse hosted an elegant dinner, at which the city's leadership (surely Giles Knight and Abel James were both in attendance) congratulated themselves on their triumph.[31] After dinner, as per tradition at such events, a long series of toasts ensued. The first round of course saluted the king, and then queen, followed by the Prince of Wales and the rest of the royal family. Another round raised a glass in the hope that the "Illustrious House of HANOVER preside over the United British Empire, to the End of Time"; this was followed by toasts to the House of Lords, the House of Commons and the "present worthy ministry." Next was honored the "Glorious and Immortal Mr. PITT," that "Lover and Supporter of Justice, Lord CAMBDEN," and the London Committee of Merchants; a gesture to America's friends in Great Britain took in anyone else they'd forgotten. Then, the by-now glowing crowd acknowledged the Virginia House of Burgesses and "All other ASSEMBLIES on the Continent, actuated by the like Zeal for the Liberties of their Country." The assembly wished "Prosperity to the Spirited Inhabitants of St. CHRISTOPHERS" (among the few West Indian islands to join in the public protest, burning the stamped paper in their port), success to the "NAVY and ARMY," and thanks to "DANIEL DULANY, Esquire" (whose political tract "Considerations on the Propriety of Imposing Taxes in the British Colonies" was apparently much appreciated). They raised a glass in the hope that "the Interest of GREAT BRITAIN and her COLONIES be always United." Next, they favored "TRADE and NAVIGATION," and then

"AMERICA's Friends in Ireland." Toast number 20 got around to "Prosperity to the Province of PENNSYLVANIA." The twenty-first and final glass was lifted to the "Liberty of the PRESS in America."

The province's cannon in the statehouse yard fired a salute as the first toast commenced, and seven guns after each succeeding. The affair concluded with bonfires, the ringing of church bells and "Strong Beer to the Populace." The proceedings, the editors of the *Gazette* assured readers, "gave general Satisfaction to every Person concerned, so much so that the assembled company unanimously resolved "to demonstrate our Affection to Great Britain, and our Gratitude for the REPEAL of the STAMP ACT, each of us will, on the Fourth of June next, being the Birth Day of our most gracious Sovereign GEORGE III, dress ourselves in a new Suit, of the Manufactures of England, and give what HOME SPUN we have to the POOR."[32]

The city's poor were still wearing the cast-off symbols of colonial patriotism when the subject of domestic manufactures rose again to widespread attention two years later when Parliament passed the Townshend Duties in June 1767. Despite the Stamp Act's hostile reception, the administration struck again a few years later when Chancellor of the Exchequer (today we might think of this office as the secretary of the treasury) Charles Townshend proposed a series of duties, again in order to raise revenue for support of colonial administration. The new plan would impose duties on glass, lead, paints, paper and tea imported into the colonies. The legislation also created the Board of Customs Commissioners to enforce customs laws, which in practice denied those accused of violating the law their cherished access to a trial by jury.

The political outcry objected once again to the implications the tax scheme held for imperial relations, but for artisans and artisans-in-training like Samuel Griscom and his daughter Betsy, these taxes had more tangible effects as well. The enumerated goods hit close to home for anyone working in trades like theirs: crown glass, plate glass, flint glass, white glass, green glass, red and white lead, painters colors, and a wide range of papers, as well as paste-, mill- and scale-boards (thin boards used in bookbinding, hatboxes and the like). The act required, for instance, that "all paper which shall be printed, painted, or stained, in Great Britain, to serve for hangings or other uses" be duted at "three farthings for every yard square, over and above the duties payable for such paper by this act, if the same had not been printed, painted, or stained; and after those rates respectively for any greater or less quantity."[33] In occupations like upholstery, which relied on wallpaper, pasteboard and other such materials in its everyday business, the consequences were worrisome, but for carpenters like Samuel Griscom, they were still more ominous: glass, paint, lead—these were essential elements of the building trades.

The duties were passed in June 1767. If the Carpenters' Company considered their implications at its regular meetings in July and October, no mention was made of this, because no minutes were kept—an omission that would become a habit as the resistance movement gathered steam.[34] But across the city, Philadelphians leaped up to denounce this most recent imperial affront to their native liberties. A long press campaign to drum up support for a renewed resistance movement began when the Philadelphia attorney John Dickinson published his *Letters from a Farmer in Pennsylvania*. (Attorneys, not much more beloved as a class then than they are now, were unappealing spokespersons, hence the adoption of the yeoman persona.) "If you ONCE admit," Dickinson warned readers, "that *Great Britain* may lay duties upon her exportations to us, *for the purpose of levying money on us only,* she then will have nothing to do, but to lay those duties on the articles which she prohibits us to manufacture—and the tragedy of *American* liberty is finished. We have been prohibited from procuring manufactures, in all cases, any where but from *Great Britain* (excepting linens, which we are permitted to import directly from *Ireland*). We have been prohibited, in some cases, from manufacturing for ourselves; and may be prohibited in others . . . If *Great Britain* can order us to come to her for necessaries we want, and can order us to pay what taxes she pleases before we take them away, or when we land them here, we are as abject slaves."[35] The legislation, Dickinson proposed, was at least in part "an *experiment made of our disposition*. It is a bird sent out over the waters, to discover, whether the waves, that lately agitated this part of the world with such violence, have yet *subsided*. If *this adventurer* gets footing here, we shall quickly find it to be of the kind described by the poet," that is, *Infelix vates*, a "direful foreteller of future calamities." Americans would have to bring this bird down, and fast.[36]

Abel James and his fellow merchants, though they condemned the revenue plan along with the rest of the city, were initially reluctant to revive the boycott. The residents of Boston had called for action as early as December 1767. During the spring of 1768, merchants in Boston and New York appealed to their Philadelphia counterparts to join in association, and New York merchants circulated their own nonimportation resolutions by August 1768. In Philadelphia, public pressure heightened in August and September when throngs rallied, urging the Pennsylvania Assembly to act. Giles Knight and his fellow Pennsylvania assemblymen agreed only to send a petition to Parliament asking its members to reconsider.[37]

Finally merchants gave in and pledged to embrace nonimportation. In February and March 1769, more than 250 merchants subscribed to a boycott of British goods, to begin April 1 and continue until they secured repeal. Both Abel James and his partner, Henry Drinker, were elected to the committee charged with enforcing the agreement. James had tried to convince his colleagues that a selective effort would prove more effective, but when they countered that the prospect for getting consensus on what to boycott and what not to were slim, James conceded the point. In a letter to merchants and manufacturers in Great Britain, the Philadelphians denounced the duties, warning that they were all but compelling Americans to "set up Manufactories of their own," devastating the balance of trade in the long run. Not only would Americans refuse to purchase the enumerated goods; they would "put a stop to the importation of [all] goods from Great Britain." The appeal asserting the travesty of the duties as an affront to American "Liberty" went out over James's signature.[38] But at the same time, behind the scenes, James and other merchants hustled to mitigate the damage to their trade, to find silver linings in this cloud of political pressure. For instance, the boycott provided a perfect opportunity for James and Drinker to unload some inferior glass; "stopping the Importation here and at New York seems the only Chance of selling such a Quality." In fact, when rumors began to circulate that the Townshend Duties might be repealed, they rushed to "push off all those articles now before [them]" before it was too late. (Indeed, at least one of James's Philadelphia counterparts would report the "very general wish amongst merchants" that the boycott "may continue at least one Year in order that they may dispose of the great Quantity of Goods on hand.")[39]

In the middle of all this, Abel James's health failed. He traveled to England, ostensibly to enjoy the restorative properties of England's north country, but perhaps, too, to advance Pennsylvania's prospects from across the Atlantic. He soon felt strong enough to help those London merchants inclined to lobby Parliament on the colonies' behalf. Meanwhile, ships filled with cargoes intended for America began returning to England, their hulls filled with goods rejected by American consumers.

Once more, people had to decide how they would respond to the protest movement. As committees emerged to enforce compliance with the nonimportation pact, the smallest choices became politically charged. Leaders of the resistance again embraced a "Buy American" campaign, allowing tradesmen to keep the pressure and spotlight on American goods. As early as January 1768, editorials began advocating the "disuse of all foreign superfluities," urging readers to patronize local businesses instead.[40] Four of the city's glass-makers took out a joint advertisement alerting readers that they would buy broken glass, which they would recycle in a new manufactory.[41] "Colonus" (in the eighteenth century it was common to take a pen name, less to conceal one's identity than to give weight to the opinions therein, which were thereby cast as broader and more enduring than the mere opinion of a single individual, and classical names were often preferred, for gravitas) observed that "it is unquestionably our highest interest to manufacture for ourselves so far as we have materials."[42]

Artisans embraced the protest movement. In October 1768, "A Trades-man" complained in the *Chronicle* that imported goods were the root of a "crowd of vices" including poverty, idleness and pride, and that artisans should follow the lead established by their New York counterparts and refuse to buy imported goods whether or not their own city's merchants continued to support the boycott.[43] More united than ever, artisans argued that merchants, by controlling the protest movement, were suggesting that working men "have no right . . . to *speak* or *think* for themselves." Craftsmen wanted their own representatives—men like them who shared their values and priorities—and a new political force gradually emerged as militant artisans allied with the most radical merchants as well as like-minded professionals.[44]

The upholsterer Plunket Fleeson was particularly incensed. The new tax on paper directly threatened his profits, since selling and hanging wallpaper was a key feature of his business. He promptly alerted readers of the *Pennsylvania Gazette* that he had in stock wallpapers as well as decorative papier-mâché moldings that had been manufactured in Philadelphia. "It cannot be doubted," he asserted, "but that every one among us, who wishes prosperity to America, will give a preference to our own manufactures."[45]

The materials from which one's clothing and furniture were made again became politically loaded. Already in 1766, a company had formed to employ Philadelphia's poor in the manufacture of linen. Abel James had been a sup-porter of this effort; from 1764 to 1767, he was one of the seven proprietors of the factory, launched with the twin aims of providing employment for the poor and profit for the owners.[46] Philadelphians also made "Numerous attempts" to establish a woolen manufactory."[47] James served on the board of another ambitious effort, as well—the Society for the Cultivation of Silk, which aimed to reduce American dependence on this desirable imported cloth.[48]

Again, the protest movement's success hinged on the support of the city's

women, "for we all know how much it is in their power to retrench superfluous expense."[49] The Quaker poet Hannah Griffits circulated a verse
titled "The Female Patriots; Address'd to the Daughters of Liberty in
America; by the same, 1768" that eventually made its way to the *Pennsylvania
Gazette*. In it, she chastised the colony's politicians for shrinking from the
challenge, and promised that their wives and daughters would rise up in
their place:

> Since the Men from a Party, for fear of a Frown, / Are kept by a Sugar-Plumb,
> quietly down / Supinely asleep, & depriv'd of their Sight / Are strip'd of their
> Freedom, & rob'd of their Right. / If the Sons (so degenerate) the Blessing
> despise, / Let the Daughters of Liberty, nobly arise, / And tho' we've no
> Voice, but a negative here / The use of the Taxables, let us forebear.

Griffits added that merchants might be reluctant to embrace nonimportation, but women would embrace nonconsumption: "Refuse all their colours,
tho richest of dye / The juice of a Berry—our Paint can supply / To humor our
fancy—and as for our houses / They'll do without painting as well as our
Spouses."[50]

The *Pennsylvania Gazette*, too, joined the campaign, praising women,
many from the "best families in this town," who pledged to lay aside their
finery. "How agreeable will they appear in their native beauty," the editors
remarked.[51] The press urged women—many of whom had never needed to
know how to spin—to get their hands on a wheel and learn.[52] Model gestures
from other colonies were widely reported in city papers. In the last *Pennsylvania Gazette* of 1767, Philadelphia women read that a "considerable number"
of Boston's "respectable Ladies" had "agreed with each other, that they will
not use any foreign teas from the tenth of December instant, to the tenth of
December 1768." "The music of the spinning wheel," the correspondent continued, "is now heard in many of our best families; and it is surprizing to
observe how many are lately set a going through the town."[53] The same paper
carried this report from Providence, Rhode Island: "It is with pleasure we can
inform the public, and the neighbouring colonies, that the resolutions of our
late town meeting are like to be productive of the most salutary effects.—The
subscription rolls, for suppressing the unnecessary and destructive importation of European goods, and foreign superfluities, and for the encouragement
of industry, economy and manufactures, are now filling up very fast, and
there is not the least doubt but that they will be unanimously signed. Three
young ladies, daughters to a gentleman of fortune in the neighbourhood of

this town, have lately clothed themselves in garments of their own spinning, from the noblest of all motives—LOVE TO THEIR COUNTRY."[54]

This second crisis, however, would develop very differently from the first. When the Stamp Act protest erupted, the principal agents of opposition were among the elite class of merchants most directly affected by the law. Now that the action shifted from merchants to consumers, the movement's center of gravity shifted out of the countinghouses and into the workrooms, beyond offices and parlors and into the streets. Everyday men and women found themselves increasingly caught up in events; politics engaged mass attention in a way that it never had before. To enforce the boycott, there had to be surveillance, lists and monitoring; transgressors had to be caught and properly (meaning publicly) scorned. Across the colonies, newspapers published detailed lists of the goods to be avoided. One broadside chastised merchants caught selling enumerated merchandise, whose base greed caused them to "subvert the grand, the glorious cause of Liberty; long ably, virtuously and successfully supported by our Brethren on the continent in general, and the truly patriotic *Philadelphians* in particular."[55] No shallow penitence would be tolerated; men who thought perfunctory apologies would suffice quickly learned how very wrong they would be. One man, dissatisfied with the account of some errant men's confessions in the *Journal,* had five hundred cards printed with the names of the "villainous" gentlemen attached. Public shaming now claimed a place in the protester's tool kit.

The strategy was rife with potential for homegrown tyranny. Whom, exactly, did these extralegal committees represent? "This," one correspondent pointed out in the local paper, "is a point in which every freeholder of this province is highly interested. And in which every one of them has a right to a voice." Just what was the source of authority claimed by "subscribers to the non-importation," who appeared to have assumed "an exclusive right to determine this matter?" It was beginning to look like the "subscribers to the non-importation have the sole right to determine a question of liberty"—in and of itself a threat to liberty—since if "those two or three hundred subscribers have a right to make the agreement voice whenever they please, it is a plain inference that they have a right to decide on a point which affects the liberties of the people of this province." Votes, this essayist insisted, not signatures, were the correct way to express the public will—a method that necessarily excluded young Betsy Griscom.[56]

Though the movement's initial efforts were successful, frightening incidents in the summer and fall of 1769 altered the city's temper. In July, a ship called the *Charming Polly* arrived at port with a load of malt. The city's brewers refused delivery, and, at a contentious public meeting, the assembled residents declared anyone in receipt of the goods an "enemy to his country." The fervor unleashed shocking brutality. In mid-October, after customs officials seized several casks of contraband wine, sailors tracked down the supposed informant, John Keats, and subjected him to street discipline. To tap the curative effect of humiliation, they tarred and feathered him and put him into a cart with a rope round his neck, to be wheeled through the city. When Keats—surely weakened—would not "get up & shew himself" as some "thought he ought," the mob pulled him out of the cart, and, when he would not or could not walk, "dragge'd him over the Stone half the length of a street." Now on his feet, Keats was driven through the street until the crowd reached the pillory, where tormentors hurled mud and stones at the supposed informer. In all, the crowd "beat and kicked" him for about four hours before leaving him at the customhouse door. Later that day, someone wrote "Woe be to the collector" on the building's wall.[57]

In the midst of such public tension, the Society of Friends' commitment to pacifism threatened to divide the city's resistance effort. Nervous about where all this upheaval was leading, Philadelphia's Quaker leadership condemned all involvement in committee activity by its members. Abel James was by this time in England, but Henry Drinker, who favored nonimportation, reluctantly retreated from active participation in the movement. (In time Drinker would decidedly oppose the continued boycott.)[58] Quaker merchants were advised to withdraw from the nonimportation agreements, and all Friends were instructed to give a wide berth to resistance activities that could lead to violence. It was a glimpse of a wedge that would fracture revolutionary Philadelphia.

By spring 1770, merchants had run through their stock. Empty shelves made them impatient. In May, Pennsylvania's colonists learned that Parliament had again given in and repealed the duties on everything but tea. While a handful of merchants urged their counterparts to maintain the boycott as a matter of principle concerning the ongoing dispute over taxation policies and colonial sovereignty, most were eager to put the whole episode behind them. But the city's artisans—many of whom had enjoyed a "fragile prosperity" while the boycott was in force—had other plans.[59] Rallied by Charles Thomson, the city's "artisans, manufacturers, tradesmen, mechanics and others" resolved "to render the non-importation, as it now stands, permanent."[60] At a mass meeting Thomson read a letter from Benjamin Franklin urging them to stay the course. A five-point program emerged that was embraced by artisans across Philadelphia: they would strive to maintain nonimportation "by all prudential ways and means"; to "exert our Influence for the Promotion of American Manufactures, both by using them ourselves, and by recommending them to others"; to boycott any merchant who breaks the agreement; to boycott those Rhode Island suppliers who had already abandoned nonimportation; and to attend a June meeting of the merchants subscribing to nonimportation and demand its continuation.[61]

When those merchants subscribing to nonimportation met in June to consider their options, they found themselves met by a mass of tradesmen, urging them on. A few days later, "A House Carpenter" (surely not Samuel Griscom, but one of his colleagues) argued in the local press that the merchants "dread a further continuance of the non-importation agreement, as [they] see with grief and astonishment, that if they continue one year longer the vend for British manufactures will be ruined in future, as industry, manufacturing and economy gain ground every hour, which will finally render English goods unnecessary."[62] Much to the dismay of many of the city's merchants, the June meeting voted to maintain nonimportation. But by the early fall, merchants began to demand an end to the protest. The Merchants Committee continued to try to enforce the measures, but did so halfheartedly—at least in the view of the newly formed Mechanics Committee, eager to extend (and so, police) the ban.

In July, New York merchants abandoned their protest. On the fourteenth, a large meeting in the statehouse yard denounced the disloyal New York merchants and pledged not to trade with that colony. But when Boston and Newport also lifted trade restrictions, Philadelphia merchants knew they must follow suit. In September, seventeen city merchants sent a letter asking the nonimportation committee to canvas the boycott's subscribers and see what they wanted to do. James and Drinker's firm was among the signatories. But a boycott only succeeds if it is unanimous, and the merchants were no longer united in the cause. When the signers met a week later, they agreed to abandon the general boycott and resume normal trade on everything but tea. Days later, a large rally gathered on the statehouse grounds to protest their decision. But the deal was done—or, rather, undone.

Abel James sailed home that fall to learn that, just weeks before docking in Philadelphia, he had been elected to the Pennsylvania Assembly, likely in rebuke to the radicals who had pressed to extend the general boycott. He disembarked at a city transformed. Plenty of opportunities for grudges had emerged, among merchants within Philadelphia and between them and merchants in other cities, between Quakers and other populations within the fractious city, and within the Quaker community itself. The artisanal community, though defeated, was galvanized. As the Quaker leadership backed away from the swelling resistance movement, the city's artisans stepped toward it. They had come to see the craft community as a force unto itself—one which no longer needed the traditional leadership or representation of the city's elites. Never again would the city's artisans assume a deferential posture when it came to formulating or expressing their collective will. When the fall elections rolled around, a "Brother Chip" editorialized that his fellow carpenters vote only for candidates who represented their interests; for the first time in recent memory, a craftsman ran for the office of sheriff, artisans were elected to four of the ten city offices on the ballot, and a tailor was voted into the Pennsylvania Assembly.[63]

The significance of these political epiphanies as a turning point for the entire Revolution cannot be overestimated. Tired of acceding to the political judgment of the ruling class, carpenters, upholsterers and other tradesmen began to see themselves as men who deserved a voice in the political arena. Before May 1770, artisans had worked collectively when circumstances called for it, but such actions were limited to those who shared a single craft, or to address a specific issue. The imperial crisis brought craftsmen—and craftswomen—together. Also, as their interests diverged from those of the merchants, who had always provided leadership on commercial questions, craftsmen had to start cultivating their own leaders.

Samuel Griscom had managed to steer well clear of controversy during these years, but the artisanal channels in which he and his family traveled had been altered—even radicalized, as historians would say today. His daughter Betsy had been just a girl when the Stamp Act crisis erupted, but by the time this second flare-up had subsided, she was eighteen. She had seen real violence come to the "first Town in America" and learned firsthand the tangible animosity that could accompany abstract political discussions. By the end of the year, routines in the city's upholstery shops were returning to normal; no sooner had the crisis resolved than the upholsterer John Mason was advertising the wares of the Crown and Cushion with his usual flair, playing on the recent political rhetoric to remind readers that he takes the "LIBERTY" of selling his "PROPERTY": furniture checks, mattresses, sacking bottoms, and the usual stocks of upholstery goods.[64]

But during the same months when a young Betsy Griscom nervously watched wrenching events unsettle the public sphere, another series of crises, eruptions and interventions unsettled more domestic equilibriums. If George III was frustrated with these unwelcome assertions of discontent among his unruly subjects, he had nothing on Samuel Griscom.

# 6

# Domestic Rebellions

While imperial government over the Atlantic colonies was unraveling, so did parental government, in the Quaker community, and in the Griscom household. The months between summer 1769 and January 1771—the same seasons that saw the province straining against imperial authority—saw the Griscom girls straining against parental and religious authority, fomenting rebellions of their own. Teenaged Betsy watched as one sister after another ran afoul of Quaker discipline: Deborah, Susannah, Mary and then Sarah found themselves facing the prospect of disownment. Month after month, members of the Philadelphia Monthly Meeting recorded in their minutes the plodding progress of earnest conversations in the Griscom parlor. It was a tutorial in resistance, and Betsy learned its lessons well.

The Society of Friends had been watching nervously for some time as its ability to control its children seemed to be on the wane. By the late 1760s and '70s, Philadelphia's Friends were embroiled in internal change and an effort to implement reforms. Quakers concerned that their community was losing the discipline that formed the core of their faith sought to restore a more uniform religious fervor that was separate from the world. Many Friends found themselves turned out of the Society as it struggled with issues of wealth and politics. A rising tide of sentiment opposed to slavery and favoring abolition was already increasing tensions; the midcentury war with France and now this looming conflict with the mother country further divided the faithful. That the Society turned inward, and in so doing became less tolerant of deviations from its core values, changed the faith forever.

The reform movement that gathered momentum in the 1760s included a reassertion of the rules pertaining to marriage. The Friends had only just produced an updated version of the *Discipline*, that "Collection of Christian and Brotherly Advices" that was part spiritual guide, part handbook for policies and procedures.[1] When the Yearly Meeting drafted a new *Discipline* in 1762, it drew on material collected in past editions, adding new advice where appropriate. The new version consumed some three hundred handwritten pages and covered topics from Burials and Arbitrations to Conduct and Conversation, Tale-Bearing and Back-Biting. Friends could consult the *Discipline* for guidance concerning Wills, Schools and Trading, and for warnings about Taverns, Gaming and Sorcery. With the new compilation of guidelines, Quaker elders also began enforcing more rigorously policies and practices concerning external unions. In the 1750s, '60s and '70s, one-third of all disciplinary cases involved "incorrect" marriages; by the late 1760s, two-thirds of these cases would end in disownment.[2]

In the same years that the mother country struggled to exert greater control over her colonial offspring, the Society of Friends worried over ongoing problems with Quaker youth, who more and more seemed to be sleeping in meetings, leaving before they were over, and engaging in other "unbecoming behaviors."[3] In 1771, elders urged parents to take a firmer hand to arrest the "sorrowful deviation among youth both in dress and address."[4] A year later, fathers and mothers still appeared to be dropping the parental ball; leaders were "painfully apprehensive that amongst some, there is too great a neglect of Quaker precepts of decency and moderation," evidenced "by the gay appearance of many of the youth among us."[5]

Apparently, young Quaker men and women were finding the strictures of the Church too binding and the world's amenities irresistible. That's not all they failed to resist. More and more often, Quaker youths were choosing marriage partners from outside the Society of Friends, to the dismay of their parents and elders. Samuel and Rebecca Griscom got their first taste of this small rebellion when Betsy's oldest sister, Deborah, married Everard Bolton in Philadelphia's First Baptist Church, "contrary," of course, to Quaker discipline. On the face of it, twenty-five-year-old Everard probably seemed like a fine choice and a promising son-in-law. The Boltons, like the Jameses and the Knights, were an old Byberry family; when Rebecca James was growing up, her father, George, had served as an overseer of the Quaker meeting alongside another Everard Bolton, the grandfather of Deborah's new husband.[6] Everard's father, Isaac Bolton, had been born in the colony in 1697. He and his wife, Sarah Jones, moved to Philadelphia in 1722, but in 1750 they returned to Abington, where Isaac farmed and also worked as a peltsmonger. With the right start and his own abilities to contribute, Isaac Bolton became extremely wealthy.[7] The Boltons were also prominent members of their local meeting; Sarah Bolton, one of Everard's older sisters, was a Byberry minister.[8]

But when they decided to marry, Deborah and Everard did not comply with Quaker strictures. For reasons now lost to history, they married in the city's newly built Baptist church instead.[9] It does not seem to have been an unplanned pregnancy that drove them in this direction, since their first child did not arrive until March 1766, two years after they exchanged vows (though of course if an earlier pregnancy ended in miscarriage we would not now know). But despite the irregular wedding, they chose to comply with procedures designed to express formal regret and repair their relationship with the community. The couple submitted a signed statement condemning their actions, a gesture that, alongside conversations Friends had had with the newlyweds, gave firm "ground to hope they are sincere in condemning their unchastity, and their transgression of our religious testimony and Discipline, by marrying by a priest, and their disobedience to their parents therein."[10] The Boltons assured the Quakers that their future conduct would prove the sincerity of their regret, and after a statement to that effect was read at the close of a first-day morning meeting, unity was restored. Having settled that unpleasant matter, the Friends turned to the next item on the agenda: a report from Abel James on efforts toward the construction of a new building. One wonders what James was thinking as his niece's apology was read before his friends and fellow faithful. Was it uncomfortable for him to sit quietly as she confessed to her errors? Was it uncomfortable for Deborah, or Rebecca, to see Uncle Abel sitting in his seat, staring ahead as the condemnation was read?

Perhaps everyone's discomfort was less than we might imagine. Deborah's marriage outside meeting was not ideal, but neither was it especially egregious; larger numbers of Quaker youth were sidestepping procedure, so Samuel and Rebecca, who had done something similar themselves, had plenty of Quaker parents to commiserate with them when their eldest violated the strictures of their faith. And then Deborah and her new husband—who was otherwise clearly a good catch for their daughter—took the steps necessary to restore their membership among the city's Friends.

In the years that followed, as the crisis over the Stamp Act and then the Townshend Duties unfolded, the whole family turned their attention to the more pressing public matters at hand. But real trouble for the Griscoms erupted again in summer 1769, during the height of the nonimportation movement, when their daughter Susannah married the mariner Ephraim Doane at Saint Paul's Church in Philadelphia, and—far worse—their daughter Mary gave birth to an illegitimate child.

Doane would have seemed a good mate for Susannah if the couple had wed through proper channels. A master mariner by the time he and Susannah met, Ephraim was the son of a prosperous Wrightstown farmer and tavern keeper who had moved with his family from Cape Cod at the tail end of the seventeenth century.[11] But Samuel and Rebecca disapproved (as their faith recommended) of Susannah's desire to wed outside the Society of Friends, making it impossible for her both to conform to the discipline *and* to marry the man of her choosing. So she married him in his own church, Saint Paul's.

In December 1769, the women's meeting asked Ann Howell and Hannah Saunders to "confer" with Susannah, "being married contrary to the rules of our discipline, to a Man of another religious profession."[12] When the women's meeting convened again the following month, Howell and Saunders reported that they had met with the new Mrs. Doane, and that she "took kindly to their visit, but required some more time for more deliberate consideration." It was a stalling tactic. Susannah was willing to admit some fault to Ann and Hannah within the safe harbor of her family's parlor, but she was not anxious to face the women's meeting itself, where she would be asked, among other things, to formally express her public regret at, if not the choice of her spouse per se, then the circumstances of her marriage. In February 1770, the emissaries again reported that Susannah "continued disposed to condemn her misconduct," but again "requested some longer time." March and April passed, and Susannah did not appear at the meeting. She agreed to come in May, but some last-minute obstacle prevented her from attending, so she asked for another extension. June came and went without any contact, the Friends noting Susannah's request for "forbearance, some considerable time since" (their own forbearance apparently beginning to wane). They agreed to delay again in July, and fully expected her to appear in August, but by the time the meeting was set, some "indisposition of the body" made it impossible once again for her to attend.

And so it went through the fall. Susannah was in no rush to bring this matter to a speedy conclusion. In December, fully a year after proceedings were initiated, the group noted that Susannah was "still declining to offer an acknowledgement of her breech of good order, notwithstanding she diverse times exprest an inclination thereto." In view of what was now an intolerable delay, they concluded themselves "at Liberty to proceed" without her. At the monthly meeting, Susannah not showing a "disposition to condemn" her breach of the discipline, two members were asked to prepare a testimony to that effect. In January 1771, they issued the following statement: "Susanna[h] Doan (late Griscom) who was educated and made Profession with Friends hath so far disregarded our Christian Testimony, and the rules of our Religious Society, as to be married by a hireling priest to a Man of another Profession without the Consent of her Parents, therefore we can no longer esteem her a Member in fellowship with us until from a Sense of her outgoing she Condemns the same to the Satisfaction of this Meeting which she may through Divine Grace be enable to do is our desire." The Philadelphia Monthly Meeting handled close to fifty cases every year; most took just under five months to resolve, and two-thirds were settled in seven, but when Anna Warner and Margery Norton finally delivered the meeting's statement to Mrs. Doane, it was an event Susannah had successfully postponed for more than a year.[13]

Mary's case unfolded more quickly, though she rode Susannah's foot-dragging as long as she could. The two cases had been introduced at the same December 1769 meeting. With Susannah's transgression introduced, the members of the women's meeting turned with a sigh to the next errant Griscom: the team of Friends dispatched to "treat with" Susannah were also to discuss Mary Griscom's "reproachful conduct, the consequence wherein being" that she was now the "mother of an illegitimate child."[14] Howell and Saunders made their way to the Griscoms' Arch Street home and settled in the parlor for a serious discussion. It is easy to picture the younger girls—seventeen-year-old Betsy, fourteen-year-old Hannah and even seven-year-old Rachel, straining to catch some of what must have been a tense conversation.

The Quaker community of course did not countenance sex outside marriage. Nevertheless, premarital intimacies would bring more than forty women before the women of the Philadelphia Monthly Meeting between 1760 and 1780.[15] Over two dozen of these were, like Mary Griscom, guilty of bastardy. Ann Howell and Hannah Saunders tried to persuade Mary to renounce her unchaste behavior, and to their relief, found her, like Susannah, cooperative: Mary seemed in a "good disposition of mind" to concede her error.[16] This time, however, it was Samuel Griscom who asked the women for more time; he did not want his daughter to face her fate until he was sure she was good and ready. Mary's case, together with Susannah's, languished through most of the year, one delay after the next. In July, however, Mary's attitude toward her situation seems to have changed. She finally reported that the fact of the matter was that she did not genuinely believe herself "so sensible of her offence, as the Nature thereof requires," and so told Ann Howell and Hannah

Saunders that the women's meeting should go ahead and do what it needed to do. She would accept disownment.

In choosing this path, Mary was like most of the other Quaker women similarly chastised in these years. Of the fifteen women the Philadelphia women's meeting "treated with" for this offense in the 1760s and '70s, fully eleven were unrepentant, choosing not to submit to Quaker discipline.[17] Perhaps the jolly little baby in Mary's arms made her feel less sorry for her actions, unlikely to consider the union that produced her beautiful new son as "evil conduct." Perhaps Deborah and Susannah, having forged their own paths away from Quaker strictures, shored up her resolve. Proceedings against her were initiated. A testimony was drafted that Mary was "so far deluded by the Enemy of her Peace, as to be guilt of Unchastity, for which she hath been often tenderly treated with, but not appearing in a suitable disposition of Mind to condemn the same, We think it our Duty, for the clearing of Truth, to declare against the Evil Conduct of the said Mary Griscomb [sic], and Disown her being in religious Fellowship with us until from a sense of her sinful Conduct and the Reproach she hath occasioned thereby, she shows proper Signs of Repentance, seeks to be reconciled with Friends, and condemns the same to the Satisfaction of this meeting."[18] By October 1770, the testimony was in Mary's hands, and she too was disowned. Samuel and Rebecca were three-for-three: Deborah, Susannah and now Mary had all been estranged from their community of faith.

Mary did not remain a single mother for long. Since she married the clock- and watchmaker Thomas Morgan in 1770, he seems the likely father of her unsanctioned child.[19] For some reason, Mary did not take the same path that many of her Quaker counterparts did, and marry Thomas quickly in order to conceal the date of the child's conception, but outside the time-consuming procedures mandated by the Friends' discipline. To some minds, this would have constituted a less grievous offense. Perhaps Thomas was away or otherwise unavailable to rescue his intended from these unseemly proceedings. He appears to have been living in Baltimore around this time; he may for some reason have been unable to return in time to spare Mary the painful process.[20] Mary went on to raise a family with Thomas, severing her ties with the Quaker community. Though they escaped the immediate scrutiny and censure of their former Friends by moving to Baltimore for the next several years—where Thomas kept a shop at the Sign of the Arch Dial—they in time returned to Philadelphia. Their sons and daughter, as we shall see, would become some of the nieces and nephews closest to their aunt Betsy.[21]

But the troubles between the Griscom girls and the women's meeting were not yet over. Just months after these awkward events, the women's meeting took up the case of Sarah Griscom, who had married William Donaldson on December 31, 1770, in Philadelphia's Christ Church. By now, Samuel and Rebecca had surely tired of sitting in their parlor watching pairs of Friends confer with their various children over their various offenses. It was only just the Friday a few days before Sarah's wedding that the Philadelphia Monthly Meeting reported its unsuccessful effort to treat with Susannah over her actions, and instructed two members to prepare a testimony to that effect, and now on Monday Sarah (perhaps emboldened by watching these conversations unfold over the previous week) had to elope with her own beau. How much of this sort of thing could parents take?

The Donaldsons were, compared to the Griscoms or the James family—or the Boltons, for that matter—new arrivals to the colony. William's parents had been born in Glasgow and Ulster; his brother Arthur had been born in Belfast, though William himself had been born in Darby, Pennsylvania, just south and west of Philadelphia.[22] The family had migrated to Britain's colonies in the mid-Atlantic, probably first to New Jersey, where Arthur Donaldson met and married Elizabeth Kaighn, Sarah and Betsy's Gloucester County cousin.[23] It seems likely that it was through the 1763 marriage of cousin Elizabeth that Sarah Griscom came to know Arthur's brother William. Sarah apparently found his Irish coloring—dark brown hair set against his "fresh" complexion—appealing.[24] The couple were eager to wed—so eager, in fact, that they too skipped the long, deliberative process favored by the Friends and married of their own accord at Christ Church.

Like Susannah, during the initial visit from the delegates from the women's meeting, Sarah had seemed contrite, "in a good disposition of mind, and very desirous to make satisfaction." Surely eyebrows were raised when Sarah asked for more time before any additional steps were taken; the Friends had seen this maneuver before. Sarah offered to come to the October 1771 meeting but then canceled. In November, she tried to escape appearing by sending along a note acknowledging her breach of discipline, but the women's meeting decided to hold off reading it until the offender could be present, to face her punishment in person. Finally, in December, Sarah made the dreaded walk to the meeting. The acknowledgment was read and sent on to the men's meeting, where it was accepted.[25] A "satisfactory report being made concerning her by some Friends who treated with her," Sarah seems to have restored her membership in the Friends' community.

Samuel and Rebecca had now watched as four of their daughters experienced the trials of Quaker discipline. It is possible that their marriage choices cast a slanting light on more than the Griscom family's spiritual commitment.

As the constraints of the Friends' discipline heightened competition for Quaker mates, children from wealthier families found themselves in a comparatively advantageous position; one study finds that the daughters of poorer parents married, on average, almost six years later than their wealthier counterparts, and sons about seven.[26] Perhaps Betsy's sisters had felt compelled to look beyond the Society of Friends when it came time for them to think about their lives outside their parents' house. The fact that Deborah and Sarah eventually chose to reconcile themselves to the Quakers after their transgressions suggests that they weren't uniformly opposed to the faith's values. But Mary and Susannah chose to forgo any effort to restore unity with the meeting; whether their unity with their parents was damaged as well we will never know.

As the Griscom girls faced these inquiries and eventual disownments, so too did ever-larger numbers of Quakers across the colony. Over the course of Betsy's young life, Pennsylvania meetings had disowned more than one in five of their members—more than fourteen hundred of those for irregular marriages.[27] And it wasn't just the headstrong youth who found themselves the targets of the revitalized faith; when Uncle Giles Knight remarried in 1770, the Abington Monthly Meeting appointed a committee to investigate whether he and his second wife, Phebe, had been "guilty of Fornication." (They had been "married by the assistance of a priest," always cause for disapproval.) A testimony disowning Knight was approved by August, and in September Phebe informed the women's meeting that she no longer desired "to be Continued under the notice" of the Abington Friends. She did not appeal her dismissal. It would be eighteen years before Giles and Phebe rethought their position and submitted an acknowledgment of their error to the Abington Monthly Meeting; at that remove, the meeting did not rush to accept it, but finally the quarterly meeting recommended that the Knights at long last be restored to membership.[28]

When Samuel and Rebecca Griscom looked around the dinner table in January 1771, they saw four more daughters—Rebecca, Betsy, Rachel and Hannah—who would either conform to discipline or reject it. Surely the girls watched these events closely, too—the quiet, earnest discussions between their sisters and their Quaker neighbors, the louder conversations with their parents, and whispered ones among the sisters. By the time Sarah's dispute was resolved, Betsy was almost twenty and surely thinking about her own marriage prospects. One man in particular had caught her eye, a hardworking fellow employee at the upholstery shop. But her parents wouldn't be pleased with her choice, the son of an Anglican clergyman. His name was John Ross.

# · 7 ·

# Union and Disunion

A<small>s</small> Betsy greeted her twenty-first birthday, a glance over the pages of the *Pennsylvania Chronicle* suggested a quiet beginning to 1773. The city was unusually still now that the Delaware River was iced over, blocking the passage of ships into or out of port. The groves of masts usually crowded along the city's waterfront were absent; buildings along the Jersey shore were curiously visible across a field of ice. "We have had 'very cold,' 'extremely cold,' 'excessive cold,' and 'exceeding cold,'" one woman wrote in the pages of her diary, but "none of these separately is sufficient to convey the idea of the temperature of this day—it needs more than the superlative degree, it would take a super-superlative degree if there is such a one."[1] People could not remember a season this cold since the winter an ox was frozen on the river. Perusing the pages of the newspaper by the warmth of a fire, Betsy little knew how ominous was a single line in the year's first editor's column: "We hear that some material changes in the government of America, and the West Indies, are now in agitation."[2] By the time New Year's would roll around again, a new crisis would reignite tensions between the Penn family and its imperial administration. Conversation would again become strained, one's choices in the city's shops once more subject to scrutiny. After three years of relative calm, a new chain of events would force Philadelphians to harden positions on imperial relations. Friendships with some would mean fallings-out with others. Betsy Griscom found herself ensnarled in large and small dramas that were all at once political, familial, economic and romantic. And one way or another, all of it was tied to East Indian tea.

———

For a young woman in love, the city's fraying nerves came at the worst possible time. After several years in the upholstery trade, Betsy had learned her craft well, having attended for several years now to the routine business of John Webster's shop: upholstering sofas and chairs; sewing slipcovers; making, trimming and mounting curtains, canopies and bed hangings; assembling window blinds; and helping customers select silks, linens, wallpapers and other materials. Between chair cases and window blinds the young craftswoman had also found some time to cultivate romance. Betsy had become increasingly attached to an ambitious and charming minister's son who worked alongside her in Webster's workrooms. In the yellow buckskin breeches, checked shirt, red flannel jacket and leather apron common to Philadelphia tradesmen, the dark and handsome John Ross was the picture of artisanal appeal. As the rest of the city braced for its biggest political storm yet, Betsy had marriage on her mind.

Ross had been born while his parents were living in Germantown, probably about the same time as Betsy, between 1750 and 1752.[3] His family, like hers, had been in the colonies for decades. At the turn of the century his grandfather George Ross, an Anglican missionary with the Society for the Propagation of the Gospel (or SPG), had emigrated from Scotland, assigned to a post in New Castle, Delaware. Indeed, the advent of the first Ross was meant to be an antidote to the first Griscom, the one Society founded to offset the other. The SPG, organized in the 1690s, was created partly to counter the wildly flourishing Society of Friends, whose prosperity and profusion threatened to dominate British North America. Its first missionary was none other than George Keith, who sailed to England to continue advocating the theological positions that failed so spectacularly in Pennsylvania, and in time converted to Anglicanism. In March 1702, he crossed the Atlantic once more, this time on the Anglican shilling. And close behind was the Reverend George Ross.[4]

Born in 1679 in Balblair, Scotland, Ross graduated from the University of Edinburgh in 1700.[5] Once ordained in the Church of England, he took a position as a chaplain on a man-of-war. Soon thereafter he accepted this post from the SPG, a missionary in the New World. He would serve congregations in both Pennsylvania and Delaware, but after 1717 was stationed in New Castle, where he remained for the rest of his pastoral career. He and his wife, Joanna Williams, welcomed six children into the world, but she died in the 1720s, and George raised them mostly on his own.

Of George's several sons, only one—Aeneas—followed him into the ministry. Born in Delaware and educated in Scotland, in 1741 and 1742 Aeneas served briefly as assistant rector in Philadelphia's renowned Christ Church before he was assigned to Saint Thomas Church in Whitemarsh and Trinity Church at Oxford just north of Philadelphia. He would eventually move to his father's church in New Castle. It was during these years that Aeneas courted a wife and started his family. He married Sarah Leech in 1744, and two years later they celebrated the birth of their first child, Aeneas Jr. Over the next decade, Aeneas and Sarah cradled five more children.[6] But these years proved difficult for the young couple. Aeneas Jr. died when he was just eleven, and three daughters—Maria, Mary and Sarah—followed him while still infants. New Castle remained a hardscrabble place; as George Ross would observe, "The town of Newcastle consisting of about fourscore houses waxes poorer and poorer, and falls into Contempt more and more, every year, having Several houses without inhabitants, & Some not fit for habitation."[7] The place's "dying Condition" was "partly owing," Ross claimed, "to an upstart village lying on a neighboring creek"; indeed, Wilmington, which enjoyed superior water access, would eclipse New Castle in the years to come, contributing to the difficult life ministers there endured.

On top of these already trying circumstances, the family endured still more difficulty as John's mother, Sarah, struggled, apparently unsuccessfully, to preserve her sanity.[8] John's experience with mental illness would resonate throughout Betsy's life—not only in shaping the man he would become but twenty years later when Betsy would watch another member of her family struggle with her own demons. By then, she would know more than she perhaps bargained for about illnesses of the mind.

Sarah Ross's mental instability emerged at least as early as the move to New Castle and perhaps earlier. Her neighbors would in time observe that she had been "bereaved of her understanding and wholly disqualified to manage her Household affairs" for as long as they'd known her.[9] Unable to care for her himself and eager to avail himself of facilities available at Philadelphia's impressive new hospital, Aeneas made the difficult decision to place his wife in institutional care. The Rosses were not in a position to pay for her treatment; when her name was first entered into the hospital's record book, it was among the "poor." Ross's parishioners, however, intervened. In a letter to hospital administrators, a number of Ross's supporters wrote to "certify . . . that Sarah the wife of the Rev'd Aeneas Ross . . . hath during her residence in this place, for near five years past, been Lunatick." At the reverend's request the men wrote to "recommend her to you as a patient proper to be admitted into your charitable institution."[10]

Sarah Ross was admitted to the Pennsylvania Hospital for the Sick Poor in August 1764 and diagnosed with "lunacy."[11] More than 220 men and women had already sought the hospital's care the year she was admitted, for a range of maladies from dislocated shoulders, frostbite and all sorts of injuries on the job (one mariner was admitted when a case of sugar fell and crushed his chest; another man was brought in when he fell into a well and broke his leg) to scurvy, dropsy, rheumatism and an array of fevers and agues. Some sixteen men with "Lues Venerea"—a venereal disease—crossed the hospital's threshold, as did others with gonorrhea.

Mental illness, however, presented special challenges. The hospital had been the idea of Dr. Thomas Bond, who in 1751 with the help of Benjamin Franklin gathered subscriptions in support of a public institution able to care for the colony's indigent residents. In a petition to the legislature, "sundry inhabitants" articulated their concerns regarding the colony's mentally unstable inhabitants, "some of them going at large, a Terror to their Neighbors, who are daily apprehensive of the Violences they may commit: and others are continually wasting their Substance, to the great Injury of themselves and Families, ill-disposed Persons wickedly taking Advantage of their unhappy condition, and drawing them into unreasonable bargains, etc."[12] Soon thereafter the Pennsylvania Assembly, in an "ACT to encourage the establishing of a Hospital for the Relief of the Sick Poor of this Province, and for the Reception and Cure of Lunaticks," chartered the effort. Eager to address the problem of mental illness, the earliest managers and physicians were nevertheless ill-equipped to treat patients effectively; the numbers of locks, chains, handcuffs and leg locks that appear in the early records suggest that confinement was the main remedy available for many patients. The hospital's plan (construction began in 1755) was designed with the needs of this population in mind, with mentally ill patients housed on the ground floor near extensive grounds available for exercise, with galleries on the first story of each ward "eighty feet in length for such of them as may be trusted to walk about." Unfortunately, these amenities also invited unwanted gawking; on Sundays, Philadelphians with nothing better to do strolled to the hospital to "see the crazy people," attention so annoying to patients and managers alike that in April 1767—Sarah's third year there—an order was reissued that "the Hatch door be kept carefully shut and that no person be admitted without paying the gratuity of Four Pence formerly agreed upon and that care be taken to prevent the throng of people who are led by Curiosity to frequent the House on the first day of the Week to the great disturbance of the Patients."[13]

Despite these shortcomings, the Pennsylvania Hospital was pathbreaking in approaching mental disorders within the larger context of bodily health rather than personal weakness or moral failing. When Aeneas brought his ailing wife to the doors of the hospital, there were already several patients in residence struggling with symptoms similar to hers, though the hospital's record concerning them was mixed. Among the forty-five cases admitted for treatment until the date of Sarah's arrival, in four instances the patient was "relieved" of his or her symptoms after several weeks' treatment, and more than a dozen were eventually declared "cured." But a far larger number found that their symptoms persisted. When Sarah arrived, the resident population of lunacy patients numbered more than twenty. Tabitha Goforth had been hospitalized for almost eight years, and Mary Boardman nearly six. Cases like these must have been discouraging for the Ross family, who surely hoped for a speedier resolution. More ominously, six of the men and women so diagnosed—including Elizabeth Poet, admitted for "melancholy lunacy"—either had died or would die in the institution.

Sarah Ross would share that fate; whatever her ailment was, it proved intractable. Year after year, the physicians unable to help her, Sarah remained within the confines of the hospital grounds. Admitted when her son John was entering his teens, Sarah had been in the hospital for some three years by the time he began his apprenticeship just a few blocks away and met his future bride. If the New Castle congregants were correct that she was ill at least as early as 1758, then John (about six when his family moved to Delaware) may have had little memory of his mother as a capable parent. What scars her illness left we can only surmise. After Sarah's death in 1770, Aeneas would remarry, to Mary Hunter, a Chester County "gentlewoman of Amiable character," but too late to provide a new parent for his adult son.[14] We can no longer know whether Betsy ever met the mother of the man she would soon marry, but the years to come would give her occasion to contemplate the madness confined within the hospital's walls.

In May 1768, the upholsterer John Webster advertised an opportunity for a "genteel boy" to land an apprenticeship in his shop; perhaps it was this very notice that brought young John Ross to the attention of young Betsy Griscom.[15] Ross was then around seventeen years old. If he inherited the "large black eyes most expressive of tenderness and melancholy" his grandmother possessed, one can imagine the attraction.[16] For five years, he and Betsy worked alongside each other, flirted, bickered and generally sized each other up as potential partners in the life ahead.

At the start of 1773, not long after Betsy's twenty-first birthday, John Ross completed his training and struck out on his own. The city of Philadelphia was enjoying a window of unusual prosperity. It had weathered the crests and falls of a wartime and postwar economy; as the 1770s began, a flourishing provisions trade and vigorous real estate market enabled fortunate Philadelphians to treat themselves to new comforts.[17] Upholstery was already a crowded field when another competitor—William Martin—arrived, and advertised proudly that he had served his own apprenticeship with "Mr. Palmeer of London." Martin's arrival prompted John Mason, the owner of the already fashionable Crown and Cushion, to remind readers that he, too, provided furniture and wallpaper "after the modern taste, and with the greatest dispatch" in his Front Street shop, where Philadelphians could acquire "mattresses or wool beds, the great utility and intrinsic virtues of which ought to be duly attended to at this season."[18] One potential rival that John Ross could dismiss, it seems, was his former master; Webster's fortunes in Philadelphia had been uneven, and in 1773, the city's assessors found no taxable assets in his possession.[19]

With this sense of the field in hand, in February, Ross took out his own, comparatively spare notice to alert potential customers to his enterprise:

> John Ross, takes this method to inform the public, that he has opened an Upholder's Shop in Chestnut Street between Front and Second, where all kinds of Upholder's business is done in the neatest and most fashionable manner, on the shortest notice, with care and dispatch.

It was an advertisement appropriate for a newcomer; having not yet developed any particular specialty, Ross invited potential customers to bring him whatever needs they had. In time, he would carve out an appropriate niche within the city's craft community, but what that would be was not yet clear.[20]

What neither John nor Betsy could have known that hard, hopeful winter was that the imperial breach that had so threatened livelihoods during the Townshend Duties crisis was about to widen once more, when members of Parliament decided to bail out the struggling East India Company. By the 1770s, the company—chartered in 1600 by Elizabeth I—had long controlled British interests in India and East Asia. Originally an importer of Indonesian spices, over the course of time the company expanded into Indian textiles and dyes, Chinese tea and porcelain, opium from Bengal and coffee from Yemen, eventually becoming the single largest commercial firm in all Britain.[21] Like the companies that established Britain's North American colonies, it also served as the government of its trading outposts. But it had become too large, and was now overextended geographically and fiscally.

News of the company's strained finances made the Philadelphia papers as early as January 1773 and would remain a topic of interest throughout the year.[22] Tea was just one of the company's many concerns, but it was among the most profitable and offered an opportunity in that it intersected with conditions in the colonies. The law required that the company be subject to a series of duties, making its tea more expensive than the Dutch tea obtained through smugglers. The Townshend Duties protests, which included a boycott on English tea, created a demand for Dutch tea that lingered after the duties were withdrawn. Tea piled up in company warehouses, and debts mounted. By the close of 1772, the company was facing bankruptcy. But it was too big to be allowed to fail (a notion familiar in our times too), and so the ministry mobilized support for some intervention in Parliament (which contained many stockholders); meanwhile, company directors, desperately needing financial assistance, asked for a £1.5 million public loan.

The ministry leaped in, using the opportunity to assert more control of the massive company and its extensive holdings. As part of the aid package, it granted the company's request that, rather than auction the tea off to merchants, it be sold directly through agents the company would select in America. Without the middlemen, the thinking went, the tea might be cheap enough to undercut Dutch competitors. The duty would remain in place, allowing the ministry to affirm its rights to collect such revenue, and to raise a little cash along the way. In May 1773, the Tea Act was approved, and company directors scrambled to get their tea into the American market. Company directors— their much-needed loan now in hand—breathed a sigh of relief, while British prime minister Lord North congratulated himself for having established both a new revenue stream and parliamentary sovereignty in one fell swoop. Naturally, the residents of Britain's mainland colonies once again took a different view of these maneuvers. Imperial administrators had failed to anticipate that the Tea Act would be immediately perceived as yet more evidence of a sinister conspiracy to constrain the colonists' freedom and drain their wallets. The men who led the protests against the Townshend Duties had hated to see consumers give in to duted company tea after the boycott was abandoned in 1770. "I told you so" now hung in the air.

Real trouble landed in Betsy's backyard when, early in October 1773, the Quaker firm James & Drinker and a handful of other Philadelphia traders received word that they had been selected to receive one of the exclusive commissions to distribute East India Company tea.[23] They were, of course, thrilled.[24] But the political winds in the city had shifted since James returned from England to find himself elected to the colonial assembly as a reward for his comparatively conservative response to the Townshend Duties crisis. In the fall elections of 1772, Abel James was passed over for an assembly seat—an oversight his colleague Joseph Galloway would blame on the "wicked and base conduct" of "mad people": the city's Whigs.[25] Now, the tea situation would test his relationship with his neighbors still further.

The city's initial public response to the act seemed mild, giving James & Drinker reason to hope that the storm would blow over and they would eventually reap the significant profits their commission promised. But it would not be so. Protests erupted across the city. A large, unsigned printed card began to circulate, tacked to doors, posts and fences. "We are informed," it read, "that you have this Day received your Commission to enslave your Native Country; and as your frivolous Plea of having received no Advice relative to the Scandalous Part you were to act in the TEA scheme can no longer serve your Purpose nor divert our Attention, we expect and desire you will immediately inform the PUBLIC by a line or two left at the COFFEE HOUSE, whether you will not renounce all Pretensions to Execute the Commission." In an ominous closing phrase, the authors warned, "We will govern ourselves accordingly."[26]

While Abel James and Henry Drinker kept an anxious eye on the mood of the city, at a protest rally on October 16, Philadelphians summarized their arguments, strenuously objecting to Parliament's "levying contributions on them without their consent," acts which constituted a "violent attack upon the liberties of America." The attorney and onetime assemblyman John Ross—the uncle of Betsy's beau of the same name—was among those who "harangued" some three hundred to seven hundred spectators at a public meeting in the statehouse yard.[27] Submitting to the tea tax, patriots asserted, had "a direct tendency to render assemblies useless and to introduce arbitrary government and slavery." All citizens were accordingly urged to demonstrate that "a virtuous and steady opposition to this ministerial plan of governing America is absolutely necessary to preserve even the shadow of liberty."[28] The large public assembly—which surely included young John Ross, and perhaps Samuel Griscom too or even Rebecca and Betsy Griscom—adopted a series of resolutions. One declared that "the duty imposed by Parliament upon tea landed in America is a tax on the Americans, or levying contributions on them without their consent"; another that "the resolution lately entered into by the East

India Company, to send out their tea to America subject to the payment of duties on its being landed here, is an open attempt to enforce the ministerial plan, and a violent attack upon the liberties of America."

The resolutions appeared in the October 16 *Gazette* and soon made their way to other colonial ports; notably, the good people of Boston would observe that "the sense of this town cannot be better expressed than in the words of certain judicious resolves, lately entered into by our worthy brethren, the citizens of Philadelphia." Years later, the physician and patriot Benjamin Rush would recall that he once heard John Adams claim that the "active business of the American Revolution began in Philadelphia" and that "Massachusetts would have received her portion of the tea had not [Philadelphia's] example encouraged her to expect union and support" in destroying it. The "flame kindled" on that October day "soon extended to Boston and gradually spread throughout the whole continent. It was the first throe of that convulsion which delivered Great Britain of the United States."[29] Philadelphians may take pride in such sentiments today, but if their 1773 counterparts—spirited though they were—had had any notion that Bostonians would interpret their example as license to destroy the company's tea, they would have scattered in a hurry.

The next day, Samuel Griscom—who by this time surely perceived his brother-in-law Abel to be a closet Tory—may well have attended a different gathering. The overseers of the Philadelphia Monthly Meeting, worried that the agitation would prove disruptive to their community of faith, called a general meeting of all men in the Society.[30] They repeated George Fox's instructions concerning the "cares of the world" (and Friends' need to steer clear of them) and read an advisory letter from their London counterparts, as well as a "cautionary minute" from the Yearly Meeting. Various Quaker leaders addressed the gathering. Afterward, the merchant and prominent Friend James Pemberton wrote acquaintances in England to say that he thought that no Quakers were contributing to the agitation. He asserted the position of the Philadelphia community of Friends: "Although we are not insensible of the incroachments of Powers and of the value of Civil Rights yet in matters contestable we can neither join with nor approve the measures which have been too often proposed by particular persons and adopted by others for asserting and defending them." However, "such is the agitation of those who are foremost in these matters," that "it appears in Vain" to interfere.[31] Samuel must have seemed conspicuous at this meeting, in view of his brother-in-law's position at the center of the action. And it is likely that Samuel, given what some evidence suggests was his conservative take on such matters, approved of Abel's actions. But Betsy was hearing another side of the story around the upholstery shop from the other man in her life. John Ross and his family had a decidedly different interpretation of these events.

Among the protestors, a committee was appointed to visit the various commissioners to get a sense of their views and maybe talk them into resigning their commissions.[32] Several nervous agents gave in, but James & Drinker held out—a decision that enraged radical Philadelphians and also estranged the two merchants from other traders who had decided to attempt some compromise.[33] Thomas and Isaac Wharton gave "[us] all the satisfaction we could desire," but "Mssrs James and Drinker," the report read, were not "so candid and explicit in their answer to the Request" as the Committee would have liked. "We have the same Ideas of the American Revenue Act with our Fellow Citizens generally," they said. They had had some "intimation" that they would be among the named commissioners, and if the tea indeed arrived and they were indeed named commissioners, their "conduct [would] be open to [their] fellow citizens." More than this they declined to say. The committee found the response evasive—and James & Drinker now cast themselves as equally puzzled. It all came down to that word *generally*: James & Drinker indicated that they had meant "widely shared," but the committeemen seem to have heard "more or less"—a difference of great import when so much was in doubt, and on the line. "We seriously declare that it never occurred to us that these words could mean or bear any other construction than this general sentiment among the people 'that if the said Act were enforced here, it would be an infringement of our common Rights as Englishmen,'" they asserted.[34] In their defense, on the following day the committeemen responded that, while they were pleased that James & Drinker had since clarified their meaning, the "ambiguity" of their statement was "striking to every Member of the Committee." What's more, they continued to find their public position "defective," since they had said more about their position on the act than what they intended to do if the tea landed.[35] Privately, Abel James expressed his derision: when he invited fellow tea agent Thomas Wharton to his home in Frankford to discuss these matters, he suggested that out there they would find "fewer of the Yahoo Race."[36] Indeed they would maintain that they had been right all along: "Men of weight & influence in this City," they later insisted, had come to regret their choices, including "sending the Tea back to England," and "approving publicly the Conduct of the Town of Boston in destroying the Tea." Now, James and Drinker opined, most say that "had we pursued the Legal, peaceable plan" that they themselves had advocated, "& adhered to it with firmness," their "conduct would have been unimpeached both here and in England."[37]

If the year had gotten off to an unseasonably cold start, it was now uncomfortably warm. Late in October, noontime temperatures were still measuring some seventy-six degrees, and each edition of the local papers carried more news and debate over the impending arrival of the *Polly,* laden with some six hundred chests of the "detested tea." The city was too hot, by any definition.

On November 4, 1773, as the city swirled with drama and intrigue, Betsy and John gave in to another kind of fever and crossed the Delaware River; they were married at Hugg's Tavern in New Jersey, their marriage license issued by Benjamin Franklin's son William and the ceremony performed by Gloucester County justice James Bowman.

Marrying outside the Society of Friends was of course still forbidden, though the marriages of Betsy's sisters hint that fewer and fewer Quaker youth found the prohibition compelling. The Quaker leadership had responded to what was apparently a worrisome spate of violations when they reminded their followers that "marriage implies union and concurrence, as well in spiritual as temporal concerns. Whilst the parties differ in religion, they stand disunited in the main point; even that which should increase and confirm their mutual happiness, and rends them meet-helps and blessings to each other. Where it is otherwise, the reciprocal obligation they have entered into becomes their burden, and the more so, as it may not be of short and transient duration." Such marriages, the Friends further observed, also complicate the spiritual prospects of the couple's children, who are forced to choose between competing sets of beliefs. To avoid the possibility of such problematic marriages, Quaker men and women were instructed to "especially avoid too frequent and too familiar converse with those from whom may arise a danger of entanglement, by their alluring passions, and drawing affections after them."[38]

This helpful advice came too late for young Betsy, whose affections had already been drawn in the spaces of the Webster shop; she had decided to risk these various difficulties when she wed John Ross. In January 1774, the Philadelphia Monthly Meeting (Northern District) reported that it "conferred" with Betsy "on occasion of her Breach of Discipline in marriage, but she wholly declines condemning her offence, and declares in her choice to attend religious worship with her husband."[39] As it happened, her childhood teacher Hannah Cathrall was head of the women's meeting at this time, and her uncle's business partner, Henry Drinker, chaired the men's meeting.[40] Receiving an admonition from Cathrall was surely awkward at best, but the bride stood her ground; having refused to concede that her marriage was inappropriate, she coolly informed the elders that she would no longer be attending the Friends' meeting.

In other words, while Betsy's parents had accepted public censure for their actions, apologized for it and so returned to the Quaker fold, and her sisters delayed the resolution of these proceedings for as long as possible, an intractable Betsy Ross promptly asserted that she preferred to leave the Society and join her husband in his Anglican congregation. For some time, the Quakers of Philadelphia's Northern District held out hope that their errant Friend would return to the fold, but it was not to be. Several months later, the Society's minutes further observe that "Elizabeth Ross late Griscom . . . for want of taking her to the Dictates of truth in her own Mind," had "so far Departed therefrom, as to be Married to a Man of another religious Persuasion and without the consent of her Parents." For her actions—which they termed both "Disorderly" and "undutiful"—she had been "tenderly treated with"; nevertheless, "[our] Labour of Love not having the Desir'd Effect; we hereby Testify that she hath thereby Disunited herself from Religious Fellowship with us; until by sincere Repentance she makes such Acknowledgement to this Meeting, as the nature of her Case requires, which through the Assistance of Divine Grace we desire she may be enabled to Do."[41] Whether Betsy found their labor loving is hard to say. Perhaps she understood the exchange to be a pro forma ritual, since her sisters Deborah, Susannah, Mary and Sarah had endured it before.

Apparently, Samuel and Rebecca Griscom actively opposed the marriage, though we don't necessarily know why. Samuel and Rebecca were hardly in a position to object overmuch to Betsy's actions, having themselves eloped to New Jersey, marrying outside Quaker tradition. But they had acknowledged the error of their ways and restored their unity with the Quaker community. Nevertheless, object they did—though perhaps it was not the young man's religion that troubled them. She was marrying reasonably well, even if it was into a comparatively poor branch of an otherwise wealthy family. As the Griscoms took the measure of young John Ross, it seems unlikely that it was only the fact of his faith that concerned them, since in choosing this path, their headstrong daughter was by no means unique, or even unusual, certainly among Philadelphia's Quaker youth, or even within the Griscom family. When Betsy eloped with John, even the consequences of her infraction were less notable. By the time she chose her fate, the proportion of breaches of unity that ended in disownment had risen. About two-thirds of such cases ended in estrangement when Sarah went through it; the less-forgiving Friends now disowned fully three-fourths of such violators.[42] Moreover, Samuel and Rebecca Griscom's opposition to their daughter's marriage was as likely to have been on political as religious grounds. The elopement encapsulates much of the tangle of union and disunion unfolding over these months. John was certainly a member of the "Yahoo Race" of whom Abel so vehemently disapproved; apparently Samuel and Rebecca Griscom disapproved as well. Just as William Franklin would (famously) become increasingly estranged from his father as the gulf between Whigs and Tories widened, Betsy's father was leaning toward William's side just as John's family was leaning toward Benjamin's. In the middle of the crises encircling her family, the Society and the city, the willful young woman bound herself to a man whose family and faith departed dramatically from her own.

While the Quaker community was struggling to contain the disorder threatened by the political crisis, certain members of the Ross family—particularly Aeneas's brothers, John's uncles, who (having chosen to become lawyers rather than ministers) had become both affluent and politically important—were becoming deeply enmeshed in the movement to resist imperial policy.[43]

By the 1770s, several members of the Ross family had already made significant marks in the colonial Mid-Atlantic region. John's uncle John Ross had studied law and was admitted to the bar in 1735; he rose to become the attorney general of Delaware and an influential lawyer in Philadelphia.[44] In 1762, he was elected to the first of three terms in the Pennsylvania Assembly as a representative of Berks County, where he served with far more vigor than the average legislator and was an active supporter of efforts in opposition to the proprietors. When controversy erupted over the Stamp Act, John Ross had been caught in the middle. He found himself praising the appointed stamp distributor for refusing to resign his post while at the same time, as a member of the assembly, championing resistance there, helping to seek the act's repeal, and to draft specific talking points that stressed the act's financial consequences. He lost his Berks County seat in 1765, only to be returned the following year as a representative of Philadelphia (defeating John Dickinson by just thirty-four votes), and served another four terms.

Assemblyman Ross was slow and halfhearted in taking any position on the unfolding imperial crisis. He "loved ease and madeira much better than liberty and strife," some said (reason enough for the Griscoms to disapprove), and was well remembered for his indifference to the political crises. He once famously remarked that no matter who was king, he would still be a subject.[45] Ross was a man of "great vivacity, wit and humor"; he liked hearty laughs over good meals. As one acquaintance would years later remark, he was "not the stuff out of which martyrs and patriots are made."[46] When war finally erupted in 1775, William Thompson, now a colonel in the Continental army serving outside Boston, asked his brother-in-law George Read to pass along his love to "brother John," and added, "I know he will be pleased to have his liberty secured to him, whatever he may say to the contrary."[47] But he was learned and eloquent in the courtroom, and beyond it was quick with a joke and as happy to laugh at himself as others, a winning combination that brought him friends from all ranks. Uncle John's point of view during the crises emerged only gradually; as John Adams noted in the pages of his diary, Ross had once been thought to be a "great Tory, but now, they say, begins to be converted."[48]

Another uncle, George Ross, also studied law, partly with his half-brother John, and in 1768 joined him in the Pennsylvania Assembly. There they came to know both Abel James and Giles Knight.[49] As a Lancaster County attorney not yet active in the assembly, George was not involved in the Stamp Act protests in any official way (though when news of its repeal reached the community in March 1766, he "promoted a great Drunken bustle by the way of Rejoicing"), but he threw his weight behind efforts to resist the Townshend Duties.[50] "We apprehend it a Duty we owe to the sacred Shrine of Freedom," he and other Lancaster worthies advised their Philadelphia counterparts; though they were not themselves residents of the seaports so directly affected, they were eager to "testify [their] Apprehension" in this "Time of Danger," and register support for the "Measures taken by the Colonies, for procuring a Repeal of those [Townshend] Acts, so destructive to that glorious Liberty handed down to them and us by our Ancestors, and which as Freemen and Descendents of Britons, we have a right to." He and other Lancaster County men pledged to enforce nonimportation in their communities, and to publish the names of any violators "as a lasting Monument of infamy."[51] If John Ross liked a good joke better than a good argument, his half-brother George was a man of a different temper—he was hot-blooded, known to throw the occasional punch in a fit of passion. But both would find themselves drawn into what they perceived as a pattern of injustice where colonial administration was concerned.

George and John served two terms together; John left the assembly in 1770, but George remained until October 1772. Those first four terms were eventful ones. The number of committee assignments and other charges he was given while a member exceeded those of many other assemblymen, and he crafted some seventeen bills. After the surprising 1772 defeat, he was returned to office in January 1773 and would serve four more terms. When George's wife, Ann, died in the summer of 1773, all six of her pallbearers were magistrates. Young John—perhaps with his bride-to-be alongside him—surely attended her funeral, which the papers reported as among the largest the city had ever seen.[52]

The women of the Ross family—John's aunts—each chose men whose careers and convictions would steer them toward leadership in the resistance movement. In 1763, Gertrude Ross had married George Read, a lawyer who that year succeeded John Ross as attorney general of the three lower counties on the Delaware, an office Read held until he was elected to the Continental Congress in August 1774. Another sister, Catherine, in 1762 had married William Thompson, who would become an aide-de-camp of George Washington; his appointment as brigadier general would be signed by John Hancock. The year before, Aunt Elizabeth had married Edward Biddle, a veteran of the French and Indian War who had become a Philadelphia attorney; by 1767, he was serving as Berks County's representative to the Pennsylvania Assembly. He would act as Speaker in 1774 and be among Pennsylvania's delegates to the first Continental Congress. Meanwhile, in the 1760s, another aunt, Mary Ross, had married Mark Bird, who together with John's uncle George was operating a blast furnace; in 1775, Bird would serve as lieutenant colonel of the Second Battalion, Berks County militia.[53] Mark's sister Rachel had recently married James Wilson, a young attorney training under another leading figure in the swelling resistance movement, John Dickinson, whose *Letters from a Farmer in Pennsylvania*, published in the *Pennsylvania Chronicle*, had galvanized colonial protest against the Townshend Duties. A member of the provincial convention of Pennsylvania, Wilson together with Dickinson would be proposed as delegates to the 1774 Congress, though Joseph Galloway opposed and then thwarted their election.[54]

What's important about this tangle of marital and political alliances is the degree to which Betsy Ross's household was enmeshed in the public dramas of the 1760s and mid-1770s. Historians have noted that the men who gathered in local and colonial assemblies and committees as the imperial crisis ensued were already familiar to one another through the course of the institutions that nurtured their political leadership and economic influence, but a notable number of them were familiar to Betsy Griscom Ross as well. As the colony sorted out its various responses to what many perceived as imperial tyranny, and John and Betsy embarked on their relationship and then marriage, his family was deeply engaged in these developments, and at the highest levels of government. John Ross's family was increasingly committed to the Whig cause, while Betsy's father opposed it.[55] Maybe Samuel and Rebecca already sensed trouble coming in the choices Ross and his uncles were making—and their daughter, as well.

But just as 1773 drew to a close and the Griscoms absorbed the news that Betsy had eloped, larger events in the ongoing political crisis also demanded their attention. There would be little time for brooding. For Betsy Griscom Ross, colonial responses to the Tea Act threatened to tear her two families apart just as she and her husband had brought them together. As the city struggled to respond to this new imperial initiative, to the radical actions of their counterparts in Boston and to London's punishing response, positions hardened. Betsy's family found themselves drawn toward the conservative line, John's to the radical.

The weeks following the elopement saw a flurry of essays in the local press as city residents struggled to respond to political events both near and far. Newspapers were drenched in vitriol. When the October mail finally arrived from New York at the beginning of December, James & Drinker together with the Whartons and Jonathan Browne received confirmation that the ship *Polly*, under the command of Captain Samuel Ayres, had sailed from London at the end of September and was carrying tea shipped under the auspices of the Revenue Act. Feeling increasingly confident that public opinion was behind them, a new committee—the city's youngest and most radical yet—started to make plans for the ship's arrival. Concentrated pressure on James & Drinker finally forced the firm to promise that it would not insist on landing the tea. Meanwhile, Samuel Griscom reluctantly trudged to a special meeting of the Carpenters' Company on December 15. Although he was not especially regular in his appearance at meetings, this was a conversation too important to miss.[56]

While the approach of the *Polly* forced Philadelphians to decide how they would handle tea in their own harbor, they also had to decide whether to condone or censure the way another colonial city had handled theirs. As the city leaders sat down to their midday meal on December 24, they learned that the self-proclaimed Sons of Liberty in Boston, Massachusetts, had thrown hundreds of tea chests overboard rather than permit them to be landed on the city's docks. By five o'clock, a broadside appeared presenting news of this "Christmas Gift" to the city. The destruction of company property was no act of political theater; it was a serious challenge and would no doubt bring imperial repercussions. Should Pennsylvanians endorse such radicalism or reject it? After serious debate, nineteen Philadelphia committeemen signed a letter approving of Boston's actions. Later that same night, they learned that the *Polly* was approaching their own wharves with the dreaded tea.

Pennsylvania's resistance movement determined to keep the ship from docking altogether. Once the *Polly* had sailed as far as the mouth of the Delaware River, protesters sent its captain a broadside which warned, "[Your] cargo . . . will most assuredly bring you into hot water." Hinting that he secure the ship "against the rafts of combustible matter which may be set on fire, and set loose against her," the broadside likewise advised Captain Ayres to "preserve" his own "Person from the Pitch and Feathers" that awaited him should he land. As the ship reached Gloucester Point, a committee met the captain and brought him to a town meeting, where between eight and ten thousand men and women—the largest crowd ever known to have assembled to date in Philadelphia—came to suggest that the tea not be landed. Fully apprised of the mood in the city, Ayres turned his ship around and headed home.

The tea crisis—in the city and for the family—unfolded over the same months that Elizabeth Griscom wed John Ross. The political landscape was shifting so fast it was hard to see a safe course. Her uncle Abel was the target of rebel threats and intimidation, her husband was in the thick of the resistance movement, and her father was trying to remain neutral. Every day for Betsy was a minefield. Public and private sentiment changed quickly and power careened around the city, dwindling and gathering with each turn of events. "New lords," one man would observe, "made new laws, created new crimes and new punishments; terrific new bulls were issued, denouncing vengeance against those who dare to cross their measures."[57] Certainly Betsy was putting her parents in a difficult position; in the coming year, both Rebecca and Samuel would have to reconcile Betsy's choices with those of Rebecca's family. And it was not just money and influence at stake for the James as well as the Griscom households; the peace testimony embraced by their faith, too, was asking them all to steer clear of the imperial rupture as much as possible.


As Philadelphians awakened to another new year, tensions were palpable. The annual New Year's verse published in the *Pennsylvania Journal* urged readers to "let BOSTON'S great Example fire your Souls to Deeds of noble and heroick daring"—but what was noble and heroic to some was treasonous and dangerous to others.[58]

Imperial policy and colonial sovereignty drifted from the newlyweds' minds as they moved into their new home together—the first in a lifetime of rented rooms around the city for Betsy Ross, who would never own her own home. Home ownership was not especially common in the eighteenth-century city. (Unlike today, neither was it necessarily the goal of most families, who often preferred to rent.)[59] John had found them space on Chestnut Street near the waterfront. Pemberton's wharf stood at the end of the street, and just beyond that, the Crooked Billet. Like most town houses across the city, the building was tall and narrow, crowded among others just like it that lined the city streets. Most houses in Walnut Ward—a comparatively affluent neighborhood—enclosed about fourteen hundred square feet. Artisanal families like John and Betsy Ross were likely to enjoy far less; just under half of the city's craftsmen lived in houses smaller than nine hundred square feet.[60] The company engaged to insure the Rosses' home against the threat of fire noted that the building was fifteen feet wide and twenty-three feet deep, and three stories high with a party wall to the garret floor. As was typical, two rooms occupied each floor; simple wooden partitions separated the interior spaces, and the house, the assessors suggested, could have used a new roof. In fact, "old" seemed to be the house's most striking quality: a separate single-story kitchen, which the surveyors also described as "old," lay behind the building. Old though it was, the house was affordable and seemed like a good place for an enterprising young couple to start their life together.[61]

As she left her father's home to begin married life, Betsy looked forward to working alongside John on behalf of their family and business. Her Quaker tradition conferred an expectation of marital partnership. John's mother's mental illness meant that she had never been a powerful figure in his upbringing (though to be sure, her absence surely had a powerful effect); he could barely remember his parents living together, much less forging a coequal union. As he entered marriage, John had very little to go on, but Betsy brought a world of insights gleaned from watching her own parents negotiate the terms of their marriage. Equally if not more important, she had the experience and advice of four older sisters who could help her learn to get through the early trials all newlyweds faced. She was ready.

Betsy was also well prepared for an economic partnership. John's training in the upholstery trades balanced Betsy's, he learning to execute some tasks and she others. Given their separate and complementary skills, they could begin to serve clients without hiring any employees. The workbench, pine table and worktable on trestles present in their home served the purposes of their upholstery work, reminding us that John and Betsy's house, like the homes of many other Philadelphians, included shop space.[62] Six days a week, the newlyweds rose, enjoyed a quick breakfast and lifted aprons (leather for John, linen for Betsy) off pegs in the shop space to start what would be a long workday—almost always some twelve or fifteen hours—longer in the winter than the summer. The demands of both the home and the craft shop were relentless. Ground-floor workshops and storefronts beneath upper-floor living rooms then as now were common along the city's streets, and the combination of one's business and home life was visible in other ways, too. Married couples—particularly among middling craftsmen and shopkeepers like the Ross household—depended on each other to promote the family's well-being.[63]

John and Betsy made their rented rooms as comfortable as possible, drawing on their earnings from the shop as well as their own craft skills. As a schoolgirl, Betsy dutifully copied verses like this one, which pledged simplicity: "My wish would bound a small retreat / In temperate air & furnish'd neat." And: "No costly Labours of the Loom / Should e'er adorn my humble room."[64] But "costly Labours of the Loom" were part and parcel of everyday life for Philadelphia upholsterers, and John and Betsy surely admired, and perhaps acquired, the fabrics also desired by their clients. The newlyweds made themselves a feather bed, sacking bottom and mattress on which to sleep, and hung curtains that were fashioned from the same checked cloth they often used in the shop. A plain pine clothes chest held their wardrobes, but four mahogany chairs and a mahogany desk—perhaps wedding gifts from more affluent relatives—ornamented their parlor. Six silver teaspoons could be brought out when the occasion called for it—though certainly not anytime soon, while the subject of tea was so highly charged. In a less formal room, a half-dozen green Windsor chairs could be pulled up to a walnut table. A dressing glass allowed them to check their appearance before the day's business began. For their kitchen, the young couple had acquired the usual assemblage of iron pots and pans, a copper kettle, earthen jars and jugs, and pewter and tin plates and dishes, though a few pieces of china were reserved for special occasions. And John's gun, bayonet and pair of pistols sat alongside his cartouche box, ready at an instant should the tumult in the streets get out of hand.

The newlyweds were not alone in their house; joining them was an African American child (no notation indicates whether the child was a boy or a girl), eight years old when the constable took his 1775 census of the Walnut Ward.[65] That the Rosses would have access to African American labor, even from one so young, should not surprise us. With few funds to hire employees, and no children of their own yet to dispatch on small errands or chores, this child surely filled some real needs.

One of a relatively small number of black children in Philadelphia (a 1775 census found fewer than one hundred born after 1766 who had survived infancy), the child who shared the Rosses' home may have been free, or may have been a slave in another household whose services the Rosses leased. (No evidence suggests that they themselves were slaveowners.)[66] Whether enslaved or not, Betsy and John's young laborer was a member of the city's significant black community, a population in flux during these years. The period between 1767 and 1775—the years of Betsy's apprenticeship and marriage—marked a significant decrease in the number of slaves held in Philadelphia. After a flurry of slave importations, in 1767 the city of 18,000 residents included some 590 slaveholders and some 1,400 slaves; one in five families lived in homes with slave labor.[67] In the years to follow, the Philadelphia Yearly Meeting channeled significant energies into an effort to end slaveholding among Quakers. While the campaign did contribute to a decline in slave ownership, the dropping numbers were largely a product of the decreasing importation of captive Africans, high slave mortality and a low rate of fertility among the enslaved population. By 1775, the city's population had climbed to 25,000, but the number of slaveholders had dropped to 376, and the population of slaves to fewer than 700.[68] The number of free blacks in the city shifted in the reverse: in 1770, as many as 200 or 300 lived in the city's wards; by 1775, that number—given the rising number of manumissions—may have doubled.[69] But even free blacks struggled to establish and preserve their autonomy. The historians Ruth Herndon and Ella Sekatau have reminded us that in the chaotic mix of early American labor systems, there was no neat division between slavery and liberty; instead people (white or black) who labored under contracts that bound them to a household or enterprise for given periods of time experienced degrees of freedom and unfreedom.[70] The small child in the Ross house is best thought of somewhere on that continuum.

Betsy and John's young laborer had some company in the neighborhood, too, and it's likely that the child's family lived nearby. Thirty-six other African Americans lived in the Walnut Ward in 1775, about a third of them in their twenties, a third younger and another third in their thirties and forties.[71] The census found them across a smattering of households, evidence that families of color rarely enjoyed the benefits of living together. (Of fifty-five slave-owning households in the Chestnut and Mulberry wards, according to the historian Gary Nash, only five had adult men and women living together.)[72] The children of marriages between enslaved blacks were also less likely to live with their parents, or even their mother, in Philadelphia than they were, say, in rural Chester County, and even among free blacks, the need to place children in households where they would be supported while perhaps earning a small wage drove families into different households.[73] But with luck, if family members weren't under the same roof, the word-of-mouth network through which laborers were found sometimes meant that they remained nearby.

For Betsy and John, both family and faith shaped their views on African labor. The Quaker tradition in which Betsy was raised had been grappling for some time with the issue of slavery as well as the conditions under which all Americans of color lived, and when Betsy's great-grandparents Andrew and Sarah lived in such comfort in the early years of the city, it was in part due to the labors of the enslaved woman whose work in the wash house and elsewhere around the property eased Sarah Griscom's own.[74] Betsy's uncle Giles

Knight was a slaveholder, and her sister Deborah's father-in-law, Isaac Bolton, held no fewer than five captive Africans.[75] Betsy's sister Mary joined a family of Maryland slaveholders when she wed Thomas Morgan, and Betsy did, too, when she married John Ross: John's uncle John Ross regularly owned between three and five slaves, and his brother George and sister Elizabeth Ross Biddle owned smaller numbers.[76]

John's views on slavery and African Americans were more directly shaped by his father, the Reverend Aeneas Ross, who had long been notable for his commitment to the spiritual lives of the slaves whose labor was making the Mid-Atlantic colonies rich. Aeneas, unlike his brothers, is not known to have owned slaves. (His meager salary would scarcely have permitted it, whatever his inclinations.) Moreover, he maintained a clear commitment to the equality of black souls. He had already been converting slaves in Delaware when he seized the opportunity of a temporary appointment in Philadelphia to "open the doors of Christ Church to the city's slaves," the historian Gary Nash has observed, as well as "a handful of free blacks." Ross had moved to Philadelphia in the early 1740s to fill in for Christ Church's ailing rector Archibald Cummings. While in the city Ross baptized some one hundred people, including twelve blacks who, Ross would report, "appear'd publickly before the Congregation & were examined in, & said their Catechisms to the Admiration of all that heard them." Seven African American men and two women were baptized in one fell swoop in January 1742—the "like sight," Reverend Ross would later reflect, was never before seen in a Philadelphia church.[77] The Anglicans established a school for blacks in 1758, and more than forty free blacks were baptized at Christ Church in the decade beginning in 1766.[78] When Betsy and John walked to Sunday services there, their young servant may well have followed along, pondering together with them the increasingly shrill rhetoric of liberty and freedom.

## · 8 ·

# Mr. and Mrs. Ross

Betsy and John were still occupied with settling their household and launching their business when, after some welcome weeks of relative peace in the wake of the tea ship's departure, public matters again took a turn for the worse. In April 1774, Philadelphians learned of the bitter assault launched on the reputation of favorite son Benjamin Franklin, attacked in England's Privy Council by Solicitor General Alexander Wedderburn after Franklin's role in the publication of some sensitive correspondence became known. Sixteen months earlier, Franklin had been shown letters written by the governor of the colony in Massachusetts, Thomas Hutchinson, in which Hutchinson asked for troops to suppress dissent. Franklin circulated the letters (which seemed to be clear evidence of Hutchinson's designs on colonial liberty) among some leaders of the protest movement, with a request—which may or may not have been genuine—that they not be leaked to the press. But of course they were, causing a public reaction so violent that Hutchinson was forced to flee. The British government naturally demanded to know the source of the leak, and when three innocent men were accused, Franklin stepped forward to acknowledge his actions. Incensed Philadelphians burned both Hutchinson and Wedderburn in effigy; for good measure, they acknowledged Franklin by setting the blaze afire with an electric spark.[1]

Betsy might have seen an omen in these unnerving events: the day after Hutchinson and Wedderburn were symbolically torched, the eighty-four-degree weather they'd been enjoying all week gave way to a spring snow that covered the tulips already in bloom.[2] Everything seemed off. Soon, Betsy together with the rest of the city learned what Bostonians had earned for their rash actions at the city's waterfront. The news was simply stunning: Parliament had closed the port of Boston to all commerce, appointed General Thomas Gage to the governor's office and dispatched four British regiments to help him keep order. In actions that came to be known as the Coercive Acts to some, and the Intolerable Acts to others, Parliament reorganized the Massachusetts colony's government, reduced the power of its assembly and clamped down on the town meetings from which so much dissent had sprung. What's more, the Administration of Justice Act allowed royal officials to transfer court cases to England, securing for themselves protection from local prosecution while undermining the principle of trial by jury. Lastly, the Quartering Act permitted the Crown to house troops in any occupied dwelling. Within days the Boston artisan-activist Paul Revere galloped to the largest of the colonial cities to deliver a request for political support and material aid for the frightened Bostonians. The severity of Parliament's response astonished not just New Englanders but their counterparts across the Atlantic colonies. To many, the attack on colonial rights seemed incomprehensible, even reprehensible. Indeed, the severity of the Crown's reaction seems to have been the last straw for Assemblyman John Ross; long on or near the political fence, Ross, having already "harangued" Philadelphians on the injustice of the Tea Act, now believed that the "[Intolerable] Acts were founded in Wrong, Injustice, and Oppression. The great Town of Boston" (Adams was especially gratified to hear) had been "remarkably punished without being heard."[3] But others believed Boston's arrogant gesture of protest to have been completely out of scale; Britain was right to demand that Bostonians pay for the destroyed tea. They'd earned every ounce of their punishment.

Philadelphia's city leaders had to determine quickly how best to respond to this latest threat to the rights of British colonists everywhere. Local radicals began planning ways to channel widespread disgust with British administration into concrete political action. Meanwhile, conservatives moved just as quickly to tamp down emotions. Both sides strained to shape the public mood, the effort to whip up the city's outrage being met with another urging cooler heads and a more measured response. Betsy watched as her husband was attracted to the Revolution's orbit and her father repelled from it. She would find her own chair cases, curtains and coverings implicated as representatives gathered in a "Continental Congress" and embraced a boycott of imported goods just as she and John at last began to receive the patronage of the colony's leading families.

In order to decide how Philadelphia should respond to Boston's request for support, a large meeting was convened on May 20, 1774, at City Tavern. Radicals had strategized beforehand, pleading with the attorney John Dickinson (though he was so useful during the Townshend Duties crisis, Dickinson had recently become a more moderate voice) to address the assembled crowd of over two hundred merchants, lawyers and other leading citizens. After the radicals stated their hope that the city would, as Boston requested, embrace a unilateral nonimportation boycott, the merchants—predictably—began shouting out their objections. In the chaos, Dickinson rose to suggest that they petition Governor John Penn (the grandson of William Penn), ask him to convene the Pennsylvania Assembly and instruct that official body to respond. The gathering also agreed to send a letter affirming their solidarity with Boston. A committee of nineteen men was appointed to correspond with both Boston (to which they would pledge their support, albeit in a tone that radicals found all too cautious, even vaguely disapproving) and the other colonies who were at that moment formulating their own responses to the crisis in Massachusetts.[4]

A dizzying array of committees and subcommittees would emerge to guide the protest movement. Betsy and John watched as the leading craftsman in their field, the upholsterer Plunket Fleeson, was among eleven men asked to work with the committee of merchants organized in May, and the following month tradesmen elected him to a seven-man committee charged with urging Philadelphia's Committee of Correspondence to call a mass meeting of the county's inhabitants intended to produce instructions to the colony's delegates to the Continental Congress. Fleeson and his colleagues were rebuffed—the committee preferred to be guided by the steadier tempers of the colony's assembly—but Fleeson prepared for the seemingly inevitable when he bought an ad in the paper reminding readers that his shop offered drums, flags and "other Military Instruments." Fleeson was so swamped with both political and military work that one observer noted that the upholsterer could provide "neither drum nor colours" for some time.[5]

The committee of nineteen men appointed at the May 20 meeting to handle the protest movement would turn out to be more tentative and conservative than the radicals preferred, so they turned their attention to more public forms of protest, politics "out of doors," as they said at the time. In an effort to galvanize public opinion against the imperial administration, radicals called for a "solemn pause"—a suspension of all business—on June 1, 1774, the day the Port Bill was scheduled to go into effect, to show that colonists were united in their disapproval of the direction policy appeared to be heading, and to encourage citizens to contemplate the future. The Society of Friends immediately announced its opposition to this action. The day before the planned "pause," Quaker leaders met at the Chestnut Street schoolhouse to draft a statement denying support of the planned observance and affirming that their peace testimony would prevent Friends from participating. As the sun rose on June 1, throughout the city flags were lowered to half-mast and shops closed to the hurry of business. Churches scheduled special services. Someone climbed the bell tower at Christ Church and rang a funeral peal on muffled bells. A mood of sorrow tinged with indignation settled over the city.[6] It seems likely that Betsy and John observed the pause, closing their shop and spending the day in anxious reflection, but that Samuel and Rebecca Griscom—following the preferences of their faith, and perhaps their politics as well—did not. The Philadelphia Meeting for Sufferings would affirm that Friends ought to "keep from mixing with the people in their Public Consultations, as snares and dangers arise from meetings of that kind."[7] What did Samuel and Rebecca make of their daughter's choices now?

The summer of 1774 proved decisive for Betsy and her husband. All around them, friends and family, neighbors and strangers, were sizing up the crisis, sizing up one another, in some cases staking out their political ground, and in other cases trying desperately not to. Despite the fact that some nine hundred citizens signed the petition to Governor Penn to convene an emergency session of the Pennsylvania Assembly, he denied the request; indeed, he had not for a moment considered anything else. For their part, the city's radicals expected nothing and had never wished for another outcome, reluctant as they were to have the comparatively conservative assembly choose men to represent Pennsylvania's interests in the crisis, rather than men like themselves who favored more extreme measures. On June 8, a week after the solemn pause, Betsy, John and their fellow artisans found broadsides plastered around town, inviting them to a mass meeting. The next day, some twelve hundred people gathered—John Ross no doubt among them, and perhaps Betsy, too. They learned that still another mass meeting was planned in a little over a week, to allow people from the countryside to attend.

The intervening days would see mad scrambles of plotting and planning.[8] On June 10 and 11, the Committee of Nineteen together with other leaders from the city's religious communities hunkered down in the Philosophical Society hall to hash out a plan. After condemning the Boston Port Act they endorsed calls for a general congress. Since Governor Penn had refused to summon the Assembly, which would have been the obvious means through which to identify delegates to send to represent Pennsylvania at any inter-colony gathering, delegates argued over what to do. In the end they agreed that the Assembly should gather unofficially and choose delegates as advised by citizen committees. To supplant Philadelphia's Committee of Nineteen with a larger body, they proposed delegates to be elected at a mass meeting in the State House yard on June 18.

On the day before the mass meeting, fifty-nine-year-old attorney John Ross gathered with an assembly of artisans and Germans at the Bunch of Grapes Inn to join them in working to push a more aggressive agenda than the city's leadership was inclined to pursue. When men from the city's artisanal and laboring communities had come together in the mass meeting of June 9, eight days earlier, Ross had accepted appointment to the committee chosen to represent their interests; in fact, he had opened the meeting and read aloud a letter from tradesmen in New York seeking a response from their counter-parts in Philadelphia.[9] Now, attorney Ross was among the spokesmen the city's mechanics and German population trusted to infuse more radical energy into the resistance movement.[10]

The men gathered around the inn's long tables would demand changes in the political complexion of the movement's leadership. The Committee of Nineteen had proposed that the new slate of nominees to be presented at the June 18 gathering include forty men to represent the colony's interests. But the radicals assembled at the Bunch of Grapes wanted a still larger committee—fifty-one men (in reference to the number elected in New York City the month before)—in an effort to add more radical voices without necessarily calling for the removal of any more conservatives members already named, save the intolerable Thomas Wharton (the onetime tea agent) and Dr. William Smith. John and Betsy watched as men they knew were proposed for the new com-mittee, including John Ross and Plunket Fleeson as well as the builder Benja-min Loxley Jr. and the carpenter James Worrell. The effort failed in most of its aims, but clearly a spirit of revolutionary unity was emerging among the city's artisanal families.

Thousands of Pennsylvanians attended the June 18 meeting. Betsy's and John's uncles squared off. As they considered the resolutions proposed, Abel James, together with Henry Drinker and other influential Friends, opposed any action beyond requesting that the colonial assembly petition Great Britain for redress. Moderates favored sending delegates to an all-colony meeting to discuss collective action; they hoped the assembly would have the right to name the representatives and draft the instructions to which they would be bound. The most radical element also wanted to send delegates to some sort of a congress but wanted them chosen by a provincial convention, believing that the popular vote would select more radical representatives and give them greater leeway.

After considerable negotiation, the Committee of Forty-Three that at last emerged proved more diverse than any of its predecessors. This new body of citizens addressed the thorny question of how to select delegates to the Continental Congress. While seven colonies held provincial conventions, and three charged their legislatures with the task, only Pennsylvania did both, leaving the Assembly formally responsible for the management of the delegates, though under the guidance of a provincial convention.

In July, a provincial convention—including some seventy committeemen—met, charged with instructing the legislature on how to react to the unfolding situation. The attorney John Ross was not there, but his half-brother George was. The gathered body drafted instructions and presented them to the assembly, but their efforts were met with silence; the assemblymen dismissed the work of the provincial congress altogether. Instead, they decided to choose for themselves the men who would represent their colony's interests to the planned intercolonial congress. On the inside, George Ross was named to an eight-member committee that drafted instructions for the deputies, allowing them to participate in the forging of some intercolonial protest strategy, but no more. "The Trust reposed in you," the instructions advised, "is of such a nature . . . that it is scarcely possible to give you particular Instructions respecting it. We shall therefore only in general direct, that you are to . . . exert your utmost Endeavors to form and adopt a Plan, which shall afford the best Prospect of obtaining a Redress of American Grievances, ascertaining American Rights, and establishing the Union and Harmony which is most essential to the welfare and Happiness of both Countries." "In doing this," the instructions continued, the delegates were "strictly charged to avoid every Thing indecent or disrespectful to the Mother State."[11]

Having participated in the drafting of the instructions, George found himself a recipient of them, too, when he was named among the colony's representatives. In July, the Pennsylvania Assembly sent a split delegation to the first Continental Congress: Joseph Galloway, Charles Humphreys and Samuel Rhoads—the latter, with Samuel Griscom, a member of the Carpenters'

Company—ranged from conservative to moderate (depending on whom you asked), while John's uncles Edward Biddle and George Ross together with Thomas Mifflin and John Morton were judged moderate to radical (again, depending on whose opinion prevailed). As a delegate to the Congress, George signed the October 24 document that, while affirming loyalty to George III and denouncing the last ten years of British imperial policy, embraced nonimportation (as of December 1) and nonexportation (beginning in September 1775, if no resolution had yet emerged). He would help advance an appeal to the people of Quebec to join the protest, and signed the long list of grievances the Continental Congress drafted and directed to George III.

A handshake away, young John Ross was working to establish himself among the city's craftsmen, especially those inclined toward the more radical corners of the resistance movement. In August and September 1774, John applied for membership in the Masonic Lodge. The Masons would be closely associated with the Revolution. Between eight and fourteen of the fifty-six men who signed the Declaration of Independence were members of Masonic lodges, and estimates of the percentage of Continental army generals who were members range from a third to nearly one half. Of the thirty-three men who would sign the U.S. Constitution, fully a third were Masons. Ross was approved for membership in mid-September and immediately agreed to spruce up the lodge's meeting space with a couple of cushions, drawing Betsy into his effort to please his new associates.[12] As the couple stuffed and stitched seats to soften John's meetings to come, they had occasion to speculate how the many connections he would make through the Masons might enhance their small shop's future prospects. By April, when the fledgling member underwent his examination and gained admittance to the Degree of Fellow Crafts, John had already assumed a minor office in the organization. Interestingly, the minutes of lodge meetings between April 1775 and February 1776— the remainder of Ross's brief Masonic career—have been torn from the record book; we can no longer know what Ross and his fellow Masons did during those tumultuous months, or who attended their gatherings. But through the lodge, Ross had the opportunity to meet influential Masons like John Cadwalader, John Dickinson and George Washington, men whose decisions were steering the colonial protest movement toward outright rebellion.[13]

While Betsy's husband threw himself into Revolutionary circles, her father found himself struggling to escape the political vortex that was already drawing in his daughter.[14] The Friends' peace testimony—their aversion to the support

of violence of any sort, and for any purpose—was severely tested by the ensuing crisis, but Friends buoyed one another in their mutual effort to remain
neutral as the estrangement between the colonies and Parliament became
increasingly severe. At the 1774 Yearly Meeting of Friends, held in Philadelphia, a letter was approved and ordered to be sent to all meetings of Friends
in America, urging members to cling to their peaceful principles and eschew
any part in the political controversy, reminding them that under the king's
government they had been favored with a peaceful and prosperous enjoy-
ment of their rights. The dispatch strongly suggested that Friends consider
disowning any members who disobeyed the orders issued by the Yearly Meeting. And indeed, most Quakers struggled to keep the resistance movement at
arm's length.

Despite these admonitions, a handful of conservative Quakers—Abel
James among them—remained active in the political machinations unfolding hour by hour across Philadelphia. As a leading merchant, James had a
tremendous stake in trying to control a resistance movement that threatened to
undermine his livelihood as well as his sources of influence in the city. At the
same time, Friends were under tremendous external pressure to support the
resistance movement in any number of ways, and men and women responded
as their own conscience and circumstances dictated. Some members, whether
as a matter of scruples, survival or something in between, "held that as they
should render duty to their Government of willing obedience, so also they
owed it their active support when threatened by invasion. While agreeing
with their elders as to the wickedness of aggressive war and needless strife,
they took the ground that it would be inconsistent to accept the support of
the Continental Congress and armies, and refuse to aid them by every means
possible."[15]

The longtime Quaker Isaac Howell, for instance, had "so far deviated"
from the peace testimony "as to manifest a disposition to contend for the
asserting of civil rights in a manner contrary to our peaceable profession
and principles, and accepted of and acted in a public station, the purpose
and intention of which has tended to promote measures inconsistent there-
with." A number of Friends tried to convince him of his error, but this
"labour of love not having the desired effect, and as the testimony of Truth
has suffered by his means, and he doth not shew a disposition to condemn the
same, We are under the necessity in order to support our Christian Testimony to declare that he hath separated himself from the Unity and fellowship
of our Religious Society." The Friends expressed their "earnest desire that he

may become sensible of his deviations so as to manifest a just sense of his error, and by a due concern for the testimony of Truth, manifested by a suitable acknowledgment, become restored into membership." Howell, "having disobeyed the precept of Yearly Meeting of 1774, and also having fallen away from correct following after Quakerism by accepting office under a government in rebellion, and by serving in a military capacity," was disowned by the Philadelphia Meeting of Friends.[16] He would find himself in increasingly good company, as the Revolutionary crisis drove numbers of Friends outside the formal structures of the Quaker meeting.

Like John Ross, Samuel Griscom found himself enmeshed in events through his membership in a local workingmen's association, the Carpenters' Company. Despite Betsy's father's opposition to the gathering resistance movement, he could scarcely avoid traveling in its orbit. As the demand for public meetings spiraled upward, the Carpenters' Company offered its new hall to gatherings associated with the protest movement. Griscom together with his fellow craftsmen (having enjoyed a decadelong construction boom through the 1760s) in 1770 had voted to build the union its own quarters. Thirty-six members purchased shares. Betsy's father bought eight and contributed labor and materials as well. As the massive frame—girders of eastern white pine—rose, the building took the form of a Greek cross. Brick walls more than a foot thick supported the two-story structure, and a massive triangular pediment topped with an octagonal cupola crowned the whole. Outside of the statehouse itself and the city's several churches, the carpenters now possessed the largest assembly space in Philadelphia.

What's more, by 1774, members of the Carpenters' Company were some of the city's most radical activists among those objecting to imperial policy. When more than fifty delegates from twelve of Britain's mainland colonies converged in Philadelphia in September and October to discuss responses to the growing crisis, the Carpenters' Company offered them use of its meeting hall, shifting the venue from the Pennsylvania statehouse, the site preferred by more conservative representatives like Joseph Galloway (the idea being that representatives meeting in the colony's formal political spaces would be hard-pressed to think in radical terms; getting out from under the architecture of empire makes it easier to contemplate dismantling it). Three of Betsy's new in-laws—John's uncles George Ross and Edward Biddle from Pennsylvania, and Delaware's George Read—were among the delegates gathered in this hall her father had helped build. The Congress "enjoined every member to keep a secret" until deliberations were completed, "to avoid needless disputations" on the streets. "This is much to the disappointment of the curious," Caesar Rodney would note, a group sure to include Betsy and John, so close and yet so far from the epicenter.[17]

When in the city, many of these delegates chose to worship at Christ Church, the locus of the Church of England in Philadelphia, and Betsy's new spiritual home. As Betsy took her place alongside John in the pews of Christ Church, one glance at her surroundings conveyed the enormity of her change in circumstances.[18] In marked contrast with the plain structures embraced by the Quakers, Philadelphia's Christ Church was a showplace, among the finest buildings certainly in the city and in the colony, and perhaps the whole of Britain's North American colonies. (Years later, Betsy's daughter Rachel could still remember her mother describing the "handsome" pews, the minister's lined with red velvet—a detail the young upholsterer of course noticed right away.)[19] John could picture his father in the pulpit, but Betsy couldn't picture hers sitting in a pew.

Christ Church was also a place where religious and political conviction fell in concert and in conflict. Members of the Society of Friends needed to attend to the advices of their discipline and eschew entanglement in political controversies; any appearance to the contrary risked censure. But in some ways Christ Church represented even trickier waters than the Quaker meeting-house. Since this was the official Church of England, siding with the revolutionaries necessarily meant renouncing one's faith, at least in the sense of its affiliation with the mother country. Rebellion could mean, in that respect, treason to God and king alike. More immediately, when Betsy looked around her before services began, she saw the men whose choices were shaping the future of not only her own colony but the colonies united in rebellion. There was no anonymity amid the red velvet cushions of Christ Church. Decisions loaded with meaning confronted the congregation almost weekly. The church defied the Crown when it embraced a fast day declared by the Continental Congress. Its assistant minister, Reverend Thomas Coombe, delivered a sermon condemning the "dark designs" of British administrators who had "sacrilegiously lifted the sword" against the British constitution, while reminding parishioners not to overlook the benefits of their connection with a "wise and powerful nation, whom we were taught, from our cradles, to look up to with filial reverence."[20] The Reverend Jacob Duché, minister of Christ Church and chaplain to the Continental Congress, noted that the American resistance movement had disavowed "any pretensions to, or even desire of independency," and prayed that God would "restore that brotherly union and concord, which ought to subsist inviolate in the great family to which we belong."[21]

Each Sunday, as Mr. and Mrs. Ross attended services, cues both subtle and overt conveyed the ever-shifting temper of the community. They would conduct themselves accordingly.

As they continued to meet and deliberate, the delegates, whom Massachusetts representative John Adams called "young, smart and spirited" at the outset, became "fearful, timid [and] skittish."[22] The initial hubris that prompted Tom Paine to toast the "collision of British flint and American steel" gave way to long hours of tedious meetings among the sequestered delegates, and mounting fear among the city's residents.[23] In September, rumors flew that British ships in Boston's harbor had fired on the city, taking down houses and killing their residents. People daily anticipated that cities along the seaboard could be destroyed.[24] The delegates responded cautiously to the growing crisis. While Joseph Galloway proposed forming an American version of Parliament that would act in concert with the existing British body, the arrival of the Boston activist Paul Revere with a number of resolves from Suffolk County, Massachusetts, objecting strenuously to the Coercive Acts galvanized the more radical contingent. Congress endorsed the resolves, signaling clearly the solidarity that was emerging among the North American colonies.

The meeting also once again embraced unified economic protest, reviving the boycotts that the colonies had harnessed during the Townshend Duties crisis. The "Continental Association" was envisioned as a vigorous attempt to force the repeal of all of this objectionable legislation by implementing a total boycott against trade with Britain, Ireland and the British West Indies. As of December 1, colonists would no longer import "any goods, wares, or merchandise whatsoever, or from any other place, any such goods, wares, or merchandise, as shall have been exported from Great-Britain or Ireland; nor will we, after that day, import any East-India tea from any part of the world; nor any molasses, syrups, paneles [brown unpurified sugar], coffee, or pimento, from the British plantations or from Dominica; nor wines from Madeira, or the Western Islands; nor foreign indigo."[25] Nonconsumption (meant to help secure nonimportation) would begin March 1, and if Parliament did not accede to colonial demands by September 1775, nonexportation would commence. Moreover, the colonists would be urged not to consume those British products already in America. This program of concerted economic pressure— nonimportation, nonexportation and nonconsumption—was to continue until the offending laws were repealed. Men and women in their "several stations" pledged to "encourage frugality, economy, and industry, and promote agriculture, arts and the manufactures of this country, especially that of wool; and will discountenance and discourage every species of extravagance and dissipation, especially all horse-racing, and all kinds of gaming, cock-fighting, exhibitions of shews, plays, and other expensive diversions and entertainments; and on the death of any relation or friend, none of us, or any of our families, will go into any further mourning-dress, than a black crape or ribbon on the arm or hat, for gentlemen, and a black ribbon and necklace for ladies, and we will discontinue the giving of gloves and scarves at funerals."

The Continental Congress recommended that communities appoint local committees to monitor economic activity. Samuel Griscom saw several of his fellow carpenters appointed to Philadelphia's crew of enforcers: Abraham Jones, Joseph Wetherill, Isaac Coats, Benjamin Loxley and William Robinson.[26] Would this be to his benefit, he surely wondered, or to his detriment?

Having decided to once again pursue an economic boycott to press their agenda, the Congress also decided to try a diplomatic effort as well, and issued a Declaration and Resolves that articulated its complaints. Betsy and John's uncle Edward Biddle helped draft the document, which asserted that the "foundation of English liberty, and of all free government, is a right in the people to participate in their legislative council: and as the English colonists are not represented, and from their local and other circumstances, cannot properly be represented in the British parliament, they are entitled to a free and exclusive power of legislation in their several provincial legislatures, where their right of representation can alone be preserved, in all cases of taxation and internal polity, subject only to the negative of their sovereign, in such manner as has been heretofore used and accustomed."[27] Whether or not Samuel Griscom's reservations were met by the tepid political response, he and Betsy both must have greeted the Continental Association with some apprehension, given the effect it would have on their livelihoods. In the sharpened atmosphere of Revolutionary Philadelphia, as the colony hurtled toward rebellion, the Griscom family hurtled with it.

As the colony careened from one crisis to the next, business went on—maybe not "as usual," but households continued to need the services craftspeople like the Rosses provided. George Haughton (with whom Betsy had worked while he was employed as John Webster's journeyman) had struck out on his own at the beginning of the year, and now competed with his colleagues for the city's business.[28] The prominent craftsman William Martin had published his intention to leave Philadelphia in the spring, urging readers of the *Pennsylvania Packet* to patronize in his place his journeyman Charles Jaffrey.[29] John Mason had arrived from South Carolina seven years earlier to take over Blanch White's Crown and Cushion, and in time took space near Betsy's parents (and would—perhaps having sensed trouble—be leaving soon), and of course Plunket Fleeson continued to capture the business of the city's wealthiest families from his shop under the Sign of the Easy Chair on Chestnut Street.

But their work was now thoroughly entangled in the political crisis. While John's uncles crafted policies of resistance (uncles George Ross and George Read, as delegates to Congress, had both signed the Continental Association), John and Betsy more literally crafted their own responses to the resistance movement as they negotiated with clients and filled their orders. Seasoned veterans of the Townshend Duties, they understood how loaded choices in the marketplace had become. As artisans whose trade depended heavily both on imported goods and on the privileged families who purchased them, the Rosses observed the unfolding crisis carefully. Although they had learned much from watching Webster navigate the Townshend Act crisis, now they had to make their own decisions about whom to work for, where to purchase materials, and which fellow craftsmen to patronize.

Curtains and chair covers may seem a far cry from tensions over imperial policy, but when protestors identified the boycotting of imported goods as the key form of resistance, such goods were thrust to the center of the debate. In the same months that the Continental Congress was meeting in Philadelphia to formulate a joint response to the looming crisis, John and Betsy were presented with an opportunity and a challenge when the wealthy Philadelphia attorney Benjamin Chew—as of April 1774 the colony's chief justice—placed a sizable order that engaged the very goods under increasing scrutiny.[30] Their work suggests the range of skills that they had cultivated under the supervision of John Webster and Ann King, hints at the promising future that seemed to await them, and suggests how fragile that future became when the sources of their livelihood became among the most politically charged objects in the Revolutionary tool kit.

Chew's daughter Elizabeth was planning her marriage to Edward Tilghman, and preparing for the household they would establish together. In fitting out his daughter's new home, Chew naturally turned to tradespeople whose work he already knew. The cabinetmaker Jacob Knor (whom Chew knew well; he had served as master carpenter for Chew's Germantown estate, Cliveden) was hired to make mahogany bedsteads as well as a variety of tables, trays and stands for the newlyweds, while the carver, gilder and framemaker James Reynolds fashioned a pair of carved oval mirrors, a pair of girandoles (sconces) and other impressive goods.

Chew—who tended toward London-trained craftsmen when hiring work for his own town house or summer home—must have been pleased with the work the Rosses provided, since he included the fledgling Ross shop among the many patronized for his daughter's setting out. He had worked with John Ross at least once before, in September 1772, when he purchased some £4 6s. 6d. worth of services from Webster's shop opposite the London Coffee House while Ross was employed there. Chew turned to Webster's shop twice more in the following year, availing himself again of John Ross's skills, and probably Betsy's as well.[31] Now, in September 1774, he hired Betsy and John to make a mattress as well as a number of furnishings for a "full trimed bed."[32] Curtains hung on three sides of the bed Chew ordered for his daughter. The couple fabricated fashionable sloped cornices and attached muslin backing to chintz valances as well as matching curtains. Chew also needed wooden rods to hang the draperies on, as well as curtain rings and braiding tape. Betsy made several window curtains, too, some to match the fabric of the bed furnishings, though three check curtains were also ordered, destined for some more functional space or for summer use. The curtains were ornamented with forty-five tassels—two sets of twelve (a dozen in white) and another set of twenty-one—perhaps purchased, though possibly of Betsy's own manufacture as well. The Rosses also fashioned paper curtains for at least three windows in the Tilghman household. In addition to curtains trimmed with braid and embellished with tassels, the firm supplied the pulley lathes, pins and hooks necessary to mount them.

Betsy also constructed some twenty chair cases. Probably fashioned of some sort of washable linen or cotton, the cases were likely of a color or pattern that matched the rest of the furnishings Elizabeth had chosen for the room.[33] The firm charged a shilling each for Betsy's work constructing these; the making of each set of three window curtains added another fifteen shillings to the bill.

Finally, the pair earned £1 making carpeting for one of the genteel newlyweds' floors, charging Chew as much for this effort as for all twenty chair cases together. Carpet was of course a luxury item; only about one in five Philadelphia households between 1720 and 1835 possessed any kind of floor covering at all, and a small percentage of those enjoyed coverings imported from Europe.[34] Wealthy families might choose Brussels carpets (looped-pile carpet with a linen warp and weft and worsted pile) or Wilton carpets (cut-pile carpets on Jacquard looms), but both came in strips and had to be sewn together to form a covering large enough for a room.[35] This, too, was work that routinely fell to women. The Rosses may have assembled the imported carpeting

Chew had purchased on his daughter's behalf from Baker & Weiss, though it's possible too that they produced some sort of strip carpeting intended for a strictly functional space.

Altogether, the Chew-Tilghman job earned Betsy and John just over £27—a handsome sum when a kitchen maid might earn half that in a year. Given the size of the order, it must have taken an all-out effort for John, Betsy and probably the African American child who worked for them as well. Their competitors also benefited from Chew's outlay: Elizabeth Lawrence, for instance, took in £8 6s. 10d. for mattress hair and wool, and forty weight of feathers, John Davis earned £7 5s. 3d. stuffing twenty-eight pounds of curled hair into ten chairs and Edward Oxley made a respectable £17 for converting close to one hundred pounds of feathers to mattresses and bolsters and pillows. Ann King addressed another aspect of the household's needs when she made a "servant's bed" filled with fifty-six pounds of cattails (yes, the plant). Even John Webster gained something, selling the household a ready-made mattress as well as ten mahogany chairs (perhaps the same ones that John Davis stuffed), two card tables and a tea table; interestingly, Webster does not seem to have provided services in upholstery per se, perhaps because he was now short two employees. The Chews were sufficiently pleased with Betsy's work to order another ten cases in the spring, possibly intended to preserve those ten chairs that the upholsterer John Davis had stuffed in November. As Elizabeth Chew Tilghman set to housekeeping, she owed her comfortable and pleasing new home at least in part to Betsy and John Ross.

Working on this large order for their colony's chief justice in the same months that the Continental Congress assembled, and that the Continental Association went into effect, brought the Ross upholstery shop ever closer to the spiraling political crisis. The adoption of the Articles of Association, the historian Benjamin Irvin has observed, "generated a frenzy of committee activity and dramatically reshaped the city's economy."[36] The Congress scheduled nonimportation to begin December 1 and nonconsumption to commence on March 1, 1775. Tilghman and his father both supported a vigorous resistance movement, as had Chew—at first. But as the protests became more radical, Chew grew uncomfortable. Confident that formal channels of remonstrance and reform held the most promise for resolving these parliamentary disputes, Chew would distance himself from the cause as support grew for a full-blown independence movement. But the Rosses' fledgling enterprise could little afford to turn away such a large contract. What's more, John and Betsy were highly motivated to complete as many orders as they could by December 1, when importation would grind to a halt.[37] Chew's

September order was one thing, but when another job came Betsy's way in April 1775—for ten calico chair cases, also for Elizabeth Tilghman—it must have given her pause: just as Quaker artisans participated as clients complied with—or violated—their faith's discipline, now Betsy was implicated too as clients chose how to interpret, or whether to comply with, the dictates of the resistance movement. Hopefully this was fabric that had been on hand for some time; otherwise, people surely looked askance as the craftswoman labored over materials that were now prohibited.[38]

Artisan households like John and Betsy's were truly torn over what to make of the crisis. In the long run, increased attention to domestic manufactures over European goods would benefit Pennsylvania's craft community, but the short run was harder to take. They could probably continue to produce sacking bottoms and mattresses from Pennsylvania materials, and maybe even Venetian blinds, and there would still be a need for them to repair and remake worn goods. But most of the market for bed hangings, window curtains and chair cases—all of the high-end and most profitable work—depended on the importation of goods from abroad. Now, the Continental Congress debated responses to perceived abuses of imperial authority while Benjamin Chew decided where to spend the serious sums of money needed to outfit his daughter's home, and John and Betsy Ross launched their fledgling firm in the middle of the greatest political and commercial crisis the city had ever seen. It is easy to imagine Betsy and John bent over the Chew household's chintzes through those highly charged weeks, reporting back and forth what they'd heard, sometimes from reliable sources, sometimes from the city streets, through Quaker channels and in the pews of Christ Church, about the deliberations of the Congress and the likely responses from the Chews and the Tilghmans.

Betsy and John Ross surely hoped that the Chews and Tilghmans were talking, too, to affluent and influential friends and family members—the Galloways, Mifflins and Whartons, among others—about their beautiful purchases and the upholsterers who made them. They hoped that members of the Chew family's circle would be impressed by the upholsterers' work and place orders of their own. As the city and the wealth of its most prosperous residents grew, the already thriving market for the tassels, chair covers, bed hangings and valances that Betsy made so beautifully would only expand, and their small shop had already found solid purchase within it. If this latest political rupture could just be resolved peaceably, their future seemed as secure as Betsy's taut stitches.

# · 9 ·

# Meditations in Trouble

As Betsy boxed up the finished chair cases for the Chew order, she was thinking about the enforcement of the Continental Association's articles every bit as
much as was her uncle Abel James. With the Continental Association in place,
a committee, a body that would become Philadelphia's Committee of Observation and Inspection, was now required to implement its policies. Choosing
the men who would fill these posts was as charged a process as anything else:
who would control the way the rebellion was policed? The city's tradesmen
submitted a slate of candidates for membership that omitted the influential
merchants who had so long dominated Philadelphia politics, choosing instead
both moderate and radical artisans, tradesmen and shopkeepers. Another
slate, submitted by moderates and conservatives, was soundly defeated. As
one historian has written, it is not so much that the majority of people had by
this time embraced the radical point of view; rather, those who held moderate
or conservative views no longer felt free to express them. The "zealous," as one
historian has observed, had "thoroughly cowed the cautious."[1]

The committee met Mondays in the American Philosophical Society
rooms and soon created subcommittees to oversee various neighborhoods.
Every day, these men walked the wharves, inspecting the cargoes of the ships
docked there, and then went on to the London Coffee Shop, where from
10:00 a.m. to 1:00 p.m. they registered each import and assigned it for "sale,
storage or reshipment in accordance with the rules of the Association."[2] Imple-
mentation came as an unwelcome surprise to Abel James. The James & Drinker

firm had not expected nonimportation to begin so soon, and when they learned in early October that the Continental Congress had set December 1 as the date after which new imports could no longer be sold for a profit, they realized they were in trouble. They and a number of other importers had hoped—expected, truth be told—that the committee would make exceptions for ships that had sailed from England as early as September but were unable to reach Philadelphia before the deadline. The committee, however, granted no such exceptions. Soon, over £1,000 of James & Drinker's goods sat in warehouses rented by the committee. The importers could sell their stock until March 1 but could only recover their cost plus shipping charges; radicals directed that any profits go toward the relief of the besieged Boston colonists.[3]

As 1774 gave way to 1775, the whole city was on pins and needles. As one observer wrote in the opening months of the year, "all was wakefulness, watchfulness, suspicion, contrivance and invention."[4] Ships that made port after the first of December were forced to deliver their goods to the ad hoc government, which sold them at auction; by February, ships were no longer permitted to unload at all and were instead sent on to the West Indies.[5] The Quakers—broadbrims, as many derided—were also meeting almost daily, trying to find a response to events that preserved their faith's peace testimony without jeopardizing the safety of Friends. Meanwhile, James Wilson, a delegate to the Pennsylvania provincial convention, argued for Massachusetts's right to resist this malicious attack on its charter, declaring that, since the means the British government had chosen to compel obedience was "force unwarranted by any act of parliament, unsupported by any principle of the common law, unauthorized by any commission from the crown," resistance was justified by "both the letter and the spirit of the British constitution"; he also, by his speech, began shifting the burden of responsibility from Parliament or the king's ministers to the king himself.[6]

"I wish we were once quietly settled for [the delegates] seem to be very firm and are waiting to know what the King and Parliament will do," one Philadelphia woman mused, since "till then things will be partly at a stand."[7] Governor Penn, eager to reconcile his colony with the British government, called the assembly into session, determined to have Pennsylvania send its own declarations, based on the "plan of union" that Joseph Galloway had proposed to the Continental Congress, despite the fact that that body had rejected it. But the colonial assembly was already sliding toward rebellion—in no small part due to the leadership of John Ross's uncles, the radical Whigs George Ross and Edward Biddle, who together with John Dickinson persuaded their colleagues to oppose Penn's preferences. Biddle took Galloway's position as Speaker, and the Continental Congress's actions were approved. The next time a delegation needed to be sent to represent Pennsylvania, it would reflect the radical position.

Those family connections ensured that the young couple would be close to events across the colonies as news came pouring in. At 5:00 p.m. on April 24, 1775, an express rider from Trenton charged toward the City Tavern and reported that shots had been exchanged in the Massachusetts countryside, in two small towns called Lexington and Concord. By morning, the news was all over town. A staggering eight thousand people gathered in the statehouse yard to find out what was going to happen next. Now that colonial blood was at last spilled, war seemed to many inevitable.

With a close eye on the ever-shifting political sands, John's father, Aeneas, still in Delaware, tread carefully. Reverend Ross's situation points up the choices that faced most colonists as the crisis of revolution hit. His family leaned toward rebellion, but his position in the Church of England demanded loyalty. In October 1777, with the British fleet floating nearby, he had to decide what to do. The rebels had insisted that clergymen forgo the prayers for the king that the Anglican liturgy traditionally involved, and, as the historian Liam Riordan notes, most Anglican rectors closed up their churches entirely rather than comply. But Reverend Ross, torn in two directions, could bring himself neither to conform to Revolutionary dictates nor to halt services altogether. Ambrose Serle, Lord Admiral Howe's personal secretary, has left us some insight into Ross's solution. Serle found Ross's church "an odd motley Service of religion." Reverend Ross "read the Liturgy" but "garbled of the Prayers for the King and Royal Family." He then turned the pulpit over to a guest clergyman inclined toward Methodism (and loyalism), who offered a "long & full Prayer for the King & a Blessing on his Arms." Thus, Aeneas Ross was able to conform to the instructions of the government in rebellion while also keeping Immanuel Church open. Perhaps he had a greater sense of responsibility than most, since the church he would have had to close was founded by his own father more than sixty years earlier. By managing to have it both ways, Ross, Riordan suggests, "may have been the most pro-Patriot Anglican minister in Delaware."[8]

Meanwhile in Philadelphia, residents began to form neighborhood militia units. The new Walnut Street prison at the corner of Sixth Street and across from the statehouse yard was converted to a powder magazine; powder and arms began flowing faster than the Delaware River. Two of the colony's six powder mills were alone producing some 2,500 pounds per week. On June

10, about eighteen hundred young men—John Ross almost certainly among them—marched in review before the Continental Congress. Over the next three weeks, some thirty companies formed and began training together. The colony's leadership explicitly endorsed the local military associations, promised to pay all soldiers who defended Pennsylvania from invasion, and ordered that 4,500 muskets be supplied to minutemen. As plans were made to defend the Delaware River, arm colonists and provision soldiers, the most important political action was the creation of the Committee of Safety—twenty-five men who would become the colony's de facto administration for the next eighteen months. George Ross and Edward Biddle joined the newly formed committee and began to attend its twice-a-day meetings; perhaps they had a direct hand in drawing their nephew into a more active role in the resistance movement. Across town, one woman wrote, "I heartily wish the Authors of all this Mischief may be brought to Justice," but it was no longer at all clear whose hands "Justice" was in.[9]

Delegates from Britain's mainland colonies returned to Philadelphia again in May 1775—George Ross once again among them—convening just as American forces under the command of Ethan Allen took the initiative and seized Fort Ticonderoga. In June, this assembly (now known as the Second Continental Congress) appointed George Washington head of the army encamped around Boston. Congress sent one last gesture for peace to England (the so-called Olive Branch Petition), at the same time drafting the "Declaration of the Causes and Necessity of Taking Up Arms" to justify the military buildup. Pointedly denying that they sought anything but redress—independence was still not their aim—the delegates assured their English audience that the "Lives of Britons are still dear to us. They are the Children of our Parents, and an uninterrupted Intercourse of mutual Benefits had knit the bonds of Friendship."[10] "When hostilities were commenced," the assembly added, "when on a late Occasion we were wantonly attacked by your Troops, though we repelled their Assaults and returned their Blows, yet we lamented the Wounds they obliged us to give." The address claimed that reconciliation was still possible, and even still the colonists' chief wish; but fewer and fewer people, George Ross included, were finding that position compelling. Ross by July 1775 was knee-deep in military and political activity—a colonel in the local militia, a member of the Lancaster County Committee of Observation and Inspection, a member of the Pennsylvania Committee of Safety and a delegate to the important Continental Congress.

War seemed increasingly inevitable. John and Betsy's emotional response to the events driving the Revolution was captured in the new artwork they acquired for their home's walls. Almost as soon it became available, they rushed out to buy the 1775 "Map of the Seat of the Civil War in New England," printed at the Philadelphia shop of Nicholas Brooks.[11] The map, "Indexed for points of interest," included a "Plan of Boston and its environs," and "A view of the lines thrown up on Boston Neck; by the ministerial army." Obviously interested in the military action unfolding in New England, they also acquired a "view of the late Battle of Charlestown." Their landlord, Hugh Henry, would later be called out as a traitor to the Patriot cause; hopefully he didn't find reason to stop by as the newlyweds hung their new treasures on the walls of their rental apartment.[12]

The prints suggest how alert Philadelphians were to events in Massachusetts. Provincials and regulars had clashed outside Boston on June 17, 1775, and by mid-September 1775, Brooks had "proposed to print an exact view of the late Battle at Charlestown . . . in which an advanced party of seven hundred provincials stood an attack made by eleven regiments, and a train of artillery of the ministerial forces, and, after an engagement of two hours, retreated to their main body at Cambridge, leaving eleven hundred of the regulars killed and wounded on the field." The map, which would be available to subscribers, would also include views of "General Putnam, a part of Boston, Charlestown in flames, Breeds hill, provincial breast-work, a broken officer and the Somerset man of war, and a frigate firing upon Charlestown." Having paid five shillings for their map (and seven and a half if in color), the Rosses could well have found irony in the fact that their purchase was "printed on a good crown imperial paper."[13] If so, they must not have objected too strongly, since they bought the new print as soon as it was available. No visitor to their home would wonder where their political sympathies lay.

Thoughts of impending war also hovered over the pews of Christ Church. The Continental Congress recommended a "general fast throughout the twelve united colonies of North-America," to take place on Thursday, July 20, 1775. On that day, Thomas Coombe ascended the pulpit and read these words from Chronicles 20, verses 11–13: "Behold, I say, how they reward us, to come to cast us out of thy possession which thou has given us to inherit. O our god, wilt thou not judge them? For we have no might against this great company that cometh against us; neither know we what to do, but our eyes are upon thee. And all Judah stood before the Lord, with their little ones, their wives and their children." The words, Coombe reminded the assembled congregation, came from a pious king who, threatened by a "great multitude" from "beyond the sea," proclaimed and then joined a fast, and thereby secured "victory without bloodshed."[14] Their own situation, Coombe declared, was "much more awful and affecting," since the enemy "thundering at [their] gates, in all the parade of war" were their "own kinsmen and brethren." Coombe rehearsed recent events and assured his congregation that "whatever measures have been entered into on our part . . . were purely *defensive*." "We asked but for peace, liberty and safety," he insisted, while Britain tried to rob them of the just fruits of their labor. From the pulpit Coombes applauded his listeners for their conduct: "[It has] demonstrated to the world around, how well you deserve that liberty for which you are contending." But make no mistake: "We are thus early called upon to maintain our ground in the rank of Freemen by open force, or to herd it in hopeless slavery to the latest generations. Instead of cultivating the gentle arts of peace, every man under his own vine and fig tree, all orders and degrees of men are employed in 'turning the battle from the gates'; the HUSBANDMAN hath 'beat his plough-shares into swords, and his pruning-hooks into spears,' the CITIZEN is called off from his quiet station in the community, to attend to the fin of arms, and the PRIEST from the altar, to weep over the distress of his country."

John and Betsy Ross did not need encouragement from their minister to embrace the cause of revolution, but it didn't hurt. John Mason (the upholsterer whose shop stood across the street from the Griscoms) also gave Betsy and John plenty of chances to talk politics and was especially likely to urge the younger man on. Mason had come to Philadelphia from South Carolina about 1767, and from time to time would publish short verses in the *Pennsylvania Packet*. In 1775, a verse from his pen, titled "Liberty's Call," pictured Fair Liberty "high on the banks of Delaware," and invited her "friends, from every land / Where freedom doth not reign" to "hither fly from every clime / Sweet liberty to gain." "Expect not that on downy beds" (Mason being a particular expert on that subject) / "This boon you can secure; At perils smile, rouse up your souls / War's dangers to endure." "Beauteous virgins," he assured young men like Ross, were even then gathering "Laurel your brows to wreathe." If not one's lovers, he added, one should think of one's parents: "Was it for this, ye mothers dear ! / Ye nursed your tender babes? / Was it for this, our yet loved sons ! / We sheathed our trusty blades."[15] Women weeping, men with swords on their thighs—Mason's poetry teemed with romance, sex and glory, themes that swirled throughout colonial society in these first heady months of outright rebellion.

Betsy together with her sisters watched as their husbands decided what to do. When called into service in 1777, Susannah's husband, Ephraim Doane, opted to hire a substitute, Jacob Lesher, to serve in George Forepaugh's Company in the Fifth Battalion. Doane as well as William Donaldson may have preferred to contribute his skills at sea.[16] Deborah's husband, Quaker Everard Bolton, is listed under "Peale's battalion" as having paid a series of fines.[17] Mary's husband, Thomas Morgan, had been active in the protest movements before the war; whether or how he contributed to any military organization is now difficult to tell.[18] Sarah's brother-in-law, Arthur Donaldson, would be charged with placing chevaux-de-frise (or, as one resident would call them, employing a certain linguistic logic, "Shiver de friezes") in the Delaware River. (In November 2007, a rare surviving piece of Donaldson's works—essentially a telephone pole that ends in a metal point—was found in the Delaware River by a contractor charged with maintaining Sunoco's Delaware River piers.)[19] Betsy, Sarah and Arthur's wife, Elizabeth, who was also their cousin, we can well imagine, gathered at the water's edge and watched as the men assembled timbers as large as the masts of the ships in the harbor and fitted them out with iron-tipped points. When the timbers, logs and points were assembled, workmen bound them as tightly as possible and covered the whole with planks and caulking. Some thirty tons of stones were loaded onto the device to sink it into position, with the points about six or seven feet under the surface of the water. Rows were "sunk sixty feet asunder from each other and another behind in their intervals, to form a range."[20] On the other side of the family, John's uncle George joined the First Battalion of his county's Associators. Some men, George Ross used to say, were "neither chip nor porridge"—no Ross wanted to be in that category.[21]

Joanna Ross, too, knew the worry of watching a husband pack his kit. In mid-October 1775, John's sister had married the former British soldier (now turned rebel) Thomas Holland in their father's New Castle church. Joanna's husband was a handsome, if portly, man in his fifties—closer to her father's age than her own.[22] His story, as he had once recounted it to an admiring fellow soldier, reads like the plot of one of the seduction novels that had just burst onto the eighteenth-century scene. But it also sheds some light on the life of Betsy's sister-in-law and lifelong friend Joanna Ross, whose wartime experiences would be every bit as grim as Betsy's own.

Holland had been a soldier all his life, having joined the British army as a young man during King George's War. He rose to the office of captain, married and settled in London. But his love for the British army soured when he intervened on behalf of the daughter of a good friend—a "modest virgin" who had "given way to the arts of seduction." Turned out of her father's house and now apparently dying, she sought out Holland and pleaded with him to help her find justice. More specifically, she wanted him to prosecute two men who "outrageously maltreated" her (and who may or may not have been the initial cause of her fall from grace). Holland's language is obscure to us today, but it seems as though the young woman was reporting either a rape or an attempted rape. The girl died, but Holland did pursue the matter; the men, "with false witnesses, false swearing, etc.," were cleared of any wrongdoing, prompting an uncle—the colonel, as it happens, of Holland's regiment—to retaliate. The colonel told Holland that if he did not resign his commission, he would be court-martialed. Holland asked whether he might sell this office instead—the commission was worth £1,000—but the colonel refused. So Holland resigned to "go to the land of liberty," he would later recount, "where a poor man is something in the scale of being."

Holland (by this time a widower) left his two small sons behind with friends and sometime in 1775 arrived in Philadelphia. He couldn't have been more welcome. Holland joined the Fourth Pennsylvania Battalion under Colonel Anthony Wayne and was commissioned a second lieutenant.[23] In mid-March he resigned that office, perhaps to relocate to New Castle where Joanna lived, since later in the spring of 1776 he was serving as an adjutant with the First Company in the Delaware regiment. An "excellent disciplinarian," Holland had a knowledge of formal tactics and procedures that would prove a boon to the Delaware troops.[24]

With Philadelphia now up to its ears in gunpowder, men everywhere raced to join all manner of military efforts. By midsummer, ever-larger numbers of Philadelphians were caught up in the ever-expanding rebellion, serving on, in addition to the Pennsylvania Assembly and the Committee of Safety, local committees of observation and other vehicles of protest. They were also drawn into plans for armed engagement. While the Committee of Safety tackled the defense of the city's waterfront, gathering weapons, ordnance and medical supplies, the Continental Congress published instructions to assist in the organization of militia outfits. The summer was filled with activity.

By fall 1775, Betsy and her husband had made their position plain. In August, when King George declared the inhabitants of his North American colonies to be in open rebellion, Elizabeth Griscom Ross was squarely among them. Whatever the preferences of her parents or the James family, she had determined to throw in her lot with the resistance movement. Her in-laws clearly drifted to the radical edge; in fact, in November 1775, when the Pennsylvania Assembly chose delegates to attend the second Continental Congress, George Ross was the only deputy to the first meeting not sent to the second—likely because instructions this time around specifically forbade the colony's delegates to support any independence movement should it emerge, and George's views were well known. ("I can't help saying," George wrote to his brother-in-law James Wilson, "Heaven seems to Smile on & favour the great Cause of Liberty, Our Successes have been equal to our most Sanguine hopes, And I think nothing but our misconduct can prevent our Triumphing over the enemies of America.")[25]

Somehow in the midst of all this agitation, probably late in 1775, Betsy's husband John Ross sustained a serious injury to his health. No clear picture survived among Betsy's grandchildren about the circumstances of her first husband's death. Some family members later came to believe that an explosion occurred while he was watching a munitions cache as a member of the citizen's guard, a notion that's been repeated often through the years. But no public record—no newspaper accounts, nor military memoranda—exists concerning any such explosion, casting doubt on this tradition. Others remembered something about a hemorrhage that came on while he was on duty, perhaps brought on by some vigorous physical activity. There's some hint that perhaps it was plain old tomfoolery among the watchmen that provoked whatever unfortunate events followed.[26]

The upholsterer John Ross may well have been engaged in some work of the Committee of Safety under the direction of his uncles; indeed, it would seem odd if the young craftsman was not somehow contributing to the military buildup transforming the city. The 1775 revival of the "Associators of the City and Liberties of Philadelphia"—initially organized by Benjamin Franklin to provide militia defense for the city—drew hundreds of men into the military effort. Five battalions of infantry and two batteries of artillery were raised in the city itself, and joined by other battalions organized across the countryside. Committed to principles of liberty and equality, the Associators reflected the ethnic and religious diversity of the city, as well as the radicalism of its workingmen. Associators agreed to elect their officers by secret ballot and in May 1775 called for a uniform that would "level all distinctions" and cost no more than ten shillings.[27] If John Ross was injured while somehow engaged in these preparations for the defense of the city, it may well have been associated with the massive effort to gather arms.

But other evidence suggests an alternate explanation. While Betsy would later regale her children and grandchildren with stories of the Revolution she knew, enough mystery surrounds John's death to hint that there was something about it she was less eager to discuss. Years later, one of Betsy's grandchildren remembered hearing about John Ross's final days, and learning that his mind was altered toward the end: "He wrote immense quantities of senseless matter," one later recalled, "thinking he was composing some impor-tant work."[28] Given what they knew about the mental illness of John's mother, Sarah, some descendants would later suspect that no specific incident at all had provoked John's death, but that it was instead related to dementia. Mem-ories were fuzzy as to how long Betsy cared for her husband in this frightening state; some thought a matter of weeks, others believed it was much longer.[29] If mental illness was a real factor in John's health, Betsy surely watched his behavior closely. Whatever scars he had borne from having grown up with-out his mother's care Betsy had learned about during their courtship and marriage. Perhaps she'd had occasion to meet Sarah on the hospital grounds when she and John first became acquainted; depending on the state of their friendship or courtship, Betsy may have attended the funeral just a few years earlier when Sarah died in 1770. The specter may have loomed in her mind all along; it certainly must have become alarming once his symptoms became glaringly apparent. Would he recover? Or would she see her husband hospi-talized for weeks or months—or, like Sarah, for years, until his death?

If the beginning of his decline is hard to see, the end is not: on Saturday, January 21, 1776, John Ross was buried in Christ Church's graveyard, where his mother had been laid to rest.[30] The young couple had been married just over twenty-six months. Whatever politics were driving the Griscom and Ross families apart were set aside as Betsy's two families gathered to console her. It wasn't just the severe cold that seemed to muffle conversation; any exchange between the Rosses and the Griscoms was surely approached with caution, not least because the talk of the town was an explosive pamphlet that had hit the streets just over a week before, claiming to bring some clarity to the increasingly complex imperial crisis. Unsigned, it was called *Common Sense*. Speculation about the identity of the author ran rampant: Was it John Adams? Benjamin Rush? Dr. Franklin? Whoever its author, the prose trans-formed the city, and with it the life of the young widow. As Betsy mourned her all-too-brief union with John Ross, Philadelphians careened toward dis-union.

# PART III

# TRUE COLORS

# Crafting Colors

Widowhood must have hit Betsy Griscom Ross like a ton of bricks. Two days after John was buried, she crossed paths again with Benjamin Chew, but it was not the happy task of a large order that brought them together now; this time it was in Chew's official capacity, to post a £500 bond to guarantee the settlement of her husband's estate.[1] It was not a task any twenty-four-year-old easily envisioned. Fewer than one in ten eighteenth-century Quakers faced the loss of a spouse before their fifth wedding anniversary; Betsy lost her husband well before their third.[2] Having tackled the painful job of dismantling her home with John Ross, she sold what was left in the shop and moved back to her parents' Arch Street house.[3]

As John Ross had lay dying in his Chestnut Street bed, a few blocks away judge Edward Shippen penned his assessment of the political situation: "A book called *Common Sense*, wrote in favor of a total separation from England, seems to gain ground with the common people; it is artfully wrote, yet might be easily refuted. The idea of an Independence, tho some time ago abhorred, may possibly by degrees become so familiar as to be cherished. It is in everybody's mouth as a thing absolutely necessary in case foreign troops should be landed, as if this step alone would enable us to oppose them with success."[4] Now, with her husband dead, Betsy was left to navigate the volatile situation on her own. Rumors careened around a city braced for invasion. As Thomas Paine's stunning pamphlet transformed public opinion around her, Betsy adjusted to life alone. The next weeks would prove pivotal, for the colony of

Pennsylvania, and for its newest widow. In six months' time, independence would be declared.

As the colony braced for violence, the machinery of war began once more to grind. Drums, cartouche boxes, haversacks—artisans across Philadelphia turned their energies toward military supply. Among them were a handful of women whose skills equipped them to make an especially valuable and necessary category of goods: the flags, ensigns and standards that would identify men assembled in defense of the colonies.

As Betsy's first months alone began to unfold, each successive season brought new and never-ending controversy. The effort to protest unwelcome innovations in colonial tax policy was hurtling toward a movement with a far-more-radical aim: independence from British rule. Just a few months ago this would have been inconceivable. But now, one observer noted, "the plot thickens; peace is scarcely thought of—Independency predominant. Thinking people uneasy, irresolute & inactive. The Mobility triumphant." "I love the Cause of Liberty," diarist James Allen would affirm, but he like many people had wanted merely to protest Parliament's excesses—not to launch a full-on rebellion. Many refused to "heartily join in the prosecution of measures totally foreign to the original plan of Resistance." The "madness of the multitude," he observed, is "but one degree better than submission to the Tea-Act."[5] If the tyranny of the king was under attack, it was the tyranny of the masses that some feared now threatened the city.

Betsy grasped the full threat of this unpredictable force all too soon when her sister Sarah Donaldson's family was engulfed in it: Arthur Donaldson was accused of being a traitor to the Patriot cause.[6] In a street-corner conversation that summer, Benjamin Randolph—the renowned cabinetmaker whose elegant chairs Betsy had from time to time embellished with protective slipcovers—had started a rumor that Donaldson, who was in New York at the request of General Washington, had not, in fact, been summoned there to consult on a "defensive work of great importance," as he claimed; instead, Randolph intimated, the summons was Washington's ruse to draw Donaldson to his headquarters, where he would be imprisoned on suspicion of treason, having allegedly supplied the British with the plans of the chevaux-de-frise he had built to protect the Delaware. The listeners were immediately skeptical. Why would the commander in chief of the Continental army need to resort to any such subterfuge to imprison a suspected traitor? When confronted, Randolph would claim that it had all been a mistake. He had been misunderstood, the incident had been misremembered, Donaldson's name might have gotten confused with someone else's, the timing of his travels and Donaldson's cleared him of any blame in the matter—Randolph's excuses were many and varied.

When Donaldson returned to Philadelphia and learned that his integrity had been questioned, he rushed to the Committee of Safety, both to confirm that its members weren't taken in by this story and to insist that they conduct an inquiry into Randolph's role in spreading the slander. "Next to the duty of detecting and punishing those who are engaged in practices injurious to the cause of liberty," Donaldson would later assert in the columns of the local newspaper, where he sought to clear his name, "is that of acquitting the innocent of false and unjust accusations."[7] Donaldson's family had been "made extremely unhappy" by the implications of Randolph's careless conversation and, to be sure, had been put in some danger themselves. As Sarah joined her in-laws in protest, Betsy saw firsthand the consequences of loose talk.

With the colony on the brink of revolt, rumors were palpably dangerous; all it took were a few heated words and an angry mob, and a man might find himself facing a bucket full of hot tar. In such times, the wise tread lightly. Betsy's family continued to tiptoe across a volatile political landscape. Even those who would become instrumental to the rebellion did not rush to foment it. John's uncle George Read was among those who took his time, wanting to be sure that all efforts toward reconciliation had been exhausted before embracing rebellion. ("I have often, when young, heard Mr. Read speak," one acquaintance recalled. "He was slow," the other man observed. "Yes," came the reply, "but sure.")[8] While a delegate to both the first and second Congress, Read attended the relentless battery of committee meetings, often all day and half the night. By January 1776, eager for a break, he returned to New Castle, only to be summoned back for the July 2 vote on independence. When his name was called, Read voted no—the only eventual signer of the Declaration to reject independence at that late hour. A month later, however, he returned with other delegates to sign the official copy of the document. (Contrary to popular imagery, the delegates did not line up to sign the Declaration at the moment Congress passed it; instead, they returned in the weeks and months that followed to sign the official version once it had been prepared.) His bridges now well and truly burned, from then on Read became a committed supporter of the Patriot cause.

On Betsy's side, Abel James and Giles Knight were still more skeptical. Abel James's Quaker faith prevented him from becoming overtly involved in the political crisis—lucky for him, since his business interests weighed in on the side of the Crown rather than the rebellion now in full swing. Giles Knight, too, was disinclined to support the protest movement. In July 1776, he contributed a musket to the effort to round up arms, but apparently it was too old or in too poor repair to be of much use to the cause.[9] Four years later, he supplied some horses, too, but on the eve of the siege at Yorktown that would signal the war's end, he submitted the promissory note to recover the £45 in value plus another £2 12s. in interest. Knight was the only man not already in office to be sent to the Pennsylvania Assembly during Bucks County's so-called Tory Election in October 1776—evidence that his neighbors had a sense of the direction he would try to steer things if given the chance.[10]

If young Betsy hoped to concentrate on her work and put some space between herself and the political crisis, she found it hard going; carrying on craftwork became tougher and tougher as the crisis spiraled out of control. Upholsterers found themselves underestimating the cost of orders as the price of scarce goods skyrocketed. Plunket Fleeson told Edward Shippen that "every material" he had occasion to buy "[was] raised in its price from its scarcity and the prevailing Exorbitance of the shopkeepers."[11] Everyone had to start—and keep—pressing one's debtors in order to stay afloat. Betsy probably spent much of the spring trying to collect the debts due her late husband. She may have reopened her shop, now under her own steam; at least William Canby would recall that her "unpretending and humble abode was once distinguished with a tin sign upon the window containing the words Elizabeth Ross Upholsterer."[12] If that's correct, it would have been right around this time that she made the move to a house very near her parents on Arch Street. It is also possible that she found work with some of her former colleagues from Webster's shop, now out on their own—Ann King, who had hung her own shingle as a tassel maker, or George Haughton, who had a year earlier opened his own enterprise. In January, just as Betsy prepared to lay John to rest, Haughton published a new ad to remind readers that he continued to make, in the "genteelist manner" and at the "most reasonable rates," various goods, including "every article in the military way," and mattresses of all sorts— goods Betsy was well used to constructing. He also offered colors.[13] Perhaps in the weeks following John's death Betsy turned to these familiar faces for the work she needed to survive.

Spring 1776 brought some unexpected opportunities to the city's upholsterers, generated by the residence of the Continental Congress. Benjamin Franklin's accounts suggest that various artisans and shopkeepers benefited from the assemblage of out-of-town delegates. On March 5, 1776, for instance, Franklin paid the upholsterer Hyns Taylor "his bill for mattresses for the Commissioners from Congress" (a hefty £40 4s. 7d.). In May, he purchased blankets and bagging for the beds (£2 17s. 6d.), and bed covers from a

Mrs. Graydon (£3 12s.); he paid another £12 7s. for sheeting—early instances of government contracts for an entity that was not yet the United States of America.[14]

In June, those men gathered in the Continental Congress edged closer to severing their colonial ties. The Virginian Richard Henry Lee introduced a resolution that the United Colonies "are, and of right ought to be, free and independent states." In expectation of a positive vote, a committee was appointed to draft a document asserting independence; Thomas Jefferson withdrew to Jacob Graff's new house on the corner of 7th and Market Street and set to work. On July 1, Congress debated the weighty resolution; an informal vote suggested that the resolution would carry, but Pennsylvania and South Carolina voted against it and, with only two of three delegates present, Delaware's vote was divided. The next day, Congress convened for its formal vote. This time, the South Carolina delegates concurred with the majority. The missing Delaware delegate, Caesar Rodney, had ridden through the night to reach Philadelphia in time to cast his vote. Robert Morris and John Dickinson, still unprepared to vote for independence but unwilling to stand in the way of consensus, stayed home; Pennsylvania now voted in the affirmative. The resolution carried 12–0 (New York abstaining). On July 2, 1776, the delegates had risen from their mattresses and declared independence.

Alongside beds and bedding, another category of textile goods now interested the colonial leadership. Among the military stores needed in this time of impending conflict were standards (military flags generally used by mounted troops), colors (military flags for ground troops), ensigns (the flag announcing the ship's nation, usually flown at the stern) and jacks (the smaller flag that flew from the ship's bow). Flags and flag makers had been no rarity throughout colonial Philadelphia. Today flags serve a largely symbolic function, but in early America their role was far more utilitarian. During times of war, flags—particularly in an era before mass-produced uniforms—helped troops both on land and at sea to identify and locate one another. Flags were also used to convey information at a distance; the white flag of surrender is the best-known example today, but for eighteenth-century seamen on both military and trading vessels, flags provided a means to communicate all sorts of information from ship to ship. As one of the busiest ports on the North American mainland, Philadelphia welcomed the Crown's vessels and supported a large commercial shipping industry, activity that generated a long-standing demand for pennants (the long narrow streamer flown from the masthead), vanes (short pennants flown at the masthead), signal flags and other markers. Since England's North American colonies had been engaged in a series of wars from the late seventeenth century onward, Pennsylvania's militiamen, too, had long needed various sorts of flags and banners. Though no artisans supported themselves by making flags alone, flags were unremarkable and steadily required goods in the seaport city throughout the eighteenth century.

Flags stood alongside other goods built from assemblages of textiles—including tents, hammocks and bedding—routinely needed by troops in the field and at sea, and generally supplied by upholsterers. In the 1750s, the upholsterer Blanch White's Crown and Cushion offered "Drums of all Sorts (made to the King Standard) Colours, Standards . . . Trench Tents, Horsemens Ditto, Field Bedsteads, Tables, Stools, Havre Sacks, Napsacks, Cartouche boxes, Matrasses made of Hair, and all Kinds of Field Equipage."[15] Years later, White's competitor George Richey reminded readers that he could supply "all sorts of tent equipage, tents and marquees, horsemen tents, square tents, with fan and square flies, camp colours, haversacks, kettle bags, valences for bedding, and mock feathers for soldiers hats."[16]

As Pennsylvania braced for fighting once more—this time, incredibly, with England itself—the conflict proved a boon (as is often the case in time of war) for such fabricators as the market for military goods expanded dramatically. As early as January 1775, the entrepreneurial Plunket Fleeson alerted prospective customers that in addition to carrying on "the Upholsterer's Business, in the most fashionable and useful manner," he "likewise continues to make and prepare, for sea or land, DRUMS and COLOURS, and other Military Instruments, of the most approved kinds, and will endeavor to execute any distant orders with the utmost dispatch"[17] George Haughton—Betsy's onetime coworker—in January 1776 offered drums, camp bedsteads and furniture, camp chairs, stools, tables and mattresses of all sorts, and colors.[18]

When the protest over imperial policy finally erupted into violence, military goods were needed—and quickly. An all-out effort commenced to secure a wide range of articles, flags among them. When Americans today think about the Revolution, one of the most enduring images is the drum, fife and flag bearer made famous in Archibald Willard's 1876 painting *The Spirit of '76*. Flags, drums, fifes—these weren't just props for holiday parades or pageant tableaux, but necessary tools essential to the movements of troops that had to be acquired from artisans who knew how to make them (and employed by men who knew how to use them). In October 1776, for instance, Philip Cole apprised the Council of Safety of expenses associated with his Northumberland County battalion; for each of the four companies within his command he noted the cost of obtaining the drum and fife, as well as the wages of the drummer and fifer (3s. 6d. each per day). His costs also included £10 5s. for the battalion's standard.[19]

Though flags seem simple affairs—certainly they did not present the construction challenges of upholstered easy chairs, for instance—fabricating them did demand excellent sewing skills, knowledge of materials and their properties, and in some cases familiarity, too, with the regulations that governed ships at sea. On land, the earliest regimental flags were made of silk or linen; for flags that would need to withstand rough weather, like those over military sites, or atop public buildings, wool was often preferred.[20] Bunting was a type of cloth with an especially loose weave (its origins can be found in cloth used to sift grain; "to bunt" once meant "to sift"); both lighter and stronger than other woolen cloths, it also unfurled pleasingly in the breeze. When flags needed to carry an outfit's logo, they might be made of a variety of fabrics, from silk to cotton, the ornamentation applied by an experienced painter. Sometimes fringe was put on for added panache, or the fabric itself could be frayed by hand, to create a similar effect.

During the rebellion, as demand for flags rose across Philadelphia, artisans were drawn into flag making. The painter and glazier James Claypoole, for example, in 1775 charged the First Troop of Philadelphia for "painting, gilding, and silvering a device, union, and motto on two colors." The Committee of Safety purchased a "flag of the United Colonies" from Hugh Stewart, an ensign from William Alliborne and two battalion standards from Timothy Berrett, an ornamental painter whose son, William, as we shall see, would become important to Betsy Ross in the years to come.[21]

The clients for these elements of military equipage included local militia units as well as colonial naval forces and, in time, the Continental Congress. Though it is hard for us to imagine in retrospect, when England's North American colonies came together to mount a rebellion, they were as separate and distinct from one another as, say, the United States and Canada are today; they had separate cultural, social and military traditions, and would express their individuality as they chose the standards under which their men would fight. In 1776, the Pennsylvania navy flew a flag with a green pine tree in the center of a white field, with the motto APPEAL TO HEAVEN; Massachusetts vessels also raised a flag with the traditional symbol of the pine tree, while South Carolina's naval forces flew the DON'T TREAD ON ME motto, over a rattlesnake.[22] The items obtained by the ship chandler James Wharton—which for one ship's flag locker included at least two ensigns, six flags, three jacks and more than a dozen pennants—suggest the demand generated among flag makers each time a vessel was added to the Continental navy.[23]

Ground forces, too, each carried distinctive flags. The battle standard of the Second Connecticut Continental Light Dragoons (the one that 225 years later would bring $12.36 million at the Sotheby's auction) is one such flag, and the "Waxhaws colors" of the Virginia regiment of Lieutenant Colonel Abraham Buford (which rounded out that same sale) are others.[24] For his part, Continental general Charles Lee proposed that American ground troops carry solid-colored flags "embroidere'd with the word liberty."[25] Many units in fact embraced this idea; as one historian observes, "American regiments astonished their enemies by marching . . . behind improvised military colors, hastily made from dress silk, window curtains, and upholstery fabrics, all proclaiming LIBERTY in large letters."[26] Flags like these were needed throughout the rebel colonies. The noted flag scholar Edward W. Richardson has suggested that "something on the order of one hundred or more regimental standards—one to two hundred division colors and several hundred or more state regimental, battalion, company and troop colors and standards—originally existed at various times for a total of at least five hundred or more."[27]

Every one of those flags had a maker, though almost none are known today. But with the growing need for flags of all kinds, it is no surprise that women across the largest city in the mainland colonies and the home of the Continental Congress found themselves engaged in flag making, and some seized the opportunity to make a significant business of the work. Some, like Betsy Ross, were women connected to furniture trades. Jonathan Gostelowe is well known today among collectors of early American furniture as a celebrated Philadelphia cabinetmaker, and to collectors of early American flags as the author of the so-called Gostelowe Return, a 1778 inventory of the "new Standards and Division Colours for the Use of the United States of America," which he monitored as deputy commissary, but little notice has been taken of the relationship between those two roles. Among other things, Gostelowe would have known, through his trade, every one of the city's upholsterers, artisans who now contributed to the massive acquisition of goods by state and continental military forces; he likely also knew the seamstresses and painters behind these articles.[28] The Pennsylvania Navy Board, for instance, paid Betsy's onetime supervisor, Ann King, £12 13s. 11d. for thirty-two and five-eighths bunting for "Colours for the fleet," and again £4 12s. 6d. for "making sundry colours for the fleet."[29] Other women included a "Mrs. Richardson," paid for making a jack for the Continental sloop *Sachem* (a British ship captured in April 1776 and refitted over the summer), and Mary McAlpine, who made, among other items, ensigns up to twenty feet long, pennants and burgees (those flags or pennants that end in two points).[30]

Among the most significant flag makers in Betsy Ross's Philadelphia were Cornelia Bridges, Margaret Manny and Rebecca Flower Young. Widowed in 1741 when her husband, Edward, died, Bridges took in boarders and ran a dry goods store. She sent two sons into the Royal Navy and apprenticed a third—Robert—to one of the city's many sailmakers.[31] By the 1770s she certainly needed the income flag making offered, and she was sufficiently enmeshed in the city's shipbuilding environment to understand the function and construction of flags: when the rebellion erupted, Cornelia was living with her son Robert in his house in the Dock Ward. She first appears as a flag maker in December 1775, when she made two ensigns for a ship's chandlery; she would also be hired to make colors for the boats *Warren* and *Bulldog*— two of the thirteen row galleys ordered by the Pennsylvania navy—and flags for the floating batteries.[32] She earned £16 3s. producing a white flag with the pine tree/APPEAL TO HEAVEN motto for the Pennsylvania navy.[33] In the spring of 1776, she was hired to make an ensign for the Continental brigantine *Lexington* as well as colors for the sloop of war *Reprisal*.[34] A surviving painting suggests that the flag Bridges fabricated for the *Lexington* was a Grand Union flag, that is, a flag with the crosses of Saint George and Saint Andrew in the canton, and thirteen alternating stripes of red, white and blue, while the *Reprisal*'s flag's stripes were red and white alone.[35]

Margaret Cox Manny claims a place in history as the maker of the first flag to fly over a United States ship. She, like Bridges, appears to have been a mature widow when she embraced flag making. The wife of the Chestnut Street sailmaker Francis Manny, Margaret—like Bridges—was well positioned to step into flag making when the opportunity arose.[36] As early as December 1774, Manny was gathering up yards of red bunting, and in June of the following year, she was paid for a jack, ensign and pennant. That same month, she also converted eleven yards of narrow bunting to a pennant for the shallop *Peter Reeves*.[37] Manny also delivered a jack, ensign and pennant for the Pennsylvania navy row galley *Experiment,* which joined its counterparts, the *Warren* and *Bulldog,* in the defense of the Delaware. When a pilot boat on the river needed a large jack, Manny made that as well.[38]

But Manny's still-more-notable contribution to the war effort came after the Continental Congress determined in October 1775 to begin forming a navy. The newly created Naval Committee bought the merchant ship the

*Black Prince* (just built at Philadelphia the year before) and renamed it the *Alfred* after the ninth-century West Saxon king who founded the English navy. The ensign Manny made for this first official flagship comprised the thirteen red and white stripes that signified the rebellion. When John Paul Jones later boasted, "I hoisted with my own hands the flag of freedom," this is the flag he meant.[39] The Naval Committee, too, reported the event in rousing terms: "Amidst the acclamation of many thousands assembled on the joyful occasion, under the display of a union flag with thirteen stripes in the field, emblematical of the thirteen united colonies," sailed "the first American fleet that ever swelled their sails on the Western Ocean, in defense of the rights and liberties of the people of these colonies, now suffering under the persecuting rod of the British ministry and their more than brutish tyrants in America."[40] Manny seems also to have delivered to the *Alfred* a flag with a rattlesnake accompanied by the motto DON'T TREAD ON ME, flown at the main-topmast during an attack, with the Continental Union at the stern and the striped jack at the bow.

Alongside the *Alfred* and commissioned at the same time were the *Andrew Doria*, the *Cabot* and the *Columbus*—each of which also acquired a suite of flags, whose makers remain unknown.[41] One of those flags received the so-called first salute when in November 1776, the *Andrew Doria* entered the Dutch port of St. Eustatius in the West Indies, and had its salute returned by the island's garrison, thus formally acknowledging the existence of the new American Republic. The event was so momentous that Britain cited it when war was declared against Holland, and the island's governor, Johannes de Graaff, was called home to answer for his actions.[42]

The following year, Joseph Hewes, one of North Carolina's delegates to the Continental Congress and a member of the Naval Committee, hired Manny to make a Grand Union flag for troops from his hometown in Edenton, North Carolina, and in 1777 she was credited again for "making a suit of colours" for the Continental navy galley *Champion*.[43] But Manny's death in 1778 meant that she would not contribute to the ongoing need to supply such vessels.[44] Others would have to fill her place.

One of those figures would be Rebecca Flower Young. Born in 1739 to Benjamin and Ruth Flower, Rebecca married William Young in 1762.[45] Her career in this trade appears to have begun sometime after General Washington appointed her brother Benjamin commissary general of military stores in 1777. Four years later, she was advertising in the *Pennsylvania Journal* that her shop on Walnut Street near Third offered colors for both the army and the navy. (In fact, no one made better use of the power of the press than the ambitious Rebecca Flower Young, who placed some thirty advertisements in 1781 and 1782 alone.)[46] In those same years she supplied at least five Continental standards to the nation's military stores, at the healthy sum of £26 9s. each.[47] Young shrewdly parlayed her connection to the commissary toward other work as well: she cut and made dozens of blankets for the military and fabricated dozens of drum cases as well.[48]

The history of the extended Young family was in many ways not unlike Betsy's, encompassing as it did stories of service, imprisonment and loss: as Caroline Pickersgill Purdy later recorded, her grandfather "William Young was a captain in the war: my uncle Col. Flower was 'Commissary General of Military Stores and Colonel of Artillery'—these both lost their lives by camp fever; I had another uncle taken prisoner by the British, and whipped through the fleet for attempting to escape: and my father-in-law, Henry Purdy, served through the war."[49] Rebecca Young, like Betsy Ross, was widowed early in the Revolutionary effort after William died in 1778, and the family went into flag making as a real business. In 1795, Rebecca's daughter Mary would wed John Pickersgill; by 1803, she chose to list her occupation in the city directory as "Ships and Military Colours Maker." But about two years after John died in 1805, Mary and Rebecca decided to relocate to Baltimore (where they had lived for a time before), leaving the U.S. Arsenal without two of its steadiest flag fabricators. (As it happens, and as we shall see, this was just about the same time that Betsy's daughter Clarissa, prompted by the death of her own husband, would leave Baltimore for Philadelphia, the two second-generation flag makers essentially swapping places. Mary Pickersgill would then be positioned to make, for Fort McHenry, the now-iconic Star Spangled Banner.)

The two families share another similarity as well: though the best archival evidence concerning Young's flag making comes some years after the season independence was declared, her descendants nurtured a claim remarkably similar to that of Ross's descendants—that their ancestor made one of the very earliest and most significant flags of the rebellion. As Caroline Purdy asserted, "My grandmother, Rebecca Young, made the first flag of the Revolution (under General Washington's direction)."[50] Young, her descendents claimed, made the Grand Union flag which General Washington raised over his Cambridge, Massachusetts, headquarters early in 1776—the counterpart to the ensign Margaret Manny produced for the ship *Alfred*. The assertion is certainly plausible, given that Young, like Ross, was connected to the Revolutionary government through the men in her life, and particularly her brother Benjamin. But as is also true with the Ross case, oral tradition is all we now have to go on.

As those women each embraced the opportunities flag making offered, Betsy Ross encountered a grim future. For Ross, events had taken an awful turn. Her worst fears had been realized: the colony and the city unraveled around her, and John Ross was dead. Her older sisters had all been there to tutor her in courtship, marriage and even dissent from her faith, but none of them could help her now—none yet knew the pain of burying a husband. But there was little time to indulge her grief; she had a living to earn. And now the city was plunged into a military buildup never before seen. Congress had approved the building of thirteen frigates, several rising from Philadelphia shipyards. Other women with skills like hers were finding a way to contribute, and earn something. It's hard to imagine that the young upholstery seamstress would be unaware of the opportunities. John's uncle George Read was a member of the Marine Committee, "for carrying into execution the resolutions of Congress for fitting out armed vessels, and George Ross, too, was knee-deep in preparations for war."[51] Cornelia Bridges lived in the Dock Ward, at some distance from Ross's Arch Street address, but Margaret Manny lived at the corner of Front and Arch, only a couple of blocks toward the water, and Rebecca Flower Young was on Walnut near Third—just three blocks south. Twenty-four-year-old Betsy Ross was far younger than any of these women. But she was also, like all of them, a widow. Alone and without access to her husband's skills and resources, without his emotional and economic partnership, she had every reason to look toward the future with real fear, and to seize any chance she found to secure it.

· II ·

# Signals of Independence

As a community of flag-making women emerged in Revolutionary Philadel-phia, did the widow Betsy Ross find footing there as well? Could she have been the first among them to make the ensign that followed the Grand Union flag, the inaugural use of the stars and stripes?[1]

When evidence is presented to that effect, two closely related events are generally cited together: on May 29, 1777, the Pennsylvania navy board paid Elizabeth Ross £14 12s. 2d. for "making ship's colours," and on June 14, 1777, just two weeks later, the Continental Congress passed its so-called flag reso-lution: "Resolved, that the flag of the United States be thirteen stripes, alter-nating red and white, that the Union be thirteen white stars in a blue field representing a new constellation." A century later, Betsy's grandsons claimed that, at the request of a committee of Congress, Betsy Ross produced a proto-type of the first Stars and Stripes, the very flag referred to in this congressio-nal resolution, and that its design—thirteen red and white stripes with thirteen five-pointed stars arranged on a blue canton—was in part the creation of the capable upholsterer. As naysayers will quickly point out, however, there are serious gaps between this family anecdote and the archival record. Though other sources amply document the craftswoman's later work in the flag trade, as well as the persistence in that work of her daughters and granddaughters (in fact, the best records of her flag-making activities, as we shall see, reside in a variety of government offices and date largely between 1801 and 1816, during which time Betsy Ross—now Elizabeth Claypoole—made dozens of garrison, militia and regimental flags and other flags, many for the U.S. government Indian Department), no records of the Continental Congress refer to Ross, the alleged committee or any "specimen" flag made by Ross and received to great acclaim by that body.[2]

The lion's share of the information concerning Ross's role in these events—the account of George Washington, George Ross and Robert Morris's visit to her Arch Street shop—is preserved not in public records but in the series of affidavits sworn by various members of the Claypoole family in the last quarter of the nineteenth century. They contain some things that are easy to document, some things that are clearly muddled and some things we may never be able to test. Here's what we know for sure: Ross was paid to make some sort of flag early on in the war effort, her upholstery business became involved in the making of flags for both Pennsylvania and the United States and made that work a specialty within the compass of her shop's trade, her descendants persisted in the work over subsequent generations and her family fondly remembered their grandmother telling them the story of the visit from the celebrated Washington. But the crux of the issue for the legend's latter-day promoters and naysayers alike has been whether or not Ross can indeed be credited with contributing to the design (and not merely the fabrication) of the very first Stars and Stripes to represent the new nation. Considering that question requires close scrutiny of each element of the story as preserved in the family affidavits, from the timing of the alleged visit to the number of points on the stars. To begin to separate the wheat from the chaff, we must take each element of the family narrative in turn.


According to Betsy's daughter Rachel Claypoole Jones Fletcher (the only daughter whose account survives, and so the witness closest to the events in question), sometime just before independence was declared, General Washington, in the company of congressional committeemen George Ross and Robert Morris, brought into Betsy's shop a rough sketch of the flag he had in mind: a square flag ornamented with six-pointed stars. Betsy suggested some changes: the flag should be rectangular rather than square (more precisely, it should be one third longer than its width), the stars should have five points rather than six, and they should be arranged "either in lines or in some adopted form as a circle, or star." The rest of the narrative describes the beginning of the flag-making business itself. The committeemen suggested that she call on "one of their members, a shipping merchant on the wharf," who provided the novice flag maker with a number of old ship's colors, so that she could learn what she needed to know about the flag's construction—presumably something about size and dimensions as well as which seaming techniques were best to join the strips, and how best to create the hoist. Some versions of the tale add that George Ross "gave her a note for a hundred pounds and an open line of credit to get started in that business," after which she "employed men to paint silk flags and women to do the sewing."[3]

The presence of George Ross is of course in many ways the most credible of all of the elements in the family narrative. By spring 1776, Ross was deeply engaged in the military build-up, including appointment to the Pennsylvania Committee of Safety, and committee work involving harbor defenses. Betsy had sacrificed a lot to marry Ross's nephew John; she had certainly become estranged from her faith and perhaps from some members of her family as well. That Betsy shortly after John's death appears (at least in family memory) to have been living at a different Arch Street address than her parents, who still occupied a large and increasingly empty house just a few doors away, hints at some continued tension, if not outright estrangement, during these years.[4] It is certainly plausible—even probable—that he was aware of any straitened financial circumstances his nephew's widow endured, and was eager to throw work her way when he could. Betsy continued to be close to her sister-in-law Joanna Ross, who could easily have reported Betsy's tenuous situation to her extended family.[5] In any event, George Ross may well have seen an opportunity to dispense whatever patronage he controlled in the young widow's direction.

But there are infelicities, too, in the Claypoole family story as it is recorded for posterity. For instance, both Rachel and Betsy's granddaughter Sophia Wilson Hildebrandt assert that a "specimen" flag was taken to Congress, where it was viewed and approved.[6] This detail is unlikely as there is no evidence of any specimen flag being reviewed and accepted—not in the records of Congress or in the correspondence of its members, or in any newspaper accounts or other documentary sources. The mention of a specimen flag is an example of the sort of detail that has given historians pause. What might Betsy have said that her descendants interpreted this way? We cannot now know.

Another aspect of the story as recorded by Betsy's descendants that raises questions is the account of its timing. Betsy's descendants recall her to have said that this visit occurred sometime in the spring preceding independence— that is, May or June 1776, and not 1777, when the oft-cited surviving receipt was drafted and the flag resolution passed. The colonial leaders, we already know, had indeed been thinking about flags; late in 1775 they began outfitting the first ships of the Continental navy in Philadelphia shipyards, work that gave Cornelia Bridges, Margaret Manny, Rebecca Flower Young and other women the chance to produce ensigns, jacks and pennants for ships constructed over the course of the winter. Washington was in Philadelphia from May 23 to June 5, 1776—the window during which, Grandmother Claypoole would later assert (at least as her descendants remembered it), the general made his visit to her shop. It is clear that he was taking the opportunity to acquire items he would need upon return to his Cambridge camp; other military articles that he acquired from Philadelphia upholsterers during those weeks include the dining, sleeping and office tents ordered from Plunket Fleeson in November 1775 and retrieved in May 1776.[7] There is no particular reason to doubt that, as he made his rounds through the city, he was with Ross and Morris, and that among other errands they stopped into Betsy Ross's shop and had a conversation about flags that involved stars, but the 1777 receipt and resolution are not easily reconciled with the accounts preserved in the affidavits.

Moreover, there is no particular reason to believe that the purpose of the men's visit was a congressional charge to secure a national flag. No evidence has been found of any congressional committee charged with such a task, though the flag scholar Edward Richardson has noted the fact that, in the accounts of the ship chandler James Wharton, entries related to the acquisition of flags are indeed gathered under a "Committee of Congress."[8] But George Ross was not a member of Congress at this time. He had served as a delegate to the Continental Congress in 1774 and 1775, but he was not a member in May 1776. Rather, he would be reappointed on July 26, one of five new delegates added to replace those (like Robert Morris) who had either abstained from the independence vote or voted against it. He would sign the Declaration of Independence in August in a bold, underscored hand, but he could not have been participating in a congressional committee in May 1776.

Here we might turn to the presence, too, of the Pennsylvania delegate Robert Morris, who in May 1776 opposed independence, which he considered premature. Though he believed an independence movement was probably inevitable, and planned to join it if and when it emerged, when the matter was put to a vote on July 1, he voted against it. (As we have seen, however, unwilling to thwart the will of the majority, he then remained absent from Congress in order to enable his delegation to support it. After he signed the Declaration in August, he was remembered to have said, "I am not one of those politicians that run testy when my own plans are not adopted. I think it is the duty of a good citizen to follow when he cannot lead.")[9] Morris had been named, over the course of the winter, to the Marine Committee, a body of the Congress charged with fitting out the fledgling Continental navy. He served there alongside George Read, whose brother-in-law was Aeneas Ross, John's father. Both Ross and Read were in a position to recall their nephew's widow's skills, as well as her need for employment.

The presence of George Washington is of course the key feature in the story as usually related, and though he was in Philadelphia at the moment in question, and talking to other upholsterers about military goods, his role must also be reconciled with other facts. Indeed, in Rachel's account, the good general appeared not once but twice: first to give the initial order and second to deliver funds necessary to commence production.[10] What's more, Rachel insisted that Washington's association with her mother predated the visit about the flag; Betsy had been "previously well acquainted with Washington," who "had often been in her house in friendly visits, as well as on business."[11]

Rachel's memory of her mother's relationship with Washington must be seen through the lens of history that unfolded in the years between the supposed conversation in the Ross shop and the recording of that story among descendants. The general was highly esteemed, to be sure, when he was selected to command the Continental army, having risen to prominence during and after his service in the Seven Years' War, but by the time Betsy's grandchildren were hearing about his visit to the Ross home, he had become nothing short of an American icon. After defeating the British forces he had returned to lead the 1787 Constitutional Convention, and then, to no one's surprise, was elected the first president of the new nation, serving two terms before settling once again into retirement. When he died in 1799, the outpouring of grief was like nothing ever before seen. In 1800, Mason Locke Weems (aka "Parson" Weems) published his *History of the Life and Death, Virtues and Exploits of General George Washington*, and John Marshall's monumental *Life of Washington* appeared in five volumes between 1804 and 1807. Over time Weems's books vastly outsold Marshall's, and by the much-enlarged fifth edition of 1806, Weems's *Life of Washington, with Curious Anecdotes Equally Honourable to Himself and Exemplary to His Young Countrymen*, the now famous—and fabricated—story of Washington and the cherry tree was introduced. When Weems died in 1825, his biography of Washington was in its twenty-ninth printing. In the second quarter of the nineteenth century, celebrations of Washington's birthday eclipsed those for the Fourth of July. When Betsy's grandchildren heard their grandmother's story in the 1820s and '30s, they surely marveled at her association with the Father of Their

Country, and she herself understandably harbored extraordinary pride in it as well.

In Rachel's version of the events, her mother and Washington were on friendly terms and knew each other both socially and through previous business transactions. "She had embroidered ruffles for his shirt bosoms and cuffs," Rachel recalled, and it was "partly owing to his friendship for her that she was chosen to make the flag."[12] In her later years, Rachel would point to an engraving based on Adolph Ulrich Wertmuller's 1795 portrait of the president and boast that it was her mother who made the strips of lace used to trim Washington's fine linen shirt, so prominently displayed there.[13]

Of the many threads of the Betsy Ross legend (pun unintended but nonetheless welcome), this one is especially difficult to understand. The lace captured in the portrait appears to be a Flemish or Alençon lace, which means that it was a needle rather than a bobbin lace. The difference is significant because, of the various sorts of laces (and there are many), bobbin lace bears some relation to the art of passementerie, or upholstery trimming. It is possible that the making of needle lace, too, indeed lay within Betsy's compass as an upholsterer, especially since this form of lace making was also taught in eighteenth-century Philadelphia schools, though bobbin lace was closer to her craft skills. But, whatever technique used in the lace's production, it is far more likely that a man of Washington's station wore imported lace—in general, and certainly for the occasion of a formal portrait. If that's the case, Betsy could possibly have applied the lace to his shirt, without having fabricated it herself, though this, too, presents a puzzle, since there's no reason Washington would hire an upholstery seamstress to work on his wardrobe. Unlike those family stories that either are possible to document or have historical plausibility, this one seems comparatively unlikely. There's no apparent reason that Betsy would be taking in this sort of work as part of her regular routine as there were plenty of clothing specialists available in British North America's largest metropolis. What's more, the ruffles Washington was wearing when painted in 1795 were certainly not twenty years old; for the story to help explain an acquaintance between the artisan and the general that predates May 1776, Rachel would have had to have been suggesting that Betsy made Washington's ruffles as early as 1776 and as late as 1795. It seems likelier that this particular family story confuses different points in time—though here again, from an artisanal perspective, it simply seems doubtful that a woman trained in the upholstery trades would be applying ruffles to any man's shirt. There may be a grain of truth at the bottom of this unusual detail in the family affidavits, but it seems impossible to recover at this remove.[14]

Other evidence does put Washington in Betsy's vicinity in the years pre-ceding 1776. In 1774 Washington, together with the members of the Conti-nental Congress, was meeting daily at Carpenters' Hall, Samuel Griscom's trade headquarters; he also may have been lodging at a tavern called the Harp and Crown, on North Third Street just below Arch, just around the corner from Betsy's parents.[15] In August, Washington records a dinner with a "Mr. Ross"—possibly John's uncle George.[16] When he returned the following year for the second Continental Congress, he lodged with Benjamin Randolph, a cabinetmaker who lived on Chestnut Street between Third and Fourth (whose aspersions on Arthur Donaldson so riled her sister Sarah's family)—just blocks from John and Betsy's home on the same street.[17] The cabinetmaker could easily have helped direct Washington to the widow Ross, whose sewing had ornamented his own creations. None of this is even remotely definitive, but certainly there were many chances for the upholsterer and the general to meet.

The next opportunity Washington and Ross would have had to cross paths—and the moment when family memory asserts that they did—was in the late spring of 1776, when Washington returned to Philadelphia in the course of his duties now as commander in chief of the Continental forces. What did Washington do during that fifteen-day stay in spring 1776? On May 24–25, he attended the gathering of delegates, noting the "great Variety of Business in which Congress are engaged."[18] Washington's visit to Congress prompted several actions that could have rippled outward toward the uphol-sterer Betsy Ross. Congress resolved to form a committee to "confer" with Washington on a "plan of military operations for the ensuing campaign," and appointed John Ross's uncle George Read a member. They also approved a "flying camp" of some 10,000 men to protect the mid-Atlantic colonies, granted Washington permission to build "as many fire rafts, row gallies, armed boats and floating batteries" as the defense of New York might warrant, and allo-cated $50,000 to the acquisition of tents and "sundry articles for the use of the continental army"—all activities that invoked the skills of flag makers and upholsterers. Colors were also on Washington's mind; on the twenty-eighth, he sent a letter to Major General Israel Putnam in New York concerning a number of military matters, and in a postscript added, "I desire you'll speak to the several Co[ls] & hurry them to get their colours done."[19] Putnam received the letter and wrote in his orderly book, in a note dated May 31, 1776, "Genl Wash has wrote to Genl Putnam desiring him in the most pressing terms to give positive orders to all colonels, to have Colours immediately completed for their respective regiments."[20]

Artisans across Philadelphia were receiving visits as Washington worked to outfit the fledgling armed services; Plunket Fleeson's tents and perhaps Rebecca Young's flag were among the many articles secured. The commander's brief visit surely put the city's various committeemen in a mad scramble. Ross, Morris and Washington shared several aims of a military sort that spring, both apart from and entangled with the Continental army. All three men, together with George Read, were involved in efforts to defend the Delaware River.[21]

As the most important port on the North American mainland and the home of the rebellion's leadership, Philadelphians rightly understood themselves to be an obvious target of Britain's considerable might. Nothing was more important than the defense of the Delaware. The priorities of both the Pennsylvania Committee of Safety and the Continental Congress converged on this point. Attention turned toward the waterfront, and John's uncle George Ross was especially active here. In June 1775, as a member of Pennsylvania's Committee of Safety he had been charged with helping to plan a system of defense for the colony. In February 1776, just weeks after he laid his nephew to rest in the Christ Church burying ground, he was appointed to other committees asked to review the rules governing the Associators; in the months that followed, he contributed to conversations on any number of subjects concerning the raising of local battalions.[22] And in May, just as his niece Betsy went to work on a flag, he was appointed to a nine-man committee asked to examine the colony's defensive fortifications, and to recommend improvements.[23] Morris, too, had been appointed in March 1776 to a committee charged with devising "ways and means" to fortify the harbor against the British warships. He would help develop alarms not only for the rebelling colony of Pennsylvania but also for New York and New Jersey. Morris, as a member of the Continental Congress's Maritime Committee, was also deeply involved in the affairs of both merchant and military ships for Pennsylvania as well as the larger cause.[24]

Alongside Ross, Morris and Washington, another figure essential to the story is the Philadelphia shipping merchant John Nixon, who in 1775 and 1776 served as an officer of the Pennsylvania Committee of Safety.[25] When thousands of residents gathered in the statehouse yard to hear the Declaration of Independence read for the first time in public, it was forty-three-year-old Nixon who did the honors. Betsy and John had reason to know Nixon; not only was he a prominent merchant, but he had been among the managers of the Pennsylvania Hospital while John's mother, Sarah, was committed there for lunacy, and was also a member, like John Ross, of the Masonic Lodge.

Nixon's accounts of the expenses associated with his committee's work contain references to several Philadelphia flag makers, none of them Elizabeth Ross.[26] But Nixon's records do shed light on the 1777 receipt. His ledgers for 1776 and 1777 indicate that large sums were allocated to "William Richards and Co." for flags destined for pilot boats and harbor defenses. But progress was slow. On August 19, 1776, in a letter to the Pennsylvania Committee of Safety, Richards wrote, "I hope you have agreed what sort of colors I am to have made for the galleys, etc. . . . , as they are much wanted." Apparently no decision was made. Another two months passed, after which Richards again wrote to report: "[The] commodore was with me this morning and says the fleet has not any colors to hoist if they should be called on duty. It is not in my power to get them until there is a design fixed on to make the colors by." Red, white and blue bunting appeared in William Richards's store on February 23, 1777—just a few weeks before Betsy Ross would submit her invoice for payment. It seems likely that the flag she fabricated in May 1777 comprised red, white and blue stripes, much like the flag that flew over Fort Mifflin in the months to come. Clearly, by spring 1777, Betsy Ross was a flag maker for the revolutionary government of Pennsylvania.[27]

Does the fact that Betsy Ross *did* make an early flag for the Pennsylvania navy mean that she did *not* make a red and white striped flag sporting thirteen five-pointed stars for the Continental navy in 1776? Not necessarily. Disentangling the May 1777 payment from the Pennsylvania navy from the question of the spring 1776 Continental flag returns us once more to the place the inquiry begins: the affidavits. It seems unlikely that Betsy, in the stories to her children and grandchildren, would have conflated the two very different clients (though perhaps her children did; it certainly would not be the first time that children muddled the stories they had heard from their parents). But what's more, the heart of her tale is the discussion of stars, its climax the moment her shears snipped the five-pointed version, persuading Washington to yield to her superior experience on this matter. And it is the presence of stars that separates the Grand Union flag in use in 1775 and 1776 from the Stars and Stripes approved by Congress in June 1777 (and of course from the flag of the Pennsylvania navy). So it is the question of stars—their design and configuration—that must occupy us now.

The subject of stars on flags representing the United States is surprisingly complex, and there are two separate issues to consider: the arrangement of the stars on the canton, and the number of points preferred. Interestingly, none of the family documents actually mention that the stars here were arranged in a circle, an element that has long been ascribed to the "Betsy Ross Flag." Betsy's daughter Rachel said only that, in Washington's sketch, "the stars were scattered promiscuously over the field, and she said they should be either in lines or in some adopted form as a circle, or a star." An early itera-tion of a design with stars encircled is William Barton's 1782 Second Seal design, in which the stars' "Disposition, in the form of a Circle, denotes the Perpetuity of its Continuance, the Ring being the Symbol of Eternity."[28] But Revolutionary-era flags with stars arranged in a circle are almost entirely unknown.[29] Among the earliest-surviving images of a flag with stars and stripes—made, curiously enough, by another man named John Ross—is that of a July 1779 "order of battle," which suggests what these flags likely looked like, the stars aligned in rows across the canton.[30] Interestingly, in the 1890s, a flag was discovered in the loft of the Arch Street house, its thirteen stars arranged in rows; the history (and veracity) of this artifact is of course entirely unknown, but it is a tantalizing hint at the craftswoman's earliest enter-prise.[31]

In the family memory, Betsy's innovation was not in the stars' arrange-ment; rather, she recommended that the rebellion adopt five-pointed stars rather than six. Family legend suggests she took great pride in sharing her cutting technique with a much-surprised commander in chief. Evidence of Washington's own affinity for six-pointed stars rests in the appearance of his personal flag.[32] The field of the surviving fragment is a single width of blue silk. Since it was at some point cut down to fit a frame, its original dimen-sions are unknown.[33] Thirteen large, six-pointed stars—their shape more like starfish than the comparatively fat stars we are used to today—are arranged in rows. The maker did not aim to align the stars uniformly; some are ori-ented as we would expect, with points directed up and down, while others are rotated to greater and lesser degrees. The flag reminds us of the range of pos-sibility in the eighteenth-century eye, and purportedly illustrates what Wash-ington envisioned when he walked into the Ross shop and Betsy, by folding a piece of paper and cutting it adroitly, changed his mind.[34]

Despite the many inquiries into the veracity of the Ross family tale, none have paused to consider the significance of this particular parlor trick in and of itself, and what it may be able to tell us about this early moment in the flag's history. Why would Betsy know, at the drop of a hat, this reasonably obscure technique? Though we will probably never be sure, some possibilities arise. One concerns John Ross's membership in the Masonic Lodge. The five-pointed star, or pentagram, is an element in Masonic symbolism, signaling the five points of fellowship.[35] We know that John Ross supplied cushions for his lodge rooms; perhaps the young upholsterers also worked on aprons, boxes or other objects that required this symbol. (Later in life, as we shall see, Betsy would supply ceremonial collars for her husband John Claypoole's lodge, too, confirming her familiarity with the specialized goods these organizations needed.) Even when the star appeared in painted or embroidered forms, a paper pattern may have been used in the process, providing a reason that the upholsterer would have come to know the technique. Another possibility, from an entirely different angle, is the tradition of *Scherenschnitte*—the decorative cutting of folded paper, like the snowflakes still made in elementary schools today—a folk art that arrived in Pennsylvania with German immigrants during the eighteenth century. Betsy could have learned to fold and cut stars as well as other simple ornamental forms from friends and neighbors who taught her these skills.[36] Also significant is the rising popularity of geometry in Philadelphia classrooms. Betsy may, as a schoolgirl, have mastered exercises involving triangles that would come in handy once she commenced her work in the upholstery trades.[37]

However Betsy learned the technique, once the preference for five points emerged, all Philadelphia flag makers had to master it. Assistants could be set to cutting squares of material in the proper dimension, and perhaps even to making the folds and cuts required to produce the stars as well. A practiced hand could fold, stack and cut several at once, speeding production just as the widow Ross intended the general to understand.[38]

Lastly, what can be made of the claim that Betsy Ross then produced the very first example of the Stars and Stripes, and that the new design was adapted thereafter as the symbol of the new nation? On the face of it, again, infelicities appear quickly. Certainly the question of what flag would represent the "United Colonies" was up in the air throughout the military engagement. Early on, Washington discovered that the flag he raised near his Cambridge encampment, the so-called Grand Union, was unsuccessful. The flag was essentially the British Grand Union, but with stripes across the red field, meant to symbolize the British colonies united in protest. But observers found it puzzlingly *too* British; some even wondered whether it was meant to signal capitulation. Another design was needed—but what would it be? As the movement became focused on independence, the question grew more acute. In April 1776, William Whipple, a member of the Marine Committee, described the "colors" as having "thirteen stripes and white for the field, and a union," but naval uniformity was still unattained in July, when New York delegate John Jay reported that Congress had so far made no decision concerning continental colors, and that captains of the armed vessels (and the makers of the flags they ordered) had "followed their own fancies."[39] Sometime in the following months, the notion emerged to retain alternating stripes, but replace the canton of the Grand Union design with a blue field carrying thirteen white stars—one for each colony in rebellion. But the 1777 flag resolution notwithstanding, flags of all sorts are described in period records and depicted in period images. Stars of five, six and eight points arranged in lines, circles and stars are all seen in early flags, and stripes were red, white, and blue, and sometimes green, in a range of combinations. In October 1778, Benjamin Franklin and John Adams in Paris sent a letter to the King of Two Sicilies reporting that the U.S. flag "consists of 13 stripes, alternately red, white, and blue; a small square in the upper angle, next the flag staff, is a blue field, with 13 white stars, denoting a new constellation."[40]

Flag sheets of the period—reference tools on which international flags were recorded—also suggest the array of possibilities in use throughout the military conflict. One large (two feet by three feet) 1781 sheet depicting flags of the world shows the naval "flag of the American Congress" to have five-pointed stars arranged 1-3-3-3-3. Another flag sheet of about the same year shows thirteen six-pointed stars in a 3-3-3-3-1 design. A third flag sheet, published in London in 1783, shows the American flag to have thirteen five-pointed stars in 3-2-3-2-3 pattern.[41] Plainly, consensus as to the single correct appearance of any "national" naval flag remained elusive for the whole of the war.

Flags for ground troops were as varied as those at sea. As late as May 1779, the War Board reported to General Washington, "[We] have been frequently applied to on the Subject of Drums and Colours for the several Regiments." In part, they complained, "It is impossible to comply with all the Requisitions for these Articles, as we have not materials to make either in sufficient numbers." But they had another problem as well: "As to Colours we have refused them for another Reason. The Baron Steuben [Frederick William Augustus, Baron Von Steuben] mentioned when he was here that he would settle with your Excellency some Plan as to the Colours. It was intended that every Regiment should have two Colours one the Standard of the United States which should be the same throughout the Army and the other a Regimental Colour which should [vary] according to the [uniform] facings of the Regiments. But it is not yet settled what is the Standard of the U. States. If your Excellency will therefore favour us with your Opinion on the Subject we will report to Congress and request them to establish a Standard and so soon as this is done we will endeavor to get Materials and order a Number made."[42]

Four months later, the board sent Washington drafts for his "Approbation, Rejection or Alteration." While they were at it, the members threw in their two cents: "The one with the Union and Emblems in the middle is preferred by us as being [a] variant for the Marine [Navy] Flag." Apparently this included on it a symbol of the rattlesnake, because in his reply the commander agreed that the "standard, with the Union and Emblems in the centre, is to be preferred," but he proposed an addition as well, that the "number of the State to which it belongs [be] inserted within the curve of the Serpent, in such place as the painter or designer shall judge most proper."[43]

But if it's clear that it took some time for the stars and stripes to take form, there remains the question of who proposed a constellation of stars in the first place. If Morris, Ross and Washington are the key figures in Betsy's storytelling, a claim for the flag's original design also comes from the attorney and dry goods merchant Francis Hopkinson.[44] As the proprietor of a shop on Front Street between Market and Arch that carried cloth, trimmings and other goods of interest to upholsterers, Hopkinson was surely known to Betsy even as she entered her trade in the late 1760s. But Hopkinson had larger ambitions. A customs collector in New Castle by May 1772 (and so likely a member of Aeneas Ross's congregation), in 1774 he moved to New Jersey, where he in time became an assemblyman for the state's Royal Provincial Council, a Crown-appointed position that he resigned when he was asked to represent New Jersey in the Continental Congress. He arrived in Philadelphia in June 1776 and in two weeks' time was appointed to the eleven-member Marine Committee. Hopkinson would be among the signers of the Declaration of Independence and would go on to serve on the Navy Board at Philadelphia in 1777. He was appointed judge of the Admiralty Court of Pennsylvania (a court for maritime matters) in 1779. Without question, in a variety of capacities, he was deeply involved in naval affairs as well as the acquisition of flags for the war effort.[45]

Hopkinson also had an interest in design, and contributed his artistic sensibilities to the cause. A poet, essayist and humorist, he designed currency for the nascent government (the forty-dollar bill he designed in 1778 depicted a circle of thirteen eight-pointed stars) and contributed to the design of the Great Seal of the United States, finalized in 1782.[46] On May 25, 1780, he sent a letter to the Continental Board of Admiralty, in which he listed several designs he had completed in previous years, including his Board of Admiralty seal, which contained a red-and-white striped shield on a blue field; the

Treasury Board seal; "7 devices for the Continental Currency"; and "the Flag of the United States of America." Hopkinson noted that he had not asked for any compensation at the time, but now felt that it was appropriate to request some sort of payment, proposing that a "Quarter Cask of the public Wine" would do the trick. The board forwarded his request to Congress, to which Hopkinson added another bill for his "drawings and devices." The first item on the list was "The Naval Flag of the United States." (Incidentally, this was not the only claim to a "first" fame that Hopkinson made. Having written the song "My Days Have Been So Wondrous Free"—a piece for voice and keyboard—Hopkinson asserted himself the "first Native of the United States who has produced a Musical Composition.")[47]

In its report to Congress of October 27, 1780, the Treasury Board denied Hopkinson's request. The board cited several reasons for its action, including the fact that Hopkinson "was not the only person consulted on those exhibitions of Fancy, and therefore cannot claim the sole merit of them and [is] not entitled to the full sum charged."[48] Congress knew then what we must understand now: there was no single maker and no one prototype. That subsequent generations have tried to bring order to these chaotic circumstances—to strive to identify a single moment and a single maker for the first United States flag—is an artifact of the way we have come to think about the Revolution itself, as the result of orderly deliberations by larger-than-life statesmen, rather than a desperate, ad hoc scramble to defeat the greatest military force in the world.

Understanding the visit of Ross, Morris and Washington to the Ross shop requires putting it in a larger context, and embracing the complexities of this moment for all three men and for flag-making women like Betsy Ross. Given the tangle of committees, boards and assignments as the rebellion's leaders struggled to attend simultaneously to the defense of their city, the province and the thirteen colonies joined in armed rebellion, it seems unlikely that these frantic committeemen were at any time really acting in only a single capacity. Morris and Ross together with Washington—all three scrambling to defend the colony as well as the union—may well have come to Betsy's shop with a variety of purposes in mind, and had a conversation that, in retrospect, would loom larger for the craftswoman Betsy Ross than the congressman Morris or committeeman Ross. To be sure, the notion that these men approached her shop with one sole and specific purpose in mind, and that Betsy Ross then produced a prototype of the flag that was reviewed and accepted by Congress and affirmed in the 1777 flag resolution, resonates neither with the archival record nor historical imagination when we consider the chaotic nature of rebellion. But, alternatively, continental forces did indeed exchange the Grand Union flag for the stars and stripes around the time Betsy recalled the encounter, and someone did indeed have to make it the first time those elements appeared in combination. Whatever happened in spring 1776, when, in coming years, the flag that emerged as the national standard indeed possessed the five-pointed stars Betsy had recommended, she reflected with pride on the afternoon General Washington came to appreciate the significance of her skills.

The Betsy Ross story is usually treated as a matter of design, but it is not—it is a matter of production. Perhaps Hopkinson (or Washington) sketched a design involving red and white stripes, a blue canton and a field of six-pointed stars, which the craftswoman Ross—more familiar than the gentlemanly lawyer or the practical planter with the imperatives of construction and fabrication—improved by demonstrating the efficiency of five points. The experienced upholsterer simply pointed out that if the rebel government needed a lot of these—and fast—then five-pointed stars were much easier to make. She was speaking as a fabricator—a prospective contractor in need of cash, who surely hoped that a large government order might come her way, as it had for Margaret Manny, Rebecca Young, Cornelia Bridges and other women she surely knew.

Much like the building of Philadelphia's "first" brick house, Hopkinson's "first" composition and countless other contested "firsts" in American history, the evidence reminds us that the did-she-or-didn't-she question is not especially useful. The naturalist Stephen Jay Gould has given us another good example to contemplate. Despite our collective and genuine affection for the story of Abner Doubleday inventing baseball in a Cooperstown cow pasture in 1839, Gould notes, most people generally concede that our national pastime "evolved slowly out of English stickball games" and that "no one invented baseball at any moment or in any spot." But, says Gould, "we seem to prefer the alternative model of origin by a moment of creation—for then we can have heroes and sacred places." "For some reason," he continues, "we are powerfully drawn to the subject of beginnings." We have a "psychic need" to identify the birthplaces of our "accomplishments and institutions" and, when the "facts seem too commonplace," we invent better stories in their place. We have "origin myths and stories for the beginning of hunting, of language, of art, of kindness, of war, of boxing, bow ties, and brassieres."[49] And flags. Many people helped form the national emblem we recognize today. That Betsy Ross was not alone does not diminish her contribution among them. The flag, like the Revolution it represents, was the work of many hands.

# 12

# The Mariner's Bride

In July 1777, readers of the *Pennsylvania Packet* lingered over an account of an extraordinary event of the week past. "Last Friday the 4th of July, being the Anniversary of Independence of the United States of America, was celebrated in this city with demonstrations of joy and festivity," the report began. About noon, all the armed ships and other vessels in the Delaware River began drawing before the city, bedecked with banners and streamers, the "colours of the United States" flying. At one o'clock, the day's festivities were launched with a discharge of thirteen cannon from each of the ships, and one from each of thirteen galleys, in honor of the thirteen British colonies—now American states—that one year ago had united in rebellion. In the afternoon, members of the Continental Congress together with the president and Supreme Executive Council (the new state's executive branch), the Speakers of the Pennsylvania Assembly, the general officers and colonels of the army and "strangers of eminence" enjoyed a sumptuous meal together. A band of Hessian soldiers (German regiments hired by the British Crown) captured at Trenton in December heightened the celebration with some "fine performances suited to the joyous occasion," while a corps of British deserters, "taken into the service of the continent by the state of Georgia, being drawn up before the door, filled up the interval with *feux de joie*." As the afternoon wore on, troops from North Carolina, in town on their way to join the Continental army, marched through Second Street and were reviewed by members of Congress. The festivities closed in the evening with the ringing of the city's bells, and at

night, a "grand exhibition of fire works" in the sky, while houses across Philadelphia were "beautifully illuminated" by lamps and candles.

The first anniversary of the Declaration of Independence found Betsy
wrestling with mixed emotions. Amid the euphoric crowds, the fledgling
flag maker surely looked at the American colors and felt proud of her own
contributions, tangible and intangible, to the war effort. The young widow
had produced at least one of the early flags needed by the Revolutionary
effort (at the very least a flag for the Pennsylvania navy); the many ships now
festooned "with the colours of the United States and streamers displayed"
undoubtedly included more of her handiwork as well. But emotions deeper
than artisanal pride resonated through the day. She had shared the early
strains of rebellion with her first love and cheered alongside him when fighting erupted in Massachusetts, but John had not lived to see independence
declared. Now in the summer of 1777, feelings of loss mingled with others of
faith, pride and expectation as Betsy basked in the glow of a new marriage,
to another man equally committed to—and so at risk in—the Revolutionary
cause.

If popular historical imagination suggests that Betsy Ross's life reached its
crescendo when she stitched her first flag, in truth, for the young craftswoman
this act was only the beginning of a new and long-running enterprise for her
shop. She could not know then what we know now, that her far-larger contribution to establishing American identity would come later, as the new nation
braced for a second war for U.S. sovereignty, two husbands and seven children
later. The first year of her colony's independence would also be the beginning
of a new chapter in her personal life. On June 15, 1777—the day after Congress
passed its resolution concerning a continental flag—at Old Swede's Church
near the waterfront, Betsy remarried, having found comfort and partnership
with the mariner Joseph Ashburn. Her brother George, by now a working silversmith, made her a gift to celebrate: a silver creamer inscribed with her new
initials, E. A.[1] She was Betsy Ross no more.

As the "middle husband," Joseph Ashburn has received comparatively slight
attention among those interested in Betsy Ross. Neither the man who conferred her famous name nor the husband with whom she raised the family
that cultivated the flag legend, Ashburn remains a shadowy figure in both
familial and national memory. In part, that is because he also left almost no
trace in the documentary record. His origins are almost wholly obscure; he
may have come from Philadelphia, but, as a mariner, it is also possible that he

sailed into that city's harbor from any port in the British Empire. Much more is known about his death than about his life.

Betsy's decision to marry Ashburn in the middle of the Revolutionary war warrants consideration. That the betrothed couple chose to marry at Old Swede's (also known as Gloria Dei)—a gathering place for the city's laboring population—might tell us something about Ashburn and his prospects as Betsy and he decided to wed. Having spent her youth in the quiet benches of the Quaker meeting, and her first marriage under the soaring spire of Christ Church, Betsy shifted spiritual allegiances along with temporal ones, sanctifying her union with Ashburn among the members of yet another religious community.

How and why Betsy came to marry Ashburn is colored by a larger question. Why remarry at all? Though Betsy's youth at the time of her widowhood might make the reasons for remarriage seem obvious, it is worth noting that while just over half of the city's women would be widowed during their lifetimes, most—more than four out of every five—would never marry again.[2] Even among those who did remarry, a period of widowhood usually unfolded first. Especially within the methodical culture of the Society of Friends (though Betsy was no longer technically a member, one might assume she remained at least somewhat influenced by the culture of her upbringing), hastening toward a second or third marriage was unusual. Most men waited 3.6 years to remarry, and 6.2 years was average for women, indicating that finding a new spouse either was not a high priority or not easily accomplished.[3] And yet Betsy remarried just a short eighteen months after John Ross's funeral. Whether this tells us that she was a woman of action quick to make up her mind, a clinging vine eager for the support and companionship of a husband, or a woman too excited about the prospect of motherhood to delay we cannot know, but the quick marriage to Ashburn, like the union with Ross, suggests a certain decisive quality.

What was it about Joseph Ashburn that attracted Betsy? Joseph was as fair as John was dark.[4] He was just about Betsy's age—maybe a year older. He stood at five feet eight inches and had the strapping arms and broad chest that comes from long days of hauling ropes and sails.[5] It is easy to picture him in the long ponytail so fashionable in those days among sailors and seamen; in fact, the vogue for the "longest possible whip of hair" was so prevalent that some mariners tied their hair up in eel skins to promote its growth.[6] One family tradition suggests that Joseph Ashburn and Betsy Griscom had been childhood playmates, but here is another place where Griscom oral history seems to break down upon closer scrutiny. There were very few Ashburns in the Philadelphia of Betsy's youth. The largest and most enduring family with that name was that of the baker and ferryman Martin Ashburn, who lived in the Upper Delaware Ward, but Joseph does not seem to have been an immediate member of this household. A George Ashburn—the likelier relative—appears briefly in the pages of the 1778 *Evening Post*, with goods for sale on Water Street.[7] Rather than grade-school playgrounds, it seems likelier that Betsy came to know Joseph through river channels.

One possibility is that the couple met through Betsy's sister Sarah and brother-in-law William Donaldson. The Donaldson family had long been involved in the waterfront, as both mariners and shipbuilders. William Donaldson was a shipbuilder on the Delaware, on Water Street between Christian and Queen Street. In fact, when ships for the Pennsylvania navy rose in Joshua Humphreys's shipyard William Donaldson was at work on the *Columbus* while a man listed as John Ashburn was decking the galley *Experiment*. Donaldson also sailed as a mariner and ship captain from time to time, and so could easily have known Ashburn through the wharves. The Donaldsons were longtime members of the Old Swede's Church, where Betsy and Joseph would themselves choose to marry. Perhaps they met through church or—alternatively—the Southwark tavern that William's mother ran in her home.[8]

An alternative is that Betsy made Joseph's acquaintance through her younger sister Hannah's husband, the Baptist shipwright Griffith Levering. When Hannah married Griff Levering, it was not a match for money: her husband's father, the malter and brewer Septimus Levering, had just recently been discharged from debtor's prison. His copper still together with his tubs, worms, spouts and other brewing apparatus had been seized by the sheriff three years before. Upon his release, having hit bottom in Philadelphia, Septimus moved to Virginia and opened a malt house and brewery there.[9] Yet despite the hardships his family faced, Griff Levering was successful on other terms. "Though fortune had not placed him in the most elevated station," one acquaintance would muse, "his virtues rendered him inferior to none." His friends found him to be charitable and humane, pious and hardworking.[10] And perhaps by the time Griff and Hannah married in 1776, things for the young shipwright were looking up; at least the city's shipyards had been frantic with activity the year before, and if this war kept up, they would stay that way for a while. The newlyweds found a house right next door to Susannah and Ephraim Doane in the Northern Liberties.[11]

Betsy's brother-in-law Ephraim Doane presents yet another route through which she may have encountered Joseph Ashburn. If it was the ship captain Doane rather than the ship carpenter Levering who brought Ashburn into Betsy's orbit, one could hardly blame her for hoping to match her sister's success; if she could only meet a man as lovely as Griff Levering, but with the wealth of Ephraim Doane, that would be just right. Hannah and Betsy together must have eyed their sister Susannah's comfortable circumstances with not a little envy. To cite just one measure, Doane's tax valuation was some £21,400 in a year when Griffith Levering's was a mere £3,000.[12] Betsy surely noticed the wealth her sister enjoyed, and the lovely (and costly) things that surrounded her.

Despite the drawbacks of life as a mariner's wife—Ephraim had sailed as master of the sloop *Sally* not much more than a week after their summer 1769 wedding[13]—Susannah had done well for herself in choosing Doane, evidenced if nowhere else in the beautiful home he provided for his family.[14] The house Betsy and John Ross had shared as newlyweds had been spartan; when Betsy walked through the rooms of Susannah's "mansion house" in the Northern Liberties, she surely noted the fair gap between her sister's material circumstances and her own.

Bedecked with gilt frames, mirrors and sconces, the Doane house glittered with prosperity. Mahogany furniture was found throughout the rooms (there would be no old-fashioned walnut for the Doanes if they could help it), some of it made by the celebrated Quaker craftsman Thomas Affleck, whose goods for other families of privilege Betsy had ornamented with slipcovers, tassels and fringe. A front room contained Ephraim and Susannah's mahogany desk, a mahogany card table and a sconce looking glass with gilt edges. A mahogany tea waiter (a small tray on which to pass cups of tea) allowed them to serve guests in the most genteel style. In a parlor stood an eight-day clock in a mahogany case "compleat"—perhaps the work of brother-in-law Thomas Morgan. A mahogany dining table and large and small tea tables were surrounded by a dozen mahogany chairs. A cradle and two low chairs next to the hearth (itself embellished with a good pair of andirons with brass heads) provided a place for mother and child to relax. A Bible and prayer book lay nearby, but when the reader's attention wandered she could contemplate pictures of the twelve seasons framed and edged with gilt.

Brother George could affirm that the household's assemblage of silver was equally impressive. The Doanes' tankard, canns (today we might see these as mugs), soup tureen, tablespoons and teaspoons, pap spoon, punch ladle and pepper box; their tea service included a silver cream jug and sugar tongs, as well as a sugar dish and cover. The whole totaled some 116 ounces, worth £49 6s.[15]

Behind the house stood still more artifacts of the family's wealth: a stable housing a mare and two cows (alongside two tons of hay to feed them); a "Riding chair and harness compleat" stood ready to ferry Susannah to her desired destinations—including the plantation of some six hundred acres the couple owned near New Castle. Apparently, there were worse things in life than marrying a ship captain, even if he was too often at sea.

If Ashburn entered the Griscom family circle through Captain Doane, now married eight years to Susannah, Doane also helped him to leave it. On March 21, 1777, Ephraim took command of the ten-gun brig *Hetty*. Two months later, the revolutionary leadership approved another voyage on the same ship. The ship's master on this second voyage was originally listed as George Ashbourn (perhaps the same man who advertised goods for sale on Water Street), but the name George was at some point crossed out, and *Joseph* written above, and it was Joseph who signed the ship's papers.[16] Joseph, like Ephraim, would seek to advance the Patriot cause by disrupting Britain's seaborne commerce. The documents were dated July 21, 1777. Betsy and Joseph had been married for three weeks.

In the same months that Betsy endured the loss of her first husband and enjoyed the early attentions of her second, her gaze turned toward the Delaware, and not just because it was Ashburn's habitat. In spring 1776, the British had evacuated Boston and turned toward the Mid-Atlantic colonies, the heart of North American shipping and commerce and the home of the Continental Congress now pulling the rebellion's many strings. Pennsylvanians held their breath as they awaited what seemed to be the inevitable arrival of the Crown's forces. The defense of the Delaware was imperative. Almost all of the colonies that were united in rebellion formed navies to protect their coastlines. (So far, at least eleven of the thirteen on the North American mainland were solidly on board. Despite efforts to cultivate others as well, the political leadership in the Caribbean colonies—far more dependent on British support and loath to risk uprisings among the slaves who so dramatically outnumbered them—had not joined the rebellion.) By the end of August 1776, the Pennsylvania State Navy counted among its resources more than seven hundred men manning twenty-seven vessels, with another twenty-one smaller vessels on order.[17] As soon as the spring thaw allowed, Philadelphia rebels—in full expectation of a British assault—worked to secure the river. Fortifications were raised at Fort Mercer and Billingsport on the Jersey shore, and at Fort Mifflin on Mud Island. A fleet of small armed vessels and fireships began patrolling the waters.[18]

Throughout the summer of 1777, fear mounted. All year long, prices had been sky-high, but now they threatened to fly out of sight. Coffee and flour were harder and harder to come by, and expensive when you could find them. By July, no salt could be had in the whole of the city. The new Mrs. Ashburn found provisions much depleted, and wise housewives began laying up what stores they could. What's more, amid scarcity grew crime. The newspapers that fall and winter were filled with accounts of theft. One woman had a cloak snatched off her very shoulders, and in broad daylight, too.[19]

As the rebellion accelerated, civil liberties became as endangered as provisions. Betsy's first marriage had unfolded while the Revolutionary conflict in Pennsylvania remained largely political; though street violence had erupted from time to time, most of the fighting had occurred around tables in public and private halls, and in the pages of the press. Her second marriage began as the war and all its horrors came in earnest to Philadelphia.

Social pressure on men to prove their commitment to the cause in order to secure female attention mounted; the *Pennsylvania Gazette* would report that at the close of one wedding ceremony, "a motion was made and heartily agreed to by all present, that the young unmarried ladies should form themselves into an Association, by the name of The Whig Association of the unmarried young ladies of America, in which they would pledge their honour, that they would never give their hand in marriage to any gentleman, until he had first proved himself a patriot, in readily turning out when called to defend his country from slavery, and also his heroism when called to battle, by a spirited and brave conduct, as they would wish not to be the mothers of a race of Slaves or Cowards."[20] To the modern ear it might sound silly or frivolous— and was perhaps meant tongue-in-cheek (sense of humor in the past being one of the hardest things to recover historically)—but the pressure on men to prove their patriotic mettle was considerable, and the pressure on women to appreciate it real. When Betsy Ross chose Joseph Ashburn, she already knew she was in no danger there.

Joseph pledged his troth to Betsy just as thousands of men—in compliance with the Test Act compelling avowals of allegiance to the rebel government— swore their loyalty to the cause. Once the colony committed to rebellion, the revolt's leaders felt they could not afford to tolerate dissent or even hesitation. Anyone unwilling to commit treason against the royal government was considered a threat to the Patriot cause. And as the independence movement gathered force, it became easier and easier for rebels to force fence-sitters into submission.[21] News of the advance of the regulars caused a good deal of panic across the colony; in response, the rebel government implemented the Test Act, requiring all white males to take an oath of allegiance to the Commonwealth of Pennsylvania. On June 13, 1777 (two days before Betsy married Joseph), the Pennsylvania legislature passed a law commanding all residents to appear before the justices or any other officer qualified to administer judicial oaths, and take an oath or affirmation of allegiance to the state of Pennsylvania and the United States, and "abjure forever" all allegiance to the king and government of Great Britain. Hundreds of men lined up in those first anxious weeks to pledge their loyalty; long lists of the compliant were kept for future reference. But for those who failed to appear, severe consequences awaited. They would be denied all rights of a citizen: they could not vote, hold public office, serve on juries or transfer property. Men who refused the oath could also be disarmed, as "persons disaffected to the liberty and independence of this state."[22] The historian Saul Cornell has speculated that these laws may have stripped citizenship privileges from as much as 40 percent of that population.[23] For his part, the Massachusetts delegate John Adams welcomed the Test Act and wrote home approvingly to his wife, Abigail, "The Tories have been tolerated, even to long Suffering. Beings so unfeeling, unnatural, ungratefull, as to join an Enemy of their Country so unprincipled, unmerciless and blood thirsty, deserve a Punishment much severer than Banishment."[24]

Members of the Society of Friends were under tremendous pressure to act. Many refused to comply with the law. Other acts of general noncompliance had long been noted by the Patriots, who began to see the Friends' neutrality as pernicious, if not treasonous. For weeks, rumors circulated that a list was being compiled of Quakers who had offended the new government. Some said it contained the names of four or five hundred people to be "secured and removed." Cooler heads dismissed all this talk as the panicky gossip of the uninformed. Then, just as the rumors were at last subsiding, in early September it started once again to seem possible—maybe there *was* a list after all. People claimed to have seen it, or to know someone who had seen it, or to have talked to someone who knew someone who had seen it.

Those rumors became real September 2, when a group of Patriot men claiming to be acting on the authority of Congress and the Supreme Executive

Council appeared at the homes of some nineteen prominent Quakers, insisting that the adult males agree to remain in their houses, do nothing that could be construed as injurious to the "united free states," and prepare to present themselves to Pennsylvania's president and council on demand.[25] Those who refused to sign a statement to that effect were escorted to the Masonic Lodge, converted to holding quarters for these dangerous citizens. The next day, another seven were similarly accosted. At Henry Drinker's house the Patriot men broke open his desk, taking with them books and papers that seemed suspicious. Before 10:00 a.m. Drinker was ensconced in the lodge. Abel James, too, topped the council's list. But James successfully warded off arrest. When the men—a committee or a mob, depending on your point of view—came to his door, he pleaded that his son was very ill, and that he could not leave his family at home alone. In exchange for his freedom he promised not to do or say anything that could appear to aid the enemy, and to appear before the Patriot authorities if asked to do so. The men searched his desk, too, but found nothing incriminating and so were content to leave James alone—for now.

It is no coincidence that, across town, Samuel Griscom "affirmed" his loyalty on that very same day, September 3, 1777. Nearly two months had passed since the Test Act had men lined up, hands raised, in various and sundry offices. Samuel Griscom had seen no need to join them all summer, but now with gangs of men ransacking Abel's office, he could no longer risk appearing diffident, let alone hostile, to the rebellion. If the list of suspected enemies to the rebellion truly was as long as five hundred, perhaps his name was on it, and his wife's brother was an obvious target. It was time to comply. Indeed, it was well past time. Griscom was the only man to seek out city commissioner Philip Boehm that day in order to make his pledge: "I do suare [sic] or affirm that I renounce and refuse all allegiance to George the Third, King of Great Britain, his heirs and successors, and that will be Faithfull and bear Sure Allegiance to the Commonwealth of Pennsylvania as a Free and Independent State. And that I will not at any time do our cause to be done, any matter of thing that will be prejudicial or injurious to the Freedom and Independence thereof, as declared by Congress, and also that I will make known to some one Justice of the Peace of the said State all Treasons or Conspiracies which now know or hereafter shall know to be Formed against this or any of the United States of America."[26] With his brother-in-law pleading for his freedom before what seemed to many Quakers an unstoppable mob, Samuel Griscom was taking no chances. He pledged his loyalty and gratefully took the certificate that would keep him clear of suspicion in the tense months to come.

Did Griscom make his own way to Boehm's door? Or was Rebecca—or Betsy, for that matter—standing outside, urging him on? It is certainly easy to imagine Rebecca, acutely aware of the pressure on her brother, unwilling to see her husband's freedom jeopardized as well. Did the Griscoms feel that their familial association with James alone drew unwanted attention, or did Samuel have other cause for concern? With war on the doorstep, Samuel was not the only man in the family whose actions could be drawing Patriot scrutiny; the Militia Act passed that same season required all males between fifteen and fifty-three to serve in the militia or face a steep fine. Samuel Griscom, now close to sixty, was no longer targeted by such declarations, but in April 1777, Betsy's brother George was sixteen years old. What did he do? Whatever choices each Griscom made, and the family made together, there's no doubt that 1777 brought a terrible, anxious summer. If nothing else, Betsy's marriage to Joseph Ashburn released her from the uncertainty of her Quaker parents' situation.

Betsy watched her family cope with this painful struggle to remain neutral (at least ostensibly so, if not at heart) in a city that could not tolerate neutrality. At the same time, she and her new husband were increasingly drawn into the rebellion. If she woke up every day with a pit in her stomach, waiting to see what would happen next, and to whom, it was only natural. But Betsy, as the wife of a mariner who perhaps was aboard ship on the Delaware or even at sea, faced many of those anxious days alone. An experienced sailor, Joseph Ashburn had turned privateer.

As the master of Blair McClenachan and John Pringle's brig *Hetty*, Ashburn oversaw a crew of sixteen men and ten guns.[27] Plenty of landsmen, lured by the potential for easy money, had signed on with privateers, but experienced seamen like Ashburn were especially willing and particularly able. When Ashburn first turned his energies toward deepwater shipping, he embarked on a career that thousands of Philadelphia men pursued before him. In fact, as one of British North America's largest port cities, most of Philadelphia was connected one way or another to maritime trades. Hundreds of ships docked every year at the city's wharves, and legions of people earned their livings at everything from building and repairing ships and their various accoutrements to carting, storing, loading and trading the goods, grains and livestock that came and went, to building the barrels and crates those goods traveled in, and the wharves at which they landed. Ashburn surely learned the ropes—literally—of the trade as a common seaman and eventually cultivated enough skills and knowledge to assume a vessel's command. According to one family historian, Ashburn's "paternal uncle's widow was the principal owner of a ship called the *Swallow*," and when Ashburn was twenty-one, this aunt gave him command of the ship, which engaged in West Indian trade.[28] Her choice was not driven by familial generosity alone; few trades were as dangerous as seafaring, and no man was entrusted with the lives and fortunes of so many out of mere kindness or loyalty. Someone must have thought Joseph Ashburn could turn them a profit.

As a mariner, Ashburn was at the epicenter of the city's rebellion; maritime resources—men, ships and the guns aboard them—were critical elements of the colony's Revolutionary equation. To be sure, the colonies would at least need to be able to defend their waters. (Any offensive strategy at sea was simply out of the question.) Opponents of the independence movement had repeatedly pointed to the futility of confronting Britain's Royal Navy—which, though once the protector of American shipping, was now making every effort to destroy it. Amid the soaring rhetoric of Thomas Paine's *Common Sense* were paragraphs (evidence that readers would be sufficiently concerned by the question of American naval forces that Paine felt compelled to address it) asserting the continent's strengths in terms of shipbuilding resources and manpower. When the American colonies declared their independence from Great Britain, the infant nation seemed to be in no position to defy what was demonstrably the world's most powerful navy. But if they could not confront the British navy head-on, they could undermine its seagoing commerce. Given their decided lack of alternatives, Americans turned to privateering, allowing, and even encouraging, private citizens to harass British shipping.

In cultivating a fleet of privateers, American officials embraced long-held European practice in which governments regularly issued documents known as letters of marque and reprisal to legitimize privately outfitted vessels. The documents authorized armed merchant ships to challenge enemy vessels that crossed their path during the course of a commercial voyage. Put another way, they allowed nonmilitary individuals to attack enemy ships, activities that would otherwise be considered acts of plain piracy and subject to prosecution.[29] Although the records are scattered and incomplete, about seventeen hundred letters of marque were issued during the American Revolution, allowing some eight hundred vessels to capture or destroy British ships. They certainly achieved their intended aim; one historian estimates that the "total damage to British shipping by American privateers was about $18 million by the end of the war, or just over $302 million in today's dollars."[30]

That's a lot of swag, appealing to anyone eager to have some adventure while profiting handsomely at the same time. About seventy thousand men would serve as privateers during the war for independence.[31] Many of them were Pennsylvanians; fully one quarter of the vessels carrying letters of marque and reprisal issued by the Continental Congress sailed from the port of Philadelphia.[32] In 1777, the first year Joseph Ashburn's name appears on surviving lists of masters and mates of privateer ships departing from the port of Philadelphia, over fourteen hundred men crewed some thirty-one vessels. Ashburn's boss, Blair McClenachan, was deeply involved in privateering; ships owned by McClenachan and/or Pringle account for one third of the vessels that received papers that year. Among others, McClenachan owned both the *Fair American* and the *Holker*, which regularly appeared in the city's newspapers advertising auctions of their captured goods.[33] Insurance rates in England skyrocketed, while American seamen lined their pockets.

The Ashburns had only just married when Joseph sailed the *Hetty* out of the city.[34] While Betsy fabricated ensigns for American ships, Joseph kept his own eyes peeled for the "red duster" of British merchant vessels.[35] He likely as not had put his own flags away—in the cat and mouse game that was eighteenth-century privateering, one need not (and should not) necessarily announce one's identity too plainly. On the wartime Atlantic, deception was essential; ships flew any flags they thought would be most advantageous, or no flag at all.[36] For instance, when it was captured in 1780, the prize brig *Hope* carried a constellation of flags that included two English ensigns, one English jack, a red pennant, a red signal jack, one white signal jack, two continental ensigns, one French jack and "sundry remnants of old colours."[37] Flags, in other words, were of deep interest to both newlyweds.

Every ship at sea, the naval historian Donald Petrie has explained, was either predator or prey—and which was which could change in an instant. You might begin to give chase, only to have the prey turn and chase back. Gun ports were disguised, crews hidden below decks. A big ship might try to conceal its capacity for speed by trailing the drogue (a device meant to increase stability during a storm); the predator, seeing the sails set, would then misjudge its prey's abilities—or agility—until it was too late. Once the gap between the ships closed, the predator fired a shot across its prey's bow, signaling that it should bring its bow into the wind and lower its sails. The predator now raised its real colors—an announcement of authority and also an important precaution, lest it turn out that both ships were in fact on the same side.

If the prey was going to try to make a break for it, this was its last chance. If the ship was near land and the crew wanted to swim for it, now was the time to jump, because the predator was about to board. The victorious officer reviewed the captured ship's papers and might interrogate (or interview, if the ship seemed neutral or was small) any crew or passengers. The holds of the prize ship were inspected, and a new crew installed, instructed to steer the captured vessel into port. Often it was necessary for the new crew to retain some of the original crew, though this was always a risk; such men could, and did, plot to overpower the privateer crew and reclaim control of their ship. And of course now the prize vessel was just as vulnerable to the predations of others.

Once safely in port, the prize was submitted to an admiralty court. The captor would "libel" the prize—meaning make a public statement, typically in the newspaper, announcing the legal capture of the ship and seeking confirmation of that determination through a trial at which anyone with an interest in the ship or the contents of its hold could contest the capture or claim the property. If the captor prevailed and the vessel and its cargo were found to be enemy property legally captured at sea, the ship and goods were "condemned," that is, made available for public sale with clear title.

While Ashburn was at sea, he remained alert to opportunity and risk; his future was no firmer than the ocean on which he sailed. By late fall 1777, the *Hetty* was "in the river of Bordeaux," its hold full of tea, bale goods and cordage, when its companion, the *Portsmouth*, seized the brig *Emperor of Germany*. The captured crewmen were offered an opportunity to "enter" the American forces, and three of the prize ship's crew took berths on the *Hetty*. Ashburn's ship headed to Philadelphia via St. Martin, where the crew planned to pick up a load of salt, but, incredibly, the three sailors from the prize ship together with four men who had come aboard at Bordeaux seized control of the ship. The captors had become captives. Ashburn would tell his story to Jonathan Williams, who relayed it to the American commissioners: "Capt. Ashburn who sailed from Bordeaux the 22d. bound to St. Martins and thence to America with a load of Salt, was risen upon the 25th by his Crew and himself with two people who continued faithfull to him were put into a Boat and sent a drift."[38] Luckily the small boat was spotted by a French sloop and rescued. Meanwhile, Ashburn's former crew helped the captors steer the ship to Dungarven, on the south coast of Ireland. Some speculated that the ship and its contents would bring perhaps £7,000 at auction.

Ashburn escaped tragedy and lived to return to Philadelphia. Even this harrowing voyage would not be enough to keep him on land for long.

# 13

# The Occupied City

While Ashburn sailed those dangerous waters, the threat of British troops converging on Philadelphia loomed over the city streets. As the anniversary of independence was celebrated in the summer of 1777, John Adams mused that "the Designs of the Enemy are uncertain and their Motions a little mis-terious."[1] Philadelphians endured painful uncertainty: "I am more Anxious, now, than ever," wrote Adams, "on another Account. The Enemy's Fleet has sailed—But to what Place, they are destined, is unknown. Some conjecture Philadelphia, some Rhode Island, and some, that they mean only a Feint and intend soon to return to the North River."[2] At the end of July, news began to reach the city of the loss of Fort Ticonderoga to the British, occasioning "loud Complaints" and "keen Resentment." By August 1, the British fleet was seen in the Delaware Bay. Some 228 ships had been spotted "in the Offing, from Cape Henlopen," and were making their way slowly upriver.[3] General Washington and the light-horsemen arrived in the city, and soon, the first two or three divisions of the Continental army began to appear.

For his part, Adams welcomed the enemy's arrival, listing for his wife the various advantages of the event: "1. It will make an entire and final Separation of the Wheat from the Chaff, the Ore from the Dross, the Whiggs [sic] from the Tories. 2. It will give a little Breath to you in N. England. 3. If they should fail in their Attempt upon Philadelphia, it will give Lustre to our Arms and Disgrace to theirs, but if they succeed, it will cutt off this corrupted City, from the Body of the Country, and it will take all their Force to maintain it."[4] No comparable missive survives to tell us how Betsy Ashburn assessed the situation. But one can easily imagine her own list: 1. It will make an entire and final separation of the wheat from the chaff, Whigs from the Tories, and so drive a decisive wedge between the people most important to me as they are forced to choose sides. 2. Whether the British succeed or fail, every neighborhood will see bloodshed. 3. My husband will take up arms and set sail. I am newly wed once again, again war has come to my home, and I may very well bury another young husband.

What's more, the mild temperatures of July had given way; the city suffered heat that could melt the marrow in a man's bones. "We have been sweltering here, for a great Number of days together, under the scalding Wrath of the Dog Star," wrote Adams. "So severe a Spell of Heat has scarcely been known these twenty Years. The Air of the City has been like the fierce Breath of an hot oven." There was no respite to be found; even the shade of the city's trees was barely tolerable.[5]

The sight of British ships on the Delaware at first appeared a false alarm; Howe's fleet vanished once again, and what their destination might be was again anybody's guess. Some said South Carolina, others Georgia; still others thought he might be headed to Rhode Island, or Halifax, or the West Indies, or back to England—almost no theory went unoffered in a city on the verge of panic. Finally, the navy appeared: more than 260 ships carrying some seventeen thousand men sailed up Chesapeake Bay and began to land. Washington had positioned the Continental army on high ground between the bay and Philadelphia, around a small town called Chadds Ford. Heavy fog on September 11 allowed the British to outflank Washington's forces. At an engagement that would become known as the Battle of Brandywine, the Americans were outmanned and outmaneuvered. In the end, their retreating forces were compelled to abandon all but three of their cannons because so many of their horses had been killed. Some four or five hundred rebels were buried on the field of battle, and another thousand were either wounded or captured.[6]

Over the course of the next two weeks, Betsy Ashburn alongside her parents, sisters and neighbors, and indeed every citizen of the city, had to decide what to do. Flee to the countryside and risk losing everything they had? Or stay in their houses to protect them from looting, and risk exposure to the enemy? What if the British accused them of treason? Which was the bigger gamble—to stay or to go? Men and women who had been to any degree supportive of the resistance movement had to be especially worried. If the British took the city, would they be jailed? Or worse? Conversations circled endlessly, coming back to just where they began. It was impossible to predict the future.

Thousands left Philadelphia. The dust from outbound wagons choked the air. Still, Betsy chose to stay.

Finally, the city fell. On September 25, residents were asked to remain "quietly and peaceably" in their homes—there would be no attacks on people or property.[7] British troops entered the city the following morning, just before the midday meal. Only three short months after Betsy married Joseph Ashburn, the Philadelphia diarist Elizabeth Drinker would write, "Well, here are the English in earnest," as she observed some three thousand men under the command of Lord Charles Cornwallis take possession of the city. Columns of regulars, weapons glittering in the early fall sun, marched up Second Street, she noted, "without opposition or interruption, no plundering on the one side or the other."[8] Years later, Betsy's niece Margaret Donaldson Boggs would remember sitting on her father's shoulders (telling us that the Donaldsons, at least, had also decided to tough it out), watching the British troops on the march; it is easy to picture Betsy alongside them, watching in anxious silence as the redcoats entered their city.[9] The fears of many were realized when several hundred citizens who had supported the rebel cause were rounded up and taken to the Walnut Street jail.[10] For the next eight months, Betsy lived in an occupied city.

Just days later, a few blocks away, Betsy's uncle Abel James was having breakfast with his brother-in-law Giles Knight in the well-appointed parlor of Elizabeth and Henry Drinker. The conversation there was just as tense as anyplace else. The rumors were impossible to track. One day, Drinker wrote, "tis reported to day that Gattes [American general Horatio Gates] has beat Burgoine [British general John Burgoyne], also that Burgoine has beat Gattes; which is the truth we know not, perhaps nither." The next day, word started trickling into the city about an engagement at Germantown, just a few miles north of the city. In the morning on the fourth, she heard that "some 1000 Regulars were slain," but in time Chalkley James—Betsy's cousin—arrived to report that he himself had been as far as Benjamin Chew's place and "could not learn of more then 30 of the English being kill'd, tho a great number were wounded & brought into this City." James had counted eighteen "Amiracans [sic] lyeing dead, in the lane from the Road to Chews House." Toward evening, they had still more news; in this "last account," Drinker heard that "the English were pursueing Washingtons troops, who are very numerous, and that they were flying before them, the Americans [sic] are divided into three different divisions, one over Schuykill, another near Germantown, and the third I know not where—so that the Army that was with us, are chiefly call'd off, and a double guard, is this Night thought nescesary; it is thought, that it was the intention, that one division should enter the City, while the troops were engaged with the others." "The apprehensions of their entering, and fears of the Gondelows & other Vessels in the River, will render this night, greveious [*sic*] to many," Elizabeth Drinker mused. "Washington is said to be Wounded in the thigh; Friends, and others, in the Jersyes, and indeed almost round the Country, are Suffering deeply."[11]

Germantown had been a disaster. Over one thousand American soldiers were killed, wounded, missing or captured, of a total of eleven thousand, while the British losses numbered half that. Wounded men poured into the city, many of them housed in makeshift quarters in the colony's statehouse. Every available building was filled with wounded men—British and American alike. Philadelphia descended into chaos. After a Hessian guard standing watch on the Race Street wharfs was fired at from what seemed to be Abel James's back store, a group of neighbors joined forces to "regulate a Nightly Watch, which has been drop'd for some time, but is thought to be again Nesessary."[12] With county vendors no longer coming into the city, scarcity grew nearly untenable; the price of mutton went sky-high, and butter became increasingly hard to find. Wood supplies depleted, with little opportunity to get more; over the weeks to come, fences, stables and even pews began to vanish into campfires and kitchen hearths. People in the countryside gossiped that desperate Philadelphians would pay five shillings for a rat—if they could get one. Things weren't quite that bad—yet—but, as Elizabeth Drinker would write, "If things dont change 'eer long, we shall be in poor plight, everything scarce and dear, and nothing suffer'd to be brought in to us."[13] To take just one measure of the deprivation the city endured, the loyalist James Allen would lose some forty-four pounds over the winter of the occupation.[14]

In the midst of this chaos, Betsy's onetime sister-in-law and still close friend Joanna Ross Holland now found herself widowed as well. It turned out to be a two-year marriage for her, too; Thomas Holland was wounded in the fighting at Germantown.[15] He was brought to a house on the Schuylkill Road, where his friends found him "lying in ruins." Some British soldiers who had once served with Holland stopped in to urge his caregivers to tend well to this "worthy" man. But nothing could be done. He was one of the "children of misfortune," one of his men would later remark, "born under a fiery planet."[16] Both women had mourned together when they buried John Ross; now Joanna knew Betsy's grief as a widow, too.

Meanwhile, the Delaware remained the center of everyone's attention. At first, it seemed that the British general Howe wouldn't be able to winter in the city. After several failed attempts, it looked very much like he couldn't get his

shipping safely up the river; the chevaux-de-frise had altered the river channel, and the sixty-four-gun *Augusta* and twenty-eight-gun *Liverpool* both ran
aground and were attacked. Hessian forces made a failed attempt on Fort
Mercer, but then, in November, Howe finally managed to demolish Fort Mifflin.
Fort Mercer collapsed in mid-November. Some three hundred sails, both
warships and merchant vessels, were soon making their way upriver. People
had just begun thinking that the British couldn't last in the city another week,
but now, with access to the homeland secured, they had a new lease on life.[17]

During the months when Philadelphia was an occupied city, Betsy Ashburn's life was highly unsettled. The Ashburns do not appear in any tax ledgers for the city until 1780, when they are listed as residents of the Mulberry
Ward; no city records, then, confirm where Betsy was living between 1775
and 1780.[18] Joseph was probably shipboard much of this time, on the Delaware or at sea. Whether Betsy chose to remain in her own home, move in
with her parents or one of her sisters, or even take refuge with her New Jersey
relatives remains something of a mystery (and of course all three may have
been true at different points in time; stability was a luxury in these turbulent
months), but most family stories make little mention of Ashburn during this
period, and place Betsy on Arch Street. The archival evidence, while slight,
suggests that is correct.

According to Betsy's daughter Jane, Betsy had been renting space in the
house next door to the shoemaker Daniel Niles, but "when the war came," she
"moved into the house next west," that of Niles.[19] What's intriguing about
this slice of family memory is a passing reference to a small gesture of kindness. Jane's account remembers that when William Niles (Daniel's son) was
burned in the "Battle of the Kegs," Betsy dressed his wounds. The Battle of the
Kegs was a minor but memorable moment in the Patriot military effort. War,
like all human experience, does sometimes see humor alongside tragedy, and
this seems to have been one of those occasions. In an attempt to harry British
shipping, a man named David Bushnell (later remembered as "America's
submarine pioneer") constructed a number of underwater mines. Attached
to kegs serving as buoys, the mines were set afloat in hopes that the river's
current would bring them into contact with enemy ships, causing explosions.
But conception didn't match execution. Not only did the kegs fail to ignite
any ships, but, set afloat from Warder's Wharf at the foot of Race Street, some
of the barrels got caught in an ebb tide, and one was carried to the foot of
Washington Avenue before the tide turned and brought it bobbing back. The
floating mines failed to destroy any ships, but as they began to detonate, the
British "in panic began firing a continuous discharge of small arms and can-

non, aiming wildly at everything in the river for several hours . . . It was said that afterwards, Lord Howe dispatched a packet to London with an account of his great victory over the kegs."[20]

The whole thing was strangely hilarious. The editors of the *New Jersey Gazette* got their licks in, noting in their account that "not a wandering ship, stick, or drift log, but felt the vigor of the British Arms. The action began about sunrise, and would have been completed by noon, had not an old market woman coming down the river with provisions, unfortunately let a small keg of butter fall overboard, which (as it was then ebb) floated down to the scene of action. At sight of this unexpected reinforcement of the enemy, the battle was renewed with fresh fury, and the firing was incessant till the evening closed the affair."[21]

The "battle" took place in January 1778 but, according to an article in the *New Jersey Gazette,* a few days earlier, at the end of December, two boys on the waterfront had spotted something strange bobbing in the water: They got in a small boat to investigate, and when they tried to haul the mysterious object into the vessel, it exploded.[22] It was their unfortunate experience that alerted others to the nature of these floating bombs a week later. Was one of these boys William Niles? Bushnell's plan failed, giving cause for both amusement and embarrassment on both sides, but the account of Betsy tending to William's powder burns helps confirm Betsy's presence in occupied Philadelphia.[23]

The affidavit of Betsy's granddaughter Susan Satterthwaite Newport (in whose childhood home Betsy spent part of her twilight years) also places the craftswoman in the city during the occupation. Late in life, Susan recalled stories about British officers quartered in Betsy's house (though the evidence supporting this claim is slim); she also remembered that they called her grandmother the "Little Rebel."[24] Other sources confirm elements of this small anecdote—at least it is true that the British army made free use of the term *rebel,* a tidbit preserved in the recollections of several residents during the occupation. They may well have called Betsy Ashburn by this name, as it was an epithet heard all around the city. But it seems unlikely that officers were quartered at this particular house, given its small size and already crowded conditions. Perhaps it was some soldiers' occupation of the house next door, however, that forced Ashburn to move in with Niles, which seems altogether plausible. Betsy had already lived in two houses along Arch Street; what was one more?

In fact, much has been made of the possibility that the house preserved today at 239 Arch Street to honor Betsy's memory may or may not have been the house she inhabited in these years, but in truth, as is often the case in the contested record swirling around Ross's legend, the forest has been lost for the trees. Arch Street was Betsy's home for at least thirty of her eighty-four years. Her childhood home stood on Arch, and she lived in at least three houses, and probably more, along that street during the heat of the rebellion. She commenced her trade in an Arch Street shop. At least two of her daughters would be wed at the Arch Street meetinghouse, and her son-in-law's hardware store would stand at the corner of Arch and Third. When her grandson Aquilla Wilson hung out his own upholsterer's shingle many years later, it dangled over yet another Arch Street door. The house at 239 Arch may be the home she inhabited in 1776, or at some point during the occupation; it may be a mirror opposite of one of those homes. But this wainscoting or that floorboard little mattered to her, and the house that stands today, lovingly preserved, certainly helps us understand her world.

While Betsy weathered the British occupation of Philadelphia as best she could, these months marked still another turning point for Samuel Griscom, for reasons both political and religious. Unable to trade with either side, Quakers found their stockpiled goods appropriated by the warring armies. Many Friends did not feel that they could accept payment for these materials, since even that act could be interpreted as supporting one side over the other, and even if payment was accepted, they certainly could not appear to profit from wartime exigency. Samuel Griscom found himself between a rock and a hard place. The British seized any available lumber to construct defensive redoubts along the city's perimeter, so anything Griscom may have had on hand before the British occupation was by now long gone.[25] What's more, Griscom found himself impressed on England's behalf: the British chief of engineering John Montresor recruited more than 260 laborers to help build the fortifications, and the master mason John Palmer together with the master carpenters Elias Smith and Samuel Griscom were "engaged" to "supervise the construction of the defenses."[26] It was not the only work Griscom would perform—whether willingly or not—for the occupying forces. On October 1, Montresor made an entry in his commonplace book: "Samuel Griscom—Master Carpenter Opposite to the Quakers burying Ground Gate—Contractor for cradles." (In the eighteenth-century, a "cradle" was not just a bed for an infant, but also a standing bedstead for wounded seamen or soldiers.) The next day he elaborated: Griscom and his "gang" would make "Cradles for the Hospitals and Barracks."[27] Only four weeks before, Griscom had affirmed his loyalty to the rebel forces; now, with the winds blowing from another direction, he found himself working for the British army.

It seems possible that Griscom was never compensated for his labor or materials; at least a list of items to which the auditors of the Treasury later took exception includes one bill for £4,380 in Pennsylvania currency for "5 items of bills of Samuel Griscomb, James C. Fisher, George Wack, William Pearson and Thomas Gouge"; his name reappears under two additional lists of questioned debts.[28] Since Griscom appears to have been neither sanctioned nor censured in the Friends' fold for this activity, perhaps his Quaker community understood him to have but little choice in the matter, and felt he'd already been punished enough. In any event, Griscom's business would never recover from these blows.[29]

But more than mere property was at risk as Betsy's family endured the occupation. Sarah and William Donaldson had also decided to ride out the storm and stay in the city—a decision that in time came with exactly the consequences people feared most. The Donaldsons were wounded by the fire of a British sentry when Sarah and William together with their infant daughter Margaret and a "negro boy" were in a yawl near the Market Street landing. (Today the term *yawl* would signal a two-masted sailboat, but in 1777–78 it likelier meant a rowboat of four or six oars; William probably rowed one pair, and the African American boy was along to handle the other.) They were apparently crossing back from the Jersey side—likely in a search for provisions, perhaps from their New Jersey relatives—when the sentry hailed the boat, telling them to land or prepare for fire. A defiant Captain Donaldson thought it was an empty threat—"why, those officers dined with us last week," his daughter would later recount him saying; "they won't do anything to harm us." William dared the man to fire, and the soldier rose to the challenge, his shot passing though Sarah's wrist, according to one account, and into William's chest, in another (with Sarah's wrist being also "shattered" by the ball). In a more dramatic telling, to a journalist on the occasion of Margaret's hundredth birthday, the "colored servant" caught baby Margaret in his arms and laid down with her in the bottom of the boat to escape further harm. With Sarah and Donald both unconscious, the boat floated downstream past the family shipmen, where workers noticed the pilotless boat and brought it safely to shore.[30] The injury to Sarah's wrist seems the most reliable element in the account of the damages, though it is possible that William was hurt as well. Whatever the details, the shooting must have been frightening for the whole family, who had already mourned enough loss to Revolutionary violence.

If the Donaldsons' encounter reminded them how suddenly a threat could appear, poverty and scarcity proved more constant enemies. How Betsy supported herself during these tense months is unclear. Many artisans benefited from the demands of the war, whichever side they served. The cabinetmaker David Evans, for instance, made hundreds of ensign and standard poles and staffs as well as camp chairs and other items; work for the war effort accounted for fully one third of his income in 1776. (Unfortunately, another feature of wartime production also reshaped Evans's work in these years: coffin production increased dramatically between 1778 and 1780, and accounted for more than half of his total revenue in 1780.)[31] The occupation for some proved no less lucrative. When the British troops arrived, several of Betsy's companions and competitors in the upholstery trades also tried to cash in on their presence, simply exchanging one clientele for another. If Betsy's onetime coworker George Haughton had any scruple about profiting from the circumstances, he set it aside in favor of the income to be gained from the arrival of hundreds of new potential customers. The English soldiers had barely unpacked when the London-trained upholsterer placed a notice in the *Pennsylvania Evening Post* looking for business among the city's newest residents. Since this was a recently arrived population, Haughton had to inform readers unfamiliar with his record that he was formerly a "workman to Mr. Trotter in London," and that he now had a shop next to the Coffee House on Front Street where "gentlemen of the army may be supplied with all kinds of CAMP EQUIPAGE on the shortest notice—tents and drums made and repaired."[32] (He was also beginning to move away from production and toward sales: in July of that year, 1777, he placed a notice that he planned to "open his house as a General repository, or Store, for all kinds of Furniture, Wares, and Merchandize, by commission." Haughton also placed notices in the *Pennsylvania Packet* announcing that he was planning to open his "House as a General Repository as a store for all kinds of furniture works.")[33] Amelia Taylor, a mantua maker turned upholsterer, also produced camp equipment, while the "Fringe and Lace Maker" James Butland alerted readers of the *Pennsylvania Gazette* that he offered "all kinds of UNIFORMS for the ARMY."[34]

Betsy Ashburn may have had to work in these shops to survive, sewing and fabricating the same sorts of domestic goods she had once made for John Webster. Plunket Fleeson's large enterprise—if indeed he remained in the city—would seem to have been the perfect home for an experienced upholstery seamstress like Betsy. Perhaps she even found work with her old colleague Haughton, who was clearly seeking out new clients. In fact, this scenario seems not just possible but plausible; it is hard to imagine her finding among the suffering community of rebellious Philadelphians enough sources of income that she could refuse on principle to fabricate tassels, mattresses, chair covers or camp equipage for enemy quarters during the entire course of the occupation.

After a comfortable winter in Philadelphia, the British left the city, their sights now set on colonies farther south. The occupation ended in June 1778, capped with the legendary "Meschianza," a stunningly elaborate—many would say egregiously so—celebration honoring Sir William Howe before he left the city. The lavish party spared no expense in a city where many were more than down on their heels. Some four hundred guests traveled by flotilla to the Wharton estate at the southern edge of the city, the site of a fanciful tournament in which fourteen "knights" performed a jousting match for the bedecked "damsels" in attendance. Among the gallants who jousted for the honor of such fair maidens as Peggy and Sarah Chew and Rebecca Franks was John Andre, who would be caught up and killed in the betrayal of Benedict Arnold, and Banastre Tarleton, who in the months to come would capture the battle standards that two hundred years later would bring millions at auction. Dancing and fireworks preceded a midnight banquet lit by three hundred candles and more than 140 mirrors. The tables were attended by two dozen slaves dressed in "oriental" costumes, silver collars and bracelets. The costumed revelers danced until nearly dawn. One wonders which craftsmen benefited from this extravaganza, every element of which had to be produced on short notice. Upholsterer's skills were invoked at every stage, from the barges and boats "lined with Cloth, covered with Awnings, and dressed out with Colours and Streamers in full naval pomp" to the tented pavilions lining the jousting field. Of the hundreds of observers who crowded the banks of the Delaware to watch the flotilla drift past, Betsy Ashburn surely marveled at the work and materials lavished on the display, for she knew better than most what it meant to produce them. Indeed, for all we know, she had.

When the British army set sail on June 18, they took with them thousands of citizens loyal to the Crown. As one observer wrote, "My head grew dizzy with the bustle and confusion; carts [and] wagons laden with dry goods and household furniture dragged through the streets by men to the wharves for want of horses."[35] If the Meschianza celebrated beauty and fantasy, the city that the army left in its wake was ugly, dirty and only too real. Before they left, the British burned ships under construction on the waterfront, together with stockpiles of building materials. The city was a shambles. The regulars left Philadelphia a cesspool of dirt and debris. There were so many flies that you couldn't drink a cup of tea; no sooner was the dish poured than flies swarmed over it.[36] The statehouse (transformed into a hospital) was virtually unusable. The enemy had dug a pit outside in which to throw trash, dead horses and dead men. When Congress returned, it had to meet elsewhere while Washington Square was deodorized; who did that distasteful work we no longer know.[37] With the flies came other pests. One man remembered the "inumerable [sic] frogs within their lines, about the size of a hickory nut, so much so as to be a very nuisance, flies never appeared thicker on a butcher's shambles than these frogs were in some places along their lines."[38]

Nevertheless, people remembered the great joy, too, that accompanied the evacuation, and the return of Patriot families to their homes. "What pleasure was shown in Whigs face as they entered the city," Charles Willson Peale would recall. "What shakings of hands" as friends recognized friends. "What variety of meetings of Friends that were once intimate, fearful and distrustfull least they should take one by the hand who played the Traitors part." Peale continued: "Most of them that stayed would amediately after they welcomed their acquaintance into the City, begin the doleful tale of their sufferings. How the tories abused them and how the whole of their Houses were taken up by either officers or soldiers, and they dare not say a word but they were called rebels and threatened with the Poison and a Halter."[39] As one of the survivors, Betsy had plenty of her own tales to tell.

Immediately, the Patriots restored to power leaped to punish others they suspected to have collaborated with the enemy during the occupation. Abel James topped their list.[40] No one wants to open the paper and see their family members impugned on its pages, but as Betsy picked up the June 3 edition of the *Pennsylvania Packet,* she read that the newly returned Supreme Executive Council charged James, among many others, with having "knowing[ly] and willingly aided and assisted the enemies of this state and of the United States of America." The council demanded that James "stand and be attained of High Treason." (Hugh Henry, a wig maker and Betsy's landlord while she was the wife of John Ross, was likewise accused. James evidently provided the council with whatever satisfaction they required, because the matter was allowed to drop.)[41] Betsy could now rest easier with her own safety assured, but she could once again begin worrying about her family's uneasy relationship to the rebel government.

If Betsy sighed with relief as she watched the last of the British ships vanish on the horizon, she couldn't know that worse was yet to come. From summer 1778 to late 1780, the city saw severe hardship, in what one historian has called "the economic nadir of the Revolution."[42] Prices skyrocketed. In January 1779, a squad of Continental army troops (under the direction of Fleeson, now back in action) squelched a mob of sailors protesting high prices and low wages.[43]

In May 1779, more than fifty militiamen took their case to the Pennsylvania Assembly. Radical leaders trying to dissipate tension called a public meeting. The morning of the meeting, residents reminded shopkeepers that they had other forms of recourse, too, when they showed up at stores with clubs, forcing merchants to lower their prices. The mass meeting affirmed that "monopolizing, hoarding, and price-gouging" were "extraordinary abuses" that the public had a right to oppose. Committees were formed to investigate allegations of hoarding and to set price ceilings. Crowds were reported clamoring for bread, and three men accused of raising prices were ushered to the city jail.[44] But the crisis was not over yet. In October 1779, five suspected Tories were arrested. In the afternoon, a crowd gathered at the corner of Third and Walnut, surrounding the home of James Wilson, who had opposed price controls. About twenty of his allies (some of the city's radical leadership) joined him there as well. Shots were fired, and before the violence subsided, five men were dead and close to twenty wounded. In the wake of the "Fort Wilson Riot," the assembly distributed flour and, for what it was worth, reasserted its disapproval of any effort to manipulate prices or to gain from the economic straits in which the city found itself. And the assembly pardoned the rioters.[45] Peace was restored—for now.

With her husband, friends and family deeply engaged in the rebellion, Betsy Ashburn joined as well. She and thousands of women like her contributed to the war effort by producing cannon cartridges, fuses, musket cartridges and other munitions.[46] In Philadelphia, dozens of women (among them fellow flag maker Rebecca Young) supplied the city's arsenal, largely producing musket cartridges, which sped the loading of muskets. Women rolled paper tubes, placed lead musket balls at the bottom and then inserted a measured charge of powder.[47] When the open end was folded into a "tail" and closed, the cartridge was complete.

In November and December 1778, for instance, Catherine Friend produced 1,000 musket cartridges every few days for the war effort—more than 35,000 in those two months alone and more than 100,000 in 1779. Sarah Cribs began working for the arsenal in these years as well, producing some 33,000 cartridges in 1778 and another 86,000 in 1779; toward the end of the war she was still extraordinarily active, earning £67 10s. for making 9,000 musket cartridges (at 20 dollars per thousand) in January 1781, another £41 5s. for 5,500 in March and, still later, as much as £240 for 16,000 musket cartridges (now at 40 dollars per thousand).[48]

Betsy joined the effort, though on a far smaller scale. On January 11, 1779, for instance, she received five hundred musket balls, which she returned on the nineteenth as cartridges. The next day, she took another five hundred out, returning them as cartridges eight days later. Betsy again contributed to the arsenal's production, producing one thousand cartridges in the span of a week. But she did not throw herself into ordnance making, perhaps because just a few weeks after she learned the work, she discovered she was at last pregnant.

It is hard to imagine the mix of joy and dread this news must have conjured, how worrisome a pregnancy must have been just then. "A ship under sail and a big-bellied woman / are the handsomest things that can be seen common"—so said Franklin's *Poor Richard's Almanack*, and surely the mariner Joseph Ashburn thought exactly that when he gazed upon his pregnant wife.[49] Joy certainly tempered the many worries the family confronted in these trying days. Twenty-six-year-old Betsy was at last expecting her long-awaited first child—with starvation rampant, supplies short and her husband at war. But her happiness was surely colored by her all-too-sure knowledge of the dangers that accompanied pregnancy and early childhood. These were lessons that came quickly for all young women in colonial America. In her own youth, Betsy had welcomed several sisters and brothers into the world only to see them die before they reached the age of five. She was too small to remember when her brother Samuel, born in April 1753, died in 1756 at three; and she was just five years old when three-year-old Martha died in July 1757. Hannah, born in November 1755, would live to the ripe old age of eighty-one, but Rebecca Griscom's next two children—Ann and a second Samuel—both had been born and died in the space of three years. The family doubly mourned in fall 1762 when the twins, Joseph and Abigail, succumbed to an epidemic sweeping the city; they, too, were just three. Six children in all were born and died before Betsy turned eleven. As she anticipated the birth of her own first child, she could not help but recall the difficulties her own mother had weathered.

At last Betsy's first child, a daughter, was born September 15, 1779. She and Joseph named her Aucilla, or "Zillah."[50] This odd choice of a name should provide some clue into Joseph and Betsy's marriage, but it raises more questions than it answers. For historians of eighteenth-century America, the proliferation of names like Betsy's own—Elizabeth—makes genealogy especially challenging; indeed there were at least three women named Elizabeth Claypoole in Betsy's Philadelphia, one of them African American. Surprisingly, then, the name Aucilla is unique. It is most often associated with a river that arises in southern Georgia (and so derives from the language and culture of the Timucuans who settled there, but its original meaning is now lost) and empties into the Gulf of Mexico along the Florida panhandle. Did Captain Ashburn find himself in this area and become smitten with the name? Did it cue for him some especially pleasant memory? Alternatively, *Aucilla* can be translated as "little bird" in Latin. Were the new parents drawing on some classical education as they chose this unusual name for their first daughter? Oddly, another Latin dictionary "designed for the use of schools" and published in 1818 defines *Aucilla* quite differently, associating it with the idea of a kitchen or nursery maid.[51] Surely the smiling parents were likelier to see a little bird than a miniature maid as they gazed on their new daughter, but the true source of the unusual choice will probably never be known.

If Betsy's residence before 1780 is not definitively known, by that year archival records do place her and Joseph in the Arch Street quarters they rented from the landlord Jesse Jones.[52] Whenever Betsy and Joseph moved into this home, it was a neighborhood she knew well, still crowded with artisanal and shop-keeping families.[53]

Betsy's parents notwithstanding, the Mulberry Ward in Revolutionary Philadelphia tended to draw the community's least successful members.[54] At just under twelve hundred square feet on average, houses here were the smallest of pre-Revolutionary Philadelphia; of those insured, nearly half were smaller than six hundred square feet.[55] Betsy and Joseph's home—a typical Philadelphia town house, almost identical to others along the street, with a large bake house on the back of the kitchen—was likely crowded as well, as the couple carved out space near other renters like themselves, men whose names and occupations must have sounded to little Aucilla like lines from a nursery rhyme, the barber Frederick Bayer and the baker Frederick Wing.

Betsy had grown up in the larger and more comfortable house her father built just a few doors away, and not all that many years before. She returned to her old neighborhood as Mrs. Joseph Ashburn, a world-wise and war-weary wife and mother, but she knew many of her neighbors from the more carefree days of her childhood. Hannah Lithgow had kept a shop in the front room of her home just next door for years, at least since the early 1760s; surely this was a shop that all of the Griscom children had known well.[56] There were some new faces in the old neighborhood, but many familiar ones, too, and in most ways it was much the same. Like every block in the city, it teemed with activity, goods and groceries rolling in and out of shops. Past the Lithgow shop was the merchant Sampson Hervey, and next to him William Sellers, publisher of the *Pennsylvania Gazette*. The influential Philadelphia attorney Robert Strettle Jones lived in the next house. Walking the street the other direction, toward the river, Betsy passed John Germon's jewelry shop, Andrew Burkhardt's shoe shop and a house shared by a number of craftsmen, including the whip makers and carpenters John and Richard Thornhull and the cordwainer Peter Walter. The scent of mustard seed—collected as a form of payment by the neighborhood shopkeeper Leonard Dorsey—filled the air. Her parents were still in the home where Betsy grew up, and perhaps sisters Rebecca and Rachel, too. When Betsy's sister Mary and her husband, Thomas Morgan, returned home from Baltimore, it was also to Arch Street, where Thomas reopened his watchmaking shop somewhere between Moravian Alley (Bread Street) and Third—practically next door to Betsy, if not in her own house.[57] It was surely a comfort to feel her sisters nearby.

And she would need them. Whatever fears Betsy harbored about the potential fragility of her child's life were borne out when little Zillah died just days before she reached her first birthday. Their little bird was gone. On September 5, 1780, Joseph steeled his resolve and walked up Arch Street to the red frame carpenter's shop of David Evans, where he ordered a child's coffin made of walnut. The small coffin, just inches shy of three feet long, was a simple affair; Joseph chose walnut rather than mahogany, declined the silver handles that would have doubled the expense, and declined too the name plate that adorned some other coffins of the day.[58] Betsy was already well along in another pregnancy when they buried their baby—cause again for both joy and apprehension. Her fears were exacerbated by Joseph's plans to head again to sea, though at least she had the company of two of her sisters in similar circumstances: Susan's husband, Ephraim Doane, was now master of the ship *Flora,* with sixteen guns and a crew of seventy-five (a vessel he owned together with William Pollard and Alexander Tod), while Sarah's husband, William Donaldson, had signed on as mate on the *Pilgrim,* a small ship of four guns crewed by fifteen men.[59] It is easy to imagine long evenings in front of Susannah's comfortable fireplace, the Griscom girls rallied round one another.

As Betsy mourned the loss of Zillah, one of the most celebrated events in this history of women and the Revolution in Philadelphia unfolded around her. On June 19, 1780, Philadelphians awoke to a new broadside, *The Sentiments of an American Woman.* Citing the long history of women's contributions to historic events up to and through the consumer boycotts just prior to the outbreak of war, Esther De Berdt Reed launched a massive campaign to raise funds for the beleagured American army. Within days, three dozen women had formed teams to canvas the city, going ward by ward and door to door, looking for anything women could contribute to the war effort. In Betsy's neighborhood, Race to Arch, some 225 women together contributed more than $13,000.[60]

Betsy's name is not present on these lists. But her mother's is. Rebecca Griscom gave the cause eight shillings six pence. The homes of Quakers were not omitted from the canvass, as organizers believed that it was easy to reconcile this "beneficent scheme" with a "beneficent religion."[61] Should we be surprised that Rebecca responded to the request, despite her faith's prescription against supporting the war? We have very little insight into what Rebecca Griscom thought of the rebellion, or in truth, what she thought of anything at all; this single line among the many columns of Reed's donors is our only tantalizing glimpse into her views. Her donation is modest when tallied alongside the amounts given by others. Perhaps Rebecca had little to offer, given the effect of the war on her husband's trade. Or perhaps she wished to give only a token amount, in the hope that it might have some benefit, however indirect, to her various sons-in-law. Or perhaps she wished to give as little as possible simply to get the women to leave; at least one Philadelphia woman—the daughter of loyalists—complained that the collectors were "so extremely importunate that people were obliged to give them something to get rid of them."[62] Any one of these motives might explain Mrs. Griscom's choice; what we know for sure is that Reed, with the help of Rebecca Griscom and some sixteen hundred women like her, raised enough money to provide more than two thousand shirts for the Continental forces.[63]

As thrilling as it would be to find Elizabeth Ashburn's name among these patriotic women, it is easy to guess why she may not have contributed. With Joseph sometimes at sea, Betsy's financial fortunes became precarious. What sources of income she found during these terrible times is unknown. It is again possible that Betsy worked as an employee of a shop, rather than a proprietor herself, or she may have been doing a little of both. Especially now, with a baby on the way, it seems likely that she would have tried to pick up some work from fellow upholsterers, rather than sustain her own enterprise.[64] Betsy's household seems to have been fairly comfortable in March 1780 when Ashburn was taxed at the rate of £70, but just a year later, in 1781, the tax bill dropped to £3 11s. 1d., with Betsy listed as taxpayer.[65] Perhaps Betsy—pregnant during some of these months—was largely unable to work. Or perhaps the outcome of Ashburn's voyage and his capture on board the *Lion* was by this time known in Philadelphia.

# 14

# Privateer to Prisoner

By December 1780, Betsy was six months pregnant. But this was not enough to keep Joseph on land. Confident that his wife could cope with another departure, he signed on as mate on the *Patty*. If all went well, he would be home long before the baby arrived. The *Patty*'s owners, Robert McClenachan and Patrick Moore, fitted out the six-gun brigantine with a crew of nineteen, under the master Frances Knox.[1] And indeed, there's no reason to doubt that Joseph was home for the birth of their second daughter, Eliza, in February 1781. Once again, Betsy took a deep breath and embraced the joys and the fears of motherhood. But it was Joseph's fortunes that would prove precarious in the months to come.

Ashburn's next berth was as master of the eighteen-gun ship *Lion*.[2] In late summer 1781, loaded with goods in Haiti, the *Lion*, under the command of Captain John Green, set sail for Nantes. They had nearly made it when, at the end of June 1781, after a fourteen-hour chase, the ship was taken off the coast of France by the forty-gun frigate *La Prudente*.[3] For a month, Ashburn and his crewmates languished in the hold of an enemy ship with precious little air or food. In time, he could compare notes with fellow prisoner William Russell, who spent weeks trapped in a three-foot-high hold some thirty feet below the water. A man could only crouch or lie down. The water was so thick with "animacules" that it was best drunk through closed teeth.[4] This was not the adventure at sea that Ashburn had hoped for.

By the end of August, a company of the *Lion*'s sailors found themselves off the coast of Plymouth, England (the same Plymouth from which the Pilgrims aboard the *Mayflower* had sailed 160 years earlier). Plymouth was the site of Mill (or Old Mill) Prison, which, together with Forton Prison, in Portsmouth, was the wartime home of hundreds of American men. That year—1781—saw the largest number of crews imprisoned at Mill Prison.[5] Ashburn was one of several Philadelphians, along with Captain John Green, who landed at the prison that day; others included William Miles, John Stewart and a man (likely African American) with the felicitous name Virtue Sweet.[6] Upon arrival in Plymouth, Ashburn and his companions submitted to a hearing in the rooms of the Fountain Inn, where British officers examined the prisoners. Where were you born? Do you have a commission from the treasonous Continental Congress? When did you sail, and when were you captured? The prisoners were then taken away and brought back individually, and subjected to the same questions. Once satisfied, the assembled judges read each man's answers back, asking him to affirm their veracity. After a third examination, the prisoners were brought together again before the panel to hear their sentence read: they would be consigned to Mill Prison for "Piracy, Treason and Rebellion against his Majesty on the High Sea."[7] Ashburn braced himself for a long term in prison, and, should the Americans lose the war, the prospect of execution.

The county of Devon in southwestern England was otherwise a pleasant, picturesque place.[8] The rugged coastline—some 150 miles of it, in a county bounded by the Bristol Channel on the north, the river Tamar (the boundary with Cornwall, on the west) and the English Channel on the south and southeast—was broken by sandy beaches and small fishing villages, while above that lay a landscape of scenic moors and forests. The prison itself was set on a windswept tidal headland. Several windmills once drove a mill at the head of the bay as early as Norman times, but these were long gone by the time Ashburn and his shipmates stumbled toward the prison. The prison outside Plymouth existed at least from the late seventeenth century, when the now out-of-date windmills were replaced with an internment facility for men taken during the War of the League of Augsburg, and harnessed again during the War of the Austrian Succession, when permanent prison facilities were built. The Mill Prison confined swelling numbers of captives taken during the Seven Years' War—almost seven thousand men by 1762—making it the largest collection of prisoners in England at the time. Mill Prison was reopened to welcome its new residents in May 1777.

Hundreds of Pennsylvania men entered the Old Mill's iron gates. As a purpose-built facility (unlike Forton Prison, for instance, which was converted from a hospital), the Mill was secure. The approaching men first saw the double stone walls that surrounded it—twenty feet apart, fourteen feet at the lowest point and twenty at the highest—all frieze-topped with broken glass. The captives passed through an eight-foot iron gate before crossing the outer courtyard, the prison offices and kitchen. Next they were led through the interior wooden gate—and past the guards with fixed bayonets who flanked it—into the inner courtyard, where they found themselves in a large yard, some 250 feet long and 158 feet wide. At night, the yard was lit dimly by a tall lamppost in the center; when necessary, the lamp also served as a whipping post. Lanterns encircled the prison yard, deterrents to nighttime escapes. Uncooperative prisoners were sent to the "Black hole." A pump near the gate afforded water. Home, for the foreseeable future, was a long, two-story, windowless hall on the courtyard's north side.

The men at Old Mill were from all over the world. France, Spain and the Netherlands were all represented among the ranks. But while the Europeans confined there were considered prisoners of war, Americans were being held on charges of either treason or piracy—an important distinction. Britain, of course, did not recognize American sovereignty, and so privateers could not, technically, be prisoners of war. Instead, they were considered rebels, and so civil prisoners. This made their status, as well as the rules governing their treatment, complicated. Civil prisoners in England necessarily had rights of their own, including, for instance, the right to be released on bail while awaiting trial—an intolerable policy when the prisoners in question have specifically rejected their national allegiance and are actively trying to throw off the bonds of government.[9] In March 1777, Parliament passed legislation that created a sort of legal purgatory, redefining captured Americans as traitors who could be held without bail, and continued to deny their status as prisoners of war. This denial would materially affect the conditions of their imprisonment. American men, for instance, received two-thirds the rations of their French counterparts. Both were divided into messes of six men, but the Americans were then given only rations for four.

The prison and its occupants became something of a local attraction. On Sundays, for a fee, Englishmen and -women could view the "American monsters."[10] Inmates took advantage of their celebrity, making tokens and souvenirs to sell for cash to buy food from the vendors who also came to the prison gate. Enterprising prisoners converted scrap wood into boxes, spoons, chairs and even model ships which they could sell to the curious visitors, and then converted those pennies and shillings into desperately wanted food to supplement their meager diets when market day came around. The work softened the hardness of prison life and relieved its crushing boredom as well.

Early on, an inmate described their daily allowance at the prison: "a pound of bread, a quarter of a pound of beef, a pound of greens, a quart of beer and a little pot-liquor that the beef and greens are boiled in, without any thickening,—per day."[11] As time went on, however, conditions at the prison deteriorated. It didn't take long for starvation to become rampant. As one man observed,

> It is enough to break the heart of a stone to see so many strong, hearty men, almost starved to death through want of provisions. A great part of those in prison, eat at one meal what they draw for twenty long hours, and then go without until the next day. Many are strongly tempted to pick up the grass in the yard, and eat it, and some pick up old bones in the yard, that have been laying in the dirt a week or ten days, and pound them to pieces and suck them. Some will pick up snails out of the holes in the wall, and from among the grass and weeds in the yard, boil them and eat them, and drink the broth. Often the cooks, after they have picked over our cabbage, will cut off some of the but-ends of the stalks and throw them over the gate into the yard, and I have often seen, after a rain, when the mud would be over shoes, as these stumps were thrown over the gate, the men running from all parts of the yard, regardless of the mud, to catch at them, and nearly trample one another under feet to get a piece. These same cabbage stumps, hogs in America would scarcely eat if they had them; and as to our broth, I know very well hogs in America would scarcely put their noses into it. Our meat is very poor in general; we scarcely see a good piece once in a month. Many are driven to such necessity by want of provisions, that they have sold most of the clothes off their backs for the sake of getting a little money to buy them some bread.[12]

Searching for ways to alleviate their suffering, inmates built a charity-box and mounted it at the prison's gate. A sign—HEALTH, PLENTY, AND COMPETENCE TO THE DONORS—invited contributions from the visitors who came to gawk at the men inside.[13] In June 1781, American prisoners submitted a petition "setting forth that they were treated with less humanity than the French and Spanish, though by reason that they had no Agent established in this country for their protection, they were entitled to expect a larger share of indulgence than others." They had "not a sufficient allowance of bread," they added, "and were very scantily furnished with clothing."[14] After considerable discussion in both houses of Parliament, an inquiry revealed that the American prisoners were indeed "allowed a half pound of bread less per day than the French and Spanish prisoners." But the petitions of the Americans failed to effect any change, and the "conduct of the Administration was equally unpolitic and illiberal"; the additional allowance that the prisoners sought "could be no object, either to Government or to the Nation, and it was certainly unwise, by treating American prisoners worse than those of France or Spain, to increase the fatal animosity which had unhappily taken place between the mother country and the Colonies, and this, too, at a period when the subjugation of the latter had become hopeless."[15] William Russell captured the sentiments of many prisoners of war in his entry for New Year's Eve, 1781: "I am 29 months from my Dear Wife & Family, & 27 months in Captivity. May the Great and Allwise God, in the midst of His Judgements remember mercy and like Israel (of Old) enjoy the Promised Land (America) w[h]ere we may sit down with our Wives and Families, each under their own vine and Fig tree, and the Sons of Violence not make them afraid."[16] A fair amount of sympathy would arise even in English households for the men held at Old Mill. Englishmen and -women donated close to thirty thousand dollars for the relief of American prisoners confined in English jails.[17]

Given the miserable conditions, it is unsurprising that some men tried to escape, and some men made it. Prisoners tunneled out and went over the wall; they bribed guards and donned costumes to get past the gates. Over the course of the war, more than a hundred escapes, attempted escapes or foiled plots drew the attention of the prison guards.[18] Few of the escapees made it home, and then far and away more officers than seamen succeeded, largely because getting out of the prison was only the first step—one still had to get out of Britain. The generous reward offered the farmers of Devon for help capturing escapees didn't help; it wasn't so much escaping the prison that kept men trapped, but the impossibility of crossing the local countryside. As one of Ashburn's fellow prisoners wrote, "The people are allowed £5 per head and they would sell their fathers for 1/2 the money."[19]

In dire circumstances, men tried to find occasions for levity. On July 4, 1781—the fifth anniversary of the American Declaration—Mr. and Mrs. Ashburn found themselves three thousand miles apart. The men of Mill Prison decorated their hats with stars and stripes, and mottoes of liberty and independence; they gave thirteen cheers, which their French counterparts answered over the yard's wall.[20] In November, Ashburn stood with his companions in the yard of the Mill and celebrated the news of Cornwallis's defeat at Yorktown. Even the cold rain could not dampen their spirits. The men made an ad hoc American flag; it's tempting to picture Ashburn directing its fabrication, imagining his wife's hands at work.[21]

Betsy had continued to sort out her own situation as the war for independence wound to a close. Early one morning in October 1781, an express rider galloped into the city with news of Cornwallis's surrender at Yorktown. Another citywide illumination was planned, and once more, the Quaker houses that remained unlit were attacked by vandals. A fireworks display was launched from the statehouse yard. In early November, of particular interest to Betsy Ashburn, twenty-four flags seized from Cornwallis were ceremonially brought to the city and delivered to Congress.[22]

These were months of transition in more ways than one. Not only did Betsy endure the absence of yet another husband; she bid farewell too to her childhood when that fall, her parents sold the Arch Street house where she grew up.[23] To be sure, the move was at least in part prompted by the emptying of that large nest; only three children (thirty-four-year-old Rebecca, twenty-year-old George, and nineteen-year-old Rachel) remained unmarried, and George was by this time out of the house (having moved to the Baltimore home of sister Mary Morgan to work in the watch and clock shop of her husband, Thomas, he may have returned with them to Philadelphia as well).[24] But less happy circumstances might also have made it necessary to sell the house. One descendant claimed that a fire destroyed Samuel Griscom's lumberyard, prompting the move.[25] But as we have seen, the business weathered other challenges, too, particularly during the occupation.[26] The years of political upheaval and warfare were certainly hard on the aging carpenter.[27] He still found work from time to time—the repair of buildings damaged during the occupation brought in some income in the summer of 1789, and he would be among the men hired to raise a new meetinghouse—but Griscom was slowing down.[28] He had all but stopped attending meetings of the Carpenters' Company, his dues in arrears mounting month after month, year after year.[29] He sold the house for £1,550 in gold and silver to Matthew Clarkson, an attorney on the rise whose seven children could now run in the halls and on the stairs once filled with Griscoms.[30] Samuel, quite unlike his daughter, had no reason to embrace the Revolution; one can only guess at the resentment he felt in its aftermath. Now, the house he had built for his budding family twenty years earlier would belong to another, its eleven rooms and nine fireplaces to be enjoyed by someone else's children. Samuel's carpenter's shop would shelter someone else's craftsmanship.

In Philadelphia, papers were increasingly filled with news of interest to the city's privateers and their anxious families. Notices from the admiralty court concerning auctions of captured ships and the contents of their holds filled the advertising columns. But with news from the prisons so intermittent, available only when someone managed to get a letter aboard a ship bound for Pennsylvania or an exchanged prisoner made his way home, Betsy simply had to watch and wait for news of her husband. How long would it be before she, like others separated from loved ones at sea, started watching to see if a gull flew over the house—a sure sign that someone was returning home from sea? Every time a knife or a fork or a pair of scissors fell and its point stuck in the floor—another clue that Joseph might be on his way—a gleam perhaps brightened her face.[31] Finally in April 1782, a man returned from Europe with a list of all the men imprisoned in the Old Mill. On the twenty-third, the *Pennsylvania Packet* began publishing the names, starting with the men who had been there the longest. Its length obligated the paper to publish this list in installments, but when Betsy picked up the paper on the twenty-fifth, there was no list. Nothing on the twenty-seventh, either. On the thirtieth the list resumed, but still contained the names of men taken in 1777, when she was yet a newlywed. Inexplicably—how many nerves were frayed as families opened paper after paper with no further information?—the press was silent on the subject until May 23, three weeks later, when the names began to appear again with regularity, but given the slow pace of publication, it wasn't until the twenty-eighth that the *Packet* printed the names of men aboard ships taken in the winter of 1780–81. Finally, on June 18, the dreaded news came: there, at the bottom of the page Betsy's eyes landed on these words: "Ship LION, taken June 29, Part of the Crew Committeed August 31, 1781." After the name of the captain, and the crewmen William Miles, Virtue Sweet and John Stewart, she saw "———Ashborn." Betsy of course knew instantly how to fill in the blank.

What she couldn't know was that the news was still worse: by the time this list appeared in the *Packet*'s columns, her husband was dead. Joseph Ashburn died March 3, 1782.[32] What killed him we do not know: smallpox, tuberculosis, dysentery, influenza—any of those maladies, which coursed through the prisons, could have done it. Whatever it was, Ashburn had plenty of company: some fifty-two American prisoners died in the Old Mill between 1777 and 1782, Joseph among the last.[33] On March 25, 1782, six months after Britain's surrender at Yorktown, and two weeks after Ashburn's death, Parliament finally passed a law converting the American captives from rebellious traitors to prisoners of war. In the following months, King George accepted the United States' independence as well.

Decades later, Susan McCord Turner (the granddaughter of Betsy's sister Sarah and William Donaldson) would assert that William Donaldson was captured alongside Ashburn and imprisoned with him at England's Old Mill. She also had a story to tell about Ashburn's death. "Our patriots," she said, "overjoyed at the news, gave vent to their feelings in repeated cheers; the jailors thought their prisoners had gone mad. All participated but Captain Ashburn, who sat quietly in his chair. When addressed, he made no reply. An examination revealed the fact that he was dead. Joy had killed him." Susan went on to add that the "sad duty" of conveying the news to Betsy "devolved on Captain Donaldson, who asked John Claypoole to inform Betsy of the second bereavement."[34] Susan's story seems among the least reliable contained in the affidavits. Most obviously, news of Cornwallis's October surrender reached the prison by November 27, 1781, when the men raised the "13 stripes" (no mention of stars) in the prison yard and gave thirteen cheers, months before Ashburn died. William Donaldson does not seem to have been a prisoner there; at least no one by that name appears on the list of prisoners published in installments in the Philadelphia paper, nor in subsequent compilations of Old Mill captives.[35] It also seems hard to reconcile this family story with others that depict John Claypoole as the bearer of the unhappy news; certainly it would have been strange for Donaldson to hand off to a third party the serious duty of informing his sister-in-law of her second widowhood.[36]

However the news came, thanks to the rare survival of an extraordinary document, we know that fellow Philadelphian John Claypoole was beside Joseph during his final illness, ten days of decline that Ashburn "bore with amazing fortitude retaining his senses till the last moment of his life."[37] Claypoole's memorandum book confirms that the man who would become Betsy's third husband knew of the death of her second months before she could. John Claypoole had better fortune and lived to return to the city and inform Ashburn's wife that she was once more a widow. Elizabeth had now lost two husbands to the Revolution in the space of six years.

Men in the English prisons well knew the suffering of the women left behind. In one well-known tune from Forton, the men sang

For there's many poor Woman that's left to distress
And many poor Child that's left fatherless
Who are overwhelmed with sorrow and grief
Pray God be their comfort and send them relief.[38]

For the widow Ashburn, relief was on the way.

# PART IV

# PEACE AND PROSPERITY

# 15

# Third Time's a Charm

Elizabeth Ashburn and John Claypoole surely had much to talk about in the weeks following Claypoole's return to the city, as the veteran apprised the widow of the events of her husband's final days. Remembered later to be a "keen observer of events," Claypoole also had a way with words; he could toss off a rhyme with ease and composed poems and songs to amuse himself.[1] He was a good companion for anyone, but particularly a young, world-weary mother who had lost two husbands already to a Revolution that had consumed much of her adult life. As the sole supporter of herself and young daughter in wartime Philadelphia, she must also have welcomed the relief this man could bring to her fragile finances. As the weeks went on, Betsy and John found themselves drawn to each other.

On May 8, 1783, Betsy gambled on marriage a third time, having just entered her thirties, with daughter Eliza turning two. It was a whirlwind romance; Betsy was widowed now for just fourteen months, and John had only been back in the city a fraction of that time. If Betsy's marriage to Ashburn came fast (she spent only seventeen or eighteen months alone, when many widows who chose to remarry waited more than six years), her marriage to Claypoole came faster.[2] Very few hints survive to tell us anything about Betsy's personality, but in things marital, at least, she seems decisive: she wed John Ross against her parents' wishes and didn't dilly-dally when well-meaning Friends initiated the customary procedure to restore unity with the Society. She married Ashburn after just a year and a half alone. Now she committed herself to Claypoole with equal confidence. Betsy seems not to have been given to equivocation. In the Myers-Briggs typology, it's a safe bet that she would have scored a solid J for "Judgment"—there would be no dawdling where John Claypoole was concerned.[3] Though today she is unremembered as Elizabeth Claypoole, it was this marriage that finally gave Betsy the enduring partnership she had so long been seeking, as well as the children and grandchildren who would carry on her business, secure her memory and establish her legend.

Born, like Betsy, in 1752, John was in his early twenties when war broke out. He also—like his wife—responded to the imperial crisis as a fourth-generation colonist deeply steeped in artisanal tradition. Like the Griscoms, the Claypoole family came from a Quaker tradition, though one inflected—again like the Griscoms—with traces of Anglicanism. The first Claypoole to emigrate, James Claypoole, was the son of wealthy Puritans who occupied Northborough Manor near Peterborough in Northamptonshire. A successful London merchant and himself a member of the Church of England, James converted to the Quaker faith sometime after the fall of Oliver Cromwell (Cromwell's daughter Elizabeth had married James's brother John).[4] A close friend of George Fox, William Penn and other leading Quakers, James was also persecuted for his beliefs and chose to leave England in 1683. He became treasurer of the Free Society of Traders and would purchase some five thousand acres of Pennsylvania land, receiving as well a large lot in the planned city, on Walnut Street stretching from Front to Second Street, where he lived in a double two-story brick house—built as likely as not by great-grandfather Andrew Griscom—that boasted four lead-framed windows in front, and the same in the rear, as well as a beautiful southern exposure, down a descending green into the pleasant Dock Creek.[5]

Given the small number of leading families in those early years of settlement, it's not surprising that Griscoms and Claypooles were intertwined from the outset. In fact, when Betsy's great-grandmother Sarah Griscom settled the accounts of her husband Andrew's estate in 1694, James's son George was among the witnesses.[6] James Claypoole, again like Andrew Griscom, had been attracted to the reforms posited by George Keith; when Keith, as a missionary of the Society for the Propagation of the Gospel, returned to the Mid-Atlantic, records of one April 1702 service indicate that "three children of James Claypool (formerly a Quaker)" had been baptized.[7] The family still remained in and around the fringes of the Quaker community, however.

Raised in the Society of Friends, John's father, William Claypoole—like Samuel Griscom—married out of unity when he wed Elizabeth Hall.[8] He chose not to reconcile with the Quaker community. Like Betsy, John Claypoole was close to Quaker tradition but no longer a member of the formal Society. The Claypooles drifted farther from the Society of Friends than the Griscoms would, but both families clearly harbored some ambivalence about the two faiths.

The Claypoole family also shared the Griscoms' interest in artisanal trades. James's son Joseph was a six-year-old boy when he arrived in Penn's fledgling city, and, as the youngest of five sons, unlikely to inherit much of the family's estate. Noting that Philadelphia was in need of both cabinetmakers and joiners, he pursued the latter trade and became one of the first joiners to be trained in the city.[9] He in turn trained two of his sons, George and Josiah, in woodworking trades. George Claypoole would reach the pinnacle of status among his counterparts; to take just one measure, in 1783 he was assessed two hundred dollars in occupational tax, a figure exceeded by only one fellow craftsman—the celebrated cabinetmaker Thomas Affleck—and matched only by Benjamin Randolph and William Cox. His son, George Jr., would carry on his trade through the rest of the eighteenth century. Work from Claypoole cabinetmakers is today highly sought after by collectors of American furniture: at a January 2006 auction at Sotheby's of New York, a mahogany dressing table attributed to the Claypoole shop sold for close to $100,000, while a high chest also "possibly" carved by Jonathan Claypoole sold for more than a quarter of a million dollars.[10]

John's father, Betsy's father-in-law, was James's grandson William—a cousin of the well-known cabinetmakers. William pursued a humbler trade, having become a tanner, and possibly a currier as well, converting animal hides to the leather necessary for apparel, furniture and other uses in the eighteenth-century city. William's brother James also pursued the tanner's trade, in Kent County, Maryland (his son, James Jr., would carry on his father's work), and there's reason to suspect that young John trained with both his father and uncle at one time or another.[11] Born while his parents were living in Mount Holly, New Jersey, John spent his youth learning the ins and outs of a business that the teenage boy assumed would be his future.

When the Revolution erupted, it is easy to imagine why John—having so far known mostly the fetid air of his family's tanyards—would have been eager to swap his scudding knife for a bayonet. When it came time to choose sides, the Claypoole family leaned toward the rebellion. John and his cousins Abraham and David each enlisted in local militia groups. David later formed a partnership with the printer John Dunlap, who had bravely taken on the job of printing the first broadside sheets carrying the Declaration of Independence in the summer of 1776. In 1778, the printing firm Dunlap and Claypoole became the official printer of the Continental Congress. From their shop, Philadelphians would purchase copies of the United States Constitution and, years later, Washington's farewell address.

John Claypoole was in the thick of the fighting from the outset. In June 1777, he swore his allegiance to the state of Pennsylvania and never looked back.[12] He served in a Pennsylvania regiment commanded by Colonel Jehu Eyre. On September 13, 1777, he was commissioned a second lieutenant.[13] Family memory places him at the Battle of Germantown in early October and believes that he was wounded there by the flying fragments of a gun carriage.[14] Family memory also follows him, later that month, to Red Bank, on the Delaware shore, alongside the four hundred American soldiers who repulsed some two thousand Hessians attacking Fort Mercer. After the battle, descendants recalled, it was Claypoole who was asked to ride thirteen miles north to General Washington's camp at Whitemarsh with the news. As John crossed the contested terrain, he encountered "numbers of wounded and dying Hessians, whose appeals for care and safety awakened his pity and commiseration."[15] It was during these battles that Claypoole asked the wounded German why he had come to America to fight men with whom he had no quarrel.[16]

Family memory also puts Claypoole among the men who spent that desperate 1777–78 winter at Valley Forge, though contemporary sources cannot confirm the assertion.[17] When John's term of service expired, he did not reenlist, perhaps because his injuries prohibited further service. He tried returning to his family's tanyard but found little motivation to continue in a trade he had never much cared for. It couldn't have helped that the career promised little advancement. In 1779, the city's tanners and shoemakers published a notice in which they observed that for years, "the prices of skins, leather, and shoes were so proportioned to each other as to leave the tradesmen a bare living profit; this is evidently proved by this circumstance well known to everybody, that [no one], however industrious and attentive to his business, however frugal in his manner of living, has been able to raise a fortune rapidly . . . Our professions rendered us useful and necessary members of our community; proud of that rank, we aspired no higher."[18] Perhaps Claypoole did harbor higher aspirations.

John spent some time casting about, trying to find the right path, and soon found himself in Chestertown, Maryland, a small town on the bank of the Chester River about twenty-five miles from where it enters the Chesapeake Bay, about fifty-five miles by water east of Baltimore. It's not surprising that Claypoole traveled to Maryland's eastern shore, where he had family and friends, and likely found work in his uncle James Claypoole's tanyard. He naturally joined them, too, in the local Masonic Lodge. In December 1779, John Claypoole made a decision that John Ross had made years earlier. James Claypoole, the secretary of Kent County's Lodge No. 7, issued a certificate certifying that his nephew "was regularly entered, passed and raised."[19] A certificate dated March 30, 1780, and signed by Grand Secretary William Smith affirms—in German, French and English—that John was a member in good standing.[20]

But John, it seems, was not ready to settle down. Later that year, anxious to see more action, he signed aboard the frigate *Luzerne*, a privateering ship bound for Port L'Orient on the west coast of France. In November, he accepted a position as the ship's steward, meaning that he would keep watch over the stores and manage the ship's meals. A congressional order required that ships granted letters of marque and reprisal crew their ships at least a third with "landsmen"; its aim was to ensure that privateers—with their promise of perhaps great financial reward—did not draw off experienced manpower needed by state and continental navies. Claypoole, having military experience but only a casual knowledge of seafaring, must have seemed ideal to the ship's captain.

Claypoole would more than get the adventure he craved, though it might not have seemed so at the outset.[21] At first, the trip was slow and tedious. Contrary winds had kept them in the Delaware for more than a week, and then, after a quick start, they stalled again at sea. When a crewman died from the "very great hardships to which he was daily exposed," the crew stitched him into a spare hammock, tied some shot to his heels and heaved him overboard—a makeshift burial at sea. Finally, in January 1781, they made Port L'Orient and unloaded their cargo: some 275 hogshead of tobacco. A "severe fit of sickness," Claypoole later remembered, "well nigh carried me off the sod"; he left his position on the ship and spent twelve weeks recovering in the home of a "Madame Lazaneck," whose three daughters doted on the weakened mariner and helped him practice his French, surely a not-altogether-unpleasant convalescence.

Finally, the *Luzerne* again set sail, a "glorious breeze" carrying them along. The crew was in high spirits, pleased at the prospect of smooth sailing and a profitable venture, when "fickle jade" threw a privateer in their path; they were captured off the coast of Ireland by the *Enterprise,* a thirty-two-gun ship under the command of Thomas Eden. Led about ten miles up the river Shannon, the ship came to anchor. The British of course tried to entice Claypoole and his shipmates to service in the British cause, but after they refused, the crew was put "under guard and in irons" (Claypoole was among four exceptions allowed to walk unshackled) and marched some seventy-two miles across Ireland.

All things considered, Claypoole found his plight "tolerable"—certainly better than the poor men and women whom he encountered on the march, where "upon the same floor and frequently without any partition," he noted in the pages of the small journal he carried with him, "are lodged the Husband & wife and the multitudinous brood of children all huddled together upon straw or rushed with the cow and the calf the pig & the horse if they are rich enough to have one." Houses of sod or mud boasted only low walls and low ceilings. "Matrimony," he noted, was their "only Solace," most girls becoming mothers by the age of sixteen, and raising "shoals of children." Claypoole was struck too by the remnants of great wealth he noticed, passing "thousands of ruined houses castles and villages . . . occasioned . . . by the war of Ireland in Oliver Cromwells Days"—surely acutely aware of his ancestors' several links to Cromwell's government.

After almost six months imprisoned aboard the *Lenox* in the Cove of Cork, in summer 1781 he and nine others were charged with high treason and consigned to Old Mill Prison. The privateers consigned there were never a high priority for the independence movement, and so prisoner exchanges intended to redeem them were few and far between, a fact Claypoole well knew: "For aught I know," he mused, "I shall be here 2 years, for I do not see any likely hood of our being exchanged, and it seems impossible to get out of this place with out the wretched alternative of entering into their Infernal service which however I find many are reduced to the Necessity of doing rather than spend all their youthfull days in this hatefull confinement." When Joseph Ashburn arrived at the Old Mill, he found John Claypoole already confined there. Ashburn and Claypoole endured several weeks of imprisonment together and had plenty of time to reminisce about the city from which they'd sailed and the loved ones they had left behind.[22]

A song Claypoole went to the trouble to preserve in the pages of his small journal offers some small insight into his world, his mind and his demeanor as a young man. "A New Song on the Princes[s] Royals Losing Her Shoe o the Birth Night Ball" was sung to the tune of "Doodle Doodle Doo." "'Twas at the birth night Ball, Sir / god Bless our gracious Queen / where people great and small, Sir / were on a footing scene," the song began. "As down the dance with heels from France a Royal couple flew / Tho well she trip'd, the lady Slip'd, and off she cast her shoe." In the chorus Claypoole sang "Doodle Doodle Doo, the Princes[s] lost her shoe / her highness [Hop'd] the difflers stop'd / Not knowing what do." In the rest of the lighthearted song, after a flurry of concern the princess's shoe was restored. But at its close, the song took a more political turn: "Perhaps is true old England too / might dance from night til noon / if ships of state among the great / were mended half so soon . . . Doodle Doodle doo / Egad tis very true / late or soon they're out of tune / and know not what to do."

If the princess's shoe mocks the frantic confusion of international relations, another song inscribed into the pages of Claypoole's journal speaks more directly to the rebel's cause and hints at other emotions. In an "American Anthem"—better known today as "Chester," among the most famous songs of the Revolution—Claypoole and his fellow prisoners raised their voices in protest: "Let Tyrants shake their Iron Rod / and Slavery clank her galling chains / we fear them not we trust in God / New Englands God forever reigns. How[e] and Burgoyne & Clinton too / with Prescot and Cornwallis join'd / together Plot our overthrow / in one infernal League combin'd. When God inspir'd us for the fight / their ranks were broke their lines were Fors'd / their ships were scatter'd in our sight / or swiftly driven from our Coast." The song ends with a reminder that Britain is old and decaying, a relic of the past, while America is full of the vigor and strength of a nation on the rise: "The foe comes on with haughty stride / our troops advance with martial Noise / their veterans fly before our youth / and Generals yield to beardless Boys."[23] Claypoole was no beardless boy, but he felt keenly the passion of his generation harnessed in this quest for liberty.

Those energies were necessarily stilled while John cooled his heels in an English prison, and no less a figure than the venerable Benjamin Franklin himself, then in France to represent the wartime interests of the United States, would be asked to intervene on Claypoole's behalf. The Philadelphia merchant Michael Hillegas had passed along to Franklin the plea of John's mother: "Altho' I am sencible of your time being so very much taken up in public business, yet knowing the goodness of your Heart I am prevailed on by a poor Widow of this City [John's father, William Claypoole, had died in 1779] to request the favour of your endeavours some way or other to obtain the Releasement or Exchange of her Son John Claypoole, who was taken Prisoner on Board the Ship called the *Luzerne* commanded by Captain Bell Bound from L'Orient for this place. [He] was carried into Ireland and from thence to England and committed to Mill Prison near Plymouth. I understand he is a clever fellow, and was the only support of his Mother—his liberation would therefore be an Act of Charity."[24]

Franklin was well known to be an energetic advocate on behalf of American prisoners in England, so his mother had real hope when she sent this message through Hillegas. But in truth, only rarely did seamen find themselves beneficiaries of prisoner exchanges. As it happens, Americans were in a poor position to bargain; they had few facilities to keep prisoners, and the British knew it. English seamen transferred to France before the formal alliance would find themselves at liberty soon enough. Franklin tried to implement a system of "paroles," an honor system whereby British sailors captured and released at sea would sign a document declaring themselves in essence captives unavailable for military service, but for obvious reasons Britain refused to acknowledge this status (correctly pointing out that American ships were simply trying to remain unencumbered by prisoners so that they could continue to harry shipping). Of course most important was the nature of the conflict itself; as rebels rather than citizens of a recognized nation, for the king's purposes the American prisoners were simply criminals. When various attempts to create exchanges failed, Franklin redirected his energies toward abetting escapes. Since the main barrier to freedom was less walls or guards than the money needed to travel, Franklin was known to have sent funds to men making plans, and to have reimbursed the expenses of others who helped them.

Whether Franklin made any particular inquires on Claypoole's behalf is unknown, but John would endure the conditions at the prison longer than Ashburn. From time to time, as we have seen, men were able to escape—Claypoole had been relieved to hear that his friends Jonathan Kemp, Alex Tindal and five others who had gotten away had arrived safely in France—but mostly the men endured long days of tedium broken by occasional gossip about the possibility of an exchange. Somehow Claypoole learned of the firm Haslam and Cleypoole, cider merchants and fruiterers at 75 Upper Thames Street in London (was Cleypoole a distant relative who might somehow be able to come to John's aid should he decide to make a break for it himself?), information the prisoner noted carefully in the back of his memorandum book. He also put down the London addresses of Benjamin West (by this time a celebrated artist, and also a friend of Benjamin Franklin) and Henry Laurens (appointed the minister to Holland, Laurens had been captured at sea and imprisoned in the Tower of London; he would be exchanged for Cornwallis himself), as well as that of Thomas Eden's shop—did he intend on paying a visit to the man whose ship had captured him?

In the wake of Cornwallis's defeat at Yorktown, a new attitude toward captured Americans necessarily emerged. At last, Claypoole was a prisoner of war rather than a mere rebel. By July, more than a thousand men were let go from the prisons at Old Mill and Forton. In August 1782, Claypoole was finally released from his "dreary mansion"—a hint that he may have barely escaped sharing Ashburn's fate, since a July 13, 1782, report to Franklin suggests that the only prisoners not yet freed at that date were about 120 men, many of whom were sick and in the prison hospital.[25]

But Claypoole survived, and after a welcome stop in Portugal, returned to Philadelphia aboard the *Symmetry*. The seven-week voyage was shared by some 216 Philadelphians "from captivity in Britian," including John Green, Ashburn's captain aboard the *Lion*.[26] If family legend is correct, it was Claypoole himself who informed Elizabeth Ashburn that her husband had not survived imprisonment. Betsy may have already had the news itself, but given Claypoole's high regard for Joseph Ashburn, he certainly sought his widow out to share his condolences and pass on any of Ashburn's last words. Amazingly, we can narrow the window in which this conversation must have occurred to a matter of days. The *Symmetry* arrived in the port of Philadelphia on August 13, and on August 16, Claypoole wrote a friend that he was "about to" join the *Hyder-Ally*, bound for a cruise. The timing seems scarcely believable. Claypoole had left Philadelphia in November 1780; he had spent seven weeks at sea, three months docked in France, and fourteen months in an English prison. And now, he was home all of three days before he was ready to depart once again. Discharging his duty to widow Ashburn was one of the very few matters he would have been able to attend to before setting once more to sea.

Claypoole sailed aboard the *Hyder-Ally*, a vessel named for Haidar Ali, the ruler of Mysore, an Indian kingdom drawn into the international warfare promoted by the American Revolution as France and Britain struggled over control of southeast Asia. Ali had recently contributed to an important British defeat on the Indian peninsula.[27] The vessel was under the command of Continental lieutenant Joshua Barney, already a larger-than-life character. Captured by the British while serving in the Continental navy, he and his shipmates had been imprisoned shipboard in three-foot-high boxes for fifty-three days with minimal food and water before they were transferred to Mill Prison.[28] Barney managed to escape from the Old Mill in May 1781—just weeks before Claypoole arrived there. His success was surely still a topic of conversation among the prisoners who remained. Upon Barney's return to Pennsylvania, he was made captain of the *Hyder-Ally*.

Claypoole must have been thrilled to join the celebrated ship's crew, and they too met with quick success. The sales of the ship *Lady Washington,* for instance, suggest the reward privateers might expect from a good capture: the auction sold some eighty barrels of much-wanted flour, while the vessel itself generated most of the profits, £270 of the total £387 8s. distributed among the owners and sailors.[29] The ship sailed out again October 1 and did "pursue, apprehend and retake the sloop called the *James* lately owned and commanded by Peter Drummond laden with lumber." The sloop *James* had been bound to the port of Philadelphia when it was captured and taken by an armed whale boat, the *Blacksnake,* commanded by Richardson Davenport; the *Lady Washington*'s crew reclaimed the ship. They were busy. They next took the *Dove* and then the schooner *Experiment.* The *Dove* carried 170 barrels and 200 hogshead of flour plus the ship's stores; its sale netted £174 17s. 2d. to the state, and the other half to the men, at £19 10s. 3/4d. per share. The schooner *Experiment* brought some £484 19s. 5d.[30] As Claypoole pocketed his share, he surely congratulated himself upon finding the perfect balance of military excitement and material reward.

Somehow between voyages, John and Betsy had tumbled toward courtship, and the couple married a little more than eight months after the *Symmetry* landed. The war was over, and she had survived it, and had found a partner once more to boot. Surely she was in the mood for a good laugh when, just a week after her wedding and with peace in view, her fellow upholsterer John Mason celebrated the treaty in his own inimitable way, announcing his plan to build "A SUPERB SOPHA, mounted on a triumphal car, drawn by six white horses, in honor to the American army." This unusual tribute would have on it "portraits of the principal officers [who] persevered in the present contest"; ladies were offered "an opportunity of displaying their ingenuity, by preparing garlands, curious knots, and artificial flowers to decorate the car." The "grand exhibition" would be accompanied by "thirteen times thirteen boys drest in white," their path illuminated by "thirteen large torches, and thirteen small ones."[31] If nothing else, Mason knew how to draw a crowd.

In the last fifteen years of the century, about fifty upholsterers were working Philadelphia, most of them gathered on Second Street near Market. The field was getting crowded, but now Betsy had, at last, a partner once more to support her own efforts. With the war over, John needed to return to business, and he naturally joined his wife in the upholstery trade. When in the fall of 1786 they covered six chair seats with moreen for Isaac Howell, charging nine pence per seat for the labor and ten and a half shillings for the materials, they were simply continuing the work that Betsy had known now for twenty years.[32] But this third marriage transformed Betsy's work. Ten years earlier, she had clearly been the junior partner when she and husband John Ross hung out their first shingle. Joseph Ashburn had been at sea for much of their marriage; there was no expectation that he would become involved in her work. But John Claypoole was another matter. One wonders how Betsy accommodated this alteration in her enterprise. In ten years' time, she had survived a war, grieved two husbands and a daughter, and raised a daughter on her own. Now she would necessarily share decision making with a husband whom law and custom made the head of a business familiar to her but new to him.

Immediately following his marriage to Betsy Ashburn in 1783, John Claypoole reported to tax assessors that his occupation was now "upholsterer."[33] His assessment that year, compared with the taxes paid by other upholsterers, is suggestive. Plunket Fleeson, of course, was at the top of his game, and so at the top of the tax rolls, too, assessed at some £150. The London craftsman Thomas Harper owed £75, and the always lively John Mason £97. John Linton (a onetime apprentice to Fleeson) and Claypoole are noted as owning no taxable property, but Claypoole's occupational tax, a figure based on annual income, was higher than Linton's—£40 as compared with just £2.[34] Claypoole had no formal training in this work. What was it that allowed his prospects to be rated so highly? His ties to the Claypooles already well established in the furniture trades? His political contacts? The accumulated experience, reputation and talents of his new wife?

Fortunately, upholstery was not an enterprise for which Claypoole was wholly unprepared, given his family's own history. John's father, as we have seen, was a cousin of the well-known cabinetmakers, but pursued a humbler trade, having become a tanner.[35] Tanning is a tough, earthy business, and reminds us again of how labor intensive obtaining the simple accoutrements of life was for early Americans. (Lest you have any doubt about the rough nature of the work, the Discovery Channel's *Dirty Jobs* tackled leather tanning in its third season. Another episode of this series also covered "Goose Down Feather Plucker," another task the Claypooles knew well.)[36] In order to transform the hides of cows, calves, horses and pigs into leathers suitable for boots and shoes, workmen's breeches, book covers, drums, rigging for ships and a hundred other purposes, the skins had to be prepared in a series of steps that unfolded over months. First, the hides were washed to clean them of blood, dung and other debris left over from the butcher's work. Next, to loosen and remove the animal's hair, the hide was soaked in vats full of lime, sometimes for as long as a year. Eventually, the hides were transferred to other vats where they were soaked in a *bate*—a noxious mixture of hen or pigeon dung (dog dung works as well), salt and water aimed at removing the lime and restoring the hide's pliability. They were then *beamed*—that is, placed over a beam for scraping. A dull, two-handled knife was applied to the exterior, a flesher to the interior, and the hide repeatedly scraped, washed and smoothed. It was hard work: scraping a dozen hides took a full day, the "hardest and most loathsome of the many unpleasant steps" needed to convert hides to leather.

With the hair removed, tanning could begin. The tanner placed dry bark on a kiln and then ground it into a coarse powder. The hides and bark were placed into pits or vats in layers, and left there to rest (though with constant agitation) while the bark was allowed to penetrate the hide. When the tanner judged them to be ready, they were removed and smoothed once more, and hung to dry slowly in a dark shed. At this point, they were transferred to a currier for finishing, but if the tanner possessed these skills, too—as John Claypoole may well have—he could have continued working the leather. The currier's job was to prepare the leather for working, softening it either by pummeling the material with wooden mallets or even trampling it underfoot. The currier scoured and cleaned the leather once again and pared it down to the desired thickness. Once shaved, the hides were worked on a bench to flatten, and infused with tallow or fish oils to make them supple. The surplus grease was then removed and the leather hung to dry. If its intended use would require the leather to be firm, it was completed at this stage, but there were other smoothing and softening techniques to apply if need be, and the currier might also add color or otherwise manipulate the leather's appearance.[37]

Tanyards like the Claypooles', then, were fairly elaborate (if noisome) affairs. The Trenton tanyard of Benjamin Biles gives a good sense of the world in which young John Claypoole first knew the end of a hard day's work. The Biles's yard boasted a bark house and bark mill, a beam house, a good stone currying shop and a leather house; he had enough vats to tan eight hundred hides in any year, and that didn't count the calfskins as well. The Lancaster tanyard of John Foulks could tan 350 hides annually.[38] In the 1740s, Benjamin Flower's Walnut Street tanyard boasted fourteen vats, two handlers and two limes, a good water pool, a mill and millhouse, and a currying shop; a Second Street tanyard in the Northern Liberties boasted no fewer than forty-two vats, eight handlers, two limes, two bates and a beam house with a pump, a bark mill and a bark house that would hold some 110 cords of the Spanish, Hemlock or Black Oak bark Philadelphia preferred. In an unusual example of vertical integration, one Kent County farm and tanyard advertised for rent in the *Pennsylvania Gazette* included the tanyard, the currier's shop and the shoemaker's shop right on the premises, converting calves to boots at a single site.[39]

It may not be chance or individual interest that distributed Claypooles across the furniture trades; cabinetmakers, tanners and upholsterers came together both in the creation of furniture and the gathering of materials. In the 1730s, Joseph Claypoole had launched his son Josiah in the joiner's trade. Josiah acquired his father's inventory and tools in May 1738 and opened a shop on Second Street, where "all Persons may be supplied with all Sorts of furniture of the best fashion," including "desks of all sorts, chests of drawers of all sorts, dining tables, chamber tables, and all sorts of tea tables and side boards." Josiah's brother George, meanwhile, kept a shop two doors down from the Coffee House on Front Street.[40] James Claypoole was a painter and glazier who painted houses, signs, ship and show boards, and in his Walnut Street shop sold window glass as well as "colours for painting" of "white lead, red lead, yellow [ochre], Venetian red, brown [oak], spanish brown," and so forth. John's adolescent training proved useful, since tanners prepared materials used by upholsterers to cover chairs and stools. They also prepared cattle and horse hairs for use as stuffings in seats and mattresses, processing the raw materials into the ropes which they then sold to upholsterers, who used the curled, elastic hair for fillings. Horns, bones and other discarded elements were boiled to make wood glue. By the time he married, John Claypoole had spent most of his adult years in the military, but he was at least marginally prepared to work with leather in the furniture trades alongside his more experienced wife.

As the work of her shop was reconfigured, so too was Betsy's household. In 1785, she had already given birth to her third daughter, the couple's first, whom they named Clarissa, after John's sister. Another girl, Susan, conveniently named after Betsy's sister as well as John's, followed in 1786. John Claypoole's pride in becoming a father is palpable in the genealogical register printed in their family Bible: after each daughter's name, he added the moment when she appeared—9:00 a.m. in the case of Clarissa, and 4:00 p.m. for Susan.[41] As the girls grew older, they could find amusement by hovering around their mother and the other women gathered around the sewing tables in the Claypoole upholstery shop. Six-year-old Eliza and the toddler Clarissa would have to be watched carefully—there were so many pins and shears for them to get into— but baby Susan could sleep safely in a cradle alongside the boxes of fringe.

Betsy had all she could do to keep her eye on the girls and her work and the shop; the Claypoole enterprise was off to a very strong start. In 1786, the tanner-turned-upholsterer John Claypoole was assessed an occupational tax of £100, fully double that of the successful joiner George Claypoole. By this year John Claypoole's taxable property included nine ounces of silver plate, a chair (or carriage) and a horse to pull it. Indeed, it is a level of prosperity that seems difficult to take in. Tax assessors in 1786 found just 755 carriages in the whole of Philadelphia—a city of some 4,600 households and 32,000 residents. In other words, only 16 percent of households (or roughly one in six) enjoyed access to this comfortable means of transportation.[42] The picture of the thirty-four-year-old craftswoman and mother Betsy Claypoole riding with her husband in the carriage is the first of a number of such images that raises as many questions as it answers. Certainly on the face of it, Betsy had chosen well in marrying John—or perhaps it was the other way around.

# 16

# For Lord and Empire

Shortly after Betsy Ashburn and John Claypoole married, the couple decided to return to the Quaker fold—though on new terms—a decision that reveals a good deal about the religious and political convictions that underlay and endured the tempests and tumult of Revolution, and that guided Betsy Claypoole. Betsy's desire to marry John Ross had long ago severed her formal ties to the faith of her childhood, and personal and political fortunes had drawn her into the congregations at Christ Church and Old Swede's, with the war all but over, she was free to follow the dictates of her conscience, to pursue choices born of quiet reflection rather than romantic passion or political exigency.

Sometime between 1781 and 1785, Betsy gravitated toward the nascent gathering of so-called Free Quakers, a collection of once-disowned men and women who came together to restore fellowship in a community of Friends.[1] Whether she was participating on her own before her 1783 marriage to Claypoole or whether the new couple found this community together is unknown, though it seems likelier that he followed her than the other way round, since John himself, unlike Betsy, had never been a practicing Quaker. No evidence suggests that she was joined in this decision by her parents, sisters or brother; other siblings would hover in the Free Quaker's orbit, but none—not even those likewise disowned—became full members.[2] This she did on her own.

The primary instigator of this effort, Samuel Wetherill Jr., had himself descended from a long line of influential Friends. He and Betsy Claypoole were linked in knots of family attachments; Betsy had known him all her life. The Wetherills lived near Betsy's childhood home, on South Alley between Fifth and Sixth streets on a lot extending from Market to Arch. Wetherill was a minister in the Bank meeting that the Griscoms attended when Betsy was young. (Dolley Payne Madison, who also attended that meeting as a young woman in the city, would long recall Wetherill as a powerful speaker there.)[3] Wetherill, like Betsy's father, was a house carpenter by trade, about twenty years Griscom's junior and the onetime apprentice of the carpenter and Quaker preacher Mordecai Yarnall (another colleague of Samuel Griscom's; years later, Betsy's nephew Aquilla Bolton would marry Mordecai's daughter, a tightening of these ties). But Wetherill was not a member of the Carpenters' Company. In fact, in 1769 he had been among the organizers of the Friendship Carpenters' Company, the upstart union of tradesmen organized to challenge the dominance of the established society. Now, just as Samuel Wetherill Jr. was launching the Free Quaker meeting, he conceded the effort and the Friendship Company was absorbed by the older body. Wetherill's associates from the carpenters' community would prove the backbone of the new Quaker meeting; there were more house carpenters among these "nonpacifist Friends" than representatives of any other occupation.[4] Not Samuel Griscom, it seems, but some twenty other building tradesmen together rejected the Friends' stance on war and the practice of disownment.

When the Pennsylvania Assembly in rebellion demanded loyalty oaths, most Quakers—as we know—refused to submit to this violation of their traditional peace testimony. They suffered for it terribly. Wetherill affirmed his allegiance publicly (though he did not actually swear an oath) and supported the resistance movement in print as well. When his actions came to the attention of the Philadelphia Monthly Meeting, Wetherill supplied the group with some twenty pages of prose defending his actions.[5]

It would not stave off disciplinary action. The Philadelphia meeting responded predictably:

> Whereas, Samuel Wetherill of this city hath many years made profession of the Truth with us, and we have grounds to hope he hath been convinced of the nature and excellency of Christian union and fellowship, but not being sufficiently attentive to the Divine principle of Gospel peace and love, which leads and preserves the followers of Christ out of contention and discord, has deviated from our ancient Testimony and peaceable principles, by manifesting himself a party in the public commotions prevailing, and taking a test of abjuration and allegiance, and hath also violated the established order

of our Discipline by being concerned in publishing or distributing a book tending to promote dissension and division among Friends: It therefore became our care to labour to convince him of the hurtful tendency of his conduct, but our brotherly concern and endeavours for him not being effectual . . . [we] declare that he hath separated from fellowship with us and become secluded from membership in our religious Society.[6]

With this, Wetherill became one of over four hundred men and women whose actions in support of the war estranged them from the Society of Friends.

Wetherill's partner in the creation of the Free Quaker meeting was his brother-in-law Timothy Matlack, whose wife, Ellen, was the sister of Wetherill's wife, Sarah.[7] Born in Haddonfield, New Jersey, a community filled with Griscom family and friends, Matlack's father had been present at Betsy's uncle Abel's wedding. But while Abel James struggled against the protest movement, Timothy Matlack embraced it. He is best remembered today as the possible engrosser of the Declaration of Independence (that is, the man in whose handwriting the famous document and its millions of facsimiles is penned), but his service to the cause was far more extensive. A leader at the local, state and national level, he was a member of the Fifth Rifle Battalion of Philadelphia Associators and served as clerk to the secretary of the second Continental Congress, storekeeper of military supplies, a delegate to the Pennsylvania Constitutional Convention, a delegate from Pennsylvania to the Continental Congress, a member of the state Council of Safety and secretary to the state's Supreme Executive Council. In 1783, Philadelphia's Committee of Safety presented him with a silver urn "for his patriotic devotion to the cause of freedom, and the many services rendered by him throughout the struggle."[8]

When Wetherill and Matlack gathered together Philadelphia men and women who had been disowned by the Society of Friends, it was the culmination of years of anger and frustration. The coming of the war had strained relationships mightily. At the peak—or nadir—of tensions, Matlack himself had caned two fellow Quakers who criticized his son for taking up arms. But Matlack—importantly, his political opponents would insist—had not been disowned for his patriotism or over any other matter of principle; he had been censured well before Revolution erupted for indebtedness, failing to attend meeting and keeping poor company. He was known to engage in horse racing, cockfighting and other distasteful activities. Though his distinguished record of service to the rebellion would indeed have secured disownment, the truth of the matter was that Matlack was out on his own merits, or lack thereof, a decade before the first rebellious shots were fired.

As the Revolutionary War went on and the number of disowned Friends increased, they became "something of a feature" in the city—that is, there were enough of them accumulating that they began to assume a gravitational force all their own. Many of them had, like Timothy Matlack, not been sanctioned for wartime activities, and were instead, like Betsy Claypoole, estranged for other sorts of infractions. Some of those so censured cultivated an objection to disownment itself, rejecting the practice on principle. Under Wetherill and Matlack's leadership, they began meeting together to compare experiences and views, at first in small numbers in private homes. After a number of meetings for religious worship, they began to consider forming a regular meeting. Toward the end of February 1781, the new Society held its initial business meeting. When they opened the cover of their first minute book, they headed the record "The Religious Society of Friends, by some styled the Free Quakers." Original members included Timothy's brother, the watchmaker White Matlack, the well-known physician Benjamin Say and the chemist and pharmacist Christopher Marshall. Colonel Clement Biddle had been disowned as early as 1775 for "studying to learn the art of war," having raised a company of soldiers composed largely of Quakers, the "Quaker Blues." He was there, too.

A celebrated figure among the female membership was Lydia Darragh, who during the war had overheard a conversation among British officers planning to surprise Washington's army encamped at Whitemarsh. Darragh is said to have (under the pretense of a need for flour) headed to the Rising Sun Tavern, where Elias Boudinot collected information from an informal network of spies, and conveyed news of the intended attack to the American army. "And thus"—as her own considerable legend goes—"probably saved it and the American cause from destruction."[9] The Darraghs were natural members of the Free Quaker meeting (and in fact Lydia's formal disciplining stemmed from her participation in those gatherings); Lydia's son Charles had served as a lieutenant in Washington's army, and so was disowned for being "too warlike in nature," while another son, John, was likewise disowned for martial activity.[10] For her part, Lydia was disciplined (technically, at least) for poor attendance at meeting.[11]

Though it seems likelier that Betsy learned of the Free Quakers by word of mouth rather than any printed notice, a broadside dated April 24, 1781, invited other unaffiliated Friends to join their counterparts in religious worship.[12] The first "public, printed utterance" of the newly gathered Society was made when five hundred copies of a pamphlet were published and distributed to defend the decision to form this new congregation. The core principle of this Society was an objection to the practice of disownment in and of itself. In "An Apology for the Religious Society called Free Quakers in the City of Philadelphia," the founders argued that excommunication is inconsistent with the Gospel. Why, they asked, in a question of particular interest to Betsy Claypoole, should "no one among them . . . marry a person of any other Society, though ever so amiable, under pain of being expelled from the body, nor even a member of their own Society, unless they accomplished their marriage agreeable to one particular form?" Would a truly just church insist "that no man should defend his own life, nor the life of his friend, nor the government under which he lived, nor pay taxes for military purposes, nor a fine for not complying with the laws in certain cases?" In part, the Free Quakers suggested that changing times should compel the Friends to reconsider their strictures: "Can it be supposed that any number of men of sound understanding would, in the present day, lay down such a plan, and make a compliance with those rules the test of Christian fellowship? If, then, it is impossible to suppose such a case, are they wise who make those rules the test of Christian fellowship, merely because they were made the conditions of fellowship by their ancestors?" For their part, the Free Quakers resolved that if a "brother should be overtaken in a fault, we will endeavour to restore such a one in the spirit of meekness, considering ourselves, lest we also be tempted; but in no case whatever, shall any one be expelled from the Society, lest it should prove his ruin."

The Free Quakers also specifically addressed disownments grounded in military activity given the unusual circumstances of the wrenching rebellion. If one admits the necessity of government itself, they argued, then "all government is essentially a defensive war for the protection of public peace, and that when the government is threatened by domestic treason or foreign invasion, it then becomes the plain duty of every man to join in the public defence by all means possible, and that war, while an extreme measure, is in such instances not merely justifiable, but right and proper."[13] The Society members believed that aiding one's government in times of crisis was in fact a duty entirely consistent with the principles of the faith.

These men and women were estranged from their spiritual community not because of any substantial theological schism; instead, they argued, it was "forced upon us, as the pride and folly of former churches, vainly attempting to abridge the rights of conscience, excommunicated their brethren from among them." They had no hope of regaining unity with their former Friends: "For they will not permit, among them, the Christian liberty of sentiment and conduct which all are entitled to enjoy, and which we cannot consent to part with. You know that many have been disowned by that people, for no other cause than a faithful discharge of those duties which we owe to our country." "We have no new doctrines to teach, nor any design of promoting schisms in religion," their declaration continued. "We wish only to be freed from every species of ecclesiastical tyranny, and mean to pay a due regard to the principles of our forefathers."[14]

All of these arguments give us a rare glimpse into Betsy's psyche, since we know at least that she found these positions compelling. And she was not alone. Already by May 1781, turnout for Free Quaker worship was reported to be "large and decent"; it could well be that Betsy Ashburn was already attending meetings, taking comfort in this new but familiar community while Joseph was at sea.[15] Perhaps these friends came to her emotional and material aid when his fate became known in the city.

The gathering of estranged men and women might have been well and good had Wetherill and Matlack left it at that, but the Free Quakers did not intend to retreat into a corner; instead, they demanded a place in the larger community of Friends. In summer 1781, a committee of Free Quakers reported that they had attended the Bank meeting and sat through the assembly for worship. After the service concluded, and someone proposed that the group proceed to business, Henry Drinker observed that "some persons were then present who did not belong to them, and as according to the good order established among them no business could be entered upon while those persons remained among them."[16] When Drinker asked the Free Quakers to leave, they responded by announcing that they had hoped to "lay before those there met a communication of the sentiments of that meeting," asking that it be read and considered. The next day, they attended the Hill meetinghouse with the same plan. Their reception here, however, was notably kinder than it had been elsewhere. The Free Quakers continued attempting to notify their brethren in the Society of Friends of their intent to form a new meeting, with mixed responses.

In part, the Free Quakers simply needed space for gatherings and saw no reason to reinvent the wheel. As a trustee at the university, Matlack had secured some temporary space there, but the new Society wanted something more formal, more established, and already paid for—access to their former assembly rooms. Matters quickly took an ugly turn. In July, another broadside (the fourth since April) appeared, this one addressed "to Those of our Brethren Who Have Disowned us."[17] It was an appeal concerning property.

The Free Quakers hinted that they were not averse to seeking legal recourse—presenting still more evidence of their different way of thinking, since established Quaker tradition preferred settling matters internally and discouraged Friends from seeking remedies through the courts. The Society of Friends elected not to respond.

In December, the Free Quakers took a new tack when they petitioned the Pennsylvania House, seeking official recognition alongside the use of property controlled by the Society, including meetinghouses, schools and burial grounds, as well as Quaker records and libraries. Alluding vaguely to the less-than-patriotic conduct of their counterparts during the Revolutionary crisis, they hoped to win the representatives over to their side, but the legislature—loath to wade into what looked like a messy internal debate—instead tabled the petition. In their own defense, the established Friends asserted that the former members now calling themselves Free Quakers were all disowned for violations of the faith's fundamental tenets and so had forfeited their membership rights. The Free Quakers replied that their contributions prior to the imperial crisis surely entitled them to some share of the community's assets.[18]

The dispute turned into a venue for Timothy Matlack (in person and by proxy) to rake his Quaker enemies once more over the coals of patriotism for their failure to contribute to the Revolution, forcing the Friends again to assert their right to live according to the dictates of their conscience. Rumors flew. The Society of Friends had weathered more than a decade of censure—many would say persecution—for its failure to support protests and then warfare against Britain. For many, those scars were just beginning to heal; they weren't anxious to have them picked at again and their reputations further impugned. Friends heard that the petition Matlack submitted to the assembly was "so very scurrilous and inflammatory" that he had trouble finding signers. In the end, Free Quakers White Matlack and Isaac Howell (word on the street said) signed it "on behalf of their brethren" to conceal the lack of signatures. Friends braced for a "torrent of detraction and abuse."[19]

In response to Matlack's charges, the Friends sent delegates to the assembly to represent their position. A huge crowd turned out to watch the proceedings. They expected fireworks, and they weren't disappointed. The established Society of Friends' opening gambit was to present a minute from the membership appointing them official representatives of that body, and asked Matlack and Howell to produce comparable credentials identifying themselves as official representatives of all disowned Quakers, which of course they could not do. More damaging was an address sent to the House from some seventy-five Friends who had also been disowned but who did not share the Free Quakers' views. When these apostates reported to the legis-lature that they respected the discipline, did not consider Matlack and Howell true representatives of any real constituency and were prepared to take the lumps due disowned Friends, the Free Quakers' case weakened considerably.[20]

Matlack and Howell rejoined that even if they were the only two who believed themselves to have been aggrieved, they had every right to seek redress, and they could produce evidence that they did in fact represent "many hundred" in their support. Matlack dove into the case at hand, the numerous instances of Quakers being disowned for various patriotic activi-ties, to which the Friends made no objection—those facts, after all, were not in dispute. Matlack droned on for no fewer than five hours, citing incident after incident. The assemblymen listened dutifully but were unwilling to weigh in. In time, the committee to review the Free Quakers' petition was dissolved and the matter postponed. "Blessed be the Lord who hath not given us a prey to their teeth," James Pemberton wrote.[21] It didn't help that Matlack was disgraced when the legislature accused him of misappropriating tax funds in his position as secretary of the council; calling him "unworthy of public trust or confidence," the assembly stripped him of his position.[22] Finally, when it became public knowledge that Matlack and at least some of the others had not, in fact, been disowned for their service to their country but rather for all sorts of "disreputable" activities, the Free Quakers' case col-lapsed. The assembly decided that the august body was just too busy to be fooling around with such a petty intrareligious dispute.

Nevertheless, in spring 1783 the Free Quakers renewed their effort, sub-mitting another petition signed by thirty-five men.[23] That John Claypoole's name is not among the signatories here suggests that he was not yet active in the organization, and since only men were asked to sign this particular docu-ment, it doesn't confirm whether Betsy was. But whether or not the Clay-pooles (either newly wed or about to be) shared in the effort, it was a last-ditch effort, and it failed.

Matlack's performance aside, the congregation was undaunted. At first, between fifty and sixty members began coming together for worship, but before long, the congregation numbered around two hundred. Soon it became clear that they would need to erect a meetinghouse. Contributions to the building fund were solicited: Washington, Franklin and a number of other distinguished patriots were among the donors. In summer 1783, just as the final terms of the peace treaty were being hammered out in Paris, plans for building began, on land purchased from the printer John Dunlap.

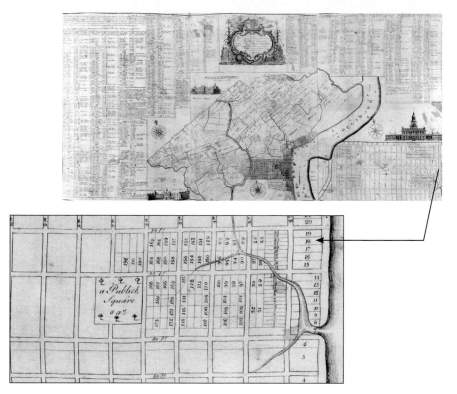

This 1774 map by John Reed notes the lot in Philadelphia that belonged to Andrew Griscom, Betsy's great-grandfather. *(Image and detail courtesy of the Winterthur Library: Printed Book and Periodical Collection. Photography by Jim Schneck.)*

This scene, from W. Birch & Son, *The City of Philadelphia: in the State of Pennsylvania, North America, as it appeared in the year 1800 . . .* (Philadelphia, 1800) depicts Arch Street between Third and Fourth (with the Second Presbyterian Church), where Betsy's father Samuel Griscom in 1764 built a large home to accommodate his growing family. *(Courtesy of the Winterthur Library: Printed Book and Periodical Collection.)*

Betsy Ross and her family were associated with sites around Philadelphia. The series of places in which she lived and worked over the course of her long life are indicated here. *(Courtesy of Patricia Nobre.)*

1  Betsy's childhood home [1764-1773]
2  Betsy's home with John Ross [1773-1776]
3  Betsy's home with Joseph Ashburn and John Claypoole [ca.1780-1787]
4  The Claypoole upholstery shop [1787-1788]
5  Betsy and John Claypoole's home and shop [1788-1792]
6  Betsy and John Claypoole's home and shop [1792-ca.1810]
7  Betsy and John Claypoole's home and shop [ca.1810-1827]
8  Jane and Caleb Canby's house, in which Betsy died in 1836
9  John Webster's first shop [1767]

Denis Diderot's engraving, from *Encyclopedie: ou Dictionnaire raisonne des sciences, des arts et des métiers par un societe de gens de letters* (Paris, 1751–65), imagines an upholstery shop interior in eighteenth-century France. The proprietor shows a client his wares and a man carries completed mattresses down the stairs while a number of women (detail) gathered around a table work on fabricating various articles for the shop. This is the sort of work Betsy Griscom learned in John Webster's Philadelphia shop. *(Courtesy of the Winterthur Library: Printed Book and Periodical Collection.)*

Portrait of Reverend Aeneas Ross, Betsy Ross's father-in-law. *(Courtesy of the Winterthur Library: Printed Book and Periodical Collection.)*

Hugg Tavern, the scene of Betsy and John Ross's elopement, as it appeared in the 1920s. *(Courtesy of the Gloucester County Historical Society, New Jersey.)*

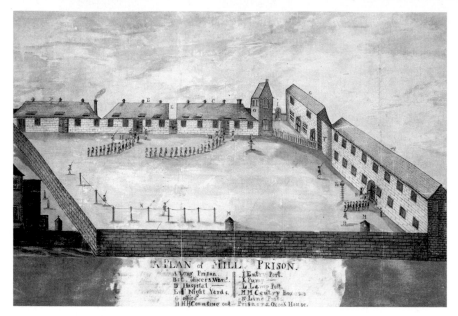

Mill Prison, Plymouth, England, where privateers Joseph Ashburn and John Claypoole, Betsy's second and third husbands, were confined during the Revolutionary War. *(Courtesy of the Peabody Essex Museum.)*

The Religious Society of Free Quakers meeting house, where Betsy Claypoole and John Ross gathered for worship beginning in the 1780s. *(Courtesy of the Library of Congress.)*

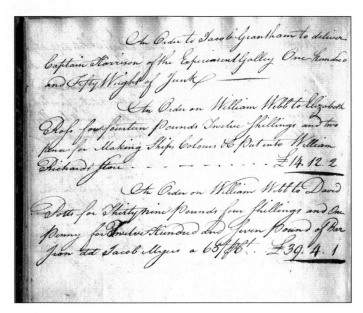

This 1777 entry in the ledgers of the Pennsylvania Navy is the earliest known record of Betsy Ross making flags for the war effort. *(Courtesy of the Pennsylvania State Archives.)*

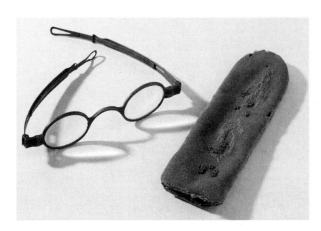

Betsy's eyesight declined over the course of her life, and by the time of her death she had lost her vision almost entirely. Her eyeglasses and case are today in the collections of the Betsy Ross House. *(Photograph courtesy of the Winterthur Library: Printed Book and Periodical Collection. Photography by Jim Schneck.)*

Betsy enjoyed taking snuff, and claimed it was good for her eyesight. Her silver snuffbox is today in the collections of the Betsy Ross House. *(Photograph courtesy of the Winterthur Library: Printed Book and Periodical Collection. Photography by Jim Schneck.)*

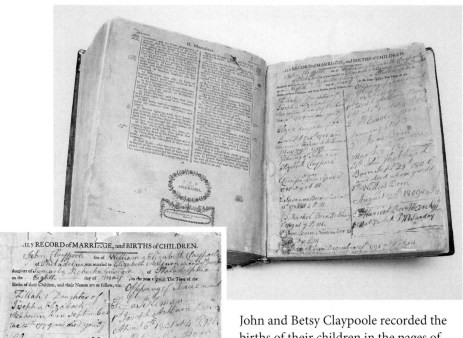

John and Betsy Claypoole recorded the births of their children in the pages of their family Bible. *(Detail courtesy of the Betsy Ross House. Photograph courtesy of the Winterthur Library: Printed Book and Periodical Collection. Photography by Jim Schneck.)*

This receipt for a "large American ensign" dates from 1813 and can be found in the collections of the Delaware Historical Society.

Contracts with the United States Indian Department for flags like this one, presented to affirm diplomatic relations with native nations, were important to Betsy's livelihood as well. *(Courtesy of the Chicago Historical Society.)*

Clarissa Claypoole Wilson had this portrait made about the time of her marriage to Jacob Wilson, ca. 1805. *(Courtesy of the Historical Society of Pennsylvania, Society Portrait Collection, artist unknown.)*

Clarissa Claypoole Wilson portrait by Joachim de Franca, ca. 1830. *(Courtesy of the Betsy Ross House. Photograph courtesy of the Winterthur Library: Printed Book and Periodical Collection. Photography by Jim Schneck.)*

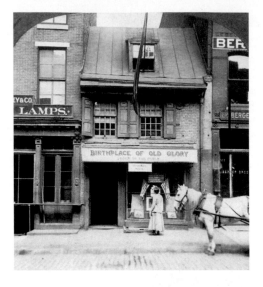

The Betsy Ross House on Philadelphia's Arch Street as it appeared about 1898, when a group of citizens established the American Flag House and Betsy Ross Memorial Association. *(Courtesy of the Library of Congress.)*

Charles H. Weisgerber's 1892 painting "Birth of Our Nation's Flag" helped propel Betsy's story to national prominence. *(Courtesy of the State Museum of Pennsylvania, Pennsylvania Historical and Museum Commission.)*

Joseph Boggs Beale was among the foremost illustrators of the nineteenth century. This image of Betsy Ross was included in a series of patriotic drawings Beale completed about 1899. *("Betsy Ross," image courtesy of the fine art collection of American National Insurance Company, Galveston, Texas.)*

The building went up in only fourteen weeks. Days after the ink on the deed dried, the timber arrived, and a few days after that the floorboards were delivered by the Water Street lumber merchants McCullogh & Peterson—at a discount, in consideration of the nature of the project. Bushels of lime began arriving by July 18, and loads of stone on the twenty-second. Some seventeen loads of sand and lengths of rope signaled the construction of scaffolding.[24] On July 29, the "Foundation Stone" was laid "in the presence of a numerous body of Spectators Friends and others."[25] In early August, the first of over a hundred thousand bricks arrived; Daniel McBride spent three and a half days just piling it. The roof was raised October 4, providing an occasion for festivities: sixty people gathered for a celebratory dinner at Samuel Wetherill's.[26] The masonry walls would be up and under their roof by winter.[27]

In mid-October, the Philadelphia stonecutter David Chambers was paid for carving the now-famous inscription that ornaments the building's north gable end.[28] The lines chosen boldly declared the group's dual allegiances—to the Lord, and to the new empire of the United States.

By General Subscription,
For the Free Quakers, erected,
In the year of our Lord, 1783,
Of the Empire 8.

Hardware, plastering, glazing and painting—the construction of the new meetinghouse engaged artisans around the city. Terrence Smith plastered the walls; John Long glazed the second-floor windows—some 140 lights in all—while his counterpart Joseph Wirt completed the ground floor.[29] Wirt also painted the cornices and Long the rest of the building. The blacksmith Jacob Elkfeldt installed a stove. And, on June 17, 1784, Betsy's uncle and cousins—as the firm Abel James & Sons—accepted payment for lead, possibly for flashing, or to protect the floor beneath the stove from sparks.[30] The final building, the historian Bernard L. Herman has observed, "complete with giant engaged pilasters . . . tapped into the worldly and academic language of classicism." The stylish elements the meeting chose conformed to both an aesthetic of restraint and contemporary architectural fashion, and so (Herman continues) were "consistent with a Quaker doctrine that emphasizes the importance of the practice of living in the world."[31]

When the building was at last ready—or ready enough—for a meeting, a "large and solemn" gathering was attended by some two hundred people, including "most of the members of our Society who resided in this city," as well as "divers of our fellow Christians of other denominations."[32] But the interior was not yet finished. The house carpenter Evan Evans still had benches to make in August; as fall went on, the building was further improved when the meeting decided to purchase a small table for the structure and to have Venetian blinds made for the back windows—tall ones on the western wall to block out the afternoon sun. This latter job went to the upholsterer John Davis, who submitted a bill of £8 for "mounting 2 Vanicion [Venetian] blines 11 feet 3 inches long."[33] Timothy Matlack bought a folio book of the "best paper, all bound in the best leather" for the recording of marriages, and the new meeting was good to go.[34]

From the beginning, the design of the building included revenue-generating space in the cellar, which was rented out immediately to a wine merchant. But when the congregation did not grow as fast or as large as its founders envisioned, plans were made to create a second floor which could also be rented out for additional income. Brick piers were installed in the cellar and wooden columns above to support another floor, and stairs built along Arch Street to reach the new door that had to be cut through the not-so-old brickwork. Soon, the schoolmaster John Poor alerted potential students to his new "Accommodations for the Instruction of Young Ladies"; some one hundred students had enrolled by the end of the year. Poor claimed that his academy was the "first in the United States, and perhaps in the world"—maybe so, for it outgrew these quarters. In Poor's wake, the upper room of the meetinghouse was rented by the Masonic Lodge, which took a nine-year lease. For those years, the meeting space was particularly convenient to John Claypoole, if he continued to attend meetings. After the lodge moved on, the space was let by Benjamin Tucker, who kept a school there for more than thirty-five years. The rents generated were used to establish a fund for the charitable relief of the Society's members in need—monies that, as we shall see, would become essential to the Claypoole household in the years to come.[35]

No longer the passionate newlywed called on the carpet for her misbehavior, Betsy—now in her thirties and a young mother—was more establishment than rebel, and she had at last found a spiritual home. By 1800, well over one hundred steady members attended Philadelphia's Free Quaker meeting. Most of them were not Friends who had become estranged from their various meetings for taking up arms; that group represented only part of the Free Quaker membership. Most, like Betsy, had been disowned for other reasons. But they found community in a gathering devoted to freedom of conscience above all.

In joining the Free Quaker community, then, Betsy made a statement about her own religious beliefs, grounded in strong respect for individual judgment in matters of faith, and a rejection of structures that placed some Christians in judgment of others. Her own disownment would have been enough to justify that view, but the experiences of her siblings also played a role. She certainly may have harbored resentment over the treatment Deborah, Susannah, Sarah and Mary had received when they were called on the plain Quaker carpet. But perhaps her anger was fresher. Betsy Claypoole embraced the Free Quakers just as other members of her family found their own relationships with the Society of Friends strained. She and John finally found a spiritual home that suited their intellectual, spiritual and social needs at the very moment when more family drama erupted as two more siblings, in fine Griscom fashion, found themselves the targets of formal Quaker disapproval.

First, Betsy's sister Rebecca, now thirty-eight, was censured by the Philadelphia Monthly Meeting Northern District for "excessive use of strong drink." In April 1785, the women's meeting reported that Betsy's sister had "for a considered time been in the practice of taking strong drink to Excess." The meeting "exercised much labor towards her" but "without the desired Effect." Drunkenness of course violated a number of Quaker tenets and had been singled out for special attention since the colonies' earliest days. Among other strategies designed to limit drinking, William Penn had stipulated 8:00 p.m. closing times for city taverns that did not cater to businessmen, and limited Philadelphia residents to one-hour visits there.[36] Drinking to excess greatly offended the Quakers' temperate sensibilities—comprising almost a quarter of disciplinary actions for "sectarian" matters—since alcohol abuse was not only an issue in and of itself but also, as the Abington meeting noted, "an inlet to many other evils." Fully half of the Friends admonished for drunkenness were also accused of some other unwelcome behavior; members who spent too much time in the tavern also tended to miss meeting, engage in bawdy conversation, get into fights, fall into financial trouble, neglect their families and commit an array of other offenses both major and minor.[37] Sometimes the Society was able to work with errant or troubled Friends and urge them to abstain from alcohol, but more often than not the subject of concern was eventually disowned.

In the era of the Revolution and the years that followed, the Quaker position slipped from objections to drunkenness to a policy of outright abstinence.

Anthony Benezet had published *The Mighty Destroyer Displayed,* igniting concerns about alcohol abuse, and a few years later Quakers articulated prohibitions against the use, manufacture or sale of hard liquor.[38] Benjamin Rush broached the subject, too, in a 1782 essay urging employers to forego using alcohol as a routine part of an employee's compensation. Two years later, his pamphlet (the eighteenth-century version of a paperback) *Enquiry in the Effect of Spiritous Liquors* had appeared.[39] Rush—who knew the consequences of alcohol abuse firsthand, having endured both a drunken father and an abusive stepfather—warned readers that spirituous beverages were a gateway vice; he believed that beer, wine and other alcoholic drinks were tolerable, but hard liquor was addictive and progressively damaging. Even opium, he contended, carried less risk. He understood that people with taxing jobs could find some relief in the occasional use of spirits, and he grasped that given the blurry line (no pun intended) between medicine and liquor, some users were in essence self-medicating, even then, but he also believed—in language that has some startling resonance today—that alcohol abuse was essentially suicide over a longer haul. He was among the first to consider alcohol abuse a disease rather than simply a failure of will, and argued that addiction was chiefly prevented through abstinence. Cold baths, a vegetarian diet, various forms of aversion therapy—all of these remedies were included in Rush's tool kit.[40]

Rebecca's case was not as prolonged as some, but the disownment when it came marks the beginning of a steady decline in her fortunes. In April 1785, while Rush's pamphlet was still hot off the presses, Joseph Yerkes and Isaac Cathrall were appointed to draw up the testimony against her.[41] "Rebekah Griscom Daughter of Samuel Griscom," they asserted, "had by birth right of Membership and made profession with us the people called Quakers but by not taking heed of the Monitions of the divine and inward Instructor she hath been drawn into the frequent practice of drinking strong Liquor to Excess for which she hath been tenderly treated with for a long time without any apparent good Effect. We therefore for the clearing of Truth from the reproach Occasioned by her evil Conduct declare that she hath disunited herself from religious membership with us, and we hereby testifie our disunion with her until through godly sorrow She manifest sincere repentance and amendment of Life and make such Acknowledgment to this Meeting as the Nature of her Case requires, which is our Desire for her."[42] Rebecca either rejected enforced temperance on principle or disagreed that her drinking exceeded acceptable bounds. Their "labour" on her behalf not having the "desired effect," a Testimony was drawn up against her asserting that her use of "strong liquor" was "frequent," but their efforts to intervene had gone "without any apparent effect."[43] Concerned about the "reproach occasioned by her evil Conduct," the Friends declared that Rebecca had "disunited herself from religious membership"; should she "manifest sincere repentance"—that is, change her ways and submit to the discipline of the Society—she would be welcomed back, but not before.

Rebecca was not the only Griscom struggling with drink in the early years of independence: Thomas Morgan, Betsy's brother-in-law, also seems to have drunk himself into poverty. Morgan had apparently never been much of a businessman. Even in an era when long-standing credit relationships were the order of the day, Morgan seems to have had trouble collecting his accounts payable. As the account book that survives him attests, only about half of his customers ever settled their debts in full. Of the close to two hundred accounts that fill the pages of his extant ledger, about 16 percent were paid only in part. Fully one third paid nothing at all.[44] In the years following his wife Mary's death (if not before), he was apparently struggling to get by. Thomas moved to the shop of the watchmaker Ephraim Clark, across the street from Betsy and John, who would have full view of his dissolution. It was from those quarters that he would later write his son George (by then an aspiring merchant in New Orleans) for help; George would in turn confess to his sister, "[I would] cheerfully put myself to any inconvenience" to send money to their father "if I thought he would be able to make any thing like good use of it, but you know (to our sorrow) how he would imploy it."[45] When he finally died, his son George would lament that the "fate of our once (but now ever happy) unfortunate father [makes my] heart bleed."[46] When George learned the sad circumstances of his father's death, the news came from the Claypooles; it was Clarissa whose letter broke the sorry news.

Rebecca did not meet the censure of the Quakers alone. The same April meeting that entertained the public reading against her also included an agenda item for her brother George. George had taxed the patience of the Quaker community when he, as the others, married out of unity. Just months earlier, George—the only son of Samuel and Rebecca's to have survived infancy—wed Kitty Schreiner in Lehigh County's Egypt Reformed Church. The couple set up housekeeping in Burlington, New Jersey. His irregular union nevertheless came to the Friends' attention, the monthly meeting noting that George had "sometime since removed to Burlington" and had married "before a Priest without the consent" of Samuel and Rebecca; while they were at it, the Friends noted too, for the record, that (no surprise) he had been neglecting the meeting for some time.[47]

George showed no particular "sense of his deviation," and since he was already living over the river it was difficult to send Friends to treat with him; the Society was ready to wash its hands of him unusually quickly. The members tasked with discussing matters with him had trouble discharging their duty, but Samuel Emlen and Henry Drinker, having occasion to travel to Burlington on business, took the opportunity to visit George and Kitty. After "some conference" with George, they confirmed that it certainly seemed to them that "there [was] little hope of Benefit by a continuance of labour with him." They apparently asked around about George's general demeanor, because they also reported that they were "informed" that "his general conduct [was] not consistent" with Quaker principles. The meeting felt compelled to give George a bit more time, instructing the "friends first named" to "endeavor to comply with their appointment" and report back when they could.[48] But George had no sense of his error, the minutes observed.[49] A month later, Emlen and Drinker reported that they had gone to Burlington yet again and had a "full and suitable opportunity of conferring" with George; they expressed some "hope that he [was] not quite insensible" (faint praise indeed) "of good Impressions, although [was in] divers respects deficient in his conduct." As "some friends feel a tenderness towards him the Committee [desires] to give further attention to his Situation and endeavor to inform themselves further respecting his general Conduct and whether any alteration takes place as to his attendance of our religious meetings."[50] By March 1786, the Friends charged with overseeing George's case reported that they saw "little prospect" that any further delay would bring him back into the fold. The patient Friends instructed the committee to make one final attempt to assess Griscom's state of mind, but when George remained indifferent, they entered their testimony against him into the minutes. George became the next Griscom to deviate from the discipline and fail to apologize for it.[51]

During the months when these crises unfolded for Betsy's sister and brother, her uncle Abel James—whose Quaker credentials were to date impressive to say the least—would also find himself under the tender care of the Quakers, his meteoric rise having ended in an equally dramatic flame-out. James, it seems, had become overly excited about the commercial implications of the end of the Revolutionary War. "On the ratification of Peace, in 1783," a magazine would later comment, "he quitted his retirement; bought and sold an immense quantity of real estate; and, at the age of sixty, launched again into the uncertain ocean of trade, with the incautiousness of a youthful adventurer."[52] He imported far more goods than demand justified, and in time his business failed. Perhaps ironically, he had just around this time

come across some early papers of Benjamin Franklin, including the beginning pages of an autobiography, and penned a now-famous letter to his old
friend urging him to publish his life story, since "no character living" has "so
much in his Power" to "promote a greater Spirit of Industry and early Attention to Business, frugality and Temperance with the American Youth."[53] But
apparently James was better at reading about these subjects than practicing
them. Disorderly conduct among the Society of Friends pertained to the
countinghouse as well as the tavern; just as the Quakers disapproved of Rebecca's intemperance with alcohol, they disapproved of intemperate trading.
James was censured for his lack of caution and for letting his accounts fall
into disarray.[54]

Interestingly, neither Rebecca nor George (and certainly not Abel), once
released from the Quaker fold, seems to have drifted toward Betsy's community of disowned Friends. Perhaps she did not try to convince them to, but
then again, she was at times an advocate of her newfound faith. Although it is
difficult to spy Betsy Claypoole in either the messy public or more intimate
private battles that surrounded the Free Quakers' founding, in time her own
actions are preserved among the Society's records. In May 1789, she added
her signature to a letter to the "Monthly Meeting of the disowned Friends at
Rochester and Aqueshinet or Long Plains, Dartmouth, State of Massachusetts Bay." Philadelphia's Free Quakers sought to strengthen connections
with these New England counterparts. "We have been long in Expectation of
being made acquainted with your religious progress," they wrote, and eagerly
anticipated getting more news of the Dartmouth group's activities. They also
urged the Massachusetts gathering to embrace the term *Free Quakers,* so that
the two groups "might be outwardly one people in name and practice." "Unity
tho at a distance" was their aim, just as the Church was at the dawn of Christianity itself. They were also pleased to report, "[The] spirit of bitterness and
ill will toward us," apparent in "conduct and conversation of the people from
whom in the course of Divine Providence we have been separated," had in
some been "restrained."[55] Betsy signed the letter on behalf of her meeting
together with a dozen women; John Claypoole signed, too, alongside sixteen
other men.[56]

If Betsy's spiritual career to date had suggested a certain absence of theological conviction—having refused to reconcile with the Society in the wake
of her first marriage, she moved through a number of religious communities
in the decade that followed—now she seems to have embraced a theology and
philosophy to which she was deeply committed. With her coreligionists she
actively sought out, and worked on behalf of, this new gathering of the faithful.

Long after other members drifted back to the Society of Friends, long after the Free Quaker meeting dwindled below viability, Betsy Claypoole continued to support the principles of this meeting for more than half a century.

Whatever comforts the Free Quaker philosophy or theology offered Betsy, they were not formally embraced by any other member of her family in these years, despite the various and sundry entanglements and estrangements that nearly all of them had endured. What was it about the Free Quaker community that appealed to Betsy, but no other Griscoms? Was it the commitment to an unusually generous freedom of conscience? In time, the Quaker community would rethink their position on outward uniformity—the Philadelphia Yearly Meeting gradually eased away from the practice; though Friends today can still be released from membership following a deliberative process much like the one Betsy knew in the eighteenth century, today this is an action of last resort—but for now, the ability to disagree without jeopardizing one's membership in the Society could be found only under the shelter of the Free Quaker meeting.[57] Unity in diversity, strength in multiplicity—these were the values the Free Quakers embraced, and that Betsy Claypoole embraced with them. When Betsy listened closely to the whisperings of the spirit, when she laid herself open to its leadings, she knew that, among this gathering of men and women who valued conviction above conformity, she had found like-minded Friends.

# 17

# Brotherly Love

When William Penn founded his city on the western banks of the Delaware River, he envisioned a community based on principles of generosity, toleration, peace and spiritual unity. He took his name for the city—Philadelphia—from the Greek words *philos* (meaning "love" or "friendship") and *adelphos* (or "brother"): the city of brotherly love. As the nation emerged from war, the Claypoole household embraced Penn's legacy and joined with other Philadelphians eager to attend to the needs of those less fortunate than themselves in a crush of voluntary and benevolent associations. At this early date, there were far more opportunities for men to exercise their charitable energies than women; the real blossoming of women's philanthropic societies was yet a few years distant, and there is no evidence that Betsy Claypoole joined the nation's first such organization, the 1795 Female Society for the Relief of the Distressed.[1] It was John Claypoole, rather than Betsy, who represented the household in a burst of civic energy that is impressive for anyone who today knows both the reward and the burden of community activism. Betsy did not attend weekly committee meetings; she did not tackle correspondence or collect unpaid dues. But John's contributions to the Pennsylvania Abolition Society and the Philadelphia Society for Alleviating the Miseries of Public Prisons cast a slanting light on Betsy's own concerns, assuming she was supportive of her husband's commitments. At the very least, John's activities hint at the stories told around the Claypoole table in these years, tales of hardship much greater than anything Betsy herself had known.

John Claypoole had already proven himself a joiner in 1779, when he followed his uncle into the local Masonic Lodge. Having entered the fraternal order in Maryland, during the war he transferred to Lodge No. 19, a military lodge designed to accommodate soldiers on the move. That lodge surrendered its warrant after the war ended, but when a new warrant was issued in 1787, John quickly affirmed his membership in the reorganized chapter. Two years later, he offered his firm's services for a small job needed by Pennsylvania's Grand Lodge, the umbrella organization for Masonic lodges around the state; Betsy found herself fabricating eight "orders" (probably the ceremonial collars officers wore) from broad and narrow blue ribbon and eighteen yards of lace.[2] Lodge No. 19 met the first and third Thursdays of each month—often enough to keep John in touch with his fellow Masons.[3]

John's initial activities stemmed from the Claypooles' spiritual community. In fall 1785, John and sixteen fellow Free Quakers joined forces to publicly oppose the reopening of the Southwark Theater, closed during the war. Quakers had long opposed theatrical productions. William Penn had tried to keep theater out of his colony from its founding; his 1686 Frame of Government deemed stage plays an "offense against God" which incited people to "Rudeness, Cruelty, Looseness and irreligion."[4] The law was abrogated in 1696, however, when William and Mary withdrew Penn's authority over the colony. Penn was in time restored, and the antitheater policy as well, but the colony's efforts to ban theaters were constantly overturned by the Crown. In 1754, when the Lewis Hallam Company arrived in Philadelphia, a press war erupted as anti- and pro-theater camps tried to influence public opinion. The governor was at last persuaded to grant the company a license, though with stipulations that nothing "indecent or immoral" would appear on a Philadelphia stage. Five years later, Hallam was dead, but his widow, Sarah Hallam, now married to David Douglass, and son, Lewis Jr., returned with the Hallam-Douglass Company (in time shrewdly renamed the American Company) and received permission to build a theater. The city's religious community was incensed; smack in the middle of the Seven Years' War, the frivolity of theater seemed particularly offensive. Petitions followed, and the governor passed yet another bill to ban theaters. This bill, like its predecessors, was repealed, but the company left the city nevertheless.

Six years later, the company returned and met opposition again, though not enough to prevent the opening of the Southwark Theater's 1766 season. As before, complaints, petitions and remonstrances ensued. This particular season of protest peaked in 1767 and 1768—the same years when citizens were acting against the Townshend Duties. The theater received no end of abuse: a "great school of debauchery," the "chair of pestilence," an "abomination before God"—no insult was too great. (Imagine young Betsy's chagrin when in January 1767, just as she was entering her trade, the company performed the farce "The Upholsterer, or, What News?")[5] The company played three seasons between October 1768 and March 1773, but by October 1774, with the Revolution firmly under way, the Continental Congress declared its own opposition to such expensive and unnecessary diversions. In 1779, the state of Pennsylvania passed legislation that would also curb such theatricals. And now, without any Crown authority to overturn colonial efforts to suppress theater, they were likelier to succeed.

In the wake of peace, attempts to reestablish theater revived. In December 1785, John Claypoole and the men of the Free Quaker meeting decided to add their voices to the opposition, drafting a memorial "To the Honorable Representatives of the Freemen of the Commonwealth of Pennsylvania, in General Assembly Met," which they published in January of the following year.[6] Noting the "considerable efforts" afoot to "establish theatrical entertainments in this city," they appealed to the assembly to stand by the policies asserted by their predecessors and uphold the ban. We "cannot stand by, and be silent spectators," they insisted, "whilst so great an evil is impending over the people." Joining with fellow "Christian brethren of other religious societies," they argued that the theater in general is a "perfect contradiction to the spirit of the Christian religion," many plays being "indecent and profane." Simply monitoring their content would never be enough; "even under the best regulations," such activities "tend to draw away the minds of the young and inexperienced into a love of dissipation and sensual pleasures . . . [T]he more we indulge our vices and passions, the less concern we must have for the interest of our country and the prosperity of the public."

The Quaker protest was picked up in January 1786 by newspapers across the United States; the *American Record and Charleston* (Massachusetts) *Advertiser*, the *Columbian Herald* (Charleston, South Carolina), *Loudon's New York Packet*, the *Independent Chronicle and Universal Advertiser* and the *Plymouth Journal and Massachusetts Advertiser* all ran copies of the Quaker appeal.[7] Matters came to a head at the end of 1788 and early 1789, when the state assembly received a petition, with some nineteen hundred signatures, to repeal the antitheater law. The religious community responded with a petition of their own—more than three thousand signatures in all—asserting that the licensing of a theater "would be impolitic and injurious to the virtue, happiness, morals and property of the citizens and productive of many vices and mischiefs."[8] But in the end, the opposition failed; on February 20, 1789, the *Federal Gazette* reported that the assembly voted 35–29 to license the theater, and the issue was settled. The Claypooles would just have to live with it.

But the vice associated with theater was not the family's only preoccupation during these years. There were more egregious sins afoot. In February 1787, the same month when the Claypooles relocated to new quarters, John joined an emerging organization that supported the abolition of slavery.[9]

Betsy Claypoole was no stranger to abolition, a topic that had suffused the Quaker community for most of her life. Her mother was a young woman in Abington when the celebrated preacher Benjamin Lay moved to a spot about a quarter mile from the meetinghouse. A radical activist for the anti-slavery cause, Lay found no gesture too outlandish if it advanced his point. To demonstrate his utter humility, Lay once threw himself on the ground before the Abington meetinghouse, compelling Friends to step over him as they left the building (a pretty showy and not particularly meek action, historians have noted, for a community that valued humility and restraint). Once, he kept the daughter of a slaveholding neighbor hostage in his own home, so that her parents might better appreciate the pain their own enslaved workers felt upon being separated from their children. Lay's most famous action occurred at one of Philadelphia's yearly meetings, when during remarks to the gathered assembly he opened his cloak to reveal a military uniform. Then, declaring that all slave-made products were products of war, he raised and plunged his sword into a hollowed-out Bible filled with pig's blood. The bleeding Bible, the spattered garments of the front-row Friends—none of this would be forgotten, which was of course Lay's aim. So many of Betsy's Philadelphia and Bucks County family were slaveholders that men and women on both sides of the issue certainly took notice of the growing public critique.[10]

The Friends' more organized response to slavery began in the mid-1770s, when the Virginian Benjamin Bannerman took delivery of an enslaved woman named Dinah Nevil and her four children.[11] Nevil insisted that she and her family were free, and asked for public support to secure her liberty. A group of Quakers filed suit on Nevil's behalf, asking the court to void Bannarman's claim to her. Eventually, the court found in favor of Bannerman, and Nevil and her children remained enslaved, but in time, the Friends provided better support to slaves working to secure freedom. In 1775, the short-lived Society for the Relief of Free Negroes Unlawfully Held in Bondage was organized, sixteen of its twenty-four founding members being Quakers.

By that year, as we have seen, Betsy and her first husband, John Ross, shared their Chestnut Street home with an eight-year-old African American child, who worked as their servant. What Betsy and John Ross felt or said about slavery can never be recovered. Nor do we know the child's legal status. But his (or her) presence in their home tied them to systems of African labor. Given Reverend Aeneas Ross's dedication to the work of baptizing slaves and free blacks, it seems certain that at least the child's afterlife was attended to by Betsy's father-in-law, if not Betsy herself.

The Quaker community would continue to keep the slavery debate alive. The chaos of Revolution interrupted their efforts, but early in 1784, the cause was revived. The immediate impetus was provided when two free blacks were accused of being runaway slaves. In summer 1783, the two men were in the Philadelphia workhouse awaiting trial when both committed suicide rather than chance enslavement. The shock to the city was enormous. The Quaker educator Anthony Benezet publicized these events, but their dramatic nature hardly made it necessary. People were eager to be mobilized.[12]

The Pennsylvania Abolition Society was reorganized in 1784, and John Claypoole was proposed for membership at the February 1787 quarterly meeting. Some forty men had assembled at John Todd's schoolhouse at Fourth and Chestnut to discuss the matters before the PAS: the work of the committee charged with proposing improvements to standard labor contracts; the presentation of a silver tankard to a loyal supporter; the election of members proposed and the names of other possible activists. John Todd was a local teacher (his son John Jr. began courting the sprightly Dolley Payne— the future Dolley Madison—right around this time) who made his school available for the PAS's quarterly meetings, and who served on its membership committee. Twelve men were proposed that evening, John Morrison sponsoring Claypoole.[13] At the general meeting that followed, Tench Coxe proposed Benjamin Franklin, and William Jackson proposed Thomas Paine. At his first meeting as a full member, John listened—alongside Benjamin Rush, Tench Coxe and others—as a committee of members was assigned the task of visiting the city's printers to ask them to forgo publishing advertisements for the sale of slaves. His work was under way.

In spring 1787, the group reorganized—with a broader membership—as the Pennsylvania Society for Promoting the Abolition of Slavery, and the Relief of Free Negroes Unlawfully Held in Bondage. Benjamin Franklin was elected its first president, with James Pemberton and Jonathan Penrose serving as his vice presidents and Benjamin Rush and Tench Coxe as secretaries. The membership directed that one thousand copies of their new constitution together with a summary of Pennsylvania's abolition laws be printed, and that the pamphlet together with a copy of Thomas Clarkson's essay on the commerce and slavery of the African be sent to each U.S. governor. "It having pleased the Creator of the world flesh, all the children of men," the constitution began, "it becomes them to consult and promote each other's happiness, as members of the same family, however diversified they may be, by colour, situation, religion, or different states of society." This is particularly true, the men continued, among those who claimed to embrace the "rights of human nature," and who call themselves Christian; for these men and women, the protection of others "detained in bondage, by fraud or violence," demanded their action.[14]

The full group met only quarterly, on the first Monday in January (when officers were elected), April, July and October. In the interim, business was conducted by the Acting Committee, six members trusted with discharging the real work of the Society between general meetings. Because the workload was onerous, two of the six members were relieved of their duties at each quarterly meeting, and two new members appointed in their place. Three months into the reorganization, John Claypoole was appointed to that committee.[15] During the course of his first meeting, the gathering discussed the more than twenty men and women who had recently come to the Society's attention. Among them was Pompey, a man of about twenty-five who had been a slave in New Jersey. His owner, Margaret Tolman, moved to Philadelphia, bringing Pompey with her, with a promise of eventual freedom. That was about four years earlier, and Pompey was still with her. John Claypoole was assigned to the team of members asked to inquire into Pompey's circumstances. The members then turned their attention to a plea that came from a free black woman named Rosannah Lux. Rosannah had signed an indenture placing her daughter Susanna in the household of R. R. Cross, but when Cross shipped Susanna off to New York without her mother's permission, Rosannah came to the Society for help. Eager to contribute to the work of his new group, John accepted Susanna's case, too, together with five others, and at the next meeting took on still more, including that of a young girl, Charity, whose mother had bound her to a widow by the name of Pancake. In her final illness, the widow Pancake transferred the balance of Charity's indenture to her son, Major Pancake, but now her time was up, Charity's mother reported, and yet the girl remained in service. Cross's treatment of another one of his servants was also under scrutiny; Cross had brought a woman named Lucky from Jamaica many years earlier, and he had neither registered her nor held her by indenture. She was among the slaves sent, with Susanna Lux, to New York.

Claypoole embraced his duties with vigor. By the end of the month, he reported to his fellow committee members that he had met with Margaret Tolman, who confirmed Pompey's story, but to no one's surprise, "on general conversation ... suggested the propriety of the Negro rendering her some more service."[16] For his part, Major Pancake claimed that Charity's indenture extended until she reached thirty-one, not eighteen. So no resolution was achieved there, either. At this same meeting, John agreed to take on yet another case: a woman named Silve, now in her midtwenties, had weathered the storms of Revolution. Her parents were free, and sometime before the fighting broke out they bound their daughter to John Watkins, a New York City blacksmith. She was hired out to a man with the British army, who took Silve with him when he sailed for Yorktown; she was captured along with him and Cornwallis at Yorktown. She fell into the hands of John Caldwell, who brought her back to Philadelphia and sold her to a tavernkeeper. Caldwell had since been arrested for robbery but managed to escape.

By August, John Claypoole was able to report that Judge George Bryant had found Susanna Lux to be a servant of R. R. Cross (as Rosannah had asserted from the outset), but that she could not legally be taken out of Pennsylvania. But Lucky was luckier; the judge found in her favor, and the manumission papers had already been filed. It was not long before he could add that his team had talked with Pompey, and, not surprisingly, he was "not willing to render her [Margaret Tolman] any more service"; since he was a man of twenty-five, the committee decided "they could not think themselves justified in urging the matter." Neither was Major Pancake willing to release Charity, but he promised to think it over. In more positive news, Judge Bryant had found in Silve's favor and declared her free, too.[17] In the end, Charity resolved her own matter; the committee reported that when they went to see how Major Pancake's contemplations were progressing, he reported that Charity "had left his service and that he relinquished all claim to her."[18] There was no further news of Silve.

Before summer ended, scandal erupted when the Society's secretary, Tench Coxe, himself became the object of the Society's scrutiny; the membership discovered that he had helped ship a woman named Peggy and her daughter Mariah to St. Croix. The Acting Committee drafted a statement chastising Coxe for his inexplicable behavior and appointed Claypoole along with John Warner to deliver the text to their errant colleague.[19] One can imagine the pair's puzzled expression when Coxe explained that he had somehow misunderstood the Society's policies; he hadn't anticipated its objection but would pledge to retrieve the two women. Claypoole reported this response to the meeting, and in time, Coxe did follow through, confirming in January 1788 that the two women had returned safely to Philadelphia. Claypoole's duties also brought him to the home of the great Benjamin Franklin himself. When the Acting Committee wanted a decision as to whether an address received by the Society's membership merited publication, they asked Claypoole to take the text to Society president Franklin for a decision. Days later, Claypoole was able to report that his team had indeed visited Franklin, who "expressed his satisfaction of the establishment of that Society" and agreed that the document should be published.[20]

And so it went. In October 1787, the committee visited the workhouse and found there a man named George who had been committed by Plunket Fleeson "after taking his free papers from him." The committee went to the magistrate, who sent George on his way.[21] Another high-profile case came Claypoole's way when in November, Stephen Girard was rumored to be about to move to the West Indies, taking several of his servants with him. Claypoole was asked to address this matter as well, and went to Girard's to investigate further. Girard admitted that, yes, he was making travel plans, and taking his slave Abram, but that it was simply a voyage and both he and Abram would be returning to the city. Just to be sure, they got that in writing.[22]

Captive African Americans were not the only people who concerned John Claypoole. The occupants of the city's prisons also endured uncertain welfare. In August 1787, John joined the Philadelphia Society for Alleviating the Miseries of Public Prisons.[23] The men who embraced prison reform tended to be the same men who worked on behalf of enslaved African Americans; the membership of both reform societies overlapped to a notable degree. And both organizations operated along similar lines, assigning members to monitor and advocate for particular cases. At times, some of the cases themselves crossed over, as a number of the men and women observed by the prison group's Acting Committee would come to the attention of the abolitionist group's Acting Committee. It was easy for men to bring business from one group to the attention of the other.

This particular reform effort was not the first time Philadelphians expressed their collective dismay at conditions in the city's jail. In February 1776, the Philadelphia Society for Assisting Distressed Prisoners formed, and a "considerable Number of Citizens cheerfully became members." The Society worked toward its mission for about nineteen months, until the following minute was entered in its record book: "The British Army having entered the City of Philadelphia in September (1777) and possessed themselves of the Public Gaols, no further service could be rendered nor was any Election held this month for the appointment of new managers, so that the Philadelphia Society for Assisting Distressed Prisoners was dissolved during this memorable period." The members of the revived Society noted this earlier episode in their own minutes to honor the laudable impulses of their fellow citizens.[24]

Organized—or reorganized, as it were—in May 1787, the newly constituted body of concerned citizens chose, on the first page of their minute book, to note the scripture that inspired them to action: "I was in prison & ye came unto me, and the king shall answer, & say unto them, verily I say unto you, in as much as ye have done it unto one of the least of these my brethren, ye have done it unto me" (Matthew 25.36.40). The Society's constitution set out its plan. Physicians would be sent into the prison to assess conditions. As with the abolitionist group, the heart of the Society was a rotating Acting Committee charged with visiting the prison at least weekly to monitor the circumstances of individual prisoners. These men would report abuses back to the group's officers. Members would pay ten shillings in annual dues and meet on the second Monday of January, April, July and October. So for John Claypoole and other like-minded Philadelphians (John Morrison, for instance, who proposed Claypoole for membership in the PAS, was a founding member of the prison reform effort as well), the first Monday of the month would be devoted to the welfare of slaves and the second to prisoners.

The organization was embraced immediately. More than eighty people joined at a single meeting at the German School House on Cherry Alley on August 13, including the luminaries Benjamin and William Temple Franklin, Philip Benezet, James Pemberton, Henry Drinker and Christopher Marshall—both Sr. and Jr. Notably, Henry Drinker had been imprisoned during the Revolutionary War, though under different circumstances as one of the Quaker men exiled to Winchester, Virginia, along with James Pemberton, Samuel Pleasants and Thomas Affleck, who also joined this Society. The cause held obvious appeal for John Claypoole, only too familiar with the plight of prisoners who had to beg for food, warmth or other basic comforts. Betsy, too, well knew the consequences of such deprivation, which had robbed her of a husband

and her daughter Eliza a father. John's stories helped her imagine it all the more vividly.

At an early meeting, the members of the Acting Committee were advised to acquire a copy of the English philanthropist John Howard's *State of the Prisons in England and Wales.* They sent Howard a letter describing their project and shared their hope that he would stay in touch. The group also sought to review the effects of recent penal law on the "criminals now at work in our streets." It was a reference to the notorious "wheelbarrow law" of 1786, which sentenced convicts to hard labor on the city's streets. The sewer running along Fourth Street from High Street to Harmony Court was allegedly dug by convicts secured by ball and chain to each other, under the watch of armed guards. Authors of the legislation hoped that giving prisoners something constructive to do would relieve the tedium of incarceration, but in time city residents came to resent, and fear, the unavoidable interaction with "wheelbarrow men," who were intimidating at best, threatening at worst.[25] In the recollection of one observer, the uniform of the jailed men itself inspired fear. Like the orange jumpsuits of today, the prison-issued apparel (one half of their jacket and pants blue, the other half drab, with the hair on their head half shaven, too) was meant to make prisoners immediately visible. And indeed, as another observer noted, they made a "horrid spectacle."[26] Benjamin Rush was among those appalled, and what's more, he thought the policy counterproductive; as these prisoners endured the humiliation of public punishment, he argued, they would only become more estranged from society, and as citizens cultivated their fear of these men, the chance that they would be absorbed back into the community at the end of their sentence grew slim.[27] The reformers hoped to assess its "influence upon Society, and whether the law is duly executed, if not to collect such observations as may assist in correcting any abuses suffered therein."[28]

A report of the Visiting Committee filed in summer 1788 offers a glimpse of the work the reformers undertook while in the jails. While on a visit, one prisoner used his blanket to climb over the wall separating the quarters for criminals from the debtor's yard. The jailer ordered him into the East Wing, but no sooner were the doors locked than he "turned with the fury of a madman with threats and language of the most abusive Nature against the committee—causing the jailer to remark that should Justice [William] Pollard ever brave the jail, it'd be at risk—at which the men in the West Wing, crowded to the windows, erupted in agreement." The "wheelbarrow men" threatened often that if Pollard should ever visit, they would "cut his hair off and disfigure him so that he should not be known." The committeemen next moved to the debtors' apartment, where the "same spirit prevailed." Most of the women they encountered appeared to be drunk, "fighting and in general confusion"; when the jailer took some of the most disruptive into another room, debtors seized the moment to tell the committeemen that thieves among them were constantly stealing their clothing—they could never take their hats off for fear of them being stolen—and asked whether those imprisoned for debt might be separated from those jailed for more violent offenses. The committeemen suggested that they submit a petition toward that end to the jailer, but the debtors were terrified that "if their names were known to the Criminals, their lives would be in danger," which, they added, the jailer well knew.

The circumstances the committeemen encountered were both tragic and predictable. People awaiting trial, for instance, often ran out of clothing—especially shirts and stockings and "warm coverings." Sometimes the clothing had simply worn out, but in other cases it was because inmates traded anything they had for liquor. More than a little of the clothing the Society provided to destitute inmates got swapped for rum. Worse, sometimes new inmates were forcibly stripped so that their clothes could be sold. Reformers argued that, because the law failed to meet the needs of distressed prisoners and could not prevent the abuse of charitable donations, these trades appeared to be an "evil without remedy," but if a prison uniform was instituted, they reasoned, it would be impossible to trade or sell. As for the prisoners' diet, working criminals received an allowance, while those awaiting trial received a half of a fourpenny loaf each day, but no provision was made for people being held as witnesses. In these cases, a "stranger accidentally present at the commission of a criminal action without friends to enter security for his appearance as evidence is committed to Gaol for the benefit of the community, and suffers more than the actual criminal."[29] Similarly, reformers noted, prisoners acquitted of their crime, but nevertheless unable to pay the associated fees, often languished without aid. The population of imprisoned women who were breast-feeding was large enough to receive notice as well, since they did not receive any additional allotment; one winter alone, the Society provided one hundred gallons of soup to this class of inmates. No bedding or straw was regularly supplied, open chimneys provided little warmth—the list went on and on.

At the January 14, 1788, meeting at the Baptist Meeting House in Lodge Alley, John Claypoole was appointed to the Electing Committee, charged with admitting new members.[30] Later that month, the Society's secretary recorded the group's petition to the Pennsylvania Assembly in which they made their case for reforming penal law.[31] Punishing criminals by "hard labor *publickly* [*sic*] & disgracefully imposed," as the preamble dictates, should be revised; punishments of "more *private* or even *Solitary* labor" would more likely "reclaim" the "unhappy objects." The latter course also would limit the exposure of "young minds" to "vicious characters" and would prevent prisoners from taking the opportunity of their temporary access to the streets to beg. They also urged the separation of men and women, and that more effort be made to keep liquor out of the mix. Perhaps because he and Betsy lived so near the publisher of the *Pennsylvania Gazette,* Claypoole was asked to serve on the committee charged with getting fifty copies of the petition published, to collect signatures, and to "attend any Committee the House of Assembly may appoint on the Said Case."

The following year, a missive to Pennsylvania's Supreme Executive Council articulated three main lines of concern: the mixing of sexes, the use of liquor and the indiscriminate confinement of debtors and criminals. The latter topic had been raised in November 1787, on a list of complaints submitted by the prisoners themselves. Men held for debt resented living alongside those whose crimes were more violent or more treacherous. The friends and wives who visit them, they noted, are "search'd, in the most insulting and indecent manner for spirituous liquour"; not that they didn't bring any—they did, and it would get seized—another cause for complaint. These prisoners also objected when a comparatively compassionate turnkey was replaced with "a couple of fellows devoid of Humanity and feelings & Hackney'd in the ways of Cruelty from a long servitude." They insulted and hit the debtors, prisoners claimed and made visitors wait in the cold while they finished their breakfast. "The interference of the Society to get humane persons to fill that station," they believed, "will greatly assist in mitigating our Sufferings & Relieve even our friends from the dread of insult."[32] Finally, the "necessaries" (that is, the outhouses) "are not fit for your committees' inspection" and may well pose a health hazard—the debtor class happily proposed making one of the criminal class clean them every third day. The committee agreed, and pressed the Supreme Executive Council to remedy their complaints—not least because they also worried that debtors who mixed with the criminal class too often became convicts themselves. They had "reason to believe" that corrupting influence had led to the ruin of many otherwise good, but unlucky, men. The same, to be sure, was true among the women; female convicts who associated with girls and young women confined temporarily by masters or mistresses as a punishment had a corrupting influence. Lastly, they conceded that criminals had little or nothing to do all day and became desperate to be in the streets—hence their recommendation that labor be assigned, but that it be solitary, so that it was clearly a punishment and not just an escape (meta-phorical or real).

John Claypoole's burst of civic activism appears to have been short-lived. The constitution of the Pennsylvania Society for Promoting the Abolition of Slavery stipulated that every member contribute ten shillings per year, with two shillings six pence due at each quarter, but by 1788, the group's membership lists note Claypoole as "unable to pay his quarterly dues"; in fact, lists of "Members in Arrears" regularly included his name.[33] This was nothing out of the ordinary; as with many such organizations (then as now), getting the membership to pay their dues occupied a great deal of the treasurer's attention. When Claypoole was noted as being in arrears for half of 1787 and all of 1788, he was in good company; fully a third of the membership had not yet managed to bring their accounts up to date. But apparently Claypoole never did. Members who failed to pay for more than two years, "upon due notice" of their delinquency, were ejected. He still remained interested—when W. W. Woodward's Front Street print shop brought out an edition of the *View of the life, travels, and philanthropic labors of the late John Howard*, Claypoole was among the subscribers—but became less active himself.[34] Claypoole would also contribute to the Philadelphia Dispensary for the Medical Relief of the Poor, but he did not become especially active in this cause.[35]

Part of the explanation for Claypoole's withdrawal from civic life may be found in the fact that the upholstery shop moved around this time. Perhaps the crowded field was proving a challenge. In February 1787, Betsy with her growing family left Arch Street and moved to a new address. That same month, a notice in the *Pennsylvania Packet*—placed of course by "John Claypoole, upholsterer"—alerted "the public in general, and his Friends and customers in particular," that the shop could now be found at a new stand on the southwest corner of Race and Second streets (today beneath the approach to the Ben Franklin Bridge), and where he would continue to carry on the upholstery business "in all its various branches."[36]

John's 1787 advertisement hints at other changes in the business as well. The notice, for instance, drew readers' particular attention to their stock of wallpapers. Whatever contribution John Claypoole was able to make to the production of upholstery goods, he would steer Betsy's enterprise in new directions, too. As the couple began papering rooms, they moved toward the cutting edge of an emerging fashion. As one memoirist recalled, "All the houses which I remember to have seen in my youth were whitewashed only;

there may have been some rare exceptions," but in general the papering of walls (despite the early efforts of the indefatigable Plunket Fleeson to promote the fashion) "was not much introduced til after the year 1790."[37] As the Claypooles stocked this new trend in wall treatments, they hoped to capture the business of Philadelphians eager to re-create their homes—and themselves—in the new Republic.

The notice also directed readers to "some very handsome mahogany furniture to be disposed of, viz. sofas, easy chairs, desks, tables, chairs, etc." This, too, creates a changing picture of the couple's enterprise. Now they required not simply a workroom with space to display materials, but also some sort of salesroom where potential customers could browse among ready-made furniture.[38] The Claypooles' decision to sell ready-made furniture was part of the larger change in the furniture market. Consumers had always been able to find already-made upholstered goods on the secondhand market, but in the decades following the American Revolution, shoppers perceived the rise of ready-made inventory—a mix of new and used—in furniture stores that began to look like something we'd recognize today. George Haughton's 1777 shop was an early example, and in 1783, John Mason called his shop "John Mason and Comp. Upholstery store," noting that customers there could examine a variety of finished goods for ready sale.[39] In 1798, Cocks & Co. advertised their "large assortment of Household Furniture, New and Second Hand. They . . . take Second Hand Furniture in exchange for New," with the "most money given for Furniture, Beds and Bedding."[40] One need not commission a piece and wait for it to be made; consumers in the early Republic could now find their desires satisfied immediately.

Picturing their shops, our limited historical imagination usually fails to conjure the crowded and cluttered nature of early American life. Neat, spare period room installations in historic house and living history museums too often cue overly tidy visions of the early American past, but if you want to picture what an eighteenth-century shop really was like, head to New York City's fashion district, where shops bursting with buttons and trims best capture the teeming nature of eighteenth-century life. An inventory of Claypooles' competitor John Davis gives us the best glimpse of what their own enterprise looked like in these years. Over five hundred pounds of curled hair lay waiting to be stuffed into seats and chair bottoms, and half again that much moss. Close to three hundred yards of assorted fringe in various colors—light blue, yellow, pea green, as well as combinations of white with yellow, green, blue or purple—lay neatly in boxes and bins, ready for their application, alongside yards of gimp—as many as twenty lengths, of every color. More than thirteen dozen tassels and close to four hundred yards of binding awaited the client's shrewd eye. Davis's shop contained more than seventy gross "colored line, cut pieces."[41] In one case were stored another thirty gross line, eleven gross lace and nineteen dozen tassels, in another almost twelve hundred tassels and close to three thousand pieces of fringe; a third held still more tassels—almost five hundred—together with yards of silk lace, four cattail mattresses, remnants of cloth, thread and paper.[42] Fabric around the shop included plain and striped satin, moreen durants and ticklenburg. The Claypoole shop also included yards of wallpaper (sold then in panels rather than the rolls so familiar today) and, in a salesroom, the array of furniture to which his newspaper notice drew attention.

A final line in the February 1787 notice that Claypoole placed in the *Pennsylvania Packet* to announce that the Claypoole shop had relocated suggests that John and Betsy may indeed have suffered some sort of financial reversal around the same time John quit paying his membership dues. If 1786 found them enjoying the luxury of a horse and carriage, 1787 found them looking for new sources of income. The ad mentioned rental space in the cellar, but of more import to Betsy was this line: "Two or three gentlemen may be accommodated with Genteel Board and Lodging on reasonable terms."[43]

Betsy now added boardinghouse keeper to her other duties around the shop and for her family. She was by no means alone; many households took in a little extra money by keeping lodgers.[44] But, like many businesses, boardinghouses in the 1780s were still sought and found by word of mouth, as boarders seeking housing simply asked around for referrals. In 1787, only a handful of homes placed notices seeking boarders.[45] That John was among them suggests that he was serious about finding some extra income—which rings true in months when he was behind on his dues for the Abolition Society. The Claypooles, it seems, were overextended. Betsy would have to augment the income she raised through the shop with work around the house as well. The duties for the women who accepted lodgers were not particularly onerous, but it was more linens to wash, more food to prepare, more dishes to do. Eliza was by now almost big enough to be of some genuine help to her mother, but Clarissa was five weeks away from the terrible twos, and Susan just fourteen weeks old. One can picture the level stare with which John's proposal was met.

Then, after only a year in the shop at Race and Second, in May 1788 John Claypoole placed another notice in the newspaper to announce to the public that the upholstery shop had moved again, this time to a new location on

Second Street.[46] The house stood just a few doors away from the City Tavern, a gathering place for the city's merchants—surely an enviable spot to attract the attention of Philadelphia's movers and shakers. John's notice assured readers that he "continue[d] to carry on the Business of an Upholsterer In all its various branches," pledging to service his customers "with care and punctuality, and on reasonable terms," while a "few gentlemen may be accommodated with Board and Lodging."

If John looked at this move as a means to improve the family's future, Betsy had in some ways returned home, or at least to her roots. The house on South Second Street appears to have been the very home that Betsy's great-grandfather, Andrew Griscom, built in the 1680s on the land granted by William Penn.[47] So posh in its day, the century-old building was well out of date. It was now owned by one of Betsy's Griscom relatives—perhaps they were getting a break on the rent. The landmark Slate House was nearly across the street, another of the many reminders of her family's long history in Pennsylvania. As she walked the rooms once occupied by Andrew and Sarah Griscom, Betsy was surrounded by evidence of the past. It's probably just as well that she could not see the future.

# · 18 ·

# Fever

As Philadelphia entered the last decade of the eighteenth century, Betsy approached her seventh wedding anniversary. Now a wife and mother well into her thirties, she was no longer the tentative young craftswoman eager to please the Revolutionary leadership, nor was she a woman alone in a city at war, or the worried wife and then widow of an active soldier. As she and John nurtured their business and threw themselves into the civic voluntarism prompted in part by their shared faith, they quietly began to provide a sense of stability for the larger Griscom clan. When trouble came—and it did— Betsy and John could be relied on to help.

Betsy's father was now a man of seventy and showing his age more every year. No longer in need of much space, the Griscoms, who had already moved once, in 1791 or 1792, downsized again, trading their house on Vine Street for still smaller quarters on McCullough's Court, near their daughter Mary Morgan and her family, which by now included three boys and a girl.[1] They kept just the essentials. The parlor still contained the old walnut high chest and matching low chest, as well as the walnut chamber table and tea table. One looking glass was broken, but another remained to reflect light and like-ness. Their bedstead, featherbed, bolster and two pillows (surely made by their girls) were cloaked with painted cotton. Three Windsor chairs sat near a walnut dining table—all they really needed now. The walnut desk where Samuel had for so long kept his accounts followed them to their new quarters, too. And of course he packed and moved his well-used tools—forty planes and his chest full of carpenter's tools—though occasions for their use came more rarely.[2]

One has to wonder what Samuel made of his circumstances as he moved into these modest rooms. Close to seven thousand houses now stood in Philadelphia. He had seen thousands rise—around 4,600, to be more precise—since he moved to the city in the 1750s.[3] The bright future that Samuel Griscom anticipated when a young builder in a booming port city had gone seriously awry as Pennsylvania severed its royal ties. In fact, he watched his whole community of tradesmen scramble and regroup. After independence the Carpenters' Company struggled to recover. After brokering a deal with the competing Friendship Carpenters' Company (an effort to protect the interests of the city's longtime carpenters against the encroachments of carpenters flooding in to rebuild the injured city), the now-united company devoted itself to the creation of a revised price book that reflected the demands of postwar building. New architectural styles necessarily transformed the nature—and the value—of the skills the trade demanded. Better and more elaborate construction also meant better and more expensive materials. But the unity among masters that made such efforts possible belied tensions between masters and journeymen; the forces unleashed by the Revolution were transforming social and labor relations in the capital city.[4] A world in which deference to one's superiors had been assumed (whether genuine or phony is something historians continue to debate) gave way to a world in which men asserted their equality as a matter of principle. The seeds of Philadelphia's labor movement had been planted.[5] Men like Samuel Griscom became artifacts of the colonial past in more ways than one.

At least he could look with pride on his hardworking children and now growing numbers of grandchildren. Betsy and John Claypoole continued to run their upholstery shop on South Second Street, and to cultivate their small garden of girls.[6] Nine-year-old Eliza was old enough to help mind little Clarissa and Susan, five and four years old now and almost ready for school. Another daughter, Rachel, had been born in February 1789 and was just now beginning to toddle around their home. Perhaps the fun of watching their youngest master her chubby little legs gave them some respite from the string of troubles her first years saw.

A spate of bad luck began when Betsy's sister Hannah lost her house on Front Street just above the Hay Scales. In fact, trouble had started even earlier, when Hannah's husband, the shipwright Griffith Levering, died in August 1788, leaving her with six children under the age of ten, including a babe-in-arms born at the end of October. Griff was just thirty-three when he died.

His illness was short and severe—though he weathered it (as the friends who placed a notice in the local papers would attest) "with that patience and resignation which can only arise from a consciousness of a life well spent."[7] The grief of his family and friends proved a "tribute due to the memory of a man, who when living meritted [*sic*] the esteem of all who knew him."[8] "By his industry," his obituary would observe, he "supported a large family, who are now left to mourn the loss of so good a husband, parent and master." But his industry must have met his family's day-to-day needs and little more. Once a member of the Baptist congregation, in time Levering had found himself drawn to the Universalist teachings of Elhanan Winchester. By the 1780s, he and Hannah appear to have been in the orbit of Betsy's Free Quaker meeting (though they do not seem to have been formal members); he would be buried under their auspices, his grave marked by a stone in their burying ground.[9]

The following spring, Hannah and her brother-in-law Everard Bolton, Griff's executors, auctioned the household's goods to satisfy his debts. One Saturday afternoon found the family gathered for the grim task of watching Hannah's home dismantled and sold to the highest bidders, themselves trying to preserve as much as possible on her behalf.[10] Everard purchased forty-seven pounds of loaf sugar, eight and a half pounds of indigo and four bottles of snuff, as well as two sets of sweeping brushes and another set of scrubbing brushes. He also rescued a tea table, eleven Windsor chairs, her kitchen furniture, a pair of andirons and some sheets and table linens. Isaac Bolton (Everard's father) attended the auction as well (presumably on Hannah's behalf rather than for his own benefit) and bought more than seventy pounds of sugar, as well as twelve pounds of Bohea tea and six pounds of hard soap; he also acquired two silver tablespoons and Levering's silver watch. Despite Samuel's own reduced circumstances, he chipped in, buying the Leverings' china and glassware, a bed, and a bureau table and chest. The Claypooles paid for a dozen sweeping brushes as well as a bed and bedstead. In a gesture only a sister could truly appreciate, Rachel spent six shillings for Hannah's only pair of window curtains.

Hannah was able to preserve a keg of gin, some vinegar, eleven pounds of chocolate and fifteen bottles of mustard. She also kept a saw and steelyards as well as six sheets of tin and Griffith's gun, the family's books and some of her husband's clothing. She watched others cart away her husband's desk, their looking glass and tea server. Samuel Fletcher, the clerk of the auction, took the opportunity to acquire the Leverings' Rittenhouse stove as well as a pair of andirons, tongs and a fireplace shovel. Hannah now began coping with the realities of widowhood. She owed back rent, and the bill for the children's schooling was overdue. By April 1790, Griff's real estate was also auctioned off.[11] In time Hannah opened a small grocery store on North Front Street.[12]

As if worrying about Hannah's future were not trouble enough, Betsy also saw her cousin Rebecca Griscom's circumstances take an unwelcome turn. Apparently, forty-four-year-old Rebecca was no longer able to maintain herself with her own income. A November 1789 edition of the *Gazette* announced, for all their friends and neighbors to see: "By virtue of a writ of Venditioni Exponas to me directed, will be exposed to sale by public vendue, at the Merchants Coffee house in Second street, on Wed the 2 day of December next, at five o'clock in the evening, a certain two story brick messuage or tenement . . . Taken in execution, and to be sold as the property of Rebecca Griscom."[13] The family braced for another auction. Rebecca seems to have been living in that home at least as early as 1772 as a relatively young woman, but she was unable to maintain it—for reasons that, as we shall see, shed light not only on the vulnerability to which unmarried craftswomen like Rebecca were necessarily subject, but also on Betsy's unfortunately long experience with loved ones grappling with mental illness.[14]

Where Rebecca spent the years immediately following is unknown. But by spring 1794, she requested permission to move to the Quaker almshouse, a request to which the meeting consented.[15] Built in 1729 on the south side of Walnut between Third and Fourth streets, the almshouse took in aged Friends without other means of support. Betsy's sister Rebecca, too, by these years was no longer able to maintain an independent living and was also forced to seek public support; having been disowned some years earlier for her dependence on alcohol, she was unable to access the Friends almshouse, so she sought admission, in 1792, to the city almshouse. Apparently she had not conquered her demons; the guardians of the poor found that she was still "addicted to liquor."[16]

A third blow to the family came when, after so many years of having survived the considerable risks associated with a sailor's life, William Donaldson was lost at sea. His wife, Betsy's sister Sarah, had died just a few years earlier, leaving William to care for their daughters Margaret, Sarah and Susanna (now thirteen, ten and Susanna still younger), though how he managed while he was working as a mariner is a mystery; the aunts and uncles must have been stepping in for some years already when Donaldson went missing. In midsummer 1790, the city's Overseers of the Poor, concerned about the welfare of William's daughter Sarah, officially assigned the girl to the household of Everard and Deborah Bolton "to be taught the art & mystery of sewing, housewifery, reading and writing."[17] Margaret moved in with Aunt Betsy and

Uncle John—another "daughter" to add to their noisy family, and Susanna found a new home, too, probably also with the Claypooles, since the first federal census in 1790 found seven women living in the household that year. Census takers also found two men in addition to John in the house—perhaps the hoped-for boarders, or apprentices to the upholstery shop.[18]

With his household expanding, John Claypoole needed to enlarge his household's income to match its enlarged demands. In addition to the evidence that the upholstery business was perhaps struggling, in truth he probably made very little material contribution there. John began looking for work, and where better than the newly arrived federal government? Like thousands of veterans, Claypoole sought a position in President Washington's administration. In early September 1790, he sent a letter to his former commander in chief, seeking a bureaucratic position: "I entreat your pardon for taking this method of presenting my petition," Claypoole wrote, "as I had not an [opportunity] of sending it in the usual way. I make bold to inclose the opinion of some of my fellow cittizens [sic] with respect to my qualifications as an officer in aid of the Customs. Wishing not to intrude on your time, I have only to promise, that should you be pleas'd to appoint me, I shall exert my best abilities in a faithfull [sic] discharge of the duties of that appointment. I take the liberty to subscribe myself with every sentiment of respect Your hum'l Serv't." He added a postscript: "If it should please you to order me to your presence before you leave this citty [sic], or send an answer I live 3 doors above the Citty tavern."[19] The names of the men who supplied Claypoole's letters of reference, and the contents of their testimonials, are no longer known, but they were not enough to secure him an immediate post. Perhaps, too, Claypoole hoped that their shared association with the Masonic Lodge would help him land a job. Apparently the fact that Claypoole was the husband of the former Betsy Ross did not spur Washington to prompt action, if he was aware of the connection. Weeks passed, and no reply arrived.

The Claypoole upholstery enterprise was of course still active. Betsy and John would seem to have been positioned well in that particular market. Few of their competitors, with the exception of John Mason, could claim the longevity—and persistence—in the community that Betsy Claypoole enjoyed, and with her marriage to John she was now allied with the prominent family of joiners and artists. That she had relocated to a spot near the famed City Tavern couldn't have hurt; by 1790, City Tavern had become as much a center of business acumen as it had once been a center of political agitation. An advertisement from these years, noting that the enterprise was under new management, announced the advent of "The Merchants' Coffee-House, and

Place of Exchange, Opened and established by the subscriptions of Merchants, Captains of Vessels and other Gentlemen at the CITY-TAVERN, in Second Street." The intent of the original subscribers was met with a vengeance, the tavern quickly becoming an epicenter of local commerce.[20]

Around this time, John did find a job with the federal government, as messenger to the Comptroller's office. It was not a big job and did not pay particularly well—he earned not quite $16.50 for work performed between January and September 1792—but it was a foot in the door.[21] In that same year, John Claypoole took other, more marked action aimed at embracing economic opportunity: he packed up his traveling chest and set to sea again, headed for South America, and more specifically to Demerara (today part of Guyana), "to look after an estate bequeathed to him by the will of an old friend."[22]

Demerara, like Pennsylvania, had been colonized by both Dutch and British settlers who hoped to profit from coffee, cotton and sugar plantations there. Demerara spirits could be had by the hogshead at George Meade's shop on Second Street at Lodge's Alley—a stone's throw from the Claypoole home.[23] England seized the opportunity of the Revolution to capture the colony from Holland (an ally of the rebelling United States). In the aftermath of the peace, it was returned. But by then, colonists who had tasted freedom and prosperity during the comparatively unfettered years of wartime trading were reluctant to submit to the rule of a Dutch trading company, and as of January 1, 1792, the company lost its charter.[24] When John Claypoole sailed there later that year, the colony reported directly to the Dutch States General. But the population included growing numbers of British planters, drawn by the promise of profit from the cotton, coffee and sugar plantations. Just who bequeathed land here to John Claypoole remains a mystery, but if it was one of the lucrative plantations outside Georgetown, it would certainly have been worth the trip to claim it. Sometime in late spring or early summer, with his wife's sixth pregnancy just starting to show, John set out.

Interestingly, Demerara was just then caught up in its own colonial struggle, also grounded in discontent over taxes and representation. Planters in Demerara had drawn up a proposal, the Concept Plan of Redress, that involved a reorganization of the government and assertion of constitutional reforms. When the Dutch West India Company's charter was allowed to expire in 1792, the Concept Plan of Redress was implemented, and Demerara and its neighboring colony, Essequibo, became the United Colony of Demerara and Essequibo, and came under the direct control of the Dutch government. Was the timing of Claypoole's trip driven at all by these dramatic events? Was he trying to get there before, or after, the collapse of the Dutch administration?

While he was away, and just before their daughter Jane was born in mid-November, Betsy moved her family into a new home on Front Street at the corner of Norris' Alley, where they would remain for the next seventeen years.[25] The brick town house was typical of the neighborhood: two stories high, with a single-story brick kitchen in the back, it was just a smidge larger than those around it—most houses in their neighborhood, the Walnut Ward, were around 900 square feet, while Betsy's home measured 936 over two floors.[26] That Betsy should make a change while John was away suggests that the move may not have been entirely voluntary. The Bank of Pennsylvania, incorporated in 1793, would over the course of the next few years rise on the site of the Claypoole's Second Street home. Perhaps they were forced to move by the sale of the building, or perhaps the growing family was simply looking for more space.

The house Betsy chose was among the city's oldest, dating from the city's infancy.[27] According to Betsy's grandson William Canby, it was a "quaint old double house (two houses in one) with gable to the street." "[The family] lived here for many years," Canby added, "when they moved into the adjoining house next door." The house appears to have been larger than that of many artisanal families (the Claypooles—all nine of them—enjoyed almost 300 more square feet than most artisanal families across Philadelphia), and the property more valuable; while the mean value of Philadelphia dwellings and lots at the time of the 1798 direct tax came in at $1,741, John and Betsy's property was worth $2,250.[28] The Philadelphia antiquarian John Fanning Watson would begin a discussion of "Rare Old Houses" with a description of this building, noting that "the only house of size now in Philadelphia with gable end front on the street, is to be seen at the south-west corner of Front Street and Norris' Alley. It formerly had a balcony and door at its second story, and its windows in leaden frames; one of which still remains on the alley side of the house."[29] Just a door or two south stood another house "remarkable for having in its foundation a large brick on which was scratched before burning—'This is the sixth house built in Philadelphia.'"[30] Perhaps these buildings, too, were the work of Andrew Griscom.

This new neighborhood on Front Street was a lot like their old one, filled with a variety of shops and artisans. On their side of the block, closer to Chestnut, one could find the goldsmith Joseph Richardson and the ironmonger Nathaniel Richardson; a bit farther along was John Elliot's looking-glass manufactory. From there one could smell the mustard manufactory John Dixon ran, and hear the forge of the brass founder Daniel King. Just their side of the merchant Samuel Coates was Margaret Fennell, a competing upholsterer, and

James Brice, yet another, was near the corner of Walnut. Across the street was the clock- and watchmaker Ephraim Clark, the hairdresser James Mathews and the tobacconist and bologna sausage maker Anthony Vitally, one of fewer than a dozen Italians in the city decades before anyone could envision an Italian market.

Baby Jane arrived in due course in November 1792, and John returned home safely to find his family ensconced in their new home. With a new house and a new shop to get settled, there was plenty of work to be done. But before they celebrated their first anniversary in the house, calamity struck.

In the late summer of 1793, yellow fever gripped Philadelphia. Before it was all over, between four and five thousand people would die. Another seventeen thousand—of the city's population of some fifty thousand—fled during the outbreak. To put the magnitude of the tragedy in perspective, one contemporary observer has noted that "it would be as if a disease were to sweep through Washington and its suburbs today killing about 400,000 people between late August and November."[31] As news of the epidemic broke, Samuel and Rebecca Griscom surely recalled the tense weeks during the fall of 1762, when the city was last ravaged by epidemic disease and they buried their twins Joseph and Abigail. Dr. John Redman, assisted by his eager apprentice, the then-seventeen-year-old Benjamin Rush, had responded to that outbreak. Redman believed that the fever originated in a cluster of "small back tenements, forming a kind of court, the entrance to which was by two narrow alleys from Front and Pine Streets, and where sailors often had their lodgings, to which a sick sailor from on board a vessel from the Havannah (where it then raged) was brought privately after night, before the vessel had come up to town, to the house of one Leadbetter, where he soon died, and was secretly buried; and I believe Leadbetter, with most of his family and many others in that court, soon after fell a sacrifice to the distemper."[32] If some of the Griscoms were exposed but recovered in 1762, it would have given them some immunity from the 1793 virus, but not everyone would be so fortunate.[33]

When faced with another epidemic at the end of the century, Rush—now a seasoned physician—also recalled the 1762 episode. In that year, he remembered, "in the months of August, September, October, November, and December, the bilious yellow fever prevailed in Philadelphia, after a *very hot summer*, and spread like a plague, carrying off daily, for some time, upwards of twenty persons. These patients were generally seized with rigors, which were succeeded with a violent fever and pains in the head and back. The pulse was full, and sometimes irregular. The eyes were inflamed, and had a yellow cast, and vomiting almost always attended. The third, fifth, and seventh days were mostly critical, and the disease generally terminated in one of them, in life or death. An eruption on the third or seventh day over the body, proved salutary. An excessive heat, and burning about the region of the liver, with cold extremities, portended death to be at hand."[34]

Betsy Claypoole, like Rush, surely remembered those days well. Though she was just ten years old at the time, the constant rumble of hearses passing through the streets of her new city was impossible to forget. A young girl who watched her mother prepare the darling twins for burial in 1762, in 1793 Betsy knew enough to brace for the worst. And her fears were realized quickly: Deborah Bolton, her oldest sister, was among the plague's first victims. Before the disease had run its course, it would take both Samuel and Rebecca James Griscom, too, and perhaps contribute to the death of sister Mary as well.

The first signs of crisis emerged on August 5, when the daughter of the physician Hugh Hodge suddenly came down with a high fever. She was jaundiced and vomiting blood. The family called Benjamin Rush, but there was nothing he could do; she died the same day. The next day, Mrs. Thomas Bradford became ill, and then the son of Mrs. McNair. McNair started to improve but then suddenly started hemorrhaging from his nose and died. Over this week, more and more cases began and ended just the same: first was the appearance of yellow eyes and skin, then purple hemorrhages into the skin, next blood began pouring from the nose and mouth. The printer and bookseller Mathew Carey (his ripped-from-the-headlines history of the events, published just days after the first fall frost killed the mosquito population and ended the outbreak, sold out immediately) observed that "if these symptoms were not soon relieved, a vomiting of matter, resembling coffee grounds in color and consistency, commonly called the black vomit, sometimes accompanied with or succeeded by hemorrhages from the nose, fauces [the oral pharyngeal passage], gums, and other parts of the body—a yellowish purple color and putrescent appearance of the whole body, hiccup, agitations, deep and distressed sighing, comatose, delerium, and finally death."[35]

Coffee grounds was an apt metaphor for the symptoms, because some believed they may have harbored the cause. In a letter to his wife, Julia, as the outbreak just began, Rush reported that there was "a malignant fever" along Water Street that had "carried off twelve persons." "It is supposed to have been produced," he suggested, "by some damaged coffee." The sloop *Amelia* from Santo Domingo had anchored with a cargo of coffee, which had spilled during the voyage. The bad coffee was dumped on Ball's Wharf (near Arch Street), where it putrefied in the sun and sent out a powerful odor discernable over a quarter mile away. Others agreed that the coffee was suspect. One observer reported to the College of Physicians that "the Sloop *Amelia* came to the Wharf the 23rd July and immediately began to discharge her Cargo—this Vessel was wholly loaded with Coffee in Bags the lower tier of which from the leaky condition of the Vessel were under water & found to be wholly rotten, and when thrown on the Wharf occasioned a most intolerable stench for several days. Two of her passengers or Crew I am informed died on board her while she lay at the Wharf."[36] According to Rush, "the fever was contained for a while to Water Street, between Race and Arch Streets, but I have lately met with it in Second Street, and in Kensington; but whether propagated by contagion, or by the original exhalation, I cannot tell . . . I have not seen a fever of so much malignity, so general, since the year 1762."[37] If death came, it was generally between the fifth and eighth day—in other words, fast.[38] By August 19, the physician Benjamin Rush declared it to be yellow fever.

Betsy's loved ones were dangerously close to the outbreak. The Hodge girl lived at 91 North Water Street, and the McNair boy at 52 North Front, and most of Betsy's family were by this time, too, gathered along the waterfront toward or in the Northern Liberties: Betsy's parents and the Morgans on McCullough's Court; Deborah and Everard's shop stood at 38 North Front Street, while Hannah Griscom Levering was just a bit farther up the street, at 334 North Front.[39] They were all clustered near the houses first affected, and just a stone's throw from Water Street, where the crisis began. The neighborhood in these years did not suggest much confidence. One visitor to the city would explain that, behind the waterfront wharves, "Water-Street . . . is the first street which you usually enter after landing, and it does not serve to give a stranger a very favourable opinion either of the neatness or commodiousness of the public ways of Philadelphia. It is no more than thirty feet wide, and immediately behind the houses, which stand on the side farthest from the water, a high bank, supposed to be the old bank of the river, rises, which renders the air very confined. Added to this, such stenches at times prevail in it, owing in part to the quantity of filth and dirt that is suffered to remain on the pavement, and in part to what is deposited in waste houses, of which there are several in the street, that it is really dreadful to pass through it."[40] The neighborhood was close, stuffy, crowded and dirty—all the ingredients for an epidemic.

Rush knew something terrible was happening. The illness, he would write to his wife, safely ensconced out of town, "comes nearer to [the Plague] in violence and mortality than any disease we have ever before had in this country." He listed its various symptoms: "Sometimes it comes on with a chilly fit and a high fever, but more frequently it steals on with headache, languor, and sick stomach. These symptoms are followed by stupor, delirium, vomiting, a dry skin, cool or cold hands and feet, a feeble slow pulse, sometimes below in frequency the pulse of health." "The eyes are at first suffused with blood," he continued, and "afterwards become yellow, and in most cases a yellowness covers the whole skin on the 3rd or 4th day. Few survive the 5th day, but more die on the 2nd and 3rd days." Sometimes the "patients possess their reason to the last and discover much less weakness than in the last stage of common fevers. One of my patients stood up and shaved himself on the morning of the day he died. Livid [bluish] spots on the body, a bleeding at the nose, from the gums, from the bowels, and a vomiting of black matter in some instances close the scenes of life."[41]

By the weekend of August 24 and 25, the city had reached a panic state.[42] People searched for a way to explain the crisis. The summer had been hot: temperatures had hovered in the high seventies through June and the mideighties in July. The "Father of American Poetry" Philip Freneau (at this point the publisher of the National Gazette and a translator in the State Department) captured the scene in verse: "Hot, dry winds forever blowing / Dead men to the grave-yards going / Constant hearses / Funeral verses; Oh! what plagues—there is no knowing!" . . . "Doctors raving and disputing, death's pale army still recruiting / What a pother / One with t'other! / Some a-writing, some a-shooting. Nature's poisons here collected, / Water, earth, and air infected / O, what a pity, / Such a City / Was in such a place erected!" Large flocks of pigeons had been noticed over the city. After the catastrophe had run its lethal course, people wondered—had the birds' presence been a clue? A comet had been seen—was it a warning? Wasn't the number of cats found dead in the street unusually large?[43] Had the city's slaves poisoned the wells? Was the outbreak somehow a product of the weather? Did the disease travel through the air from some single source, or was it being carried from person to person? Had it come somehow with the two thousand refugees—French colonists as well as their slaves—lately arrived in the city from the Caribbean slave revolt?

Philadelphians did not know it at the time, but what they were seeing was epidemic liver failure. Mosquitoes from the Caribbean had brought to the city yellow fever, a viral disease that invades and destroys the organ. (Today we know that the disease does not travel from person to person, but rather is spread by the *Aedes aegypti* mosquito, which has been wiped out in North America but is still found elsewhere in the world, particularly in West and Central Africa and among South American forestry and agricultural workers. An effective vaccine has been available since the 1930s.)[44] Carried aboard ships from the West Indies, the mosquitoes thrived along the waterfront, in marshes, Dock Creek—even rain barrels. Some Philadelphians whose speculations about the disease's source fell closer to the mark suspected that it came aboard Henry Drinker's ship *Mary*, arriving from Cape François.[45] Given the relatively short range of the insects that carried the virus, the men and women most likely to be affected (infected) were residents of waterfront neighborhoods—putting Betsy and her family straight in harm's way.

The College of Physicians published its own set of guidelines for preventing the progress of the fever: Residents of the city should avoid "all unnecessary intercourse" with the infected, and put markers on the doors or windows of houses where those infected dwelled. Anyone showing signs of the disease should be placed in the center of large and airy rooms, in beds without curtains, and Philadelphians needed to "pay the strictest regard to cleanliness, by frequently changing their body and bed linen; also, by removing, as speedily as possible, all offensive matters from their rooms." The streets and wharves of the city, too, were to be kept as clean as possible. The physicians also urged the city to "provide a large and airy hospital, in the neighbourhood of the city, for the reception of such poor persons as cannot be accommodated with the above advantages in private houses." In order to do what they could to minimize the despair settling over the city they "put a stop to the tolling of the bells" and asked residents to "bury such persons as they die of this fever in as private a manner as possible." Also, since the "contagion of the disease may be taken into the body and pass out of it without producing the fever, unless it be rendered active by some occasional cause," the physicians urged Philadelphians to "avoid all fatigue of body and mind"; "avoid standing or sitting in the sun, also in a current of air, or in the evening air"; "accommodate the dress to the weather, and to exceed rather in warm than in cool clothing"; and "avoid intemperance, but to use fermented liquors, such as wine, beer and cyder with moderation." They observed that fires were a "very ineffectual, if not dangerous" means of checking the fever, and "have reason to place more dependence upon the burning of gunpowder." The "benefits of Vinegar and Camphor," they added, "are confined chiefly to infected rooms, and they cannot be used too frequently upon handkerchiefs, or in smelling bottles, by persons whose duty calls them to visit or attend the sick."[46]

Once the nature of the crisis became clear, thousands fled. Those who stayed in the city tried any and all remedies that came their way. The smell of gunpowder, burned tobacco, nitre and sprinkled vinegar was inescapable, and families incessantly scoured and whitewashed their rooms. Any who ventured out pressed vinegar-soaked handkerchiefs or sponges to their noses; others carried pieces of tarred rope in their hands or pockets, or tied camphor bags around their necks. By September, the city was strangely empty. Some churches were nearly deserted, and others simply closed. The coffeehouses shut down, as did the city library, and most of the public offices. Three of the city's four daily papers were discontinued.[47] Why didn't the Griscoms leave? Was it Deborah's early sickness that prevented them from escaping the epidemic themselves? Did Betsy and John leave the city despite the family calamity? Or did they stay and ride out the epidemic together? The horror stories flying through the streets could not have helped their state of mind. One man died in the night, accompanied by no one except his wife, who went into labor while her husband lay dying; she opened a window and called out for help, but no one in the street answered. The next morning someone went in to see how they had fared, and found the man and woman both dead, and the newborn child alive and alone.[48]

Doctors scrambled to treat the ill. At first, Rush preferred a fairly moderate approach to the disease, inducing "gentle vomits" and prescribing "physics," such as tea and broth, to settle the patient's stomach, or in some cases, more "powerful cordials," like ipecac and wine. In time, however, he began taking more aggressive measures, including bloodletting and purgatives. By mid-September, when the Griscoms began to need care, Rush had fully embraced these strategies. Sometimes he might draw upwards of sixty ounces of blood (in twenty-ounce increments) from a patient, and even up to eighty. The idea was to remove the disease's sources of strength; the purging and bleeding, accompanied by a reduced diet, was meant to eliminate possible hosts.[49] By early October, Rush wrote, "I continue to use mercury in large doses, with great success. I have found 40 grains necessary in the course of the day to open the bowels. I rely upon no evacuations until they are large & bilious." He added, "I have only lost one patient who took mercury on the first day in the manner I have mentioned, & I think I have saved two in a very advanced stage of the disorder by it."[50]

Deborah Griscom Bolton was fifty-three years old, the mother of five living children, the youngest just nine years old when fever struck. She was already dead when Betsy's father started showing symptoms in the first week of September. The fever ravaging the city had appeared to subside, but in early September caught a second wind. By now, the city had marshaled its forces in an organized response. A small red flag—on the order of the Board of Health—was posted on the Griscoms' door to alert neighbors to the presence of disease. (In the end, one in five of the residents of McCullough's Court died in the epidemic).[51] Seventy-six-year-old Samuel Griscom was buried on September 15—just about the time his widow began to feel a fever coming on.[52] The household, impoverished as it was in these years, looked for aid to give Samuel a proper burial; the Carpenters' Company paid £3 10s. "for a walnutt [sic] coffin made for our ancient member Saml Griscom."[53] Seventy-two-year-old Rebecca was buried a week later, on the twenty-third. The Carpenters' Company does not appear to have come to the rescue this time.[54] (News of the Griscom family's tragedy reached Elizabeth Drinker by the twenty-seventh, when she recorded that Samuel Griscom was dead; she added to that "and wife," and then crossed it out to correct herself—"and daughter"—not yet aware that all three were gone.) Samuel was one of fifty-six dead in one day; Rebecca was one of sixty-eight. Betsy Claypoole found herself orphaned in the space of a week, but in the context of the city writ large, her parents were two among thousands.

Indeed, the residents of the city were falling so fast that it was difficult to keep up. "They are a Dieing on our right hand & on our Left," one man wrote in dismay and despair; "we have it oposit us, in fact, all around us, great are the number that are Calld to the grave . . . we live in the midst of death."[55] A thick stack of "Orders for Interment" captures the sadly busy weeks the Free Quakers' gravedigger Jacob Karcher put in during September and October of that year.[56] More than one thousand people were buried in the city's "potter's field," today Washington Square, sometimes in trenches.[57] The city's graveyards, some said, looked more like freshly plowed fields than burying grounds.[58]

Work stopped. Among other things, in November, the committee appointed to "prevent the introduction and spreading of infectious disease in this city" confirmed "health is restored to the city of Philadelphia"; but neighboring communities worried that a "real danger is still to be apprehended from the bedding and clothing of those who have been ill of the malignant fever." Having learned that "numbers of valuable, but infected, beds" had been given to the nurses and attendants of the sick, residents of New York City published their concern that some of these might be offered for sale; they had already learned, to their alarm, that attempts had been made to freight "considerable quantities" of beds and bedding into their city. New Yorkers determined not to admit "beds and bedding of any kind, or feathers in bags"; they also excluded "second hand wearing apparel of every species, coming from places infected with the yellow fever." They urged their New Jersey neighbors to do the same. Whatever materials the Claypoole shop might have had on hand that fall, they were of little value now.[59]

One of Betsy's granddaughters had a curious recollection related to this episode that suggests that Betsy had strong opinions about the care given to the epidemic's victims. While no other descendant commented on Betsy's interest in medicine or healing, Susan Satterthwaite remembered that her grandmother's "knowledge of the science of medicine was remarkable," and further, that she was an "Anti-Rushite and antagonistic to the use of calomel as a drug, and to the practice of bleeding."[60] Apparently, Betsy was among the many critics of the physician Benjamin Rush. (Rush, by the way, had been baptized by Betsy's first father-in-law, Aeneas Ross, but there's no evidence that she knew Rush particularly well.)[61] When the epidemic emerged, Rush was of course among the first to the scene; his "aggressive regimen" of "copious bloodletting" alongside doses of mercury and jalap to induce purging was highly controversial from the outset.[62] In fact, as the virus raged through the city, Philadelphia's medical establishment took their debate over various forms of treatment to the pages of the press; as the disease increased in its virulence, so did their debate.[63] Rush himself launched the public debate when he began publishing his observations and recommendations in the paper in order to respond more efficiently to the hundreds of queries that poured into his office. But as soon as Rush's column advising residents on the virtues of purging and bleeding appeared in the paper, Dr. Adam Kuhn responded with his own column denouncing Rush's approach and recommending less aggressive techniques. Drs. Thomas Rushton and William Currie weighed in against Rush, and Robert Annan in his support. The constant barrage of dissenting opinions did nothing to reassure the people of the distressed city, who themselves began to write to the paper to express their disgust over the physicians' press war.

Betsy could easily have been among the readers whose opinion of Rush was settled by these columns alone. Or perhaps her contact with the famed physician was more direct. Rush lost three of the first dozen patients—was Betsy's sister Deborah among them?[64] Did he treat her parents? Of the fifty men, women and children definitely known to have been treated by Rush, thirty-nine recovered; if another twenty-two possible patients are included, many of whom died, his overall recovery rate still hovers over 50 percent.[65] But Rush treated thousands; it is impossible to gather any meaningful statistics about his success rate. Rush complained bitterly about the accusations of his critics, noting that they said the few patients he lost were "all killed by mercury and bleeding."[66] Were the Griscoms among these? Betsy's feelings about his medical practices were strong enough that her granddaughter recalled them decades later. Why? The calomel to which she specifically objected was a mixture of six parts mercury to one part chlorine; Rush had patented pills (some fifty dozen would be sent with Lewis and Clark on their westward expedition) that combined calomel with jalap to produce a purgative effect. That these came to be called "Thunderclappers" suggests to a degree their effect. Did Rush use these medicines on Betsy's sister or parents? Did she blame the famous physician for their deaths?

David Newport, married to Betsy's granddaughter, would years later claim that Betsy was "famous in Old Philadelphia as a 'wise woman.'" Newport also claimed that the "wisdom and discernment of her nature" meant that "in sickness and physical ailments, her advice was largely sought. Her faith in the *vis medicatrix naturae* [that is, the healing power of nature] was unbounded."[67] A medicine chest that survives today in the home of descendants suggests that her children thought enough of this particular artifact after her death to take the trouble to preserve it.

In the wake of the catastrophe, Betsy's whole family was reconfigured. The past few years had already seen some unwelcome changes. Betsy's sister Sarah Donaldson had died in 1785 at the age of forty-six, and then her sister Susannah Doane died in April 1788, at forty-five.[68] The following year, the mariner William Donaldson's luck at last ran out when he was lost at sea.[69] At least one of the Donaldson girls had been taken in by the Boltons, but now with Deborah dead, too, Sarah moved yet again, this time in with the Claypooles, where she would stay until the time of her own marriage in 1797. Lastly, there's a chance that Mary Griscom Morgan was another member of Betsy's family who succumbed to the fever; at least in March 1794, George Morgan wrote home from New Orleans to respond to the news of the loss of their "dear mother." If Mary did not die in the fever epidemic per se, she died in the months that immediately followed.[70] Her daughter Rebecca Morgan seems to have moved in with the Claypooles as well, at least for a time; perhaps her father Thomas was already drinking and the Claypoole home seemed more stable.[71] As Betsy made room now for fourteen-year-old Sarah, and perhaps twenty-year-old Rebecca as well, her own newest arrival, baby Jane, marked her first birthday. The Front Street house, already close, was getting downright crowded.

When the fever at last subsided, Philadelphians set about putting the city to rights. All those mattresses, curtains, furniture and other infected articles had to be cleaned, walls whitewashed and rooms scrubbed from floor to ceil-ing. Rush put his own bed and furniture outdoors in the hopes that a frost might quash any remaining infection.[72] Betsy and her sister Rachel surely had their hands full helping families salvage what they could of their mattresses and replacing those that were beyond consideration. As something like normalcy returned to the city, there were some new features as well. The same ships that had brought the fever brought new populations of residents, who carried with them new styles and new preferences. Tomatoes, along with artichokes and okra, became known in the city—at first for medicinal purposes and then as part of the city's everyday diets.[73] Betsy was notably fond of tomatoes, these strange souvenirs of terrible times.

Another souvenir of the fever would shortly arrive to provide some comfort. Years earlier, when Samuel's stepsister, Sarah Holloway, wrote her will, she expressed her wish that a Bible be given to each of the children of her several brothers and sisters, with funds that would become available after the death of her brother Samuel. As the Griscoms went about the many sad chores associated with dismantling their parents' household, someone went to a city bookseller to purchase the large number of Bibles the bequest required. One of them came to Betsy Claypoole. John got out the thirty-year-old Bible he had received from his own mother, and began copying the family records into the volume's pages, beginning with the 1657 marriage of James Claypoole while a Quaker missionary in Bremen, Germany. He entered the births of his daughters with Betsy. Strangely, no one inscribed the names of Samuel, Rebecca or Deborah, lost so recently, and in such a cataclysmic way. The Claypooles, apparently, were not ones to dwell upon grief. They left those sorrowful columns for another hand to complete.

# 19

# The Federal Edifice

If Americans today pin the apex of Betsy Ross's life to 1776, she for her own part surely looked at the 1790s as the years when long-deferred hopes were at last realized. To be sure, the fever epidemic had been a devastating episode. But the 1790s, despite this rocky start, were generally fair sailing. She was at last married and raising a family under a peacetime government, and she considered herself acquainted with the most famous man in the emerging nation, soon to become its first president. The years of Washington's tenure in the Executive Office must have been thrilling for Betsy. Residents of the new nation's capital, she and John would hitch their wagon to the federal star and hope it would lead them to good fortune. John parlayed his war record and contacts into an enviable job with the customs service, and soon their daughters were attending a fashionable school, having their portraits made and accumulating the various accomplishments of well-raised young women.

Nowhere in the newly united states was more exciting to live than Philadelphia, which served as the national capital from 1791 to 1800. City, state and nation here blended into one swarming metropolis. Some forty-four thousand people crowded the streets. The economy pulsed with activity. Much of the new nation's shipping moved in and out of this port. At the ferry terminal at the foot of Arch Street was moored John Fitch's steamboat, the first of its kind in the new nation. Charles Willson Peale invited Philadelphians to see his unparalleled and unprecedented collection of natural and human history. It was a city of wonders.

Just a few years earlier, in the summer of 1788, five thousand Philadelphians had assembled at the corner of Third and South streets to celebrate the ratification of the new federal Constitution. Pennsylvania had been the second state to vote for ratification, late in 1787, but the deal was not sealed until the following summer when successful conventions in New Hampshire and Virginia gave Philadelphia Federalists something to celebrate. The night before, the city's street commissioners had seen that along the route the streets were neatly swept and the trees trimmed. At 9:30 a.m. on July 4, people began lining up. The weather was perfect. "Clouds blocked out the hot July sun, and a cooling breeze blew all day," notes one historian of the day. "In the evening the sky was illuminated by a beautiful Aurora Borealis." All of nature seemed to bless the proceedings.[1]

The highlight of the procession was the "Federal Edifice," a massive float designed to celebrate the new terms of union. On a carriage drawn by ten white horses (the number of ratifying states to date) passed the

grand federal edifice ... the dome supported by thirteen Corinthian columns, raised on pedestals proper to that order; the frieze decorated with thirteen stars; ten of the columns compleat and three left unfinished—on the pedestals of the columns were inscribed, in ornamented cyphers, the initials of the thirteen American states. On the top of the dome, a handsome cupola surrounded by a figure of Plenty, bearing her cornucopia's, and other emblems of her character. The dimensions of this building were as follows: ten feet diameter, eleven feet to the top of the cornice, the dome four feet high, the cupola five feet high, the figure of Plenty, three feet six inches; the carriage on which it was mounted, three feet high; the whole thirty-six feet in height. Round the pedestal of the edifice were these words, "in union the fabric stands firm."[2]

Behind the Federal Edifice marched artisanal Philadelphia. A large part of the parade included representatives from more than forty trades and professions, each under the banner of their craft, reflecting the pride that the marchers attached to their skills. Cordwainers, coach painters, cabinet and chair makers walked, as did brick makers, painters and porters. Bricklayers, tailors, whip manufacturers, wheelwrights, tin-plate workers, bookbinders, saddlers, tobacconists, stocking manufacturers, curriers, barbers—every imaginable occupation was represented. Some 450 architects and house carpenters joined the procession. Had Samuel Griscom been among them? Betsy's brother-in-law Thomas Morgan was likely among the watchmakers, and perhaps her brother George with the silversmiths. Upholsterers marched last among the furniture trades. John Mason and John Davis headed the group. Their display included a patriotic emblem of peace and liberty—a dove with an olive branch in its mouth carried on a cushion with its drapery, followed by a cabriole sofa. Their motto? "Be Liberty thine."[3]

Trades that were generally female—milliners and lacemakers, glove and mantua makers—had not been invited to march. But Elizabeth Claypoole was a member of a more encompassing craft that involved both male and female practitioners. Did John join the parade? Surely. Did Betsy Claypoole walk alongside him and their fellow upholsterers? Probably not. But it is certainly tempting to imagine Mrs. Claypoole helping to make the banner under which they walked, and she may well have done more. At least it seems likely that the Claypooles were among the ardent Federalists rejoicing at the success of the new Constitution. Charles Willson Peale, whom John knew from his days in Maryland tanyards and also through the Masonic Lodge, was deeply involved in the planning, "laying out the route of the parade, providing flags of all of America's allies, suggesting costumes, banners, and mottos for the participating groups, and, of course, working on the Grand Federal Edifice."[4] John and Betsy were hardly likely to sit out this spectacular event in which their politics and trade so beautifully converged.

By this time (and probably for many years before, and perhaps all along), Betsy's sister Rachel was also working in the upholstery business.[5] Ten years younger than Betsy, Rachel had surely trained at her sister's side, if not in her shop. She may have begun learning the upholsterer's craft when John Ross was still alive, and continued helping her sister out through the difficult years between his death and Betsy's marriages to Joseph Ashburn and then John Claypoole. By the 1790s, Rachel was regularly working for families around town, including the wealthy and influential Drinkers, business partners of Uncle Abel's. Elizabeth Drinker's diary captures several glimpses of Rachel at work. In May 1794, for instance, Drinker noted that "Rachel Griscomb [sic] work'd here yesterday, she made up a Bed tick and put in the feathers, preparatory to our going out of town." In summer 1796, Rachel Griscom was again there, "making up a bedtick and putting in the feathers." Later that year, once again Drinker wrote, "Rachel Griscomb [sic] here putting up beds."[6]

It is worth noting that Drinker does not associate Rachel in any of these entries with the Claypoole household; in fact, Drinker's voluminous diary makes not a single reference to John or Betsy Claypoole, though other

Griscoms attracted her attention. Many years before, Rebecca Griscom had been close to the Drinker family circle. When Sally Drinker was laid low by the "fall fever" of 1783, "Becky" Griscom was one of the family friends, along-side Rebecca Waln, who had sat up all night at Sally's bedside.[7] When Betsy's family was hard-hit by the 1793 fever epidemic, Drinker wrote, "[My neigh-bor] Waln spent this evening with me—she mention'd many affecting Cir-cumstances that have lately occur'd—Everard Bolton's wife dy'd some time ago, she was a Daughter of Saml and Rebecca Griscomb [sic] who are also both gone." Betsy's sister Deborah was on the minds of Drinker and Waln, as were Samuel and Rebecca, and Rachel was a routine presence in their household in the course of her work as an upholsterer, but at no time does Drinker suggest any particular awareness of Betsy Claypoole. Perhaps it was—at least in part—Betsy's departure from the Society of Friends, and her alliance with the Free Quakers, that put her beyond Drinker's view.

By the 1790s, Betsy's cousin Rebecca came to Drinker's full attention. The fifty-year-old mantua maker had fallen on hard times. Having lost her home in 1789, five years later she was adrift—economically, socially and apparently spiritually as well. And she seems to have nursed a long-standing grudge against the Quaker "chiefs" who persecuted her—the Drinkers among them.

By the winter of 1795, Rebecca had become "very troublesome" at meet-ing.[8] Betsy's sister, also named Rebecca, had become estranged from her own meeting ten years earlier for alcoholism (in 1792 she had been admitted to the city almshouse),[9] and now apparently cousin Rebecca, too, had developed a serious quarrel with the Society of Friends.[10] She became disruptive in meet-ings, talking out of turn and sitting and standing in the wrong places and at the wrong time. She seemed threatening, provocative. She made people ner-vous. She was also accused of "neglecting the proper means of procuring a livelihood." By July, women Friends had "long and tenderly treated with" Rebecca "on account of her disorderly conduct, not only in using reviling language," but "more particularly disturbing our public meeting by unseemly noise to the interruption of approved ministering Friends in the Exercise of their gifts and manifesting a Spirit contradictory to the general sense of Friends by keeping her Seat in Times of Prayer." They "kindly remonstrated" with her to "convince her to the Evil of her perverse and unbecoming demeanor," not merely by "rejecting Friends' loving advice," but—more mad-deningly—"in return thereof endeavoring to asperse the body of Friends by writing and otherwise."[11]

Apparently they were entirely unsuccessful, for in August Rebecca had to be removed forcibly from Quaker worship.[12] The women's meeting suggested that more intervention would be necessary. Henry Drinker, John Webb, Edward Garrigues, Jacob Tomkins, Jonathan Drinker and Isaac Cathrall—an unusually large committee, perhaps because this was an unusually difficult matter—were appointed to further consider her case. By early September, the Friends convened a meeting in the Drinkers' front parlor, requiring Rebecca to attend. Also summoned were John Webb, Joseph Drinker and wife, Sarah Bacon, Thomas Morris, Henry Drinker and other leaders of the Friends community.[13] Now still more Friends were involved in this mounting effort to set Rebecca straight.

But their intervention apparently had little effect, or at least little good effect. The next week, according to Elizabeth Drinker, Rebecca again was "very troublesome and talkative this forenoon in meeting," and in the weeks to follow would be disruptive and/or removed from each week's meeting. On September 22, she was "carried out of meeting again this forenoon, but not yet excommunicated." On the twenty-ninth, Rebecca was once again "troublesome at meeting," and the good Friends had had enough; this time, they carried her off to jail. A small guard of Quakers was stationed at the meetinghouse gate to prevent her from returning, but they found this a "difficult business, and therefore thought fitt [sic] to confine her." Even this intervention had no effect. Two weeks later, when another member became "troublesome," causing Henry Drinker to "[take] him to task," it "set R. Griscomb a going in the old way, in meeting."[14] A month later, the Friends once more endured "a very great rumpus" from Rebecca—"she was twice carried out forcibly," Elizabeth Drinker reported. One week later, like clockwork, she was removed again and again the following week as well.[15]

In Rebecca's mind, her cause was just. About a dozen years earlier, when she was in her midthirties, she would testify, she had become aware of her spiritual shortcomings.[16] She had been neglecting "public worship" and resolved to do better in the future. But she found life a struggle. Though she had inherited the property in which she lived, it was all she could do to keep the house in good repair and the taxes paid.[17] "Being somewhat embarrassed in [her] Circumstances," she was "very diligent" in her "endeavors at [the] Needle" to "extricate" herself from debt. But this proved impossible—and she believed it was because "two women who filled some pretty high stations" had it in for her. They claimed that she started it, that for some reason she avoided them in the street, and they began gossiping that Rebecca would urge "S D-k-r," a "lovely young creature then under [her] care" [perhaps Sally Drinker, whom

Rebecca had helped nurse through the fever], to "treat them with the same or as much contempt" as Rebecca herself did. They reported a general "uneasiness" with her conduct. Rebecca sought each woman out, begging to know what she had done to offend her; naturally each denied that she had been gossiping, and insisted that she had "nothing against" her—but warned, too, that Rebecca should "leave off writing." Indeed, this "writing" was a real problem. Apparently Rebecca had been sending long letters to various overseers articulating her concerns—a practice that itself tested the Friends' forbearance. This latter reference may include, for example, the June 1785 letter that Rebecca sent James Pemberton, objecting to the Quakers' efforts to remove a "much loved relative and companion" from her home, ostensibly because it would be inconvenient for this relative to get to school, though she strongly suspected that other motives were afoot.[18]

Rebecca came to believe that the prejudice of these women had also ruined her business. Their conduct "occasioned a shock that [her] tender nerves had never before experienced," so that she was "not in a capacity to dispatch much" in the way of employment. "I made it my daily care to seek employment & do what I could," she insisted, but for some seven years from the first "slanderous insinuations" of "uneasiness," Rebecca earned almost nothing from any Quaker client—not "three pounds worth of work from all the Members of our Meeting put together." And so Rebecca in time lost her house and was forced to apply for "public assistance." She entered the Quaker almshouse in March 1794.[19]

Acutely embarrassed, resentful and angry, Rebecca began sending missives to the printer Richard Folwell "in order publickly to testify [her] disunity." She resented hints that, in gratitude for this financial support, she should withhold her considerable critique; £15 in room and board would not "bribe me to silence on subjects which I think of the highest importance," she wrote.[20] Furthermore, she claimed, when she tried to move to a more hospitable meeting she was denied the necessary certificate—more evidence, she believed, of egregious discrimination against the poor, unwelcome by others who feared taking on their needs.

The chip on Rebecca's shoulder grew as she nurtured a growing sensitivity to class privilege among Friends. Soon she developed a new preoccupation—with seats in the meetinghouse. In another letter she observed that while the tenets of the faith declare that no seat in the meeting for worship is "more consecrated or holy than another," yet she had seen a man quietly take a seat among those traditionally reserved for a meeting's leadership and then be seized by arm and leg and dragged not simply out of the seat but out of the building altogether. "For my own part," she continued, "in condescension to their Choice (in a seat for me) I long since relinquished the Individual's right (to choose) &"—in a gesture reminiscent of Benjamin Lay's showy activism— "sat upon the footstool."

In time, she confronted her persecutors more directly. On November 24, 1795, Elizabeth Drinker wrote, "After the first meeting broke up Nancy Skyrin called. RG had been exclaiming, in a friendly stile, against several, then, in meeting, HD and Isaac Potts among the rest, whom she called instigators— and threatened with having their names soon in print, &c." Two weeks later, Rebecca Griscom paid a "visit of accusation" to Henry Drinker at his counting-house ("Gervis Johnson gently moved her out"), and then, on December 14, a letter from Rebecca to Henry Drinker arrived at the house. On the twenty-second, Elizabeth Drinker again noted that Rebecca had "vociferated" at meeting.[21]

At the business meeting following the "vociferation," a "report was made that a copy of the testimony concluded on in the case of Rebecca Griscom hath been delivered to her & that, on being informed of her privilege to appeal, she declared her Intention to avail herself of it." (Imagine their joy.) The meeting appointed four men, including Henry Drinker, to "attend such committee as the quarterly meeting may appoint to her objections" and to "attend the case in such other Manner as may be found needful and proper."[22] All this upheaval was clearly wearing even the capable Henry Drinker out; in a letter otherwise dedicated to business, he wrote, "My time is much taken up, more so than is pleasant at this advanced stage . . . there are certain duties which we owe to the community at large and to individuals in religious communion, which seem to fall to the lot of some in a much greater degree than others."[23]

In January 1796, Rebecca turned her attention to racial equality. On the twenty-first, Elizabeth Drinker wrote, "I read a piece of twelve pages, published by Rebecca Griscomb, on the propriety of taking people of colour into society."[24] Rebecca had begun scolding her fellow Friends for their reluctance to admit African Americans to membership. Friends had long welcomed men and women of color into their worship services. As early as 1698, the Philadelphia Monthly Meeting invited masters to bring their slaves with them to meeting. William Penn himself proposed a monthly meeting for slaves, and by the 1750s a quarterly meeting at the Bank meetinghouse had commenced.[25] When the "Great Meetinghouse" at the corner of Market and Second was renovated and enlarged in 1756, planners were asked to "allot some suitable places" for men and women of color "to sit in our common meetings."[26] But men and women of color had not yet been accepted as full members of the Quaker meeting.

The first known case of an application for membership from a mixed-race worshipper is that of Abigail Franks. In 1781, Franks—a woman of European, Native American and African American descent—applied for membership in Birmingham, in Pennsylvania's Delaware County. The matter was eventually referred to the quarterly meeting, which, in typical Quaker fashion, appointed a committee "to inquire more minutely into the disposition, color and circumstances of the individual on whose account the application took its rise." Three months later, the committee reported that her "disposition" indeed seemed "worthy of Friends' notice; and her color appeared to them not darker than some who are esteemed white." Her great-grandmother, they learned, had been Native American and her great-grandfather of African descent; their son had married an Indian woman, and their son—the applicant's father—had formed a union with a white woman, the applicant's mother. Having ascertained all of this, the body forwarded the matter to the yearly meeting, and after "weighty and edifying deliberations"—and despite "mountains of opposition"—the 1784 Yearly Meeting accepted her application.

By the mid-1780s, as the number of manumissions grew, the increasing numbers of freed slaves in the city made their church membership an increasingly pressing question. By 1796, progressive members of the Philadelphia Yearly Meeting were able to insert the following statement into the meeting *Discipline*: "Meetings are at liberty to receive such [convinced persons] into membership, without respect of nation or color." African American membership was now possible, but meetings remained cautious—some might say exceedingly so—on the subject.[27]

When the question came to a head in Philadelphia, Rebecca was ready to express strongly held beliefs. Enough discussion had unfolded by 1794 that Joseph Drinker undertook the writing of an essay on the topic, which he finished in January 1795 and began to circulate among friends. That same year, Quaker tolerance was tested when Hannah Burrows, a light-skinned woman of color who had been active among the Society of Friends as a preacher, sought full membership with the Society of Friends. A March 1795 conference in the back parlor of the Drinker house, with Henry Drinker, James Pemberton and others in attendance, suggests that the issue was under consideration by the spring of that year—just about the time Rebecca Griscom's disruptive behavior commenced.[28] The Quakers' other good efforts on behalf of African Americans aside, Burrows's application for membership tested the limits of their broad-mindedness because, as Joseph Drinker recognized, if blacks were admitted full church membership, intermarriage might not be far behind, and the congregation was simply not ready to take so radical a step.[29] Drinker was troubled to see his otherwise tolerant friends, and Friends, balk at the admission of people of color, which he saw as in direct conflict with their "Fundimental [sic] Principles" that "God is no respector of Persons, that in every Nation Such as fear him, and work Righteousness are accepted of him, and that what God hath Cleansed no man Should call common or Unclean." Christ promised that there was one Shepherd and one Sheepfold; "he did not say there should be one fold for black sheep and other fold for white sheep, as some of our friends would have it." Indeed he declared the Friends, in spite of their "Noble Testimony" and principles clearly among the most enlightened in the world, to be only people he knew "who [made] any objections to the Blacks or People of Color joining them in church Fellowship."[30]

Rebecca apparently found all this talk frustrating. Given her own experiences on the margins of Quaker society, she was acutely sensitive to prejudice within the Friends' ranks. Her behavior suggests that she sought to make her impatience visible and unavoidable, and that her fellow Friends found the gestures unwelcome, much as they had Benjamin Lay's political theater many years before. That Griscom's paper apeared the same month that Drinker's essay was released makes plain that she was acting in response to him, or perhaps he to her.[31] What we don't know is what she wrote; despite Elizabeth Drinker's reference to Griscom's essay being "published," no copy is known to have survived. Is the paper she published what she had in mind back in November 1795, when she threatened Henry Drinker that he would see his "name soon in print"? It's clear that these writings themselves were unwelcome: the Friends were well and truly tired of these screeds, which had apparently begun to appear by autumn 1794 and continued on now for several months. Printer Richard Folwell was surely dismayed when they began to appear at his door, not least because the letters that do survive suggest that—however passionate and correct her perceptions—Rebecca was indeed becoming unhinged.

Of course passionate protest is not to be confused with illness or instability, but there are hints that perhaps something more was afoot than religious or political zeal alone. Rebecca refers to herself in one of these missives as a "lunatick," and asserts that the "extraordinary conduct" of her fellow Quakers, so shocking to her "tender nerves, had compromised her capacity for work." There is a quality to these letters that suggests she had begun to see evidence of conspiracy all around her. Whether Quaker collusion had indeed deprived her of income or whether some sort of nervous breakdown prevented her from working, Rebecca had apparently exhausted her means of supporting herself and—tellingly—did not find it convenient or possible, when she made application to the Quaker almshouse, to join the household of any of her cousins (or perhaps they were reluctant to add this volatile figure to their own households). If Rebecca Griscom was indeed grappling with any kind of disorder, Betsy had at least her knowledge of Sarah Ross's struggle, if not John's own, to guide her own response to the situation.

At this remove of course it's impossible to assess Rebecca Griscom's state of mind, but plainly she felt passionately compelled to challenge meeting authority and procedure, and to confront the "chiefs" who abused their privilege and authority as they sat in judgment over their less fortunate neighbors. Rebecca stood by her beliefs. The letters teem with quotations from the *Discipline* and the queries to the membership that regularly appear there. When censured by the Northern District meeting, she replied that she intended to appeal. A committee of four (including Henry Drinker) was appointed to respond, and the meeting added another ten names to it; apparently they anticipated needing some assembled strength to meet Griscom's own considerable force. In May 1796, Rebecca was defeated; but, undaunted, in August she took her case still higher, to the yearly meeting, the last court of appeal in the Quaker community. In September, the Philadelphia Yearly Meeting confirmed the original judgment: Rebecca Griscom was formally and decidedly in the wrong.[32]

By this point, the Friends had taken all that even these very patient people could take. Their statement accompanying her disownment notes her disruptive presence at meetings, "where it has been her common practice to manifest her Opposition to the united Sense of friends by keeping her Seat in time of Prayer," and "showing her dislike to approved ministering Friends during the exerxise of their Gospel Service by making indecent & offensive Noises, and frequently interrupting the Solemnity of our said meetings by an impertinent & unsavory clamour of Words." Despite the best efforts of Friends to talk with her, Rebecca, "persisting in her evil Demeanor & perverse self will, not only rejected the tender counsel offered and slighted our kind forbearance, but returning therefore vilifying & groundless Charges against individual members in good esteem among us." Having "likewise attempted both with Tongue & Pen to asperse the Body of our christian Community," as well as her "disreputable reglect of the proper means of procuring a livelihood," the meeting disowned her.[33]

Cousin Rebecca's case seemed hardly past when sister Rebecca again claimed the attention of both Betsy Claypoole and Elizabeth Drinker. In

August 1798, Betsy's sister died. Elizabeth Drinker, with compassion, wrote that "poor Becky Griscomb" was "gone, she died in Friends Almshouse."[34] Rebecca Griscom's course ended when another yellow fever epidemic—the second in just five years—ravaged Philadelphia. This epidemic, too, came up from the wharves and was (for what it's worth), as the physician Samuel Powel Griffits would observe, "much more violent & contagious than in '93."[35] Betsy braced herself for more loss. Rebecca no longer lived in the waterfront neighborhood that was the epidemic's epicenter, but, her physician noted with disapproval, she was "a woman who went every where." She had been sick for three days already when she finally broke down and called for a doctor. Griffits at first believed that her fever was in abeyance, but this wasn't the sign of hope one might think; it was already too late. "Those who are properly attended & seen," Griffits would opine, "in time generally recover," but he could not give Rebecca the course of care he generally recommended. His "plan," as soon as he was called, was normally to bleed the patient "largely," accompanied by regular doses of calomel to encourage "purging." (If this was all a little too much for someone already so ill, he also prescribed a little opium to take the edge off. "Women certainly do not bear the medicines nor the disease as well as men," Griffits noted, suggesting that Rebecca requested and received the painkiller.) This course—bleeding and purging—continued for three days, and was followed by the application of blisters to the wrists in cases of nausea, weakness or fever, and to the stomach if vomiting came on. But Rebecca called too late, and none of these measures were enough to save her. By August 20, she was dead. Apparently Rebecca was not altogether estranged from her community of faith; she was buried in the Friends burying ground.[36] With Rebecca's death, Betsy was now the oldest living of Samuel Griscom's daughters.

Betsy's feelings as she watched both Rebeccas' painful declines, though not preserved in any archival record, are easy to imagine. But with her own family growing every year, the prospects of her shop demanded attention as well. As Philadelphia became the seat of the national government, craftsmen of all sorts enjoyed the benefits of government contracts, and upholsterers were no exception. When Congress Hall was erected, for instance, the upholsterer David Evans got the contract for the blinds, and Samuel Benge upholstered the red morocco leather and crimson moreen chairs.[37] He also supplied the canopy and hangings in the Senate chamber, converting damask lined with silk into fashionable interior decoration.[38] When that hall was enlarged a few years later, Benge landed one of the best contracts: forty-four chairs upholstered in black leather for the House and one in red for the Senate.[39] John Claypoole sought out such opportunities for his own shop and found them. In 1789, Betsy and John produced "sundry furniture for the council chambers"; the following spring they took a small job covering the desks in the secretary's office at the statehouse, taking in £2 11s. 18d. for covering three desks with the green coverings so familiar to us today.[40]

With the new nation's capital in the city, John and Betsy could consider themselves a handshake away from the first president, George Washington. Claypoole family memory preserves a number of stories suggesting that Betsy Claypoole and the president remained acquainted during these years. Rachel Claypoole Jones Fletcher did not say so in her formal affidavit, but in a separate interview with her nephew, she asserted that Betsy, who in the 1770s had attended Christ Church with John Ross, "afterwards [attended alongside] General Washington, who sat in their pew, it was a very handsome pew—the ministers—lined with red velvet. General Washington owned a seat in it. They all went together. He and the Ross Family, Johanna [Joanna] and Betsy."[41] Whether Betsy continued to attend Christ Church after John Ross's death is not known. A century later, when Betsy's niece Margaret Donaldson Boggs was a celebrated centenarian, she described attending Christ Church with Betsy in the years before Betsy joined the Free Quaker meeting, where they occupied the pew adjoining General Washington, and "never failed to receive a polite bow."[42] But these various accounts of Betsy's attendance alongside Washington are conflicting and difficult to reconcile, since Boggs was born in 1776 and Betsy joined the Free Quakers in the early 1780s. If Betsy, Margaret and Washington indeed exchanged nods at Christ Church, it would seem to have been during Washington's presidency.

Part of the understanding of Betsy's relationship with Washington also concerns Betsy's onetime sister-in-law Joanna Ross Holland. Widowed like Betsy early in the war, Joanna had remained Betsy's lifelong friend. Years later, Betsy's daughter Jane would recall that Joanna often visited her mother and still called her "Sister Betsy" almost a quarter century after they buried John Ross.[43] Betsy was perhaps pleased when, in late January 1789, Joanna remarried, to a man named James Armstrong.[44] Her onetime father-in-law, Aeneas Ross, performed the ceremony at his church in New Castle, Delaware.

Several family histories comment on Armstrong, but in ways that are difficult to reconcile with the archival record. Betsy's daughter Rachel remembered that Betsy had sat near General Washington at Christ Church, an "intimacy . . . caused by her being sister-in-law" to Armstrong, who, she claimed, had served as Washington's aide-de-camp. This would place Betsy and Joanna in church with the general sometime after Joanna's 1789 wedding, during Washington's two terms as president—years during which Betsy was presumably worshipping with her fellow members of the Free Quaker meeting. What's more, Rachel recalled, Armstrong had "saved General Washington's life in battle and lost his own by so doing. He interposed himself between Washington & the bullets of the enemy and was shot & killed & the same shot killed Washington's horse."[45] Given the date of the marriage, Armstrong could not have died protecting his commander in chief. Betsy's grandson, William Canby, searched Washington Irving's biography of the general "for all points indicated by Armstrong in the index," and found no mention of the "affair" that Rachel mentioned. He consulted his mother, Jane Claypoole Canby, about this tale, and she said that she did "not recollect that Armstrong was killed, but that he saved General Washington's life and the horse was shot."[46] This latter version is easier to reconcile with larger historical narratives, and allows the relationship in the pews of Christ Church to unfold in the 1790s, but still does not explain why Betsy might have attended services there in those years—or indeed why Joanna did, since she and James seem to have lived in Delaware.[47]

For the insight it provides into women's lives in the early Republic, it is worth noting that another set of records suggests a seamier side to Joanna Holland's union with James Armstrong. In 1790, both Joanna and a woman named Catherine Armstrong sent petitions to Pennsylvania's Supreme Executive Council seeking release from jail. Catherine Armstrong was accused of helping steal six shawls. In her defense, she claimed that she was merely in the store when the goods were taken; the shopkeeper rushed out to seize her after he noticed the shawls missing, but she had nothing hidden. However, the court believed that she was an accessory to the crime, distracting the shopkeeper while her accomplice grabbed the goods. Convicted of larceny in December 1789 by the Mayor's Court of Philadelphia, she was fined £1 10s. and sentenced to one year in jail. It was from there that Catherine, in March 1790, submitted a petition that described how she, newly arrived in the United States and naive, was innocent of the charges against her. In a second petition, she asked that the fine be remitted, again so she might be released from prison. Joanna Holland's petitions do not survive, so the events leading to her own incarceration are unknown, but it seems likely that she too was imprisoned for reasons stemming from her poverty. And perhaps the companionship of a woman with the same name as the man she was about to marry is simply a coincidence. But it seems possible that the two impoverished women were somehow caught up together in the same downward spiral that ended in the Philadelphia jail.[48]

If Joanna was already on the skids when she formed her union with

Armstrong, things got no better after that marriage. Whatever heroism he once displayed on the battlefield, he apparently was not without flaws. Ross descendants have stories of their own, and one is that Armstrong was a terrible partner who "through indolence and idleness . . . wasted all of [Joanna's] property," leaving her to die in "extreme poverty."[49]

The moment seems rife with paradox: just as poverty drove her friend Joanna into the city jail, Betsy enjoyed at least some proximity to President Washington. A claim that Betsy had a hand in the ruffles Washington wore as he sat for Adolph Ulrich Wertmuller's 1795 oil portrait suggests that the two maintained at least a nodding acquaintance in these years, though as we've seen, there is some confusion among the evidence itself.[50] If Betsy did contribute to Washington's 1795 appearance, she was still in contact with him during his presidency—and, in fact, would have been in touch with him just as her husband John Claypoole at last secured a coveted position with the federal Customs Service.

As an essential source of revenue to the fledgling United States, few arms of the new national government were as important as the Customs Service. After securing independence, the government immediately faced bankruptcy; desperately in need of funds, on July 4, 1789, in an act hailed by the press as "the second Declaration of Independence," Congress passed the Tariff Act, authorizing the collection of duties on imported goods. Four weeks later, Congress established the Customs Service and determined its ports of entry. Federalists in the 1790s, seeking to expand their political base, appointed numbers of middling and working-class men to civil service jobs. By 1792, customs offices had been established in fourteen states and employed close to 150 officers and more than 300 subordinates. The former group included collectors of customs, naval officers (deputy collectors), surveyors of customs, and civilian masters (captains), while the lesser positions included revenue cutter crews, inspectors of customs, gaugers, weighers, measurers and boatmen.[51] Unsurprisingly, the customhouses in New York, Baltimore and Philadelphia, as the monitors of the bulk of the nation's commercial traffic, "dominated the federal civil establishment in the Middle Atlantic." Philadelphia's leadership had a keen interest in using these positions to advantage, since the Federalists and their opposition were more evenly matched there than in other cities.[52] Employees were generally Federalists of middling status, like former seamen and craftsmen. Indeed, civil service was, in the nation's first capital city, filled with supporters of the Federalist cause, and the Customs Service a prime source of party employment; with the customs collector Sharp Delany at its head, the customs office employed almost forty men.[53]

In 1794, four years after his letter to Washington, John Claypoole finally landed the long-wished-for position as a customs official; he would be an inspector of incoming vessels. Ships from around the world brought Philadelphians the fruits of the globe: limes, oranges, cordials, sweetmeats, coffee, sugar, cigars from the West Indies, indigo from the Haitian port Anse-à-Veau, and Liverpool coal by the ton. Sugar, cotton and coffee flowed into port from across the West Indies. John's job was to confirm that the items in each ship's hold corresponded to the manifest filed, checking to see that there was nothing aboard not stated on the manifest, and nothing listed on the manifest not present in the hold. Claypoole's work as a ship's steward certainly gave him familiarity with ships' stores. Probably more important, Delany was a neighbor on Second Street.[54] In time, Claypoole parlayed both his experiences and contacts into a government position. The work schedule posted in the 1794 city directory suggests that the customhouse opened for business at 9:00 a.m. and remained open until 3:00 p.m., while the warden's office was open from 10:00 a.m. to 1:00 p.m. every day but Sunday, and Saturdays between 3:00 p.m. and 5:00 p.m. for the clearance of vessels. Between his duties for the customhouse and his work around the upholstery shop, John likely worked every day but Sunday.[55]

John's first assignment was the ship *Diana* from Haiti's Saint-Marc.[56] The ship carried a cargo that included forty-five hogsheads of sugar, forty-four bales of cotton, as well as forty-six casks, five barrels and five bags of coffee. Claypoole found that the ship's manifest and the actual contents of the hold "compared and agreed," except for one bag of coffee "more in manifest than delivered," as well as a keg of snuff, a cask of linen, thirty-one reams of paper, a bale of nankeen (a cotton fabric), and some other goods "delivered that are not on manifest." The *Arethusa*, coming in from New Castle, England, likewise "compared and agreed, except for one hundred dozen broken beer bottles"—out of some 13,100.[57] When the sloop *Nelly* pulled in, John looked over the list submitted and found the hogsheads of sugar, casks of indigo, bags of coffee, and 5,600 weight of logwood all to be in good order, but the "3 barrels women's cloths" piqued his curiosity. He inspected further and "found them to have been in use." When the schooner *Hope* docked after its voyage from Haiti's Cape François, he found that the lists agreed except for two barrels of "orrangs" [*sic*] which had gone totally rotten.[58]

Work at the customhouse put John Claypoole at a hub of international trade, something he would have had an interest in not only as a man whose livelihood (and wife's occupation) depended on international commerce, but also as someone who was himself well traveled and worldly. John appears to have taken considerable pride in his work. Beginning in 1797 (the same year John Adams was inaugurated as president, which may have meant some changes in staffing and in status), he noted his title as "Inspector of the Customs for the District of Pennsylvania" in the pages of the city directory.[59] To be sure, positions were highly politicized, and of the country's customhouses, the nation's capital of course saw the most action and tension. The most highly placed officials were all decided and influential Federalists. Inspector of Customs Alexander Boyd, who leaned toward Thomas Jefferson, was dismissed; he subsequently claimed that he lost his $400-a-year, part-time job because he had the temerity to vote for a candidate who was not Federalist. Another inspector, Jonas Simonds, insisted that he had to leave off politics in order to keep his job. Being Republican, he claimed, "was a great crime at the customs house."[60]

Other evidence, too, suggests that Claypoole must have been a party supporter in order to get—and keep—this appointment. A handful of men at the top of the Customs Service firmly enforced the Federal line. Sharp Delany, an Irish immigrant who had served in the Pennsylvania legislature during the years of confederation, was a decided nationalist. His tenure came to an unexpected and unpleasant end when it was discovered that he had embezzled some $86,000 from the national coffers, but his replacement, George Latimer, was just as reliable among the party faithful. Latimer had been an officer in the Continental army, a Pennsylvania assemblyman and a member of Pennsylvania's ratifying convention in 1788; while in his post at the customhouse, he also served as a "regular member of the electioneering committee" in Philadelphia, and from time to time chaired Philadelphia's Federalist Committee of Correspondence.[61] The naval officer William McPherson had been promoted to this civil service position from his job as a surveyor. McPherson had, like Latimer, served in the Continental army and attended Pennsylvania's ratifying convention; he was also a member of the influential Society of Cincinnati. Surveyor of Customs William Jackson was another former army officer and had served as secretary to the 1787 Constitutional Convention. Another member of the Society of Cincinnati, Jackson had also worked as private secretary to President Washington.

For John Claypoole, landing a position with the federal government must have seemed a blessing. Customs officials had been at the center of the rebellion that Betsy and John Claypoole helped foment twenty years earlier, and ironically now they themselves were intimately connected with that hot spot of international policy. They had gone from "rebels" to "establishment." They certainly welcomed with no small relief the salary the position commanded;

compensation ranged from several hundred dollars annually for part-time inspectors to almost two thousand dollars for full-time weighers and gaugers. The nature of Claypoole's compensation is not known, but these years seem to have been ones of prosperity for Betsy. At last, those years of struggle began to seem worth it, as the upholstery shop expanded its trade and John landed this comfortable job with the federal government.

Such prosperity inclined them to position their daughters for even greater social—and with any luck, material—success. Their daughter Rachel years later would recall with pride that she (and so presumably her sisters as well) attended what she called the "Pennsylvania Academy for Young Ladies"—but what was probably the Young Ladies' Academy of Philadelphia.[62] Established by June 1787, the academy was chartered in January 1792, making it the first such institution of higher education for women in the nation.[63] It had its origins in the same school that once occupied the chambers of the Free Quaker meeting, adding plausibility to Rachel's claim to having attended this school; the city directory of 1802 lists the school at 9 Cherry Street and notes James A. Neal as principal.[64] Though the school was nondenominational, Benjamin Say (Betsy and John's coreligionist in the Free Quaker meeting) was among the founders, which perhaps helps account for the Claypooles' ability to educate their girls there, but the school's prestige provided motive enough to attract any parent with aspirations on their children's behalves. The student body included the daughters of Pennsylvania's chief justice and the treasurer of the United States, while the trustees were prominent doctors, lawyers and scholars, past and present members of Congress, trustees and faculty from the University of Pennsylvania, and other leading figures. They included Benjamin Rush, who—Betsy's feeling about his healing philosophy aside—was indisputably the leading spokesman for female education in the new nation.[65] Each year, more than one hundred young scholars attended classes in a curriculum that included, in addition to the basics, courses in rhetoric, geography, chemistry, astronomy, history and natural philosophy. The progressive agenda made the academy highly fashionable in Philadelphia and well beyond.

When Ann Loxley—the daughter of Benjamin Loxley, Samuel Griscom's colleague and competitor in the building trades—gave the valedictory address in 1790, she declared that the curriculum aimed not to produce "docile women willing to assume subordinate roles in life," but rather encouraged women to cherish autonomy.[66] A culture of independence took hold. Students urged one another to " 'be emulous to excel' at endeavors quite apart from marriage," and not to put all their eggs in the matrimonial basket. One student "implied that the Revolution was not complete until women cast off their own shackles, and explicitly embraced radical feminist Mary Wollstonecraft as women's answer to Thomas Paine." First Lady Martha Washington attended the 1794 commencement exercises, along with most members of Congress and the Pennsylvania Assembly—and perhaps Betsy and John Claypoole as well.[67]

Betsy's daughters certainly enjoyed this foray into fashionability. They traveled in social circles high enough that at "one of the courtly private assemblages" of 1794—perhaps associated with the school's closing exercises—Betsy's niece Margaret (Sarah's daughter, then just eighteen) found herself dancing the *minuet de la cour* with none other than President Washington. The family went all out for the event: the train of Margaret's silk gown was so long that it had to be carried as she walked.[68] Her hair was piled in front, and elsewhere fell in curls down to her shoulders. Washington took the young woman's hand and led her to the floor. The musicians began to play. After Washington made a "profound salutation" to the company, he led his partner ahead. Three slow steps were taken, and the couple made an "equally grave salutation" to each other. Washington led Margaret to her place on the floor, and the couple began the "series of slow, graceful evolutions by which the imaginative old French masters who perfected this dance intended to represent the varying relations of two newly formed acquaintances to each other in good society." The stately president and young Margaret were at times as much as ten paces apart, and then approached and passed each other "gracefully but gravely" two or three times, as if they were intrigued by each other but reluctant to meet. Then they advanced slowly and joined hands—only to part again ("coquettishly," when younger dancers were on the floor, but surely not so on this particular occasion) and even turn away from each other as the dance continued. In the end, however, the two partners in this small play came together, faced each other and smiled—and surely Margaret beamed at the president, though it seems unlikely that he beamed back.

Whether or not it was the appealing new fashions or the turn around the floor with the president that helped make the match, one of Betsy's first chicks now left the nest: in July 1794, Margaret Donaldson married the scrivener, conveyancer and broker Joseph Boggs.[69] Boggs had early on worked at an ancient trade; scriveners were professional copyists, employed to reproduce documents by hand. They also acted as notaries, and in time, Boggs drifted toward an emerging career managing financial transactions in a booming commercial sphere. A specialist in the business of transferring properties tangible and intangible, he was surely a catch for the daughter of a mariner lost at sea. Opening what appears to be his first ledger in November 1791, he drew the deeds, bonds, mortgages and leases needed in exchanges of buildings and land, and also bought and sold on commission public securities, bank stock and bills of exchange.[70] As he opened this ledger, Boggs tallied the ready money on hand, seventeen notes due him and miscellaneous debts. He had also accumulated a fair amount of funded and unfunded Pennsylvania state stock, state debt of New Jersey and Delaware, and unfunded debt of the United States. His total assets rose to not quite $31,200. Unfortunately, his total debts rose to $31,840. But young Boggs was undeterred. He recorded these entries in the large bold hand of a man who was confident in his abilities and optimistic about his future. Soon he would be trading too in the stock of companies formed to build canals, like the one planned to link the Schuylkill and Susequehanna rivers. From time to time he sold tickets for the New Jersey lottery.[71] In August 1794, he also staked out new occupational territory when he filed claims asserting his authorship of a new city directory for the ensuing year, 1795.[72]

Boggs was a newlywed that August; the young couple had just married in the First Baptist Church the previous month. But their joy was short-lived and the directory never published: in August 1795, Joseph died while on a trip to South Carolina.[73] His ledger came into the hands of John Reed and Standish Forde, Philadelphia merchants whose firm transacted business across England, France, Spain, Holland, Portugal, the West Indies, and the French and Spanish port of New Orleans. That Thomas Morgan, Betsy's nephew, was a ship captain in the firm's employ hints at how Margaret may have met her groom and reminds us how deeply the rising generation around Betsy Claypoole were becoming engaged in the substantial risks of international trade. But however Margaret and Joseph first found their way toward marital bliss, now young Margaret was widowed, and already the mother of an infant son. Betsy could certainly be sympathetic to a bride whose expectations were dashed so soon after marriage, and she welcomed Margaret back into her home and to the work of her shop.[74] Margaret also joined Betsy in the fold of the Free Quaker meeting.[75] In time, Margaret Boggs would become like another of Betsy's daughters and—though no one could have known it yet—would come to play a formative role in the creation of her legend.

As 1795 drew to a close, Thomas Morgan wrote to his brother George, reporting that "Aunt Claypoole's family" was "brave & hearty."[76] Morgan's use of the word *brave* just then may have referred to his aunt's advanced pregnancy; forty-three-year-old Betsy was eleven days away from delivering her seventh daughter. John's record in the family Bible notes that baby Harriet arrived at 5:00 a.m. on the morning of December 20. It's all too easy to picture the long night of labor preceding Harriet's birth, and soon they had an extraordinary good-luck charm—the seventh daughter of a seventh daughter. But luck was not with them after all; in October, John Claypoole walked the same path Joseph Ashburn had so many years earlier to ask David Evans to make a coffin for his child. Now with the ability to indulge in such luxuries, Betsy and John chose mahogany for the baby, not walnut.[77]

Harriet was Betsy's last pregnancy. She was by then around the common age for menopause in the eighteenth century. She was, perhaps less eager, too, to add to her crowded family. As Betsy looked around, she saw her family in many ways changed. Her parents were now dead, as was her oldest sister, Deborah (and the Bolton house on Front Street was eventually lost in a sheriff's sale). Susannah and her husband, Ephraim Doane, were both gone, as were Sarah and her husband, William Donaldson. The family had buried Mary Morgan, and Thomas, too. The two Rebeccas—Betsy's cousin and sister—were both residents of almshouses. (Betsy would send them little packets and parcels—tea and bread—from time to time.)[78] Niece Sarah Donaldson moved out after her May 1797 marriage to James Lownes, but as Sarah's sister Margaret quickly filled her place, Betsy increasingly became the head of a large family that encompassed not only her daughters but also her nieces, and their children as well. The number of Griscoms who shared her childhood memories was shrinking, but there were still brothers and sisters who could reminisce with Betsy about those halcyon years, before the rupture of the Revolution, when all of them were gathered under the sturdy roof Samuel built for them on Arch Street. She and her younger sisters Hannah and Rachel held steady together, sharing what came, good or ill.

But although many loved ones were gone, new ones were filling their place. Sister Hannah, the widow of Griffith Levering, had recently remarried, to a man named William McIntire, and had also been drawn into the work of Betsy's shop, taking discarded remnants from the shop goods as well as worn-out clothing and cutting them into strips from which she made rag rugs.[79] In these same years, too, Betsy began to see the future take shape in the marriages of her own girls. In May 1799, Eliza, her oldest living daughter, married ship captain Isaac Silliman.[80] If Betsy's family tree was filled with artisans, the in-laws tended to come by sea. Betsy's first son-in-law, like her several brothers-in-law, was a mariner. Isaac captained the brig *Nancy,* which sailed to Cádiz, Sanlúcar and other ports across the Atlantic.[81] Eliza's husband, like her father, Joseph Ashburn, would make his living on the water. It seems that the couple moved—perhaps immediately—out of Philadelphia or even went to sea.[82]

Isaac was only the first to take one of Betsy's daughters away from home. Others would soon follow. The children began to scatter to the winds. Soon,

Clarissa would move to Baltimore, Mary's boys would be in New Orleans and Hannah's sons would launch a business in the new capital on the banks of the Potomoc and head to someplace far west with the unlikely name of Kaskaskia, Illinois. But family trumped geography; as distance stretched between them, these cousins nevertheless remained devoted to one another and to their several aunts and uncles. A particularly revealing letter that George Morgan wrote to his sister Rebecca from New Orleans nicely captures the family's warmth in these years. He notes that he mailed packets home to "Uncle Bolton," and suggests that his cousin Abel Bolton might send down some chocolate. He asks to be remembered to his various aunts, as well as cousins Jane Doane and Sammy Levering, and he mentions that, upon receipt of the three fans he sent to her, Rebecca is to keep one and give the other two to Sarah Donaldson and Jane Doane. He also mailed an unusual treat, a keg of exotic nuts called paccands (otherwise known as pecans), that Rebecca was instructed to share with everyone on Front Street.[83] Other letters suggest ways that the family worked together on matters of business. They stayed abreast of one another's activities and needs, and sent their concern by mail when they weren't there to deliver it in person.

But not yet perceptible to the family were other developments that threatened to undermine their happiness. Most immediately, John Claypoole's government appointment ended in 1800 with the exit of John Adams and the inauguration of Thomas Jefferson. John Claypoole's dismissal from the Customs Service may have been over a disagreement about some policy matter, or perhaps he saw the writing on the wall and left of his own accord. It could also have been a product of his declining health. These years may have been invigorating politically for the Claypoole household, but the family faced both acute and ongoing health crises at the same time. Meanwhile, the consequences of the Revolution continued to reverberate for Betsy's family, in ways both intimate and global.

PART V

---

# ENDINGS AND

# BEGINNINGS

# 20

# War, Redux

One night John Claypoole dreamed that he was walking through a country neighborhood when he came upon a church. Inside, he could hear voices. "Why should we mortals vex ourselves with trouble, care and woe," the choir sang, "when so much pleasure we can find walking to and fro?"[1] As John's health declined, and he could no longer work productively, he would recall these lines from his sleeping mind, and they gave him comfort. And comfort would be something Betsy's household sorely needed as the eighteenth century gave way to the nineteenth.

Ironically, perhaps, these difficult years—both the highs and the lows—are among the best documented in Betsy's life. The demand for flags in the early nineteenth century brought the knowledgeable craftswoman once more to the attention of government agents and agencies eager to contract for her services. Whether she was working more in this period or whether the record of her efforts is simply richer or more accessible we can't know, but the vast majority of extant references to Betsy's work as a flag maker date to these years. At the same time, her husband's declining health attracted the kind attention of the Free Quakers, who found more and more occasion to enter into their own records various disbursements meant to help keep the Claypooles afloat. Yet, as the documentary record becomes more ample, it becomes more contradictory. The first decade of the nineteenth century, like other moments in Betsy's life, seems marked by both affluence and scarcity. For instance, portrait miniatures made about 1806 suggest the pride the Clay-pooles had in their beautiful girls, and the couple's desire (and ability) to capture and display their hard-won gentility to their friends and neighbors.[2] The likeness of daughter Rachel (which may have been painted by a member of the Peale family, with whom the Claypooles were distantly related and had been associated for some time) captures a family eager to embrace the latest trends. They remind us, too, that parenting teenage girls in some ways has changed little over time. Betsy was the mother of young daughters just as a scandalous new fashion swept Philadelphia. As the new Republic found its footing, designs inspired by ancient Roman and Greek culture became wildly popular. Betsy had already seen these new preferences reshaping trends in upholstery; new forms for chairs demanded new fabrics, and drap-eries took new shapes. On the whole, the look was spare and clean; demand for tassels dropped off sharply, and other sorts of trimmings took their place. Women's clothing was utterly transformed as well, and as is often the case, it was the youth who took the new aesthetic logic to its most extreme forms. Girls aspired to look like the classical statues they were seeing every-place. Gowns became sheerer and sheerer, clingier and clingier. High-waisted dresses emphasized the bustline, while airy fabrics just barely suggested the shape of the thighs. Stories were passed around of girls who refused to wear coats over such revealing clothes and caught their deaths as a result. At least Rachel Claypoole, if not her sisters, was apparently undeterred; the miniature shows her decidedly à la mode. That Rachel's likeness was made in the same years that Betsy's flag making approached its zenith should not surprise us; that these same years saw the Claypoole household begin to receive the char-itable support of the Society of Free Quakers is difficult to explain. But these records of fortune and fragility, laid alongside one another, remind us just how capricious life could be for working women and their families in the early Republic.

Many might say that the eighteenth century officially came to a close with the December 1799 death of George Washington. When the aged statesman died in his home at Mount Vernon, the nation plunged into mourning. The level of national grieving was unprecedented and extraordinary. Genuine outpour-ings of sorrow were manifested in gestures small and large around the coun-try. "Our Washington is no more!" exclaimed Congressman John Marshall. "The hero, the sage, and the patriot of America—the man on whom, in times of danger, every eye was turned and all hopes were placed, lives now, only in his own great actions, and in the hearts of an affectionate and afflicted people." "More than any other individual," he continued, "and as much as to one individual was possible, has he contributed to found this our wide spreading empire, and to give to the western world its independence and its freedom." Washington, his mourners avowed, had forged plowshares from swords and voluntarily sank the soldier in the citizen; in advancing the Constitution he rescued a failing federal system, and so preserved the Union; he accepted the presidency when the nation demanded it, and later in great humility declined it as well. Upon word of his death, the members of Congress resolved to wear black; they shrouded their chambers and furniture in black as well.[3] The city's bells were muffled for three days. Ships wore their colors at half-mast; officers donned crepe bands on the left arm, below the elbow, which they retained for months.[4]

On December 26, by congressional decree, Philadelphia held a mock funeral, and there can be no doubt that Betsy Claypoole was among the deep rows of the bereaved lining the city streets. As soon as it was light, sixteen cannons began firing to mark each hour. A procession formed at the statehouse and marched to the beat of muffled drums. A riderless horse "trimmed with black—the head festooned with elegant black and white feathers"— carried an empty saddle, holsters, pistols and boots reversed in the stirrups. Pallbearers carried a draped empty bier. Given the reverence and esteem Betsy Claypoole harbored for Washington, she surely strained alongside some four thousand men and women to hear the Virginian "Light Horse Harry" Lee deliver his funeral oration. To take still better measure of the nation's grief, this solemn occasion was only one of three mock funerals held that same day, among no fewer than fifteen held in Philadelphia between December 22, 1799, and February 22, 1800.[5]

The death of Washington seems like an obvious moment for Betsy Claypoole to begin regaling her family with her own personal knowledge of the heroic leader, if she had not already. And John Claypoole had his own tales to tell. Just as the children would later recall Betsy telling the story of making the flag, John recounted his own experiences in the war—though hers would become legendary, his must have been livelier at the time—describing the battle at Germantown, his days at sea and his own brush with greatness when he was selected to carry dispatches to General Washington with news of the military success at Red Bank. After Washington's death, the Claypooles were among the thousands of American households to acquire some memento of his life: a large framed engraving depicting a statue of the fallen leader upon a pedestal carrying the famous words from Lee's eulogy: FIRST IN WAR, FIRST

IN PEACE, FIRST IN THE HEARTS OF HIS COUNTRYMEN. "We loved him," Betsy Claypoole would say, "as we shall never love another."[6]


Another terrible turn of events brought Betsy's grieving still closer to her Front Street home.[7] Even as Betsy mourned the death of Washington, she faced more personal tragedy when John suffered a "stroke of paralysis" which some sources say left him an invalid.[8] A token of regard left behind from Isaac Silliman sheds some light on this unhappy event and at the same time speaks of both the familial affection the mariner maintained for his wife's family and the travels that carried him around the globe. Despite the effects of the stroke, he was still at least somewhat mobile ten years later when Isaac Silliman presented his father-in-law with a gift: a bamboo cane with a steel tip.[9] Embellished with the head of a dog, the cane also carried some Masonic imagery. Marked IS TO JC, 1810, the cane also bore the inscription JOHN E. CLAYPOOLE, 74 S. FRONT STREET—lest the old man leave it behind someplace. If John's stroke had impaired his mobility, apparently he was still able to walk with assistance, and traveled far and often enough from home that Isaac worried he might accidentally leave the cane behind.

But he was apparently unable to work, and as John's health declined, so did more material fortunes. By 1802, a committee of Free Quakers was appointed to call upon several Friends, including Betsy and John Claypoole, "to examine into their circumstances and relieve them, either with money or wood in such quantity as the committee in their discretion may think proper."[10] The Claypooles had long watched their meeting care for its less fortunate members; now they were among them.[11] In March 1803, the Claypoole household was still in need. A "committee appointed to distribute some money among certain members of the society" presented ten dollars each to four struggling members, while John Claypoole and another man received fifteen.[12] It wasn't enough. John swallowed his pride and sent a petition for aid to his fellow Masons, despite having resigned his membership some six years earlier; they sent ten dollars, every penny of which Betsy put to good use.[13]

There's no evidence that the Masons continued to keep an eye on the Claypooles, but the Quakers did. Just a few months later, a "private conference" of members of the Society (hinting that this conversation occurred outside the church's regular deliberations about its members in need) decided to present another fifteen dollars to Claypoole "on account of his extreme disability of Body."[14] In December 1804, George Kemble was appointed to visit John and to "take his afflicted situation into consideration and to assist him as he may appear to need." Just a couple of months later, the meeting paid "for clothes for Jon. Claypoole": three and a half yards of velvet, three-fourths yards linen, silk and twist, and the cost of "making a pair of pantaloons."[15] In the years that followed, the congregation from time to time provided him with pairs of shoes.[16] In November 1811, they would set aside some fifty dollars "for cloathing J Claypole" (among the highest allocations), one of a number of contributions that were ongoing and much needed.[17]

With John unable to work, and Betsy with four daughters between the ages of fifteen and eight to support, the upholsterer had her hands full. Now with Eliza newly married, Clarissa would have to take charge of the domestic affairs. Certainly all those girls could keep the housework going while Betsy attended to the shop, but she still had to feed and clothe a large household. Betsy's niece Margaret Donaldson Boggs also helped, but it was a lot to handle. Betsy barely had time to catch her breath as she crossed another of those watershed moments in a woman's life. In April 1801, she had become a grandmother when her oldest daughter, Eliza, gave birth to her own first child—a son, whom she named Joseph Ashburn Silliman after her long-dead father.[18] The choice surely was bittersweet for the new grandmother, a reminder of those frightening times, and a touching gesture for a daughter who never knew the man for whom her son was named. A daughter, Amelia, named for Isaac's mother in Connecticut, followed in 1803, and two years later like clockwork they cradled another daughter, Jane.

Then in June 1805, twenty-year-old Clarissa married. She chose the merchant and accountant Jacob Wilson and soon thereafter moved to Baltimore.[19] There was a natural relationship between these two port cities, and merchants and artisans moved easily between them, more and more so as Baltimore hit its stride toward the turn of the nineteenth century. In 1752, the year Betsy was born, just twenty-five houses had stood along the harbor that would become Baltimore: the population of Baltimore doubled between 1790 and 1800, and nearly doubled again in the next decade, reaching over forty-six thousand in 1810.[20] By the time Clarissa and Jacob Wilson moved to Conowago Street, it was a boomtown.

In 1806, Betsy welcomed more grandchildren into the world when Clarissa had twins—which then, as now, tend to skip a generation. When the babies were born, they were so tiny the family feared they would not survive; people said that their heads were so small they could have fit in a teacup. Betsy rushed to Baltimore to meet little Sophia Berg Wilson and Elizabeth Griscom Wilson—the latter named in clear tribute to her grandmother.

Clarissa, like her cousin Margaret, had found herself a mate who worked with his mind rather than his hands. In 1807, Jacob Wilson instructed the compilers of the city directory to list his occupation as "accomptant." It was the dawn of accountancy as an occupation. As the middle class emerged in early American cities, Clarissa and Jacob aimed to be in it.[21] Betsy's own father had supported his family by the sweat of his brow and the strength of his shoulder; he wore a leather apron to work. Jacob Wilson wore a dark suit—the emerging uniform of the middle class. Like his father-in-law, Wilson was a supporter of strong government; when his own daughter Clarissa was born during a visit home to Philadelphia in 1809, she was baptized by the Lutheran pastor Justus Henry Christian Helmuth, a "devoted Federalist who had long used his pulpit for political sermons."[22] For his wife Clarissa's part, there were several upholstery shops in Baltimore; if need be, she could find work in any one of them. Or perhaps she aimed from the outset to extend the family flag-making business into another port city.[23]

By 1810, the Wilsons had moved to the corner of Saratoga and Liberty streets—both named to celebrate the Revolution, honoring liberty itself as well as the 1777 victory that turned the war's tide. (After only a couple of years there, they moved once more, this time to Greene Street, named in honor of a hero of the Revolution, General Nathanael Greene.) Clarissa had a houseful of charges to attend to: the third federal census found her and Jacob Wilson together with two boys under ten (only one of them known to be a son, Aquilla), their three small daughters, and also another girl in her early teens, a woman between twenty-six and forty-four (perhaps one of Clarissa's sisters) and also another "free" person, probably a servant engaged to help with the housework.[24]

Betsy now had to make do without Clarissa's help, but she may have been little missed in a household that continued to swap daughters for nieces. The daughters of Betsy's sister Sarah Donaldson (Margaret, Sarah and Susanna) became increasingly important in these years. These girls and their own children (when sister Sarah's namesake Sarah Donaldson Lownes came to Betsy's home, she brought three and maybe four children from her marriage to James Lownes) also received help from the Free Quaker meeting.[25] In November 1807, "a son of Margaret Boggs who attends our meetings pretty regularly being in want of school" received funds enough for one year of schooling—the first of several contributions toward the young boy's education.[26] For the next twenty years, members of the Claypoole household continued to receive regular assistance from the Society of Free Quakers. The meeting put shoes on their feet and coats on their backs, and helped send Betsy's grandchildren to school.

The summer after Clarissa wed Jacob Wilson, another daughter left the nest when seventeen-year-old Rachel married the ship captain Edward Jones. Betsy kissed another girl farewell and good luck. With Eliza's husband, Isaac Silliman, also making a living on the water, men at sea became the family's focus. Betsy's niece Rebecca Morgan had been married a dozen-plus years now to the ship captain Samuel Pile; a double portrait taken around 1809 shows the couple in the Canary Islands, with the volcano Pico de Teyde looming in the distance behind them.[27] The network of mariners proved useful to one another. Silliman, writing from Lisbon, could advise Pile that a cargo of salt might sell well in Brazil, that sugar could be had cheap in Pemambuco as well as El Salvador, and hides, coffee and cocoa would be profitable, too. Other letters to and from Liverpool, Madeira and Calcutta kept one another abreast of kin and commerce alike.[28] The specter of William Donaldson's disappearance must have hovered over each of these marriages, though women in seaport cities were used to this particular brand of worry.

Betsy herself had bid a husband farewell never to see him again, so she knew all too well the risks of unions with sailors. Her children's families hedged their bets, several joining the Society for the Relief of Poor, Aged, and Infirm Masters of Ships, their Widows and Children. In an age before life insurance, disability or workmen's comp, groups like this one formed to create some sort of safety net for families associated by occupation. A fund was created from regular dues, from which payments could be made to needful applicants. At least if something happened to Samuel Pile, Edward Jones or Isaac Silliman, Rebecca, Rachel, Eliza and their families left behind might find some support, however small.[29]

Betsy must have been relieved that some of her daughters chose men whose work tied them more tangibly to the city. The hardware dealer Abel Satterthwaite affords a small glimpse into Betsy's home in these years. Though he had not yet married Betsy's daughter Susan, he was already part of the family circle. His mother was Betsy's cousin Mary Knight, the daughter of Uncle Giles; born in 1779, he was probably named for Uncle Abel James as well. About 1803, he had moved from Abington to Philadelphia, opening a store in Betsy's old neighborhood, near the corner of Third and Arch, and became a familiar presence in Betsy's parlor. A letter Abel sent to Rebecca's husband, Samuel Pile, then aboard the *Perseverance* off New Castle, opens a window into Betsy's house on Front Street. Abel wanted to let Samuel know that he and Pile's daughter (probably Elizabeth), who had been traveling together, had returned safely to Philadelphia: "Both the child and my self," he writes, "were heartily tired of [traveling] and I thought I should be (and you will give me credit for this) more happy at Aunt Betsy's." "I immediately carried her there and kicked Susan up [Betsy's daughter] who as usual rec'd us very friendly and when I left her Susan informed [me] that Mary & Emma [Samuel's other daughters] appear to be perfectly at their ease."[30]

As Betsy watched the changes that came gradually and naturally to her household as her daughters grew up, she also witnessed watershed moments in larger histories: Washington replaced Philadelphia as the nation's capital, and Republicans replaced Federalists as the party in power. Betsy—surely like her husband a Federalist at heart—probably hated to see both. But it would be during Thomas Jefferson's administration that Betsy would make her greatest contribution to the making of U.S. flags, at least so far as the documentary record can affirm. In many respects Betsy Claypoole was a government contractor, and these would prove especially lucrative years. Margaret Donaldson Boggs would later remember that her aunt Betsy made "all the flags" for the "United States in Philadelphia, and largely for other naval stations"—which could be tempting to dismiss as filial exaggeration, but appears to be true at least for a time in the early nineteenth century, and Boggs—who had been living and working with Betsy for several years, now—was in a position to know.[31]

In these years, Betsy's fortunes were directly entwined with those of another flag-making family, the Youngs. Rebecca Flower Young's daughter Mary had wed John Pickersgill, but after his death about 1805, the two widows decided to return to Baltimore, where they had lived for a time before, leaving Philadelphia's arsenal without two of its steadiest flag fabricators.[32] Constructed about 1800 to store ammunition and other military supplies, the Schuylkill Arsenal also supplied clothing and textile goods to military operations. (By 1818, the facility had shifted away from ordnance and was dedicated solely to manufacturing, storing and distributing clothing and textile articles.)[33] Flags were among the items the arsenal supplied. But with the Youngs absent, the facility would have to look elsewhere for these things, creating an opening for Betsy Claypoole.

The appointment of Tench Coxe as purveyor of public supplies at this very moment would prove a boon to the Claypooles.[34] Coxe's grandfather had been the first purveyor, appointed in 1794 when the office was created, and a decade later—in 1803—Jefferson gave the nod to Tench Coxe. Coxe and John Claypoole had known each other through both the prison reform movement and the Pennsylvania Abolition Society; it had been John Claypoole who delivered the news when Coxe was chastised for what appeared to be an attempt to participate in the slave trade.[35] Just a few years later, when Coxe ordered new ladders, cords and tassels for seven Venetian blinds in his family's posh Second Street home, he engaged the Claypooles to fabricate them, and to paint and mend slats as well. On another occasion, he invited them back to stuff and mend six chair seats.[36] It's no surprise, then, that in the run-up to another war with Britain, when the purveyor of public supplies needed flags, he steered the business toward the Claypooles, though by now it was clearly Betsy, and not John, whose work he hired.

Flag making had altered somewhat in the decades since the rebellion. After two new states, Vermont (1791) and Kentucky (1792), joined the blossoming union, raising the magic number from thirteen to fifteen, Betsy's shop absorbed the implications of the Second Flag Act. In late December 1793, Vermont senator Stephen R. Bradley, eager to see his home state included on the national flag, introduced a bill to update the Flag Act of 1777; the flag should now have, he argued, fifteen stars, and fifteen stripes. The measure was controversial; as some observed, revisions to the flag could go on forever (and indeed, expansionists hoped they would). A countereffort was launched to "fix" (that is, to settle) the flag, but it failed. Bradley's bill passed in the House of Representatives narrowly in January by a vote of 50–42, and Betsy began to factor in two additional stars and two additional stripes to her new orders.[37] Fortunately, when Tennessee was admitted in 1796, or Ohio in 1803, no comparable calls were made: the fifteen-star, fifteen-stripe flag would stay on the books for the next twenty-three years.

Opportunities for flag makers were of course tied to the fortunes of the U.S. military, and as international tensions over impressments and trade grew in the first decade of the nineteenth centry, the need for flags rose. When Britain went to war with Napoleon's empire in France, American ships were inevitably drawn in, since Britain had no intention of allowing the United States to trade with the enemy; what's more, the Royal Navy aggressively searched U.S. ships for alleged deserters to refresh its own ranks. An attack on the USS *Chesapeake* in June 1807 heightened the nation's state of alert; Jefferson responded with an embargo on international trade. Jefferson and his successor, James Madison, took a different approach to naval forces than had their predecessors, preferring a number of small boats to large investments in frigates (essentially more eggs in more baskets).[38] In time, contracts would go out to private firms for more than two hundred small gunboats, which in turn meant flags for each ship. Betsy didn't need to read the newspapers to track the growing threat to American sailors. In spring

1808, her son-in-law Isaac Silliman had occasion to warn fellow mariners that American vessels were "very much exposed" to capture and that it was advisable "not to sail without a convoy."[39] His family surely knew just how much danger he was in.

In April that same year, in a flurry of military activity, Congress also authorized the creation of five infantry regiments, as well as regiments of light dragoons, light artillery and riflemen. Work at the purveyor's office suddenly tripled.[40] In May, Secretary of War Henry Dearborn contacted Purveyor Coxe to let him know that he was eager to supply seven regiments, and each would need two flags: colors announcing the regiment's identity, and standards that identified the nation for which they fought. Even at this date, the Stars and Stripes was not yet the national standard for all branches of service "bearing what purported to be the Great Seal or coat of Arms of the United States."[41]

Seals cannot easily be fashioned out of cloth; for these flags, Betsy needed to work together with an experienced painter who could apply the needed design onto the banner she sewed. In her affidavit, Betsy's daughter Rachel remembers her mother drawing on the skills of the Philadelphia painter William Berrett. In Rachel's memory, Betsy hired Berrett "to paint the coat of arms of the United States and of the State [of Pennsylvania] on silk flags." Rachel called Berrett "an artist who lived on the North side of Cherry Street above Third Street, [in] a large three story brick house on the West side of an alley which ran back to the Pennsylvania Academy for Young Ladies," kept by James A. Neal in the Free Quaker meetinghouse; in her mind, his shop was associated with her school, which is not suprising, since she and Berrett's daughter Anna both attended.[42] Whether the upholsterer Claypoole hired the painter Berrett or vice versa is unclear (and perhaps immaterial, and probably alternating), but Berrett certainly maintained a close relationship with the Pennsylvania treasurer's office to produce flags into the second quarter of the nineteenth century, and there's no reason to doubt Rachel's memory of their association.

Ornamental painters like William Berrett were the same artisans who created those memorable shop signs—the easy chairs and stays—as well as tavern signs, coaches and so forth. The "remarkably beautiful signboards with backgrounds of different colors speckled with gold or silver" that marked the sites of Philadelphia's shops and craftsmen were the work of these hands.[43] Ornamental painters sustained close relationships with upholsterers and other artisans in the furniture trades. Next door to Plunket Fleeson, for instance, stood the shop of George Rutter, a sign painter who ornamented "fire buckets, landscapes, carriages and show boards." Rutter also painted the "Arms" of Pennsylvania "&c" over the seat of the Supreme Court of Judicature.[44] William's father, Timothy, was an ornamental painter as well, and when the fashion for japanned furniture (that is, furniture whose decoration is inspired by Asian lacquerwork) flourished in the middle decades of the eighteenth century, the senior Berrett applied this embellishment to desks and high chests made in the city's cabinet shop. He also added gilding to carriages and wagons, and even worked on houses from time to time; while Betsy was at work on the Cadwalader furniture, Timothy Berrett was adding painted ornamentation to the house itself. When work in the shop was slow, he offered drawing lessons to children of privilege.[45] He also found work in government contracts: in 1776, the Pennsylvania Committee of Safety purchased two battalion standards from Timothy Berrett.[46]

Though William Berrett was purchasing paint supplies in Philadelphia as early as 1785 (on his father's account), the first clear indication that he was out on his own came in 1793, when he asked the compilers of Hardie's city directory to list him as a painter on Mulberry Street. A second listing suggests that he also performed coach painting from a shop on Lombard. By 1800, he had moved to the address at 9 Cherry Alley, where he would remain for the next twenty-five years. The census for that year finds him in a household comprising five men and a youth, a young woman and two girls, and two other "free persons." Ten years later, the household comprised Berrett together with no fewer than seven men between the ages of twenty-six and forty-five, and two between sixteen and twenty-six; also present were a girl between ten and sixteen years old, two women in their late teens or early twenties, and one woman between twenty-six and forty-five years old, as well as two free blacks, for a total of sixteen. It seems that Berrett had rather a large operation that housed several employees.[47]

The earlier Berrett shop on Arch Street between Second and Third was very near the house in which Betsy grew up, as well as the home she had shared with Joseph Ashburn and then John Claypoole in the 1770s and '80s.[48] William and his parents, Timothy and Mary, were surely well known to Betsy for many years before they first collaborated on a flag.[49] Betsy's association with Berrett may also suggest how he came to donate his workmanship to the renovation of Immanuel Church in New Castle, the pulpit of Betsy's onetime father-in-law Aeneas Ross. The painter applied the Ten Commandments, the Apostle's Creed, the Lord's prayer and other scriptural passages in gold to tablets on the west end near the pulpit and chancel.[50]

The earliest known evidence of Berrett painting flags (and so potentially the earliest evidence of his collaboration with Betsy Claypoole) appears in 1801, when he charged the state of Pennsylvania more than $1,700 (well more than twice the size of the next largest flag maker's account) for colors for the militia.[51] Five stands of colors for the Franklin County militia in that year brought in just over $600; another five the following summer netted even more.[52] A steady stream of payments to Berrett would flow from Pennsylvania coffers over the ensuing decades.[53]

The months that followed the 1807 assault on the *Chesapeake* and ensuing embargo acts heightened martial activity across the armed services. In May 1808, when Secretary Dearborn contacted Coxe about the seven sets of standards he wanted, he described very carefully what he had in mind. The regimental colors—five feet on the hoist and six on the fly—should be plain, buff-colored silk, with the appropriate lettering applied to designate the regiment. Cords and tassels would also be required. The standards each regiment would need—two yards on the hoist and two and a half yards on the fly— were to have a "deep blue field with full spread Eagle in the Centre surrounded by 17 stars, hansomely [*sic*] wrought in needle work with yellow silk for the Artillery and white silk for the infantry on both sides. Under the Eagle should be the number of the Infantry Regiment, . . . those for the Artillery designated 1st Regt Lt. Artillery—the one for the Rifle Regiment 1st Rifle Regt.—U.S. should be on the breast of the Eagle, in white silk needle work." The Eagle "ought to be so large, that the extent from tip to tip of his wings" should be two and a half feet—that is, filling the whole field. The eagle's head should be white, and the whole "handsomely wrought in the real Colors" of the bird, if at all possible.[54]

The contract for at least some of the work went to Anna and Eliza Leslie, who billed Coxe for embroidering a flag for the light artillery, but painted flags were obtained from William Berrett, and so, likely involved Betsy Claypoole too.[55] Six months after those directives were issued, in November 1808, Coxe recorded in his day journal that eleven yards of blue "Kershaw" (probably kersey, a woolen cloth) were en route, to be converted into standards; several weeks later (in February 1809), Philadelphia's military storekeeper informed Coxe that "Mrs. Claypoole charges for making 2 garrison and 2 silk flags and 7 regimental colors."[56]

In addition to flags for the army and militia, Coxe and the military stores he supervised supplied the needs of the Indian Department, an agency as old as the nation itself, formed immediately to coordinate relations with the nations bordering to the west. These flags, too, involved both fabric and painted elements, and so also involved both Betsy Claypoole and William Berrett. Presentation goods were an important part of international diplomacy, and flags were among the goods that symbolized respect. In the wake of the Louisiana Purchase, Thomas Jefferson equipped a number of exploratory expeditions with red-and-white-striped flags with an eagle painted in the canton. When Lewis and Clark were dispatched to the Missouri River, they carried among other things just over two dozen flags to present to native nations along the route.[57] Philadelphia's George Hunter and his companion William Dunbar headed to the Ouachita River—Choctaw territory (today Arkansas and Louisiana)—and they too needed flags, so in January 1804, Philadelphia flag makers delivered five flags for the Indian Department (the flags noted as being intended "for Choctaw Indians"), each measuring nine feet by six feet and carrying seventeen stars and seventeen stripes, "with the eagle."[58]

At least some of these flags were supplied by longtime flag maker Rebecca Flower Young, but a cryptic line in a letter to Tench Coxe late in 1803 suggests that something was amiss in her world.[59] Young wanted Coxe to "please observe that any Colours sent to my son, do not come under my direction." The order for the five presentation flags for the Choctaws had come just three days before Rebecca penned the puzzling note. Apparently there had been some estrangement between Rebecca and her oldest son, William, and Rebecca wanted the Purveyor's office to know that orders sent to him may no longer engage her expertise. William indeed produced the flags ordered, as well as (over the course of the next thirty months) ten U.S. ensigns (three yards square with a painted eagle), five garrison flags (each with dimensions of eighteen feet by thirty-six feet), bound to St. Louis for "western forts," four other garrison flags (these with dimensions of ten feet by thirty-one feet), for Fort Jay, and two smaller "boat flags," all delivered to the Indian Department or the Quartermaster General. If Rebecca Young was not directing the work, who was? Was this a moment of particular opportunity for Betsy Claypoole? It's certainly tempting to imagine her slipping into any breach within the longstanding Young enterprise, and along the way establish her own connection with Coxe, one that would bear fruit in the not too distant future. Certainly the next chapter in Rebecca Flower Young's life shaped Betsy's as well, since after her daughter Mary Pickersgill's husband died in 1805, Rebecca and Mary relocated to Baltimore, leaving the field in Philadelphia wide open for Elizabeth Claypoole.

Whether Betsy had any role in the flags delivered between 1804 and 1806, by 1810 she was certainly making goods for diplomatic exchange. An "inventory of flags on hand" made in December 1810 notes sixteen "fields" from "Mrs. Claypoole," fourteen embellished with painting in Berrett's hand. Berrett and Claypoole may have been working together as early as those orders in 1801 for various stands of regimental colors (giving us perhaps some insight into the portrait miniatures and the stylish young women captured there, which such orders may have made possible), but they were definitely teamed up by the end of the nineteenth century's first decade. The year 1811 saw Betsy fabricate no fewer than twenty-seven flags for the Indian Department.[60] Because they involved far less sewing (the work was really in the painting), these were much less remunerative—less than half the income per flag than garrison flags.[61] (A rare surviving example of an Indian presentation flag in the collections of the Chicago Historical Society—one of only about a half dozen known to be extant—suggests how these flags appeared and the work involved in their fabrication. Like standard U.S. flags, this flag has fifteen red and white stripes, but the canton carries painted ornamentation, seventeen gold six-pointed stars surrounding an eagle.) That work would, like garrison flags, prove steady. Some years later, Superintendent of Indian Affairs Thomas McKenney wrote to Henry Simpson in Philadelphia asking him to "have made twelve small flags with an eagle painted on each side." He told Simpson, "Mr. Bronaugh once purchased such as I now want from a Mr. Claypoole of Philadelphia, from whom you can get every information respecting them." Two weeks later, the flags were almost done, and by the first week of June they were in McKenney's hand, earning Betsy and her family about twelve dollars each for their fabrication.[62]

It was a productive relationship: while Betsy Claypoole landed contracts for garrison and regimental flags, Berrett landed contracts for knapsacks and other ornamented supplies, on a single occasion painting no fewer than 3,500 knapsacks for the army.[63] Along the way, both developed and sustained vital contacts. Berrett, for instance, was engaged by John Jones, brigadier inspector of the Pennsylvania militia, to supply fifes and drums; in his correspondence about the order, Berrett added, "If you should want any colours for the use of your brigade I should be glad to supply you." In a follow-up message confirming delivery, Berrett again noted, "If at any time colours should be wanted your order shall be punctually attended to"; the next words, *by me,* are crossed out in Berrett's letter.[64]

In 1810, Claypoole also contracted for six 18-by-24-foot garrison flags for the military installation at New Orleans, which she delivered in January 1811. The enormity of this order is breathtaking. Even one flag of this size required a tremendous amount of labor. (For some sense of this size flag, look around your own house; few living rooms today could even accommodate a flag of these dimensions. Betsy's whole home around this time occupied just 468 square feet per floor; an 18-by-24-foot flag unfolds to 432 square feet.)[65] Each article demanded some twenty-four feet of seams for each of the thirteen stripes (and these seams were felled, which means the length was stitched twice), not to mention the assembly of the canton, the application of the stars, and so forth. In all, each flag required more than one hundred thousand stitches.[66] And of course that was to make just one; the full order demanded some six hundred thousand stitches. Betsy's six flags joined two dozen drums and fifes as well as another dozen snare drums for the installation (made by the Philadelphia upholsterer Thomas Jaquet), as well as boxes and barrels of saws, axes, nails, window glass, some five hundred yards of mosquito netting—all destined for the Gulf Coast fort.[67]

Those six flags may have seemed like the largest contract Betsy could hope either to land or to fill. Surely it meant the constant attention of not just Betsy but also her niece Margaret, her daughters, her sister Rachel and whoever else could be set to work. But in spring 1811, Coxe contracted with Betsy once again, this time for a tremendous order—no fewer than forty-six garrison flags—which she was to deliver "with all dispatch" to the U.S. Arsenal on the Schuylkill. The number seems incredible. The work was commissioned on March 19. Tensions with Britain were once again high; though the embargo acts were revoked in 1809, relations had remained strained, and on March 2, just seventeen days earlier, Madison had banned trade with England. It seems impossible to imagine that any one firm would be engaged to make forty-six flags the size of those she sent to New Orleans. Later that year, in September, Betsy was paid over $70 for eight garrison flags ($48 of it her labor in assembly, or $6 per flag), each consuming 161 yards of materials, not including the forty yards of muslin needed for the stars.[68] This may mean that her shop fabricated more than fifty garrison flags in 1811, though it seems possible that those recorded in September were among the forty-six Coxe reported in March, and not a separate order. If so, the full order perhaps generated just over $400, maybe $276 for labor.

When Betsy Claypoole filled these large orders for garrison flags, the arsenal was bracing for a second war with the world's most powerful military. That same month when Betsy started cutting close to seven hundred strips of bunting and an equal number of stars, Coxe ordered from Walter Kendrick some 2,500 felt wool caps, and from Sebastien Saladé nearly eight hundred epaulettes (both white cotton and yellow silk) and no fewer than three thousand white cotton hat cords with tassels, while the upholsterer Thomas Jaquet provided three dozen drums painted with the arms of the United States, and three dozen fifes to go with them. For his part, William Berrett applied the U.S. arms to sixteen hundred knapsacks.[69]

The shop did benefit from wartime contracts, apart from the purveyor of public supplies. On March 28, 1811, just nine days after Betsy landed the enormous contract for forty-six flags, Coxe was legislated out of office. Though the purveyorship would not be abolished officially until May 1812, the creation of the Quartermaster Department eliminated the need for Coxe's post. Other men assumed responsibility for purchasing, and Betsy Claypoole's name appears less frequently in public accounts. Her name is notably absent from the secretary of war's statement of contracts for 1812, though Berrett's remained on the parchment directories of the right officers. By March of that year, he would be painting another batch of knapsacks—now five thousand, at ten cents a sack. He also painted six blue silk standards; perhaps Betsy Claypoole's work to stitch the necessary panels and channels (essentially a subcontractor) is cloaked under Berrett's name as the provider of these articles.[70]

Nevertheless, Betsy and Clarissa found other clients during the war, making among other things a "large American ensign" for Caesar A. Rodney.[71] They were surely glad for the business; other family members observed the depressed nature of commerce in general during the war. Aquila Murray (one of Betsy's sister Susannah Doane's grandsons) tried his hand at trade in New York, but the stagnation associated with the war meant it was a tough time to be starting out. He wrote his cousin Jane Claypoole, still at home in Betsy's care, that business there appears at "lowest ebb," yet the "people are as gay and lively as a Frenchman after a victory of his sovereigns; amusements which delight & fascinate (to use the words of the newspapers) are daily offered and the avidity with which they are followed by all classes raises a doubt in my mind, whether the distress they complain of can be real or only an ebullition of a contradictory and discontented spirit."[72]

Betsy's client, Caesar Augustus Rodney, was the nephew of the more famous Caesar Rodney who represented Delaware at the Continental Congress. The attorney general for both Jefferson and Madison, the younger Rodney had resigned the job when he was passed over for the Supreme Court, and when war broke out with England in 1812, he served as captain of a rifle corps which became the Delaware First Artillery. When the British blockaded the Delaware River in spring 1813, Rodney swung into action in defense of Wilmington, Delaware. After a British ship captain threatened to attack a shoreside town that refused to sell provisions, communities up and down the river scrambled to prepare for like provocations. Fort Union quickly rose on the site of previous fortifications outside Wilmington. In March, Wilmington men sent a request to Alexander Murray, the commanding naval officer in Philadelphia, seeking the use of a gunboat to help defend the city. Murray consented.[73] The ensign Betsy and Clarissa delivered to Rodney was likely intended for the vessel's stern.

On April 7, 1813, Rodney was commissioned captain of the Second Company of Artillery attached to the First Brigade, stationed at Fort Union. Twelve weeks later, a member of the Company, Louis M'Lane, made a Fourth of July oration to Rodney's assembled company; in it, he gestured to the flag under which they served.[74] "Shall that flag now unfurled from the standard around which we rally," he thundered, "be furled in ignominious defeat, and heighten the splendour of an enemy's trophies?"[75] The fort, M'Lane suggested, would be the "Thermopylae of our village," and the "invader shall march to our town" only "over the slain of its defenders."

That same summer, in Baltimore, another pair of flag makers, Rebecca Young and her daughter Mary Pickersgill, would commence work on a much larger flag for the installation at Fort McHenry. Rebecca Young's descendants would later claim that she had made the "first flag of the Revolution (under General Washington's direction) and for this reason [Mary Pickersgill] . . . was selected by Commo. Barney and General Stricker, (family connections), to make this 'Star Spangled Banner' which she did, being an exceedingly patriotic woman."[76] Commander George Armistead wanted a garrison flag "so large that the British will have no trouble seeing it from a distance."[77] The enormous flag Pickersgill made for Fort McHenry measured thirty feet by forty-two feet and consumed hundreds of yards of bunting. She completed work on this flag and a smaller storm flag with the help of both family and servants within six weeks, by working, as her daughter would later recall, into the wee hours night after night.

Betsy Claypoole would not produce anything during the war of 1812 to match the grandeur of the flag we now know as the Star Spangled Banner, though she surely appreciated Mary Pickersgill's success. Fort McHenry was attacked, but the banner survived, and became revered in its own right when Francis Scott Key saw "by the dawn's early light" the same flag that anxious observers "so proudly . . . hailed at the twilight's last gleaming." Just weeks after the battle, the Philadelphia bookseller and publisher Moses Thomas published Key's lyrics in the November 1814 issue of Philadelphia's *Analectic Magazine*, in a volume edited by Washington Irving.[78]

Betsy and Clarissa surely noted with interest the attention given to the flag made by their longtime acquaintances Mary Pickersgill and her mother, Rebecca Young. They must have marveled at its size, since they knew better than most the labor behind such a huge undertaking. The "large American ensign" Claypoole and Wilson delivered to Rodney in May 1813 was by no means as spectacular; neither flag nor fort was as impressive as those made famous at Fort McHenry. But American success at the Wilmington garrison was as important to Betsy Claypoole and Clarissa Wilson as anyone whose fortunes were so closely tied to the emerging nation's. Flags Betsy made— those dozens produced between 1810 and 1812—flew over land and sea, across the United States and beyond. From the mouth of the Mississippi to the Delaware Valley, and probably to the Great Lakes and into the western interior as well, Claypoole and Wilson's flags announced and advanced the aims of the young Republic.

# A Port in the Storm

In January 1812, Betsy turned sixty. In the year that followed, Jefferson made his formal declaration of war against Great Britain, the second such declaration the aging craftswoman lived to see. With peace in 1815, the future of the Republic now seemed secure. But Betsy could already perceive how very different her grandchildren's world would be from her own. Philadelphia was no longer the United States' leading port, eclipsed first by New York and later New Orleans. (At least she could take comfort that her Morgan nephews, Mary's sons, were thriving there.) The nation's capital had moved to the banks of the Potomac in Virginia. When Monroe succeeded Jefferson in March 1817, he was the first president to have no real connection to Betsy Claypoole's Philadelphia. Penn's city was no longer the nation's center of political, economic or cultural gravity. In September 1814, Betsy's and John's hearts rose as the legislature debated moving the nation's capital back to Philadelphia (the motion failed in the House by a close vote, just 83–74), but it was not to be.[1] The world was beginning to pass them by. Their home on Second Street had been dismantled to make way for the Bank of Pennsylvania, erasing not just the scene of her family's early joys but also the evidence of great-grandfather Andrew Griscom's importance to the city's birth. Even the momentous events in which they took part were fading from memory: in 1813 and again in 1816, the Pennsylvania State House—the scene of so much drama over the last half century—was itself nearly demolished to make room for more profitable city development.[2] By the fiftieth anniversary of independence in 1826, at

Philadelphia, "the very last place where the anniversary of the Declaration of Independence should pass by unhonored," no celebration was planned.[3]

If most women assumed that at age sixty their domestic duties would at last be diminishing, Betsy's household was strangely growing at this late point in her life as her home continued to absorb children, grandchildren and nieces when circumstances demanded. For the many grandchildren of Samuel and Rebecca Griscom, in the early nineteenth century, the Claypoole home was a port in the storm. Margaret Donaldson Boggs was still there with her son and Betsy's household had expanded once again—and again due to the fortunes of national war—after Clarissa, her first daughter with John Claypoole and a young mother now in her late twenties, was widowed. On the first Sunday of 1812, in the pages of a small diary Abel Satterthwaite kept while traveling from Philadelphia to Washington, he noted that he visited "Cousin Clarissa Wilson & sister" in Baltimore on his way to Washington, "her husband having gone to sea."[4] The "husband" was probably Jacob Wilson, and the unnamed sister presumably the object of Abel's courtship, Susan, who may have traveled south to be with her sister, now about four months pregnant, while her husband was absent. Just a few weeks later, Jacob would be dead. Clarissa, expecting their sixth child, moved her family home from Baltimore to her mother's house on South Front Street, where her daughter Rachel—named for Clarissa's aunt, another of Betsy's sisters—was born in June.[5]

Clarissa returned home with five children under seven years old. Her first pregnancy had brought her twin girls, whom she and Jacob named Sophia and Elizabeth, and next she and Jacob had welcomed a son, Aquilla, and then a daughter, Clarissa, named for her mother. Another girl, Susan, arrived next. But then Jacob died, and Clarissa couldn't both care for and support all those small children, so she, like many women in similar circumstances, returned home. For Betsy, it was like starting all over again; Clarissa's twins were just six, and the rest toddlers, and now here was another infant to care for. Clarissa may have been able to help Betsy and Margaret tend to her failing father, but with her own children underfoot, it was more a matter of trading off the sorts of caregiving work needed in the family, rather than reducing the amount of it.

What's more, others continued to join the household. A mysterious series of references in the records of the Free Quaker meeting indicates that Betsy's family welcomed still more members about this time. Between 1810 and 1812, Betsy received a series of payments from the Free Quaker coffers in support of a "J. Thomas" and child. When the child died in spring 1812, Betsy was reimbursed for the cost of the coffin and burial, and J. Thomas vanishes from the record. Not long thereafter, a reference in September 1812 introduces a new name to the constellation of people under her roof. In this year, an "R. Ludley" became a member of the household.[6] Ludley's identity remains a mystery, but the Quaker community recognized the need for his (or her) ongoing support for some thirteen years to follow, regularly delivering to Betsy small sums to cover the expense of board. Their final allocation on Ludley's behalf came in March 1825, when they delivered funds for a "coffin for R. Ludley."[7] Was Betsy receiving needy boarders in these years, with the help of the Free Quaker community? It's hard to say, but given that she and John began seeking boarders for income more than twenty years earlier, it's not hard to imagine her deciding to take someone in if they brought with them some source of support.

Such generosity was possible in part because Betsy was still launching daughters into the world. In November 1812, her daughter Susan—now in her midtwenties—married the thirty-three-year-old Philadelphia hardware merchant Abel Satterthwaite. Susan's union affirmed long-standing family ties in Abington. And Betsy couldn't have missed noticing that Susan chose a man much like her own father. John Claypoole surely approved when his son-in-law turned out to be equally engaged in social causes. Abel was already a supporter of the Adelphi School, a school in the Northern Liberties dedicated to the "instruction of poor children," and would soon join the Board of Managers for the Society for the Establishment and Support of Charity Schools.[8] He also became involved in the Asylum for the Relief of Persons Deprived of the Use of Their Reason (apparently organizations all founded before the invention of acronyms), proposed to the 1811 Philadelphia Friends Yearly Meeting; in the 1820s, Abel would serve for several years among the asylum's managers.[9]

For her part, daughter Jane married Caleb Canby in 1818. Another plumber and hardware dealer, he was the sort of steady man any woman is glad to see her daughter marry. He was careful, thoughtful and memorably judicious. "Mr. Canby takes out his words and looks at 'em, 'fore he speaks," one acquaintance would later say.[10] Susan's and Jane's weddings suggest that the family had reconciled at least in part with the larger Quaker community; both took place at the Arch Street meetinghouse.[11] Each of the girls had been "received by request" into the Philadelphia meeting just a few months before their marriages.

With Clarissa now home and Margaret Donaldson Boggs still working in the shop alongside her aunt, the business became a still-larger family operation.

Clarissa became integral to the shop's operations, while Betsy's younger sister Hannah—when not behind the counter of her grocery store—contributed to the enterprise by converting scraps of leftover fabric to rag rugs.[12] Sister Rachel, too, continued to work as an upholsterer, either within Betsy's shop or on her own—and probably both. The grandchildren helped out in various ways, both in the shop and around the house, to free their mothers for more remunerative work.

Betsy had her hands full with a business to run, a large household to support and a new generation of children to raise. Clarissa's youngest daughter Rachel, born in the Claypoole house, years later would remember her grandmother having an active role in her rearing. The Free Quaker meeting helped Betsy meet the additional expense of educating Clarissa's children, year after year committing funds for their tuition.[13] And surely Clarissa was an asset to the shop. But given John's health, Betsy seems to have become the family's anchor.

At some point in these years, perhaps as a result of all these changes in the household, Betsy and John packed up their things once more, shifting just a block south down Front Street (between Walnut and Chestnut).[14] This new house was well appointed; as Betsy's grand-niece would remember, it was "quite large with commodious parlors" and boasted, among other things, "large dining, butler's room and kitchens," and even a "bath-room, not so common an apartment as now."[15] The references to the butler's room and bathroom are indeed puzzling; this description of Betsy's comfortable quarters seems at odds with other evidence about the family's circumstances.[16] Betsy and John still advertised their shop on South Front, though it seems unlikely that John was contributing much to the enterprise; funds continued to flow to Betsy for John's ongoing care. In September 1812, for instance, the amount of $72 (with an additional $2.25 specifically set aside for shoes) was transferred to "E Claypoole" and described as "for boarding J. Claypoole," suggesting the degree to which John's health had by then deteriorated.[17] The Free Quakers were essential in other ways, too. Whenever they could, these Friends threw work Betsy's way. In 1813, for instance, they hired her to make a bench cushion and pillows. The surviving receipt credits the upholsterer for obtaining some thirty pounds of "curled hair," sixteen and a half yards of linen, nineteen yards of cotton cassimere, fifty yards of binding, thread silk worsted as well as "two small pillows"—suggesting that those plain Quakers were not above sitting on an overstuffed superfine wool cushion with silk bindings, with pillows supporting their backs.[18]

But more direct assistance was forthcoming as well. In June 1813, Samuel Wetherill, one of the founders of the Free Quakers, added a codicil to his will that must have stunned the family. In the original document, he had included a bequest of one hundred dollars to a domestic servant who had served the family well. But when she left "without cause," Wetherill decided to redirect those funds to Margaret Donaldson Boggs. What's more, he instructed his executors to add the interest from a bond as well. Margaret Donaldson Boggs, her sister Sarah Donaldson McCord and Clarissa Wilson would each receive sizable bequests—as much as $300 in a year when the wages of a domestic servant averaged around $1.50 a week—from the aged Friend, legacies he considered a token of his "regard for them," and for their "sober and exemplary conduct."[19] It was a windfall sorely needed, from a revered Friend.

In the summer of 1817, Elizabeth Claypoole was widowed for the last time when her husband of a quarter century died on a Sunday morning in early August. John Claypoole was sixty-five years old. Notices announcing his death appeared in newspapers near and far, from Loudon's *American Daily Advertiser* to New York's *Commercial Advertiser* and the *Spectator*, as well as the *Essex Register* out of Salem, Massachusetts.[20] The family perceived that friends in these various places would want to know of John's death, or perhaps that his creditors would.

With a large family to support her (and to support), widowhood looked very different this third time around. The year before, Susan and her husband, Abel, had taken their two boys and moved back to Abington, and though their day-to-day presence was surely missed, Philadelphia was now downright crowded with Betsy Claypoole's children, grandchildren, nieces and nephews who looked on her with respect and affection.[21] Like other early American women in an era long before retirement plans or social safety nets, Betsy worked well into advanced age—through some ten years of her third widowhood. She continued to have both Margaret and Clarissa—the latter now in her early thirties and a single mother herself—by her side, as well as Clarissa's several children, but Betsy remained at the head of her shop.

After John's death, Betsy and Clarissa ran the business as Claypoole & Wilson. Clarissa's twins were eleven years old now, big enough to help out in the shop, and baby Rachel was already five. In time, those various granddaughters became employees of the business as well.[22] As a firm, Claypoole & Wilson remained alert to developments on the national and state levels that affected their livelihood. Most important among these was the third major Flag Act, passed in 1818. After Mississippi was admitted as a state in 1817, debate about how the flag would accommodate the ever-changing union was

revived. The number of states had reached twenty, and one proposal suggested that seven stars hereafter represent the added states, with the thirteen
stripes always signaling the original thirteen. Another congressman suggested
twenty stars and twenty stripes. Luckily, others whose design skills were perhaps more acute observed that either the flag would have to get bigger and
bigger or the stripes narrower and narrower—and that neither would do.
Finally, a solution emerged: the stripes would remain stable at thirteen but
one star would be added for each new state (for the first time, it was also specifically articulated that the stripes be horizontal). Fabricators like Claypoole & Wilson were acutely interested in the outcome of these discussions,
given the potential impact on their time and labor. The craftswomen surely
read with interest the January 21, 1817, edition of *Poulson's Daily Advertiser*
announcing that the U.S. government had decided not to try to add stripes as
states joined the union, but to let the stars alone evolve. What a relief; there
would be a lot less seaming after all.[23] Eager to receive contracts for the making of these flags, the mother-daughter partnership sent a letter to the commissioners of the navy to remind them of "their services in all the different
branches of colormaking." Noting their "large stock of first quality bunting"
in terms of both colors and durability, the two women added that their "work
has always met the approbation of the Department both for strength and
neatness."[24]

The shop, then, continued to produce flags for the government and mattresses for the ships on the Delaware River.[25] Orders for militia colors continued to flow to Berrett, and perhaps Betsy as well.[26] She and Clarissa also
continued to draw residential clients, some from as far away as Wilmington,
Delaware. In the spring of 1822, for instance, when Henry Latimer Jr. and
Sally Bailey (the daughter of the president of the Bank of Delaware) were
planning to wed, Sally chose the partnership of Claypoole & Wilson to supply
window cornices, muslin, fringe and draperies for her new home.[27] Just as she
and John Ross had sought the patronage of the Chew and Tilghman families
fully a half century earlier, Betsy still found opportunities among the region's
most privileged families, whose weddings meant new homes to ornament,
new orders to fill.

Making up the Latimer order, Betsy may well have noted how little had
changed about this work over the years. The style of the Latimer draperies
might have differed slightly, but she was still stitching long hems and channels
and applying yards of fringe to embellish them. But although the work remained
the same, much of the work environment was altered. Now there was far more
competition, as well as new modes of production and new priorities for con-

sumers. The shifting circumstances of Betsy's life in the early nineteenth century reflected changes in the larger economy. Among other things, many more women competed for attention in the marketplace. Now, for instance, Mary Butland made and sold tassels and fringes at her Spruce Street shop, and a few years later, Charlotte Beckman advertised her services as a lace and fringe weaver on Sassafras. Mary Watson was an upholsterer on Union and later Fourth Street, Sarah Nicholson worked on Federal and then Key's Alley, and Ann Wevill invited customers to her shop at the corner of Chestnut and Fifth.[28]

Another subtle change in the artisan's world is reflected in the columns of the 1799 city directory. For many years, directories listed residents alphabetically, but in 1799, for the first time, readers could turn to pages that grouped people by occupation. What seems like a small alteration in format actually tells us much about the evolving landscape of Philadelphia commerce. Alphabetical listings suggest that readers are likely to know the name of the person they are trying to find, and simply need to confirm their location. It suggests word-of-mouth referrals to individual shops. Listings gathered by occupation suggest a different relationship between artisans and clients, one that was more likely to be anonymous. If someone needed an upholsterer, he or she could simply flip to that page and choose one from the names listed. Though the 1799 innovation was not definitive, a world in which clients were cultivated by reputation and referral was giving way to another grounded in advertisements and impersonal exchange. By 1825, the whole volume would tellingly be titled the *Philadelphia Directory and Stranger's Guide*.[29]

More ominous was the challenge mounted by the new machines creeping into her trade. Betsy and Clarissa were still advertising their joint enterprise on South Front Street, but the world of domestic interiors was transforming around them.[30] Betsy had long offered clients work assembling carpets, and her sister fabricated rag rugs, but as the eighteenth century gave way to the nineteenth, carpets entered the factory, removing this particular object from Betsy's product line. The first carpet manufactory to appear in the United States opened in Philadelphia in 1791, when Betsy was not quite forty years old. By 1810, some ten thousand yards of carpeting were manufactured in the United States, three-quarters of it in Philadelphia.[31] Isaac MacCauley for some years ran an oilcloth business at the corner of Broad and Filbert streets; by 1820, he would buy the James Hamilton mansion "Bush Hill" and convert it to a factory. In time he added buildings around Eighteenth and Morris (now Spring Garden) streets and begin manufacturing carpets by the yard.

Very few of the arenas of the eighteenth-century upholsterer were not challenged by America's industrial revolution. In 1825, for instance, the Boston cabinetmaker Charles B. F. Adams patented his "Windlass Beam Bedsteads"; sold to Philadelphians by the firm John Hancock and Company, the innovation allowed a bed to be "tightened any time in one second," keeping the sacking bottom comfortably taut.[32] More important, the firm provided furniture supported by iron-wire springs—an innovation as pleasing to consumers as it was cost-effective for upholsterers eager to avoid the inconveniences and expense of curled hair fillings.[33]

The fortunes of Betsy's household in these years, then, seem somewhat fragile. One report that "at Aunt Claypoole's they are generally well" seems lukewarm assurance; there's a hint that the true meaning is "as well as can be expected."[34] And all would not remain well. In November 1823, Betsy absorbed bad news when her oldest living daughter, Eliza Ashburn Silliman, was herself widowed. Isaac Silliman died in Charleston, South Carolina; that their eleven-year-old son, Willis, was with him, in life and in death, doubled the blow.[35] Isaac's funeral would be carried out at the home of his brother John, also a ship captain in that city. A newspaper reference to Silliman's "late residence in Mazyckborough," a neighborhood in Charleston, suggests that perhaps the family was in the process of moving there (Isaac and Willis had been there since January), but Eliza (and presumably Jane) seems to have been still in Philadelphia when the dreaded news came.[36]

Tragedy would beget tragedy. Isaac Silliman's death threw his eighteen-year-old daughter Jane into deep despair. When news reached her at their aunt Jane Canby's (where she was then living) she "took to her bed, gradually weakened, and died" three weeks later, immersed in regret that she "had not in early life chosen a religious course."[37]

First Margaret Donaldson Boggs's husband and then her daughter Clarissa's, and now Eliza's—Betsy lived to see too many girls become widows, and now she mourned two grandchildren in the space of a month as well. Eliza and her children would have to shift for themselves. Some sources suggest that she, too, moved home to her mother's and lent a hand in Betsy's shop.[38]

Eliza's situation was precarious; with her husband and provider suddenly gone, she turned to the community of maritime families for help. Isaac Silliman's membership in the Society for the Relief of Poor, Aged, and Infirm Masters of Ships, their Widows and Children had been steadily maintained over some sixteen years; the keeper of its dues book now noted "dead" next to his name. His dues were up to date as of just the past October. But as it happens, this organization would provide no relief for Eliza and her family. Though she applied for assistance, her name is among a handful of women who submitted applications but "rec'd nothing this quarter." Why Eliza Silliman was not among the fifty-plus women who regularly received a few dollars in aid remains a mystery; certainly Isaac had been diligent about paying his dues regularly in the event of just such misfortune. But by the 1820s, the Society had implemented a system in which members visited applicants in order to assess their needs. Perhaps they found Eliza's circumstances to be less desperate than the other women seeking their help. Other applicants whose situations were more favorably reviewed by the Society's managers were found to be in poor health, unable to work or dependent on children who had little themselves to spare; perhaps the Society noted whatever Eliza had been able to set aside, and her ability to find work in her mother's shop, and decided she would make it on her own. For whatever reason, despite years of payments, Eliza's name never appears among those widows granted relief.[39]

Eliza was not the only one of Betsy's girls to have grieved—as Betsy had—the loss of a sailor. By this time, Betsy's daughter Rachel Jones, too, had been left a widow when her first husband, the ship captain Edward Jones, died. Rachel must have been spending a lot of time with Susan's family in Abington, because when she remarried, she chose John Fletcher, a son of an old Abington family. They married in the Abington Monthly Meeting. In fact, seventy-one-year-old Betsy made her way to the marriage ceremony, as did her sister Rachel, and several of her own children, including Clarissa, Jane and Caleb Canby, Abel and Susan Satterthwaite, and also Margaret Donaldson Boggs.[40] In good times and in bad, Betsy could count on her children coming together.

Jane and Susan had married particularly well and were able to provide Betsy with some financial support in her twilight years, but money remained a constant source of worry. Betsy's sister Rachel Griscom had witnessed the strain on Betsy as well as Hannah Levering McIntire in these latter years, and when in 1824 she began making plans for her own death, she hoped to alleviate it. In that year, "mindful" of her own mortality, Rachel wrote a will that would reflect her affection and concern for the women of her family.[41] She chose Caleb Canby, Betsy's son-in-law, to serve as her executor. As she penned the opening words—"I, Rachel Griscom, of the City of Philadelphia, upholsterer"—she embraced a craft identity that had sustained both her and Betsy through the years. Her first thoughts were to providing a permanent home for Betsy and Hannah, to whom she bequeathed her house at 53 Race Street. She asked that her sisters open the home as well to their great-niece Jane Murray (the never-married granddaughter of Susannah Griscom and Ephraim Doane) as well as her "namesake" Rachel Griscom Murray (Jane's younger sister), and instructed her executor to be sure that her sideboard be returned to the house (from where, we don't know) for the use of the planned occupants. To Hannah she also left her best cloth cloak, with the remainder of her clothing to be divided between her two living sisters and great-niece Jane Murray— like this house itself, to "share and share alike." Few words so beautifully capture seven decades of sisterly affection, competition and concern.

As her namesake, Rachel Murray was first in her mind as she considered the distribution of her other possessions. Young Rachel received her best bed, bedstead, bolster, pillows sheets, blanket, "comfortable" (that is, comforter), along with the bed quilt and curtains that went with it. Surely there was no more meaningful gift for the upholsterer to bestow. She also left Rachel her looking glass, together with six silver teaspoons marked *RG*—perhaps gifts from brother George, like the creamer he gave Betsy so many years before. To Betsy's daughter Susan Satterthwaite, she left a pair of silver tea tongs. To Clarissa Wilson, she left a bedspread with a yellow star in the center, as well as her mahogany candlestand. Her nephew, Deborah's oldest son Aquilla Bolton, together with Catharine Warren and Lawrence Johnson, witnessed as Rachel struggled to add her signature.

The will accounted for nearly every possession Rachel had. When she died in November 1825, only a silver watch and her silver spectacles, six Windsor chairs, two bureaus and a trunk of sewing cottons went unaccounted for as she had tenderly thought through the disposition of her worldly goods. She had apparently been ill for a time before she finally passed away, as a nurse and doctor appear among her estate's final creditors. These accounts also make plain that her various nieces and nephews were supporting Rachel in her old age. Jane Murray submitted a bill for "sundries" amounting to some $43 (the combined value of Rachel's household goods totaled only $66), and Clarissa was owed a balance of $28.81. Abel Satterthwaite had signed a bond of mortgage in the amount of $500, on top of more than $150 in personal loans; her executor, Caleb Canby, had apparently loaned her another $12 as well. Rachel's estate, it seems, was insolvent. Betsy and Hannah would not get to keep the house their sister so lovingly bequeathed; it was sold, bringing some $1,250 toward the settling of the accounts.

As Rachel's estate was at last settled, Betsy began making alternate plans. She remained active in the Philadelphia business until at least 1827, but, having reached her seventy-fifth year, she at last decided to leave the work to others. Her vision was failing, and she could no longer keep up with the younger women in the shop. Betsy had continued to count on the ongoing aid of the Free Quakers; long after John's death, she accepted regular disbursements from the Free Quakers, as did Clarissa and her children. In 1818 alone, the household needed more than $100 in aid for Betsy, and a nearly equal amount for Clarissa and the children. As we have seen, R. Ludley continued to be both a member of this family and a recipient of Free Quaker largesse until his (or her) death in March 1826, when the disbursements to Betsy stop. Interestingly, at just about the same time, Betsy packed up and moved to the Satterthwaite household. Was the death of the mysterious Ludley a factor in the timing of the move? It seems so.[42]

Released from this lingering caretaking responsibility in the city, Betsy relocated to Abington, to the comfortable home Susan and Abel Satterthwaite had built a few years earlier. Apparently Betsy had been traveling back and forth to Abington for some time; one account suggests that she "would travel out old Second Street Pike by stage to Fox Chase," where she would wait at a local inn for one of the Satterthwaites to come meet her.[43] Family tradition holds that, rather than carry a more traditional basket of sewing tools, Betsy would simply take a drawer out of her sewing table and carry it with her on trips like this one. Certainly materials associated with the Philadelphia shop traveled back and forth to Abington and elsewhere. Edwin Satterthwaite, Betsy's nephew, later remembered that during his childhood in the 1820s, there were "quantities of red, white and blue bunting all about the little shop"; he also carried scraps of leftover bunting out to his mother in Abington, where she wove them into rag rugs, as Hannah Griscom Levering had done years earlier.[44]

Betsy remained in Abington for several years, and her various grandchildren spent summers there. But after a serious bout of dysentery left her weakened, the Satterthwaites felt they were no longer able to provide the best care. Someone else would have to take a turn. Betsy moved back to Philadelphia, to her daughter Jane's household on Cherry Street. The Canby home, with its light, airy side yard, would prove a comfortable place for the aging craftswoman to spend her days.[45] Susan McCord particularly remembered her great aunt's presence there during these years, and especially the charity Betsy showed to Philadelphians less fortunate; she regularly sent loaves of bread and parcels of tea to the residents of the city's Bettering House, surely at least in part in memory of her cousin Rebecca. Susan McCord and her sister Harriet were sent to deliver such packages as late as the 1820s. Betsy apparently kept up these small gifts some twenty years after her Rebecca died in her almshouse bed.[46]

Perhaps it was the insecurity of these uncertain times that convinced Betsy to at last open an account in the Philadelphia Saving Fund Society (PSFS). It is hard for us today to imagine a world before banks, but in the early Republic, they were not yet familiar institutions. In time, the threat posed by growing numbers of indigents prompted public officials to create ways to encourage saving.[47] As Thomas Malthus's *Essay on Population* gained an audience, policy makers came to believe that relief to the poor undermined natural systems that checked the population of the impoverished. Public relief and charity, Malthus asserted, "create the poor which they maintain." New institutions were invented to help families save for the future—the idea being that, rather than turning to public support, families would save up their own money to see them through rough patches, and to draw on in times of sickness or in their old age.

When the Philadelphia Saving Fund Society opened in 1816—the first institution of its kind to appear on this side of the Atlantic—the Claypooles were not among its members. They were apparently unpersuaded by the logic such an institution presented, despite the efforts of fellow Free Quaker Clement Biddle, who helped found the enterprise. In December 1816, the group placed an "Address to the Public" in the *Freeman's Journal and Philadelphia Mercantile Advertiser* explaining that the goal of the new institution was to "promote economy and the practice of saving amongst the poor and laboring classes of the community." In the PSFS, mechanics, servants, tradesmen, laborers and others would find a "secure and profitable mode of investment for small Sums." To ensure that the fund would benefit the "poor and industrious classes of our fellow citizens" as it was intended to do, initial deposits could not exceed $500, to prevent wealthy men from speculating.[48] One promoter used the pages of the *Commerical Advertiser* to assert that "a more desirable mode of promoting the benefit of the poor cannot perhaps be devised"; by 1830, approximately one in ten Philadelphians had opened accounts.[49]

A cousin of Nicholas Biddle (president of the Second Bank of the United States), Clement Biddle had nurtured a long interest in and understanding of economics. A lawyer by training, Biddle served on the PSFS Board of Directors and in 1834 was elected president, an office he held for the next twenty years, overseeing the institution's evolution from a comparatively small voluntary organization into a large, professionally managed financial powerhouse.[50] The year after Betsy's death, it would be Biddle's skill and savvy that allowed the PSFS to survive the damaging Panic of 1837.

Betsy's account was opened on May 24, 1830, by her son-in-law Caleb Canby. Perhaps she was too frail at that point to personally appear at the bank's offices on Sixth Street between Market and Chestnut to open an account, sign the signature book and list her street address and occupation. So Canby opened an account for her. The bylaws required that she deposit at least one dollar; Betsy opened her account with $200.[51] She—together with her niece Margaret Donaldson Boggs and great-niece Sarah McCord—was in good company; more than 60 percent of the bank's customers were women (and 15 percent were African Americans at a time that the city's population was about 18 percent African American, suggesting that the bank achieved its aim of reaching out to the laboring classes). But fourteen years had elapsed since the PSFS opened. What prompted them to join just when they did?

Perhaps Biddle, being a key member of the main source of Betsy's charitable aid to date, the Religious Society of Free Quakers, at last convinced her to take action; as late as January 1829, Betsy was still receiving support from the congregation's funds "for the relief of the poor."[52] Whatever the impetus, in its first year, her PSFS account had begun to pay off, earning $4.67 in interest. Another lump sum, again $200, was deposited in 1832, and together with interest earned drove the balance up to $414. After that, no additional deposits on Betsy's behalf were made; the account was allowed simply to accrue interest, reaching close to $485 by 1836, the year of her death. Where did this money come from, and why was it deposited by Caleb in her name? The account of Margaret Donaldson Boggs offers a small clue. Margaret opened her account on the very last day of 1827, a Monday morning.[53] Taking a more typical pattern with regular deposits, Margaret's account was opened with $25, with another $10 added right away in January. The fund grew steadily in 1828. Almost every Monday morning that summer, Margaret appeared at the bank to make her deposit—anywhere from $40 (the largest) to $5 (the smallest). A handful more deposits followed in the fall, so that by the end of the year she had accumulated just over $239.

Then, on September 21, 1829, she emptied nearly the whole account. By the end of the year, her balance had grown once more, to $171.55. And then, on May 13, 1830, she took out $125—almost three-quarters of her accumulated money. Just eleven days later, Caleb would enter the bank's doors with $200 to open an account under Betsy's name. Was Margaret trying to provide some security for her aging aunt, transferring funds on which Betsy might draw in her old age? Given the many years of support Betsy provided for Margaret, it seems natural that she would want to respond in kind. Did Margaret try offering the money to her aunt, only to have it declined? Did she then ask Caleb simply to put it in the bank under Betsy's name, in order to overcome any prideful objections?

In these latter years, Betsy's family hovered around her. In 1829, daughter Rachel's twins, Mary and Daniel, were born, some twenty-three years after Clarissa's twins arrived. In the end, Betsy welcomed over two dozen grandchildren into the world. The children of the nieces she cared for also came to think of Aunt Claypoole in a grandmotherly way. All of these children would remember her fondly many years later.[54] But even as she welcomed the affection of these new members of her ever-growing family, a page turned when Betsy outlived one of her adult daughters—in February 1833, she faced the terrible task of burying fifty-two-year-old Eliza Ashburn Silliman. Her children, grandchildren, niece and nephews were all there to comfort her—and one another.

She continued to rely, too, on her community of faith. In the decades following the American Revolution, many of the men and women who had been disowned by their Quaker meeting gradually repaired these relationships and were absorbed back into their congregations. The Claypoole family, however, continued their connection with the Free Quakers. In 1828, the Free Quakers noted having received $12 for the "burial of William Pile he being considered a member," alongside what looks like Betsy Claypoole's very struggling signature.[55] Receipts from 1828 show the congregation still funding the schooling of the McCord children and Betsy's niece Sarah Donaldson McCord was regularly paid (two dollars a month) for cleaning and opening the meeting-house. David McCord hauled and sawed wood for the Quakers' stove. Margaret Donaldson Boggs, too, appears in these accounts, receiving ten dollars here and there for services unrecorded.[56]

Clarissa made application for membership in the Free Quaker Society in the summer of 1832, at last joining officially the religious community that had for so long sustained her mother, and her own family.[57] And, as a formal member now of the pacifist Society of Friends, Clarissa consciously abandoned the government contracts that had sustained the family for so long, "lest her handiwork should be used in time of war."[58] It may not be a coincidence that this was the summer the nation witnessed what has come to be known as the Nullification Crisis, when South Carolinians—in protest over a protective tariff signed into law by President Andrew Jackson but reviled by many southern states indignant that it favored industrial interest at the expense of agriculture—declared the tariff null and void in their state. By February, Congress passed the Force Bill (aka Jackson's Bloody Bill or War Bill, in the South), authorizing Jackson to use military force against the state. In the end, Henry Clay and John Calhoun brokered a compromise, but they were tense months that may well have given Clarissa every reason to anticipate sectional war.

In 1834, the Free Quakers again threw work toward the aging upholsterers when they paid Clarissa $10.25 for rattinet for repairing blinds—perhaps blinds that Betsy herself had mounted when the meetinghouse was first built a half century earlier.[59] Clarissa by this time had taken on a role in distributing the meeting's funds for the support of the poor; perhaps those involved realized her awkward situation and channeled funds to her via other means.[60]

Even in these twilight years, Betsy continued to try to attend the Free Quaker meeting. The Philadelphia group watched with regret as their counterparts in Maryland, Massachusetts and Ohio either passed away or rejoined their original communities of faith. Philadelphia's Free Quakers had been held together mainly by the "talent and exertions" of founder Samuel Wetherill. Wetherill served as clerk until September 1808, when at seventy-two he at last resigned and turned the office over to his son. He continued to be active in the ministry, but after he died in 1816 in his eighty-first year, the membership slowly scattered, and the numbers at worship slowly dwindled, from twenty, to twelve, and finally down to just a handful.

Even as the Free Quaker movement declined, another glimpse into Betsy's own convictions came through in her tenacity and determination to continue to meet with her community of faith. In 1834, some stories say, only two Quakers still attended the meetinghouse: Samuel Wetherill's son, John Price Wetherill, and Betsy Claypoole. While other members of this community in time drifted back toward other affiliations, Betsy Claypoole, having made a commitment, stuck to it until the very last. "No one who puts his hand to the plow and looks back is fit for service in the kingdom of God," said the New Testament that lay more and more often in Grandmother Claypoole's lap; indeed, she seems not to have been a woman given to self-doubt. She held out to the last, her resolve born of committment to the tenets of her faith and probably a good deal of loyalty to the Wetherills, too, who had shown her family so much support through the years. Eventually the pair concluded that two did not a meeting make, and this chapter in the history of the Free Quakers came to a close.[61]

Betsy's grandson William Canby, who was eleven when she died, recalled her during these latter years as a "bustling active woman, yet full of sweet womanly dignity and grace."[62] In her old age, her eyesight fading, Betsy wore spectacles. One of her "valuable formulas," granddaughter Susan Satterthwaite Newport later recalled, was for an "excellent eye-wash," suggesting that as she aged, the active needlewoman had begun looking for ways to preserve her fading vision.[63] She also started taking snuff, which someone had recommended to her as a remedy for her weakening eyes. Though taking snuff was considered "fashionable" in those days, Betsy found it distasteful (her mother-in-law used snuff, though, and, when Betsy received a silver snuffbox from her granddaughter Sidney Satterthwaite, she was so envious that she pleaded with Betsy to swap, pointing out that for now "Betsy could have hers, and it would not be long before she could have both").[64] Nevertheless, when her grandson William was sent out to acquire some on her behalf and came home with a large bladder full of Scotch snuff, he watched her laugh as she pocketed the "monster." On some evenings in these twilight years, William remembered, "the conversation then turned, as it did on other occasions, to the various battles by sea and land, and we listened with interest to all that she told us of the incidents of those times."[65] Wouldn't we now like to know what other stories she had to tell?

In time, Betsy became increasingly frail. When the sun was high, her eyesight was good enough for her to read the Bible without her glasses, but after a while she was content to simply keep the "good book" near her; the heavy volume would lie for hours, unopened, on her lap. Sometimes her grandchildren would sit on a stool near her feet and read to her from it.[66] Now "a little old woman, bent with years," Grandma Claypoole's storytelling days were coming to a close. Hardly a wrinkle marked her "smooth white face, about which, despite the lack of luster in the sightless eyes, and the sunken lips over a toothless mouth, there always seemed to shine a soft, mild radiance."[67] She continued to wear the accoutrements of her trade—the silver hook at her waist from which her scissors and pin-ball still dangled—but she was no longer able to sew. Her restless fingers traveled constantly around the edges of a large handkerchief.[68]

One winter night, the grandchildren were awakened, first by loud cries, then by heavy footsteps up and down the stairs. Finally, voices subsided into whispers. When morning came, the grandchildren were called in to see her. The next three days were quiet and cheerless. The children tiptoed around the house, and in and out of the back parlor where the "apparently lifeless form" of their grandmother lay upon her bed. Finally, they were brought in for final farewells, "and so gently, so like her life," she passed away, so peacefully that the children thought she was still sleeping. Betsy died at the Cherry Street home of her daughter Jane Canby on January 30, 1836.[69] She was buried next to John in the Free Quaker burying ground. Her obituary in the *American Daily Advertiser* made no reference to the making of the first United States flag.

# Epilogue

On January 1, 1836, John Fanning Watson, as was his custom, made his annual round of New Year's visits to his friends and acquaintances—as many as twenty families.[1] Philadelphia's leading antiquarian spent the day noting the great changes that he had witnessed over the course of his life, and concluded that he could no longer devote himself to marking the many transformations in every corner of society, because "the change from the olden time is so entire, and the traces of the past are so wholly effaced, that there is now scarcely any vestige left" of the colonial city. Watson pined for simpler days when the race for wealth did not consume families, when tradesmen did not "dwell in palaces" and merchants did not build houses designed only for "luxury and cumbrous pomp."

Across town, Betsy Claypoole was celebrating her birthday for what would be the last time. In a few short weeks, in the parlance of the age, she would finish her course with joy and leave this life for the next. In those final days, she could contemplate the same revolutions that preoccupied Watson, but considered them from a different vantage point. Where Watson mourned a certain gentility eroded by the Revolution and its aftermath, undermined as more middling men and women enlarged their claims in the infant Republic, Betsy Claypoole saw herself among the very families that so bemused the antiquarian. The daughter of a house carpenter, she had been the wife of a customhouse officer. She had lived in the nation's capital and could greet the men who ran the county by name; she rode in a carriage and had portrait miniatures made to capture the grace of her children. Her niece danced with the president. Not for a moment did she forget the high price she paid for her nation's independence, but when all was said and done, the strains of her last thirty years did not taint the pride in the fifty that came before.

When Betsy told her children, grandchildren, nieces and nephews about those terrible, exciting years, she spoke with satisfaction of the direct contribution she herself had made to it. She had known Washington and was clever enough to convince him of one simple point—or, rather, five of them. A thousand things had happened during the Revolution and the years that followed, but when she told her children about those times, nothing matched the shimmer of that one day in 1776.

But it was not in fact Betsy who gave us that tale. The story of how one family's anecdote about the making of the "first flag" became the stuff of national memory—the 1870 speech by Betsy's grandson William Jackson Canby to the Historical Society of Pennsylvania, the saving of Philadelphia's Flag House, and the twentieth-century career of Betsy Ross as an icon of American history—is well known.[2] The birth of the Ross legend has been plausibly seen as a story about centennial pride, a growing post–Civil War preoccupation with the flag as a symbol of national unity, and an element of resistance to the women's suffrage movement engaging the nation's attention in the last quarter of the nineteenth century. And, to be sure, those are critical contexts for the mythical figure we know today. But the Ross legend can also be spotted years earlier and seen as a story of sectional crisis and filial pride. If the story took root with Canby's 1870 presentation, and blossomed as the country prepared to celebrate its centennial, its seeds were planted in 1857. And they were planted not by Betsy Griscom Ross Ashburn Claypoole, but by her daughter Clarissa.

While it is true that Canby gave the story public life when he delivered his now-famous lecture, these events were first committed to paper thirteen years earlier, when Clarissa Wilson, anticipating a move west to Iowa, sat her nephew down and asked him to record this important story, for posterity's sake. The seventy-two-year-old flag maker was about to leave Philadelphia, never to return; she wanted the story to live on there without her. It was the same year that her mother left the city as well; in 1857, Betsy Claypoole's mortal remains were moved from the Free Quaker burial ground on Fifth Street to the newly created Mount Moriah Cemetery in southwest Philadelphia, along Cobbs Creek. Betsy's remains would in time return, to a hero's welcome. Clarissa would not, but if she set out to secure her mother's place in history, she achieved her aims—more than she ever dreamed possible.

After Betsy's death, a few belongings were meted out among the survivors. A pair of glasses, her snuffbox, a quilted petticoat, a silver creamer—what few things she kept with her in Jane's home found their way to other owners. A couple of yardsticks survived inadvertently, the only tangible traces now of her work as an upholsterer. Clarissa Wilson claimed the family Bible. William Canby found himself heir to a small joke—a bladder of snuff he had once bought for his grandmother; it turned out that the laughter he remembered after handing it over was the result of his mistake, having bought Scotch snuff (brown and unscented) instead of Rappee (black, scented and moist). Rather than hurt the small boy's feelings, Betsy had set it aside in a drawer, still there for him to receive now that she had passed. He would cherish that story, arbitrary as it may seem, for the insight, however oblique, it gave him to the revered grandmother he would never altogether know. No papers were saved. Clarissa may or may not have had the Claypoole shop's ledgers still with her when she moved to the Midwest, but if so, she didn't preserve them. More than eight decades after Elizabeth Griscom Ross first took up her upholsterer's tools, her workroom's long run came to a close.[3]

Other events marked the passage of time, the constant churning of the new and the old. As it happens, the Pennsylvania State House bell, mounted in the year of Betsy's birth to celebrate the colony's achievements in the cause of religious freedom, was christened the Liberty Bell on the eve of her death by abolitionists outraged at the obvious discrepancy between the bell's inscription and a nation that countenanced slavery. In 1835, volume 1, number 2 of the *The Anti-Slavery Record* asked, "May not the emancipationists in Philadelphia, hope to live to hear the same bell rung, when liberty shall in fact be proclaimed to all the inhabitants of this favored land? Hitherto, the bell has not obeyed the inscription; and its peals have been a mockery, while one sixth of 'all inhabitants' are in abject slavery." Thus the statehouse bell became the Liberty Bell, and began life anew.[4]

That mounting tension over abolition in the last years of Betsy's life, and the appearance of the newly christened Liberty Bell, remind us that while her life was shaped by the events of the American Revolution, her legend was born amid the coming of the Civil War. The story of Betsy Ross and the making of the first flag to mark the colonies united in Revolution is among many other things an artifact of another impending crisis of disunion.

As early as 1820, the strain of slavery threatened the fabric of the nation. Betsy was still at work in her shop when the nation weathered the Missouri crisis and ensuing compromise. The constant creation of new states—Alabama, Maine and now Missouri—meant that the nation had to continually revisit its position on enslaved labor; the decision to admit Missouri as a slave state but prohibit slavery from the remainder of the territory provided at best an illusion of resolution. Thomas Jefferson, having reached the venerable age of seventy-seven, wrote about the question of slavery's expansion: "Like a fire bell in the night, this question awakened and filled me with terror. I considered it at once as the knell of the union. It is hushed, indeed, for the moment. But this is a reprieve only, not a final sentence . . . I regret that I am now to die in the belief, that the useless sacrifice of themselves by the generation of 1776, to acquire self-government and happiness to their country, is to be thrown away by the unwise and unworthy passions of their sons, and that my only consolation is to be, that I live not to weep over it."[5] Did Betsy, herself now pushing seventy, fear that her own sacrifices, and those of John Ross, Joseph Ashburn and John Claypoole, would be useless as well? And the sacrifices of her parents and siblings, too? She, like Jefferson, would not live to weep over it. But Clarissa would.

When she began to make flags, Betsy Claypoole founded a family business that endured over generations. After her mother's death, Clarissa kept the shop going for some thirty more years, and her own children and cousins would continue on independently as well. Years later, Betsy's grandson William Canby would write, "The old stand at the S.W. corner of Front St. and Norris' Alley was retained as a flag and color store for many years by Clarissa, after her mother became, through the infirmities of years, unfitted for carrying on the business which was afterwards removed to a situation in the next square near Dock St. on the same side of Front St. where Clarissa, then a widow, (Mrs. Wilson) continued for a number of years longer to make flags for the United States Government."

By 1850, Clarissa had restyled her listing in the city directory to call herself a maker of ship's colors—a gesture reflecting, as we shall see, growing uneasiness with the nation's political direction. She still maintained the Front Street shop, but the seventh federal census that year found Clarissa in a large Prune Street household (now part of Locust Street, between Fourth and Sixth) with her daughters and grandchildren; just as had her mother before her, Clarissa had taken in her own daughters when they found themselves without husbands to support them. Sixty-five-year-old Clarissa shared a home with her twins, Elizabeth Campion and Sophia Hildebrandt, as well as Elizabeth's nineteen-year-old daughter. Clarissa's daughter and namesake, Clarissa Hanna, and her own several children also shared the home, baby Alice just a year old.[6]

Just as Betsy brought Clarissa into the business, Clarissa brought yet another generation of upholsterers and flag makers into the family trade. By 1854, Clarissa's daughter Sophia Hildebrandt and her son Aquilla Wilson were both working as upholsterers, at 154 Arch Street.[7] When Sophia assembled and installed forty-two yards of Brussels carpeting in Mary Cresson's entryway and front parlor in 1846, she was completing a task not unlike the one that her grandmother had performed for John Cadwalader and Benjamin Chew so many years before.[8] Meanwhile Charles McCord, whose grandmother was Betsy's sister Sarah Donaldson, established a branch of the family business in another port city: Mobile, Alabama.[9]

The Claypoole family, like most American families in these decades, also began to watch the rising generations scatter across the country in search of new opportunities. Some were now just outside Philadelphia. The Boltons and the Piles had moved out to Chester County. The marriage and move of Susan Satterthwaite returned one branch to their Abington roots, while George's family did the same for the New Jersey Griscoms. Jane Claypoole Canby and her family put down roots in Maryland, and Aquilla Bolton moved to Virginia.

But despite their increasingly far-flung nature, the children and grandchildren stayed as close as geography permitted. Even before fortune began luring young men and women away from Philadelphia, the names Betsy's family chose for their children suggest a conscious effort to knit generations together. It's hardly surprising that Betsy's daughter Eliza named her first son Joseph Ashburn Silliman, that Clarissa named a daughter Elizabeth Griscom Wilson or that Margaret Donaldson's sister would keep the Boggs name alive among her own children after Margaret's husband and son both died. Even Betsy's granddaughter Amelia Silliman Boyd, when she had her own first child in 1828, named her Elizabeth Ashburn after her beloved grandmother.[10] When Mary and Thomas Morgan's daughter Rebecca named a son Morgan Griscom Pile, her parents and grandparents would both be honored. For a while, those gestures and others helped keep the family close. Hannah Levering's children and grandchildren stayed in touch with the Canby and later Balderston cousins; Hannah Levering Franklin's family, in particular, were constant companions of the Canbys and doted on the aging Margaret Donaldson Boggs. In the 1870s, Betsy's granddaughter Catherine Canby Balderston would make a trip that took in visits to the Leverings in Ohio, her Albright cousins in Iowa and others along the way.[11] The Pile family papers document numerous exchanges among Betsy's family and the children of her sisters Mary and Hannah.[12] For a time, the grandchildren and great-grandchildren of Samuel and Rebecca James Griscom continued to share a family identity, but eventually the branches would become too scattered to sustain that sense of commonality. People lost touch; memories dimmed.

These routine developments in any family's story—waning ties among new and growing progenies, as John Fanning Watson would say—were accompanied by other, more profound alterations. In time, family memory asserts, "conscientious motives" compelled Clarissa to give up government work and accept orders only for the "mercantile marine."[13] The reference is vague and indistinct, but raises the possibility that Clarissa objected to government policies that were increasingly belligerent, to both enslaved men and women at home, and to her neighbors to the south. Clarissa had been raised in the community of Free Quakers that her parents helped create, and for the twenty years after she returned to Philadelphia newly widowed she was the recipient of the Free Quakers' largesse, but she herself did not become a formal member until 1832.[14] Given the clearly articulated Quaker position on slavery, it may have been that membership alone was enough to cause her to rethink the nature of her steadiest clients. Or perhaps events in the public sphere became so problematic that she could no longer in good conscience support her government's activities. An extant flag believed to have been made by Clarissa between 1845 and 1848 suggests that she may still have been accepting government contracts at this time; perhaps concern gave way to conviction when the highly controversial war erupted with Mexico.[15] Or possibly any one of a sadly long series of incidents concerning the nation's policy on slavery was what finally gave her pause. For whatever reason, at some point the actions of the federal government had departed so far from Wilson's belief system that she would no longer accept its money, no matter how much she needed it.[16]

The year of Clarissa's move and the first effort to record the story of the first flag was also a year of moment for a nation hurtling toward disunion. In the Dred Scott decision of 1857, Chief Justice Roger B. Taney declared that African Americans—slave or free—were not citizens of the United States. Years before, Betsy's cousin Rebecca Griscom had been physically removed from the Quaker meeting in a dispute over the membership of people of color in their community; as a formal member of the Quaker community that had accepted the full membership of blacks in the wake of Rebecca's demonstrations, surely Clarissa objected to the Supreme Court's decision now. In 1857, as Americans braced themselves for what seemed to many an inevitable national rupture, Clarissa Wilson was preoccupied with her mother's contribution to the union, and took obvious pride in that effort. She sat her nephew William down so that her memory, and her mother's, would not be lost.

The 1857 removal of Betsy's mortal remains from their original burial ground at South Fifth Street to Mount Moriah Cemetery is itself a document of economic and social change. As the nineteenth century passed the midway mark, pressure to develop center-city land became great; at the same time, the flowering of a fashion for cemeteries that were at least as aesthetically pleasing as they were functional provided a timely excuse to create scenic rural idylls for the dead and their mourners, while making way for more productive spaces on the city blocks these cemeteries once occupied.[17] The dislocation of Betsy's remains in some ways only made tangible other sorts of dislocations that had been afoot for Philadelphia's artisanal community for several decades. To take just one example, by the second quarter of the nineteenth century the cotton industry was booming, partly thanks to Eli Whitney's invention of the cotton gin, but largely because the end of the Napoleonic Wars abroad reconfigured the global marketplace. As the historian Daniel Walker Howe writes, "In response to an apparently insatiable world demand for textiles, U.S. cotton production soared from seventy-three thousand bales in 1800 to ten times that in 1820. In 1801, eight percent of the world's cotton came from the USA and sixty percent from Asia. Half a century later, the United States provided sixty-eight percent of a total world production three times as large."[18] As those thousands of bales headed toward more thousands of looms, yardage spilled off power-driven looms in immense quantities barely imaginable when Betsy Claypoole, or even Clarissa Wilson, was a girl. Across the city, buildings raised by Griscom men were replaced by factories that occupied entire city blocks.

Handwork gave way to mechanization in any number of onetime crafts. Betsy's good friend Samuel Wetherill Jr. had been in on the ground floor of this phenomenon and in fact had begun helping to bring it about as early as 1784, when he placed an ad in the *Pennyslvania Gazette* unveiling his vision of a fully mechanized cotton factory—no fewer than five stories high and containing some one thousand spindles—where the "whole operation of carding, roping, spinning and reeling is done by machinery."[19] Fifty years later, that vision had been superseded, many times over, as the city's artisanal trades found themselves relegated to the margins as industrial production supplanted handwork at almost every stage of the trade Clarissa had for so long known. The fabrication of trimmings, once the principal contribution Betsy and women like her made to the upholstery trade, was completely revolutionized. Long gone were the days when Betsy and a half-dozen coworkers gathered around tables to fabricate an order of tassels; by the second quarter of the nineteenth century, Philadelphia was quickly becoming the "chief seat of the general manufacture of Trimmings in the United States." By the eve of the Civil War, some twenty firms were engaged in various branches of this industry, churning out carriage laces, regalia and upholstery. The largest, William H. Horstmann & Sons, established in 1815, had grown from a small enterprise that made "a few patterns of coach laces and fringes" to occupy a huge factory at Fifth and Cherry—just up the street from where Betsy lived with her daughter Jane Canby in those last years of her life—that "embraced a wide circle of fabrics, of silk, silk and wool, silk and cotton; and included some that were not made elsewhere in this country."[20]

Gradually, in the final years of her life, Betsy Claypoole witnessed the crafts she had labored to master yield to the economies of mechanization. Horstmann introduced plaiting or braiding machines in 1824; the following year, Jacquard machines appeared. Gold laces were factory-produced in Philadelphia earlier than they would be in Europe, and the use of power to make fringes "may be said the company claimed to have been first generally adopted" there as well. Horstmann & Sons were also the "first in any country" to use machine power to cut fringe apart. One trade association account boasted, "Fringes, it is well understood by the trade, are woven together, and then cut apart with scissors; but this machine does the work most accurately, and about twenty times as fast as by hand." It was an acceleration hardly comprehensible to a woman who first picked up her own shears in the 1760s. Some 180 power looms alongside dozens of plaiting and braiding machines now churned out goods at a rate Betsy could scarcely imagine. Sadly, and perhaps ironically, the Friends meetinghouse would in time be converted into a "spacious salesroom" for this very enterprise.[21]

Indeed, Betsy and then Clarissa watched as every element of their artisanal world was transformed by factory production in the manufacture of cotton and wool carpeting. By the 1850s, some one hundred individual manufacturers employing 1,500 hand looms (the largest manufacturer employing 150 looms at work on his fabrics) found places in Philadelphia. Each loom churned out around 4,320 yards yearly, for an annual production of almost 6.5 million yards. At the same time, another 1.7 million yards of rag and list carpeting flowed annually from the city's industrial buildings—a far cry from the rag rugs Hannah once braided from the scraps of bunting the flag trade left behind.[22] About eight manufactories produced awnings, bags, sacking bottoms and so forth, as well as garden and field tents, and "verandahs" for windows. Westward expansion provided impetus for other innovations, and soon Philadelphia manufactories were also producing canvas wagon covers. As one observer wrote in those years, "Military tents were, during the Mexican War, and until a recent period, made here to a very large amount for the U.S. Army, but are now all made at the U.S. Arsenal in this city. Wagon covers and sacking bottoms form considerable items in the business here; and of the former, two extensive Wagon buildings established in this city necessarily require many for their Mexican and Southern customers." Even flags, by mid-century, had entered the factory, New York City's Annin and Co. becoming among the largest such ventures.[23]

Upholsterers found still more about their trade altered. As the nineteenth century progressed, clients no longer wanted mattresses stuffed with cattails or horsehair; now, spring support was all the rage. George Sturges and vendors like him offered customers the "Improved Spiral Spring Mattress." He also altered hair mattresses into Spring Beds, and made "Spring Bolsters, Pillows, Carriage Seats and Pew Cushions" too.[24] The foundations of upholstery itself were no longer the by-products of natural processes associated with allied trades—feathers plucked from geese intended eventually for dinner tables, or hair recovered from animal hides en route to becoming boots and shoes. Now the mattresses that cradled antebellum spines were themselves objects of industrial production.

The transformation of production brought transformations, too, in the organization of labor. Betsy Claypoole withdrew from the upholstery trades in the same years that journeymen house-carpenters launched a strike that persisted over two building seasons and put hundreds of men out of work.[25] Just a few years later, having spent more than half a century working twelve- and fifteen-hour days over a six-day week, Betsy lived to see Philadelphia craftsmen win the ten-hour day. It was 1835, and the now-eighty-three-year-old glimpsed a world in which relations between labor, capital, skill and machines were seeing revolutions of their own. She saw another change as well: when Edward Hazen published his *Panorama of professions and trades: or, Every man's book*—nineteenth-century Philadelphia's answer to Campbell's *London Tradesman* of a century earlier—he described the work of stuffing mattresses, fabricating curtains and assembling carpets, and noted that a "great proportion" of this work was "performed by females."[26] A clipping preserved in the research files of Independence National Historic Park provides a tantalizing glimpse into her descendants' response to these developments in a claim that the city's first upholsterer's union was born in the spaces of Claypoole & Wilson's shop in the summer of 1853.[27]

When Betsy hung up her shears in the late 1820s or early 1830s, and when she passed away nearly a decade later, very little of the city she knew as a craftswoman survived intact. Benjamin Franklin's house was demolished in 1812; George Washington's presidential mansion faded into oblivion in 1832. When Clarissa strove to secure her mother's story in 1857, she was also memorializing an era evanescing before her very eyes. As she left Philadelphia, Carpenters' Hall had fallen into a shambles, the ground floor holding an auction house cluttered with secondhand goods people were forced to sell. The illustrious City Tavern had been demolished in 1854. The famed Slate House—in her grandfather's day the home of the city's leading citizens—was collapsing into ruin. It was time to go. When her son Aquilla died in September 1856, Clarissa began making plans to join her daughter Rachel Albright in the fresh environs of the West.

As she prepared to leave Philadelphia for good, Clarissa hoped to establish her mother's life within the emerging history of the Revolution. Neither Clarissa nor her mother would have expected to see Betsy's name in some of the very earliest chronicles of the nation's founding, David Ramsay's *History of the American Revolution* (1789), or Mercy Otis Warren's three-volume *History of the Rise, Progress and Termination of the American Revolution* (1805). But other histories hit a little closer to home and began inscribing the names of prominent Philadelphians into official narratives of these momentous events. John Fanning Watson's *Annals of Philadelphia* first appeared in 1830 and included among the earliest tellings of how Lydia Darragh was the "cause of saving Washington's army from great disaster."[28] The Claypooles knew the Darraghs well; Lydia and William had joined the Free Quaker meeting a few years before John and Betsy. When Darragh's actions were recounted in Watson's *Annals*, she achieved a certain sort of immortality and became a fixture in the history of the Revolution in the city even to today. Perhaps Clarissa wanted her mother's contribution to find equal footing. (After all, it was Darragh's daughter Ann who had committed her mother's story to posterity years after the events allegedly occurred, though—as was the case with Betsy Ross, too—"since Ann's telling has some information which doesn't gibe with other accounts," one contemapry narrator noted, "some historians have dismissed it outright as a concocted tale.")[29] Lydia had died years earlier, in 1789; Ann had contributed her mother's account to the March 1827 issue of the *American Quarterly Review*, a new magazine of history and culture. Now that it had appeared in Watson's *Annals* as well, as Clarissa could plainly see, Darragh's place in accounts of the Revolution was secure.

Then, in 1848, Elizabeth Fries Ellet published her two-volume work, *The Women of the American Revolution*, and still more Philadelphians saw their roles in the rebellion acknowledged and preserved. Ellet had spent two years gathering information, collecting manuscripts and interviewing witnesses. When her book finally appeared, it was so successful that she brought out a third volume two years later. Both Betsy and Clarissa would have known several of the women profiled there, including Rebecca Biddle and Margaret Morris. Lydia Darragh made these pages as well, as did Mary Worrell Knight, lionized for her aid to Washington's troops at Valley Forge, one of those "devoted women who aided to relieve the horrible sufferings of Washington's army . . . cooking and carrying provisions to them alone, through the depths of winter, even passing through the outposts of the British Army in the disguise of a market woman." She was remembered as once having hidden her brother Isaac Worrell, an officer in the rebel forces, for three days, concealing him in a cider barrel in her basement and feeding him through the bunghole (a feat that was surely more miraculous for Worrell than for the widow Knight). Betsy and Clarissa surely knew Mary Knight, who was part of the extended family of the Griscoms' Bucks County cousins.[30] Clarissa understood her own mother's story to be just as valuable as those now enshrined in Ellet's pages, and wanted to see it, too, achieve the immortality publication confers.

While attention to women's contributions to the Revolution grew, so too did interest in early flags. In February 1844, an unidentified author placed an article in the *Philadelphia North American* ruminating on the strange absence of information on the subject.[31] Recalling that, before and during the battle of Germantown, a flag with thirteen stripes and stars flew from a liberty pole in the middle of Manheim Street, the essay mused how "curious" it was that "none of the historians of the contemporary period" discussed the "characteristics of our colors—either by land or sea." "Perhaps some of the ancients," the author added, encouragingly, "who may remember some of our public vessels of the Revolution, may communicate something decisive on the subject. Do none remember the Flag of our ships, the *Trumbull, Delaware, Randolph,* and *Hyder Alley!*" "We wish to be informed of the colors used in the Flag," he continued—questions asked "on behalf of a historical laborer, who is collecting information on this subject in connection with other matters of revolutionary times." Apparently neither the article's author nor the historical laborer (quite possibly J. Franklin Reigart, whose mother was Betsy's niece, and who published his *United States Album* that year) received the hoped-for replies—at least no publication appeared in the wake of the query reporting them—but perhaps this article, too, helped Clarissa apprehend the significance of her mother's story.[32]

Another piece of the puzzle may be the 1852 appearance of Schuyler Hamilton's *History of the National Flag of the United States of America*.[33] The author, a grandson of Alexander Hamilton, opened the volume by observing that, "as nearly as we can learn, the only origin which has been suggested for the devices combined in the national colors of our country is, that they were adopted from the coat of arms of General Washington," but quickly added that Washington's well-known "modesty," not to mention the "spirit of the times in which the flag was adopted," cast doubt on this assertion. Hamilton was eager to set the story straight while memory was still comparatively fresh, but he was also motivated by the deteriorating political situation. If nothing else, his book would remind readers how passionately that founding generation was "attached to the idea of Union." Hamilton had no interest in tracking the makers of these early flags, but—citing mainly John Trumbull's 1822 painting of Burgoyne's October 1777 surrender—he does seem to be the first to propose in print that the "new constellation" of stars stipulated in the 1777 Flag Act meant stars arranged in a circle, suggesting perpetuity. The book was published by Lippincott, Grambo and Co., a large Philadelphia enterprise with salesrooms so big and impressive that they were featured in the magazine *Godey's Lady's Book* that same year.[34] Clarissa may well have made her way to the publisher's shop at Fourth and Race and noted with interest this effort to narrate the early history of an article that had become so essential to her livelihood. Hamilton's description of the flag's fuzzy origins may have prompted Clarissa to set down what she knew about those events.

Whatever the catalyst, somewhere in these years—we don't know just when—Clarissa sat young William Canby down and asked him to find a tablet. An intriguing clue rests in an entry made in the diary of Joseph Boggs Beale, whose mother, Louise McCord, was the granddaughter of Betsy's sister Sarah, his grandmother one of the children Betsy took in after the death of her sister and brother-in-law.[35] Born in 1841, Beale never knew Elizabeth Claypoole, but he knew both Clarissa and "Aunty" Margaret Donaldson Boggs (whose dead husband had supplied his own name) quite well.[36] Beale would remain friendly with his cousins, the various children and grandchildren of Betsy's sisters, and in time became one of the nation's most influential illustrators. Many years later, he too would gather with his sisters and brothers to swear out an affidavit affirming that they'd often heard Aunt Margaret tell the story of her aunt Betsy and the making of the first flag.[37] In the 1850s, Beale was still an art student. His diary describes the usual comings and goings of a young man and the doings of his extended family. On February 19, 1857, he recorded that Margaret Donaldson Boggs went to Clarissa's house on Race Street below Fourth. In the evening when he and his father went to bring her home, they were invited to stay for tea and lingered until 9:30 p.m. Jane Canby and her daughter "Mrs. Balderston" were there, as were Anne and Kate Albright and "several others." In other words, most of the family still in Philadelphia was gathered. Could this have been Clarissa's going-away party? Oddly, though the artist's diary contains no other sketches or doodles, at the bottom of this page, drawn in heavy ink, is a five-pointed star.

Once she had safely transferred her mother's legacy to the rising generation in Philadelphia, Clarissa packed up the Claypoole family Bible and moved to Fort Madison, Iowa, where she joined her daughter Rachel Albright. Rachel's husband, Jacob Albright, and his brother William had grown up in Pennsylvania, but when they became men had begun looking westward for opportunities.[38] The Albrights were a political family; after Jacob had first moved out to the Midwest, he helped launch the *Daily Evening Herald,* which was published for a few months in 1835. He would later boast that, though the first paper to be established west of the Mississippi was the 1808 *Missouri Gazette,* he had founded the first *daily* paper west of the Mississippi (another "first" to add to the family annals). But Albright's paper was unable to compete with the established papers and was unprofitable. William established a dry goods store in Fort Madison, in 1839, where R. W. Albright—another of Jacob's brothers—founded the *Lee County Democrat* in the 1840s.

By the late 1850s, the family was prosperous enough to build an elaborate duplex to house two households. They chose a design based on the work of the noted Philadelphia architect Samuel Sloan (from the 1852 plan book, *The Model Architect*), exporting this slice of East Coast culture to their adopted midwestern home, completed in 1858. Two years later, when the Civil War at last erupted, the house was full. Under that ample roof lived Jacob and Rachel, their children Catharine, Clarence, Jacob and Daniel, and of course the elderly Clarissa as well as Rachel's sisters, fifty-four-year-old Sophia Hildebrandt (the former upholsterer now working as a milliner), her twin sister Elizabeth Campion, and their eighteen-year-old servant girl, Anna Staab. Fort Madison must have felt, to Clarissa at least, like the Wild West. Iowa had only achieved statehood in 1846; she had grandchildren older than that. Born in the nation's putative capital in the wake of Revolution, she had come a long way indeed. Clarissa Wilson died in Fort Madison in 1864.

William Canby's notes from his original conversation with Aunt Clarissa have not survived. What we have left is the text of the speech he delivered thirteen years later. In 1870, the legend of the making of the first flag was first shared publicly when Canby read a paper before the Historical Society of Pennsylvania. He was eleven when Betsy died in 1836, and thirty-two when Clarissa left in 1857. By the late 1860s, the Canby brothers (at least) were discussing their grandmother's story with other historically minded friends.[39] As the centennial of independence approached, the Claypoole family's attention once again turned to their grandmother's role in the founding, and this time offered her story to a receptive nation.

Almost immediately, Canby's story—not a "tradition," but a "report," he liked to emphasize, from the lips of immediate observers—came into question. As early as 1872, George Henry Preble's *Our Flag: Origin and Progress of the Flag of the United States of America* questioned the details of Canby's story, and in the decades since then, many others have followed, either recounting the story while offering some skepticism about its veracity, or omitting it altogether.[40] No edition of Watson's *Annals of Philadelphia*, published and republished throughout the nineteenth century, incorporated the claim. When J. Thomas Scharf and Thompson Westcott unveiled their monumental *History of Philadelphia* in 1884, the canon of women important to Philadelphia's revolution had assumed the shape it largely holds to this day—Sarah Franklin, Deborah Logan, Sally Wister, Esther De Berdt Reed—and Betsy Ross was not among them.[41] Meanwhile, friends and family members produced their own books affirming the family story. Not to be outdone by his Canby cousins, in 1878 J. Franklin Reigart was the first in print, offering *The History of the First United States Flag, and the Patriotism of Betsy Ross, The Immortal Heroine That Originated The First Flag of the Union*. Preble called the work a "ridiculous pamphlet" and a "literary curiosity" repudiated even by Mr. Canby himself—a not unsurprising reaction given the Canby family's more direct relationship to the family story and the wild claims Reigart made—that Betsy also named the nation itself when she marked her flags "United States of America," that her own "War Song of Independence" inspired the Marseillaise Hymn, and other flights of fancy guaranteed to undermine the Canbys' comparatively modest assertions.[42] A more measured work is that of Addie Guthrie Weaver, who became interested "through a family relationship with one of the descendents"; her *Story of Our Flag* followed twenty years later, just as attention turned toward the Arch Street house.[43]

The Canbys would prompt the founding of the Betsy Ross House, the key event that would establish Betsy Ross in the canon of Revolutionary women. (Only Abigail Adams, I would argue, rivals her place today.) As Canby's speech gained fame, so too did the little house on Arch Street where these events were believed to have transpired. Owned in the last quarter of the nineteenth century by the Munds, German immigrants who ran a tailor's shop and cigar store there, in the wake of Canby's speech the house at 239 Arch Street became a tourist attraction. The entrepreneurial Munds posted a sign reading FIRST FLAG OF THE US MADE IN THE HOUSE. An 1876 advertisement read: "Original Flag House, Lager, Wine and Liquors. This is the house where the first United States flag was made by Mrs. John Ross." For some twenty years, the Munds capitalized on their association with Betsy Ross. But then, as the Arch Street neighborhood began to collapse, and building after building razed to make way for industrial expansion, Philadelphians began to worry that this landmark, too—if comparatively newly discovered—would be lost.

Not coincidentally, these were years during which Americans cultivated what the historian Robert E. Bonner has called a "uniquely flag-centered patriotism." Its seeds planted in the War of 1812, a fascination with the flag emerged over the course of the nineteenth century and blossomed in the wake of the Civil War. A symbol of union drenched in the sacrifice of hundreds and thousands of men, the United States flag, in the decade of the nation's centennial, came to signal the "patriotic ideal." As the century marched on, the flag took on new meanings, too, in a nation struggling to accept the arrival of new populations of immigrants, and new political philosophies that threatened the status quo. By the 1890s, the flag had become a powerful symbol of American nationalism in ways that it had never been before. The Pledge of Allegiance was penned in 1892, and in 1896 pioneering political operative Mark Hanna distributed hundreds of thousands of flags to supporters of his candidate, William McKinley. By the last decade of the nineteenth century, American interest in the national flag was higher than ever before.[44]

It was in this particular political climate that the Betsy Ross house would galvanize national attention. This phase of the legend's life—the part of the story that is best known today—is largely attached to the energies of Charles H. Weisgerber, who is mainly remembered as the chief developer of the Betsy Ross House museum and the advocate who took the baton from the Canby family and carried it into the twentieth century. Weisgerber was a successful artist at the moment the flag legend crossed his path. A biographical dictionary published just before attention focused on the preservation of the Arch

Street property lists him as among Philadelphia's foremost pastel artists, whose portraits hang in the "handsomest mansions in the United States."[45] Born in New York City, Weisgerber trained both in formal academies and with private tutors. By 1890, he was best known for having executed the largest pastel painting yet attempted in the United States, *The Modern Gladiator*. One biographer called him "unassuming, serious and tenacious of purpose." Tenacity would indeed prove his most valuable asset.[46]

In 1892, the thirty-six-year-old artist was casting about for a subject to enter into a citywide competition for the best rendering of a historical event. George Canby (William's younger brother) persuaded Weisgerber to create a scene based on the Ross story. The now-famous canvas *Birth of Our Nation's Flag*, depicting Betsy Ross presenting the flag to Washington, Morris and Ross, was displayed at the World's Columbian Exposition in Chicago (millions have seen the painting today: in 1952, it was reproduced on 116 million three-cent postage stamps commemorating the two hundredth anniversary of Betsy Ross's birth).[47] Weisgerber sensed an opportunity in the wind, and perhaps a livelihood more stable than securing commissions for portraits. Six years later, when the house was threatened with demolition, he and the other founding members of the American Flag House and Betsy Ross Memorial Association raised funds to buy it. They sold lifetime memberships to the association for ten cents and presented members with a certificate bearing Weisgerber's scene. Individuals who formed "clubs" of thirty or more members would receive a ten-color chromolithograph of the painting (suitable for framing, as they say) as well as certificates for each club member. In time, some 2 million Americans would respond to that call. In 1898, the site opened to visitors, with the famous moment interpreted in the back parlor, and the front room devoted to souvenir sales. It became a tremendous success that to this day attracts hundreds of thousands of visitors annually. For his part, Weisgerber was so pleased with himself that he named a son Vexil Domus—Latin for "Flag House."[48]

Weisgerber was not the only one to see opportunity in the story of the "first flag." Rachel Wilson Albright embraced her grandmother's legacy more materially as she made and sold small commemorative flags. Caroline Hutch, a niece, was a widow living with her parents next door to Aunt Rachel. Rachel had made a small flag for "some society to which she belonged" (William Canby thought it was perhaps the Daughters of the American Revolution), and shortly thereafter began to receive requests from other organizations for similar flags—requests with which she complied for a small fee.[49] Eventually Caroline approached Charles Weisgerber to capitalize on her family's legend. Rachel, now ninety-two years old, accepted a contract to make small flags for the Columbian Exposition, and, as William Canby confided to George, "from the peremptory manner in which Callie [Caroline] inquires who makes the flags that float over the house day & night one might suppose they were going into the business."[50] Others did likewise. Betsy's great-granddaughter Sarah Wilson made and sold flags from the East Wing of Independence Hall—their thirteen stars arranged in the circle that by this time was firmly associated with the Betsy Ross flag—into the second decade of the twentieth century, capitalizing on the patriotic resonance to add luster to their souvenir trade.

Betsy's grand-nephew Joseph Boggs Beale in time made his own contribution to the dissemination of the Ross tale when he began painting scenes for "Magic Lantern" shows, large spectacles in which slides were projected onto screens. As the images changed every thirty seconds or so, they illustrated (together with the help of a live showman, musicians and often the audience as well) stories or songs, often on holiday themes like Christmas or Halloween, and eventually (once it became possible to transfer photographs to the slides) scenic views from around the world. It was the nineteenth-century precursor to IMAX. Beale became the country's foremost artist of Magic Lantern scenes. Over the course of his career (brought to a close with the advent of film), he painted about two thousand images for the lantern. Very few were historical, but in 1899, he rendered one of Betsy Ross showing the flag she made to the men assembled in her parlor. It would be one of the earliest imaginings of that event. Beale's version places Washington's proposed six-pointed star prominently in the scene's foreground, scraps of fabric with five-pointed stars cut out of them subtly in the background, at the feet of the seamstress portrayed at the completion of the project, displaying the large flag with thirteen five-pointed stars arranged in a circle. The image contributed to Beale's series of historical and patriotic paintings, shown to thousands of schoolchildren as well as church and lodge members. It was later purchased and heavily merchandized. Among other things, it was printed in the 1930s on a Homer-Laughlin plate that sold so well that it is routinely found today in antique stores, flea markets and on eBay.[51]

Indeed, while the story of the first flag continued to attract scrutiny, the legend of Betsy Ross flourished independently of academic discussion. Alongside the Homer-Laughlin plate could be found a stunning array of Betsy Ross products. Consumers could buy Betsy Ross pincushions and sewing machines, as well as (less predictably) tea and berry bowls, in addition to (believe it or not) golf irons, bakelite knives and even pianos. More formal recognitions persisted as well. When the body of President William McKinley traveled in state from Washington to Ohio in 1901, the casket lay draped under a flag made by a descendant of Betsy's shop, a flag requested by the president while living and completed in time for this solemn service.[52] When Rear Admiral Richard Byrd made his historic 1927 flight from New York to France, Rodman Wanamaker (the son of Philadelphia department-store founder Lewis Rodman Wanamaker) gave him a scrap of bunting allegedly from the flag maker's shop to carry with him.[53] The story lent itself to any variety of purposes—part of its wide appeal. Just as it could advance a range of agendas during the struggle over suffrage, in later generations it was harnessed again and again for political purposes. A 1942 episode of the radio program *Cavalcade of America*, for instance, presented a highly fictional version of Betsy's life, but gave the character of George Washington occasion to note that "in times like these . . . the smallest task may mean the difference between defeat and victory. The most menial assignment can become a solemn responsibility," words meant to encourage keepers of World War II–era Victory gardens and collectors of rubber tires to keep up the good work.[54] She was put to political purposes again in the 1970s when Vietnam Veterans Against the War occupied the Betsy Ross House and turned the flag in front of the building upside down, while feminist producers invoked her legend in the theme song to the hit sitcom *Maude*.[55] When a new bridge from Philadelphia to Pennsauken, New Jersey, opened in the bicentennial year 1976, it was named in honor of the flag maker.

Here in the twenty-first century, hundreds of thousands of visitors still crowd the museum dedicated to Ross's memory, while scholars continue to debate her meaning and relevance. Although historians and most of the general public today take the story of the making of the first flag with a grain of salt, Canby's version of events gained support in the early twentieth century, when a paper star pattern with a Wilson family signature on it (and labeled BETSY ROSS PATTERN FOR STARS) was discovered.[56] The star's mysterious discovery and subsequent disappearance seem symbolic of the larger story it represents, shaped as it has been by similar moments of affirmation, mystery and loss. In his best-selling book *Lies My Teacher Told Me*, James Loewen echoes a familiar refrain when he suggests that her descendants "invented the myth of the first flag" in an effort to "create a tourist attraction." Eager to hammer a decisive nail in the flag tale's coffin, Loewen goes so far as to declare outright: "Betsy Ross never did anything."[57]

He is not alone, as other scholars have raced to assert Ross's insignificance. But surely the historical value of Betsy Ross need not be a zero-sum game. As the bride of a privateer, and then the wife of a wounded war veteran who would eventually land a job in the U.S. Customs Service, and as the recipient of government contracts for the rest of her life, she found her fortunes to be inextricably tied with those of the federal government. Skeptics—or cynics—who dismiss Ross altogether as a source of historical insight because no conclusive evidence confirms that single conversation in the upholsterer's parlor have lost the baby with the bathwater. If the legend indeed tends to overstate the known facts (as legends by definition do), the life does not. Over a sixty-year career, Betsy Ross fabricated hundreds of curtains, mattresses and tassels, and countless yards of fringe. She produced dozens of colors, ensigns and standards—those hundred or so recorded in known archival sources representing just a fraction of her total output. We cannot know whether any of the flags that today survive from early-nineteenth-century military installations or from diplomatic overtures to western tribes were the work of her hands, but given her grip on contracts from the Schuylkill Arsenal for several years after the century's turn, they may well be.

Betsy Ross "never knew what it was to want employment," as she herself would say. Her life gives us a view not just into the life behind the Betsy Ross legend, but into the lives of working women across Revolutionary America whose labors made the new nation possible.[58] To be sure, the tangible traces of her life scattered over time, obscuring historical truths and making way for myths and legends. Only a few possessions survive for inspection today. The places where she was born, where she grew up, where she first learned her trade and where she raised her young family are all gone. Hugg's Tavern, the scene of her elopement, was torn down in 1929. The buildings on Front Street that for so many years sheltered her shop and family were demolished.[59] The neighborhood in which she died was razed in the 1950s to make way for—ironically enough—Independence Mall. The Arch Street house that survives today must stand for houses and workrooms all over Philadelphia that once sheltered her considerable enterprise.

Betsy Griscom Ross Ashburn Claypoole may indeed seem elusive, but her life nevertheless helps us to contemplate the Revolution and its aftermath in new ways. She is important to our understanding of American history not because she made any one flag, however iconic that moment may have become, but because she was a young craftswoman who embraced the resistance movement with vigor, celebrated its triumphs and suffered its consequences. Her life is significant not only for what it teaches us about the soldiers and sailors, assemblymen and privateers whose orbits traversed Betsy's own, but also for what it reveals about people who summoned the courage to dissent from their faiths and to challenge their government when they believed it had transgressed its bounds. Her story is worth knowing for what it tells us, too, about the working women and men who built early America's cities, furnished its rooms and clothed its citizens—families who fomented, endured and remembered the upheaval of the Revolution. And lastly she helps us imagine more ordinary times, the familiar cares of everyday life, and the pleasure taken in the simple comforts of beautiful and functional things made by capable hands.

# KEY FIGURES

*Joseph Ashburn* (ca. 1750–81). Betsy's second husband and the father of her eldest surviving daughter, Eliza Ashburn Silliman; a privateer who died in the Old Mill Prison near Plymouth, England.

*Joseph Boggs Beale* (1841–1926). Betsy's great-nephew, an artist who would go on to fame as an illustrator of Magic Lantern slides.

*William Berrett* (ca. 1770–1850). Philadelphia painter and Betsy's collaborator in the flag business.

*Margaret Donaldson Boggs* (1776–1876). Betsy's niece, the daughter of her sister Sarah Donaldson; the wife of Joseph Boggs.

*Deborah Griscom Bolton* (1743–93). Betsy's eldest sister, she married Everard Bolton and died in the 1793 yellow fever epidemic.

*Everard Bolton* (1731–1839). Betsy's brother-in-law, married to her oldest sister, Deborah.

*Caleb Canby* (1789–1852). Betsy's son-in-law, the husband of daughter Jane; a hardware dealer who would later help manage Betsy's affairs.

*Jane Claypoole Canby* (1792–1873). Betsy's sixth daughter; it was in Jane's Cherry Street home that Betsy spent her final years.

*William Canby* (1825–90). Betsy's grandson, who delivered the 1870 lecture that launched the story of the first flag.

*John Claypoole* (1752–1817). Betsy's third husband, a onetime tanner, upholsterer and employee of the Customs Service.

*Susannah Griscom Doane* (1744–88). Betsy's sister, married to the ship captain Ephraim Doane.

*Sarah Donaldson* (1749–85). Betsy's sister, married to the mariner William Donaldson; the mother of Margaret Donaldson Boggs.

*William Donaldson* (1748–89). Betsy's brother-in-law, married to sister Sarah; the father of Margaret Donaldson Boggs.

*Plunket Fleeson* (1712–91). Eighteenth-century Philadelphia's leading upholsterer.

*Rachel Claypoole Jones Fletcher* (1789–1873). Betsy's fifth daughter, the only one to record her mother's story in an affidavit.

*Andrew Griscom* (d. 1694). Betsy's great-grandfather, a house carpenter who emigrated from the British Isles to New Jersey in about 1680.

*George Griscom* (1761–1835). Betsy's only brother who survived into adulthood, a silversmith in Philadelphia and New Jersey.

*Rachel Griscom* (1762–1825). Betsy's youngest sister, a never-married fellow upholsterer.

*Rebecca Griscom* (1746–97). Betsy's sister, never married, who died in a Philadelphia almshouse.

*Rebecca Griscom* (1745–1807). Betsy's cousin, a mantua maker in the Northern Liberties.

*Rebecca James Griscom* (1721–93). Betsy's mother, the daughter of shop-keeper George James and the sister of merchant Abel James.

*Samuel Griscom* (1717–93). Betsy's father, a Philadelphia house carpenter.

*Sarah Dole Griscom* (d. 1703). Betsy's great-grandmother, who later married John Kaighn.

*Sarah Griscom* (1693–1773). Betsy's great-aunt, a Philadelphia staymaker.

*Abel James* (1724–90). Betsy's uncle, among the leading merchants of Phila-delphia.

*Elizabeth Knight* (1719–66). Betsy's aunt, her mother's sister, and the wife of Giles Knight.

*Giles Knight* (1719–99). Betsy's uncle, a Bucks County farmer and assemblyman.

*Griffith Levering* (1753–88). Betsy's brother-in-law, a ship carpenter married to her sister Hannah.

*Hannah Griscom Levering* (1755–1836). Betsy's sister, a grocer; she married Griffith Levering and later William McIntire.

*Mary Griscom Morgan* (1750–ca. 1793). Betsy's sister, who married the clock- and watchmaker Thomas Morgan.

*Thomas Morgan* (ca. 1750–1800). Betsy's brother-in-law, a clock- and watch-maker from Maryland.

*George Read* (1733–98). Betsy's uncle through her marriage to John Ross, a signer of the Declaration of Independence representing Delaware.

*George Ross* (1730–79). Betsy's uncle through her marriage to John Ross, a signer of the Declaration of Independence representing Pennsylvania.

*John Ross* (ca. 1750–76). A Philadelphia upholsterer and Betsy's first hus-band, the son of Reverend Aeneas Ross and Sarah Leech Ross.

*John Ross* (1714–76). Betsy's uncle through her marriage to John Ross; an attorney and a signer of the Declaration of Independence.

*Susan Claypoole Satterthwaite* (1786–1875).  Betsy's fourth daughter, the wife of hardware dealer Abel Satterthwaite.

*Eliza Ashburn Silliman* (1781–1833). Betsy's only surviving daughter by Joseph Ashburn; she married ship captain Isaac Silliman.

*Clarissa Claypoole Wilson* (1785–1864). Betsy's oldest daughter with John Claypoole; the wife of Jacob Wilson, she carried on Betsy's business until 1857.

# NOTES

ABBREVIATIONS

APS   American Philosophical Society

BRH   Betsy Ross House, American Flag House and Betsy Ross Memorial

EDD   Elizabeth Drinker, *The Diary of Elizabeth Drinker*, Elaine Forman Crane, ed., 3 vols. (Boston: Northeastern University Press, 1991).

FHL   Friends Historical Library, Swarthmore College Library

GCHS   Gloucester County Historical Society, Woodbury, New Jersey

HSP   Historical Society of Pennsylvania

INHP   Independence National Historical Park, National Park Service

JDC   Joseph Downs Collection of Manuscripts and Printed Ephemera, H. F. du Pont Winterthur Museum

LCP   Library Company of Philadelphia

LOC   Library of Congress

NARA   National Archives

NDAR   *Naval Documents of the American Revolution*, William Bell Clark, William James Morgan and Michael J. Crawford, eds. (Washington, D.C.: Department of the Navy, 1964–2005).

PA   *Pennsylvania Archives*

PCA   Philadelphia City Archives

PEP   *Pennsylvania Evening Post*

PG   *Pennsylvania Gazette*

PJ   *Pennsylvania Journal*

PMHB   *Pennsylvania Magazine of History and Biography*

PMMM   Philadelphia Monthly Meeting Minutes (consulted on microfilm at the QCHC)

**PMMMND**   Philadelphia Monthly Meeting Minutes—Northern District (consulted
on microfilm at QCHC)
*PP   Pennsylvania Packet*
**PSA**   Pennsylvania State Archive
**QCHC**   Quaker Collection, Haverford College

## PROLOGUE

1. See "Sotheby's to Sell Four Battle Flags Captured During the Revolution,"
*Internet Antiques Guide*, 5 June 2006 (accessed 25 May 2007); Richard Pyle, "Sotheby's
Auctions Rare Revolutionary War Flags," http://www.Boston.com, 14 June 2006
(accessed 25 May 2007); and Monica Almeida, "Remnants of Revolution, $17 million,"
*New York Times*, 15 June 2006 (accessed at www.flagresearchcenter.com on 25 May
2007). Scott A. Miskimon provides an account of the auction in "Sacred Relics Unfurled
for Auction," *Southern Campaigns of the American Revolution*, vol. 3, nos. 6–8 (June–
August 2006), 3–6 (accessed at www.southerncampaign.org on 25 May 2007). The
standing record for an American flag at auction, set in May 2002, had been the $163,000
paid for a Grand Union flag made about 1800. At that same Sotheby's auction, a banner
believed to date from George Washington's inaugural sold for $262,500. See the *New
York Times*, 4 July 2002. I am grateful to Sotheby's vice chairman David Redden for
inviting me to attend this exciting auction just at the time I was embarking on this project, and for providing the auction catalog, "Four Battle Flags of the Revolution" (2006),
on which this discussion draws.

2. Glenn Collins, "Stars, Stripes and Dollar Signs," *New York Times*, 11 November
2005. For a list of surviving flags, see the "Preliminary Census of American Revolutionary Battleflags," in "Four Battle Flags of the Revolution," 33–34.

3. See Benjamin H. Irvin, "Benjamin Franklin's *Enriching Virtues*: Continental
Currency and the Creation of a Revolutionary Republic," *Common-Place* 6, no. 3 (2006),
http://www.common-place.org.

4. The Sotheby's catalog describes the stars in the canton as "arranged as a triangle of three stars within a circle of eight stars, with two further stars at the upper left
and right corners of the canton." The triangle and circle are somewhat in the eye of the
beholder; the maker may have begun to execute the 3-2-3-2-3 pattern typical at the time
and failed in the application of the elements.

5. In 1999, the *Boston Globe* reported, "Of the six other known chairs, four are in
museum collections, the Metropolitan Museum of Art, the Winterthur Museum, the
Philadelphia Museum of Art, and Colonial Williamsburg. The two remaining chairs
are in private collections." See Virginia Bohlin, "George Washington Gets Outranked,"
*Boston Globe*, 3 October 1999.

6. Lita Solis-Cohen, "Record American Chairs Top October Americana Auction," *Maine Antiques Digest*, December 1999.

7. Heidi L. Berry, "American Furniture Gathers in Strength; Recent High Prices
Spotlight Appeal of Antique American Pieces," *New York Times*, 5 February 1987.

8. Solis-Cohen, "Record American Chairs."

9. These receipts and others are reproduced in Mark J. Anderson et al., "Cadwalader Study" (unpublished research report, H. F. du Pont Winterthur Museum, 1995).

10. Nicholas B. Wainwright, *Colonial Grandeur in Philadelphia: The House and
Furniture of General John Cadwalader* (Philadelphia: HSP, 1964), 51; John Cadwalader's

waste book, 12 February 1772, HSP; Linda Baumgarten, "Protective Covers for Furniture and Its Contents," in Luke Beckerdite, ed., *American Furniture* (Hanover, N.H.: University Press of New England for the Chipstone Foundation, 2000), 3–14; and Lerroy Graves and Luke Beckerdite, "New Insights on John Cadwalader's Commode-Seat Side Chairs," in Luke Beckerdite, ed., *American Furniture* (Hanover, N.H.: University Press of New England for the Chipstone Foundation, 2000), 153–68.

11. The first printed reference to the story, in the wake of William J. Canby's paper before the Historical Society of Pennsylvania, was in the *Philadelphia Press*, 15 March 1870.

12. Michael Frisch, "American History and the Structures of Collective Memory: A Modest Exercise in Empirical Iconography," *Journal of American History* 75, no. 4 (1989): 1130–55. Visitation figures provided by the Betsy Ross House staff. There is some generational change afoot; Ross does not fare as well in more recent studies, which indicate that Rosa Parks—ironically, another much-misunderstood "seamstress"—has come to supplant her in terms of general historical literacy. See Sam Wineburg and Chauncey Monte-Santo, "'Famous Americans': The Changing Pantheon of American Heroes," *Journal of American History* 94, no. 4 (2008): 1186–1202.

13. A heroic effort to recover that material can be found in the digital editorial project "Papers of the War Department, 1784–1800," which makes available "some 55,000 documents of the early War Department many long thought irretrievable but now reconstructed through a painstaking, multi-year research effort available online to scholars, students, and the general public." See http://wardepartmentpapers.org/index.php.

14. Charles Hardy evaluates the quality and plausibility of the affidavits in "Betsy Ross: Tracing the Evolution of a National Creation Story," unpublished report prepared for *History Now*, 17 March 1996, BRH.

15. For histories of the United States flag as well as the Ross legend, see George Henry Preble, *Our Flag: Origin and Progress of the Flag of the United States of America* (Albany, N.Y., 1872); Addie Guthrie Weaver, *The Story of Our Flag* (Chicago, 1898); Lloyd Balderston and George Canby, *The Evolution of the American Flag* (Philadelphia: Ferris and Leach, 1909); James Alfred Moss, *The Flag of the United States: Its History and Symbolism* (Washington, D.C.: United States Flag Association, 1930); Edwin S. Parry, *Betsy Ross: Quaker Rebel* (Philadelphia: John C. Winston, 1930); Theodore D. Gottlieb, *The Origin and Evolution of the Betsy Ross Flag, Legend or Tradition* (Newark, N.J., 1938); Whitney Smith, "Face to Face with Betsy Ross" (Winchester, Mass.: Flags Research Center, 1975); William Rea Furlong, Byron McCandless and Harold D. Langley, *So Proudly We Hail: The History of the United States Flag* (Washington, D.C.: Smithsonian Institution Press, 1981); Edward W. Richardson, *Standards and Colors of the American Revolution* (Philadelphia: University of Pennsylvania Press, 1982); William B. Timmons, *Betsy Ross: The Griscom Legacy* (Salem, N.J.: Salem County Cultural & Heritage Commission, 1983); Scot M. Guenter, *The American Flag, 1777–1924: Cultural Shifts from Creation to Codification* (Rutherford, N.J.: Fairleigh Dickinson University Press, 1990); Henry W. Moeller, *Shattering an American Myth: Unfurling the History of the Stars and Stripes* (Mattituck, N.Y.: American House, 1992); Michael Corcoran, *For Which It Stands: An Anecdotal Biography of the American Flag* (New York: Simon and Schuster, 2002); John Harker, *Betsy Ross's Five Pointed Star* (Melbourne Beach, Fla.: Canmore Press, 2005); and Marc Leepson, *Flag: An American Biography* (New York: St. Martin's Press, 2006). Lonn Taylor also addresses the Betsy Ross story in *The Star Spangled Banner* (New York: Smithsonian Books/HarperCollins, 2008), 68–69.

16. Richard White, *Remembering Ahanagran: Storytelling in a Family's Past* (New York: Hill and Wang, 1998), 21.

17. Avi Decter, "Folklore Perspectives on Oral Traditions," memo to Interpretive Planning Team, 1996, BRH.

18. See Karal Ann Marling, *George Washington Slept Here: Colonial Revivals and American Culture, 1876–1986* (Cambridge, Mass.: Harvard University Press, 1988). There is far more scholarship on the career of the Ross legend than on Ross's actual life. The best place to begin is Allan E. Peterson, "Cherished and Ignored: A Cultural History of Betsy Ross" (M.A. thesis, San Diego State University, 2001).

19. James Duffin, "Transcription of Notes of Interview with Margaret (Donaldson) Boggs, 1776–1876," BRH.

20. James Duffin, "Transcription of 1870 Affidavit of Sophia B. (Wilson) Hildebrandt," BRH.

21. Rebecca Iron Graff, *Genealogy of the Claypoole Family in Philadelphia* (Philadelphia, 1893), 69.

22. James Duffin, "Transcription of the Recollections of William Jackson Canby (1825–1890) of His Grandmother," BRH. The descendant and researcher John Balderston agrees that it was the visit of Washington, rather than the "firstness" of the flag, that was the point of Betsy's story. Ross, he maintained, "never to the end of her life was particularly interested in the idea that she made the first flag, although she said she had; to her the highlight of the story of her life was always that to her, a poor seamstress, came the great gentleman and general-in-chief of the armies, Mr. Washington, and talked to her in her shop." See John L. Balderston to George Hastings, 21 March 1939, GCHS.

23. Canby's affidavit is confusing on this point: it is unclear who is pointing to what engraving. Irving's *Life of Washington* was not published until 1855; if Elizabeth Claypoole herself gestured toward this engraving while she made this claim, it is likelier to have been the version reproduced in Benjamin Franklin French's *Biographia Americana* (New York, 1825).

24. Eleanor Parke Custis Lewis to Elizabeth Bordley, 28 October 1820, in Patricia Brady, ed., *George Washington's Beautiful Nelly: The Letters of Eleanor Parke Custis Lewis to Elizabeth Bordley Gibson, 1794–1851* (Columbia: University of South Carolina Press, 1991), 287, as presented in North American Women's Letters and Diaries, subscription database, Alexander Street Press.

25. Marla R. Miller, *The Needle's Eye: Women and Work in the Age of Revolution* (Amherst: University of Massachusetts Press, 2006), 4.

26. See Alfred Young, *Masquerade: The Life and Times of Deborah Sampson, Continental Soldier* (New York: Knopf, 2004); Alfred Young, *The Shoemaker and the Tea Party* (Boston: Beacon Press, 1999); and Laurel Thatcher Ulrich, *A Midwife's Tale: The Life of Martha Ballard, Based on Her Diary, 1785–1812* (New York: Knopf, 1991).

27. Of course, substantive unpublished work is contained among the in-house research materials that supports interpretation at the BRH. Particularly important among these are Debra Jean Force, "Betsy Ross, Upholsterer and Flag-Maker: A Proposal to Furnish Her Home" (unpublished report, Betsy Ross Foundation, 1976); Stephanie Grauman Wolf, "Betsy Ross: American Woman of the Revolutionary Generation" (unpublished report, Betsy Ross Foundation, 1996); and Sandra Lloyd, "Betsy Ross and Women in Revolutionary Philadelphia" (unpublished report, Betsy Ross Foundation, 1998), BRH. Among the published studies listed in note 15, the most attentive to the full sweep of Betsy Ross's life is Timmons, *Betsy Ross*.

28. "Save the Birthplace of Freedom's Flag," *Philadelphia Inquirer*, 14 May 1893.

29. Other objects today associated with Ross are also known, but their connection to her is difficult to verify. Plausible but unverified are elements of a silver tea service that remains in family hands, as well as a chatelaine that once belonged to Sarah Holloway (the stepsister of Betsy's father, Samuel); both are illustrated in Timmons, *Betsy Ross*, 160, 120. Examples of less plausible artifacts include a pair of shoes and an embroidered sash in the collections of the Pennsylvania Museum of Art and said by the donor to be worn by Ross at a ball held in Fredericksburg, Virginia, in 1781, celebrating the victory at Yorktown. However, the shoes do not appear to date from the last quarter of the century, and Ross is not known to have traveled to Fredericksburg.

30. On the snuff, see Duffin, "Transcription of the Recollections of William Jackson Canby (1825–1890) of His Grandmother"; on the tomatoes, see the Lydia S. Parry reminiscence, 13 February 1936, GCHS.

31. James Duffin, "Transcription of 1909 Affidavit of Susan (Satterthwaite) Newport (1827–?) and Mary Satterthwaite (1824–?)"; Duffin, "Transcription of the Recollections of William Jackson Canby (1825–1890) of His Grandmother"; and Duffin, "Transcription of William J. Canby's Lecture on Betsy Ross and the Flag," all at BRH.

## 1. THE LIGHT WITHIN

1. William B. Timmons, *Betsy Ross: The Griscom Legacy* (Salem, N.J.: Salem County Cultural & Heritage Commission, 1983), 9, 98, 272 n. 2.

2. Anna Griscom genealogy, 1869, GCHS; Timmons, *Betsy Ross*, 272 n. 10; and Griscom Family folder, Chester County Historical Society, West Chester, Pennsylvania. The Griscom line in the United Kingdom is indeed difficult to track. While traveling in England in the nineteenth century, John Griscom L.D., John Denn Griscom and David Griscom "could find no trace of the name." Some evidence places the Griscoms in London around the time of Andrew's emigration. The *Proceedings of the Old Bailey* (courtesy of the British Library and HRI Online Publications, accessed 4 June 2008) note that, on 31 August 1681, "William Wats was Tryed for a Fellony and Burglary committed in the Parish of Stepny, in July last on the House of Andrew Grescom [*sic*]." But the record does not necessarily require Griscom to have been present at the time; perhaps his mother was still in residence when William Wats was accused of burglary; indeed, perhaps it was Griscom's absence that tempted the alleged thief. Additionally, *Marriage Licences, 1611–1828* (as available via http://www.Ancestry.com), as well as the *Calendar of Marriage Licence Allegations, 1597–1648*, book 15, 5 March 1632–33, note the union of a Tobias Powell and a Grizel Grisham ("of St Andrew's, Holborn, Spinster, 20, daughter of Richard Gresham, deceased; consent of mother Elizabeth Gresham; at St Andrew's, Holborn"); though their relationship to Andrew Griscom is unknown, the appearance of the names Tobias, Grizel and Gresham in constellation with one another makes some association seem likely. Friends Quarterly Meeting records of London and Middlesex also include a reference to an Andrew Griscom (Parish of St. Paul's Shadwell), whose infant daughter, Sarah, died 25 October 1681 and was buried in Ratcliffe; see English Friends Records, Quarterly Meetings of London and Middlesex, transcribed in Griscom Family: Vital Records, GCHS. Whether this is the daughter of the same Andrew Griscom may never be known. Andrew's bride, Sarah Dole, seems to have come from Wales by way of Bristol, which may account for the association of Andrew Griscom with Wales, too. Later generations muddied the waters

further, having come to believe Griscom was born on the Isle of Man (the point of origin of his widow's second husband, John Kaighn), though indexes at the Manx National Heritage Library today contain no references to this surname. My thanks to Manx National Heritage Library archivist Wendy Thirkettle and (London) Library of the Religious Society of Friends archivist Jennifer Milligan for their help with this query.

3. The account that follows is drawn from Pink Dandelion, *The Quakers: A Very Short Introduction* (New York: Oxford University Press, 2008); David Hackett Fischer, *Albion's Seed: Four British Folkways in America* (New York: Oxford University Press, 1989); and Barry Levy, "Quakers, the Delaware Valley, and North Midlands Emigration to America," *William and Mary Quarterly*, 3rd series, 48, no. 2 (1991): 246–52.

4. Isaac Penington to Thomas Walmsley (1670), *The Works of the Long Mournful and Sorely Distressed Isaac Penington*, WWW edition (http://www.qhpress.org/texts/penington/index.html, accessed 4 June 2008).

5. For the 1680 date, see Timmons, *Betsy Ross*, 9 and 272 n. 2.

6. William Penn, as quoted in Clive E. Driver, comp., *Passing Through: Letters and Documents Written in Philadelphia by Famous Visitors* (Philadelphia: Rosenbach Museum and Library, 1982), 4.

7. Fischer, *Albion's Seed*, 421, 441.

8. Timmons, *Betsy Ross*, 9 and 272 n. 2, citing Francis B. Lee, *The Genealogical Memorial History of the State of New Jersey* (New York: Lewis, 1910), 1205; see also John Clement, *Sketches of the First Immigrant Settlers of Newton Township, Old Gloucester County, West New Jersey* (Camden, N.J., 1877), and Thomas Shourds, *History and Genealogy of Fenwick's Colony* (Bridgeton, N.J., 1876). Griscom may have purchased the land directly from Samuel Norris, of London's Watlin Street, though no deed has ever been found; see Elizabeth J. Harrell, "The Quaker Ancestry of Samuel Griscom (1787–1849) and His Wife Ann Powell (1789–1850)," unpublished typescript in the GCHS.

9. "The present state of the colony of West-Jersey, 1681," in Albert Cook Myers, ed., *Narratives of Early Pennsylvania, West New Jersey and Delaware* (New York: Barnes and Noble, 1912), 195.

10. William Penn, *Some Account of the Province of Pennsylvania . . . for the Information of such as are or may be disposed to transport themselves or servants into those parts"* (London, 1681), as quoted in Myers, *Narratives of Early Pennsylvania*, 204, 209.

11. Between July 1681 and March 1685, close to six hundred people bought some 715,437 acres of land from William Penn; these "first purchasers" were joined by another 194—Andrew Griscom among them—whom the historians Richard Dunn and Mary Dunn call "reputed first purchasers," people who either purchased land from Penn (but whose transactions are not comparably documented) or bought land from a first purchaser. See Richard Dunn and Mary Dunn, eds., *Papers of William Penn*, 4 vols. (Philadelphia: University of Pennsylvania Press, 1981–87), 2:660. See also Andrew Griscom/Henry Flower (1683, book 2, 188); Andrew Griscomb/William Campson (1685, book La, vol. 4, 7); Andrew Griscom/Jason Whitehall (1687, book IH9, 119).

12. Susan Mackiewicz, "Philadelphia Flourishing: The Material World of Philadelphians, 1882–1760" (Ph.D. dissertation, University of Delaware, 1988), 147–50.

13. Gary B. Nash, "City Planning and Political Tension in the Seventeenth Century: The Case of Philadelphia," *Proceedings of the American Philosophical Society* 112, no. 1 (1968): 54–73; 61, 63.

14. Hannah Benner Roach, comp., in the "Philadelphia Business Directory, 1670," *Pennsylvania Genealogical Magazine* 23 (1963): 106–8, finds nine master carpenters in the city before 1690, Griscom among them.

15. Gary B. Nash, *Quakers and Politics: Pennsylvania, 1681–1926* (1968; Boston: Northeastern University Press, 1993), 50.

16. Susan E. Klepp, "Encounter and Experiment: The Colonial Period," in Randall M. Miller and William Pencak, eds., *Pennsylvania: A History of the Commonwealth* (University Park: Pennsylvania State University Press, 2002), 64.

17. Penn, *Some Account of the Province of Pennsylvania*, as quoted in Myers, *Narratives of Early Pennsylvania*, 211.

18. Mackiewicz, "Philadelphia Flourishing," 176–77.

19. "Early Pennsylvania Land Records, Minute Book D, "Minute Book of Propriety Commencing the Seventh Day of the Twelfth Month, 1689–90," http://www.ancestry.com.

20. William Penn to George Saville, as quoted in Mackiewicz, "Philadelphia Flourishing," 195.

21. On Robert Turner and the 1667 legislation, see ibid., 199.

22. Timmins, *Betsy Ross*, 11, cites Anna Griscom's 1869 family tree, which itself quotes "Leeds Almanac" (New York, 1694), as stating, "It is now 11 years since Andrew Griscom built the first brick house in Philadelphia." But the origin of this quotation is puzzling. Anna Griscom probably relied on John Fanning Watson's 1830 *Annals of Philadelphia* (Philadelphia, 1830), where Watson refers (413–14) to the Second Street house of a D. Griscom, pulled down to make way for the Bank of Pennsylvania, allegedly the "first built house of brick" in Philadelphia; in an asterisked note, he quotes *Leeds Almanac*. Oddly, though, Daniel Leeds's 1694 almanac does not include any reference to the city's first brick house, or to Andrew Griscom, and no other publication included in Early American Imprints contains similar language. The source of Watson's note remains a mystery, but I have been unable to locate any alternate source for the assertion. On Richard Cantril's claim, see http://homepages.rootsweb.com/~lcompton/myfamily/d0002/g0000114.htm (accessed 14 May 2007). Citations to Watson's *Annals* will always prefer the earliest edition in which the relevant material appears of this often-republished work.

23. Harrell, "The Quaker Ancestry of Samuel Griscom," 12.

24. As quoted in Watson, *Annals of Philadelphia*, 414.

25. Hannah Benner Roach, *Colonial Philadelphians* (Philadelphia: Genealogical Society of Pennsylvania, 1999), 38, 39, 60 n. 63, 66 n. 129.

26. "An Account of Pennsylvania and Its Improvements by William Penn," 1684, reprinted in *PMHB* 9, no. 1 (1885): 66–67; and Robert Turner to William Penn, 3 August 1685, cited in ibid., 74, both as quoted in John M. Bacon, "Cellars, Garrets, and Related Spaces in Philadelphia Homes, 1750–1850" (INHP, National Park Service, September 1991), 11.

27. Charles Pickering to Anne Harrison, 15 April 1689, and Alexander Beardsley to William Penn, 1690, both as quoted in Mackiewicz, "Philadelphia Flourishing," 224–25.

28. Gabriel Thomas, *An historical and geographical account of the province of Pennsylvania* (London, 1698). See also Roger William Moss Jr., "Master Builders: A History of the Colonial Philadelphia Buildings Trade" (Ph.D. dissertation, University of Delaware, 1972), 29–31.

29. See Andrew Griscom, will, 1694, file 102, PCA; and Julian Hartzfelder to Andrew Griscom, recited in a deed from Cunrads to Shoemaker, Deed Book G 11.382, PCA.

30. See PMMM, 1 April 1685, 5 August 1685; and Myers, *Narratives of Early Phila-delphia*, 271.

31. PMMM, 2 June 1686, 29 August 1686.

32. Robert Turner to William Penn, 3 August 1685, as quoted in Mackiewicz, "Philadelphia Flourishing," 283–84.

33. PMMM, 26 September 1686. Some years later, a dispute emerged concerning his payment; see PMMM, 27 November 1692 and 26 March 1693. The building may have been completed, but the city didn't in fact reach it; the Quakers sold the building in 1700 to William Penn, who later gave it back to the congregation, which disman-tled it and reused materials in a second structure to house the Bank meeting, built in 1702.

34. Mackiewicz, "Philadelphia Flourishing," 284.

35. John F. Watson and Willis P. Hazard, *Annals of Philadelphia*, vol. 1, 358.

36. Anna Griscom family tree, 1869, GCHS; Walter Lee Sheppard Jr., *Passengers and Ships Prior to 1684* (Welcome Society, 1970), 41–43; and "Ancestors Approved for Membership," Welcome Society, http://www.welcomesociety.org/Welcome_ancestors .htm.

37. Timmons, *Betsy Ross*, 12; see also the Pennsylvania Land Office, *Minutes of the Board of Property of the Province of Pennsylvania*, William Henry Egle, ed. (Harrisburg, 1893), 1:514, 519, which discusses fifty acres of headland granted to Dole on 25 Septem-ber 1684, and another fifty granted on 9 October, on "Ridley Creek at a corner of Chas. Whitacre's land," which Sarah conveyed to Randall Vernon in 1702.

38. PMMM, 3 December 1684, 7 February 1685; and William Montgomery Clem-ens, *American Marriage Records Before 1699* (Pompton Lakes, N.J.: Biblio, 1926).

39. Recounted in Mackiewicz, "Philadelphia Flourishing," 173–74.

40. See Andrew Griscom, will, 1694, file 102, PCA; Richard Morris, will, file 77, PCA; and receipt, JDC, no. 75 x 110.3.

41. Julie Winch, *A Gentleman of Color: James Forten* (New York: Oxford Univer-sity Press), 9; see also Gary B. Nash, "Slaves and Slaveowners in Philadelphia," *William and Mary Quarterly* 30, no. 2 (1973): 223–56; *Minutes of the Provincial Council, Colo-nial Records*, vol. 1 (Philadelphia and Harrisburg, 1852–53); and Gary B. Nash, *Forging Freedom: The Formation of Philadelphia's Black Community, 1720–1840* (Cambridge, Mass.: Harvard University Press, 1991).

42. Winch, *A Gentleman of Color*, 10.

43. See Nash, "Slaves and Slaveowners in Philadelphia," 225.

44. The description that follows of the Griscom home is based on Andrew Griscom, probate inventory, 1694, file 102, PCA.

45. On Matthias Jewell, see Timmons, *Betsy Ross*, 14, and Roach, "Pennsylvania Business Directory."

46. The total value of Andrew Griscom's estate in 1694 was £814 8s. ½d. See file 102, PCA. By comparison, the carpenter whose estate came closest to Griscom's—John Harris's—was valued at £722 5s. 3d., with £196 5s. 3d. in household goods. Of the eight men whose estates were inventoried in 1694, the average total estate value was £241 14s. (just over a quarter of Griscom's), with the average value in household goods being £83 10s. 8d. Even if one takes all of the estates probated between 1685 and 1700, Griscom's is nearly twice the average, £409 4s. 5d. in total estate value, and half again the wealth in household goods, £104 5s. 7d. See Ruth Matzkin, "Inventories of Estates in Philadel-phia County, 1682–1710" (M.A. thesis, University of Delaware, 1959), 98.

47. Ibid., 58, 85, 159.

48. The following account is drawn from Nash, *Quakers and Politics*, 144–61.

49. Ibid., 153.

50. According to ibid., 156 n. 52, "Twenty-one of Keith's followers signed his tract *Some Reasons and Causes of the Late Separation . . .*" (Philadelphia, 1692); the names of twenty-eight adherents who signed a defense of Keith dated 3 July 1692 are given in Charles P. Keith, *Chronicles of Pennsylvania* (Philadelphia, 1917), 1:223. Sixty-six Keithians signed another paper titled "Declaration of the Yearly Meeting at Burlington, the 4th, 5th, 6th and 7th days of the Seventh Month, anno 1692," in *Parrish Collection, Proud Papers*, vol. 2, 42; other partisans are identifiable in a variety of sources listed in *Inventory of Church Archives, Society of Friends in Pennsylvania* (Philadelphia, 1941), 198–201.

51. Nash, *Quakers and Politics*, 160; the account that follows relies heavily on Nash's discussion of the rupture, 144–61. For an alternate view, see Jon Butler, " 'Gospel Order Improved': The Keithian Schism and the Exercise of Quaker Ministerial Authority in Pennsylvania," *William and Mary Quarterly*, 3rd series, 31, no. 3 (1974): 431–52.

52. See Craig W. Horle, Joseph S. Foster and Laurie M. Wolfe, eds., *Lawmaking and Legislators in Pennsylvania: A Biographical Dictionary* (University Park: Pennsylvania State University Press, 2005), vol. 1, appendix 6: "The Keithian Controversy and Factions in Philadelphia County."

53. Yearly Meeting, minutes, 27–28 February 1793, in Records of the Salem, New Jersey, Abstract of Monthly Men's Meeting Minutes, 1676–1744, 172–77, HSP.

54. See Timmons, *Betsy Ross*, 14, and Clement, *Sketches of the First Emigrant Settlers*, 217.

55. See Shourds, *History and Genealogy of Fenwick Colony*, 393; Shourds's assertion that Griscom "reconciled" with the Society of Friends contradicts my findings.

56. Harrell, "The Quaker Ancestry of Samuel Griscom."

57. According to documents filed in the Philadelphia City Archive, his personal estate was valued at another £243, including his carpentry tools (£27) and his "negro woman" (£20). For his probate inventory and will, see file 102, PCA.

58. Grizell Griscom Morris, like her son, was considered outside the Quaker community at the time of her death, her name also appearing among the thousand or so listed in an early "account of burials of such not as Friends within this town of Philadelphia." See Harrell, "The Quaker Ancestry of Samuel Griscom," 12, and William Wade Hinshaw, comp., *Encyclopedia of American Quaker Genealogy*, vol. 11 (New Jersey and Pennsylvania Monthly Meetings) (Baltimore: Genealogical Publishing, 1978), 444.

59. Kaighn was born on the Isle of Man, perhaps at Ballacragga, a town on the island's southeast coast where his mother lived with his brother Charles before removing to Kirk Andrew to the north. The year of Kaighn's emigration is unknown, but by 1694 he was living and working as a carpenter in Byberry, Pennsylvania, and married to Ann Albertson Forrest. See Clement, *Sketches of the First Emigrant Settlers*, 149–57.

60. See ibid., 151.

61. Debra Jean Force, "Betsy Ross, Upholsterer and Flag-Maker: A Proposal to Furnish Her Home" (unpublished report, Betsy Ross Foundation, 1976), 2. See also Griscom Family: Indentures, at the GCHS.

62. Gary B. Nash, *The Urban Crucible: The Northern Seaports and the Origins of the American Revolution* (Cambridge, Mass.: Harvard University Press, 1979), 110.

**63.** 30 November 1735–36, Deborah Read Franklin Shop Book, 1737–39, Benjamin Franklin Papers, APS.

**64.** The two brothers were not alone; their stepsisters Abigail and Sarah Holloway moved into the city when they were placed (apparently at their own request) under the guardianship of the Philadelphia joiner George Wilson. See Orphans Court Records, 1716–55, 30 April 1742, PCA; and Timmons, *Betsy Ross*, 51.

**65.** Morrison H. Heckscher, "Philadelphia Furniture, 1760–90: Native-born and London-Trained Craftsmen," in Francis J. Puig and Michael Conforti, eds., *The American Craftsman and the European Tradition* (Minneapolis: Minneapolis Institute of Arts; Hanover, N.H.: distributed by the University Press of New England, 1989), 92–111.

**66.** Fanny Salter repeated this recollection of her grandfather in "Fanny Salter's Reminiscences of Colonial Days in Philadelphia," *PMHB* 40, no. 2 (1916): 187. For a similar sentiment, see the "Diary of James Allen, Esq.," *PMHB* 9, no. 2 (1885): 176–96.

**67.** Tobias bought share number 27 from Thomas Potts Jr. See "A Chronological Register of Names of the Members of the Library Company of Philadelphia," LCP, and Dorothy Grimm, "A History of the Library Company of Philadelphia, 1731–1835" (Ph.D. dissertation, University of Pennsylvania, 1955), 33, 38.

**68.** See Moss, "Master Builders," 93. As Moss notes, several men were members of both the Library and Carpenters' Company, and eventually the Library Company housed the latter's collection—which by 1789 included some twenty titles on "Civil Architecture"—on the second floor of Carpenters' Hall.

## 2. A NURSERY TO THE LORD

**1.** William B. Timmons makes this observation in *Betsy Ross: The Griscom Legacy* (Salem, N.J.: Salem County Cultural & Heritage Commission, 1983), 98, 125, following Addie Guthrie Weaver, *The Story of Our Flag* (Chicago, 1898), 71, and the Claypoole family Bible; for a description of this last, see Lewis D. Cook, "Family Records from the Bible of 'Betsy Ross' of Philadelphia," *Genealogies of Pennsylvania Families from the Pennsylvania Genealogical Magazine*, vol. 3 (Baltimore: Genealogical Publishing, 1982), 905–6.

**2.** The meaning of the bell and its inscription is a matter of some debate. One of the best accounts is by David Kimball, who notes that the inscription lauds the achievement of liberty, and nods toward the fiftieth year, yet bears the date 1752, when the jubilee of the Charter of Privileges was in 1751. See David A. Kimball, *Venerable Relic: The Story of the Liberty Bell* (Philadelphia: Eastern National Park Association, 1989), 19.

**3.** Ibid., 14.

**4.** It seems likeliest that they met in Philadelphia, but it is possible that there is some Byberry connection here, too, since Andrew Griscom held land in what would become Byberry; see Grantee-Grantor Records, book F-8, 200, PCA.

**5.** A great deal of confusion surrounds Rebecca James's parentage, but it is entirely understandable, because the genealogical record is indeed perplexing and has become more so as errors have been introduced and perpetuated over time. According to Wynne James III, "James Families of America Since 1630" (typescript, Bucks County Historical Society, 1990), a George James of South Wales had moved to Chester County before 1692, while another George James, the son of James James, probably of Radnorshire, had moved to Radnor, Pennsylvania, before 1690. This family genealogy asserts that the "first clear evidence" of this George James "was his listing as an overseer at Byberry meeting in 1695"; however, this too may be another George James, since the father of Abel and Rebecca had only recently completed his term of indentured servitude when he moved to Bensalem in 1715. The name Hinkson is also uncertain; though most sources repeat it, others also suggest that was the daughter of a Quaker preacher named Abel Kingstone.

6. "Minutes of the Abington Monthly Meeting, Pennsylvania, 1682–1746," 26 October 1715 and 25 January 1717, Joseph E. Gillingham, comp., 1893, HSP, 92, 98. See also James, "James Families of America Since 1630"; and David Haugaard, "Abel James," in Craig W. Horle, Joseph S. Foster and Laurie M. Wolfe, eds., *Lawmaking and Legislators in Pennsylvania: A Biographical Dictionary* (University Park: Pennsylvania State University Press, 2005), 3:757.

7. "Minutes of the Abington Monthly Meeting, Pennsylvania, 1682–1746," HSP, 227, 229. Joseph received his clearance to marry Martha Livesay from the Philadelphia meeting; see PMMM, 28 July 1741.

8. Haugaard, "Abel James," 3:757.

9. George James, inventory, 1746, file 145, PCA.

10. On Quaker discipline and marriages, see Barry Levy, *Quakers and the American Family: British Settlement in the Delaware Valley* (New York: Oxford University Press, 1988); J. William Frost, *The Quaker Family in Colonial America: A Portrait of the Society of Friends* (New York: St. Martin's Press, 1973); and Jack D. Marietta, *Reformation of American Quakerism, 1848–1783* (Philadelphia: University of Pennsylvania Press, 1984).

11. "Minutes of the Abington Monthly Meeting, Pennsylvania, 1682–1746," 24 February 1738, 222, HSP.

12. Archives and History Bureau, New Jersey State Library, 6 February 1741, Licenses of Marriages Applied for, 76; in Timmons, *Betsy Ross*, 279 n. 48.

13. Timmons, *Betsy Ross*, 95, citing PMMM, 26 September 1742.

14. Timmons, *Betsy Ross*, 99.

15. PMMM, ca. 29 August 1742.

16. PMMMND, 26 November 1742.

17. *Journal of Thomas Chalkley* (Philadelphia, 1808), 33.

18. Ibid., 49.

19. This discussion of James's relationship with the Chalkley family is from Haugaard, "Abel James," 3:757.

20. For the marriage certificate of Abel James and Rebecca Chalkley, which also lists Rebecca Griscom and Elizabeth Knight among the groom's family, and Samuel Griscom and Giles Knight among the guests, see PMMM, Marriage Certificates, 1672–1759, 9 February 1747.

21. This latter point is made in Haugaard, "Abel James," 3:757–58.

22. Abel James, marriage certificate, 9 February 1749, PMMM.

23. For insight into Abel and Giles's friendship, see Abel James to Rebecca James, 11 June 1770, Thompson Papers, box 9, folder 8, HSP; and EDD, 30 January–3 February 1766 and 15 July 1799. On the other hand, the single time that Samuel Griscom appears in the surviving James papers is in a small notebook that Abel kept while on a trip to drain a swamp in which he had some interest; Samuel is listed among about a dozen men along on the trip, and if a reader didn't already know that Griscom was James's brother-in-law, there would be no reason to notice the name at all. See Abel James,

diary, Henry Drinker Papers, HSP. Likewise, when Elizabeth Drinker recorded in the pages of her diary that Samuel Griscom had "come up before dinner with one of his Boys: he and Is[rael] Warrel are building a barn for us," one would never know that this was the brother-in-law of her husband's longtime mentor and best friend. See EDD, 23 January 1767. Evidence from the Quaker meeting records also hints at Griscom family relations. When Elizabeth and Giles's children began to marry, Abel and Rebecca James were reliably at nearly every ceremony, but Rebecca James Griscom and her children rarely so. Samuel Griscom's name never appears on these marriage certificates, and neither, for that matter, does his daughter Betsy's. When Abigail Knight married in April 1764, Rebecca went to see her niece wed, and Rebecca's daughter Susannah signed the marriage certificate as well; the following year, when Susannah Knight married, the only Griscom to sign the certificate was Susannah. In another two years, it was Rebekah Knight's turn; this time, Betsy's mother was the only Griscom to make the trip from Philadelphia. When Giles himself remarried in 1767, the only Griscom in attendance was, again, Betsy's sister Susannah. When Mary Knight married William Satterthwaite the following year, only Sarah Griscom went. See Abington Monthly Meeting records, 107, 109, 118, 121, 125. The evidence is slender but gives us some hint of the shape of the family's interactions in these years.

24. Anna Griscom family tree, GCHS.

25. The discussion of Knight's political career and wealth in this paragraph and the next are drawn from Robert E. Wright and Laurie M. Wolfe, "Giles Knight," in *Lawmaking and Legislators*, 3:821–28.

26. Joseph C. Martindale, *History of the Townships of Byberry and Moreland* (Philadelphia, 1867), 303.

27. Ibid., 112.

28. *Universal or Columbian Magazine* 5, no. 5 (1790): 287–88; see also Haugaard, "Abel James," 768, for the intriguing suggestion that James suffered from bipolar disorder. Henry Drinker described an "instability of conduct" to which James was given, at least by the 1780s: "Sometimes his spirits are so elevated, that he is carried away beyond the line of prudent Circumspection & apprehends he is in the Road to surmount all his troubles, when in fact he can be brought to do little to good effect; at other seasons he is attended with great Dejection, Despondency & unfitness for almost any business, giving every thing over as irretrievably lost."

29. *Universal or Columbian Magazine*, ibid.

30. William B. Timmons suggests that Betsy Ross was likely born in this house in *Betsy Ross: The Griscom Legacy* (Salem, N.J.: Salem County Cultural & Heritage Commission, 1983), 36. A photograph of the house appears here as well.

31. "Cold Winters and Deep Snows," from the *Baltimore Sun*, republished in the *American Quarterly Journal of Agriculture and Science* 1 (1845): 350.

32. William Burke, *An account of the European settlements in America. In six parts ... In two volumes*, ... 4th ed. (Dublin, 1762), 198; see also Dell Upton, *Another City: Urban Life and Urban Spaces in the New American Republic* (New Haven, Conn.: Yale University Press, 2008), 22.

33. As quoted in Carl Bridenbaugh, *Cities in Revolt: Urban Life in America, 1743–1776* (New York: Oxford University Press, 1970), 224; Carole Shammas suggests that 228 houses appeared each year in "The Space Problem in the Early United States," *William and Mary Quarterly*, 3rd series, 57, no. 3 (2000): 512.

34. Grantee-Grantor Records, book H-17, 495–99; and book D-14, 47, PCA.

35. See Timmons, *Betsy Ross*, 97; and Grantee-Grantor Records, book I-7, 503, and book H-5, 413, PCA.

36. *PG*, 12 December 1754.

37. Ibid., 15 July 1762.

38. Hannah Benner Roach, comp., "Taxables in the City of Philadelphia, 1756," *Pennsylvania Genealogical Magazine* 22 (1961): 3–41.

39. *Independent Gazetteer*, 15 October 1782. Susan McCord Turner recalled that Griscom had a lumberyard at this site as well; see James Duffin, "Transcription of the 1909 Affidavit of Susan Jacobs (McCord) Turner," BRH.

40. Philadelphia Contributionship Digital Archives (http://www.philadelphia buildings.org/contributionship/), no. 978. The number of rooms and fireplaces is mentioned in a later advertisement concerning the house's sale: see *PG*, 16 October 1782. Though it takes up a slightly later period, an excellent place to begin exploring Philadelphia architecture is Bernard L. Herman, *Town House: Architecture and Material Life in the Early American City, 1780–1830* (Chapel Hill: University of North Carolina Press, 2005). On midcentury buildings, see Frank Cousin and Phil Madison Riley, *The Colonial Architecture of Philadelphia* (New York: Little, Brown, 1920).

41. "A Chronological Register of Names of the Members of the Library Company of Philadelphia," LCP.

42. Dorothy Grimm, "A History of the Library Company of Philadelphia, 1731–1835" (Ph.D. dissertation, University of Pennsylvania Press, 1955), 49.

43. Timmons, *Betsy Ross*, 79.

44. Ibid., 129. Though Jones was already teaching when Betsy reached school age, she had not yet converted; Jones's Quaker school opened its doors when Betsy was about nine, so Betsy probably began her schooling in another of the several Quaker classrooms across the city. The extant records for Jones's school in association with the Society of Friends begin in 1763 and do not include any references to Betsy Griscom or any of the other Griscom children, though these lists appear to be incomplete; see "Rebekah Birchall's Account of Free Scholars," 1760, in Teachers Accounts, William Penn Charter School Archives, QCHC; and Debra Jean Force, "Betsy Ross, Upholsterer and Flag-Maker: A Proposal to Furnish Her Home" (unpublished report, Betsy Ross Foundation, 1976), 18–19.

45. William J. Allinson, comp., *Memorials of Rebecca Jones* (Philadelphia, 1849).

46. Betty Ring, *Girlhood Embroidery: American Samplers and Pictorial Needlework, 1650–1850* (New York: Knopf, 1993), 2:337; and Allinson, *Memorials of Rebecca Jones*, 5.

47. Allinson, *Memorials of Rebecca Jones*, 17.

48. Ibid., 14.

49. See, e.g., 1792 in Grantor-Grantee Records, book EF-8, 393, PCA.

50. This discussion is drawn from Nancy F. Rosenberg, "The Subtextual Religion: Quakers, the Book, and Public Education in Philadelphia, 1682–1800" (Ph.D. dissertation, University of Michigan, 1991), 339–42.

51. Allinson, *Memorials of Rebecca Jones*, 17.

52. *Extracts from divers antient testimonies of Friends and others* (Wilmington, Del., 1766), 34.

53. Allinson, *Memorials of Rebecca Jones*, 21.

54. On Quaker needlework, the best place to begin is Carol Humphrey, *Friends, A Common Thread: Samplers with a Quaker Influence* (Witney, Oxon, U.K.: Witney

Antiques, 2008); and Betty Ring, *Girlhood Embroidery: American Samplers and Pictorial Needlework* (New York: Knopf, 1993).

55. *Extracts from divers antient testimonies*, 28–29.

## 3. PINS AND NEEDLES

1. James Duffin, "Transcription of Notes of Interview with Rachel (Claypoole) Jones Fletcher (1789–1873)," 7 March 1870, BRH. There is an element of error in Fletcher's account. She believed that her mother's visit to Webster's shop occurred when Betsy was thirteen—that is, about 1765, two years before Webster appears to have been in the city. Betsy may have misremembered her age when she told her daughter the story, Rachel may have misremembered this detail, or Betsy may have begun work at another shop and only later moved over to Webster's employ, a fact that Rachel perhaps never knew or had forgotten. Canby, it should be said, also interviewed Betsy's daughter Clarissa, who worked alongside her mother for many years and was likelier to have more accurate knowledge of her mother's training; unfortunately, no notes from this exchange are known to survive.

2. In 1766, for instance, Polly Gion, a "maid" in the Coates family, earned £2 10s. per quarter; in 1767, Rachel Baremore earned £3 per quarter. See Deborah Morris, Account Book, 1760–69, vol. 125, Coates-Reynall Family Papers, HSP. On women's wages in midcentury Philadelphia, see Billy G. Smith, *The 'Lower Sort': Philadelphia's Laboring People, 1750–1800* (Ithaca, N.Y.: Cornell University Press, 1990); and Joan R. Gunderson, *To Be Useful to the World: Women in Revolutionary America, 1740–1790* (New York: Twayne; London: Prentice Hall International, 1996). It's possible that Webster was a fellow Quaker, smoothing the way for Rebecca Griscom to accept his offer.

3. For a beautiful introduction to the material world into which Betsy Griscom was born, see Jack L. Lindsey et al., *Worldly Goods: The Arts of Early Pennsylvania, 1680–1758* (Philadelphia: Philadelphia Museum of Art, 1999). On eighteenth-century constructions of gentility, see Richard L. Bushman, *The Refinement of America: Persons, Houses, Cities* (New York: Knopf, 1992).

4. In 1721, Sarah Griscom applied to Newton Monthly Meeting for a certificate of transfer to Philadelphia Monthly Meeting; see William B. Timmons, *Betsy Ross: The Griscom Legacy* (Salem, N.J.: Salem County Cultural & Heritage Commission, 1983), 34.

5. Isabella Potts James, *Memorial to Thomas Potts, Jr.* (Cambridge, Mass., 1874), 377.

6. *PG*, 29 January 1736. Five years later, the *PG* again announced that "ALL persons indebted to Sarah Griscom, of the City of Philadelphia, by Bond, Bill, or otherwise, are desired forthwith to pay their respective Sums, or give farther security for the same. And all Persons who have any Accts against her, are desired to bring them in order to have them adjusted, n.b. Very good Stays for women and children, are made and sold at reasonable rates, by the said Sarah Griscom." *PG*, 12 March 1741.

7. Ibid., 7 April 1737, 27 January 1742, 1 March 1748, 24 December 1751, 7 January 1755.

8. Robert Campbell, *The London Tradesman* (1747; reprint, London: David and Charles Reprints, 1969), 224–25. See also the discussion of staymaking in Marla R. Miller, *The Needle's Eye: Women and Work in the Age of Revolution* (Amherst: University of Massachusetts Press, 2006), 67, 141.

9. On craft skill and marital status, see Marla R. Miller, "'My Part Alone'": The World of Rebecca Dickinson," *New England Quarterly* 71 (3): 341–71.

10. Clare Haru Crowston, *Fabricating Women: The Seamstresses of Old Regime France, 1675–1791* (Durham, N.C.: Duke University Press, 2001), 36. Here I'm drawing, too, on my own previous discussion of this craft in *The Needle's Eye*, 56–88 and 134–62.

11. Campbell, *London Tradesman*, 227.

12. *The Book of Trades, or Library of the Useful Arts*, vol. 3 (Whitehall, Pa., 1807), 31.

13. *PG*, 3 October 1765.

14. Gunderson, *To Be Useful to the World*, 70. See also Carole Shammas, "The Female Social Structure in Philadelphia in 1775," *PMHB* 107, no. 1 (1983): 71–73.

15. My thanks to Robert Blair St. George for urging me to think more about Betsy Ross and the creation of an "urban vernacular gentility." See also John Styles and Amanda Vickery, eds., *Gender, Taste and Material Culture in Britain and North America, 1700–1830* (New Haven, Conn.: Yale Center for British Art, 2006).

16. Campbell, *London Tradesman*, 170.

17. Ibid.

18. Ibid.

19. Patricia Chapin O'Donnell, "The Upholsterer in Philadelphia, 1760–1810" (M.A. thesis, University of Delaware, 1980), 3.

20. Ibid., 12; and Jeffrey L. Scheib, "Plunket Fleeson," in Craig W. Horle, Joseph S. Foster and Laurie M. Wolfe, eds., *Lawmaking and Legislators in Pennsylvania: A Biographical Dictionary* (University Park: Pennsylvania State University Press, 2005), 3:501–6.

21. Scheib, "Plunket Fleeson," in *Lawmaking and Legislators*, 3:502.

22. O'Donnell, "The Upholsterer in Philadelphia," 5.

23. Trade Cards, H. F. du Pont Winterthur Museum; and *PG*, 26 July 1769; see also *PJ*, 7 August 1760.

24. Patricia Chapin O'Donnell, "Richard Wevill, Upholsterer," in Edward S. Cook Jr., ed., *Upholstery in America & Europe from the Seventeenth Century to World War I* (New York: Norton, 1987), 114–30.

25. Susan Laura Garfinkel, "Discipline, Discourse and Deviation: The Material Life of Philadelphia Quakers, 1762–1781" (M.A. thesis, University of Delaware, 1986), 6–7.

26. John Reynall to Daniel Flexney, 25 November 1738, John Reynall Letter Book, quoted in Garfinkel, "Discipline, Discourse and Deviation," 5. See also Frederick B. Tolles, "'Of the Best Sort but Plain': The Quaker Esthetic," *American Quarterly* 11, no. 4 (1959): 484–502. John Adams cast a wry eye over such affluence when he noted that he had "Dined with Mr. Miers Fisher, a young Quaker and a Lawyer. We saw his library, which is clever. But this plain Friend and his plain tho pretty wife, with her Thee's and Thou's had provided us the most costly entertainment—Ducks, Hams, Chickens, Beef, Pig, Tarts, Creams, Custards, Gellies, fools, trifles, floating islands, Beer, Porter, Punch, wine a long &c." See Adams, 7 September 1774, *Diary and Autobiography of John Adams*, L. H. Butterfield, ed. (Cambridge, Mass.: Harvard University Press, 1961), vol. 2, *Diary, 1771–1781*, 126, as quoted in Garfinkel, "Discipline, Discourse and Deviation," 6.

27. William Penn, *No Cross No Crown*, as quoted in William S. Dye, "Pennsylvania Versus the Theatre," *PMHB* 55, no. 4 (1931): 336–37.

28. J. William Frost, "From Plainness to Simplicity: Changing Quaker Ideals for Material Culture," in Emma Jones Lapsansky and Anne A. Verplanck, eds., *Quaker Aesthetics: Reflections on a Quaker Ethic in American Design and Consumption, 1720–1920* (Philadelphia: University of Pennsylvania Press, 2003), 24–26. For such prescriptions gathered in a published source, several relevant to the furniture trades, see *Extracts from divers antient testimonies of Friends and others* (Wilmington, Del., 1766), 70–79.

**29.** "A Collection of Christian and Brotherly Advices given forth from time to time by the yearly-meetings of Friends of New Jersey & Pennsylvania . . . 1762–1794," 1762, 207–8, FHL.

**30.** Ibid.

**31.** Ibid. The quotations throughout this paragraph are drawn from this source.

**32.** The total absence of references to excesses in upholstery in Quaker texts is somewhat surprising, given the close relationship between textiles and furniture and the degree to which both depended on the consumption of never-ending displays of the luxurious fabrics constantly spilling from European manufacturers. In fact, fabric drove the very shape and style that furniture could take, its widths off the loom literally determining the dimensions the furniture could take. See Susan Garfinkel, "Quakers and High Chests: The Plainness Problem Reconsidered," in Lapsansky, *Quaker Aesthetics*, 65.

**33.** John Fanning Watson, *Annals of Philadelphia* (1830), 183.

**34.** See John E. Crowley, *Invention of Comfort: Sensibilities and Design in Early Modern Britain and Early America* (Baltimore: Johns Hopkins University Press, 2001), 7, 75.

## 4. CRAFTING COMFORT

**1.** *PJ*, 20 August 1767, quoted in Alfred Coxe Prime, *Arts and Crafts in Philadelphia, Maryland and South Carolina*, series 1 (Philadelphia: Walpole Society, 1929), 214–15.

**2.** *PG*, 26 July 1759.

**3.** Ibid., 29 November 1770.

**4.** Ibid., 13 June 1765.

**5.** Ibid., 20 July 1738, 10 May 1739, 17 May 1763, 17 May 1764.

**6.** Ibid., 18 October 1770.

**7.** Susan Prendergast Schoelwer, "Form, Function and Meaning in the Use of Fabric Furnishings: A Philadelphia Case Study," *Winterthur Portfolio* 14, no. 1 (1979): 25–40, esp. 28. Schoelwer finds that the proportion of households containing a bedstead rose over time, reaching over 70 percent by the eve of the Revolution, but the percentage of those with bed hangings never exceeded 40 percent. See also Aimee E. Newell, "Household Textiles in Philadelphia, 1720–1840" (unpublished paper, INHP, 1995); and Abbott Lowell Cummings, *Bed Hangings: A Treatise on Fabrics and Styles in the Curtaining of Beds, 1650–1850* (Boston: Society for the Preservation of New England Antiquities, 1961).

**8.** Schoelwer, "Form, Function and Meaning," 38.

**9.** Ibid., 29; Andrew Griscom, inventory, 1694, file 102, PCA.

**10.** John E. Crowley, *Invention of Comfort: Sensibilities and Design in Early Modern Britain and Early America* (Baltimore: Johns Hopkins University Press, 2001), 7. See also Catherine Thomas Masetti, "Bed Form and Placement in Chester County, Pennsylvania, 1683–1751" (M.A. thesis, University of Delaware, 1987).

**11.** For an example of a sacking bottom, see the collections of the H. F. du Pont Winterthur Museum, 69.2932.

**12.** *PG*, 17 May 1764. Ticking was not strictly used for mattresses, at least among the laboring classes; runaway servants throughout the century wore ticking breeches and trousers; see *PG*, 17 June 1742 and 10 June 1795. A runaway slave named Jack wore a ticking waistcoat—surely not as notable as his "old dimity Coat . . . with Buttons of Horse teeth set in Brass"; see *PG*, 13 August 1730.

13. Ibid., 12 December 1765.

14. See David H. Conradsen, "Ease and Economy: The Hancocks and the Development of Spring-Seat Upholstery in America" (M.A. thesis, University of Delaware, 1998), 21. As late as twentieth-century Boston, an apprentice upholsterer filled down cushions in a screened area dubbed the Chicken Coop; see Andrew Passeri, "My Life as an Upholsterer," in Gerald W. R. Ward, ed., *Perspectives in American Furniture* (New York: Norton, 1988), as quoted in Conradsen, "Ease and Economy," 29.

15. See Elaine Forman Crane, ed., in EDD, citing invoice for goods, 16 November 1756 and 14 August 1756, HSP. The Drinkers were vending imported Irish feathers as late as the 1780s, "in such quantities as may suit housekeepers, and others"; see, e.g., *PG*, 3 December 1788 and 5 August 1789. For other importers of European feathers, see, e.g., *PG*, 18 November 1742 and 6 June 1765. The Philadelphia merchants Moulder and Clayton sold feathers at two shillings a pound, sometimes in lots of fifty or more pounds; see Moulder and Clayton Account Book, 1726–63, Nathaniel Falkner account, August 1757, 383, HSP. On the country trade, see, e.g., *PG*, 27 December 1753 and 31 March 1773. On the contemporary industry, see *Business Daily Update*, 3 December 2008.

16. *PG*, 12 June 1740.

17. Ibid., 16 September 1736, 12 November 1741, 10 May 1744, 4 February 1755, 23 September 1742; see also 16 April 1741.

18. Ibid., 19 September 1754.

19. Valerie Davies and Sherry Doyal, "Upholstered Mattress Construction and Conservation," in Ann French, ed., *Conservation of Furnishing Textiles: Post-Prints of the Conference Held at the Burrell Collection, Marcy, 1990* (Glasgow: Scottish Society for Conservation and Restoration, 1990), 59.

20. Ibid., 59–60.

21. EDD, 9 May 1794, 27 July 1796, 6 October 1796.

22. See Hannah Haines to sister, 6 September 1810, Wyck Papers, series 2, box 12, folder 65, APS.

23. *PG*, 14 May 1730.

24. Schoelwer, "Form, Function and Meaning," 27–29; and Griscom, inventory, 1694, file 102, PCA.

25. As the eighteenth century wore on, window curtains became increasingly common but remained a mark of privilege; fewer than 9 percent of Philadelphia households at the turn of the eighteenth century for which inventories survive contained window curtains, and as late as 1775, the number had risen to just 15 percent. See Schoelwer, "Form, Function and Meaning," table 2, p. 30.

26. *PG*, 9 July 1761.

27. Ibid., 14 July 1763.

28. The following discussion of window dressings is based on Florence M. Montgomery, "Eighteenth-Century American Bed and Window Hangings," in Edward S. Cooke Jr., ed., *Upholstery in America and Europe from the Seventeenth Century to World War I* (New York: Norton, 1987), 162–74.

29. *PG*, 6 May 1768.

30. Linda Baumgarten, "Protective Covers for Furniture and Its Contents," in Luke Beckerdite, ed., *American Furniture* (Hanover, N.H.: University Press of New England for the Chipstone Foundation, 2000), 3–14.

31. *PJ*, 17 May 1775. In the late eighteenth century, one study notes "large numbers of women recorded in the 1790 census in the households of the upholsterers with the

highest occupational assessments"; see Patricia Chapin O'Donnell, "The Upholsterer in Philadelphia, 1760–1810" (M.A. thesis, University of Delaware, 1980), 19.

32. *Federal Gazette*, 15 May 1794, as cited in O'Donnell, "The Upholsterer in Philadelphia," 59.

33. *PG*, 14 April 1773. For another example, see also *PG*, 8 October 1778, and *PP*, 17 April 1787.

34. See, e.g., the ca. 1761 flounced chair slipcover in the collections of the H. F. du Pont Winterthur Museum, acc. no. 55.15.5, and the snug-fitting trio of cotton covers, acc. no. 59.90.1–3.

35. Receipt, 23 September 1774, Ms.Doc.S, Cadwalader Collection, HSP.

36. *Pennsylvania Chronicle*, 27 March 1769; see also the ad of his competitor John Williams, 10 April 1769.

37. *PJ*, 17 May 1775.

38. For Richey's advertisement, see *PG*, 17 October 1771.

39. See Denis Diderot's treatment of the trimmings maker's shop in *Encyclopédie, ou dictionnaire raisonné des sciences, des arts et des métiers* (Neufchastel, 1764), vol. 2. King was not alone among female tassel makers in the city; on Second Street at the corner of Pear, her competitor Mary Scouvemont made and sold, in both wholesale and retail quantities, "French Trimmings and Tassels" intended to ornament women's apparel; *PG*, 29 August 1765.

40. May Berkouwer, "The Conservation of Tassels and Trimmings from Castle Coole," in French, ed., *Conservation of Furnishing Textiles*, 96–98.

41. Brock Jobe, "The Boston Upholstery Trade, 1700–75," in Cooke, *Upholstery in America and Europe*, 76; Robert Campbell, *The London Tradesman* (1747; reprint, London: David and Charles Reprints, 1969), 171.

42. In his interview with Rachel Fletcher, William Canby records his aunt's recollection that Webster's "large establishment" stood "on the East side of 2nd Street below Chestnut," rather than on Chestnut itself, as other recollections indicate; he also inserts a notation that "the house was afterwards occupied by Catharine Morris & her brother Israel Morris," and was "about half way between Chestnut Street and Gray's alley." In 1870 it was "there yet."

43. See *PJ*, 20 August 1767; and also *PG*, 26 May 1768.

44. See O'Donnell, "The Upholsterer in Philadelphia," 56.

45. *PJ*, 17 May 1775; see also O'Donnell, "The Upholsterer in Philadelphia," table 4A.

46. *PJ*, 17 May 1775.

47. See Nicholas B. Wainwright, *Colonial Grandeur in Philadelphia: The House and Furniture of General John Cadwalader* (Philadelphia: HSP, 1964).

48. Lita Solis-Cohen, "John Cadwalader's Easy Chair Gift to [the Pennsylvania Museum of Art]," *Maine Antiques Digest*, April 2002; and *New York Times*, 1 February 1987.

49. Florence Montgomery, *Printed Textiles: English and American Cottons and Linens, 1700–1850* (New York: Viking Press, 1970), 55–56. Fleeson's shop trimmed other beds for the Cadwaladers as well, of a dark chintz and Saxon blue furniture check with matching curtains and cases. He upholstered a number of chairs for Cadwalader, but rather than fitting them with some expensive imported fabric, Fleeson's shop only finished the chairs in canvas, a not-uncommon technique that served until permanent upholstery was nailed on or slipcovers were made to match the room furnishings. Between October 1770 and January 1771, Fleeson charged Cadwalader £33 3s. 10d. for labor and materials for no fewer than thirty-two chairs, three sofas and an easy chair,

all of which he "finish'd in Canvis." See Montgomery, *Printed Textiles*, 55–56, and Baumgarten, "Protective Covers," 3–14.

**50.** John Cadwalader to John Webster, 26 May 1771 and July 1771, Cadwalader Collection, HSP, account notations reproduced in Mark J. Anderson et al., "Cadwalader Study," H. F. du Pont Winterthur Museum, 1995.

**51.** See Baumgarten, "Protective Covers"; Leroy Graves and Luke Beckerdite, "New Insights on John Cadwalader's Commode-Seat Side Chairs," in Luke Beckerdite, ed., *American Furniture* (Hanover, N.H.: University Press of New England for the Chipstone Foundation, 2000), 152–68; and Wainwright, *Colonial Grandeur*, 51.

**52.** John Cadwalader to John Webster, 27 October and 27 November 1772, and 18 January, 22 April, 12 and 27 May 1773, Cadwalader Collection, HSP, account notations reproduced in Anderson et al., "Cadwalader Study."

**53.** Account notations reproduced in Anderson et al., "Cadwalader Study"; and Billy G. Smith, "The Material Lives of Laboring Philadelphians, 1750–1800," in Robert Blair St. George, ed., *Material Life in America, 1600–1860* (Boston: Northeastern University Press, 1988), 244, 246.

**54.** Silas Deane to Elizabeth Deane, 3 June 1775, Silas Deane Online. Work on the other end of the spectrum generated income as well. For instance, in those same weeks, the shop collected £1 18 "in full for 2 sackin bottoms" from attorney Edmund Physick; see Nancy Goyne, "Furniture Craftsmen in Philadelphia, 1760–1790: Their Role in a Mercantile Society" (M.A. thesis, University of Delaware, 1963), 25.

**55.** Sarah Griscom died in West Chester, Pennsylvania, a "poor Friend" in the care of the Goshen Monthly Meeting. See Goshen Monthly Meeting records, 7 October 1773. My thanks to Jennifer Turner for passing along this reference.

**56.** My thanks to Robert Blair St. George for positing these questions.

## 5. COMBUSTIBLE MATTERS

**1.** N. D. Mereness, ed., "Journal of Lord Adam Gordon, 1764–65," in *Travels in the American Colonies* (New York: Macmillan, 1916), 410–11, as cited in Aimee E. Newell, "Household Textiles in Philadelphia, 1720–1840" (unpublished paper, INHP, 1995).

**2.** As quoted in Benson Bobrick, *Angel in the Whirlwind: The Triumph of the American Revolution* (New York: Simon and Schuster, 1997), 29.

**3.** Peter D. G. Thomas, "The Grenville Program, 1763–1765," in Jack P. Greene and J. R. Pole, eds., *Companion to the American Revolution* (Malden, Mass., and Oxford, England: Blackwell, 2000, 2004), 119.

**4.** Don Cook, *The Long Fuse: How England Lost the American Colonies, 1760–1785* (New York: Atlantic Monthly Press, 1995), 56.

**5.** My understanding of Knight and the imperial crisis is informed by Robert E. Wright and Laurie M. Wolfe, "Giles Knight," in Craig W. Horle, Joseph S. Foster and Laurie M. Wolfe, eds., *Lawmaking and Legislators in Pennsylvania: A Biographical Dictionary* (University Park: Pennsylvania State University Press, 2005), 3:821–28; and Gary B. Nash, *The Unknown American Revolution: The Unruly Birth of Democracy and the Struggle to Create America* (New York: Viking, 2005), 27–32.

**6.** See David Haugaard, "Abel James," in *Lawmaking and Legislators*, 3:757, and also the entry for John Smith; also James and Drinker Letterbooks, 1756–62, HSP; and Thompson Family Papers, series 6: Abel James, HSP. For early descriptions of James's enterprise, see *PG*, 5, 12 and 26 October 1749.

7. As quoted in Haugaard, "Abel James," in *Lawmaking and Legislators*, 3:758.

8. Ibid.

9. Thomas, "The Grenville Program, 1763–1765," 121.

10. *Votes and proceedings of the House of Representatives of the province of Pennsylvania, met at Philadelphia, on the fifteenth of October, anno Domini 1764, and continued by adjournments* (Philadelphia, 1765), 60; on the votes, see Wright and Wolfe, "Giles Knight," in *Lawmaking and Legislators*, 3:825.

11. *Votes and proceedings*, 68–69.

12. *Pennsylvania Journal*, 10 October 1785. An excellent account of the Stamp Act protests in Philadelphia is found in Edmund S. Morgan and Helen M. Morgan, *The Stamp Act Crisis: Prologue to Revolution* (Chapel Hill: University of North Carolina Press, 1962 [1995]), 248–68.

13. John Hughes to Governor Penn, 8 October 1765, and Hughes to John Swift, Alexander Barclay and Thomas Graeme, 5 November 1765, Manuscripts Related to Non-importation Resolutions, vol. 1 items 9 and 10, APS.

14. James and Drinker to David Barclay and Sons, October 14, 1765, James and Drinker Letterbook, 1764–66, Henry Drinker Business Papers, HSP, as quoted in Jane Merritt, "Tea Trade, Consumption, and the Republican Paradox in pre-Revolutionary Philadelphia," *PMHB* 123, no. 2 (2004): 133. This discussion of James and the imperial crises of the 1760s follows Merritt's.

15. *PG*, 31 October 1765.

16. Quoted in H. W. Brands, *The First American: The Life and Times of Benjamin Franklin* (New York: Doubleday, 2000), 369.

17. Jeffrey L. Scheib, "Plunket Fleeson," in *Lawmaking and Legislators*, 3:502.

18. *PG*, 26 December 1765, as quoted in T. H. Breen, *Marketplace of Revolution: How Consumer Politics Shaped American Independence* (New York: Oxford University Press, 2004), 224.

19. *PG*, 9 January 1766, and *PJ*, 2 January 1766, as quoted in Breen, *Marketplace*, 225–26.

20. Breen, *Marketplace*, 226.

21. *PG*, 28 March 1765.

22. Unidentified author, "Good effects of the Patriotism of Women," ca. 1765, Manuscripts Related to Non-importation Resolutions, vol. 1, item 1, APS.

23. "As no Licences for Marriage could be obtained since the first of November, for want of stamped Paper, we can assure the Publick, several genteel Couples were published in the different Churches of this City last Week; and we hear that the young Ladies of this Place are determined to join Hands with none but such as will to the utmost endeavour to abolish the Custom of marrying with Licence." See *PG*, 5 December 1765.

24. Ibid., 3 April 1766. See also Laurel Thatcher Ulrich, "'Daughters of Liberty': Religious Women in Revolutionary New England," in Ronald Hoffman and Peter J. Albert, eds., *Women in the Age of the American Revolution* (Charlottesville: University of Virginia Press, 1989), 211–43; and Alfred F. Young, "The Women of Boston: 'Persons of Consequence' in the Making of the American Revolution," in Harriet B. Applewhite and Darlene G. Levy, eds., *Women and Politics in the Age of Democratic Revolution* (Ann Arbor: University of Michigan Press, 1990), 181–226.

25. James and Drinker to Neate, Pigou and Booth, 17 December 1765, in Merritt, "Tea Trade," 133.

26. *PG*, 23 May 1765, 3 October 1765.

27. Ibid., 13 March 1766.

28. The business would be sold to Joseph Allardepe and Co.; see ibid., 11 December 1766.

29. See EDD, 19 May 1766; and *PG*, 22 May 1766.

30. *Universal or Columbian Magazine* 5, no. 5 (1790): 287–88.

31. *PG*, 22 May 1766.

32. Ibid.

33. The Townshend Act can be found at the Avalon Project: Documents in Law, History and Diplomacy, Lillian Goldman Law Library, Yale Law School, http://avalon .law.yale.edu/.

34. Roger William Moss Jr. suggests that there is a pattern to these silences in "Master Builders: A History of the Colonial Philadelphia Building Trades" (Ph.D. dissertation, University of Delaware, 1972).

35. John Dickinson, *Letters from a Farmer*, in *The Political Writings of John Dickinson*, vol. 1 (Wilmington, Del., 1801), 163.

36. Ibid.

37. Merritt, "Tea Trade," 134.

38. "Letter from a Committee of Merchants in Philadelphia to the Committee of Merchants in London, 1769," as quoted in Merritt, "Tea Trade," 135, and Haugaard, "Abel James," in *Lawmaking and Legislators*, 3:762.

39. James and Drinker to Lancelot Cowper, 9 April 1769, James and Drinker Letterbook, HSP; Thomas Clifford to Thomas Pennington, 23 November 1765, Thomas and John Clifford Letterbook, 1759–66, Clifford Family Papers, HSP, both as quoted in Merritt, "Tea Trade," 135–36.

40. Charles S. Olton, *Artisans for Independence: Philadelphia Mechanics and the American Revolution* (Syracuse, N.Y.: Syracuse University Press, 1975), 28.

41. *Pennsylvania Chronicle*, 24 July 1769.

42. *PJ*, 12 January 1769.

43. *Pennsylvania Chronicle*, 10 October 1768, as quoted in Olton, *Artisans for Independence*, 41.

44. Steven Rosswurm, *Arms, Country and Class: The Philadelphia Militia and the "Lower Sort" during the American Revolution* (New Brunswick, N.J.: Rutgers University Press, 1988), 42.

45. Jeffrey L. Scheib, "Plunket Fleeson," in *Lawmaking and Legislators*, 3:504. See also *PJ*, 17 May 1775.

46. Haugaard, "Abel James," in *Lawmaking and Legislators*, 3:759–60, and Olton, *Artisans for Independence*, 30 and 130 n. 64; and *PG*, 9 January 1766.

47. Olton, *Artisans for Independence*, 30.

48. See *PG*, 8 March and 8 November 1770, 14 November 1771. Also *PA*, series 8, vol. 8 (Harrisburg, Pa., 1931–35): 6684–86; and Haugaard, "Abel James," in *Lawmaking and Legislators*, 3:759–60. Abel James's passing interest in the Philosophical Society revolved around similar concerns. A member from 1768 to 1770, he served on the committees on trade and commerce as well as husbandry and American improvements, but apparently his attention flagged fairly quickly, and he moved on to other matters. See Haugaard, "Abel James," *Lawmaking and Legislators*, 3:760, and Whitfield J. Bell Jr., *Patriot Improvers: Biographical Sketches of Members of the American Philosophical Society* (Philadelphia: American Philosophical Society, 1997), 2:5–9.

49. *Pennsylvania Chronicle*, 28 December 1767, as quoted in Breen, *Marketplace*, 230.

50. Catherine La Courreye Blecki and Karin A. Wulf, eds., *Milcah Martha Moore's Book: A Commonplace Book from Revolutionary America* (University Park: Pennsylvania State University Press, 1997), 172–73; and *Pennsylvania Chronicle*, 18–25 December 1769.

51. *PG*, 14 January 1768 and 23 March 1769.

52. Ibid., 12 November and 31 December 1767.

53. Ibid., 31 December 1767.

54. Ibid., 14 January 1768.

55. Anonymous, *To the Public . . .* (Philadelphia, 1770), as quoted in Breen, *Marketplace*, 255–56.

56. Cato essay, see *Pennsylvania Chronicle*, 4 June 1770, as quoted in Breen, *Marketplace*, 275–76.

57. See *PG*, 12 October 1769, and Rosswurm, *Arms, Country and Class*, 32.

58. See Richard Alan Ryerson, *The Revolution Is Now Begun: The Radical Committees of Philadelphia, 1765–1776* (Philadelphia: University of Pennsylvania Press, 1978), 29–30, 78.

59. See ibid., 31; Olton, *Artisans for Independence*, 41–47; and Eric Foner, *Tom Paine and Revolutionary America* (New York: Oxford University Press, 1977), 28–66.

60. As quoted in Ryerson, *Revolution Is Now Begun*, 31.

61. *Pennsylvania Chronicle*, 28 May 1770, in Olton, *Artisans for Independence*, 43.

62. *Pennsylvania Chronicle*, 18 June 1770.

63. Ryerson, *Revolution Is Now Begun*, 33.

64. *PG*, 8, 15, 18 and 22 October 1770, 29 November and 20 December 1770.

## 6. DOMESTIC REBELLIONS

1. See, e.g., "A Collection of Christian and Brotherly Advices," 1762, FHL

2. Jack D. Marietta, *Reformation of American Quakerism, 1848–1783* (Philadelphia: University of Pennsylvania Press, 1984), 6–7, 63. Among other things, the new policies immediately strengthened the influence of the women's meeting itself, since the monitoring of marriage procedures fell under their purview; see Margaret Hope Bacon, "A Widening Path: Women in the Philadelphia Yearly Meeting Move Toward Equality, 1681–1929," in Margaret Hope Bacon, ed., *Friends in the Delaware Valley: Philadelphia Yearly Meeting, 1681–1981* (Haverford, Pa.: Friends Historical Association, 1981), 189; see also William J. Frost, *The Quaker Family in Colonial America* (New York: St. Martin's Press, 1973). Jay Fliegelman posits a larger rupture in family relations in the latter half of the eighteenth century in *Prodigals and Pilgrims: The American Revolution against Patriarchal Authority* (Cambridge: Cambridge University Press, 1982).

3. Philadelphia Quarterly Meeting minutes, August 1773, November 1773, August 1770.

4. Ibid., August 1771.

5. Ibid., August 1772. See also Philadelphia Quarterly Meeting minutes, August 1773 and August 1774.

6. The Boltons were long-standing members of the Quaker community, and Everard's grandfather served as treasurer of Abington Meeting for nearly forty years. For the Bolton family history, see "The Family of Everard and Elizabeth Bolton," typescript, n.d., Enders Collection, HSP.

7. Ibid.

8. Joseph C. Martindale, *History of the Townships of Byberry and Moreland* (Philadelphia, 1867), 95, 238–39.

9. They married 13 February 1764; see "Pennsylvania Marriages Prior to 1810," in *PA*, series 2, vol. 8 (Harrisburg, Pa., 1895): 764.

10. PMMM, 22 February 1763.

11. *The Doane Family*, vol. 1, 2nd ed. (Boston: Alfred Alden Doane, 1960), 79. (Originally published in 1902.)

12. The story of Susannah's breach can be tracked in the PMMM and Philadelphia Monthly Meeting of Women Friends minutes for December 1769 through January 1771. All the quotations below are drawn from this source.

13. Marietta, *Reformation*, 27, 55.

14. Philadelphia Monthly Meeting of Women Friends, 29 December 1769.

15. Clare A. Lyons, *Sex Among the Rabble: An Intimate History of Gender and Power in the Age of Revolution, Philadelphia, 1730–1830* (Chapel Hill: University of North Carolina Press, 2006), 83.

16. For the breach between Mary Morgan and the Society of Friends, see PMMM, 29 December 1769–31 August 1770.

17. Lyons, *Sex Among the Rabble*, 84–85.

18. PMMM, 31 August 1770.

19. See "Ancestors of John Walker Taylor," 20; my thanks to John W. Taylor for making this available to me. Morgan is mentioned in a handful of works that discuss artisans in Baltimore. See Wilbur C. Plummer, "Consumer Credit in Colonial Philadelphia," *PMHB* 66, no. 4 (1942): 385–409; Carl Bridenbaugh, *The Colonial Craftsman* (New York: Dover Publications, 1990), 142; Tina H. Sheller, "Freeman, Servants, and Slaves: Artisans and the Class Structure of the Revolutionary Baltimore Town," in Howard B. Rock, Paul A. Gilje and Robert Asher, *American Artisans: Crafting Social Identity, 1750–1850* (Baltimore: Johns Hopkins University Press, 1995), 19; and William Voss Elder III, *Maryland Queen Anne and Chippendale Furniture of the Eighteenth Century* (Baltimore: October House for the Baltimore Museum of Art, 1968).

20. Thomas is listed among the members of the "Mechanical Company of Baltimore," an association of tradesmen, in 1769 and 1770. See Henry C. Peden Jr., *Inhabitants of Baltimore County, 1763–1774* (Westminster, Md.: Heritage Books, 2007), 9.

21. On Morgan in Baltimore, see J. Thomas Scharf, *History of Baltimore City and County* (1881; Baltimore: Regional Publishing, 1971), part 1, 432; and Plummer, "Consumer Credit in Colonial Philadelphia," 392. For notices concerning his business, see Alfred Coxe Prime, *The Arts and Crafts in Philadelphia, Maryland and South Carolina*, series 1 (Philadelphia: Walpole Society, 1929), 256–58.

22. William Donaldson was born 28 March 1748, according to Katharine Dougherty Beale Barclay's Lineage Form for membership in the Welcome Society of Pennsylvania, 1977, in the Griscom Family: miscellaneous file, GCHS. See also Patricia Ruth Manning Miller Donaldson, *Donaldson* (Georgetown, Ohio: P. R. Donaldson, 1978), 207–8.

23. Elizabeth and the Griscom girls shared a grandmother, Andrew Griscom's wife, Sarah Dole; Elizabeth descended from one of Sarah's sons after her second marriage, to John Kaighn.

24. William Donaldson is described in *PA*, series 5, vol. 1 (Harrisburg, Pa., 1906): 631.

25. PMMM, 23–27 December 1771.

26. See Barry Levy, *Quakers and the American Family: British Settlement in the Delaware Valley* (New York: Oxford University Press, 1988), 143. Levy also found that "disobedient poor children" in the meetings he studied, Chester and Radnor between the 1680s and the 1740s, "were disowned at a much higher rate than disobedient wealthy children."

27. Levy, *Quakers and the American Family*, 252; see also Marietta, *Reformation*, 55.

28. Robert E. Wright and Laurie M. Wolfe, "Giles Knight," in Craig W. Horle, Joseph S. Foster and Laurie M. Wolfe, eds., *Lawmaking and Legislators in Pennsylvania: A Biographical Dictionary* (University Park: Pennsylvania State University Press, 2005), 3:826.

## 7. UNION AND DISUNION

1. "Extracts from the Journal of Miss Sarah Eve: Written While Living Near the City of Philadelphia in 1772–73," *PMHB* 5 (1881): 19–36, 191–205, entry for 21 February 1773, in North American Women's Letters and Diaries, subscription database, Alexander Street Press.

2. *Pennsylvania Chronicle*, 2 January 1773.

3. According to Nelson Waite Rightmyer, *The Anglican Church in Delaware* (Philadelphia: Church Historical Society, 1947), 23, the Ross family's initial plan was that Aeneas would assist his father, George, in his ministry, attending in particular to Anglican adherents in Bristol, White Clay Creek and Fogg's Manor, but after the death of Christ Church rector Reverend Archibald Cummings left the pulpit there vacant, Aeneas remained until he was replaced by the Reverend Robert Jenny. For fifteen years thereafter (that is, between 1742 and 1757), Aeneas Ross served churches at Oxford and Whitemarsh, choosing to live at Germantown, in the middle. He received an appointment to his father's former church in New Castle in 1758 and remained there until his death in 1782.

4. Barry Levy, *Quakers and the American Family: British Settlement in the Delaware Valley* (New York: Oxford University Press, 1988), 173; and Rightmyer, *The Anglican Church in Delaware*, 7.

5. E. L. Pennington, *The Reverend George Ross, SPG Missionary of New Castle, Delaware* (Proceedings of the American Antiquarian Society, October 1936).

6. For the 3 January 1744 marriage, see Marriage Records, 1709–1800, 420, Christ Church Archives, Philadelphia.

7. George Ross, letter of 27 March 1750, as quoted in Rightmyer, *The Anglican Church in Delaware*, 21.

8. William J. Canby to William T. Read, 21 February 1870, BRH.

9. Signatories to managers, 28 September 1763, as quoted in Thomas G. Morton, *The History of the Pennsylvania Hospital, 1751–1895* (ca. 1895; reprint, New York: Arno Press, 1973), 133.

10. Ibid.

11. Most of the repeated references to Sarah's stay indicate that she was admitted 22 August 1764, though one list, dated 28 April 1770, notes that she is among those diagnosed with "lunacy," and that she was admitted 22 October 1763. See Manager Minutes, 1769–77, Pennsylvania Hospital Archives. The following discussion is based on Morton, *History of the Pennsylvania Hospital*, and the "List of patients in the Penn-

sylvania Hospital for year ending 30 April 1764," in Manager Minutes, 1757–64, Pennsylvania Hospital Archives.

12. As quoted in Morgan, *History of the Pennsylvania Hospital*, 3.

13. As quoted in ibid., 54. Unwanted spectators had been an ongoing problem; in May 1760, a "palisade fence" was built to protect the windows, and in 1762, the "hatch door" implemented to reduce intrusions by charging a "gratuity" to enter. See Morgan, *History of the Pennsylvania Hospital*, 130–31.

14. *PG*, 21 May 1772. The couple did not marry at Christ Church; the notice of their wedding appears to place it in Philadelphia, but they may have married at Trinity Church in Oxford.

15. Ibid., 26 May 1768.

16. See William Thompson Read (senior warden, Immanuel Church, New Castle), "Biographical Notice of the Rev Aeneas Ross . . . by His Grand Nephew," draft, June 1851, Read Manuscripts, Collection 537, HSP.

17. Eleanore Parker Gadsden, "From Traditional Cabinetmaking to Entrepreneurial Production: David Evans (1748–1819)" (M.A. thesis, University of Delaware, 2000), 22; and Thomas M. Dorflinger, *Vigorous Spirit of Enterprise: Merchants and Economic Development in Revolutionary Philadelphia* (Chapel Hill: University of North Carolina Press for the Institute of Early American History and Culture, Williamsburg, Va., 1986), 262.

18. *PG*, 15 March 1770, 29 June 1774.

19. County Tax Duplication, 1773, PCA.

20. *PG*, 24 February 1773. On Ross's business and this notice, see Debra Jean Force, "Betsy Ross, Upholsterer and Flag-Maker: A Proposal to Furnish Her Home" (unpublished report, Betsy Ross Foundation, 1976); and Stephanie Grauman Wolf, "Betsy Ross: American Woman of the Revolutionary Generation" (unpublished report, Betsy Ross Foundation, 1996).

21. See Linda Colley, *Captives* (New York: Pantheon, 2002), 247–48; John Keay, *The Honourable Company* (New York: Macmillan, 1994); and Anthony Farrington, *Trading Places: The East India Company and Asia, 1600–1834* (London: British Library, 2002).

22. *Philadelphia Chronicle*, 9 January 1773.

23. William B. Timmons, *Betsy Ross: The Griscom Legacy* (Salem, N.J.: Salem County Cultural & Heritage Commission, 1983).

24. For their effusive thanks, see James and Drinker to Pigou and Booth, 27 August 1773, discussed in Jane Merritt, "Tea Trade, Consumption, and the Republican Paradox in Pre-Revolutionary Philadelphia," *PMHB* 123, no. 2 (2004): 143.

25. As quoted in David Haugaard, "Abel James," in Craig W. Horle, Joseph S. Foster and Laurie M. Wolfe, eds., *Lawmaking and Legislators in Pennsylvania: A Biographical Dictionary* (University Park: Pennsylvania State University Press, 2005), 3:764.

26. Manuscripts Related to Non-importation Resolutions, vol. 2, APS; Philadelphia Resolutions published in the *PG*, 1773.

27. Craig W. Horle, "John Ross," in *Lawmaking and Legislators*, vol. 3: 1264.

28. Morrill Jensen, ed., *English Historical Documents*, 9: 773–74, in *American Colonial Documents to 1776* (London: Eyre and Spottisworde, 1955).

29. Benjamin Rush to John Adams, 14 August 1809, in Lyman H. Butterfield, ed., *Letters of Benjamin Rush*, vol. 2 (Princeton, N.J.: published for the APS by Princeton University Press, 1951), 1014.

**30.** Arthur J. Mekeel, *The Relation of the Quakers to the American Revolution* (Washington, D.C.: University Press of America, 1979).

**31.** James Pemberton to Dr. John Fothergill and others, 30 October 1773, as quoted in Jack D. Marietta, *Reformation of American Quakerism* (Philadelphia: University of Pennsylvania Press, 1984), 217 n. 335.

**32.** See Notice, 2 December 1773, Manuscripts Related to Non-importation Resolutions, vol. 2, APS.

**33.** See Toby Ditz, "Secret Selves, Credible Personas," in Robert Blair St. George, ed., *Possible Pasts: Becoming Colonial in Early America* (Ithaca, N.Y.: Cornell University Press, 2000), 219–42.

**34.** James and Drinker, 22 October 1773, Manuscripts Related to Non-importation Resolutions, vol. 2, APS.

**35.** "Reply of the Committee to Mssrs James and Drinker, 23 October 1773," in ibid.

**36.** Loose letter, dated 16 October 1773, in 1773 folder, 1771–1820 box, Thomas Wharton Sr. Collection, HSP, as cited in Richard Alan Ryerson, *The Revolution Is Now Begun: The Radical Committees of Philadelphia, 1765–1776* (Philadelphia: University of Pennsylvania Press, 1978), 18, who notes that James may have been casting his aspersion on Germans, Presbyterians or the laboring classes in general.

**37.** James and Drinker to Pigou and Booth, 31 May 1774, in Merritt, "Tea Trade," 146 n. 109.

**38.** "The Epistle from the Yearly Meeting in London," 19 May 1777, "to the Quarterly and Monthly Meetings of Friends in Great Britain, Ireland, and Elsewhere" (Philadelphia, 1777).

**39.** The PMMM for the Northern District was established in 1772 by the Philadelphia Quarterly Meeting by dividing the PMMM. Its territory included the south side of Mulberry (Arch) and northward into the Northern Liberties.

**40.** Edwin S. Parry, *Betsy Ross: Quaker Rebel* (Philadelphia: John C. Winston, 1930), 43–45.

**41.** PMMM, 1773–74, 38–47.

**42.** Jack D. Marietta, *Reformation of American Quakerism 1748–1783* (Philadelphia: University of Pennsylvania Press, 1984), 63.

**43.** Force, "Betsy Ross, Upholsterer and Flag-Maker," 4.

**44.** On John Ross's political career, see Craig W. Horle, in *Lawmaking and Legislators*, 3:1256–67.

**45.** Alexander Graydon, *Memoirs of His Own Time: With Reminiscences of the Men and Events of the Revolution*, John Stockton Littell, ed. (Philadelphia, 1846), 118.

**46.** William Thompson Read, *Life and Correspondence of George Read* (Philadelphia, 1870), 45.

**47.** William Thompson to George Read, 10 September 1775, in ibid., 112–13.

**48.** John Adams diary, 25 September 1775, as quoted in Craig W. Horle, "John Ross," in *Lawmaking and Legislators*, 3:1264.

**49.** When, the following year, members of the assembly rose to the defense of their member George Ross—threatened by ruinous gossip alleging that he had approved of taxing Lancaster stills—publishing a testimonial on Ross's behalf, Giles Knight was among them. *PG*, 16 October 1769.

**50.** This discussion of Ross's political career to the time of Betsy's marriage is taken from the entry in *Lawmaking and Legislators*, 3:1237–55.

**51.** As quoted in Craig W. Horle, "George Ross," in *Lawmaking and Legislators*,

3:1241–42, George Ross was also involved in some efforts that would be especially relevant to his niece Betsy, including the 1769 passage of legislation confirming the process by which *femmes coverts*—that is, married women in business under their own names—secured land rights, legislation aimed to assist women in trade whose husbands were at sea (as Betsy would in time be).

52. *Pennsylvania Chronicle*, 7 June 1773.

53. Force, "Betsy Ross, Upholsterer and Flag-Maker," 4.

54. From 1775 to 1777, however, James Wilson would serve as a member of Congress.

55. Rachel Albright to Nellie Chaffee, 27 October 1903, BRH.

56. Minutes of the Carpenters' Company of the City of Philadelphia, 15 December 1773, on deposit at the library of the APS.

57. John Drinker, *Observations on the Late Popular Measures* (Philadelphia, 1774).

58. *PJ*, 1 January 1774.

59. See Sharon V. Salinger and Charles Wetherell, "Wealth and Renting in Prerevolutionary Philadelphia," *Journal of America History* 71 (1985): 837–40; and Carole M. Shammas, "The Space Problem in the Early United States," *William and Mary Quarterly*, 3rd series, 57, no. 3 (2000): 529. Shammas found that only about 20 percent of people paying property and poll taxes in 1769 owned their dwelling, and most (80 percent) of those owed rent on the land on which the home stood.

60. Sharon V. Salinger, "Spaces, Inside and Outside, in Eighteenth-Century Philadelphia," *Journal of Interdisciplinary History* 26, no. 1 (1995): 1–31, 22. See also Emma Jones Lapsansky, "South Street in Philadelphia, 1762–1854: A Haven for Those Low in the World" (Ph.D. dissertation, University of Pennsylvania, 1975).

61. In 1775, Philadelphia tax records list John Ross, "upholder," in Walnut Ward; for the description of the house, see Philadelphia Contributionship for the Insurance of Houses from Loss by Fire, Insurance Survey S01708.

62. John Ross, probate inventory, 1776, BRH.

63. On marriage and economic partnership, see Lisa Wilson Waciega, "A 'Man of Business': The Widow of Means in Southeastern Pennsylvania, 1750–1850," *William and Mary Quarterly*, 3rd series, 44, no. 1 (1987): 40–64, esp. 51–52; and Claudia Goldin, "The Economic Status of Women in the Early Republic: Quantitative Evidence," *Journal of Interdisciplinary History* 16, no. 3 (1986): 375–404.

64. See Ann Flower, Commonplace Book, QCHC.

65. Constable's Returns to the Assessor, Philadelphia [Walnut Ward], 1775, PCA.

66. Gary B. Nash, *Forging Freedom: The Formation of Philadelphia's Black Community, 1720–1840* (Cambridge, Mass.: Harvard University Press, 1988), 34; Nash notes that this figure—fewer than one hundred African American children—is "hardly half" of the number one might expect given the population of fourteen hundred blacks in Philadelphia in the mid-1760s.

67. See Nash, "Slaves and Slaveowners in Philadelphia," *William and Mary Quarterly*, 3rd series, 30 (1973): 236, 243.

68. Nash, *Forging Freedom*, 33.

69. Ibid., 36.

70. Ruth Herndon and Ella Sekatau, "Pauper Apprenticeship in Narragansett Country: A Different Name for Slavery in Early New England," *Slavery/Anti-Slavery in New England* (2003 Proceedings of the Dublin Seminar for New England Folklife), Peter Benes, ed. (Boston: Boston University Scholarly Publications, 2005), 56–70.

71. Four are listed as "of age"; no ages are indicated for another three. See Constable's Returns to the Assesor, Philadelphia [Walnut Ward], 1775, PCA. Thirty-two bound servants also appear on the return.

72. See Nash, "Slaves and Slaveowners in Philadelphia," 239.

73. Jean R. Soderlund, "Black Women in Colonial Philadelphia," *PMHB* 107, no. 1 (1983): 50–68, esp. 55–59.

74. Andrew Griscom, inventory, 1694, file 102, PCA.

75. See Wright and Wolfe, "Giles Knight," in *Lawmaking and Legislators*, 3:821–28; and Isaac Bolton, will, file 1775–01455.

76. On Morgan, see the Thomas Morgan ledger, 1771–1803, HSP. In 1767, John Ross's tax assessment in the High Street Ward ranked him in the ninety-seventh percentile, his entry showing four slaves. His 1769 proprietary tax showed five servants, and his 1774 assessment three. George Ross "consistently" owned a slave, and a "mulatto girl" was in his possession in 1779; Elizabeth and Edward Biddle held at least one in bondage. On George and the other Rosses, see *Lawmaking and Legislators*, 3:1264, 1258, 1252 and 340.

77. All as discussed and quoted in Nash, *Forging Freedom*, 20; Ross's comments are found in Ross to Secretary of SPG, 15 March 1742, as quoted in William S. Perry, ed., *Papers Relating to the History of the Church in Pennsylvania* (Hartford, Conn., 1871), 230.

78. See Nash, "Slaves and Slaveowners in Philadelphia," 240.

## 8. MR. AND MRS. ROSS

1. As told in Richard Alan Ryerson, *The Revolution Is Now Begun: The Radical Committees of Philadelphia, 1765–1776* (Philadelphia: University of Pennsylvania Press, 1978), 40. The discussion below is drawn especially from 25–115.

2. EDD, 3 and 4 May 1774.

3. John Adams, diary, 25 September 1775, as quoted in Craig W. Horle, "John Ross," in Craig W. Horle, Joseph S. Foster and Laurie M. Wolfe, eds., *Lawmaking and Legislators in Pennsylvania: A Biographical Dictionary* (University Park: Pennsylvania State University Press, 2005), 3:1264.

4. Ryerson, *Revolution Is Now Begun*, 40–43.

5. Ibid.; and Jeffrey L. Scheib, "Plunket Fleeson," in *Lawmaking and Legislators*, 3:504.

6. Christopher Marshall, diary, 1 June 1774, William Duane, ed., *Extracts from the Diary of Christopher Marshall, 1774–1781* (New York: New York Times, 1969).

7. Arthur J. Mekeel, *The Relation of the Quakers to the American Revolution* (Washington, D.C.: University Press of America, 1979), 72.

8. Ryerson, *Revolution Is Now Begun*, 40–64.

9. William Duane, ed., *Extracts from the Diary of Christopher Marshall*, 9 June 1774.

10. The effort made to add Ross to the citywide committee of forty-three, though, failed. See Craig W. Horle, "John Ross," in *Lawmaking and Legislators*, 3:1264, and Ryerson, *Revolution Is Now Begun*, 49–52.

11. Ibid., and Craig W. Horle, "George Ross," in *Lawmaking and Legislators*, 3:1243.

12. Minutes Lodge No. 2, A.Y.M., 14 September 1774, as published in Norris Stan-

ley Barratt and Julius Friedrick Sachse, *Freemasonry in Pennsylvania, 1727–1907* (Philadelphia, 1908), 276; and Steven C. Bullock, *Revolutionary Brotherhood: Freemasonry and the Transformation of the American Social Order, 1730–1840* (Chapel Hill, N.C.: University of North Carolina Press, 1996).

13. Debra Jean Force, "Betsy Ross, Upholsterer and Flag-Maker: A Proposal to Furnish Her Home" (unpublished report, Betsy Ross Foundation, 1976), 15.

14. It didn't help that as the political crisis escalated Samuel Griscom was also having trouble with his servant William Kelly to put the two men at odds in the Court of Common Pleas. See Court of Common Pleas Appearance Docket, RG 20.2, PCA; in June, a judgment of "Sur Rule to plead, cont Non assumpt and issue" was filed. In May 1773, "William Kelly last from London, servant" was bound to "Samuel Griscom House-carpenter of Philadelphia"; see "Record of Servants and Apprentices Bound and Assigned Before Hon. John Gibson, Mayor of Philadelphia," 5 December 1772 to 21 May 1773, *PMHB* 34, no. 1 (1910): 225. See also EDD 23 January 1767.

15. Charles Wetherill, *History of The Religious Society of Friends Called by Some The Free Quakers, in the City of Philadelphia* (Philadelphia, 1894).

16. Ibid.

17. Caesar Rodney to Thomas Rodney, 12 September 1774, as quoted in Edmund Cody Burnett, ed., *Letters of Members of the Continental Congress*, vol. 1 (Washington, D.C.: Carnegie Institution, 1921), 30.

18. A plaque is mounted in Christ Church to mark the spot where Betsy sat; however, the source of this attribution is unknown at the time of this writing. See James Duffin, "Transcription of Notes of Interview with Rachel (Claypoole) Jones Fletcher (1789–1873)," 7 March 1870, BRH, on Betsy's church attendance.

19. James Duffin, "Transcription of the 1870 Affidavit of Rachel (Claypoole) Jones Fletcher, 1789–1873," BRH.

20. As quoted in Deborah Mathias Gough, *Christ Church, Philadelphia: The Nation's Church in a Changing City* (Philadelphia: University of Pennsylvania Press, 1995), 135.

21. As quoted in ibid., 135.

22. John Adams, diary, 30 August 1774, in Edmund Cody Burnett, ed., *Letters of Members of the Continental Congress* (Washington, D.C.: Carnegie Institution, 1921), 1:1; and John Adams to Abigail Adams, 25 September 1774, also in Burnett, *Letters*, 1:47.

23. John Adams, diary, 3 September 1774, in Burnett, *Letters*, 1:3.

24. Eliza Farmar, 19 September 1774, in *Letters of Eliza Farmar to Her Nephew* (Philadelphia: HSP, 1916).

25. This phrase and the next from the Articles of Association vol. 1 (Washington, D.C.: Government Printing Office, 1907), 74–80, as published in the *Journals of the Continental Congress, 1774–1789*.

26. Roger William Moss Jr., "Master Builders: A History of the Colonial Philadelphia Buildings Trades" (Ph.D. dissertation, University of Delaware, 1972), 178.

27. Declaration and Resolves of the First Continental Congress, October 1774; Charles C. Tansill, comp., *Documents Illustrative of the Formation of the Union of the American States* (Washington, D.C.: Government Printing Office, 1927).

28. *PP*, 30 January 1775.

29. Ibid., 13 March 1775.

30. Records of Chew's order with John and Betsy Ross are transcribed in Nancy E. Richards, "The City Home of Benjamin Chew, Sr., and His Family: A Case Study of the

Textures of Life," unpublished typescript, Cliveden, National Trust for Historic Preservation, 1996, 81–82, 86, available online at http://www.cliveden.org/Content/Research/Benjamin%20Chew%20townhouse.pdf.

31. Chew Receipt Book, 1770–1809, 41, 47, 55, as transcribed in Nancy E. Richards, "Benjamin Chew's Receipt Book, 1770–1809," unpublished paper, n.d., Cliveden, National Trust for Historic Preservation, available online at http://www.cliveden.org/Content/Research/Benjamin%20Chew%20Receipt%20Book.pdf.

32. Richards, "City Home of Benjamin Chew," 81–82.

33. Linda Baumgarten, "Protective Covers for Furniture and Its Contents," in Luke Beckerdite, ed., *American Furniture*, (Hanover, N.H.: University Press of New England for the Chipstone Foundation, 2000), 3–14.

34. Aimee E. Newell, "Household Textiles in Philadelphia, 1720–1840" (unpublished paper, INHP, 1995), 38–40. See also EDD, 15 January 1796: "Betsy Lang here this forenoon measuring a carpet, which she promises to come, next fourth day to make up."

35. Newell, "Household Textiles in Philadelphia," 38–40.

36. Benjamin H. Irvin, "The Streets of Philadelphia: Crowds, Congress, and the Political Culture of Revolution, 1774–1783," *PMHB* 129, no. 1 (2005): 7–44.

37. Though nonexportation was scheduled to begin on September 10, 1775, most upholsterers exported comparatively little, so this would have been of less concern to the budding Ross firm.

38. The term calico in this period did not necessarily mean the printed fabric we know today; rather, it signaled a plain cotton. My thanks to textile curator Linda Eaton for drawing my attention to this distinction.

## 9. MEDITATIONS IN TROUBLE

1. Richard Alan Ryerson, *The Revolution Is Now Begun: The Radical Committees of Philadelphia, 1765–1776* (Philadelphia: University of Pennsylvania Press, 1978), 96.

2. Ibid., 98.

3. Ibid., 98–99.

4. J. Thomas Scharf and Thompson Westcott, *History of Philadelphia, 1609–1884* (Philadelphia, 1884), 293.

5. "Letters of Eliza Farmar to Her Nephew," *PMHB* 40, no. 157 (1916): 199–207.

6. James DeWitt Andrews, ed., *The Works of James Wilson, Vol. II* (Chicago: Callaghan and Company, 1896), 564.

7. "Letters of Eliza Farmer to Her Nephew," 203.

8. *American Journal of Ambrose Serle* (San Marino, Calif.: Huntington, 1940), 257, 259–60, as quoted in Liam Riordan, *Many Identities, One Nation: The Revolution and Its Legacy in the Mid-Atlantic* (Philadelphia: University of Pennsylvania Press, 2007), 64–65.

9. "Letters of Eliza Farmar to Her Nephew," 203.

10. "A declaration by the representatives of the United Colonies of North America . . . setting forth the Causes and Necessity of their taking up arms" (Philadelphia, 1775).

11. John Ross, probate inventory, BRH; and *PG*, 20 September 1775.

12. On Hugh Henry, see *PEP*, 25 June 1778.

13. *PG*, 20 September 1775.

14. Thomas Coombe, *A Sermon, Preached before the Congregations of Christ Church and St. Peter's, Philadelphia, on Thursday, July 20, 1775, Being the Day Recommended by the Honorable Continental Congress for a General Fast . . .* (Philadelphia, 1775).

15. *PP*, 23 October 1775.

16. *PA*, series 6, vol. 1 (Harrisburg, Pa., 1906), 15, 337; and Robert T. Williams and Mildred C. Williams, *Soldiers of the American Revolution* (Newton, P.A.: Will-Britt Books, 1987), 205, HSP. On William Donaldson, see *PA*, series 6, vol. 1 (Harrisburg, Pa., 1906), 478.

17. See *PA*, series 3, vol. 5 (Harrisburg, Pa., 1896), 440, 454, 496; Williams and Williams, *Soldiers of the American Revolution*, 81, HSP; and *PA*, series 6, vol. 1 (Harrisburg, Pa., 1906), 369.

18. Given the common nature of Thomas Morgan's name, it is almost impossible to determine with certainty whether a given reference denotes the man who was Betsy's brother-in-law. But on his earlier activities, see Henry C. Peden, *Inhabitants of Baltimore County, 1763–1774* (Westminster, Md.: Heritage Books, 1989), 9–10, which notes that members of the "Mechanical Company of Baltimore," to which Morgan belonged, were deeply engaged in the protest movements of the 1760s.

19. The only extant section of the chevaux-de-frise is on display at Red Bank Battlefield, in National Park, New Jersey. "Revolutionary War Artifact from the Depths of the Delaware River," Independence Seaport Museum, http://www.phillyseaport.org/cheval-de-frise.shtml, accessed October 2, 2008. For the "shivers," see receipt for logs drawn, 1 September 1775, in the Council of Safety Accounts, 1776–77 and undated (15 folders) (series 27.7), PSA.

20. See http://www.ushistory.org/march/other/cheveaux.htm.

21. For quote, see Craig W. Horle, "George Ross," in Craig W. Horle, Joseph S. Foster and Laurie M. Wolfe, eds., *Lawmaking and Legislators in Pennsylvania: A Biographical Dictionary*, vol. 3 (University Park: Pennsylvania State University Press, 2005), 1244.

22. Holland's biography is recounted in Henry Hobart Bellas, ed., "Personal Recollections of Captain Enoch Anderson: An Officer of the Delaware Regiments in the Revolutionary War," *Papers of the Historical Society of Delaware*, 16 (Wilmington, Del., 1896), 46–50; see also William B. Timmons, *Betsy Ross: The Griscom Legacy* (Salem, N.J.: Salem County Cultural & Heritage Commission, 1983), 135; and James Duffin, "Transcription of Notes of Interview with Rachel (Claypoole) Jones Fletcher (1789–1873)," BRH.

23. See *PA*, series 2, vol. 10 (Harrisburg, Pa., 1880), 120.

24. Bellas, ed., "Personal Recollections of Captain Enoch Anderson," 7.

25. As quoted in Horle, "George Ross," *Lawmaking and Legislators*, 3:1247.

26. For the munitions story, see, e.g., Edwin S. Parry, *Betsy Ross: Quaker Rebel* (Philadelphia, P.A.: John C. Winston Company, 1930), 70–73. It is possible that the events that caused Ross's death were triggered by his involvement in militia activities. The flag scholar Henry Moeller has asserted that Ross was "engaged in Colonial espionage activities, as a muster master in the Delaware River beacon network," and that it was in the course of these duties that Ross sustained the injuries that killed him. But Moeller has the wrong man; the John Ross appointed muster master is not the same man who was married to Elizabeth Griscom Ross, but rather the forty-nine-year-old merchant of the same name. See Henry W. Moeller, *Shattering an American Myth: Unfurling the History of the Stars and Stripes* (Mattituck, N.Y.: Ameron House, 1992), 100.

27. David Hackett Fischer, *Washington's Crossing* (New York: Oxford University Press, 2004), 27; see also Eric Foner, *Tom Paine and Revolutionary America* (New York: Oxford University Press, 2005), 63–67.

28. See James Duffin, "Transcription of Notes of Interview with Rachel (Claypoole) Jones Fletcher (1789–1873)," BRH; and "William J. Canby (1825–1890) to William T. Read Concerning John Ross," BRH.

29. See Fletcher and Canby documents cited in note 28 above.

30. Burial Records, 1709–85, 3183, 3247, Christ Church.

## 10. CRAFTING COLORS

1. John Ross estate papers, 23 January 1776, BRH.

2. Robert V. Wells, "Quaker Marriage Patterns in a Colonial Perspective," *William and Mary Quarterly*, 3rd series, 29 (1972): 421–22; 1.9 percent of people were married under a year, and 5.5 percent less than 4.9 years. More than 60 percent of marriages lasted 25 years or more.

3. James Duffin, "Transcription of Notes of Interview with Jane (Claypoole) Canby, 1792–1873," BRH.

4. Edward Shippin to Jasper Yeates, 19 January 1776, as quoted in Lawrence Lewis Jr., "Edward Shippen, Chief-Justice of Pennsylvania," *PMHB* 12, no. 1 (1883): 24.

5. "Diary of James Allen, Esq.," *PMHB* 9, no. 2 (1885): 176–96.

6. Arthur Donaldson was Sarah's brother-in-law and the husband of cousin Elizabeth Kaighn.

7. *PEP*, 10 October 1776.

8. William Thompson Read, *Life and Correspondence of George Read* (Philadelphia, 1870), 15.

9. See Robert E. Wright and Laurie M. Wolfe, "Giles Knight," in Craig W. Horle, Joseph S. Foster and Laurie M. Wolfe, eds., *Lawmaking and Legislators in Pennsylvania: A Biographical Dictionary* (University Park: Pennsylvania State University Press, 2005), 3:821–28.

10. Ibid.

11. Edward Shippen to Jasper Yeates, 19 January 1776, as quoted in Lewis, "Edward Shippen," 24.

12. James Duffin, "Transcription of William J. Canby's Lecture on Betsy Ross and the Flag," BRH. The plausibility of Canby's recollection concerning the sign is unknown; I was unable to determine whether tin signs were indeed employed in the 1770s.

13. *PG*, 10 January 1776.

14. Memorandum Book, 1757–76 (see entries for March–June 1776), Franklin Papers, APS.

15. *PG*, 4 August 1757, 26 July 1759.

16. Ibid., 17 October 1771.

17. Ibid., 18 January 1775.

18. Ibid., 10 January 1776.

19. Michael Smith, a captain of a company in the Fourth Battalion of Associators in Bucks County, likewise submitted a bill to the fledgling state of Pennsylvania for expenses associated with regular musters—weekly in March, April and May and then more sporadically through September; his fife and drum men cost three shillings each per muster. Constant use apparently took its toll; at the end of marching

season, Smith billed the state for a new drum and drum heads and for two shillings "cash paid' for "mending the colours." For both the Cole and Smith receipts, see the Council of Safety Accounts, 1776–77 and undated (series 27.7), PSA.

20. The discussion here is developed from Debra Jean Force, "Betsy Ross, Upholsterer and Flag-Maker: A Proposal to Furnish Her Home" (unpublished report, Betsy Ross Foundation, 1976), chapter 7, "Flag-Making." For more on regimental flags, see Gherardi Davis, *Regimental Colors in the War of the Revolution* (New York: Gilliss Press, 1910); and Donald W. Holst, "Regimental Colors of the Continental Army," *Military Collector and Historian* 20, no. 3 (1968): 69–73; Donald W. Holst, "Liberty or Death on Military Colors," *Military Collector and Historian* 38, no. 1 (1986): 7–11; Donald W. Holst, "Notes on the Standards of the Continental Light Infantry," *Military Collector and Historian* 42, no. 1 (1990): 138–40; Donald W. Holst and Marko Zlatich, "A Return of Some Continental Army Regimental Colors of 1778," *Military Collector and Historian* 19, no. 1 (1967): 109–15.

21. *State of the accounts of John Nixon, Esquire, from the 26th of October, 1775, till the 7th of August, 1776, as treasurer of the Committee of Safety, State of Pennsylvania* (Philadelphia, 1786), 12, 27, 34. Though many sources (including this one) use the spelling "Barrett," the correct spelling for Timothy and William is "Berrett."

22. John W. Jackson, *The Pennsylvania Navy, 1775–1781: The Defense of the Delaware* (New Brunswick, N.J.: Rutgers University Press, 1974), 17; Edward W. Richardson, *Standards and Colors of the American Revolution* (Philadelphia: University of Pennsylvania Press, 1982), 90–91, 66–67.

23. Richardson, *Standards and Colors*, 61–72. On their uses, see George Henry Preble, *History of the Flag of the United States of America*, 3rd edition (Boston, 1882), 233.

24. Sotheby's vice chairman David Redden, noting that this is the earliest example of five-pointed stars on a Revolutionary battle flag, suggests that this latter flag may have been made by Betsy Ross. The attribution is of course highly tentative, but not impossible. See Scott A. Miskimon, "Sacred Relics Unfurled for Auction: Revolutionary War Flags Fetch More Than $17,000,000," *Southern Campaigns of the American Revolution* 3, nos. 6–7–8 (2006), http://www.southerncampaign.org/newsletter/v3n678.pdf, accessed June 17, 2008.

25. David Hackett Fischer, *Liberty and Freedom: A Visual History of America's Founding Ideas* (New York: Oxford University Press, 2005), 128.

26. On liberty flags, see Richardson, *Standards and Colors*, 13–16; and Fischer, *Liberty and Freedom*, 128.

27. Richardson, *Standards and Colors*, 4.

28. Among Jonathan Gostelowe's most celebrated works are the mahogany communion table and baptismal font he made for Christ Church in the 1780s, but church accounts also reveal that his wife, Elizabeth Tower Gostelowe, also performed upholstery work for the congregation; see the Cash Book, 1708–1833, in the archives of Christ Church. Given her skill set, she should be considered a possible maker of the flags enumerated, too. The Return is published in Richardson, *Standards and Colors*, 43.

29. "Minutes of the Navy Board from February 18, 1777 to September 24, 1777," *PA*, series 2, vol. 1 (Harrisburg, Pa., 1896), 221, 153; see also *PJ*, 17 May 1775.

30. See Henry W. Moeller, "Pennsylvania Flag Makers, 1775–1777" a paper delivered at "Flag Manufacture in the 18th and 19th Centuries," Sixth Annual Flag Symposium, Harrisburg, Pa., 28–29 March 2003, unpublished typescript in the collections of the BRH.

31. See Julie Winch, *A Gentleman of Color: The Life of James Forten* (New York:

Oxford University Press, 2002), 18; and James Duffin, "Summary of Research on Known Flag Makers" (unpublished report prepared for *History Now*, 1996), BRH.

32. *State of the accounts of John Nixon*, 9, 17, 18.

33. See the Committee of Safety Receipt Book, Pennsylvania navy, as cited in Pat Pilling, "Early Flag Makers," research report, Star Spangled Banner Flag House, Baltimore, M.D., 2003.

34. The *Lexington* was a ship bought and refitted by the Continental forces at Wharton and Humphrey's Philadelphia shipyard in March; *Reprisal* was purchased in March and left Philadelphia 29 April 1776. On the former, see the Continental navy in account with the brigantine *Lexington*, NDAR 4 (1969): 549, and Continental navy in account with the ship *Reprisal*, NDAR 4 (1969): 1316–18. William Rea Furlong, Byron McCandless and Harold D. Langley indicate that these were Grand Union flags in *So Proudly We Hail: The History of the United States Flag* (Washington, D.C.: Smithsonian Institution Press, 1981), 91–92. On the flag of the *Reprisal*, see also *So Proudly We Hail*, 91; and Boleslaw Mastai and Marie-Louise D'Otrange Mastai, *The Stars and the Stripes* (New York: Knopf, 1973), 23.

35. See Furlong, McCandless and Langley, *So Proudly We Hail*, 91–93.

36. For her 1747 marriage, see "Pennsylvania Marriages Prior to 1790," *PA*, series 2, vol. 2 (Harrisburg, Pa., 1897), 60. On Francis Manny, see PG, 21 June 1750, and Minutes of the Provincial Council of Pennsylvania, 12 February 1747, *PA*, series 1, vol. 5 (Harrisburg, Pa., 1851), 197.

37. See Moeller, "Pennsylvania Flag Makers."

38. Moeller, "Pennsylvania Flag Makers" and *Shattering an American Myth*, 102.

39. Jones's claim is the subject of some controversy. See George Henry Preble, *History of the Flag of the United States of America* (Boston, 1894), 229–30; and "John Paul Jones on the *Alfred* first raised the United States flag" (excerpt from *Navies of the American Revolution*, posted at http://www.geocities.com/CollegePark/Den/7812/alfred.html, and accessed 7 June 2007). On Manny's work, see Richardson, *Standards and Colors*, 63–64.

40. Quoted in John J. McCusker, *The First Continental Flagship, 1775–1778* (Washington, D.C.: Smithsonian Institution Press, 1973), 8–9.

41. A Union flag and ensign for the *Columbus* both appear in James Wharton's daybooks, but no maker is identified. Wharton also notes providing a pennant for the thirty-two-gun *Effingham*. See James Wharton Daybooks, vol. 11, 1775–83, HSP, entries for 12 and 23 December 1775 and 9 March 1776.

42. See Andrew Jackson O'Shaughnessy, *Empire Divided: The American Revolution and the British Caribbean* (Philadelphia: University of Pennsylvania Press, 2000), 214–17.

43. On the "suit of colours," see Woodhouse Papers, HSP, cited in Moeller, "Pennsylvania Flag Makers." Also Furlong, McCandless and Langley, *So Proudly We Hail*, 90–91.

44. *PP*, 26 September 1778.

45. The best work on Rebecca Flower Young and Mary Young Pickersgill is Pat Pilling, "Documents of a Flag-making Family," *Flag Bulletin* 201 (2000): 19–24; and Lonn Taylor et al., *The Star-Spangled Banner: The Making of an American Icon* (New York: HarperCollins, 2008).

46. See Furlong, McCandless and Langley, *So Proudly We Hail*, 136–37.

47. For Young's advertisements, see, e.g., *PP*, 28 June and 17 July 1781 through 13 July 1782; on the receipts, see Pat Pilling, "Early Flag Makers."

**48.** Furlong, McCandless and Langley, *So Proudly We Hail*, 136–37.

**49.** Caroline Pickersgill Purdy to Georgiana Armistead Appleton, 1876, Appleton Family Properties, Massachusetts Historical Society.

**50.** Ibid.

**51.** Gardner Weld Allen, *Naval History of the American Revolution* (New York: Houghton Mifflin, 1913), 31.

## 11. SIGNALS OF INDEPENDENCE

**1.** Several books on the history of the United States flag by historians, curators and collectors have tackled various elements of this history. Of twentieth-century scholarship, the best places to begin, arranged chronologically, are John Henry Fow, *The True Story of the American Flag* (Philadelphia: William J. Campbell, 1908); Grace Rogers Cooper, *Thirteen Star Flags: Keys to Identification* (Washington, D.C.: Smithsonian Institution Press, 1973); William Rea Furlong, Byron McCandless and Harold D. Langley, *So Proudly We Hail: The History of the United States Flag* (Washington, D.C.: Smithsonian Institution Press, 1981); Edward W. Richardson, *Standards and Colors of the American Revolution* (Philadelphia: University of Pennsylvania Press, 1982); Henry W. Moeller, *Shattering an American Myth: Unfurling the History of the Stars and Stripes* (Mattituck, N.Y.: Ameron House, 1992); Nancy Druckman and Jeffrey Kenneth Kohn, *American Flags: Designs for a Young Nation* (New York: Harry N. Abrams, 2003); and Peter Keim and Kevin Keim, *A Grand Old Flag: A History of the United States Through Its Flags* (New York: DK Publishing, 2007). The most recent inquiry into the validity of the Ross legend itself is by descendant John Harker. See *Betsy Ross's Five-Pointed Star* (Melbourne Beach, F.L.: Canmore Press, 2005).

**2.** Even information about the site at which the work is said to have occurred is now muddied. For obvious reasons, no tax records from 1776, 1777 or 1778 Philadelphia survive, so it is hard to know exactly where Ross was then living. Three of the affidavits sworn by descendants say Ross had moved out of her parents' house and was living on "Arch Street below Third," on the north side, above Bread Street, when these events occurred, in a house where she was certainly living by 1780 (and possibly occupied at least as early as December 1777), when the documentary record resumes. James Duffin conducted title searches for the entire 200 block of Arch Street to clarify information gathered from tax records, and found that, by 1780, Betsy Ross can clearly be found living with her second husband, Joseph Ashburn, and later her third husband, John Claypoole, at the present site of 241 Arch Street in a house that was likely gone by the mid-nineteenth century, and that shared a party wall with 239, the site of the present-day Betsy Ross House, a mirror image of the dwelling at 241. See Duffin, "Investigation of Revolutionary Era Tax Records for Betsy Ross" (unpublished report prepared for *History Now*, 1996), BRH. It is worth noting that public records clearly place Ross in at least two houses on Arch Street (this one and her childhood home), and the affidavits suggest that during the British occupation she moved from one Arch Street house to another as well, placing her in at least three houses on this street between 1776 and 1780.

**3.** James Duffin, "Transcription of the 1870 Affidavit of Rachel (Claypoole) Jones Fletcher, 1789–1873," BRH; and "Transcription of Notes of Interview with Rachel (Claypoole) Jones Fletcher (1789–1873)," BRH.

**4.** Both ibid. and James Duffin, "Transcription of Notes of Interview with Jane (Claypoole) Canby, 1792–1873," BRH, mention that Betsy returned only briefly to her parents, and describe Betsy's subsequent proximity to "Grandfather Griscom's" home in these years.

5. On Betsy's friendship with Joanna Ross, see "Letter from William J. Canby (1825–1890) to William T. Read concerning John Ross," 21 February 1870, BRH. What's more, George Ross appears to have stopped at Betsy's brother-in-law Thomas Morgan's shop for "show" and knee buckles on 27 May, during the narrow window of time in which the visit would have had to occur; the reference is somewhat puzzling, since newspaper advertisements suggest that Morgan did not return to Philadelphia until 1779, but the coincidence seems notable. See Thomas Morgan, Ledger, 1771–1803, 27 May 1776, 79, HSP; and Alfred Coxe Prime, *Arts and Crafts in Philadelphia, Maryland and South Carolina*, series 1 (1929), 256–58.

6. James Duffin, "Transcription of the 1870 Affidavit of Rachel (Claypoole) Jones Fletcher, 1789–1873," BRH; and "Transcription of the 1870 Affidavit of Sophia B. (Wilson) Hildebrandt," BRH.

7. News release, "Washington's Campaign Tents to Be Displayed at Yorktown," National Park Service, 22 February 2003; there is some question now as to how the extant tents associated with Washington are related to one another, and to surviving receipts: some may date from this campaign season, and others from a later moment in time. For the receipt at issue here, see George Washington Papers at the LOC, 1741–99: series 5, Financial Papers, Plunket Fleeson to George Washington, 11 May 1776, Revolutionary War Accounts, Vouchers, and Receipted Accounts 2, 1775–1783.

8. Richardson, *Standards and Colors*, 270–71.

9. See Moeller, *Shattering an American Myth*, 101–4; and Clarence Lester Ver Steeg, *Robert Morris, Revolutionary Financier* (New York: Octagon Books, 1976).

10. James Duffin, "Transcription of Notes of Interview with Rachel (Claypoole) Jones Fletcher (1789–1873)," BRH.

11. James Duffin, "Transcription of the 1870 Affidavit of Rachel (Claypoole) Jones Fletcher, 1789–1873," BRH.

12. Ibid.

13. Duffin, "Transcription of Notes of Interview with Rachel (Claypoole) Jones Fletcher, 1789–1873," BRH. It is unclear just where the engraving was when this story was told. Canby notes that Rachel, "when she saw the picture in the front of Irving's *Life of Washington* said 'those ruffles on his shirt were made by mother.'" Irving's multivolume biography began to appear in 1855, long after Betsy Claypoole was dead, so if Betsy showed her daughter this particular image and made this particular claim, it must have been from some other, earlier work. Alternatively, Rachel could have meant that her mother fabricated ruffles in general, and Canby misunderstood her to mean those particular ruffles pictured. In any case, it's a puzzling corner of family history. Interestingly, though, one version of Wertmuller's portrait was engraved by Henry Bryan Hall (1808–84) and published in New York by G. P. Putnam in the 1850s, just about the time Clarissa was asking William to record these events.

14. What's more, there's doubt as to whether Washington actually sat for the portrait. Though Wertmuller claimed that he had been granted a single sitting, George Washington Parke Custis (stepgrandson and adopted son of George Washington) claimed that he was with the family every day in 1795, and no such sitting occurred. See George Washington Parke Custis and M. Russell Thayer, "George Washington Parke Custis's Opinion of Portraits of Washington," *PMHB* 18, no. 1 (1894): 81–84.

15. Donald Jackson, ed., and Dorothy Twohig, assoc. ed., *The Papers of George*

*Washington*, vol. 3, *The Diaries of George Washington* (Charlottesville: University Press of Virginia, 1978), 276.

16. Ibid., 19 August 1774, 279.

17. Ibid., 329.

18. George Washington to Israel Putnam, 28 May 1776, in John C. Fitzpatrick, ed., *The Writings of George Washington from the Original Manuscript Sources, 1745-1799* (Washington, D.C.: Government Printing Office, 1964). On the actions of Congress during Washington's visit, see *Journals of the Continental Congress*, vol. 4 (Washington, D.C.: Government Printing Office, 1906), 391, 406-7.

19. Ibid.

20. As quoted in Furlong, McCandless and Langley, *So Proudly We Hail*, 116.

21. This discussion of the flags and the defense of the Delaware River relies on Moeller, *Shattering an American Myth*, 97-109.

22. Craig W. Horle, "George Ross," in Craig W. Horle, Joseph S. Foster and Laurie M. Wolfe, eds., *Lawmaking and Legislators in Pennsylvania: A Biographical Dictionary* (University Park: Pennsylvania State University Press, 2005), 1243.

23. Ibid.

24. On Morris's committee assignments, see Moeller, *Shattering an American Myth*, 101.

25. The below is drawn from Henry W. Moeller, "Pennsylvania Flag Makers, 1775–1777" a paper delivered at "Flag Manufacture in the 18th and 19th Centuries," Sixth Annual Flag Symposium, Harrisburg, Pa., 28–29 March 2003, unpublished typescript in the collections of the BRH; and Moeller, *Shattering an American Myth*, 97–109. It is possible that Nixon is in fact the "shipping merchant" mentioned in the family affidavits, noted for supplying Betsy with a flag to use as a model.

26. Some of Nixon's accounts can be found in the publication *State of the accounts of John Nixon, Esquire, from the 26th of October, 1775, till the 7th of August, 1776, as treasurer of the Committee of Safety, State of Pennsylvania* (Philadelphia, 1786). Henry Moeller discusses Nixon's records in "Pennsylvania Flag Makers, 1775-1777."

27. Henry Moeller concludes that these are signal flags; see "Pennsylvania Flag Makers, 1775–1777" a paper delivered at and his *Shattering an American Myth*, 103. For an illustration of the Fort Mifflin flag, see Furlong, McCandless and Langley, *So Proudly We Hail*, 114. Alternatively, Richardson suggests that the 1777 flag Betsy fabricated was the white flag with the pine tree used by the Pennsylvania navy in 1775; see *Standards and Colors*, 112–13.

28. Furlong, McCandless and Langley, *So Proudly We Hail*, 138; see also Richard S. Patterson and Richardson Dougall, *The Eagle and the Shield: A History of the Great Seal of the United States* (Washington, D.C: Department of State, 1998).

29. Far and away more common are flags on which the stars are arranged in rows, either of 4-5-4 or (less commonly) 3-2-3-2-3. The earliest surviving images of American flags—1779 drawings of the ensigns aboard John Paul Jones's ships the *Alliance* and *Serapis*—include one of each. Preserved originally in the shipping offices of Texel in Holland, they are now at the Chicago Historical Society. For images and discussion, see Richardson, *Standards and Colors*, 28; Furlong, McCandless and Langley, *So Proudly We Hail*, 129–30, 145n; and David Martucci, "The 13 Stars and Stripes: A Survey of Eighteenth-Century Images," *NAVA News*, no. 167 (April–June 2000); addenda in nos. 168 (July–September 2000), 178 (April–June 2003) and 188 (October–December 2000) available at http://www.vexman.net.

30. Richardson, *Standards and Colors*, 57.

31. "An Old-Time Flag Brought to View," *Philadelphia Inquirer*, 7 September 1896. Charles Weisgerber's iconic painting, discussed here in the epilogue, also advanced the notion that the Ross flag carried a circle of stars.

32. Richardson, *Standards and Colors*, 28.

33. Today the flag measures about twenty-seven and a half inches by thirty-five and a half inches. See Furlong, McCandless and Langley, *So Proudly We Hail*, 119–20.

34. In *Liberty and Freedom: A Visual History of America's Founding Ideas* (New York: Oxford University Press, 2005), 160, David Hackett Fischer suggests that perhaps the flag Betsy recalled was Washington's headquarters standard.

35. *Masonic Symbols in American Decorative Arts* (Lexington, Mass.: Museum of Our National Heritage, 1976), 52.

36. My thanks to Aimee Newell, director of collections at the National Heritage Museum in Lexington, Mass. for suggesting both of these possibilities to me.

37. A fascinating set of drawings by the Philadelphia author, editor and Historical Society of Pennsylvania member Charles J. Lukens, made for the flag historian George Henry Preble, in which Lukens works to demonstrate the angles and degrees of the Ross star, survives today in the collections of the American Antiquarian Society; see Manuscripts Departments, George Henry Preble, Papers, October 1873, vol. 3 (1873–1880), 183. My deep thanks to Linda Eaton for emphasizing the curricular issue and to Jessica Lepler for passing this find on to me. Lukens, interestingly enough, was a friend of George Canby; see below, Epilogue, n. 39.

38. For her help in puzzling out the mysteries of star production, I am deeply indebted to Linda Eaton, curator of textiles at the H. F. du Pont Winterthur Museum. There is a curious side note to the presence of stars in the Ross legend that merits some attention. Another family with a "first flag" tradition that attaches to and extends the Ross family story was preserved by the family of Rebecca Prescott Sherman. According to a niece, once Mrs. Sherman (the wife of congressman Roger Sherman) learned that Washington had commissioned Betsy Ross to make a flag, "nothing would satisfy" her "but to go and see it in the works, and there she had the privilege of sewing some of the stars on the very first flag of a Young Nation. Perhaps because of this experience, she was chosen and requested to make the first flag ever made in the State of Connecticut which she did, assisted by Mrs. Wooster. This fact is officially recorded." In Katharine Prescott Bennett's retelling of the tale, however, the event is cast "a little later" than the Declaration of Independence, rather than before, as in Ross's narrative. See Bennett, "American Mothers of Strong Men," *Journal of American History* 3, no. 1 (1909): 51.

39. For Whipple, see NDAR, vol. 4 (1969), 1313; Jay is quoted in Preble, *History of the Flag of the United States of America* (Boston, 1882), 212.

40. As quoted in Cooper, *Thirteen Star Flags*, 3–4.

41. Cooper, *Thirteen Star Flags*, 4.

42. As quoted in Furlong, McCandless and Langley, *So Proudly We Hail*, 118.

43. As quoted in ibid., 118.

44. Furlong, McCandless and Langley state that "in the minds of authors of this volume, there is no question that [Hopkinson] designed the flag of the United States"; see *So Proudly We Hail*, 101. Richardson calls Hopkinson the "likely designer of the Stars and Stripes," in *Standards and Colors*, 22. For alternative views, see John Harker, *Betsy Ross's Five Pointed Star* (Melbourne Beach, Fla.: Canmore Press, 2005), and Robert

Morris, "Francis Hopkinson: Did He Design Our American Flag?" (typescript, 1983), David Library of the American Revolution, Washington Crossing, Pa.

45. Morris, "Francis Hopkinson."

46. See Paul M. Zall, *Comical Spirit of Seventy-Six: The Humor of Francis Hopkinson* (San Marino, Calif.: Huntington Library, 1976). On the close relationship between the iconography of currency and flags, see Richardson, *Standards and Colors*, 47–49; Benjamin H. Irvin, "Benjamin Franklin's '*Enriching Virtues*': Continental Currency and the Creation of a Revolutionary Republic," http://www.common-place.org, vol. 6, no. 3 (April 2006); and Patterson and Dougall, *Eagle and the Shield*.

47. Barrymore Laurence Schere, *A History of American Classical Music* (Naperville, Ill.: Sourcebooks, 2007), 15.

48. Gaillard Hunt, ed., *Journals of the Continental Congress, 1774–1785*, vol. 18, 1780 (Washington, D.C.: Government Printing Office, 1910), 984.

49. Stephen Jay Gould, ed., "The Creation Myths of Cooperstown," *Natural History* 98, no. 11 (1989): 14–24, 45–48.

## 12. THE MARINER'S BRIDE

1. Carl Williams to Robert Yarrington, 14 September 1977, in Griscom Family: Miscellaneous file of the GCHS. Williams suggests that the pitcher was made not on the occasion of the wedding, but in the period between Ashburn's death and Betsy's marriage to John Claypoole. What evidence survives to indicate the timing of the gift is not indicated, and in its absence, it seems likelier that the gift would have coincided with the wedding. Another family story suggests that George converted coins into this pitcher during the war as a means to protect the silver. Nothing is known about George Griscom's training or career as a silversmith.

2. See Susan E. Klepp, "Philadelphia in Transition: A Demographic History of the City and Its Occupational Groups" (Ph.D. dissertation, University of Pennsylvania, 1980); Karin A. Wulf, *Not All Wives: Women of Colonial Philadelphia* (Ithaca, N.Y.: Cornell University Press, 2000); and Lisa Wilson, *Life after Death: Widows in Pennsylvania, 1750–1850* (Philadelphia: Temple University Press, 1992).

3. Robert V. Wells and Michael Zuckerman, "Quaker Marriage Patterns in a Colonial Perspective," *William and Mary Quarterly*, 3rd series, 29, no. 3 (1972): 415–42, 424–25.

4. Ashburn is described in *PA*, series 5, vol. 1 (Harrisburg, Pa., 1906), 631.

5. See Debra Jean Force, "Betsy Ross, Upholsterer and Flag-Maker: A Proposal to Furnish Her Home" (unpublished report, Betsy Ross Foundation, 1976), appendix 3.

6. John Fanning Watson, *Annals of Philadelphia* (Philadelphia, 1830), 174.

7. Hannah Benner Roach, ed., "Taxables in the City of Philadelphia, 1756," in *Colonial Philadelphians* (Philadelphia: Genealogical Society of Pennsylvania, 1999), 105–46; NDAR, vol. 2, 1222; and *PEP*, 3 January 1778.

8. The centenarian Margaret Donaldson Boggs reports her father's occupation in the San Francisco *Daily Evening Bulletin*, 20 January 1876; his directory listing is in *The Philadelphia Directory*, by Francis White (Philadelphia, 1785), 17. On Donaldson and Ashburn's December 1775 work in the Humphreys shipyard, see NDAR, vol. 3 (1968), 609; and vol. 2 (1966), 1222. See also Patricia Ruth Manning Miller Donaldson, *Donaldson* (Georgetown, Ohio: P. R. Donaldson, 1978), 199–200.

9. *PG*, 10 March 1763, 4 November 1772; votes of the House of Representatives,

from 29 December 1773 (Philadelphia, [1774]), 79, 81, 85, 92, 95, 97; and Richard Henry Spencer, ed., *Genealogical and Memorial Encylopedia of the State of Maryland* (New York: American Historical Society, 1919), 618; John T. Phillips, *Historian's Guide to Loudoun County, Virginia* (Leesburg, Va.: Goose Creek Productions, 1996), 344. See also John Levering, *Levering Family History and Genealogy* (Indianapolis, Ind., 1897), 119.

10. *PP*, 26 May 1788.

11. At least the assessors charged with collecting the effective supply tax noted the respective valuations of Susannah Doane and Griffith Levering side by side. See the *PA*, series 3, vol. 14 (Harrisburg, Pa., 1897), 354.

12. Ibid.

13. For Ephraim Doane and the sloop *Sally*, see *PA*, series 2, vol. 2 (Harrisburg, Pa., 1890), 560.

14. Ephraim Doane, 1780 estate inventory, file 31, PCA.

15. Ibid.

16. Records of Pennsylvania's Revolutionary Governments, Register of Letters of Marque, 1776–77, RG 27, PSA; and *PEP*, 3 January 1778.

17. Charles Oscar Paullin, *The Navy of the American Revolution* (Cleveland, Ohio, 1906), 376–79.

18. John W. Jackson, *The Pennsylvania Navy, 1775–1781: The Defense of the Delaware* (New Brunswick, N.J.: Rutgers University Press, 1974); and Harry M. Tinkcom, "The Revolutionary City, 1765–1783," in Russell F. Weigley, ed., *Philadelphia: A 300-year History* (New York: Norton, 1982), 109–54.

19. *PEP*, 6 January 1778.

20. *PG*, 17 June 1778.

21. See Henry Y. Young, "Treason and Its Punishment in Revolutionary Pennsylvania," *PMHB* 90, no. 3 (1966): 287–313.

22. Saul Cornell, "Commonplace or Anachronism: The Standard Model, the Second Amendment, and the Problem of History in Contemporary Constitutional Theory," *Constitutional Commentary* 16, no. 2 (1999): 228. The act was subsequently reinforced and toughened, when it provided that noncompliance triggered the forfeiture of goods and chattels to the state, and allowed violators to be fined, imprisoned or exiled. See Wayland F. Dunaway, *A History of Pennsylvania* (New York: Prentice-Hall, 1935), 193–94.

23. Cornell, "Commonplace or Anachronism," 228.

24. John Adams to Abigail Adams, 16 July 1777, in *Adams Family Papers: An Electronic Archive*, Massachusetts Historical Society, http://www.masshist.org/digitaladams/.

25. See Thomas Gilpin, *Exiles in Virginia* (Philadelphia, 1848), 71 and 264.

26. Oaths of Allegiance, 1777–90, series 27.36, Pennsylvania's Revolutionary Governments, PSA. None of Betsy's brothers-in-law appear on these long lists, though a man named Thomas Morgan, the same name as Mary Griscom Morgan's husband, does appear on a list from 18 August 1778. See also Thomas Westcott, *Names of Persons Who Took the Oath of Allegiance to the State of Pennsylvania* (Baltimore: Genealogical Publishing, 1965), 42.

27. On the *Hetty*, see n 16. Ashburn was also somehow associated with the brigantine *Achilles*. See Force, "Betsy Ross, Upholsterer and Flag-Maker," 16–17; and Samuel C. Morris Receipt Book, 1769–1781, JDC. Neither the owner nor the master of the *Achilles* in 1778 when letters of marque were granted the ship (in April and August) for two voyages, Ashburn nevertheless collected (in August and September) more than £1,400 from

Samuel C. Morris for debts associated with "the use of the Brigantine *Achilles.*" Regarding the *Hetty*, the association with McClenachan is significant. Born in Ireland, McClenachan immigrated to Philadelphia at an early age. He engaged in mercantile pursuits as well as banking and shipping. When the imperial crisis erupted, he also became active in the resistance movement: McClenachan helped found the First Troop of Philadelphia Cavalry; in 1780 he sent a large sum of money to help the American forces and aided the Continental Congress with money and credit. McClenachan would serve as a member of the state House of Representatives from 1790 to 1795, and was elected as a Republican to the fifth Congress.

28. William B. Timmons, *Betsy Ross: The Griscom Legacy* (Salem, N.J.: Salem County Cultural & Heritage Commission, 1983), 144, from Parry, *Quaker Rebel*, 23, 126. Ray Thompson, in *Betsy Ross: Last of Philadelphia's Free Quakers* (Fort Washington, Pa.: Bicentennial Press, 1972), 17, indicates that it was Ashburn's widowed mother who owned the ship, and that she lived on South Fourth Street. No conclusive archival references to the *Swallow* or this aunt or mother have yet been located.

29. John Frayler, "Privateers in the American Revolution," *The American Revolution: Lighting Freedom's Flame*, http://www.nps.gov/revwar/about_the_revolution/privateers.html.

30. Ibid.

31. Francis D. Cogliano, "'We All Hoisted the American Flag': National Identity among American Prisoners in Britain during the American Revolution," *Journal of American Studies* 32, no. 1 (1998): 19–37.

32. Jackson, *Pennsylvania Navy*, 13.

33. The historians Jesse Lemisch and Marcus Rediker have demonstrated the key contributions of sailors to the ideology of American Revolution and to the struggle for independence. See Jesse Lemisch, "Jack Tar in the Streets: Merchant Seamen in the Politics of Revolutionary America," *William and Mary Quarterly*, 3rd series, 25, no. 3 (1968): 371–407; Marcus Rediker, "A Motley Crew of Rebels: Sailors, Slaves, and the Coming of the American Revolution," in Ronald Hoffman and Peter J. Albert, eds., *The Transforming Hand of Revolution: Reconsidering the Revolution as a Social Movement* (Charlottesville, Va.: University of Virginia Press, 1996), 155–98; and Peter Linebaugh and Marcus Rediker, *The Many-Headed Hydra: Sailors, Slaves, Commoners and the Hidden History of the Revolutionary Atlantic* (London: Verso, 2000).

34. For the 31 July 1777 bond, see NDAR, vol. 10 (1966), 1066.

35. Philip Chadwick Foster Smith, "The Privateering Impulse of the American Revolution," *Essex Institute Historical Collections* 119, no. 1 (January 1983), 50.

36. Donald A. Petrie, *The Prize Game* (Annapolis, Md.: Naval Institute Press, 1999); the description of privateering here and below is drawn from Petrie's engaging account.

37. Admiralty Court Papers, 1780: January–June (box 3), col. 1389, HSP.

38. Jonathan Williams Jr. to the American Commissioners, 29 November 1777, as transcribed in the Benjamin Franklin Papers, http://www.franklinpapers.org/franklin/framedVolumes.jsp; and London *Chronicle*, 13–16 December 1777, as quoted in NDAR, vol. 10 (1996), 1066.

## 13. THE OCCUPIED CITY

1. John Adams to Abigail Adams, 8 July 1777, *Adams Family Papers: An Electronic Archive*, Massachusetts Historical Society, http://www.masshist.org/digitaladams/.

2. John Adams to Abigail Adams, 26 July 1777, ibid.

3. John Adams to Abigail Adams, 1 August 1777, ibid.

4. Ibid.

5. John Adams to Abigail Adams, 4, 13 and 14 August 1777, ibid.

6. David G. Martin, *The Philadelphia Campaign, June 1777–July 1778* (Conshocken, Pa.: Combined Books, 1993), 76; Thomas J. McGuire, *The Philadelphia Campaign*, vol. 1, *Brandywine and the Fall of Philadelphia* (Mechanicsburg, Pa.: Stackpole Books, 2006), 269.

7. "Diary of Robert Morton," *PMHB* 1, no. 1 (1877): 7.

8. EDD, 26 September 1777.

9. [San Francisco] *Daily Evening Bulletin*, 20 January 1876.

10. John W. Jackson, *With the British Army in Philadelphia, 1777–1778* (San Rafael, Calif.: Presidio Press, 1979), 17.

11. EDD, 4 October 1777.

12. Ibid., 16 October 1777.

13. Ibid., 18, 20 October and 1, 12 November 1777.

14. "Diary of James Allen, Esq.," 11 May 1778, *PMHB* 9, no. 2 (1885): 9, 4.

15. Four years later, Joanna would seek and receive compensation from the state of Delaware, having petitioned for some £40. See the records of Holy Trinity (Old Swedes) Church, Wilmington, Del., from 1697 to 1773, and "Minutes of the Council of Delaware State," 10 November 1781, Papers of the Historical Society of Delaware, no. 6, 672–73.

16. Henry Hobart Bellas, ed., *Personal Recollections of Captain Enoch Anderson*, Papers of the Historical Society of Delaware, no. 16 (Wilmington, 1896), 48.

17. "Diary of James Allen, Esq.," 9, 4.

18. James Duffin, "Investigation of Revolutionary Era Tax Records for Betsy Ross," BRH.

19. James Duffin, "Transcription of Notes of Interview with Jane (Claypoole) Canby (1792–1873)," BRH. The shoemaker William Niles later lived at 95 Arch Street; he appears to have moved there sometime after MacPherson's city directory of 1785 was compiled, but before the compilers of Biddle's 1791 edition made their rounds. Between 1775 and 1784, the house at 95 Arch Street was owned by the family of Ann LeGay. See also John MacPherson, *MacPherson's Directory* (Philadelphia, 1785), and Clement Biddle, *Philadelphia Directory* (Philadelphia, 1791). According to the Sons of the American Revolution, "William Niles . . . served from 1776 to 1783 as a Private in Captain Jeremiah Fisher's and Captain John Mitchel's Company, Colonel William Bradford's Regiment, of the Philadelphia Militia. He was with Washington at Valley Forge and the campaign in New Jersey, making the famous crossing of the Delaware on Christmas Eve. He continued service until the end of the war. His home was at 95 Arch (Mulberry) street in Philadelphia, a few doors from Betsy Ross's home." See the SAR Web site at http://www.sar.org/passar/graves/patriots/nileswil.html.

20. Sara L. Johnson, "The Battle of the Kegs," *Musical Rambles through History*, http://www.kitchenmusician.net.

21. Ibid.

22. *New Jersey Gazette*, 21 January 1778, as quoted in Frank Moore, *Diary of the American Revolution*, vol. 2 (New York, 1860), 6.

23. James Duffin, "Transcription of Notes of Interview with Jane (Claypoole) Canby (1792–1873)," BRH.

24. James Duffin, "Transcription of 1909 Affidavit of Susan (Satterthwaite) Newport (1827–?) and Mary Satterthwaite (1824–?)," BRH.

25. According to William B. Timmons, *Betsy Ross: A Griscom Legacy* (Salem, N.J.: Salem County Cultural & Heritage Commission, 1983), 112, in the first edition of his *Annals* John Fanning Watson asserts that wood for the redoubts was stolen from Samuel Griscom, but neither the 1830 edition nor later editions appear to make that claim.

26. Jackson, *With the British Army in Philadelphia*, 22.

27. G. D. Scull, ed., "The Montresor Journals," *Collections of the New-York Historical Society for the Year 1881* (New York, 1882), 128–29.

28. Ibid., 541–52, and Samuel C. Morris receipt book, 21 April 1779, 18 September 1780, JDC, no. 52, 72–76.

29. Family stories include a reference to a fire that consumed Griscom's lumberyard. No records of either the lumberyard or the fire have been located, but certainly the burning of a lumberyard—whatever was left of it given the constant predations of both armies—would be plausible while the war raged in Pennsylvania. For the reference, see James Duffin, "Transcription of the 1909 Affidavit of Susan Jacobs (McCord) Turner," BRH.

30. Ibid., and "A Hundred Years Ago—Mrs. Boggs' Centennial Year," *Daily Evening Bulletin*, 20 January 1876.

31. Eleanore Parker Gadsden, "From Traditional Cabinetmaking to Entrepreneurial Production: David Evans (1748–1819)" (M.A. thesis, University of Delaware, 2000), 32–33.

32. *PEP*, 23 October 1777.

33. Ibid., 1 July 1777; *PP*, 8 July 1777.

34. Nancy Goyne, "Furniture Craftsmen in Philadelphia, 1760–1790: Their Role in a Mercantile Society" (M.A. thesis, University of Delaware, 1963), 112.

35. Carl G. Karsch, "The Battle for Philadelphia," http://www.ushistory.org/carpentershall/history/battle.htm.

36. Sandra Mackenzie Lloyd, "Autobiographical Letters of Peter S. Duponceau," *PMHB* 40, no. 1 (1916): 184.

37. Sandra Mackenzie Lloyd, "Revolutionary Women Interpretative Tour Outline," 2004, BRH.

38. Owen Biddle, diary, 25 February 1779–21 June 1779, box 3, Biddle Family Papers, FHL.

39. Charles Willson Peale, diary, 18 June 1778 (APS), as quoted in INHP card file: Phila., City of; Manners & Mores, General.

40. *PP*, 3 June 1778.

41. James "surrendered" and was "discharged." See ibid., 17 June 1778; Horle, "Abel James," 767; and *Black list: a list of those Tories who took part with Great-Britain, in the revolutionary war, and were attainted of high treason* (Philadelphia, 1802).

42. Thomas M. Doerflinger, *A Vigorous Spirit of Enterprise: Merchants and Economic Development in Revolutionary Philadelphia* (Chapel Hill: University of North Carolina Press, 1986), 210.

43. Jeffrey L. Scheib, "Plunket Fleeson," in *Lawmaking and Legislators*, 3:504.

44. See Steven Rosswurm, *Arms, Country and Class: The Philadelphia Militia and the "Lower Sort" during the American Revolution* (New Brunswick, N.J.: Rutgers University Press, 1987); and Barbara Clark Smith, "Food Rioters and the American Revolution," *William and Mary Quarterly* 51, no. 1 (1994): 3–38.

45. See John K. Alexander, "The Fort Wilson Incident of 1779: A Case Study of the Revolutionary Crowd," *William and Mary Quarterly*, 3rd series, 31, no. 4 (1974): 589–612; and Smith "Food Rioters and the American Revolution."

**46.** The Board of Ordnance was established in June 1776, and worked at the corner of Market and Fourth streets. In 1777 the Commissary General of Military Stores, Benjamin Flower, assumed responsibility for arms and ordnance production in Pennsylvania.

**47.** "Cartridges made by Male & Female Employees/Ordnance Account with Female Employees, 1779 and 1780," Revolutionary War & Miscellaneous Numbered Records, 20421–20542, M859 roll 65, 1778–79, NARA.

**48.** See ibid.; Records of Women in Production at Philadelphia Arsenal, 1780–81, National Historic Site, INHP, microfilm roll 217, extracted by Richard Colton, historian, Springfield Armory, 12 May 2005; and NARA microcopy M859, roll 65, manuscript 453. This is the only numbered record that lists an Elizabeth Ashburn.

**49.** Van Wyck Brooks, ed., *Poor Richard: The Almanacks for 1733–1758* (New York: Heritage Press, 1964), 29, as quoted in Susan E. Klepp, "Revolutionary Bodies: Women and the Fertility Transition in the Mid-Atlantic Region, 1760–1820," *Journal of American History* 85, no. 3 (1998): 910.

**50.** See "Family Record of Marriage and Births of Children," Claypoole family Bible, BRH.

**51.** Robert Ainsworth, *An abridgement of Ainsworth's dictionary, English and Latin [microform] by Thomas Morell carefully corrected and improved from the last London quarto edition by John Carey* (Boston, 1818).

**52.** James Duffin, "Investigation of Revolutionary Era Tax Records for Betsy Ross" (typescript, n.d.), BRH. James Duffin compared tax records to Arch Street deeds and found that the home that Betsy and Joseph occupied in 1780, 1781 and 1782 would now be numbered 241 Arch Street, that is, just next to the present Betsy Ross House, and a mirror image of it.

**53.** Ibid.

**54.** Sharon V. Salinger, "Spaces, Inside and Outside, in Eighteenth-Century Philadelphia," *Journal of Interdisciplinary History* 26, no. 1 (1995): 8.

**55.** Ibid., 19.

**56.** Mrs. Lithgow died in the fall of 1779.

**57.** Wilbur C. Plummer, "Consumer Credit in Colonial Philadelphia," *PMHB* 66, no. 4 (1942): 392. For Morgan's movements, see Alfred Coxe Prime, *Arts and Crafts in Philadelphia, Maryland and South Carolina*, 1 (1929): 256–58. Soon the Morgans moved to Water Street between Christian and Queen; see Francis White, *Philadelphia's Directory* (Philadelphia, 1785).

**58.** David Evans Daybooks, 1774–1812, HSP. These choices were of course shaped by financial concerns. In 1796, though late for Ashburn, a master earned thirty-six dollars per month, while a mate earned thirty dollars. Ordinary seamen earned much less, prior to 1790 from £1 5 s. to £3 12 s. per month. The Ashburn household, one researcher concludes, was "more prosperous" than that of "most ordinary seamen, especially with additional income from the upholstery business." See Debra Jean Force, "Betsy Ross, Upholsterer and Flag-Maker: A Proposal to Furnish Her Home "(unpublished report, Betsy Ross Foundation, 1976), 16–17, 26.

**59.** Doane's bond is dated 18 October 1777; the document for Donaldson's ship, owned by Robert Knox together with John Wharton & Co., is dated 21 April 1781. See LOC, *Naval Records of the Revolution* (Washington, D.C.: Government Printing Office, 1906), 294, 415. The *Flora* was one of 104 ships granted a letter of marque in 1779; by 1781, when Donaldson shipped out on the *Pilgrim*, that number had risen to 134. See *PA*, series 5, vol. 1 (Harrisburg, Pa., 1906), 614–26.

60. The lists of canvassers and contributors can be consulted in the Esther De Berdt Reed/Joseph Reed Papers, 1757–85, at the New-York Historical Society.

61. Anna Rawle to Rebecca Shoemaker, as quoted in Mary Beth Norton, *Liberty's Daughters: The Revolutionary Experience of American Women, 1750–1800*, (Ithaca, N.Y.: Cornell University Press, 1996) 180.

62. Ibid.

63. For more on Reed's effort, see Gregory Duffy and Kathryn Kish Sklar, "How Did the Ladies Association of Philadelphia Shape New Forms of Women's Activism during the American Revolution, 1780–1781," in Kathryn Kish Sklar and Thomas Dublin, eds., *Women and Social Movements in the United States, 1600–2000*, accessed through the University of Massachusetts, Amherst, 23 September 2009.

64. If Betsy continued to ply her trade on her own, she was perhaps aided in part by a legal identity created for just such circumstances, as *feme sole* trader. Originally a London legal custom, *feme sole* status had been codified by Pennsylvania in 1718 and was specifically designed to assist mariners' wives such as Betsy Ashburn. In an era when women's legal identities were "covered" at the time of their marriage by their husbands—preventing married women from entering into binding contracts or from exercising control over property—the act enabled creditors to, "with certainty and safety, transact business with a married woman." A *feme sole trader*, in other words, was a married woman who had secured formal permission to conduct business on her own, with her husband's consent but without his help. See Marylynn Salmon, *Women and the Law of Property in Early America* (Chapel Hill: University of North Carolina Press, 1986); Patricia A. Cleary, "'She Merchants' of Colonial America: Women and Commerce on the Eve of the Revolution" (Ph.D. dissertation, Northwestern University, 1989) 83, 106–8; and *The charters and acts of Assembly of the province of Pennsylvania* (Philadelphia, 1762).

65. See Force, "Betsy Ross, Upholsterer and Flag-Maker," 26. The Effective Supply Tax for 1780 assessed Ashburn's value at £6,000, and for the following year at just £45. But the former figure represents wildly depreciated paper currency, corrected in the latter year; the drop is not wholly or necessarily attributable to some dramatic change in material circumstances.

## 14. PRIVATEER TO PRISONER

1. Some narratives state that Ashburn shipped out in October, but according to LOC, *Naval Records of the American Revolution* (Washington, D.C.: Government Printing Office, 1906), 410, Ashburn was mate on the *Patty*'s voyage of 7 December 1780; see also Charles Eugene Claghorn, *Naval Officers of the American Revolution: A Concise Biographical Dictionary* (Metuchan, N.J.: Scarecrow Press, 1988), 8; *PA*, series 5, vol. 1 (Harrisburg, Pa., 1906), 631.

2. Marion J. and Jack Kaminkow, *Mariners of the American Revolution* (Baltimore: Magna Carta Books, 1967), 7, 228; and Claghorn, *Naval Officers of the American Revolution*, 8.

3. Sheldon Samuel Cohen, *Yankee Sailors in British Gaols: Prisoners of War at Forton and Mill, 1777–1783* (Newark: University of Delaware Press, 1995), 51.

4. Francis D. Cogliano, *American Maritime Prisoners in the Revolution: The Captivity of William Russell* (Annapolis, Md.: Naval Institute Press, 2001), 41.

5. Cohen, *Yankee Sailors in British Gaols*, 166.

**6.** "List of Americans Committed to Old Mill Prison," *New England Historical and Genealogical Register* 19, no. 3 (1865): 209.

**7.** The above description of the hearing is taken from Cogliano, *American Maritime Prisoners*.

**8.** This and below are drawn from Cohen, *Yankee Sailors in British Gaols*, 33–39.

**9.** This and the following draw on Cogliano, *American Maritime Prisoners*, 44.

**10.** Timothy Connor, "A Yankee Privateersman in Prison in England, 1777–1779," *New England Historical and Genealogical Register* 30 (1877): 286; quoted in Francis D. Cogliano, "National Identity among American Prisoners in Britain during the American Revolution," *Journal of American Studies* 32, no. 1 (April 1998), 24.

**11.** Charles Herbert, ed., *A Relic of the Revolution, Containing a Full and Particular Account of the Sufferings and Privations of All the American Prisoners Captured on the High Seas and Carried into Plymouth, England, During the Revolution . . .* (Boston, 1847), June 6. Diaries of onetime prisoners include: Connor, "Yankee Privateersman"; Samuel Cutler, "Prison Ships and the 'Old Mill Prison,' Plymouth, England, 1777," *New England Historical and Genealogical Register* 32 (1878): 42–44, 184–88, 305–8, 395–98; Jonathan Haskins, "A Revolutionary Prison Diary: The Journal of Dr. Jonathan Haskins," Marion S. Coan, ed., *New England Quarterly* 17, no. 2 (1944): 290–309, 424–42; George Thompson, "Diary of George Thompson of Newburyport, Kept at Forton Prison, England, 1777–1781," *Essex Institute Historical Collections* 76 (1940): 221–42; William Widger, "Diary of William Widger of Marblehead, Kept at Mill Prison, England, 1781," *Essex Institute Historical Collections* 73 (1937): 311–47 and 74 (1938): 22–48, 142–58. See also John K. Alexander, "'American Privateersmen in the Mill Prison During 1777–1782': An Evaluation," *Essex Institute Historical Collections* 102 (1966): 322–26; and John K. Alexander, "Jonathan Haskins' Mill Prison 'Diary': Can It Be Accepted at Face Value?" *New England Quarterly* 40, no. 4 (1967): 561–64. Memoirs published long after the war was over include: Joshua Barney, *A Biographical Memoir of Commodore Joshua Barney*, Mary Barney, ed. (Boston, 1832); Nathaniel Fanning, *The Life of Commodore John Paul Jones; and Memoirs of Captain Nathaniel Fanning* (Lexington, Ky., 1826); and Andrew Sherburne, *Memoirs of Andrew Sherburne: A Pensioner of the Navy of the Revolution* (Providence, R.I., 1831).

**12.** Herbert, 31 August 1777, *Relic of the Revolution*, 59.

**13.** Ibid., 11 June 1777, 45.

**14.** *British Annual Register*, 1781, 152, as quoted in Danske Dandridge, *American Prisoners of the Revolution*, 158.

**15.** Ibid.

**16.** Russell, "Journal," 4:14–15, as quoted in Cogliano, "We All Hoisted the American Flag," 37.

**17.** Herbert, *Relic of the Revolution*, 10.

**18.** Cogliano, *American Maritime Prisoners*, 95.

**19.** As quoted in ibid., 96.

**20.** Ibid., 84.

**21.** For a stunning example of these flags, see the "prisoner's flag" illustrated in Boleslaw and Marie-Louise D'Otrange Mastai, *The Stars and the Stripes* (New York: Knopf, 1973), 62.

**22.** *Extracts from the diary of Jacob Hiltzheimer of Philadelphia, 1765–1798*, (Philadelphia, 1893) 3 November 1781.

**23.** *PG*, 16 October 1782.

**24.** See the Thomas Morgan ledger, 1771–1803, HSP.

25. James Duffin, "Transcription of the 1909 Affidavit of Susan Jacobs (McCord) Turner," BRH.

26. Timmons, *Betsy Ross*, 112.

27. Griscom's assets appear to have declined in the years following the occupation and preceding the peace treaty. To take just one measure, the city's Effective Supply Tax List listed his valuation at £38,000 in 1780 (a year when the median in Mulberry Ward West was closer to £8,000; Griscom was among the top 10 percent of the ward's residents in that year), £780 in 1781 and a mere £60 in 1782. Adjusting for depreciation tempers this picture—values were in wild flux during the war—suggesting that Griscom's fortunes fell at a rate comparable to many of his neighbors'. But if it is true that the Griscom lumberyard was destroyed by fire, perhaps it happened in these years. See Debra Jean Force, "Betsy Ross, Upholsterer and Flag-Maker: A Proposal to Furnish Her Home" (unpublished report, Betsy Ross Foundation, 1976), 4.

28. See EDD 11 and 18 July 1789.

29. Carpenters' Company, minutes, 1769–93, housed at the APS. Nevertheless, the company came to Griscom's aid in 1791 when its "much indisposed" colleague was in need of some financial relief; see 16 December 1791.

30. On the sale of the Griscom house to Matthew Clarkson, see Grantee-Grantor Records, book D-5, 417–19, PCA. By 1791, the house was numbered 109, with Clarkson still the occupant.

31. See Sarah Eve, journal entry for 13 November 1773, in *Extracts from the Journal of Miss Sarah Eve: Written While Living Near the City of Philadelphia in 1772–73* (Philadelphia, 1881), 34.

32. Charles Francis Jenkins, ed., *John Claypoole's Memorandum Book*, PMHB 16 (1892): 179.

33. Cogliano, *American Maritime Prisoners*, 69.

34. Duffin, "Transcription of the 1909 Affidavit of Susan Jacobs (McCord) Turner," BRH. Sarah McCord was Betsy's niece, Sarah Donaldson's daughter. She had married James Lownes 26 May 1797 and David McCord 2 July 1807.

35. Donaldson's name does not appear among those compiled in the "List of Americans Committed to Old Mill Prison," *New England Historical and Genealogical Register* 19, no. 3 (1865): 209. On the celebration, see Cogliano, "We All Hoisted the American Flag," 27, and Cohen, *Yankee Sailors*, 166, 251.

36. The family had also mourned by this time mariner Ephraim Doane; see *PG*, 7 July 1780.

37. Jenkins, ed., *John Claypoole's Memorandum Book*, 188.

38. Forton Prison, 1 August 1778, in George Gibson Carey, *A Sailor's Songbag: An American Rebel in an English Prison, 1777–1779* (Amherst: University of Massachusetts Press, 1976), 68.

## 15. THIRD TIME'S A CHARM

1. Rebecca Iron Graff, *Genealogy of the Claypoole Family in Philadelphia* (Philadelphia, 1893), 68.

2. Robert Wells, "Quaker Marriage Patterns in a Colonial Perspective," *William and Mary Quarterly*, 3rd series, 29, no. 3 (1972): 415–42, 424–25.

3. On Myers-Briggs personality types, see Rowan Bayne, *The Myers-Briggs Type Indicator* (Cheltenham, U.K.: Chapman & Hill, 1997).

4. Andrew Brunk, "The Claypoole Family Joiners of Philadelphia: Their Legacy and the Context of Their Work," in Luke Beckerdite, ed, *American Furniture*, (Hanover, N.H.: University Press of New England for the Chipstone Foundation, 2000), 147–73.

5. Ibid., 149.

6. Andrew Griscom, inventory, 1694, file 102, PCA.

7. Nelson Waite Rightmyer, *The Anglican Church in Delaware* (Philadelphia: Church Historical Society, 1947), 7.

8. Edwin Parry asserts that John's sisters Susannah, Martha and Clarissa were "old school friends" of Elizabeth's (see Parry, *Betsy Ross: Quaker Rebel* [Philadelphia: John C. Winston, 1930], 76), but this seems unlikely, in part because the children seem unlikely to have attended Quaker schools, and also because the Claypooles lived in Burlington, New Jersey, and Mount Holly, New Jersey, for several years while the children were growing up. But they must have known many people in common.

9. Brunk, "The Claypoole Family Joiners," 151.

10. For information from the January 2006 Sotheby's auction, see http://www.art fact.com.

11. James Claypoole's Kent County tanyard is discussed in Christine Daniels, "From Father to Son," in Howard B. Rock et al., eds., *American Artisans: Crafting Social Identity, 1750–1850* (Baltimore: Johns Hopkins University Press, 1995), 10, 15.

12. "Names of Persons who took the Oath of Allegiance . . . , " *PA*, series 2, vol. 3 (Harrisburg, Pa., 1875), 9.

13. "Return of Field Officers of the Philadelphia Artillery, 25 August 1777," *PA*, series 2, vol. 13 (Harrisburg, Pa., 1887), 594, lists Claypoole as a second lieutenant of the Fourth Company Artillery Battalion. See also *PA*, series 6, vol. 1 (Harrisburg, Pa., 1906), 208, 519, 527, and 573.

14. Graff, *Genealogy of the Claypoole Family*, 69; and Parry, *Betsy Ross: Quaker Rebel*, 171.

15. "Return of Field Officers of the Philadelphia Artillery, 25 August 1777" indicates that the Fourth Company Artillery Battalion was stationed to protect the Delaware.

16. Graff, *Genealogy of the Claypoole Family*, 69.

17. See http://valleyforgemusterroll.org/overview.htm, accessed 29 June 2009.

18. *To the Inhabitants of Pennsylvania in General, and Particularly Those of the City and Neighborhood of Philadelphia* (Philadelphia, 1779), LCP, as quoted in Gary B. Nash, "Artisans and Politics in Eighteenth-Century Philadelphia," in Ian B. Quimby, ed., *The Craftsman in Early America* (New York: W. W. Norton, 1984), 67.

19. As quoted in Jonathan W. Barry, "The Story of Old Glory," in *The Builder*, October 1916.

20. The location of the certificate is no longer known, but a photograph of it served as the frontispiece of *The Builder* in August 1916.

21. This discussion of Claypoole's travels and imprisonment is all drawn from his memorandum book as published in the *PMHB* 16, no. 2 (1892): 178–90.

22. On Claypoole's "great esteem" for Ashburn, see "memorandum" to the fly leaf in the family Bible, 3 January 1897, BRH.

23. My thanks to Gary Nash for identifying this classic tune.

24. Michael Hillegas to Benjamin Franklin, 29 April 1782. See also Catherine M. Prelinger, "Benjamin Franklin and the American Prisoners of War in England during the American Revolution," *William and Mary Quarterly*, 3rd series, 32, no. 2 (1975):

261–94. Genealogical sources contain errors as to the date of William Claypoole's death. Some sources give 1799 as the year of his death, and others 1779. Somewhere, a transcription error has been made and repeated. The Claypoole family Bible notes the 1779 date (see Lewis D. Cook, "Family Records from the Bible of 'Betsy Ross' of Philadelphia," *Genealogies of Pennsylvania Families from the Pennsylvania Genealogical Magazine*, vol. 3 [Baltimore: Genealogical Publishing, 1982], 905); given that and Hillegas's letter, this study takes 1779 as correct.

25. William Hodgson to Benjamin Franklin, 13 July 1782, as quoted in Prelinger, "Benjamin Franklin and the American Prisoners of War," 291 n. 114.

26. *Independent Gazetteer*, 17 August 1782.

27. See *PP*, 11 April 1782, and John A. McManemin, *Captains of the State Navies During the American Revolution* (Ho-Ho-Kus, N.J.: Ho-Ho-Kus Publishing, 1984), 260. On Claypoole's voyage, see his memorandum book, 16 August 1782.

28. Cohen, *Yankee Sailors in British Gaols*, 185–86.

29. Court of Admiralty Records, 17 September 1782, coll.1389, HSP.

30. Ibid., 16 and 19 October 1782. See also *Freeman's Journal*, 21 August 1782, and *PP*, 21 September 1782.

31. *PG*, 14 May 1783.

32. Receipt, Isaac Howell to John Claypoole, 19 September 1786, BRH.

33. See William MacPherson Hornor Jr., *Blue Book: Philadelphia Furniture* (Washington, D.C.: Highland House, 1935 [1977]); "Philadelphia Craftsmen—1783: Comparative Positions of the More Important Cabinet- and Chair-Makers," 317; and also Patricia Chapin O'Donnell, "The Upholsterer in Philadelphia, 1760–1810" (M.A. thesis, University of Delaware, 1980), 14, 18.

34. O'Donnell, "The Upholsterer in Philadelphia," 17, 15.

35. James Claypoole's Chestertown tanyard is discussed in Christine Daniels, "From Father to Son," in Rock et al., eds., *American Artisans*, 10, 15.

36. See http://dsc.discovery.com/fansites/dirtyjobs/dirtyjobs.html.

37. The discussion of tanning is drawn from Peter C. Welsh, *Tanning in the United States to 1850* (Washington, D.C.: Smithsonian Institution Press, 1964); and Marion Kite and Roy Thomson, *Conservation of Leather and Related Materials* (Burlington, Mass.: Elsevier, 2006).

38. *PG*, 22 November 1750, 28 May 1747, 25 December 1750.

39. See, e.g., 16 June 1742, 28 February 1798; *Pennsylvania Chronicle*, 6 March 1769; and *PP*, 17 April 1784.

40. Alfred Coxe Prime, *Arts and Crafts in Philadelphia, Maryland and South Carolina*, series 1 (Philadelphia: Walpole Society, 1929); see also Anne Castrodale Golovin, "Daniel Trotter: Eighteenth-Century Philadelphia Cabinetmaker," *Winterthur Portfolio* 6 (1970): 151–84.

41. See "Family Record of Marriage and Births of Children," Claypoole family Bible, BRH. In summer 1786, John had a local carpenter build a "dividing pole," perhaps an effort to create some additional space or privacy; see David Evans Daybooks, 1774–1812, HSP.

42. Hornor, *Blue Book*, 322. In 1786, of six upholsterers identified by Hornor, Claypoole was assessed far and away more occupational tax than any competitor. For comparisons with other artisans, see Golovin, "Daniel Trotter," 155; and Nancy A. Goyne, "Francis Trumble of Philadelphia: Windsor Chair and Cabinetmaker," *Winterthur Portfolio* 1 (1964): 240–41. On carriages and the population of Philadelphia in 1786, see

Richard E. Powell Jr., "Coachmaking in Philadelphia: George and William Hunter's Factory of Early Federal Period," *Winterthur Portfolio* 28, no. 4 (1993): 249; and John Bach McMaster, *A History of the People of the United States*, vol. 1 (New York, 1900), 64.

## 16. FOR LORD AND EMPIRE

**1.** The membership list of 2 February 1785 includes thirty-two men and thirty-four women, including John and Elizabeth Claypoole. See Membership Book, Religious Society of Free Quakers, APS.

**2.** References to relatives do appear occasionally in the Religious Society of Free Quakers, Financial Records: Receipt Book, 1781–1839, APS, but they do not appear to have joined formally in these years.

**3.** Edwin S. Parry, *Betsy Ross: Quaker Rebel* (Philadelphia: John C. Winston, 1930), 228; and Henry Simpson, *Lives of Eminent Philadelphians* (Philadelphia, 1859), 942.

**4.** Kenneth Alan Radbill, "Socioeconomic Background of Nonpacifist Quakers" (Ph.D. dissertation, University of Arizona, 1971), 34.

**5.** Susan Garfinkel, "This Separation Forced Upon Us: Philadelphia's Free Quakers and the Political Uses of Print," paper presented at "The Atlantic World of Print in the Age of Franklin," Philadelphia, September 2006.

**6.** For Wetherill's disownment, see Charles Wetherill, *History of the Religious Society of Friends Called by Some the Free Quakers, in the City of Philadelphia* (Philadelphia, 1894), 16. This discussion of Quakers, Free Quakers and disownment is also informed by Jack D. Marietta, *The Reformation of American Quakerism*, and Radbill, "Socioeconomic Background of Nonpacifist Quakers" (Philadelphia: University of Pennsylvania Press, 1984).

**7.** Many years later he married—interestingly enough—another woman named Elizabeth Claypoole: Elizabeth Claypoole Copper, the widowed sister of John's cousin, the printer David Claypoole. The daughter of James Claypoole and Mary Chambers, this Elizabeth was born in 1751 and had married Captain Norris Copper in 1774.

**8.** Rebecca Iron Graff, *Genealogy of the Claypoole Family in Philadelphia* (Philadelphia, 1893), 160.

**9.** Wetherill, *Religious Society of Friends*, 20. Many books today include Darragh's story; see, e.g., Melissa Lukeman Bohrer, *Glory, Passion, and Principle: The Story of Eight Remarkable Women at the Core of the American Revolution* (New York: Simon and Schuster, 2003); and Carol Berkin, *Revolutionary Mothers: Women in the Struggle for America's Independence* (New York: Knopf, 2005).

**10.** Henry Darrach, "Lydia Darragh, of the Revolution," *PMHB* 23, no. 1 (1899): 89.

**11.** Ibid.

**12.** See Wetherill, *Religious Society of Friends*, 47–49.

**13.** Ibid.

**14.** Broadside, 24 April 1781, in Joseph Scattergood album, An Account of the Free Quakers, 1781–1885, FHL.

**15.** Ibid.

**16.** Ibid.

**17.** Wetherill, *Religious Society of Friends*, Appendix 3.

**18.** Marietta, *Reformation of American Quakerism*, 246–48.

**19.** James Pemberton, 1 and 7 September 1782, Joseph Scattergood album, FHL.

20. Radbill, "Socioeconomic Background of Nonpacifist Quakers," 62, 65, 100; and Marietta, *Reformation of American Quakerism*, 246–48.

21. James Pemberton to John Pemberton, 20 September 1782, 10 November 1782, Pemberton Papers, 37:36–37, 92, in Marietta, *Reformation of American Quakerism*, 246–48.

22. Marietta, *Reformation of American Quakerism*, 248.

23. Scattergood album, FHL.

24. Charles E. Peterson, "Notes on the Free Quaker Meeting House" (typescript, 1966), I-B-1–3, HSP. Plans survive in the Seymour Adelman Collection, HSP.

25. Christopher Marshall diary, 29 July 1783, HSP.

26. Ibid., 4 October 1783.

27. Peterson, "Notes on the Free Quaker Meeting House," I-B-1.

28. Ibid.

29. Peterson, "Notes on the Free Quaker Meeting House," I-D-2.

30. Ibid.

31. Bernard L. Herman, "Introduction" to "Quakers and Producers," in Emma Jones Lapsansky and Anne Verplanck, *Quaker Aesthetics: Reflections on a Quaker Ethic in American Design and Consumption* (Philadelphia: University of Pennsylvania Press, 2003), 150.

32. Minutes, 5 July 1784, Religious Society of Free Quakers, APS; Christopher Marshall, diary, 6 June 1784.

33. Peterson, "Notes on the Free Quaker Meeting House," I-E-1 and 2; and minutes of 17 June 1784, loose pages, 1781–86, Religious Society of Free Quakers, box 1, folder 3, APS.

34. Rough minutes at 11 November 1790 and 6 December 1798, loose pages, 1789–1804, Religious Society of Free Quakers, box 1, folder 4, APS. None of the extant records indicate the presence of a separate women's meeting within the Free Quaker community.

35. On the School, see *PP*, 12 August 1788 and 10 December 1788. On the rentals, see Peterson, "Notes on the Free Quaker Meeting House," I-G-1.

36. Sharon V. Salinger, *Taverns and Drinking in Early America* (Baltimore: Johns Hopkins University Press, 2002), 116. For Rebecca Griscom's censure, see PMMND 26 April 1785.

37. The above discussion of drunkenness and Quaker culture is drawn from Marietta, *Reformation of American Quakerism*, 19–21 and 105–10; the quotation from the Abington meeting appears on p. 19.

38. Mark Edward Lender and James Kirby Martin, *Drinking in America: A History* (New York: Simon and Schuster, 1987), 35; Barry Levy, *Quakers and the American Family* (New York: Oxford University Press, 1992), 253.

39. By 7 March 1785, an excerpt appeared in the (Hartford, Connecticut) *American Mercury*; and see William L. White, *Slaying the Dragon: The History of Addiction Treatment and Recovery in America* (Bloomington, Ill.: Chestnut Health Systems, 1998), 1–4.

40. On resonances between Rush and contemporary attitudes toward alcohol abuse, see White, *Slaying the Dragon*, 3.

41. PMMMND, 26 April 1785.

42. Ibid., 26 May 1785.

43. Ibid., 26 April 1785.

44. Wilbur C. Plummer, "Consumer Credit in Colonial Philadelphia," *PMHB* 66, no. 4 (1942): 398.

45. George W. Morgan to Rebecca Pile, 17 August 1799, Pile Family Papers, HSP.

46. George W. Morgan to Rebecca Pile, 28 April 1800, Pile Family Papers, HSP.

47. See PMMND 24 January, 28 March and 23 May 1786.

48. PMMMND, 1 November 1785, 24 January 1786.

49. Ibid., 22 November 1785.

50. Ibid., 21 February 1786.

51. Ibid., 28 March, 25 April, 23 May, and 27 June 1786. George and Kitty nurtured some interest in the Episcopal Church in Burlington; at least in 1786, when donations were sought to attract a clergyman to a position at St. Mary's, the Griscoms contributed to the effort. In time, he would bring his family back to the city, reuniting Betsy not only with her brother and sister-in-law, but with her nephew George Jr. and nieces Catherine and Rebecca. George had also followed family tradition by taking up a craft; by 1791, he was a silversmith working on Wood Street in the Northern Liberties. See Carol Williams to Robert Yarrington, 14 September 1977, correspondence in the Griscom Family: Miscellaneous file of the GCHS; and Maurice Brix, *Philadelphia Silversmiths and Allied Artificers from 1682 to 1850* (Philadelphia: privately printed, 1920).

52. *Universal or Columbian Magazine* 5, no. 5 (1790): 287–88.

53. As quoted in Gordon S. Wood in *The Americanization of Benjamin Franklin* (New York: Penguin, 2004), 202.

54. See PMMMND, 5 April 1785, 24 April 1787, 26 February 1788, 9 November 1790; see also David Haugaard, "Abel James," 769–70.

55. May 1789 letter from Religious Society of Free Quakers in Philadelphia to monthly meeting of Religious Society of Free Quakers in Dartmouth, box 7, APS.

56. Minutes: loose pages, 1781–86, Religious Society of Free Quakers, box 1, folder 1, APS.

57. My thanks to HPI's Bill Robling for bringing this point to my attention and suggesting that the Free Quakers were taking a "bit more ecumenical approach" than their counterparts elsewhere in the Society of Friends. Robling to author, 3 July 2008.

## 17. BROTHERLY LOVE

1. On the history of voluntarism in this period, see Bruce Dorsey, *Reforming Men and Women: Gender in the Antebellum City* (Ithaca, N.Y.: Cornell University Press, 2002); Anne M. Boylan, *The Origins of Women's Activism: New York and Boston, 1797–1840* (Chapel Hill: University of North Carolina Press, 2002); and Albrecht Koschnik, *"Let a Common Interest Bind Us Together": Associations, Partisanship, and Culture in Philadelphia, 1775–1840* (Charlottesville: University of Virginia Press, 2007).

2. Receipt, 1789, the Grand Lodge of Free and Accepted Masons of Pennsylvania, archives, the Masonic Library and Museum of Pennsylvania.

3. Alexander H. Morgan, *History of Montgomery Lodge, No. 19* (Lancaster, Pa., 1887). Mysteriously, John would resign from the Masonic Lodge in February 1797. What had happened to cause him to take this step? Further research into the lodge may reveal an interesting tale. See *By-Laws of Montgomery Lodge* (Philadelphia: Lyon and Armor, 1926), 203.

4. As quoted in Harrold C. Shiffler, "Religious Opposition to the Eighteenth Century Philadelphia Stage," *Educational Theatre Journal* 14, no. 3 (1962): 215–23. The follow-

ing paragraphs are drawn from Shiffler's essay as well as William S. Dye, "Pennsylvania *Versus* the Theatre," *PMHB* 55, no. 14 (1931): 333–72; and Heather Shaw Nathans, "Forging a Powerful Engine: Building Theaters and Elites in Post-Revolutionary Boston and Philadelphia," *Pennsylvania History* 66, no. 5 (1999): 113–43. See also Jared Brown, *The Theatre in America During the Revolution* (Cambridge: Cambridge University Press, 1995).

5. *PG*, 22 January 1767.

6. See *Minutes of the first session of the tenth General Assembly* (Philadelphia, 1785–1786), 91.

7. The notice appeared in multiple papers, including the 2 January 1786 *New-York Packet* and the 12 January 1786 *Independent Chronicle and Universal Advertiser* (Boston).

8. *PP*, 16 February 1789.

9. Pennsylvania Abolition Society, general meeting minutes, 1784–1824, series 1, reel 1, HSP.

10. Both stories are recounted in Theodore W. Bean, *History of Montgomery County* (Philadelphia, 1884), 680. See also Donna McDaniel and Vanessa Julye, *Fit for Freedom, Not for Friendship: Quakers, African Americans, and the Myth of Racial Justice* (Philadelphia: Quaker Press, 2009), 22–24. On Betsy's family, Giles Knight, for instance, had been a slaveholder at least as early as 1774, when he sold a twenty-eight-year-old man who had been "brought up to Plantation work all his time." See *PG*, 26 January 1774. (Knight also had bound white servants; in September 1770, Knight posted a reward for Edward Marshall, a seventeen-year-old Irish servant who "speaks a good deal on the brogue." See *PG*, 6 September 1770.) Fourteen years later, Knight agreed to free an enslaved man named Robert Bayley. Bayley was not trying to leave the Knight household, but simply to alter his status there and secure his liberty: after receiving his freedom, Bayley indentured himself to Knight for another four and a half years. Pennsylvania Abolition Society Manumission Records, book B (1788–95), 139, reel 20; and Indentures, book C (1758–95), 71, HSP.

11. Gary B. Nash and Jean R. Soderlund, *Freedom by Degrees: Emancipation in Pennsylvania and Its Aftermath* (New York: Oxford University Press, 1991), 80.

12. Ibid., 115; and McDaniel and Julye, *Fit for Freedom*, 29.

13. Pennsylvania Abolition Society, general meeting minutes, 1784–1824, series 1, reel 1, HSP.

14. *The Constitution of the Pennsylvania Society, for Promoting the Abolition of Slavery, and the Relief of Free Negroes, Unlawfully Held in Bondage. Begun in the year 1774, and enlarged on the twenty-third of April, 1787. To which are added, the acts of the General Assembly of Pennsylvania, for the gradual abolition of slavery* (Philadelphia, 1787).

15. Pennsylvania Abolition Society, General Committee minutes, 26 July 1787.

16. Ibid.

17. Ibid., 10 August 1787.

18. Ibid., 23 August 1787.

19. Ibid., 6 September 1787.

20. Ibid., 13 September 1787.

21. Ibid., 25 October 1787.

22. Ibid., 29 November 1787. Claypoole seems to have rotated off Active Committee duty sometime in spring 1788, but his service to the Society had not concluded: in

September, Claypoole was also appointed to a committee charged with collecting subscriptions to Clarkson's essay on the slave trade, which Francis Bailey would be reprinting. He also helped the Society obtain a translation of Jacques Pierre Brissot de Warville's oration before the nascent Société des Amis des Noirs (the Society of the Friends of the Blacks) in Paris, also to be printed by Bailey. Soon Claypoole was promoting the work, *An essay on the impolicy of the African slave trade. In two parts. By the Rev. T. Clarkson, M.A. To which is added, an oration, upon the necessity of establishing at Paris, a society to promote the abolition of the trade and slavery of the Negroes. By J.P. Brissot de Warville* (Philadelphia, 1788).

23. Peter P. Jonitis and Elizabeth F. Jonitis, "Members of the Prison Society: Biographical Vignettes" (typescript, 1982), QCHC. See also Negley K. Teeters, *They Were in Prison: A History of the Pennsylvania Prison Society, 1787–1937* (Philadelphia: John C. Winston Company, 1937).

24. See Philadelphia Society for Alleviating the Miseries of Public Prisons, minutes, 12 October 1789, HSP.

25. See Michael Meranze, *Laboratories of Virtue: Punishment, Revolution and Authority in Philadelphia, 1760–1835* (Chapel Hill: University of North Carolina Press, 1996), 95; Peter Okun, *Crime and the Nation: Prison Reform and Popular Fiction in Philadelphia* (New York: Routledge, 2002), xii.

26. Samuel Hazard, *Hazard's Register of Pennsylvania* (Philadelphia, 1828), 287.

27. Dorsey, *Reforming Men and Women*, 22.

28. Philadelphia Society for Alleviating the Miseries of Public Prisons, minutes, 16 August 1787, HSP.

29. Philadelphia Society for Alleviating the Miseries of Public Prisons, Representation to the Supreme Executive Council, minutes, 12 January 1789, HSP.

30. Philadelphia Society for Alleviating the Miseries of Public Prisons, minutes, 14 January 1788, HSP.

31. Ibid., 29 January 1788, HSP.

32. Ibid., July–December 1787, box 1, folder 2, HSP.

33. "List of Members in Arrears" (1788), reel 17; see also "List of Members in Arrearages to the Pennsylvania Abolition Society" (1789), reel 18, Pennsylvania Abolition Society, HSP.

34. John Aiken, *A view of the life, travels, and philanthropic labors of the late John Howard, Esquire L.L.D. F.R.S.* (Philadelphia, 1794).

35. *Plan of the Philadelphia Dispensary for the Medical Relief of the Poor* (Philadelphia, 1787).

36. *PP*, 26 February 1787.

37. John Fanning Watson, *Annals of Philadelphia* (Philadelphia, 1857), vol. 1, 205.

38. See also *PP*, 10 March 1787.

39. *PEP*, 1 July 1777; and *Independent Gazetteer*, 22 March 1783, as cited in Patricia Chapin O'Donnell, "The Upholsterer in Philadelphia 1760–1810" (M.A. thesis, University of Delaware, 1980), 74.

40. *Federal Gazette*, 14 July 1798.

41. John Davis inventory, W246/1793. My thanks to David Conradsen for sharing his transcription of the document as well as much more information on Philadelphia upholsterers with me.

42. Catharine Richardson did at least some of the "women's work" in Davis's shop; thanks again to David Conradson, who noted Richardson's work.

**43.** *PG*, 26 February 1787; *PP*, 10 March 1787.

**44.** See Bernard L. Herman, *Town House: Architecture and Material Life in the Early American City, 1780–1830* (Chapel Hill: University of North Carolina Press, 2005); and Wendy Gamber, *The Boardinghouse in Nineteenth-Century America* (Baltimore: Johns Hopkins University Press, 2007).

**45.** See, e.g., *Independent Gazetteer*, 6 January and 25 May 1787; *Pennsylvania Herald and General Advertiser*, 5 September 1787; and *Pennsylvania Mercury*, 28 September 1787.

**46.** *PP*, 24 May 1788.

**47.** Watson, *Annals of Philadelphia*, vol. 1 (Philadelphia, 1855), 476; and William B. Timmons, *Betsy Ross: The Griscom Legacy* (Salem, N.J.: Salem County Cultural & Heritage Commission, 1983), 154. The house seems to have stayed in the family; some evidence suggests it was once owned by Abel James, and later by a "D. Griscom."

## 18. FEVER

**1.** William B. Timmons, *Betsy Ross: The Griscom Legacy* (Salem, N.J.: Salem County Cultural & Heritage Commission, 1983), 115. The Griscoms were located at 54 Vine Street in 1791; see Clement Biddle, *Philadelphia Directory* (Philadelphia, 1791).

**2.** Samuel Griscom, estate inventory, 1793, JDC, no. 75x110.1.

**3.** Dell Upton, *Another City: Urban Life and Urban Spaces in the New American Republic* (New Haven, Conn.: Yale University Press, 2008), 22.

**4.** On transformations in the building trades in these years, see Donna J. Rilling, *Making Houses, Crafting Capitalism: Builders in Philadelphia, 1790–1850* (Philadelphia: University of Pennsylvania Press, 2000); and Roger William Moss Jr., "Master Builders: A History of the Colonial Philadelphia Buildings Trades" (Ph.D. dissertation, University of Delaware, 1972), esp. 183–84.

**5.** Moss makes this point in "Master Builders," 185. See also "An Address of the Journeymen Carpenters," *American Daily Advertiser*, 11 May 1791, in John R. Commons et al., *A Documentary History of American Industrial Society* (Cleveland, 1910), 5: 81–84. For the larger story of these transformations, see Bruce Laurie, *Artisans into Workers: Labor in Nineteenth-Century America* (Champaign: University of Illinois Press, 1997); and *Working People of Philadelphia, 1800–1850* (Philadelphia: Temple University Press, 1980).

**6.** John Claypoole, upholsterer, is listed at 80 South Second Street in Biddle, *Philadelphia Directory* (Philadelphia, 1791).

**7.** *Independent Gazetteer*, 25 August 1788. See also John Levering, *Levering Family History and Genealogy* (Indianapolis, 1897), 140.

**8.** *Independent Gazetteer*, 25 August 1788.

**9.** On Griffith Levering's interment, see Financial Records: Treasurer's Book, 1786–1846, Religious Society of Free Quakers, box 5, APS. In November 1805, Hannah received a charitable donation intended for the hands of A. Tripp, suggesting that she was in the congregation's orbit, if not a formal member. See Financial Records: Treasurer's Accounts, Religious Society of Free Quakers, box 5, APS. On Levering's Baptist affiliation, see *An address from the Baptist Church, in Philadelphia, to their sister churches of the same denomination, throughout the confederated states of North America. Drawn up by a committee of the church, appointed for said purpose* (Philadelphia, 1781), 10, For the headstone in the burying ground on the west side of Fifth Street below Locust, see "Inscriptions on the Tombstones in the Free Quakers' Graveyard," *Publications of the Genealogical Society of Pennsylvania* 3, no. 2 (1907): 135–38.

**10.** *PP*, 4 April 1789. The documents pertaining to the vendue sale are found with Griffith Levering's probate records, Philadelphia Registry of Wills, file 60, PCA.

**11.** Two adjoining houses on Green Street in the Northern Liberties were sold, one at the instruction of the shipwright John Drinker, who had gone in on the land and buildings together with Levering, but had never received proper title. *PP* and *Daily Advertiser*, 30 April 1790.

**12.** Hannah Levering appears as a grocer at 334 North Front Street in the 1791 and 1794 city directories; see Biddle, *Philadelphia Directory*; James Hardie, *Philadelphia Directory and Register* (Philadelphia, 1794).

**13.** *PG*, 25 November 1789. The property was located on the east side of Front Street between Vine and Callowhill streets in the Northern Liberties. The first federal census of 1790, dated 2 August 1790, finds Griscom still living alone in the Northern Liberties.

**14.** William Rakestraw, will, 26 October 1772, PCA. Rakestraw may have helped Rebecca Griscom purchase the property; at least his will, in addition to describing her land as adjacent to his, also forgives her debt of approximately £46.The will of her father makes no specific reference to property in Philadelphia but does name Rebecca his sole beneficiary of any assets that remain after his debts were settled; see the will of Tobias Griscom, 29 March 1751, Kent County Probate Records, Delaware State Archives.

**15.** Philadelphia Northern District Women's Monthly Meeting, minutes, 1791–96, 25 March 1794, 155; and PMMM, 1789–95, 1 April 1794, 313.

**16.** 1 December 1792, Guardians of the Poor, Daily Occurrences, March 1792–June 1793, PCA.

**17.** Overseers of the Poor, RG35.5, ledger of indentures, 1751–87, Sarah Donaldson/Everard Bolton, 15 July 1790, PCA.

**18.** Philadelphia: Water Street, East Side, First Census of the United States, 1790, NARA.

**19.** John Claypoole to George Washington, 4 February 1790, Applications, series 7, George Washington Papers, LOC.

**20.** As quoted in Constance V. Hershey, Historic Furnishings Plan, City Tavern, INHP, 1974, 23. Though few receipts are known from Betsy's residential commissions, for a surviving record of a mattress signed by Elizabeth Claypoole in these years, see 25 August 1792 receipt book of William Wister, Wister & Ashton, & Miles & Wister, in the Wister family papers, collection 94, 56×17.3, JPC. My thanks to Jeanne Solensky for sharing this reference.

**21.** *The treasurer of the United States, accounts of payments and receipts of public monies, from the 1st of January to the 30th of September, 1792. Presented to the House of Representatives, November 6, 1792* (Philadelphia, 1793), 25.

**22.** The source of the legacy is not known; no calendar of wills in either Philadelphia or New Jersey includes a reference to such a bequest, but given the far-flung nature of Claypoole's acquaintances, the decedent could have come from almost anywhere.

**23.** See *PP* and *Daily Advertiser*, 1 April 1789.

**24.** See James Rodway, *History of British Guiana* (Georgetown, 1891). For a more contemporary history of the colony, see Johannes Postma, *The Dutch in the Atlantic Slave Trade, 1662–1805* (Cambridge: Cambridge University Press, 1990).

**25.** James Duffin, "Transcription of Notes of Interview with Jane (Claypoole)

Canby, 1792–1873," BRH; and Edmund Hogan, *Prospect of Philadelphia* (Philadelphia, 1795).

26. Duffin, "Transcription of Notes of Interview with Jane (Claypoole) Canby, 1792–1873," BRH. The 1798 Federal Direct Tax lists a value of $2,250 for the property, just below the Walnut Ward average ($2,577) and just above the median ($2,000).

27. The 1793 tax rolls show their dwelling worth £350, with personal property valued at £50. See Patricia Chapin O'Donnell, "The Upholsterer in Philadelphia, 1760–1810" (M.A. thesis, University of Delaware, 1980), table 1B. The house was owned at the time of the 1798 Federal Direct Tax by Samuel Baker; this discussion of the dwelling is developed from 1798 Federal Direct Tax, compiled and edited by Bernard L. Herman and available at "Places in Time: Historical Documentation of Place in Greater Philadelphia," accessed at http://www.brynmawr.edu/iconog/frdr.html.

28. See Stuart M. Blumin, *Emergence of the Middle Class: Social Experience in the American City, 1760–1900* (Cambridge: Cambridge University Press, 1989), 43–44; Carole Shammas provides the mean value of Philadelphia dwelling and lots in "The Space Problem in Early United States Cities," *William and Mary Quarterly*, 3rd series, 57, no. 3 (July 2000), table 6, 535. The square footage of the Claypoole House is recorded in the 1798 Federal Direct Tax, compiled and edited by Bernard L. Herman and available at "Places in Time."

29. See John Fanning Watson, *Annals of Philadelphia*, vol. 1 (1850), 445; and William J. Canby, in "The History of the Flag of the United States, a paper read before the Historical Society of Pennsylvania" (March 1870), BRH.

30. Watson, ibid.

31. Marc Micozzi, executive director of the College of Physicians of Philadelphia, offered this comparison in Gina Kolata, "When Bioterror First Struck the U.S. Capital," *New York Times*, 6 November 2001.

32. John Redman, *An Account of the Yellow Fever as It Prevailed in Philadelphia in the Autumn of 1762* (Philadelphia, 1865), 12, as quoted in Suzanne M. Schults, "Epidemics in Colonial Philadelphia from 1699–1799 and the Risk of Dying," *Early America Review* 7, no. 3 (2007), www.early america.com.

33. See J. Worth Estes, "The Yellow Fever Syndrome and Its Treatment in Philadelphia, 1793," in J. Worth Estes and Billy G. Smith, eds., *A Melancholy Scene of Devastation: The Public Response to the 1793 Yellow Fever Epidemic* (Philadelphia: LCP, 1997).

34. Benjamin Rush, "An Account of the Bilious Remitting Yellow Fever, as It Appeared in the City of Philadelphia in the Year 1793," in *Medical Inquiries and Observations*, 4 vols., 4th ed. (Philadelphia, 1815), 2:255–61.

35. Mathew Carey, *A Short Account of the Malignant Fever, Lately Prevalent in Philadelphia*, 3rd ed. (Philadelphia, 1793), 23.

36. Major Samuel Hodgson to the College of Physicians, 9 November 1793, College of Physicians of Philadelphia.

37. Rush, "An Account of the Bilious Remitting Yellow Fever," 17.

38. Estes, "The Yellow Fever Syndrome and Its Treatment," 1–18.

39. Timmons, *Betsy Ross*, 77.

40. Isaac Weld, *Travels Through the States of North America . . . During the Years 1795, 1796 and 1797*, 3–4, as quoted in Bob Arnebeck, *Destroying Angel: Benjamin Rush, Yellow Fever and the Birth of Modern Medicine* (http://www.geocities.com/bobarnebeck/ch1.html).

**41.** Benjamin Rush to Julia Rush, 29 August 1793, in Lyman H. Butterfield, ed., *Letters of Benjamin Rush*, vol. 2 (Princeton, N.J.: published for the APS by Princeton University Press, 1951), 644.

**42.** Carey, *Short Account*, 30.

**43.** Martin S. Pernick, "Politics, Parties and Pestilence: Epidemic Yellow Fever in Philadelphia and the Rise of the First Party System," *William and Mary Quarterly*, 3rd series, 29, no. 4 (1972): 559–86.

**44.** Kolata, "Bioterror"; and the Centers for Disease Control Web site discussion of "Yellow Fever—Disease and Vaccine"; R. E. Dyer, "The Role of Immunization in Wartime Advances in Medicine," *Proceedings of the American Philosophical Society* 88, no. 3 (1944): 182–88.

**45.** Peter P. Jonitis and Elizabeth W. Jonitis, "Henry Drinker," in "Members of the Prison Society: Biographical Vignettes," 2 vols. (typescript, 1982), 975A, QCHC.

**46.** *PG*, 28 August 1793.

**47.** Carey, *Short Account*, 22.

**48.** EDD, 16 September 1793.

**49.** Chris Holmes, "Benjamin Rush and the Yellow Fever," *Journal of the History of Medicine* 40, no. 3 (1966): 246–63.

**50.** Benjamin Rush to Dr. Samuel Powel Griffits, 2 October 1793, College of Physicians.

**51.** Edmund Hogan, *The Prospect of Philadelphia* (Philadelphia, 1795), 25.

**52.** PMMMND, Death Records, FHL.

**53.** Carpenters' Company, minutes, 18 January 1794, APS.

**54.** Rebecca Griscom was buried by the Northern District, 23 September 1793; PMMMND, Death Records, FHL.

**55.** Isaac Heston, 19 September 1793, as quoted in Billy G. Smith, "Disease and Community," in J. Worth Estes and Billy G. Smith, eds., *A Melancholy Scene of Devastation: The Public Response to the 1793 Philadelphia Yellow Fever Epidemic* (Canton, Mass.: Science History Publications, 1997), 147.

**56.** Religious Society of Free Quaker Meeting records, APS.

**57.** Watson, *Annals*, 1:405–7.

**58.** Carey, *Short Account*, 71.

**59.** *PG*, 27 November 1793.

**60.** James Duffin, "Transcription of 1909 Affidavit of Susan (Satterthwaite) Newport (1827–?), and Mary Satterthwaite (1824–?)," BRH.

**61.** George W. Corner, ed., *The Autobiography of Benjamin Rush* (Princeton, N.J.: Princeton University Press, 1948).

**62.** Jacquelyn C. Miller, "Passions and Politics: The Multiple Meanings of Benjamin Rush's Treatment for Yellow Fever," in Estes and Smith, *A Melancholy Scene*, 79–95.

**63.** This discussion of published debates during the fever epidemic is drawn from David Paul Nord, "Readership as Citizenship in Late Eighteenth-Century Philadelphia," in Estes and Smith, *A Melancholy Scene*, 19–44.

**64.** See Benjamin Rush to Julia Rush, 21 August 1793, *Old Family Letters Relating to Yellow Fever*, series B (Philadelphia, 1892), 3.

**65.** Holmes, *Benjamin Rush and the Yellow Fever*, 251.

**66.** Benjamin Rush to Julia Rush, 17 October 1793, in Butterfield, *Letters*, 2:716–17.

**67.** *Friends Intelligencer*, 16 September 1893. The records of George James's family are too slight to confirm that Rebecca James Griscom was a seventh child, but the notoriety would have extended powerfully to Betsy's own daughter Harriet, had she lived.

68. Susannah had remarried by the time of her death, and was then Susannah Davis. See Dorothy Davis Smith, *Davis Directory of Pennsylvania* (Baltimore: Gateway Press, 1991).

69. Family Bible Records, Mrs. C. Barclay of Wynnewood, Pa., as cited in Timmons, *Betsy Ross*, 159, 291.

70. See George Morgan to Rebecca Morgan, March 1794, Pile Family Papers, HSP.

71. Beginning in June 1794, the Morgan brothers began addressing their letters to sister Rebecca to the Claypoole house at 72 South Front Street. It may be that Rebecca was in residence there; however, in these years people also received mail at the home of any relative they thought could receive mail reliably. In some cases, the recipient would have to pay the postage due to obtain the letter. Since these were comparatively flush years for the Claypooles and meager ones for Thomas Morgan, it's possible that John Claypoole (who wrote often to his nephews in New Orleans) suggested they send her mail through him, because he was better positioned than Thomas to accept it. At any rate, in August 1794, Rebecca married Samuel Pile, and presumably moved out— though Pile's work as a ship captain may have made it convenient for her to remain with Aunt Claypoole sometime after the nuptials as well.

72. See, e.g., Benjamin Rush to Julia Rush, 28 October 1793, in Butterfield, *Letters*, 2:728–29; and 11 November 1793, in 2:744.

73. John F. Watson and Willis P. Hazard, *Annals, Philadelphia* (Philadelphia, 1881), vol. 1, 223.

## 19. THE FEDERAL EDIFICE

1. John C. Van Horne, "The Federal Procession of 1788," talk delivered to the quarterly meeting of the Carpenters' Company, July 20, 1987, posted at http://12.164.69.10/carpentershall/history/procession.htm and accessed June 2008.

2. An account of the procession appeared just days later in the *Massachusetts Gazette*, 18 July 1788.

3. Nancy Goyne, "Furniture Craftsmen in Philadelphia, 1760–1790: Their Role in a Mercantile Society" (M.A. thesis, University of Delaware, 1963), 140; and Samuel Hazard, ed., *Hazard's Register of Pennsylvania* (Philadelphia, 1828), 423.

4. Van Horne, "The Federal Procession of 1788."

5. Rachel was at least the third Griscom girl to work as an upholsterer, on the assumption that at least one older sister was present in the Webster shop, as per Rachel Claypoole's affidavit.

6. EDD, 9 May 1794, 27 July 1796, 6 October 1796.

7. Ibid., 12 September 1783. Years later, when she wrote her 1797 will, Rebecca Waln remembered Rebecca Griscom with a bequest of £6. See no. 63, PCA.

8. EDD, 27 January 1795.

9. "Guardians of the Poor, Almshouse Admissions, 1791–1797," PCA; another volume, "Guardians of the Poor, Daily Occurrences, March 1792–June 1793," notes that "Rebecca Griscom an elderly woman addicted to liquor" had entered the facility. According to the "Guardians of the Poor, Almshouse Admissions Book, 1785–1806," this Rebecca Griscom died in the almshouse 17 March 1807. The date is puzzling, since

most genealogies attribute the 1807 death date to Betsy's cousin, rather than her sister. It is difficult to disentangle the histories of these two women, both of whom were born in the mid-1740s and entered almshouses in the 1790s. The Rebecca Griscom who died in the city almshouse may have been Betsy's sister, with cousin Rebecca Griscom being the woman of that name who died in the Quaker almshouse in 1798.

10. Cousin Rebecca's story can be tracked in Philadelphia Northern District Women's Monthly Meeting, minutes, 1779–86, 193, 201, 203, 209, 212, 219–20; and Philadelphia Northern District Women's Monthly Meeting, minutes, 1791–96, 155, 235–36, 243, 249.

11. Philadelphia Northern District Women's Monthly Meeting, minutes, 1791–96, 24 July 1795, 235.

12. EDD, 3 August 1795.

13. Ibid., 8 September 1795.

14. Ibid., 22 and 29 September, and 13 October 1795.

15. Ibid., 20 and 27 October, and 2 November 1795.

16. This discussion of Rebecca's quarrel with the Quakers draws on Rebecca Griscom to Richard Folwell, 25 October 1794, Marian S. Carson Collection, box 42, LOC. The letter indicates that its author was about thirty-four or thirty-five "in or near the year 1781," making the author's birth date in 1746 or 1747. Betsy's sister was born in January 1746/47; the Philadelphia Monthly Meeting shows the birth date of Rebecca Griscom, daughter of Tobias and Grace, as "10th mo. 29, 1745." This would seem to suggest that the author of these letters is her sister rather than her cousin. But the additional references to the property inherited seem to confirm that the author is Rebecca's cousin, who owned a building in the Northern Liberties.

17. On the property, see Tobias Griscom, will, 18 March 1751; *Calendar of Kent County Delaware Probate Records 1680–1800* (Westminster, Md.: Heritage Books, 1944), 143.

18. Rebecca Griscom to James Pemberton, 16 June 1785, Pemperton Papers, vol. 44, HSP.

19. Philadelphia Northern District Women's Monthly Meeting, minutes, 1791–96, 25 March 1794, 155.

20. Rebecca Griscom to Richard Folwell, November 1794, Marian S. Carson Collection, box 42, LOC.

21. EDD, 24 November, 9 December, 14 December, and 22 December 1795.

22. PMMM, 22 December 1795.

23. Henry Drinker, draft of a letter to Mathew Cowper, 14 January 1796, Henry Drinker Letter Book, 1790–93, HSP.

24. EDD, 21 January 1796. Gary Nash also mentions this publication in *Forging Freedom: The Formation of Philadelphia's Black Community, 1720–1840* (Cambridge, Mass.: Harvard University Press, 1991), 191. For a history of African American membership among the Quakers, see Donna McDaniel and Vanessa Julye, *Fit for Freedom, Not for Friendship: Quakers, African Americans, and the Myth of Racial Justice* (Philadelphia: Quaker Press, 2009), and Henry J. Cadbury, "Negro Membership in the Society of Friends," *Journal of Negro History* 21, no. 2 (1936): 151–213.

25. Cadbury, *Journal of Negro History*, 152.

26. PMMM, 1751–56, 213, as quoted and cited in Henry J. Cadbury, "Negro Membership," 168.

27. See Cadbury, "Negro Membership," 171–72; and McDaniel and Julye, *Fit for Freedom*, 189–90.

28. EDD, 11 March 1795.

29. Joseph Drinker, discussed in Nash, *Forging Freedom*, 180. See also Thomas E. Drake, "Joseph Drinker's Plea for Admission of Colored People to the Society of Friends, 1795," *Journal of Negro History* 32, no. 1 (1947): 110–12.

30. For this text, see Drake, "Joseph Drinker's Plea," 111–12.

31. EDD, 21 January 1796.

32. Philadelphia Yearly Meeting, men's minutes, 1796 (A 1.4): report from Philadelphia Quarterly Meeting, minutes, 27 August 1796 and 30 August 1796. My thanks to Ann Upton at the QCHC for her particular help with this query.

33. PMMMND, Miscellaneous Papers, 1795, QCHC.

34. EDD, 21 August 1798.

35. Samuel Powel Griffits, diary, 20 July–30 November 1798, College of Physicians of Philadelphia.

36. *Gazette of the United States*, 1 October 1798.

37. "Furnishing Plan for the Second Floor of Congress Hall (October 1965)," part D, 37, section 3, INHP.

38. Ibid., part D, 57, section 3.

39. Ibid., part D, 131, appendix 3.

40. Records of the Office of the Comptroller General, entry 3444, RG 4, PSA, reel 3553; Register of Accounts, 1790, manuscripts in Records of Secretary of Commonwealth, Division of Public Records; and State House Papers, both noted in INHP card file.

41. James M. Duffin, "Transcription of Notes of Interview with Rachel (Claypoole) Jones Fletcher (1789–1873)," BRH.

42. Debra Jean Force, "Betsy Ross, Upholsterer and Flag-Maker: A Proposal to Furnish Her Home" (unpublished report, Betsy Ross Foundation, 1976); and *San Francisco Daily Evening Bulletin*, 20 January 1876.

43. William J. Canby to William T. Read, letter concerning John Ross, BRH, 21 February 1870.

44. According to *A Register of Marriage, in the Parish of New Castle, on Delaware, by Aeneas Ross, Missionary from ye 1st day of October, 1758*, the license for James Armstrong and Joanna Holland is dated 20 January 1789; New Castle County, Delaware, Marriages, 1645–1899, indicates that they were married nine days later.

45. James Duffin, "Transcription of Notes of Interview." The name James Armstrong is a common one and is attached to at least two other Revolutionary soldiers, one a colonel in North Carolina and another from Pennsylvania who went on to serve in Congress. There is also a James Armstrong who served in the Third Pennsylvania Regiment, which saw action in the battles of Valcour Island, Brandywine, Germantown, Monmouth and Springfield. Perhaps this is the Armstrong in question, and his service to Washington, if indeed it occurred, took place during one of these events.

46. Canby appends his mother's comments to his "Notes of Interview with Rachel (Claypoole) Jones Fletcher, 1789–1873."

47. At some point after Armstrong's death—which occurred before 1808—Joanna moved to Wilmington, Delaware; she may have lived in Philadelphia during these years, but whether or for how long is unknown, narrowing the opportunity for these events still further. The will of Philadelphia's Ann Murray, written in May 1808, refers to Joanna Armstrong as a widow living in Wilmington; see *Philadelphia County, Pennsylvania Wills, 1682–1819*, 3:342.

**48.** *Minutes of the Supreme Executive Council* vol 16 (Harrisburg, 1853), 547. Catherine Armstrong's petitions and summary of the charges are in the Clemency Files of the Supreme Executive Council (RG 27). My thanks to Aaron McWilliams of PSA for making this information available to me.

**49.** William B. Timmons reports this story in *Betsy Ross: The Griscom Legacy* (Salem, N.J.: Salem County Cultural & Heritage Commission, 1983), 136 and 288 n. 20. Joanna was clearly using every tool at her disposal to obtain support; in 1783 she petitioned the Delaware Assembly, and in 1796 wrote again concerning half-pay due her. See the *Votes of the House of Assembly of the Delaware state. Dover, Monday, January 6. 1783* (Wilmington, Del., 1783), 23; and *Journal of the House of Representatives of the state of Delaware, at a session commenced at Dover, on Tuesday, the fifth day of January, in the year of our Lord one thousand seven hundred and ninety-six, in conformity to the fourth section of the second articles of the constitution of this state, and in the twentieth year of the independence of the United States* (Wilmington, Del., 1796), 25.

**50.** James Duffin, "Transcription of Notes of Interview with Rachel (Claypoole) Jones Fletcher (1789–1873)," BRH; and Duffin, "Transcription of the 1870 Affidavit of Rachel (Claypoole) Jones Fletcher, 1789–1873," BRH.

**51.** Carl E. Prince, *The Federalists and the Origins of United States Civil Service* (New York: New York University Press, 1977), 14.

**52.** See Stephen G. Kurtz, *The Presidency of John Adams: The Collapse of Federalism* (Philadelphia: University of Pennsylvania Press, 1957); and Harry M. Tinken, *The Republicans and Federalists in Pennsylvania, 1790–1801* (Harrisburg: Pennsylvania Historical and Commission Museum, 1950).

**53.** Prince, *Federalists and the Origins of United States Civil Service*, 86–94.

**54.** Townsend Ward, "South Second Street and Its Associations," *PMHB* 4, no. 1 (1880): 55.

**55.** Force makes this point; see "Betsy Ross Upholsterer and Flag-Maker," 18; and James Hardie, *Philadelphia Directory and Register* (Philadelphia, 1794). There's some hint, too, that Claypoole was putting in time at the printing shop of his cousin David Claypoole; at least he was the man on hand to sign a receipt for cash received from Benjamin Chew in May 1795. See Nancy E. Richards, "Benjamin Chew's Receipt Book, 1770–1809," unpublished research report, Cliveden, available at http://www.cliveden.org/Content/Research/Benjamin%20Chew%20Receipt%20Book.pdf.

**56.** Inward Foreign Manifests, 17 November 1794, NARA RG 36.

**57.** Ibid., 18 July 1796, 25 November 1796, NARA RG 36.

**58.** Ibid., 20–25 March 1797, 27 April 1797 and May 1797, NARA RG 36.

**59.** Cornelius William Stafford, *The Philadelphia Directory for 1797* (Philadelphia, 1797).

**60.** Prince, *Federalists and the Origins of United States Civil Service*, 86.

**61.** Ibid., 92.

**62.** James Duffin, "Transcription of Notes of Interview with Rachel (Claypoole) Jones Fletcher," BRH. No school known as the Pennsylvania Academy for Young Ladies turns up in searches of Philadelphia newspapers; also, as we shall see, the daughter of Betsy's colleague the flag painter William Berrett attended the Young Ladies' Academy of Philadelphia, lending credence to Rachel's statement.

**63.** This discussion of the Young Ladies' Academy of Philadelphia is based on Margaret A. Nash, "Rethinking Republican Motherhood: Benjamin Rush and the Young Ladies' Academy of Philadelphia," *Journal of the Early Republic* 17, no. 1 (1997):

171–91; Ann D. Gordon, "The Young Ladies' Academy of Philadelphia," in Carol Ruth Berkin and Mary Beth Norton, eds., *Women of America: A History* (Boston: Houghton Mifflin, 1979), 68–91; Marion B. Savin and Harold J. Abrahams, "The Young Ladies' Academy of Philadelphia," *History of Education Journal* 8, no. 2 (1957): 58–67; and Joseph Pilmore, "Address," in *Rise and Progress of the Young Ladies' Academy of Philadelphia* (Philadelphia, 1794).

64. James Robinson, *Philadelphia Directory* (Philadelphia, 1802), 185.

65. Gordon, "The Young Ladies' Academy of Philadelphia," 73–80.

66. Nash, "Rethinking Republican Motherhood," 186.

67. On Martha Washington, see James A. Neal, *Essay on the Education and Genius of the Female Sex*, 14, as discussed in Carolyn Eastman, "The Female Cicero: Young Women's Oratory and Gendered Public Participation in the Early American Republic," *Gender and History* 19, no. 2 (2007): 263.

68. A newspaper article describing this event says that the train was carried by "her maids," but these "maids" were surely just friends. Since Margaret married in July 1794, she may have been the object of this particular celebration, and hence meriting this special attention; it's also possible that this has something to do with the commencement at the Young Ladies' Academy. See the *Cincinnati Daily Gazette*, 28 February 1876.

69. *Philadelphia Inquirer*, 11 January 1876. In 1793, Boggs's name appeared in a list of debts of the Pennyslvania Treasury, though the record does not indicate what services were rendered. See the State Treasurer's Reports, March 1793, RG 4.59, PSA.

70. Joseph Boggs Waste Book, 1791–92, in Reed and Forde Papers, col. 541, HSP.

71. See, e.g., *Federal Gazette* and *PEP*, 17 August 1791 and 22 April 1793, and *The Mail; or, Claypoole's Daily Advertiser*, 23 January 1792. For his waste book, 1791–92, see the Reed and Forde Papers, col. 541, HSP.

72. See *The Gazette of the United States*, 8 August 1794; *PG* and *Universal Daily Advertiser*, 14 August 1794.

73. For the marriage of Margaret Donaldson and Joseph Boggs, see Clarence M. Busch, comp., *The Record of Pennsylvania Marriages Prior to 1810, Vol. 1, PA*, series 2, vol. 8 (Harrisburg, Pa., 1895).

74. See Timmons, *Betsy Ross*, 239.

75. Membership Book, Religious Society of Free Quakers, box 6, APS.

76. Thomas Morgan to George Morgan, 9 December 1795, Pile Family Papers, HSP.

77. David Evans Daybooks, 1774–1812, HSP.

78. James Duffin, "Transcription of the 1909 Affidavit of Susan McCord Turner," BRH.

79. Hannah married William McIntire in November 1794 at Gloria Dei; she continued to run the Front Street grocery store until 1798, when the couple moved to 40 Chestnut Street—the house in which William died later that year, leaving Hannah a widow yet again. A "widow McIntire" is listed as a head of household in the Northern Liberties in the 1800 federal census. Her 1794 marriage is recorded in Busch, *Record of Pennsylvania Marriages*. For William's probate files, see Philadelphia Wills, 1798, file 10. James Duffin, "Transcription of the 1909 Affidavit of Susan McCord Turner." On Hannah's marriage, see also George W. Morgan to Rebecca Pile, 31 March 1795, Pile Family Papers, HSP.

80. See "Family Record of Marriage and Births of Children," Claypoole family Bible, BRH. The Sillimans were an old Connecticut family; historians of early America may be interested to learn that Isaac's aunt and uncle, Mary Fish Silliman and Gold

Selleck Silliman, are the same Sillimans as those portrayed in the noted book *The Way of Duty* and the subsequent film *Mary Silliman's War* ("the true story," the film's PR says, "of a remarkable woman, whose husband, a patriot leader, was kidnapped from their home by a band of tories"). Eliza and Isaac, like so many of their generation, were apparently surrounded by stories of the Revolution's trials. Isaac was born 3 July 1770 to Hezekiah Silliman and Amelia Hubbard in Fairfield, Connecticut; see Elizabeth Hubbell Schenck, *The History of Fairfield: Fairfield County, Connecticut* (New York, 1889–1905), 2:501: "First Extant Parish Record of Christ Church." On the trials of his wife, Mary Fish Silliman, see Joy Day Buel and Richard Buel, *The Way of Duty: A Woman and Her Family in Revolutionary America* (New York: Norton, 1984).

81. See, e.g., Disbursements, brig *Nancy*, Unger Watermark Collection, col. 69, JDC.

82. Isaac and Eliza Silliman appear to be absent from the whole of the 1800 United States census. By 1806, they seem to have returned to reside in Philadelphia; at that time Isaac took out a membership in the Society for the Relief of Poor, Aged, and Infirm Masters of Ships, Their Widows and Children (see the society's dues book, 1807–8, HSP). They could have returned anytime between 1802 and 1806; the society's dues books for those intervening years are not preserved. The 1810 federal census finds the Sillimans in Philadelphia's South Ward, but a decade later they again cannot be located in the census.

83. George Morgan to Rebecca Morgan, [illegible] March 1794, Pile Family Papers, HSP.

## 20. WAR, REDUX

1. Rebecca Iron Graff, *Genealogy of the Claypoole Family in Philadelphia* (Philadelphia, 1893), 75.

2. In *The Evolution of the American Flag* (Philadelphia: Ferris and Leach, 1909), 107, Lloyd Balderston suggests that two portrait miniatures were made about 1806 by Rembrandt Peale, but the source of the date and attribution are unknown. Other references suggest that Anna Peale was the artist. The miniatures, however, could not be located for this study, though a photo of Rachel's portrait is found in the Canby papers, box 2, folder 27, Huntington Library, San Marino, California.

3. *PG*, 24 December 1799.

4. Ibid.; Albert J. Beveridge, *Life of John Marshall*, vol. 2 (Boston: Houghton Mifflin, 1919), 441. Hannah Marshall Haines to Reuban Haines, 2 December 1799, Wyck Association Collection, series 2, box 12, folder 59, APS.

5. On the death of George Washington, see Gerald E. Kahler, *The Long Farewell: Americans Mourn the Death of Washington* (Charlottesville: University of Virginia Press, 2008).

6. James Duffin, "Transcription of the Recollections of William Jackson Canby (1825–1890) of His Grandmother," BRH.

7. Between 1793 and 1817, directories list John Claypoole at 70 or 72 South Front. By 1817, Betsy is listed at 74 South Front (under Elizabeth Claypoole or Claypoole & Wilson) until 1828, when the address becomes 112 South Front, as it continues to 1833. Interestingly, in 1813, the upholsterer George Breidenhart insured 117 South Front Street, with "the front room occupied as an upholsterer's shop." The building is described on the Philadelphia Contributionship for the Insurance of Houses survey form S03569.

8. Peter P. Jonitis and Elizabeth F. Jonitis, in "Members of the Prison Society: Biographical Vignettes" (typescript, 1982), QCHC, indicate that this stroke and the

ensuing invalidism occurred in 1797, but the original source for this very specific date is not indicated. The date is hard to reconcile with his work for the Customs Service at that time, but the year of his stroke is otherwise unknown.

9. John Claypoole cane, 1810, private collection.

10. Rough minutes, 11 November 1802, loose papers, 1789–1804, Religious Society of Free Quakers, box 1, folder 4, APS.

11. Ibid., 10 December 1795, 6 April 1796, 13 May 1802.

12. Ibid., 13 May 1802 and 10 March 1803.

13. John Claypoole Petition to R. W. Grand Committee of Charity, 15 August 1803, the Grand Lodge of Free and Accepted Masons of Pennsylvania archives, the Masonic Library and Museum of Pennsylvania, Philadelphia, Pa.

14. Rough minutes, 4 August 1803, loose papers, 1789–1804, Religious Society of Free Quakers, box 1, folder 4, APS.

15. Financial Records: Treasurer's Book, 1786–1846, Religious Society of Free Quakers, box 5, APS. Also, it's worth noting that in April 1805, a man by the name of Joseph Knight (very possibly Betsy's cousin) indicated that he was "desirious of joining" the meeting; George Kemble, Samuel Wetherill and—interestingly—John Claypoole were asked to visit with him and report back to the meeting. The charge was repeated in September 1805, but when they eventually reported, it appears that Claypoole did not in fact accompany them.

16. See, e.g., minutes, 5 February 1807, Minute Book, 1804–11, Religious Society of Free Quakers, box 1, APS.

17. Financial Records: Treasurer's Book, 1786–1846, Religious Society of Free Quakers, box 5, APS.

18. See "Family Record of Marriage and Births of Children," Claypoole family Bible, BRH.

19. Clarissa and Jacob Wilson were married in Bucks County, 4 June 1805, by Reverend James Boyd of the Presbyterian church at Newtown. Jacob was the son of Robert and Sophia Wilson, and born in Lancaster on 4 January 1785 (genealogy in collection of Kent Buehler). Wilson is identified as a merchant on the Anna Griscom family tree, GCHS.

20. See Camilla D. Townsend, "Doing a Day's Business in a New Nation" (Ph.D. dissertation, Rutgers University, 1995), 67; and Gregory R. Weidman, *Furniture in Maryland, 1740–1940* (Baltimore: Maryland Historical Society, 1984), 85.

21. William Fry, *The Baltimore Directory, for 1810* (Baltimore, 1810), 191; *Fry's Baltimore Directory, for the year 1812* (Baltimore, 1812), 83; and John Thomas Scharf, *History of Baltimore, City and County* (Philadelphia, 1881), 769.

22. Wilson family genealogy, private collection; and Paul Douglas Newman, *Fries's Rebellion: The Enduring Struggle for the American Revolution* (Philadelphia: University of Pennsylvania Press, 2004), 156.

23. James McHenry, *Baltimore Directory and Citizens' Register for 1807* (Baltimore, 1807).

24. Fry, *Baltimore Directory, for 1810*, 191; *Fry's Baltimore Directory, for the year 1812*, 83; and Scharf, *History of Baltimore*, 769; 1810 U.S. Federal Census, Philadelphia, Pennsylvania. Digital scan of original records in the National Archives, Washington, D.C., subscription database (http://www.ancestry.com), accessed September 2009.

25. In summer 1807, Sarah would marry David McCord, and they would have

another seven—two of whom were named for Joseph Boggs, attesting to the closeness among those sisters as well.

26. Minutes, 12 May 1808, Minute Book, 1804–11, Religious Society of Free Quakers, box 1, APS. Again in 1809, his tuition and books, to N. A. Smith & Son; see Financial Records: Treasurer's Book, 1786–1846, Religious Society of Free Quakers, box 5, APS.

27. Nicholas B. Wainwright, *Paintings and Miniatures at the Historical Society of Pennsylvania* (Philadelphia: Historical Society of Pennsylvania, 1974), 212, 221, 107.

28. Isaac Silliman to Samuel Pile, 5 March 1811, Pile Family Papers, HSP.

29. Society for the Relief of Poor, Aged, and Infirm Masters of Ships, Their Widows and Children Records, col. 1415, HSP.

30. Abel Satterthwaite to Captain Samuel Pile, 1 November 1810, Pile Family Papers, HSP.

31. James Duffin, "Transcription of the 1870 Affidavit of Margaret (Donaldson) Boggs," BRH. Though less is known about this aspect of her work, Betsy also did business with commercial vessels. For an 1808 receipt for bunting sold to Stephen Girard, see George Canby and Lloyd Balderston, *Evolution of the American Flag* (Philadelphia: Ferris and Leach, 1909), 106.

32. Rebecca Flower Young worked heavily for the arsenal in 1804; the comparatively few receipts from 1805 suggest that she may have moved in that year. In 1803, Young advertised "ready made colours for all nations" at 126 North Front Street, Philadelphia. In 1804, she and her daughter made several flags for both the army and the Indian Department, including ten U.S. ensigns, four large garrison flags and five flags for the Indian Department; the following year, they made two U.S. ensigns. By 1807, Rebecca Young was renting space on Albemarle Street in Baltimore. Interestingly, a 29 December 1803 letter to Tench Coxe suggests that she may have been aware of flags coming from another supplier. See research files, Flag House Museum, Baltimore; and Pat Piling, "Documents of a Flagmaking Family," *Flag Bulletin*, no. 201 (2000): 19–24.

33. The arsenal's modern-day successor, the Defense Supply Center of Philadelphia, continues to provide military clothing and textiles; in 2006, sales of clothing, textiles and equipment to military personnel worldwide topped $2.2 billion. See the Web site of the Defense Supply Center of Philadelphia, http://www.dscp.dla.mil/, accessed July 1, 2008.

34. Jacob E. Cooke discusses the political circumstances surrounding Coxe's appointment in *Tench Coxe and the Early Republic* (Chapel Hill: University of North Carolina Press for the Institute of Early American History and Culture, 1978), 390–405.

35. Pennsylvania Abolition Society, Acting Committee minutes, 6 September 1787, HSP.

36. The first job earned them £6 2s. 6d.; the second £12 4s. 6d. See Tench Coxe papers, bills and receipts, reel 116, HSP, under Claypoole-John (for May and June) and Claypoole-Elizabeth (when she collects against Coxe's account on 12 July 1792).

37. Marc Leepson, *Flag: An American Biography* (New York: Macmillan 2006), 57.

38. Stephen Howarth, *To Shining Sea: A History of the United States Navy, 1775–1998* (Norman: University of Oklahoma Press, 1999), 85–86.

39. On Silliman, see the *Reports of Cases Adjudged in the Supreme Court of Pennsylvania* (Philadelphia, 1809–15), 3:460.

40. Cooke, *Tench Coxe and the Early Republic*, 427.

41. Edward C. Kuhn, "U.S. Army Colors and Standards of 1808," *Military Affairs*

5:4 (1941): 263–67. For more on the evolution of the Great Seal, see Richard S. Patterson and Richardson Dougall, *The Eagle and the Shield* (Washington, D.C.: Department of State, 1976).

42. James Duffin, "Transcription of the 1870 Affidavit of Rachel (Claypoole) Jones Fletcher, 1789–1873," BRH; on Anna M. Berrett (born about 1798), see the address she delivered at a school exhibition in 1801, Marian S. Carson Collection, box 26, folder 22, LOC.

43. Kenneth and Anna M. Roberts, eds., *Moreau de St. Méry's American Journey, 1793–1798* (Garden City, N.Y.: Doubleday, 1947), 176.

44. Alexandra Alevizatos Kirtley, "The Painted Furniture of Philadelphia: A Reappraisal," *Magazine Antiques* 169, no. 5 (2006): 134–45; see also *PP*, 5 January 1782.

45. See, e.g., receipts, 8 May 1771, Pemberton Papers, vol. 22, 146; and 23 July 1771, Cadwalader Collection; and 31 December 1774, Norris Family Accounts, vol. 2, 28, all HSP. The elder Berrett was in Philadelphia at least as early as 1770, when he painted a desk for Christ Church; see Charles E. Peterson, FAIA, "The Building of Christ Church," at http://www.christchurchphila.org. "Timothy Barrett [sic], painter," appears in the effective supply tax for 1780, in Mulberry Ward, as does Samuel Griscom; see the "Effective Supply Tax of Philadelphia, 1780," *PA*, series 3, vol. 15 (Harrisburg, Pa., 1897), 292.

46. Henry Moeller, "List of Pennsylvania Flag-Makers," Pennsylvania Committee of Safety Records, 26 October 1775 to 7 August 1776, 12, 34.

47. See James Hardie, *Philadelphia directory and register* (Philadelphia, 1793), 10; and Cornelius William Stafford, *Philadelphia directory, for 1800: containing the names, occupations, and places of abode of the citizens, arranged in alphabetical order* (Philadelphia, 1800), 20. See also city directories between 1801 and 1825. As late as 1831, Berrett was still working for the state of Pennsylvania; according to the *Report of the State Treasurer on the Finances* (Harrisburg, Pa., 1831), 213, the state paid Berrett $204.50 "for two stands of colours for use of the first brigade, sixteenth division, Pennsylvania militia." In 1835–36, he earned another $153.75 for "colours"; see *Hazard's Register of Pennsylvania*, vol. 16 (Philadelphia, 1835–36), 25.

48. *PG*, 2 December 1772.

49. For Mary Berrett's obituary, see the *Philadelphia Repository*, 19 June 1802; and the *Gazette of the United States* for the same date.

50. Thomas Holcomb, *Sketch of the Early Ecclesiastical Affairs in New Castle, Delaware and History of Immanuel Church* (Wilmington, Del., 1890), 146. William's father had painted the pulpit in Philadelphia's Christ Church; see http://www.christchurch phila.org/Historic_Christ_Church/Church/Scholarly_Articles/The_Building_of_ Christ_Church/160/.

51. *Journal of the Senate of the Commonwealth of Pennsylvania [microform] which commenced at Lancaster, the seventh day of December, in the year of our Lord, one thousand eight hundred and two* . . . (Lancaster, Pa., 1802 [i.e., 1803]); *Report of the Register-General on the state of the finances of the commonwealth* (Lancaster, Pa., 1804), 18. Other men debited for militia "colors" here include Earnest [sic] Benoit, Benjamin W. Henry, Isaac Heston and John Fisher, as well as a William Clark, whose bill is the only one higher than Berrett's, a stunning $2,151.34. Howard Michael Madaus, in "The U.S. Flag in the American West," *Raven: A Journal of Vexillology*, vol. 5 (1998), 56–78, says that William Berrett painted army standards before and during the War of 1812 and painted scrolls on regimental colors and coats of arms of the United States until "at least the 1830s." He received most of the contracts for painting until 1844, Madaus continues,

but Samuel Brewer, another Philadelphian, "replaced him as the War Department's chief artist for decorating colors for the army" by 1845.

52. *Journal of the Senate of the Commonwealth of Pennsylvania*, 13:6, 154.

53. E.g., see also *Receipts and expenditures in the treasury of Pennsylvania* (Lancaster, Pa., 1803), 16; *Report of the Register-General*, 31 (Huntington County standards); *Receipts and expenditures in the treasury of Pennsylvania* (Lancaster, Pa., 1807), 142; *Report on the finances of the Commonwealth of Pennsylvania, for the year 1809* (Lancaster, Pa., 1809), 19 (nine stands for the first and second brigade to the tune of nearly $1,000); *Receipts and expenditures in the treasury of Pennsylvania* (Lancaster, Pa., 1809), 78, 101, 128, 153; *Report on the finances of the commonwealth of Pennsylvania for the year 1810* (Lancaster, Pa., 1810), 21. I also find him in 1827 making a battalion flag for the Pennsylvania militia; see *Report of the State Treasurer on the Finances by Pennsylvania Treasury, Pennsylvania* (1827), 329. Also, *Hazard's Register of Pennsylvania*, 16:25.

54. Secretary of War to Tench Coxe (Secretary of War, Miscellaneous Letters Sent), 3:249–50, NARA, as quoted in Kuhn, "U. S. Army Colors," 263–65.

55. Tench Coxe Papers, RG 92, NARA, box 17, as described in Howard Michael Madaus, "The U.S. Flag in the American West, 1777–1876": 74 n. 54.

56. Kuhn, "U. S. Army Colors," 265.

57. The U.S. Arsenal on the Schuylkill helped outfit the Lewis and Clark expedition; the Philadelphia upholsterer Richard Wevill landed the contract for the tents, and the expedition also carried a red flag, a white flag, a U.S. flag and flags for gifts to native communities, but the makers of these latter articles are not known. For the debts to Richard Wevill, see Reuben Gold Thwaites, ed., *Original Journals of the Lewis and Clark Expedition: 1804–1806* (New York: Dodd, Mead & Co., 1904–05) parts 1 and 2, vol. 7, appendix, 245.

58. Consolidated Correspondence File of the Quartermaster General, NARA RG 92, as quoted in Madaus, "The United States Flag in the American West," 71 n. 42.

59. Pat Pilling analyzes this letter in "Documents of a Flagmaking Family," *Flag Bulletin*, no. 201 (2000): 19–24; for the flags produced between 1804 and 1806, see Pilling, "Early Flag Makers," research notes for the Star Spangled Banner Flag House in Baltimore, Maryland.

60. Ledger, PPS, 1809–12, Coxe Family Papers, vol. 29, 101, HSP.

61. A flag for the Indian Department brought just under three dollars, while garrison flags were bringing six dollars. See Ledger, PPS, 1809–12; Coxe Family Papers, vol. 29, HSP.

62. Thomas L. McKenney to Henry Simpson, May 1816, Letters Sent, Office of Indian Trade, NARA RG 75, vol. D, 29, as quoted in Madaus, "The U.S. Flag in the American West," 74.

63. *Letter from the Secretary of War transmitting statements of contracts made by him and the Purveyor of Public Supplies in the year 1811* (Washington City, 1812).

64. William Berrett to John Jones, 22 July 1816 and 26 September 1816, col. 588, John Jones Papers, 1814–64, HSP.

65. The square footage of the Claypoole house is recorded in the 1798 Federal Direct Tax, compiled and edited by Bernard L. Herman and available at "Places in Time: Historical Documentation of Place in Greater Philadelphia," accessed at http://www.brynmawr.edu/iconog/frdr.html.

66. It's easy to imagine that Betsy needed to avail herself of some larger space, as Mary Pickersgill would avail herself of Claggett's Baltimore brewery to lay out the Star

Spangled Banner. See Caroline Pickersgill Purdy to Georgiana Armistead Appleton, 1876, Appleton Family Papers, Massachusetts Historical Society, as quoted in Lonn Taylor, *The Star-Spangled Banner* (New York: Smithsonian Books/HarperCollins, 2008), 67.

67. "List of Camp Equipage & Tools Required in the Southern District," 28 January 1811, Tench Coxe Papers, HSP.

68. *Letter from the Secretary of War transmitting statements of contracts made by him and the Purveyor of Public Supplies in the year 1811* (Washington City, 1812). For the record of payment for eight garrison flags in September 1811, see bill of Elizabeth Claypoole, 2 September 1811, Tench Coxe Papers, RG 92, NARA, box 17, as quoted in Madaus, "The U.S. Flag in the American West," 73–74.

69. *Letter from the Secretary of War . . . in the year 1811.*

70. *Letter from the Secretary of War, transmitting a statement of the contracts which have been made during the year 1812* (Washington City, 1813), 5, 8.

71. The receipt, dated 28 May 1813, is housed in the Rodney Collection, box 5, folder 9, Delaware Historical Society; the job earned the pair twenty-seven dollars, equivalent to roughly three weeks' wages for a domestic servant. See Donald R. Adams, "Wage Rates in the Early National Period," *Journal of Economic History* 28, no. 3 (1968): 404–26, appendix table 7.

72. Aquila Murray to Miss Jane Claypoole (addressed to her at 74 South Front), from New York City, 27 July 1814, FHL.

73. See William Jones to Alexander Murray, 22 March 1813, Rodney Collection, box 5, folder 9, Delaware Historical Society.

74. Louis M'Lane, *Oration delivered before the Artillery Company of Wilmington, commanded by Captain Rodney, on the 5th of July, A.D. 1813* (Wilmington, Del., 1813).

75. M'Lane gestured particularly here to a flag presented to the company by the "Ladies of Wilmingon"; whether this was a company flag or a garrison flag of the United States is not entirely clear.

76. Caroline Pickersgill Purdy to Georgiana Armistead Appleton, Baltimore, 1876, Massachusetts Historical Society.

77. Taylor, *Star-Spangled Banner*, 63.

78. See also *The American Muse; or Songster's Companion* (New York, 1814); on the history of the poem and song, see Taylor, *Star-Spangled Banner*, 39–62.

## 21. A PORT IN THE STORM

1. Daniel Walker Howe, *What Hath God Wrought: The Transformation of America, 1815–1848* (New York: Oxford University Press, 2007), 10, 67.

2. Gary B. Nash, *First City: Philadelphia and the Forging of Historical Memory* (Philadelphia: University of Pennsylvania Press, 2002), 2.

3. *New Bedford [Massachusetts] Mercury*, 14 July 1826. See also Len Travers, *Celebrating the Fourth: Independence Day and the Rites of Nationalism in the Early Republic* (Amherst: University of Massachusetts Press, 1999), 218–27.

4. "Journey to Washington in 1812; Abel Satterthwaite's Narrative," *Old York Road Historical Society Bulletin*, 23 (April 1962), 25, FHL.

5. See Wilson family genealogy, private collection; and William B. Timmons, *Betsy Ross: The Griscom Legacy* (Salem, N.J.: Salem County Cultural & Heritage Commission, 1983), 252. Of course it could also be that Abel's reference was instead to Clarissa's stepsister Eliza, since it would make sense for the phrase "her husband having

gone to sea" to mean Captain Isaac Silliman. Perhaps Eliza had taken her family to Baltimore while Isaac was abroad.

6. Financial Records: Treasurer's Book, 1786–1846, Religious Society of Free Quakers, box 5, APS. The first reference, in September 1812, is to an R. Ludlow (right after J. Thomas vanishes from the household), but soon and consistently becomes R. Ludley.

7. Ten years before R. Ludley took a place in Betsy's home, a Sarah Ludley was running a boardinghouse on Shippen Street; R. Ludley may have been her son or daughter, though Sarah was still living in 1819, by now identified as a widow in residence on Bidell's Alley. *The Philadelphia directory, city and county register, for 1802 . . .* ([Philadelphia, 1802?]), 152. See also James Robinson, *The Philadelphia directory, for 1816 . . .* (Philadelphia, 1816), n.p.; and John Adamas Paxton, ed., *The Philadelphia directory and register, for 1819* (Philadelphia, 1819).

8. Philadelphia Association of Friends for the Instruction of Poor Children, *A sketch of the origin and progress of the Adelphi School in the Northern Liberties* (Philadelphia, 1810); John Adams Paxton, *The Philadelphia directory and register, for 1813* (Philadelphia, 1813), civ.

9. *Account of the rise and progress of the asylum . . . for the relief of persons deprived of the use of their reason* (Philadelphia, 1814); and Patricia D'Antonio, *Founding Friends: Families, Staff, and Patients at the Friends Asylum in Early Nineteenth-Century Philadelphia* (Bethlehem, Pa.: Lehigh University Press, 2006), 181. Susan and Abel lived during these years at 107 Race Street.

10. Ruth B. Lippincott, ed., *The Balderston Family, Colora Branch* (Colora, Md.: privately printed, 1959), 32.

11. William Wade Hinshaw, *Encyclopedia of American Quaker Genealogy* (Baltimore: Genealogical Publishing, 1969), 2:487.

12. Timmons, *Betsy Ross*, 161. According to Jane Bowne Haines, "scrap" carpet (such as appropriate for her "stove room") could be purchased "either in Market or at the Prison"; see Haines to Reuban Haines, 15 October 1820, Wyck Papers, series 2, box 20, folder 167; also Haines to mother, 4 December 1820, ibid.

13. Financial Records: Treasurer's Book, 1786–1846, Religious Society of Free Quakers, box 5, APS.

14. At least daughter Jane would later recall that she was about seventeen "when they moved from the Norris Alley house," and Susan McCord Turner described the "commodious" home on Front Street *below* Walnut. See James Duffin, "Transcription of Notes of Interview with Jane (Claypoole) Canby, 1792–1873," and Duffin, "Transcription of the 1909 Affidavit of Susan Jacobs (McCord) Turner," both BRH. There's some uncertainty about this final location. William Canby mentions this site on Front between Walnut and Spruce in his narrative, Clarissa is indeed listed at 112, 114 and 118 South Front in various sources later in her career, and Jane's recollection of a move ca. 1810 would suggest that the relocation a block south occurred around this time, but city directories continue to place Elizabeth Claypoole at the 70–74 South Front address to at least 1825.

15. Duffin, "Transcription of the 1909 Affidavit of Susan Jacobs (McCord) Turner," BRH.

16. The reference here to a bathroom is especially curious, since bathrooms were still highly novel through the first quarter of the nineteenth century. Some middle-class families did without indoor plumbing even into the 1840s. My thanks to architectural

historian Doug McVarish and archaeologist Rebecca Yamin for fielding my query on this subject.

17. See Financial Records: Treasurer's Book, 1786–1846, Religious Society of Free Quakers, box 5, APS. In summer 1813, she received $28 for John Claypoole's boarding, and another $14 for boarding Clarissa; by January of the following year, the Friends set aside another $46 for John and $23 for Clarissa, in addition to the $10 spent on schooling John Boggs, and $8.66 on Clarissa's children. Midyear saw additional installments of $28 and $14, and by July another $32, plus $16.

18. Financial Records, loose receipts, March 1813, Religious Society Free Quakers, box 4, APS. Betsy billed the Free Quakers $15 for thirty pounds of curled hair, and another $14 for sixteen and a half yards of linen, nineteen yards of cotton cassimere and fifty yards of binding—she charged just $3.50 for making up two small cushions.

19. Codicil to Will of Samuel Wetherill, no. 119, 1816, Marian S. Carson Collection, oversize box 15, LOC. My thanks to John Harker for mentioning Wetherill's will to me. For wages in 1816, see Donald R. Adams Jr., "Wage Rates in the Early National Period: Philadelphia, 1785–1830," *Journal of Economic History* 28, no. 3 (1968): 404–26.

20. *Loudon's American Daily Advertiser*, 5 August 1817; *Commercial Advertiser*, 6 August 1817; *New-York Spectator*, 8 August 1817; *Essex Register*, 13 August 1817.

21. For Susan and Abel's move to Abington see William Wade Hinshaw, *Encyclopedia of American Quaker Genealogy*, vol. 2 (Baltimore: Genealogical Publishing, 1969), 643.

22. James Duffin, "Transcription of 1870 Affidavit of Sophia B. (Wilson) Hildebrandt," BRH.

23. *Poulson's American Daily Advertiser*, 21 January 1817; Kevin Keim and Peter Keim, *A Grand Old Flag* (New York: DK Publishing, 2007), 63; and Leepson, *Flag*, 77–81. Interestingly, Ross's entry in *The Twentieth Century Dictionary of Notable Americans* vol. 9 (Boston, 1904) claims that it was his wife Mary who "presented the flag to General Washington at Philadelphia in 1777."

24. Claypoole & Wilson to Commissioners of the Navy, 1820; photocopy at BRH.

25. James Duffin, "Transcription of Notes of the 1909 Affidavit of Margaret (McCord) Smith," BRH.

26. For Berrett's receipts for colors for several militia regiments in 1825 and 1826, see the Papers of James Trimble (1755–1837), Arthur Bining Collection, HSP.

27. Betsy and Clarissa employed more than twenty yards of muslin and sixty yards of fringe to complete the order. See receipt, Claypoole & Wilson to Miss Bailey, Latimer Family Papers, box 1, folder 3, JDC, no. 52.72.16.

28. James Robinson, *Philadelphia Directory* (Philadelphia, 1810); Robinson, *Philadelphia Directory* (Philadelphia, 1811); John Adams Paxton, *Philadelphia directory and register* (Philadelphia, 1813); *Kite's Philadelphia Directory* (Philadelphia, 1814); James Robinson, *Philadelphia Directory* (Philadelphia, 1816).

29. Thomas Wilson, *Philadelphia Directory and Stranger's Guide* (Philadelphia, 1825).

30. For a fascinating introduction to Philadelphia's industrial history, see Oliver Evans Chapter of the Society for Industrial Archaeology, *Workshop of the World* (Wallingford, Pa.: Oliver Evans Press, 1990).

31. John Fanning Watson and Willis P. Hazard, *Annals of Philadelphia*, vol. 3 (Philadelphia, 1884), 125.

32. David H. Conradsen, "Ease and Economy: The Hancocks and the Development of Spring-Seat Upholstery in America" (M.A. thesis, University of Delaware, 1998), 56.

33. Ibid., 35.

34. Samuel F. Pile to Joseph M. Pile, 15 March 1821, Pile Family Papers, HSP.

35. For these death dates, see Lewis D. Cook, "Family Records from the Bible of 'Betsy Ross' of Philadelphia," *Genealogies of Pennsylvania Families from the Pennsylvania Genealogical Magazine,* vol. 3 (Baltimore: Genealogical Publishing, 1982), 905–6. One Claypoole family Bible identified the boy as "Jacob," but he seems to have been known as Willis or Wyllis, born 20 August 1809 and named after Isaac's brother in Connecticut. See Brent Holcomb, comp., *Passengers Arriving at the Port of Charleston, 1820–1829* (Baltimore: Genealogical Publishing, 1994), 41, and also the "Record of marriage and births of children."

36. "Marriage and Death Notices from the City Gazette of Charleston," *South Carolina Historical Magazine* 54, no. 3 (1953): 163.

37. William Kite, *Memoirs and Letters of Thomas Kite* (Philadelphia, 1883), 142–43.

38. *American Monthly Magazine,* June 1898, 10; and Addie Guthrie Weaver, *The Story of Our Flag* (Chicago, 1898). Eliza's movements are hard to track; though Isaac Silliman and family appear in the 1810 federal census as residents of the city's South Ward they do not appear there (or in any U.S. city) in 1820, nor do they appear in city directories of the 1810s. The last city directory that mentions Isaac Silliman was James Robinson's *Philadelphia directory for 1806,* at which time the family was at 407 South Front Street (while her parents were still at 72 South Front). Oddly, this same director lists at that latter address "Claypoole, widow of William, upholsterer." John Claypoole at that time was still living but not listed. Somehow, unless Betsy's mother-in-law, also named Elizabeth, had also joined her firm and now was for some reason living there and considered the head of household, compilers conflated Elizabeth, the wife of John, with her mother-in-law, the widow of William, in an entry that reminds us of the fallibility of such sources.

39. Society for the Relief of Poor, Aged, and Infirm Masters of Ships, Their Widows and Children, Dues Books, 1807–1923; and Minute Books, 1822–33, col. 1415, HSP.

40. Records of Abington Monthly Meeting, 10 April 1823 (Joseph Gillingham, ed., 1894), 272, HSP.

41. Rachel Griscom, will, 1824, recorded in Will Book no. 8, 524, 1826, PCA.

42. Financial Records: Treasurer's Book, 1786–1846, Religious Society of Free Quakers, box 5, APS. This is not, however, the end of the charitable support of Betsy's family from the Free Quakers; there is a report regarding an appropriation of some $200 in "clothing etc for the relief of the poor commencing January 1829" that includes cash disbursements to Margaret Donaldson Boggs, her sister Sarah McCord and also to Elizabeth Claypoole. See Financial Records: Receipts and Dorcas Reports, 1810–47, Religious Society of Free Quakers, box 5, APS. Another from the following year mentions Margaret Donaldson Boggs but no other family member.

43. Ray Thompson, *Betsy Ross: Last of Philadelphia's Free Quakers* (Fort Washington, Pa.: Bicentennial Press, 1972), 67.

44. Edwin Satterthwaite Parry, *Betsy Ross: Quaker Rebel* (Philadelphia: John Winston Company, 1930), xii. For the tradition about the sewing table I am indebted to Nancy Balderston Conrad.

45. Anna Coxe Toogood, "Historic Resource Study, Independence Mall, The 18th-Century Development, Block Three," INHP, January 2004.

46. Duffin, "Transcription of the 1909 Affidavit of Susan Jacobs (McCord) Turner," BRH.

47. My understanding of the Philadelphia Savings Fund Society (PSFS) is informed

by R. Daniel Wadhwani, "The Demise of Thomas Dyott: Experimenting with Popular Finance in Jacksonian Philadelphia," paper presented at *The Panic of 1837*, Program in Early American Economy and Society conference, LCP, October 2007.

**48.** *Franklin Gazette*, 5 March 1818.

**49.** Thomas Eddy, Zachariah Lewis and James Eastburn, "A Bank for the Poor," *Commercial Advertiser*, 28 November 1816, quoted by Wadhwani, "Demise of Thomas Dyott," 11.

**50.** Wadhwani, "Demise of Thomas Dyott," 26.

**51.** Acct. 14069, PSFS Records, 1816–1990, Hagley Museum and Library, vol. 8. See also Michael Nash, "Research Note: Searching for Working-Class Philadelphia in the Records of the Philadelphia Savings Fund Society," *Journal of Social History* 29, no. 3 (1996): 683.

**52.** Religious Society of Free Quakers Records, Dorcas Report, January 1829, box 5, APS.

**53.** Register no. 2, 31 December 1827, Hagley Museum and Library.

**54.** Duffin, "Transcription of the 1909 Affadavit of Susan Jacobs (McCord) Turner," and Duffin, "Transcription of the 1909 Affadavit of Margaret McCord Smith," both BRH.

**55.** Receipt Book, 1828–38, Religious Society of Free Quakers, box 5, APS. William Pile's name does not appear in family genealogies; perhaps he was an infant whose birth is not elsewhere recorded, or possibly this is some other member of the Pile family.

**56.** Receipt Book, 1828–38, Religious Society of Free Quakers, box 5, APS; and loose accounts, Free Quaker meeting, Marian S. Carson Collection, box 28, folder 14, LOC.

**57.** Minutes, 6 July 1832 and 6 December 1827, Minute Book, 1804–11; 1827–84, Religious Society of Free Quakers, box 1, APS. Clarissa's daughter Sophia Hildebrandt would also become a member of the Free Quakers by the mid-1840s.

**58.** *Harper's Weekly*, 13 July 1872, 554.

**59.** Receipt, 17 May 1834, Religious Society of Free Quakers, box 4, APS.

**60.** Receipt Book, 1828–38, Religious Society of Free Quakers, box 5, APS.

**61.** For the 1834 date, see Edwin Satterthwaite Parry, *Betsy Ross, Quaker Rebel* (Philadelphia: John C. Winston Company, 1932). Charles Wetherill suggests that "meetings for religious worship ceased about 1836" in *History of the Religious Society of Friends Called by Some the Free Quakers, in the City of Philadelphia* (Philadelphia, 1894), 42. But the end of regular meetings did not mean the end of the community. The remaining members concluded that "a religious sense of devotion may be as well expressed in an honest life and in charitable works as by formally attending church or meeting at fixed intervals of time." They decided that they would "in some organized and distinct form . . . work as a charity, thereby recognizing that charity conducted on a proper motive is religion and worship, which Friends have always believed." The Religious Society of Free Quakers survives in Philadelphia as a philanthropic body even to today.

**62.** James Duffin, "Transcription of the Recollections of William Jackson Canby (1825–1890) of His Grandmother," BRH.

**63.** James Duffin, "Transcription of the 1909 Affidavit of Susan (Satterthwaite) Newport (1827–?) and Mary Satterthwaite (1824–?)," BRH.

**64.** James Duffin, "Transcription of Notes of Interview with Margaret (Donaldson) Boggs, 1776–1876," BRH.

**65.** Duffin, "Transcription of the Recollections of William Jackson Canby." Though

J. Franklin Reigart's *History of the First United States Flag and the Patriotism of Betsy Ross, the Immortal Heroine That Originated the First Flag of the Union* (Harrisburg, Pa., 1878) is suspect in every way, it's worth noting that it suggests that the 1824 return of the Marquis de Lafayette was a particular impetus to Betsy's storytelling, one of the few plausible notions in Reigart's book.

66. Duffin, ibid.

67. Ibid.

68. Ibid.

69. *American Daily Advertiser*, 1 February 1836: "Died, on Saturday afternoon, the 30th instant, Elizabeth Claypoole of this city, aged 84 years. Her friends are particularly invited to attend the funeral from the residence of her son-in-law C.H. Canby, No. 63 Cherry Street above 5th, this afternoon at 3 o'clock."


EPILOGUE

1. John Fanning Watson, *Annals of Philadelphia* (Philadelphia, 1857), 249.

2. Considerations of the Ross legend include Allan E. Peterson, "Cherished and Ignored: A Cultural History of Betsy Ross" (M.A. thesis, San Diego State University, 2001); JoAnn Menezes, "The birthing of the American flag and the invention of an American founding mother in the image of Betsy Ross," in Jean Pickering and Suzanne Kehde, eds., *Narratives of Nostalgia, Gender, and Nationalism* (New York: New York University Press, 1996); and Laurel Thatcher Ulrich, "How Betsy Ross Became Famous: Oral tradition, nationalism, and the invention of history," *Common-Place* 8 no. 1 (October 2007), www.common-place.org.

3. William J. Canby, "The First American Flag and Who Made It," Lloyd M. Balderston Collection, Huntington Library, San Marino, Calif. On the Bible, see Lewis D. Cook, "Family Records from the Bible of 'Betsy Ross' of Philadelphia," *Genealogies of Pennsylvania Families*, vol. 3 (1982), 905. The affidavits made no mention of any papers or records associated with Betsy Ross or kept as an effort to preserve her memory. In 1893, however, some Claypoole family papers were discovered in a store at Fourth and Spruce; they were delivered to the city's Orphan's Court upon discovery, and claimed by George Canby, *Philadelphia Inquirer*, 16 December 1893. The nature of these materials and their subsequent history is not known.

4. David A. Kimball, *Venerable Relic: The Story of the Liberty Bell* (Philadelphia: Eastern National Park Association, 1989).

5. Thomas Jefferson to John Holmes, 22 April 1820, as quoted in Daniel Walker Howe, *What Hath God Wrought: The Transformation of America, 1815–1848* (New York: Oxford University Press, 2007), 157.

6. William J. Canby, in "The History of the Flag of the United States," a paper read before the Historical Society of Pennsylvania (March 1870), BRH, says the house stood on the southwest corner of Front Street and Norris' Alley. According to city directories, the "situation . . . near Dock St. on the same side of Front" was probaby 112 (or 114 or 118—all turn up one place or another) Front Street, where Clarissa appears about 1828, and remained until 1833. If Jane's memory is correct, Betsy was in this space as early as 1809. The evidence on this move is conflicting, to be sure. In the 1850 directory, Clarissa lists her business address as 114 South Front, and home at 11 Prune. She listed no occupation in the 1850 Federal Census. For that record and the information on her family discussed below, see 1850 U.S. Federal Census, Philadelphia, Pennsylvania, Dock Ward,

14. Digital scan of original records in the National Archives, Washington, D.C., subscription database (http://www.ancestry.com/), accessed September 2009.

7. *McElroy's Philadelphia Directory for 1854*. Clarissa seems to have moved into a house that her brother-in-law Caleb owned at 36 Branch Street. Branch was a small street that ran from Third to Fourth streets between Sassafras and New. See Insurance Survey S08636, Philadelphia's Contributionship Digital Archives.

8. Mary Cresson Receipt Book, 1832–62, JDC.

9. James Duffin, "Transcription of the 1909 Affidavit of Susan Jacobs (McCord) Turner, 1819–1910," BRH.

10. Lewis D. Cook, "Family Records from the Bible of 'Betsy Ross' of Philadelphia," *Genealogies of Pennsylvania Families from the Pennsylvania Genealogical Magazine*, vol. 3 (Baltimore: Genealogical Publishing, 1982), 905–6.

11. See Ruth B. Lippincott, ed., *The Balderston Family, Colora Branch* (Colora, Md.: privately printed, 1959), 21, 28, 70. The Albrights were the family of Clarissa's daughter Rachel.

12. Pile Family Papers, 1793–1836, HSP.

13. James Duffin, "Transcription of William J. Canby's Lecture on Betsy Ross and the Flag," and Duffin, "Transcription of the 1909 Affidavit of Susan (Satterthwaite) Newport (1827–?) and Mary Satterthwaite (1824–?)," BRH. Some family members asserted that she made flags for the government until 1857, others that she worked until 1857 but that in her latter years accepted orders only from the merchant marine, having left government work earlier.

14. See Charles Wetherill, *History of the Religious Society of Friends Called by Some the Free Quakers, in the City of Philadelphia* (Philadelphia, 1894), appendix 12.

15. Flag in the collections of the BRH, evaluated by the H. F. du Pont Winterthur Museum, spring 2009. A perplexing notice in the annals of the Frankford Historical Society complicates the issue. According to an address later delivered to the society, about the same time that Clarissa withdrew from government contracts the original Ross flag was presented to the State Library of Pennsylvania along with a few other items. In 1847, it was supposed to have been "borrowed" by a Captain Williams of the Second Pennsylvania (Cameron Guards) to carry into battle in the Mexican War. The address describes Williams's role at Chalpultepec, leading the charge wrapped in Betsy Ross's flag, where he captured the commander of that fortress and had him lead the way to the top of the structure so that the flag could be flown there. The address does not relate what happened to the flag after that dramatic moment. But the (unidentified) speaker then claims—as the tale itself suggests—that this story of the flag's origin was known decades before Betsy's grandson asserted it in 1870. It is hard to know what to make of this anecdote, since it is difficult to believe that any such flag ever existed; no such artifact is ever mentioned among the family recollections, and if this important relic had actually survived the Revolution and been returned to them or was otherwise known, surely some mention of it, or at least its loss, would have been made in the several affidavits Canby later gathered. But it is also difficult to imagine what possible events could have served as the basis for this address. Was some Revolutionary-era flag associated with Ross's shop in fact carried by Williams in this war? Did Clarissa object to seeing the product of her mother's shop harnessed in a war that many found ill-advised at best, if not downright abhorrent? Edward W. Richardson, *Standards and Colors of the America Revolution* (Philadelphia: University of Pennsylvania Press, 1982), 35, illustrates a flag with thirteen red and white stripes and twelve stars encircled

on the canton (the thirteenth placed at the circle's center) carried by Maryland volunteers in the Mexican War. Perhaps some similar flag was carried by Pennsylvanians, giving rise to this story.

16. In Maryland, Betsy's granddaughter Catherine Canby and her husband, Lloyd Balderston, would also sacrifice for their pacifist commitment, having refused to pay war-related taxes. See Lippincott, *The Balderston Family*, 41.

17. William A. Kingston and Linda A. Fisher state that Betsy's remains were moved in 1857 "due to the construction of a city building" in "Authenticity of the Betsy Ross House," typescript, 1975, BRH.

18. Howe, *What Hath God Wrought*, 128.

19. *PG*, 17 January 1784.

20. Edwin T. Freedley, *Philadelphia and Its Manufactures: A Hand-book exhibiting the Development, Variety and Statistics of the Manufacturing Industry of Philadelphia* (Philadelphia, 1858), 244–46, 255. See also Susan Garfinkel, "Genres of Worldliness: Meanings of the Meetinghouse for Philadelphia Friends, 1755–1830" (Ph.D. dissertation, University of Pennsylvania, 1997).

21. Freedley, *Philadelphia and Its Manufactures*, 246.

22. Ibid., 239–40.

23. Ibid., 275, 399; and Marc Leepson, *Flag: An American Biography* (New York: Macmillan, 2006), 86.

24. George Sturges, 92 Walnut Street SW, corner at Baltimore and Frederick streets (Baltimore), Trade Card Collection, JDC.

25. Roger William Moss Jr., "Master Builders: A History of the Colonial Philadelphia Buildings Trades" (Ph.D. dissertation, University of Delaware, 1972), 186. On the strike, see Louis H. Arky, "The Mechanics Union of Trade Associations and the formation of the Philadelphia Workingmen's Movement," *PMHB* 76, no. 2 (1952): 142–76.

26. Edward Hazen, *Panorama of professions and trades: or, Every man's book* (Philadelphia, 1836), 224.

27. *Philadelphia Inquirer*, 7 July 1963, clipping file, INHP. To date, no other evidence can be located to affirm the assertion.

28. John Fanning Watson, *Annals of Philadelphia* (Philadelphia: 1850), 327. *The Female Review*, Deborah Sampson Gannett's memoir of her experience as a soldier in the Continental Service, was available at Mathew Carey's shop; see *The Constitutional Diary and Philadelphia Evening Advertiser*, 10 December 1799. Interestingly, Watson seems to have been acquainted with the Canby family (see *Annals*, 434) and surely encountered the Morgans in the two years (1804–6) that he spent attempting to launch a business in New Orleans; if they recounted any stories to him about the making of the first flag, he did not include them in his publications.

29. See the biography of Darragh on the Web site of the Independence Hall Association, http://www.ushistory.org/March/bio/lydia.htm, accessed 14 July 2008.

30. See Elizabeth Fries Ellet, *Women of the American Revolution*, vol. 3 (New York, 1856), 382.

31. The *Philadelphia North American* article was republished in the Albany, New York, *Evening Journal* of 16 February 1844, accessible at http://www.fultonhistory.com. William Rea Furling, Byron McCandless and Harold D. Langley discuss this article in *So Proudly We Hail: The History of the United States Flag* (Washington, D.C.: Smithsonian Institution Press, 1981), 114.

32. J. Franklin Reigart, *The United States Album, Embellished with the Arms of*

*Each State . . . , Containing the Autographs of the President and Cabinet . . .* (Lancaster City, Pa., 1844).

33. Schuyler Hamilton, *History of the National Flag of the United States of America* (Philadelphia, 1852).

34. *Godey's Lady's Book* 45 (November 1852).

35. Joseph Boggs Beale (1841–1926) diary, in the Joseph Boggs Beale Papers, 1852–82, HSP.

36. Margaret and Sarah Donaldson had both grown close to their aunt Betsy after their parents, Sarah and William Donaldson, died, and when Margaret reached an advanced age in the 1840s, she moved in with Sarah's daughter Louise McCord. Margaret apparently had a strong effect on those children. Louise would name her first son after Margaret's long-deceased spouse, and it was Charles McCord who opened a branch of the family enterprise on the Gulf Coast of Alabama.

37. "Affidavit of the Children of Stephen and Louisa Boggs Beale," 12 January 1909, Bucks County Historical Society, Doylestown, Pa.

38. This account of the Albrights is drawn from http://www.fmiowa.com/albright/, a Web site created by Rob and Carol Davis, the present owners and restorers of the Albright house in Fort Madison. I am deeply grateful for their generosity and willingness to share information they've gathered.

39. Charles J. Lukens describes learning about the five-pointed stars from George Canby about 1867 in a letter to George Henry Preble, 22 July 1872, Manuscripts Department, Preble October, vol. 3, 183, American Antiquarian Society, Worcester, Mass. I am grateful to Jessica Lepler for passing on this reference.

40. George Henry Preble, *Our Flag: Origin and Progress of the Flag of the United States of America* (Albany, 1872), 192–94.

41. See J. Thomas Scharf and Thompson Westcott, *History of Philadelphia, 1609–1884* (Philadelphia, 1884), vol. 2, chap. 41, "Prominent Women in Philadelphia History."

42. J. Franklin Reigart, *The History of the First United States Flag, and the Patriotism of Betsy Ross, the Immortal Heroine That Originated the First Flag of the Union* (Harrisburg, Pa., 1878); George Henry Preble, *History of the Flag of the United States of America*, 2nd ed. (Boston, 1880), 267. On Reigart's book, see also the *Boston Evening Transcript*, 12 February 1879.

43. Addie Guthrie Weaver, *The Story of Our Flag* (Chicago, 1898).

44. See Robert E. Bonner, "Star-spangled Sentiment," in *Common-Place* 3, no. 2 (2003), www.common-place.org; Stuart McConnell, "Reading the Flag: A Reconsideration of the Patriotic Cults of the 1890s," in John Bodnar, ed., *Bonds of Affection: Americans Define Their Patriotism* (Princeton, N.J.: Princeton University Press, 1996), 102–19, and Marc Leepson, *Flag: An American Biography* (New York: Macmillan, 2006), 148–49.

45. *Philadelphia and Popular Philadelphians: Illustrated with Many Views and Portraits* (Philadelphia, 1891), 227.

46. Ibid.

47. *Philadelphia Inquirer*, 27 September 1997.

48. Leepson, *Flag*, 46.

49. Rachel's daughter Kate Albright Robinson reported some of this to William J. Canby; he describes the activity to George Canby in an undated letter, ca. 1876, ALS, Lloyd M. Balderston Collection, HM 41760, folio 20-B, Huntington Library, San Marino, Calif., transcription in the collections of the BRH. See also *Daughters of the American Revolution Magazine* 22 (1903): 659.

50. Canby, undated letter, ca. 1876.

51. My thanks to Terry Borton, director of the American Magic-Lantern Theater, which re-creates Beale's shows, for providing this information on Beale's image.

52. Rupert Griscom to Oliver Randolph Parry, 16 January 1909, Betsy Ross files, Bucks County Historical Society, Doylestown, Pa.

53. Edwin Satterthwaite Parry, *Betsy Ross: Quaker Rebel* (Philadelphia: John Winston, 1930).

54. Norman Rosten, "The Lady and the Flag," episode 283, 15 June 1942; my deep thanks to Anne Boylan for sharing her notes on this episode with me.

55. *New York Times*, 28 December 1971; Lynn C. Spangler, *Television Women from Lucy to Friends: Fifty Years of Sitcoms and Feminism* (Westport, Conn.: Praeger, 2003), 121.

56. For an account of its discovery, see Robert Morris, *The Truth about the Betsy Ross Story* (Beach Haven, N.J.: Wynnehaven, 1982), 115–16. Morris cites Reeves Wetherill, clerk of the Religious Society of Free Quakers, who reported that "one day, about 1925" his father invited him to watch a safe blower open a safe once belonging to Samuel Wetherill, "and in it we found the star with the notation." The star was at rest in the Free Quaker meetinghouse until 2004, when it was discovered to be missing. But the signature on it, H. C. Wilson, is not obviously associated with Clarissa Wilson or her children; the signer's identity remains unknown. For one analysis of the star, and an illustration of it, see John Harker, *Betsy Ross's Five Pointed Star* (Melbourne Beach, Fla.: Canmore Press, 2005).

57. James Loewen, *Lies My Teacher Told Me* (New York: Simon and Schuster, 1996), 31.

58. For this phrase, see Canby, "History of the Flag in the United States," BRH.

59. For the transformation of Front Street, see the 1951 Sanborn map, illustrated in Meghan MacWilliams, "A Case Study of Philadelphia's Preservation Policy: The Square Block of Chestnut, Walnut, Front and Second Streets" (M.S. thesis, University of Pennsylvania, 1999).

# ACKNOWLEDGMENTS

This book began in the office of Lisa Moulder, then curator and now director at the Betsy Ross House. Without her immediate support and generosity, the project would never have progressed beyond the idea stage, and it certainly would not have been as much fun without her ongoing collegiality and good humor. I am deeply grateful to her for making this work possible, and also to Lisa's colleagues Michelle Budenz and Megan Harris, who were no less cheerful or capable in fielding my many queries. Lori Rech, then director of the Betsy Ross House, also offered early encouragement, as did Stephanie Grauman Wolf, who urged me to dig deeper into Ross's world to give her story the telling so long overdue. Debra Force's excellent research report in support of interpretation at the museum provided the bedrock of the initial project; late in the work, she proved invaluable once again, bringing her expertise in early American art to bear on the study. The unpublished research of James Duffin also proved essential to the project's inception; like Debra, James also offered additional aid as the project evolved. I also want to acknowledge Avi Decter and all the other scholars who have contributed to interpretation at the Betsy Ross House through the years. Without their early, unpublished research, none of this would have been possible. One of these historians—Sandra Mackenzie Lloyd—merits a separate and special thanks: her especially thoughtful and thorough interpretive materials, as well as her enthusiasm and support for this book, proved both delightful and instrumental, especially in the project's formative months.

Dan Richter and the McNeil Center for Early American Studies got the project off to a great beginning, allowing me to enter a community of scholars who proved invaluable during that first year of research. Jessica Lepler, Rose Beiler, Cathy Kelly, Michelle McDonald and Randy Mason provided especially welcome camaraderie and hospitality during a sabbatical year in Philadelphia; on a subsequent fellowship at the H. F. du Pont Winterthur Museum and Library, I was fortunate to enjoy the sociability, intellectual companionship and encouragement of Kasey Grier, Jeanne Solensky, William Donnelly and Ryan Grover, all of whom made my numerous research trips to Delaware as enjoyable as they were productive. I am particularly grateful to the Winterthur curator Linda Eaton for proposing that we undertake an exhibit on Betsy Ross; she has become more than an ally, and in many ways a true partner, in the ongoing search for Betsy Ross's story. Searching for artifacts that inform this story was enormously enlightening in all sorts of scholarly ways, but for someone who has long thought of Winterthur as the absolute pinnacle of material culture study, the opportunity to work with the staff and collections there was a dream come true.

Archivists, curators and historians in Philadelphia and beyond of course proved extraordinarily generous. Special thanks are most certainly due to the staff of the Historical Society of Pennsylvania, including David Haugaard and particularly Sarah Heim, who became a most welcome, familiar and supportive face in the reading room there. Other Philly archivists and historians who proved exceptional resources include Stacey Peeples at the Pennsylvania Hospital; Valerie-Ann Lutz and Roy Goodman at the American Philosophical Society; Connie King at the Library Company of Philadelphia; Don Smith at Christ Church; Patricia O'Donnell at Swarthmore's Friends Historical Library; Ann Upton at the Quaker Collection at Haverford College; Karen Stevens and Karie Diethorn at Independence National Historical Park/National Park Service; John Pollack at the University of Pennsylvania Rare Book and Manuscript Library; Glenys Waldman at the Masonic Library and Museum of Pennsylvania; Bruce Laverty at the Philadelphia Athenaeum; Doug McVarish, principal architectural historian at John Miller Associates; and Paul Kesler at the Library of the Defense Supply Center, Philadelphia. I am grateful to Bill Robling at Historic Philadelphia, Inc., for his comments concerning Betsy's religious convictions. Beyond the City of Brotherly Love, I am indebted to Rich Colton of the Springfield Armory National Historic Site, Aimee Newell at the National Heritage Museum in Lexington, Massachusetts; and Olga Tsapina at the Huntington Library. I thank Martha Rowe at the Museum of Early Southern Decorative Arts in Old Salem, North Carolina, for her unfailingly prompt replies to my constant queries; and Eric Voboril at the Star Spangled Banner/Flag House Museum for an event-filled day prowling through those archives. Thanks, too, are due to Tony Roberts at the Baltimore City Archives; John Ferguson at the American National Insurance Company; and Terry Borton, director of the American Magic-Lantern Theater. Most especially, I am indebted, again, to Jeanne Solensky at Winterthur, who was very generous with her time and talent, both when I was in residence at Winterthur and in the months to follow.

Material culture scholars also allowed me to impose on their time and knowledge. David Conradsen graciously shared his research on Philadelphia upholsterers. Marcia Goldberg provided insight into nineteenth-century portraiture, and Jeffrey Kohn, Harry Langley, Claude Harkins and Marilyn Zoidis helped navigate the world of standards and ensigns. Others who were liberal with their expertise include several scholars who generously agreed to review all or part of the work in progress. These lovely friends and colleagues include Linda Baumgarten, Gary Nash, Elaine Crane, Laura Moore, Bob St. George and Susan Garfinkel. Carol Berkin has been especially supportive along the full course of this project, from conception to completion. I am indebted to everyone for their willingness to share their insights and knowledge with me.

One of the true delights of this work has been meeting many of Betsy Ross's descendants, who have been just as warm and generous in the twenty-first century as I've found their ancestors to be in the nineteenth. My sincere thanks to John Harker, Jim Balderston, Kent Buehler, Ron Lord, Cathy Gaskill, Leonard and Nancy Balderston Conrad, Bill and Carole Telfair, and the Balderston family at Colora Orchards. Rob and Carol Davis in Fort Madison, Iowa, have become wonderful stewards of Betsy's family memory there and also freely shared their knowledge.

Several students provided essential research assistance along the way. Sandy Perot, Jen Turner, Amanda Goodheart and Laura Miller at the University of Massachusetts all provided capable support for this project; Laura Johnson furnished invaluable help in tracking down family records in the Philadelphia Savings Fund Society records at the Hagley Library; Rachel Guberman and Greg Ablavsky tackled deed research at the Philadelphia City Archives; and Claire Long surveyed naval records at the National Archives.

The project was brought to completion in the comfortable quarters of the C. V. Starr Center in Chestertown, Maryland, streets once walked by John Claypoole himself. I am so grateful to Adam Goodheart, Jill Ogline Titus, Michael Buckley, Jenifer Endicott and the folks associated with the center for the leap of faith they showed by offering me a home in which to complete this work and to plant new seeds from it.

A handful of people, in particular, helped transform this idea from something I "ought" to do into the book now in hand. I will never forget getting a call from George Hodgman, then at Henry Holt, and having him ask, "Are you really writing a book about Betsy Ross?" I of course gave him a firm and enthusiastic yes—though at the time my thinking hadn't evolved much beyond "I really ought to write a book about Betsy Ross." I have my friend and former colleague Kevin Boyle to thank for taking this idea out of my head and ushering it into the world at large, and bringing me into George's orbit. George Hodgman introduced me to Brettne Bloom, who believed in this project from the outset. And finally, George's capable successor, David Patterson, together with the extraordinary and hardworking staff at Henry Holt, especially Kathleen Cook and Allison McElgunn, brought the project to successful and timely conclusion.

Two other people urged me to go forward at that same moment, and helped convert "should" to "am." My UMass colleague Dave Toomey enthusiastically insisted I take on this project, and he has been a wonderful source of support and advice along the way. My brother-in-law P. J. Horgan, too, grasped immediately the importance of this story and urged me to plunge ahead. His support together with that of the rest of my family—Roger and Phyllis Miller, Todd Miller, and the Peck, Horgan, and Novak clans—sustained me through these years of research and writing. Of these, perhaps no one was as downright excited about this book than my father; I will miss giving him his weekly updates, and am glad he was able to see the project through nearly to completion. And finally I am grateful to Stephen K. Peck, who makes all things possible.

# INDEX

Abington meetinghouse, 247, 256

Abington Monthly meeting, 37, 39, 335

abolition movement, 32, 98, 126, 256–60, 345

Abram (enslaved African), 260

Adams, Abigail, 13, 189, 357

Adams, Charles B. F., 334

Adams, John, 13, 114, 119, 128, 137, 178, 189, 196–97, 301, 306

Administration of Justice Act (Britain, 1774), 128

Admiralty Court of Pennsylvania, 179

Affleck, Thomas, 4, 73, 186, 225, 261

African Americans, 9, 27–28, 32, 124–26, 141, 203, 257–60, 292–94, 339, 348

Alabama, 346

Albright, Anne, 355

Albright, Catharine (great granddaughter), 355

Albright, Clarence (great grandson), 355

Albright, Daniel (great grandson), 355

Albright, Jacob, 355

Albright, Jacob (great grandson), 355

Albright, Kate, 355

Albright, Rachel Wilson (granddaughter), 355, 358–59

Albright, R. W., 355

Albright, William, 355

Alfred (ship), 164–65

Allen, Ethan, 146

Allen, James, 156, 199

Alliborne, William, 161

Amelia (ship), 278

American Daily Advertiser, 342

American flag, first. See Claypoole, Betsy Griscom Ross Ashburn; Flag, first American; flags, early

American Flag House and Betsy Ross Memorial Association, 358

American Philosophical Society Hall, 131, 143

American Quarterly Review, 352

American Record and Charleston Advertiser, 255

American Revolution. See also Continental Congress; Flag, first America; and specific events and individuals
accusations of treason during, 156–58
Betsy and lives of artisans and women in, 9–15, 344, 361–62
Betsy and mythology of, 5–6
British advance on Delaware, 174, 187–88
British fleet occupies Philadelphia, 197–207
Carpenters' Company and, 135–36
civil liberties and, 188–90
Clarissa Wilson hopes to establish mother's life in history of, 352–55
defeat of Cornwallis at Yorktown ends, 217, 219

American Revolution (*cont'd*)
  first battles in, 145–52, 155–56
  flag making for, 161–66
  flags of, sold at Sotheby's auction house, 1–3
  hardships and scarcities during, 188, 206–9
  John Claypoole and, 9, 224–32
  John Ross's family and, 119–20, 128
  Joseph Ashburn as privateer and prisoner in, 192–95, 212–17
  Masons and, 133
  Mysore and, 231
  Quaker opposition to, 134–35, 239–40
  resistance to taxation leading up to, 78–80, 96, 113–14, 127–29, 133
  Test Act and oath of allegiance during, 189–91
  Willard's *The Spirit of '76* and, 160–61
  women raise funds for, 210–11
Amherst, Gen. Jeffery, 42
*Analectic Magazine*, 325
Andre, John, 205
*Andrew Doria* (ship), 164
Anglicans. *See* Church of England
*Annals of Philadelphia* (Watson), 352–53, 356
Annan, Dr. Robert, 283
*Anti-Slavery Record, The*, 345
"Apology for the Religious Society called Free Quakers, An," 241
*Architect: by And Palladio*, 35
*Arethusa* (ship), 300
Armistead, Comm. George, 325
Armstrong, Catherine, 298
Armstrong, James, 297–99
Armstrong, Joanna Ross Holland (sister-in-law), 149–50, 169, 199, 297–99
Arnold, Benedict, 205
Articles of Association, 141
artisans, 12. *See also* flags, early; upholstery trade
  Betsy's family as, 19, 22–23, 52–55
  British occupation of Philadelphia and, 203–5
  building of Philadelphia and, 23–24, 34
  cabinetmakers, 204, 225, 235
  Claypoole family and, 225
  Continental forces outfitted by, 156, 158–66, 174
  furniture and furnishing, 4–5, 28–29, 57, 58–60, 91–92, 186, 235, 266

  government contracts and, after Revolution, 296–97
  homes of, 275
  house carpenters, 12, 22–26, 34, 51, 89, 95, 238, 270, 288, 351
  industrial revolution and, 333–34, 349–51
  joiners, 225, 235–36
  mantua makers, 53–55
  Quaker plain style and, 59
  ratification of Constitution procession and, 287–88
  resistance and nonimportation and, 86, 91, 94–97, 131, 138–43
  silversmiths, 59–60, 186–87, 288
  staymakers, 52–54
  textiles and, 28, 38, 85–86, 92, 160, 349–51
  women as, 11, 52–55
Ashburn, Aucilla "Zillah" (daughter), 208–10
Ashburn, Elizabeth Griscom. *See* Claypoole, Elizabeth Griscom Ross Ashburn "Betsy Ross"
Ashburn, Eliza (daughter), 212, 223, 235, 262, 305–6. *See also* Silliman, Eliza
Ashburn, George, 185
Ashburn, Joseph (second husband), 9, 14, 233, 242, 288, 319, 346
  birth of children and, 208–10
  death of, 218–19
  imprisonment of, 211–18, 228–31
  marries Betsy, 183–87
  as privateer, 187, 191–96, 200
Ashburn, Martin, 185
Associators of the City and Liberties of Philadelphia, 151, 174
Asylum for the Relief of Persons Deprived of the Use of Their Reason, 329
Atwater Kent Museum, 49
*Augusta* (ship), 200
Ayres, Capt. Samuel, 121

Balderston, Catherine Canby (granddaughter), 347–48, 355
Ballard, Martha, 13
Bank meetinghouse, 26, 238, 242, 292
Bank of Pennsylvania, 275, 327
Bannerman, Benjamin, 256
Barney, Commodore Joshua, 231, 325
Barton, William, 176
Baumgarten, Linda, 69, 73
Bayer, Frederick, 209
Beale, Joseph Boggs (great-nephew), 354–55, 359

Beale, Louise McCord (great-niece), 354
Beckman, Charlotte, 333
Benezet, Anthony, 46, 48, 248, 257
Benezet, Philip, 261
Benge, Samuel, 69, 296–97
Bernard, Nicholas, 4
Berrett, Anna, 318
Berrett, Mary, 319
Berrett, Timothy, 161, 319
Berrett, William, 161, 318–22, 324, 332
Betsy Ross Bridge, 360
*Betsy Ross* (film), 5
Betsy Ross House, 3–6, 319, 344, 356–58, 360–61
Bettering House, 337
Biddle, Clement, 240, 338–39
Biddle, Edward (uncle of John Ross), 120, 126, 133, 135, 138, 144–46
Biddle, Elizabeth Ross (aunt of John Ross), 120, 126
Biddle, Nicholas, 338
Biddle, Rebecca, 353
Biles, Benjamin, 234
Birchall, Rebeckah, 48
Bird, Mark (uncle of John Ross), 120
Bird, Mary Ross (aunt of John Ross), 120
*Blacksnake* (whale boat), 232
Boardman, Mary, 110
Boehm, Philip, 190, 191
Boggs, Joseph, 303–4
Boggs, Margaret Donaldson (niece), 14, 198, 203, 272–73, 297, 303–4, 313–14, 316, 323, 328–31, 334–35, 338–40, 347, 354–55
Bolton, Abel, 306
Bolton, Aquilla (nephew), 238, 336, 347
Bolton, Deborah Griscom (sister), 43, 50, 55, 86, 105, 126, 149, 272, 278
  death of, 277, 281–83, 289, 305
  marriage of, to Everard Bolton, 98–100, 103, 117, 247
Bolton, Everard, elder, 100
Bolton, Everard, younger (brother-in-law), 50, 55, 86, 99–100, 149, 271, 278, 289
Bolton, Isaac, 100, 126, 271
Bolton, Sarah, 100
Bolton, Sarah Jones, 100
Bond, Dr. Thomas, 109
Bonner, Robert E., 357
*Book of Discipline*, 58–60, 99, 295
*Book of Trades, The*, 54–55

Boone, Daniel, 5
Boston, 34, 57, 71, 89, 92, 95, 114, 121, 128–29, 137, 144, 147
Boston Port Act (Britain, 1774), 130–31
Boudinot, Elias, 240
Bowman, James, 116
boycotts, 83–85, 90–96, 112, 137–40
Boyd, Alexander, 301
Boyd, Amelia Silliman (granddaughter), 347
Boyd, Elizabeth Ashburn (great granddaughter), 347
Bradford, Mrs. Thomas, 277
Bradley, Stephen R., 317
Brady, Alice, 5
Brandywine, Battle of, 197
Breeds Hill, Battle of, 147
Breen, T. H., 84
Brice, James, 276
Bridges, Cornelia, 163, 166, 170, 181
Bridges, Edward, 163
Bridges, Robert, 163
British Army, 128, 144, 149–50, 196–207
British merchant vessels, 192–94
British Parliament, 80, 84, 86, 88, 90, 94, 111–14, 128, 137, 144, 214, 216, 219
British Privy Council, 127
British Royal Navy, 163, 192, 196–207, 317, 324
Bronaugh, Mr., 322
Brooks, Nicholas, 147
Brown, Rachel, 66
Browne, Jonathan, 121
Bryant, Judge George, 259
Budd, John, 57
Buford, Abraham, 2, 162
*Bulldog* (ship), 163
Burgoyne, Gen. John, 198, 354
Burkhardt, Andrew, 210
Burrows, Hannah, 293–94
Bushnell, David, 200–201
Butland, James, 204
Butland, Mary, 333
Butz, Richard, 4
Byles, Thomas, 52
Byrd, Rear Adm. Richard, 360

*Cabot* (ship), 164
Cadwalader, Elizabeth Lloyd, 72–73
Cadwalader, John, 3–4, 57, 61, 70, 72–73, 133, 259, 319, 347
Calhoun, John, 340
Cambden, Lord, 87
Camerarius, Joachim, 2

Campbell, Robert, 53–54, 56, 71, 351
Campion, Elizabeth Wilson (granddaughter),
    313–14, 328, 331, 346–48, 355
Canby, Caleb (son-in-law), 329, 335–39
Canby, Catherine (granddaughter, *later*
    Balderston), 347–48
Canby, George (grandson), 5–6, 358
Canby, Jane Claypoole (daughter), 200,
    275–76, 284, 297–98, 324, 329, 334–35,
    337, 347, 350, 355
Canby, William Jackson (grandson), 5–7, 14,
    50, 158, 275, 298, 341–42, 344–46, 349,
    354–61
Cantril, Richard, 24
Carey, Mathew, 277
Carpenters' Company, 34, 44, 89, 121, 132–33,
    135–36, 138, 217, 238, 270, 282
    Hall, 135, 173, 352
Cathrall, Hannah, 47, 49, 116
Cathrall, Isaac, 248, 290
*Cavalcade of America* (radio program), 360
Center meetinghouse, 25–26, 31
Chalkley, Thomas, 40–41
*Chalkley* (ship), 41
Chambers, David, 245
*Champion* (ship), 164
Charity (indentured African), 258–59
Charles I, King of England, 20
Charles II, King of England, 20, 22
Charlestown, Battle of, 147
*Charming Polly* (ship), 94, 121–22
*Chesapeake*, USS (ship), 317, 320
Chew, Benjamin, 139–43, 155, 198, 332,
    347
Chew, Peggy, 205
Chew, Sarah, 205
Chicago Historical Society, 322
Choctaw Indians, 321
Christ Church, 104, 108, 126, 130, 136–37,
    147–48, 152, 237, 297–98
Christie's (auction house), 3
Church of England (Anglican Church),
    20–21, 32, 107, 117, 126, 145, 224
city almshouse, 289, 305, 337
City Tavern, 273–74, 352
Civil War, 345, 348–50, 355–57
Clark, Ephraim, 249, 276
Clarkson, Matthew, 217
Clarkson, Thomas, 258
Clay, Henry, 340
Claypoole, Abraham (cousin of John
    Claypoole), 225

Claypoole, Clarissa (daughter). *See* Wilson,
    Clarissa
Claypoole, David (cousin of John Claypoole),
    225
Claypoole, Elizabeth, number of women with
    name of, 208
Claypoole, Elizabeth Cromwell (ancestor of
    John Claypoole), 224
Claypoole, Elizabeth Griscom Ross Ashburn
    "Betsy Ross"
  abolition and, 256–60
  African American child living with John
    Ross and, 9, 124–26, 257
  Arch street homes of, 3–6, 13, 44–45, 61,
    155–56, 176, 201–2, 209–10, 217–18, 319,
    356–58, 361 9 (*see also* Betsy Ross
    House)
  artisanal work by women and, 4–5, 8–9,
    11, 52–56
  auction of items made by, at record-setting
    prices, 3
  Bible of, 285
  biographies of, 13–14
  birth and childhood of, 36–37, 43–45, 49
  birth of daughter Aucilla Ashburn, 208–9
  birth of daughter Clarissa Claypoole and,
    235
  birth of daughter Eliza Ashburn and, 212
  birth of daughter Harriet Claypoole,
    304–5
  birth of daughter Jane Claypoole and,
    275–76
  birth of daughter Susan Claypoole and,
    235
  *Birth of Our Nation's Flag* painting
    depicting, 358
  boarders taken in by, 267–68, 328–29
  brother-in-law Thomas Morgan's decline
    and, 249
  brothers and sisters born, 44
  Cadwalader order and, 3–5, 72–74
  charitable giving by, 337
  Chew order and, 139–42
  Constitution ratification and, 288
  Cornwallis defeat at Yorktown and, 217
  cousin Rebecca Griscom moves in with, 46
  daughter Clarissa Claypoole Wilson and,
    165, 306, 313–14, 328
  daughter Eliza Ashburn Silliman and, 235,
    305–6, 313, 334–35
  daughter Jane Claypoole Canby and, 284,
    329

daughter Rachel Jones Fletcher and, 50, 315, 335

daughters' education and, 286, 302–3

daughters' portraits and, 310

daughter Susan Claypoole Satterthwaite and, 329

death and burial of, 339, 342, 344–45, 349

death of daughter Aucilla Ashburn and, 210

death of daughter Eliza Ashburn Silliman, 340

death of great-aunt Sarah Griscom and, 74

death of husband John Claypoole and, 331

death of husband John Ross and, 151–52, 155, 166

death of husband Joseph Ashburn and, 218–20, 231

death of sister Hannah's husband and, 270–72

death of sister Rachel and bequest of, 335–37

death of sister Rebecca and, 295–96

descendants of, 306, 313–14, 339–40, 347–48

education of, 46–49, 51

family background of father and, 19–35

family background of mother and, 37–43

family life and household of, 9, 270, 272–73, 284, 303–6, 314–16, 331

Federalists and, in early nation, 301–2

finances of, 12, 211, 236, 265–68, 270, 335–39

first Continental Congress and, 132–38

first Independence Day celebration and, 183

flag legend and, 3, 5–7, 344

flag legend and, canon of Revolutionary women and popularization of, 357–62

flag legend and, commercial products celebrating, 6, 358–60

flag legend and, evidence weighed, 177–81

flag legend and, family stories on, 5–15, 168, 170, 175, 304, 344–45, 348, 354–55

flag legend and, preserved by daughter Clarissa Wilson, 344–46, 348–49, 352–55

flag legend and, preserved by grandson William Canby, 344–45, 356–57

flag legend and, scholarly debate over, 360–61

flags made by, 3, 12–13, 193

flags made by, and approach of War of 1812, 12–13, 309–10, 316–26

flags made by, and Revolutionary War, 155–56, 159, 162, 166–81

flags made by, with painter Berrett, 161, 318–22

Free Quakers aid, 9, 312–14, 328–29

Free Quakers and religious beliefs of, 237–47, 251–52, 297, 340–41

Front Street home of, 275, 330, 346

handkerchief vision of, in youth, 7, 11

husband John Claypoole's community activism and, 253–54

husband John Claypoole's Customs Service job and, 286, 299–302, 306

husband John Claypoole's illness and, 9, 309, 312–13

husband John Claypoole's travels to Demerara and, 274–75

husband John Ross's mental illness and, 108, 110

husband Joseph Ashburn as privateer and, 191–95

husband Joseph Ashburn's imprisonment and, 212–17

Joanna Ross Holland Armstrong and, 149–50, 169, 199, 297–98

legacy of, 360–62

Magic Lantern show on, by great-nephew Beale, 359

marriage of, to John Claypoole, 9, 223–24, 232–33

marriage of, to John Ross, 9, 105, 120–24, 186, 223

marriage of, to Joseph Ashburn, 9, 183–89, 191, 223

marriages of, 7, 11

Masons and, 133, 254

medicine and healing wisdom of, 283–84

meets John Ross, in Webster shop, 107–8, 110–11, 116–18

Nixon and, 174–75

old age of, 327–29, 336–44

personality and tastes of, 8, 13–15, 223–24, 285, 341–42

prison reform and, 261–62, 264

Quaker censure of brother George and, 249–50

Quaker censure of sisters and, 98–105

Quaker censure of uncle Abel James and, 250–51

Quaker family members and Test Act and, 189–91

Quakers disown, 32, 247

Claypoole, Elizabeth Griscom Ross Ashburn
"Betsy Ross" (cont'd)
resistance to British and political
awakening of, 77–81, 84–86, 88–89, 93,
96, 106, 112–15, 120–22
Revolution and, 343–44
Revolutionary War and, British
occupation of Philadelphia, 197–207
Revolutionary War and, defense of
Delaware, 188–89
Revolutionary War and, husband John
Ross's family, 145–52
Revolutionary War and, tensions with
Quakers, 11, 43, 127–36, 139, 156–58
Revolutionary War and, women's
manufacturing, 207–11
sister Rachel in upholstery trade and, 288
sister Rebecca's drinking and disownment
by Quakers, 247, 272, 289–95
slavery crises and, 346
theater reopening and, 254–56
upholstery apprenticeship of, in Webster's
shop, 4, 50–51, 57, 60–74
upholstery craft of, mechanized near end
of life, 350–52
upholstery shop of, 12
upholstery shop of, and Revolutionary
War, 158–59
upholstery shop of, and War of 1812,
324–27
upholstery shop of, with daughter Clarissa,
329–34
upholstery shop of, with John Claypoole,
232–36, 265–68, 273–74, 313
upholstery shop of, with John Ross, 122–24
upholstery shop of, with Philadelphia as
seat of government, 296–97
upholstery skills of, endure more than
other identities, 51–52, 55–56, 59
Washington and, 10, 167–81, 286, 297–99,
303, 310–12, 344
Wetherill bequest to nieces and daughter
and, 330–31
yellow fever and, 9, 276–85
Claypoole, Elizabeth Hall (mother-in-law),
225, 229
Claypoole, George, Jr. (grandson of Joseph
Claypoole), 225
Claypoole, George (son of John Claypoole's
great-grandfather James), 224–25
Claypoole, George (son of Joseph Claypoole),
235–36

Claypoole, Harriet (daughter), 304–5
Claypoole, James, elder (great grandfather of
John Claypoole,), 224–25, 285
Claypoole, James, Jr. (son of James Claypoole,
younger), 225
Claypoole, James, younger (uncle of John
Claypoole), 225, 227
Claypoole, James (painter and glazier), 161,
235
Claypoole, Jane (daughter). See Canby, Jane
Claypoole
Claypoole, John (great great-uncle of John
Claypoole), 224
Claypoole, John (third husband), 14, 346
abolition and, 256–60, 267
Betsy's nieces Margaret and Susanna
Donaldson and, 273
Bible and family records of, 235, 285
births of children of, 276, 235, 305
community activism and, 253–60, 329
Constitution ratification and, 288
Customs Service job of, 286, 299–302,
306
death of, 331
death of Joseph Ashburn and, 219
Demerara, South America, travels of,
274–76
education of daughters and, 302
family background and youth of, 224–32
financial problems of, 236, 265–68
Franklin and, 260
Free Quakers and, 237–38, 244, 246
government contracts and, 297, 316–17
government job of, in Comptroller's office,
273–74
marries Betsy, and joins upholstery trade,
9, 223–24, 232–36
Masonic Lodge and, 177
old age and illness of, 9, 309, 312–13, 328,
330
personality of, 223
prison reform and, 260–65
Revolutionary War privateering by, and
imprisonment, 9, 224–32
Southwark Theater reopening and, 254–56
tanning trade and, 12, 225, 233–35
upholstery trade and, 273–74
Washington and, 10, 311
yellow fever epidemic and, 281
Claypoole, Jonathan, 225
Claypoole, Joseph (son of John Claypoole's
great grandfather James), 225, 235

Claypoole, Josiah (son of George Claypoole, elder), 225

Claypoole, Josiah (son of Joseph Claypoole), 235

Claypoole, Rachel (daughter). *See* Fletcher, Rachel Claypoole Jones

Claypoole, Susan (daughter). *See* Satterthwaite, Susan Claypoole

Claypoole, William (father-in-law), 225, 229, 233–34

Claypoole & Wilson, 331–32, 345, 352

Coasts, Isaac, 138

Coates, Samuel, 275

Coersive (Intolerable) Acts, (Britain, 1774), 128, 137

Cole, Philip, 160

Columbian Exposition (1893), 5, 358–59

*Columbian Herald*, 255

*Columbus* (ship), 164

*Commercial Advertiser*, 331, 338

Committee of Forty-Three, 132

Committee of Nineteen, 129–31

Committee of Observation and Inspection, 143–44, 150

Committee of Safety, 146, 151, 157, 161, 239

*Common Sense* (Paine), 152, 155, 192

Concept Plan of Redress (Demerara proposal), 274

Concord, Battle of, 145

Congress Hall, 296–97

"Considerations on the Propriety of Imposing Taxes in the British Colonies" (Dulany), 87

Constitutional Convention, 171, 301

Continental Army, 2, 133, 196–97, 206–7, 210–11, 240, 301
  flags for, 162–66

Continental Association, 137–39, 141–43

Continental Board of Admiralty Seal, 179

Continental Congress
  first (1774), 120, 129, 132–38, 141–42, 144–45, 157, 173
  second (1775–80), 3, 74, 146–48, 150–51, 157–59, 161–71, 173–74, 177–80, 182, 189–90, 193, 206, 213, 217, 226, 239, 255, 324

Continental currency, 180

Continental Navy, 162–64, 170–71, 192, 231

Coombe, Rev. Thomas, 136, 147–48

Copley, John Singleton
  portrait of Paul Revere, 11

Cornell, Saul, 189

Cornwallis, Lord Charles, 198, 217, 219, 230–31

Council of Safety, 160–61, 239

Court of the Quarter Sessions, 26

Cox, William, 225

Coxe, Tench, 257–60, 316–18, 320–21, 323–24

Cresson, Mary, 347

Cromwell, Elizabeth, 224

Cromwell, Oliver, 20, 224, 228

Cross, R. R., 258–59

Cummings, Archibald, 126

Currency Act (Britain, 1764), 79

Currie, Dr. William, 283

Customs Service, 299–302, 306, 360

*Daily Evening Herald*, 355

Darragh, Ann, 352

Darragh, Charles, 240

Darragh, John, 240

Darragh, Lydia, 240, 352–53

Darragh, William, 352

Daughters of the American Revolution, 358

Davenport, Richardson, 232

Davis, John, 141, 246, 266–67, 288

Deane, Silas, 74

Dearborn, Henry, 318, 320

Declaration and Resolves, 138

Declaration of Independence, 133, 157, 159, 170–71, 174, 179, 183, 216, 226, 239, 328

"Declaration of the Causes and Necessity of Taking Up Arms," 146

Delany, Sharp, 299–301

Demerara, 274

*Diana* (ship), 300

Dickinson, John, 89, 118, 120, 129, 133, 144–45, 159

Dickinson, Jonathan, 24

*Dirty Jobs* (TV series), 233

Dixon, John, 275

Doane, Ephraim (brother-in-law), 101, 148–49, 185–87, 210, 305, 335

Doane, Jane, 306

Doane, Susannah Griscom (sister), 50, 98, 101–3, 105, 117, 148–49, 185–87, 210, 247, 284, 305, 324, 335

Dole, John (great great-uncle), 27, 32

Donaldson, Arthur, 104, 149, 156–57, 173

Donaldson, Elizabeth Kaighn (cousin), 104, 149

Donaldson, Margaret (niece). *See* Boggs, Margaret Donaldson

Donaldson, Sarah Griscom (sister), 50, 98, 103–5, 117, 149, 156–57, 173, 185, 203, 210, 219, 247, 272, 284, 305, 347, 354

Donaldson, Sarah (niece). *See* McCord, Sarah Donaldson Lownes

Donaldson, Susanna (niece), 272–73, 314

Donaldson, William (brother-in-law), 104, 149, 185, 203, 210, 219, 272, 284, 305, 315

Dorsey, Leonard, 210

Doubleday, Abner, 181

Douglass, David, 254

Douglass, Sarah Hallam, 254

*Dove* (ship), 232

*Dred Scott* decision, 348

Drinker, Elizabeth Sandwith, 65, 198–99, 282, 288–90, 292, 294–96

Drinker, Henry, 64–65, 77, 81, 83, 90, 94, 113, 115–16, 131, 190, 198, 242, 250, 261, 280, 288, 290, 292–95

Drinker, Jonathan, 290

Drinker, Joseph, 290, 293–94

Drinker, Sally, 289–91

Drinker, Sarah Bacon, 290

Drummond, Peter, 232

Duché, Rev. Jacob, 136

Dulany, Daniel, 87

Dunbar, William, 321

Dunlap, John, 225–26, 244

Dutch West India Company, 274

East India Company, 111–14, 137

Eden, Thomas, 230

Elizabeth I, Queen of England, 111

Elkfeldt, Jacob, 245

Ellet, Elizabeth Fries, 353

Elliot, John, 275

Embargo Acts (1807), 320

Emlen, Samuel, 250

*Emperor of Germany* (ship), 194

*Enquiry in the Effect of Spiritous Liquors* (Rush), 248

*Enterprise* (privateer), 9, 228

*Essay on Population* (Malthus), 338

*Essex Register*, 331

Evans, David, 204, 210, 296, 305

Evans, Evan, 246

*Evening Post*, 185

*Everyln's Parallels of Ancient and Modern Architecture*, 35

*Experiment* (ship), 163, 232

Eyre, Col. Jehu, 226

*Fair American* (privateer), 193

*Federal Gazette*, 256

Federalists, 287–88, 299, 301, 314, 316

"Female Patriots, The" (Griffits), 92

Female Society for the Relief of the Distressed, 253

Fennell, Margaret, 275

First Battalion of County Associators, 149

First Troop of Philadelphia, 161

Fisher, James C., 203

Fitch, John, 286

flag, first American. *See also* flags, early
  Betsy Ross and question of, 3–8, 167–81
  Betsy Ross legend of, popularized, 357–62
  *Birth of Our Nation's Flag* painting, 357–59
  change in, with admission of new states, 15, 317, 331–32
  Clarissa Wilson's desire to immortalize mother's contribution, 344–46, 348–49, 353–54
  Continental Congress and, 3, 167, 170, 180
  five- vs. six-pointed stars and, 5, 8, 168, 175–76, 181, 355, 359
  Hopkinson and, 179–80
  Nixon records on payment for, 175
  receipts and ledger entries and, 15
  rectangular vs. square, 168
  star arrangement and, 175–77, 179, 354
  as symbol of national unity, 344, 345–46, 357
  Washington discusses, with Putnam, 173

Flag Act (1777), 3, 317, 354

Flag Act (1793), 317

Flag Act (1818), 331–32

Flag Day, 2–3

flags, early, 12–13
  Clarissa Wilson makes, after Betsy's death, 346–48
  Continental forces and, 2, 59–66, 174, 178–79
  Cornelia Bridges and, 163, 170, 181
  Fort McHenry "Star Spangled Banner," 325–26
  increased demand for, in early nineteenth century, 309–10
  Indian presentation, 320–22
  industrialization and manufacturing of, 351
  Margaret Manny and, 163–65, 170, 181
  New Orleans garrison, 322–23
  privateers and, 193–94

rattlesnake symbol, 179
Rebecca Flower Young and, 163, 170, 181, 321, 325–26
types of, 159–61
War of 1812 and, 167–68, 316–26
William Young and, 321
women artisans and crafting of, 162–66
flag sheets (1781, 1783), 178
Fleeson, Plunket, 4, 57, 63, 65, 67, 73, 84, 91, 129, 131–32, 139, 158, 160, 170, 174, 204–7, 233, 260, 266, 318
Fleming, William, 72
Fletcher, Daniel (grandson), 339
Fletcher, John (son-in-law), 335
Fletcher, Mary (granddaughter), 339
Fletcher, Rachel Claypoole Jones (daughter), 6, 8, 10, 50, 136, 168–69, 171–72, 176, 297, 302, 310, 315, 318, 335, 339
Fletcher, Samuel, 271
*Flora* (ship), 210
Flower, Benjamin, elder, 164
Flower, Benjamin, younger, 164–65
Flower, Benjamin (tanner), 234
Flower, Ruth, 164
Folwell, Richard, 291, 294
Force Bill (1832), 340
Forde, Standish, 304
Forepaugh, George, 149
Fort McHenry, 325–26
Fort Mercer, 188, 200, 226, 231
Fort Mifflin, 175, 188, 200
Forton Prison, 213–14, 219–20
Fort Ticonderoga, 146
Fort Union, 325
Fort Wilson Riot, 207
Foulks, John, 234
Fourth Pennsylvania Battalion, 150
Fox, George, 20–22, 224
Frame of Government (1686), 254
France, 78–79, 98–99, 317
Franklin, Benjamin, 2, 13, 34–35, 41, 43, 45, 52, 83, 87, 95, 109, 118, 127, 151, 158–59, 178, 229–30, 244, 251, 257–58, 260–61, 208, 352
Franklin, Deborah, 34, 52
Franklin, Hannah Levering, 347
Franklin, Sarah, 356
Franklin, William, 87, 116, 118
Franklin, William Temple, 261
Franks, Abigail, 293
Franks, Rebecca, 205

*Freeman's Journal and Philadelphia Mercantile Adviser*, 338
Free Quakers, 9, 15, 237–47, 251–52, 254–56, 271, 282, 289, 297–98, 302, 304, 309–10, 312–14, 328–31, 336–41, 348, 352
burial ground, 342, 344, 349
Free Society of Traders, 224
French and Indian War, 42, 120. *See also* Seven Years War
Freneau, Philip, 279
Friend, Catherine, 207
Friendship Carpenters' Company, 270

Gage, Gen. Thomas, 128
Galloway, Joseph, 83, 113, 120, 132, 135, 137, 142, 144
Garrigues, Edward, 290
Gates, Gen. Horatio, 198
George (free black), 260
George III, King of England, 88, 97, 133, 150, 190, 219
Germantown, Battle of, 198–99, 226, 311, 353
Germon, John, 210
Girard, Stephen, 260
*Godey's Lady's Book*, 354
Goforth, Tabitha, 110
Gordon, Lord Adam, 78
Gostelowe, Jonathan, 162
Gostelowe Return, 162
Gouge, Thomas, 203
Gould, Stephen Jay, 181
Graaff, Johannes de, 164
Graff, Jacob, 159
Grand Union flag, 163–65, 167, 175, 181
Graydon, Mrs., 159
Great Britain (England)
emigration of Quakers from, 20–22
Intolerable Acts and, 129–32
Napoleonic wars and, 317–18
taxation of colonies by, 78–80
trade with, in early nation, 300
War of 1812 and, 323
Great Seal of the United States, 179, 318
Green, Capt. John, 212–13, 231
Greene, Gen. Nathanael, 314
*Griffen* (ship), 21
Griffitts, Hannah, 92
Griffitts, Samuel Powel, 296
Griscom, Abigail (sister), 45, 208, 276
Griscom, Andrew (great-grandfather), 19–32, 34, 43, 52, 55, 57, 64, 125, 224, 268, 275, 327, 349

Griscom, Andrew (uncle), 33
Griscom, Anna (family genealogist), 41
Griscom, Ann (sister), 45, 208
Griscom, Deborah Gabitas (grandmother).
    See Holloway, Deborah Griscom
Griscom, Deborah (sister). See Bolton,
    Deborah Griscom
Griscom, Elizabeth. See Claypoole, Elizabeth
    Griscom Ross Ashburn "Betsy Ross"
Griscom, George (brother), 12, 45, 51, 183,
    186, 217, 249–51, 288, 336, 347
Griscom, Grace Rakestraw (aunt), 45–46
Griscom, Hannah (sister). See McIntire,
    Hannah Griscom Levering
Griscom, Joseph (brother), 45, 208, 276
Griscom, Kitty Schreiner (sister-in-law),
    249–50
Griscom, Martha (sister), 45, 208
Griscom, Mary (sister). See Morgan, Mary
    Griscom
Griscom, Rachel (sister), 45, 66, 102, 105, 113,
    210, 217, 285, 288–89, 323, 330, 335
    death and will of, 295–96, 335–37
Griscom, Rebecca (cousin), 46, 51, 53–55
Griscom, Rebecca James (mother), 208, 249,
    269, 276, 289, 348
    Betsy's apprenticeship and, 49–51
    Betsy's marriage to John Ross and, 116–18,
        120
    birth of Betsy and, 37, 43–44
    death of, 277–78, 282–83
    education of, 48
    marriage of, 37–41
    marriage of daughters and, 99–105
    Revolution and, 130, 191, 210–11
Griscom, Rebecca (sister), 105, 210, 217, 272,
    305, 337
    disownment of, 247–49, 251, 289–95,
        348
Griscom, Samuel, first (brother), 45, 208
Griscom, Samuel, second (brother), 45, 208
Griscom, Samuel (father), 41, 49, 173, 238,
    249, 288, 302, 314, 348
    Betsy's marriage to John Ross and, 116–18,
        120
    birth of Betsy and, 37, 43–44
    childhood of, 33–34
    death of, 276–78, 282, 283, 289
    as house carpenter, 12, 34–35, 37, 44–45
    marries Rebecca James, 37–41, 43, 225
    marriage of daughters and, 97, 99–105
    old age of, 269–70

Revolution and, 88–89, 96, 113–15, 121,
    128–30, 132–36, 138, 190–91, 202–3, 210
sale of Arch Street house and, 217–18
Griscom, Sarah Dole (great grandmother,
    later Kaighn), 26–29, 32–33, 43, 52, 57,
    64, 125, 224
Griscom, Sarah (great-aunt), 27, 33–35, 45,
    51–53, 55, 74
Griscom, Sarah (sister). See Donaldson, Sarah
    Griscom
Griscom, Susannah (sister). See Doane,
    Susannah Griscom
Griscom, Tobias (grandfather), 27, 33
Griscom, Tobias (uncle), 33–35, 44–46

Haines, Hannah Marshall, 66
Haiti, 9, 300
Hall, Elizabeth. See Claypoole, Elizabeth Hall
Hallam, Lewis, 254
Hallam, Lewis, Jr., 254
Hallam, Sarah, 254
Hamilton, Alexander, 354
Hamilton, James, 333
Hamilton, Schuyler, 354
Hancock, John, 120
Hanna, Mark, 357
Hard, Elizabeth, 27
Hard, William, 27
Harlow, Shalom, 6
Harper, Thomas, 233
Haughton, George, 72, 138, 158, 160, 204,
    266
Havannah (ship), 276
Hazen, Edward, 351
Helmuth, Justus Henry C., 314
Henry, Hugh, 147, 206
Herman, Bernard L., 245
Herndon, Ruth, 125
Hervey, Sampson, 209
Hetty (privateer), 187, 191–95
Hewes, Joseph, 164
H. F. du Pont Winterthur Museum, 73
Hildebrandt, Sophia Wilson
    (granddaughter), 8, 169, 347, 355
Hillegas, Michael, 229, 230
Historical Society of Pennsylvania, 344, 356
History of Philadelphia (Scharf and Westcott),
    356
History of the American Revolution (Ramsay),
    352
History of the First United States Flag, The
    (Reigart), 356

*History of the Life of General George Washington, The* (Weems), 171

*History of the National Flag of the United States of America, The* (Hamilton), 354

*History of the Rise, Progress and Termination of the American Revolution, The* (Warren), 352

Hodge, Dr. Hugh, 277

*Holker* (privateer), 193

Holland, Joanna Ross (sister-in-law). *See* Armstrong, Joanna Ross Holland

Holland, Thomas (brother-in-law), 149–50, 199

Holland (country), 164, 274

Holloway, Abigail (aunt), 33

Holloway, Deborah (aunt), 33, 45

Holloway, Deborah Gabitas Griscom (grandmother), 32–33

Holloway, Mary (aunt), 33

Holloway, Sarah (aunt), 33, 285

Holloway, Tobias (father's stepfather), 33, 40

Holme, Thomas, 23

Home-Laughlin plate, 359

*Hope* (brig), 193

*Hope* (schooner), 300

Hopkinson, Francis, 179, 181

Horstmann, William H., & Sons, 350

Howard, John, 262

Howe, Daniel Walker, 349

Howe, Sir William, Lord Admiral, 145, 197, 199–201, 205

Howell, Ann, 101–3

Howell, Isaac, 134–35, 232–33, 243–44

Hudson, William, 26

Hughes, George Robert Twelves, 13

Hughes, John, 82–83

Humphreys, Charles, 132

Humphreys, Joshua, 185

Hunter, George, 321

Hutch, Caroline, 358–59

Hutchinson, Thomas, 127

*Hyder-Alley* (ship), 231, 353

Independence National Historic Park, 351

*Independent Chronicle and Universal Advertiser*, 255

Indian Department, 168, 320–22

industrial revolution, 349–52

*In Old Chicago* (film), 5

Irvin, Benjamin, 141

Irving, Washington, 298, 325

Jackson, Andrew, 340

Jackson, William, 257, 301

Jaffrey, Charles, 138

James, Abel (uncle), 14, 37, 40–43, 77–78, 81–90, 94–96, 100, 113, 115, 117–19, 131–32, 134, 143–44, 157–59, 190–91, 198–99, 206, 239, 245, 250–51, 288, 315

James, Chalkley (cousin), 41, 198

James, Elizabeth (aunt). *See* Knight, Elizabeth James

James, George (grandfather), 37–39, 81, 99–100

James, Joseph (uncle), 37

James, Rebecca Chalkley (aunt), 41

James, Rebecca (mother). *See*, Griscom, Rebecca James

James, Sarah Townshend (step grandmother), 39

James, Thomas Chalkley (cousin), 41

James & Drinker, 81, 95, 112–13, 115, 121, 143–44

James II, King of England, 22

*James* (ship), 232

Jaquet, Thomas, 323–24

Jay, John, 178

Jefferson, Thomas, 159, 301, 306, 316–17, 321, 324, 327, 346

Jeffersonian Republicans, 301, 316

Jewell, Matthias, 29

John Hancock and Company, 334

Johnson, Gervice, 292

Johnson, Lawrence, 336

Jones, Abraham, 138

Jones, Edward (son-in-law), 315, 335

Jones, Jesse, 209

Jones, John, 322

Jones, John Paul, 164

Jones, Mary Porter, 46–47, 49

Jones, Rachel Claypoole (daughter). *See* Fletcher, Rachel Claypoole Jones

Jones, Rebecca (teacher), 46–49

Jones, Robert Strettle, 209

Jugiez, Martin, 4

Kaighn, Ann (step-daughter of Sarah Dole Griscom), 33

Kaighn, Elizabeth (cousin). *See* Donaldson, Elizabeth Kaighn

Kaighn, John (second husband of Sarah Dole Griscom), 33, 52

Kaighn, John (son of Sarah Dole Griscom), 33

Kaighn, Joseph (son of Sarah Dole Griscom), 33

Kaighn, Sarah Dole Griscom (great grandmother). *See* Griscom, Sarah Dole

Karcher, Jacob, 282

Keats, John, 94

Kegs, Battle of the, 200–201

Keith, George, 29–32, 107, 224

Keithian Schism, 29–32

Kemble, Elizabeth, 71

Kemble, George, 312–13

Kemp, Jonathan, 230

Kendrick, Walter, 323

Keno, Leigh, 3

*Kent* (ship), 21

Key, Francis Scott, 325

King, Ann, 69, 70–72, 139, 141, 158, 162

King, Daniel, 275

King George's War, 149

Knight, Elizabeth James (aunt), 37–44

Knight, Giles (uncle), 14, 38–43, 77, 78, 80–82, 84, 87, 89–90, 105, 119, 125–26, 157–58, 198, 315

Knight, Joseph (cousin), 42

Knight, Mary (cousin), 315

Knight, Mary Worrell, 353

Knight, Phebe (aunt), 105

Knor, Jacob, 139

Knox, Frances, 212

Kuhn, Dr. Adam, 283

labor movement, 270, 351–52

*Lady Washington* (ship), 232

*La Prudente* (ship), 212

Latimer, George, 301

Latimer, Henry, Jr., 332

Latimer, Sally Bailey, 332

Laurens, Henry, 230

Lawrence, Elizabeth, 69–70, 141

Lawrence, Thomas, 69

Lay, Benjamin, 256, 292, 294

Lee, Gen. Charles, 162

Lee, Harry "Light Horse," 311–12

Lee, Richard Henry, 159

*Lee County Democrat*, 355

*Lenox* (ship), 228

Lesher, Jacob, 149

Leslie, Anna, 320

Leslie, Eliza, 320

*Letters from a Farmer in Pennsylvania* (Dickinson), 89, 120

Levering, Griffith (brother-in-law), 185–86, 270

Levering, Hannah Griscom (sister). *See* McIntire, Hannah

Levering, Sammy, 306

Levering, Septimus, 185

Lewis, Eleanor Parke Custis, 10

Lewis and Clark expedition, 284, 321

Lexington, Battle of, 145

*Lexington* (ship), 163

Liberty Bell, 36–37, 345

"Liberty's Call" (Mason), 148

*Lies My Teacher told Me* (Loewen), 360

*Life of Washington* (Marshall), 171

*Life of Washington* (Weems), 171

Linton, John, 233

*Lion* (ship), 211–12, 218, 231

Lithgow, Hannah, 209

*Liverpool* (ship), 200

Lloyd, Thomas, 31

Loewen, James, 360

Logan, Deborah, 356

London Rebuilding Act (Britain, 1667), 24

*London Tradesman* (Campbell), 53, 56, 71, 351

Long, John, 245

Longfellow, Henry Wadsworth, 11

*Loudon's American Daily Advertiser*, 331

*Loudon's New York Packet*, 255

Louisiana Purchase, 321

Lownes, James, 305, 314

Lownes, Sarah Donaldson (niece). *See* McCord, Sarah Donaldson

Loxley, Ann, 302

Loxley, Benjamin, 45, 302

Loxley, Benjamin, Jr., 131–32, 138

Lucky (enslaved African), 259

Ludley, R. (boarder), 329, 337

Lux, Rosannah, 258–59

Lux, Susanna, 258–59

*Luzerne* (privateer), 9, 227, 229

MacCauley, Isaac, 333

Madison, Dolley Payne, 13, 238, 257

Madison, James, 317, 324

Maine, 346

Malthus, Thomas, 338

Manny, Francis, 163

Manny, Margaret Cox, 53–55, 163–64, 166, 170, 181, 204

"Map of the Seat of the Civil War in New England" (1775), 147

Mariah (enslaved African), 259–60
mariners, 191–92, 315, 318, 335
Marshall, Christopher, Jr., 261
Marshall, Christopher, Sr., 240, 261
Marshall, John, 171, 310–11
*Martha* (ship), 21
Martin, William, 63, 138
Mary, Queen of England, 80, 254
*Mary* (ship), 21, 280
Mason, John, 63, 96, 138–39, 148, 232,
    266, 273, 288
Masonic Lodge, 133, 174, 176–77, 190,
    227, 246, 273, 288, 312
  Grand Lodge, 254
Massachusetts, 114, 127–28, 145, 147, 161
Mathews, James, 276
Matlack, Ellen, 239
Matlack, Timothy, 239–40, 242–43, 246
Matlack, White, 240, 243–44
*Maude* (TV program), 360
*Mayflower* (ship), 213
McAlpine, Mary, 163
McBride, Daniel, 245
McClenachan, Blair, 191, 193
McClenachan, Robert, 212
McCord, Charles (great-nephew), 347
McCord, David, 340
McCord, Louise (great-niece). *See* Beale,
    Louise McCord
McCord, Sarah Donaldson Lownes (niece),
    272, 284, 305–6, 314, 331, 331, 340
McCord, Sarah (great-niece), 337–39
McIntire, Hannah Griscom Levering (sister),
    45, 102, 105, 185–86, 208, 270–72, 278,
    305–6, 330, 335–37, 347–48
McIntire, William (brother-in-law), 305
McKenney, Thomas, 322
McKinley, William, 357, 359–60
McNair boy, 277–78
McPherson, William, 301
Meade, George, 274
Mifflin, Thomas, 133, 142
*Mighty Destroyer Displayed, The* (Benezet),
    248
Miles, William, 213, 218
Militia Act (1777), 191
Mill Prison (England), 213–19, 228–31
*Minerva* (ship), 86
Mississippi, 331
Missouri Compromise, 346
*Missouri Gazette*, 355
M'Lane, Louis, 325

*Model Architect, The* (Sloan), 355
Monroe, James, 327
Montcalm, General, 78
Montresor, John, 202
Moon, John, 23
Moore, Patrick, 212
Morgan, George (nephew), 249, 284, 306
Morgan, Mary Griscom (sister), 44, 50,
    98, 101–3, 105, 117, 126, 149, 217, 247,
    249, 269, 277–78, 284, 305–6,
    347–48
Morgan, Rebecca (niece). *See* Pile, Rebecca
    Morgan
Morgan, Thomas (brother-in-law), 103, 126,
    149, 186, 217, 249, 284, 288, 305, 347
Morgan, Thomas (nephew), 304
Morris, Grizell Griscom (great great-
    grandmother), 27–29, 32
Morris, Margaret, 353
Morris, Richard (step-father of Andrew
    Griscom), 27
Morris, Robert, 5, 159, 168, 170, 174, 179, 180,
    358
Morris, Thomas, 290
Morrison, John, 257
Morton, Thomas, 133
Mund family, 357
Murray, Alexander, 325
Murray, Aquila (great-nephew), 324
Murray, Jane (great-niece), 335–36
Murray, John, 24
Murray, Rachel Griscom (great-niece),
    335–36

*Nancy* (ship), 305
Napoleonic Wars, 317, 349
Nash, Gary, 23, 30, 125–26
*National Gazette*, 279
Native Americans, 293, 320–22
Navy Board, 179
Neal, James A., 302, 318
*Nelly* (ship), 300
Nevil, Dinah, 256
New Jersey, 174
*New Jersey Gazette*, 201
New Jersey Royal Provincial Council,
    179
New Orleans, 306, 322–23, 327
Newport, David, 284
Newport, Susan Satterthwaite
    (granddaughter), 13–14, 201, 283–84,
    341

New York, 85, 89, 91, 95, 131, 174, 282, 351
Nicholson, Sarah, 333
Niles, Daniel, 200–201
Niles, William, 200–201
Nixon, John, 174
*No Cross No Crown* (Penn), 58
nonimportation, 86, 90–95, 101, 133, 137, 141–45
North, Lord, 112
Norton, Margery, 102
Nullification Crisis, 340

Ohio, 317
Old Swede's Church, 183–85, 237
O'Leary, Molly, 5
Olive Branch Petition, 146
ornamental painters, 318–19
*Our Flag* (Preble), 356
Overseers of the Poor, 272
Oxley, Edward, 141

Paine, Thomas, 13, 155, 192, 257, 303
Palmer, John, 202
Pancake, Major, 258–59
Pancake, widow, 258
*Panorama of professions and trades* (Hazen), 351
Parsons, John, 23
Parsons, William, 34
*Patty* (ship), 212
Peale, Charles Wilson, 206, 286–88
Peale portrait of Rachel Claypoole, 310
Pearson, William, 203
Peggy (enslaved African), 259–60
Pemberton, James, 114, 244, 258, 261, 291, 293
Penn, John, 129, 130, 131, 144
Penn, Sir William, 22
Penn, William, 19, 22–26, 31, 36–37, 58, 224, 253–54, 292
Pennsylvania
  British taxation and, 84
  colonial government of, 31–32, 37, 42
  Constitutional ratifying convention of 1788 in, 301
  established, 22–24
  flags for, 318
Pennsylvania Abolition Society (PAS), 253, 257
Pennsylvania Academy for Young Ladies, 318
Pennsylvania Assembly, 37, 42, 77, 80–84, 89–90, 95–96, 109, 113, 118–20, 129–33,
    144–45, 150, 158, 174, 182, 207, 238, 255–56, 263–64, 301, 303
Pennsylvania Charter of Privileges, 36–37
*Pennsylvania Chronicle*, 91
Pennsylvania Committee of Safety, 146, 150, 169, 174, 175, 319
Pennsylvania Constitutional Convention, 239
*Pennsylvania Evening Post*, 204
*Pennsylvania Gazette*, 52–53, 66, 83–85, 87–88, 91–92, 114, 188, 204, 209, 235, 264, 349
Pennsylvania Hospital for the Sick Poor, 109–10
Pennsylvania House, 243–45
*Pennsylvania Journal*, 93, 122, 164
Pennsylvania militia, 160, 320, 322
Pennsylvania Navy, 161–63, 167, 183, 187–88
*Pennsylvania Packet*, 138, 148, 182, 204, 206, 218, 265, 267
Pennsylvania provincial convention, 132, 144
Pennsylvania Society for Promoting the Abolition of Slavery, 257–60, 265, 267
Pennsylvania State House, 36–37, 131–32, 205–6, 327, 345
Pennsylvania Supreme Court of Judicature, 319
Penrose, Jonathan, 258
*Perseverance* (ship), 315
*Peter Reeves* (ship), 163
Petrie, Donald, 193
Peyton, Catharine, 46–47
Philadelphia
  abolitionism in, 256–60
  African Americans in, 124–25
  artisans in, 52–60
  British occupation of, 11, 196–207
  building of early, 12, 22–26, 34–35, 41–42, 44
  as capital under Washington presidency, 286–88, 296–97
  celebration of ratification of Constitution in, 287–88
  changes in, after 1815, 327–28, 333–34, 352, 357, 361
  charitable associations in, 253–54
  customhouse and, 299–301
  founding of, by Penn, 19, 23, 253
  Independence Day celebration of 1777, 182–83
  industrial revolution and, 349–52
  lives of ordinary women, 13
  prison reform in, 260–65

resistance and Revolution in, 78–79,
    82–90, 94–96, 106, 111–16, 121–22,
    127–30, 145–52, 156, 174, 188, 193
slavery in, 28
social and labor relations in, after
    Revolution, 270
theater bans in, 254–56
yellow fever epidemic, 276–84
Philadelphia Committee of Correspondence,
    129–30
*Philadelphia Directory and Strangers' Guide*,
    333
Philadelphia Dispensary for the Medical
    Relief of the Poor, 265
Philadelphia Library Company, 34–35, 41, 45
Philadelphia Meeting for Sufferings, 130
Philadelphia Monthly Meeting, 31–32, 102–4,
    114–16, 238–39, 292–93
Philadelphia Museum of Art, 73
*Philadelphia North America*, 353
Philadelphia Provincial Council, 28
Philadelphia Saving Fund Society (PSFS),
    337–39
Philadelphia Society for Alleviating the
    Miseries of Public Prisons, 253, 260–65
Philadelphia Society for Assisting Distressed
    Prisoners, 261
Philadelphia Yearly Meeting, 30, 99, 125, 134,
    252, 293, 295, 329
Pickering, Charles, 25
Pickersgill, John, 165, 316
Pickersgill, Mary Young, 165, 316, 321, 325–26
Piesley, Mary, 46
Pile, Elizabeth (great-niece), 315–16
Pile, Emma (great-niece), 316
Pile, Mary (great-niece), 316
Pile, Morgan Griscom (great-nephew), 347
Pile, Rebecca Morgan (niece), 284, 306, 315,
    347
Pile, Samuel, 315
Pile, William, 340
*Pilgrim* (ship), 210
Pitt, William, 87
Pleasants, Samuel, 261
Pledge of Allegiance, 357
*Plymouth Journal and Massachusetts
    Advertiser*, 255
Poet, Elizabeth, 110
Pollard, John, 4
Pollard, William, 210, 262
*Polly* (ship), 116
Pompey (enslaved African), 258–59

Poor, John, 246
*Poor Richard's Almanack* (Franklin), 208
*Portsmouth* (privateer), 194
Potts, Isaac, 292
*Poulson's Daily Advertiser*, 332
Pound Ridge, Battle of, 2
Powell family, 41
Preble, George Henry, 356
Presley, Elvis, 5
Preston, Samuel, 24
Pringle, John, 191, 193
prison reform, 260–65
privateers, 192–93, 214–19, 227–28, 231–32
Purdy, Caroline Pickersgill, 165
Purdy, Henry, 165
Puritans, 20–21
Putnam, Gen. Israel, 147, 173

Quaker Blues, 240
Quakers (Society of Friends). *See also* Free
    Quakers
  African Americans and, 125–26, 256,
      292–94, 348
  almshouse of, 272, 291, 295, 296, 305
  Betsy disowned by, 9, 116–18
  burying ground, 44
  censure and disownment by, 45–46,
      98–105, 247–50, 289–95, 340
  Christ Church vs., 136
  Claypoole family and, 224–25
  drinking and, 247–48
  education and, 46–48
  family reconciles with, 329
  Free Quakers split with, 238–44
  Keithian Schism and, 29–32
  marriage policies of, 38–40, 99–100, 123,
      184
  plain style, 48–49, 58–59
  resistance and peace testimony of, 94, 96,
      114–15, 118, 130, 133–35, 144, 189–91,
      238
  Revolutionary War and, 202–3, 211
  settlement of, in Pennsylvania, 19–22,
      25–26
  theater opposed by, 254–55
Quartering Act (Britain, 1774), 128
Quartermaster Department, 324

Ramsay, David, 352
Randolph, Benjamin, 4, 156–57, 173, 225
Read, George (uncle of John Ross), 14, 118,
    120, 135, 139, 157, 166, 171, 173, 174

Read, Gertrude Ross (aunt of John Ross), 120
Red Bank, Battle of, 226, 311
Redden, David, 2
Redman, Dr. John, 276
Reed, Esther De Berdt, 210–11, 356
Reed, John, 304
Reigart, J. Franklin (great-nephew), 353–54, 356
*Reprisal* (ship), 163
Revere, Paul, 5, 11, 128, 137
Reynell, John, 58, 60
Reynolds, James, 4, 139
Rhoads, Samuel, 132
Richards, William, 175
Richardson, Edward W., 162, 170
Richardson, Joseph, 275
Richardson, Mrs., 162–63
Richardson, Nathaniel, 275
Richey, George, 71, 160
Riordan, Liam, 145
Robinson, William, 138
Rodney, Caesar, elder, 136, 159, 324
Rodney, Caesar Augustus, younger, 324–26
Ross, Aeneas, Jr., 108
Ross, Ann (wife of George Ross), 119
Ross, Rev. Aeneas, Sr. (father-in-law), 107–8, 110, 118, 126, 145, 171, 179, 257, 283, 297
Ross, Betsy. *See* Claypoole, Elizabeth Griscom Ross Ashburn "Betsy Ross"
Ross, George (uncle of John Ross), 5, 14, 119, 132–33, 135, 139, 144–46, 149–51, 166, 168–70, 173–74, 179–80, 191
   *Birth of Our Nation's Flag* painting of, 358
Ross, Gertrude (wife of George Read), 120
Ross, Rev. George (grandfather of John Ross), 107
Ross, Joanna (sister-in-law). *See* Armstrong, Joanna Ross Holland
Ross, Joanna Williams (grandmother of John Ross), 107
Ross, John (first husband), 288, 346
   African American child servant and, 257
   Chew order and Continental Congress and, 139–42
   Continental Congress and, 135–37
   death of, 9, 151–52, 158, 183
   family background and youth of, 107–8, 117–20
   marries Betsy and partners in her upholstery trade, 9, 105, 107, 110–11, 116–18, 121–26, 169, 233
   Masons and, 133, 176–77

mental illness and, 108, 152, 295
resistance and Revolution and, 113, 115, 128–33, 139–40, 144–48
slavery and, 126
Washington and, 297
Webster's upholstery shop and, 72
Ross, John (uncle of husband John Ross), 14, 113, 118–20, 128, 131–32
Ross, Maria (sister-in-law), 108
Ross, Mary Hunter (stepmother of John Ross), 110
Ross, Sarah Leech (mother-in-law), 108–10, 123, 152, 174, 295
Ross, Sarah (sister-in-law), 108
*Royal Charlotte* (ship), 82
Rush, Dr. Benjamin, 114, 248, 257–58, 262, 276–79, 281, 283–85
Rush, Julia, 277
Rushton, Dr. Thomas, 283
Rushton and Beachcroft, 4, 73
Russell, William, 212, 216
Rutter, George, 318–19

*Sachem* (ship), 163
Saladé, Sebastien, 323
*Sally* (ship), 186
Sampson, Deborah, 13
Sandwith, Mary, 65
Satterthwaite, Abel (son-in-law), 315–16, 328–29, 331, 335–37
Satterthwaite, Edwin (nephew), 337
Satterthwaite, Sidney (granddaughter), 341
Satterthwaite, Susan Claypoole (daughter), 235, 315–16, 328–29, 331, 335–37, 347
Satterthwaite, Susan (granddaughter), 283–84
Saunders, Hannah, 101–3
Say, Dr. Benjamin, 240, 302
Scharf, J. Thomas, 356
Schuylkll Arsenal, 12, 316, 323, 361
Second Company of Artillery, First Brigade, 325
Second Connecticut Continental Light Dragoons, 1–2, 162
Sekatau, Ella, 125
Sellers, William, 209
*Sentiments of an American Woman, The*, 210
Serle, Ambrose, 145
Seven Years' War, 78–79, 98, 171, 213, 254
*Shield* (ship), 21
Shippen, Edward, 24, 155, 158
Silliman, Amelia (granddaughter), 313, 347

Silliman, Eliza Ashburn (daughter), 305–6, 313, 315, 334–35, 340, 347

Silliman, Isaac (son-in-law), 305–6, 312, 315, 318, 334

Silliman, Jane (granddaughter), 313, 334

Silliman, John (Isaac's brother), 334

Silliman, Joseph Ashburn (grandson), 313, 347

Silliman, Willis (grandson), 334

Silve (indentured African), 259

Simonds, Jonas, 301

Simpson, Henry, 322

Skyrin, Nancy, 292

slavery, 9, 57, 98, 124–26, 256–60, 317, 345–46, 348

Sloan, Samuel, 355

smallpox, 45

Smith, Elias, 202

Smith, John, 81

Smith, Terrence, 245

Smith, Dr. William, 131

Smith, William (brazier), 23

Smith, William (Grand Secretary of Masons), 227

Society for the Cultivation of Silk, 91

Society for the Establishment and Support of Charity Schools, 329

Society for the Propagation of the Gospel (SPG), 107, 224

Society for the Relief of Free Negroes Unlawfully Held in Bondage, 257

Society for the Relief of Poor, Aged, and Infirm Masters of Ships, 315, 334–35

Society of Cincinnati, 301

Sons of Liberty, 121

Sotheby's (auction house), 1–4, 162, 225

South Carolina, 161, 340

Southwark Theater, 254–55

*Spectator*, 331

Staab, Anna, 355

Stamp Act (Britain, 1765), 77–78, 80–87, 93, 100, 118–19

Stamp Act Congress (New York, 1765), 81–82

*State of the Prisons in England and Wales* (Howard), 262

Steuben, Frederick William Augustus, Baron von, 178

Stewart, Deborah Griscom (cousin), 20

Stewart, Hugh, 161

Stewart, John, 213, 218

*Story of Our Flag* (Weaver), 356

Stricker, General, 325

Sturges, George, 351

Sugar (Revenue) Act (Britain, 1764), 79, 81

Supreme Executive Council, 182, 189–90, 206, 264, 298

*Swallow* (ship), 192

Sweet, Virtue, 213, 218

*Symbolorum ac Emblematum Ethico-Politicorum* (Camerarius), 2

*Symmetry* (privateer), 231–32

Taney, Roger B., 348

tanners, 225–27, 233–35

Tariff Act (1789), 299

tariffs of 1832, 340

Tarleton, Banastre, 1–2, 205

Taylor, Ameia, 204

Taylor, Hyns, 58, 158

Tea Act (Britain, 1773), 112–16, 120–22, 127, 156

Tennessee, 317

Test Act (1777), 188–91

Thomas, J. (boarder), 329

Thomas, Moses, 325

Thompson, Catherine Ross (aunt of John Ross), 120

Thompson, Col. William (uncle of John Ross), 118, 120

Thomson, Charles, 94–95

Thornhull, John, 210

Thornhull, Richard, 210

Tilghman, Edward, 139–41

Tilghman, Elizabeth Chew, 139–42, 332

Tindal, Alex, 230

Tod, Alexander, 210

Todd, John, 257

Todd, John, Jr., 257

Tolman, Margaret, 258–59

Tomkins, Jacob, 290

Tories, 118–19, 189, 207

*To the Representatives of the Free Men of this Province of Pennsylvania* (1692), 31

Townshend, Charles,, 88

Townshend Duties (Britain, 1767), 77, 88–96, 100, 111–13, 119–20, 129, 139, 255

Treasury Board, 180, 203

Trotter, Daniel, 47

Trumbull, John
Burgoyne's surrender painting, 354

*Tryal* (ship), 81

Tucker, Benjamin, 246

Turner, Robert, 24, 26

Turner, Susan McCord (great great-niece), 219

United Colony of Demerara and Essequibo, 274
*United States Album* (Reigart), 354
U.S. Army, 317–18, 320
U.S. Congress, 3, 299, 302, 303, 311, 318, 340
U.S. Constitution, 133, 226, 287–88, 311
U.S. House of Representatives, 297, 317
U.S. Navy, 317–18
U.S. Senate, 297
U.S. Supreme Court, 348
"Upholsterer" (farce), 255
upholstery trade, 4–5, 56–71. *See also* flags, early
  beds and bedding, 28, 63–67, 69, 142, 282–83, 334, 351
  Betsy and, 50–51, 158–59, 275–76, 302, 317, 361
  British occupation and, 204
  carpets and rugs, 140–41, 333, 350–51
  celebration of Constitution and, 288
  chair and sofa covers, 68–70, 142
  Clarissa Wilson and, 340–41, 346–47
  fashions and, 310
  government contracts and, 296–97, 302
  industrial revolution and, 332–34, 350–52
  John Claypoole and Betsy in, 232–36, 265–67
  John Ross and Betsy in, 111, 123–24, 139–42
  knapsacks, 322, 324
  lace, 172
  Revolution and, 88–89, 96–97, 204, 207–8, 232–33
  trimmings and tassels, 70–71, 161, 172
  yellow fever and, 282–83

Valley Forge, 226, 353
Vermont, 317
Vietnam Veterans Against the War, 360
*View of the life, travels, and philanthropic labors of the late John Howard*, 265
Virginia House of Burgesses, 87
Virginia regiment, Waxhaws colors of, 2, 162, 205
Vitally, Anthony, 276

Wack, George, 203
Waln, Rebecca, 289
Walter, Peter, 210

Wanamaker, Lewis Rodman, 360
Wanamaker, Rodman, 360
War Board, 178
War Department, 6
Warner, Anna, 102
Warner, John, 260
War of 1812, 12–13, 323–27, 357
War of the Austrian Succession, 213
War of the League of Augsburg, 213
Warren, Catharine, 336
Warren, Mercy Otis, 352
*Warren* (ship), 163
Washington, D.C., capital moved to, 327
Washington, George, 3, 13, 156–57, 244
  Betsy and John Claypoole and, 120, 226, 273, 297–99, 303, 344
  *Birth of Our Nation's Flag* and, 358
  *Cavalcade of America* and, 360
  death of, 310–11
  first flag and, 5, 8, 10, 168, 170–73, 176–81, 311–12, 354
  John Ross and, 133
  Magic Lantern show and, 359
  presidency of, 171, 226, 286, 301, 303, 352
  Rebecca Young and, 164–65, 325
  Revolutionary War and, 146, 173, 196–98, 226, 240, 352–54
  Wertmuller portrait of, 10, 172, 299
Washington, Martha, 10, 13, 303
Watkins, John, 259
Watson, John Fanning, 275, 343, 348, 352–53, 356
Watson, Mary, 333
Waxhaws colors, 1–3, 162, 205
Wayne, Col. Anthony, 150
Weaver, Addie Guthrie, 356
Webb, John, 290
Webster, John, 4, 7, 50–51, 55–56, 61–62, 68–74, 84, 79, 107, 110–11, 139–41, 158, 204
Wedderburn, Alexander, 127
Weems, Mason Locke "Parson," 171
Weisgerber, Charles, H., 357–59
  *Birth of Our Nation's Flag*, 358
  *The Modern Gladiator*, 358
Weisgerber, Vexil Domus, 358
Wertmuller, Adolph Ulrich
  Washington portrait, 10, 172, 299
West, Benjamin, 230
Westcott, Thompson, 356
West Indies, 79, 81, 87, 192, 260, 280
Wetherill, John Price, 341

Wetherill, Joseph, 138
Wetherill, Samuel, Jr., 237–39, 242, 245, 330–31, 341, 349
Wetherill, Sarah, 239
Wevill, Ann, 333
Weyman, Edward, 65
Wharton, Isaac, 115, 121
Wharton, James, 161–62, 170
Wharton, Thomas, 115, 121, 131, 142
Whig Association of the unmarried young ladies of America, 188
Whigs, 118, 120, 206
Whipple, William, 177–78
White, Blanch, 58, 62–63, 139, 160
White, Richard, 6
Whitney, Eli, 349
Willard, Archibald
    *The Spirit of '76*, 160
William, King of England, 80, 254
Williams, Jonathan, 194
*Willing Mind* (ship), 21
Wilson, Aquilla (grandson), 202, 314, 328, 347, 352
Wilson, Clarissa Claypoole (daughter), 14, 249, 235, 306, 313–15, 324, 326, 331, 340–41, 356
    death of husband and work with Betsy, 328–31, 334–37
    flag story and, 344–49, 352–56
Wilson, Clarissa (granddaughter), 314, 328
Wilson, Clarissa Hanna (granddaughter), 347
Wilson, Elizabeth Griscom (granddaughter). *See* Campion, Elizabeth
Wilson, Jacob (son-in-law), 313–14, 315, 328
Wilson, James, 120, 144, 151, 207
Wilson, Rachel Bird, 120
Wilson, Rachel (granddaughter), 328, 330–31

Wilson, Sarah (great-granddaughter), 359
Wilson, Sophia Bert (granddaughter), 313–14, 328, 331
Wilson, Susan (granddaughter), 328
Wilson, Woodrow, 3
Winchester, Elhanan, 271
Wing, Frederick, 209
Wirt, Joseph, 245
Wister, Sally, 356
Wollstonecraft, Mary, 303
women
    as artisans, 11–13, 52–54, 57, 69–70, 162–63, 288, 333–34, 361
    education of, 48, 302–3
    fashions and, 310
    imprisoned, 263–64
    philanthropic societies and, 253
    Revolution and, 77, 85–87, 91–93, 188, 207–8, 210–11, 352–53, 356
    savings accounts and, 339
    widowhood and, 184
*Women of the American Revoluton, The* (Ellet), 353
women's suffrage, 344, 360
Woodward, W.W., 265
World War II, 360
Worrell, Isaac, 353
Worrell, James, 131–32

Yarnall, Mordecai, 238
yellow fever, 9, 276–84, 296
Yerkes, Joseph, 248
Yorktown, Battle of, 158, 217, 219, 231, 259
Young, Mary. *See* Pickersgill, Mary Young
Young, Rebecca Flower, 163–66, 170, 174, 181, 207, 316, 321, 325–26
Young, William, 164, 165, 321
Young Ladies' Academy of Philadelphia, 302–3

# ABOUT THE AUTHOR

MARLA R. MILLER is a member of the history department at the University of Massachusetts Amherst, and the director of the Public History program there. She won the Organization of American Historians' Lerner-Scott Prize for the Best Dissertation in Women's History and the Walter Muir Whitehill Prize in Colonial History. In 2009, she was awarded the Patrick Henry Writing Fellowship from the C. V. Starr Center for the Study of the American Experience.